COUNTRY LIVING
MAGAZINE

Guide to Rural England

THE SOUTH
OF ENGLAND

Bedfordshire, Berkshire, Buckinghamshire,
Gloucestershire, Hampshire, Hertfordshire,
Isle of Wight, Oxfordshire and Wiltshire

By Peter Long

© Travel Publishing Ltd

Published by:
Travel Publishing Ltd
7a Apollo House, Calleva Park
Aldermaston, Berkshire RG7 8TN
ISBN 1-904-43456-8
© Travel Publishing Ltd
Country Living is a registered trademark of The National
Magazine Company Limited.

First Published: 2001
Second Edition: 2004
Third Edition: 2006

COUNTRY LIVING GUIDES:

East Anglia	Scotland
Heart of England	The South of England
Ireland	The South East of England
The North East of England	The West Country
The North West of England	Wales

PLEASE NOTE:

All advertisements in this publication have been accepted in good faith by Travel Publishing and they have not necessarily been endorsed by *Country Living* Magazine.

All information is included by the publishers in good faith and is believed to be correct at the time of going to press. No responsibility can be accepted for errors.

Editor:	Peter Long
Printing by:	Scotprint, Haddington
Location Maps:	© Maps in Minutes ™ (2006) © Crown Copyright, Ordnance Survey 2006
Walks:	Walks have been reproduced with kind permission of the internet walking site www.walkingworld.com
Walk Maps:	Reproduced from Ordnance Survey mapping on behalf of the Controller of Her Majesty's Stationery Office, © Crown Copyright. Licence Number MC 100035812
Cover Design:	Lines & Words, Aldermaston
Cover Photo:	Cotswold Cottages at Arlington Row, Bibury © www.picturesofbritain.co.uk
Text Photos:	Text photos have been kindly supplied by the Pictures of Britain photo library © www.picturesofbritain.co.uk and © Bob Brooks, Weston-super-Mare

Foreword

From a bracing walk across the hills and tarns of The Lake District to a relaxing weekend spent discovering the unspoilt hamlets of East Anglia, nothing quite matches getting off the beaten track and exploring Britain's areas of outstanding beauty.

Each month, *Country Living Magazine* celebrates the richness and diversity of our countryside with features on rural Britain and the traditions that have their roots there. So it is with great pleasure that I introduce you to the *Country Living Magazine Guide to Rural England* series. Packed with information about unusual and unique aspects of our countryside, the guides will point both fair-weather and intrepid travellers in the right direction.

Each chapter provides a fascinating tour of the South of England area, with insights into local heritage and history and easy-to-read facts on a wealth of places to visit, stay, eat, drink and shop.

I hope that this guide will help make your visit a rewarding and stimulating experience and that you will return inspired, refreshed and ready to head off on your next countryside adventure.

Susy Smith

Susy Smith
Editor, Country Living magazine

PS To subscribe to *Country Living Magazine* each month, call 01858 438844

Introduction

This is the 3rd edition of the *Country Living Guide to Rural England - The South of England* and we are sure that it will be as popular as its predecessors. Regular readers will note that the page layouts have been attractively redesigned and that we have provided more information on the places, people, and activities covered. Also, in the introduction to each village or town we have summarized and categorized the main attractions to be found there which makes it easier for readers to plan their visit. Peter Long, a very experienced travel writer has, of course, completely updated the contents of the guide and ensured that it is packed with vivid descriptions, historical stories, amusing anecdotes and interesting facts on hundreds of places in Bedfordshire, Berkshire, Buckinghamshire, Gloucestershire, Hampshire, Hertfordshire, Isle of Wight, Oxfordshire and Wiltshire.

The coloured advertising panels within each chapter provide further information on places to see, stay, eat, drink, shop and even exercise! We have also selected a number of walks from walkingworld.com (full details of this website may be found to the rear of the guide) which we highly recommend if you wish to appreciate fully the beauty and charm of the varied rural landscapes and coastlines of the South of England.

The guide however is not simply an "armchair tour". Its prime aim is to encourage the reader to visit the places described and discover much more about the wonderful towns, villages and countryside of the South of England. In this respect we would like to thank all the Tourist Information Centres who helped us to provide you with up-to-date information. Whether you decide to explore this region by wheeled transport or on foot we are sure you will find it a very uplifting experience.

We are always interested in receiving comments on places covered (or not covered) in our guides so please do not hesitate to use the reader reaction forms provided at the rear of this guide to give us your considered comments. This will help us refine and improve the content of the next edition. We also welcome any general comments which will help improve the overall presentation of the guides themselves.

For more information on the full range of travel guides published by Travel Publishing please refer to the order form at the rear of this guide or log on to our website (see below).

Travel Publishing

Did you know that you can also search our website for details of thousands of places to see, stay, eat or drink throughout Britain and Ireland? Our site has become increasingly popular and now receives monthly over 160,000 visits. Try it!

website: www.travelpublishing.co.uk

Contents

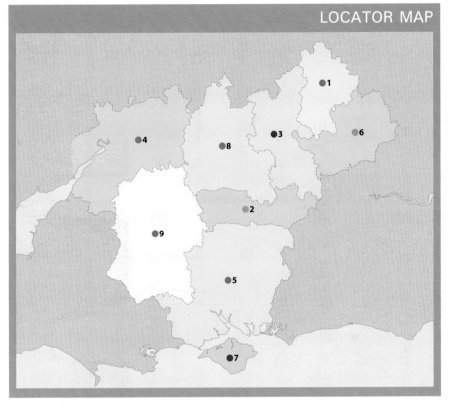

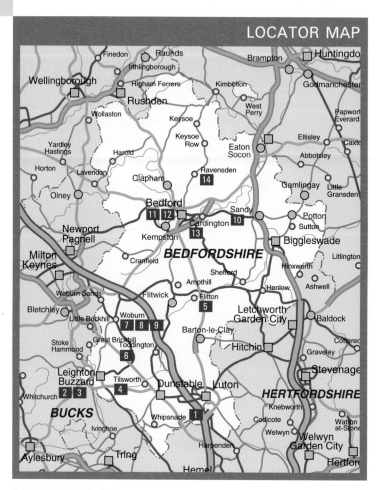

LOCATOR MAP

ADVERTISERS AND PLACES OF INTEREST

🏛 historic building   🏛 museum   🎬 historic site   🌿 scenic attraction   🌱 flora and fauna

1 | Bedfordshire

Bedfordshire is a county of multifarious delights, all within easy reach of London and major road and rail networks. In the Bedfordshire heartlands are to be found two of England's leading animal attractions, Woburn Safari Park and Whipsnade Wildlife Park. There are picturesque villages and historic houses, transport and heritage museums, mills and farms, woodland and nature reserves, great views from the Chilterns escarpment and well-established walking and cycle routes.

The Great Ouse and the Grand Union Canal, once commercial arteries, are finding a new role as leisure attractions, with miles of scenic walks or leisurely cruises to be enjoyed. The south of the county is dominated by the towns of Luton and Dunstable, while the central region of Bedfordshire is an area of ancient settlements and a rich diversity of places to see. Here is perhaps the most impressive dovecote in the country, with nests for 1,500 birds, while just outside Sandy are the headquarters of the Royal Society for the Protection of Birds. At nearby Cardington the skyline is dominated by the huge hangars where the R100 and R101 airships were built. Houghton House at Houghton Conquest is widely believed to have been the inspiration for the House Beautiful in John Bunyan's *Pilgrim's Progress*. Bunyan was born in the village of Elstow, a little way south of Bedford, and many of the places most closely associated with the writer can be visited, in both the town and the village. Bedford, the county capital, offers a blend of history and modern amenity, all set against the backdrop of the River Great Ouse, which passes through the town and many pleasant villages on its journey across the county.

Harrold Odell Country Park, near Bedford

Luton

🏠 Luton Hoo 🏛 Museum and Art Gallery

🏛 Stockwood Craft Museum 🏛 Someries Castle

The largest town in Bedfordshire and perhaps best known for Luton Airport, Vauxhall cars – and, for those with long memories of radio days, the Luton Girls Choir. Although the town has expanded rapidly from a market town in the early 19th century to a major industrial centre by the mid-20th century, it still boasts more than 100 listed buildings and three Conservation Areas.

Luton first began to prosper in the 17th century on the strength of its straw plaiting and straw hat making industries. These activities are amongst those featured at the **Luton Museum and Art Gallery,** housed within a delightful Victorian mansion in **Wardown Park**, a traditional town park with tennis and bowls. The park was opened to the public in the early years of the reign of Edward VII, but not the house, which was first a restaurant and then, during World War I, a military hospital. It was not until 1931 that the town's museum and art gallery, originally housed in the library, moved here. As well as featuring a re-creation of a Victorian shop and pub, the museum is also home to a range of collections covering the hat trade, costume, local history, archaeology and childhood. As lace making was one of the two main cottage industries in Bedfordshire, visitors will not be surprised to learn that the museum also has the largest collection of lace anywhere in the country outside London.

Visitors can also take a step back in time by seeking out **Stockwood Craft Museum and Gardens**. Occupying a Georgian stable block, the museum has a collection of Bedfordshire craft and rural items enhanced by frequent craft demonstrations. The walled garden is equally impressive and the Period Garden includes knot, medieval, Victorian, cottage, Dutch and Italian sections. The Hamilton Finlay Sculpture Garden showcases six pieces of sculpture by the internationally renowned artist Ian Hamilton Finlay in a lovely natural setting. Also here can be found the **Mossman Collection** of over 60 horse-drawn vehicles, the largest of its kind on public display in Britain. The story of transport comes into the 20th century in the Transport Gallery, whose exhibits include bicycles, vintage cars and a model of the Luton tram system. Replicas of some of the vehicles on display here have found their way into such films as *Ben Hur* and *Out of Africa*.

Just to the south of the town is the magnificent house **Luton Hoo**, originally designed by Robert Adams and set in 1,500 acres of parkland landscaped by Capability Brown. Construction of the house began in 1767, though it was extensively remodelled in 1827 and again in

Someries Castle, Luton

🏠 historic building 🏛 museum 🏛 historic site 🌳 scenic attraction 🌿 flora and fauna

1903, when the interior was given a French style for Sir Julius Wernher, who installed his fabulous art collection in the house. Luton Hoo is now a private hotel and is no longer open to the public.

Just southeast of Luton is **Someries Castle**, the remains of a fortified medieval manor house dating from the middle to late 15th century. The earliest surviving brick building in the county, both the gatehouse and chapel have survived and are still a very impressive sight. The original castle on this site belonged first to the de Someries family and then to the Wenlocks, and the house, of which only a romantic ruin remains, may have been built for the Lord Wenlock who died at the Battle of Tewkesbury in 1471, when the Yorkist victory ended the Wars of the Roses.

Around Luton

SLIP END
1 mile S of Luton on the B4540

⚑ Woodside Animal Farm

Woodside Animal Farm (see panel below) is home to more than 200 different breeds and there are hundreds of animals and birds to see and feed. The farm's many attractions include a walk-through monkey house, red squirrel enclosure, alpaca family, fabulous flamingos and hand-reared racoons. There are indoor and outdoor picnic and play areas, crazy golf, pony and tractor rides, a bouncy castle, farm shop, craft shop and coffee shop. New for 2006 is Professor Peabody's indoor heated play barn.

WOODSIDE ANIMAL FARM & LEISURE PARK

Slip End Village, Luton, Bedfordshire LU1 4DG
Tel: 01582 841044 Fax: 01582 840626
website: www.woodsidefarm.co.uk

'Something for all ages all year round' – that's the promise of **Woodside Animal Farm & Leisure Park**. On the southern outskirts of Luton a short drive from the M1 (J10), it offers a day of non-stop fun down on the farm with hundreds of birds and animals to see and feed. There are donkeys and llamas, monkeys and prairie dogs, ibis and wallabies, racoons, rabbits to cuddle, cranes and hornbills, pelicans and flamingos and rheas, iguanas and terrapins, and many more.

A traditional country fair has a helter-skelter, teacup ride, coconut shy, hook a duck, trampoline and bouncy castle, and among other attractions are tractor rides, crazy golf and an indoor heated play barn.

The Farm Shop sells chickens and eggs (which customers can also collect in the egg barn), jams and honeys, chutneys, relishes and biscuits, and everything for pets is available in the Pet Shop. Cards, candles and photo frames are just a few of the things sold in the new Gift Shop, and visitors can take a break from all the activity over a drink and a snack in the Coffee Shop

🎬 stories and anecdotes   🐦 famous people   🎨 art and craft   🎭 entertainment and sport   🥾 walks

WHIPSNADE

5 miles SW of Luton off B489

🌳 Whipsnade Tree Cathedral   🐾 Wild Animal Park

This small village with a charming, simple church is surrounded by common land on which stands **Whipsnade Tree Cathedral** (National Trust). After World War I, a local landowner, Edmund Kell Blyth, planted a variety of trees which have grown into the shape of a medieval cathedral, with a nave, transepts, cloisters and chapels. Designed as a memorial to friends of Blyth killed in the war, it's a curiously moving place. During the summer, services are held here.

To the south of the village can be seen the white silhouette of a lion cut into the green hillside, which is reminiscent of the much older White Horse at Uffington. A magnificent landmark, the lion also advertises the whereabouts of **Whipsnade Wild Animal Park**, the country home of the Zoological Society of London. Whipsnade first opened its doors in 1931, attracting over 26,000 visitors on the first Monday, and in the 70 years since it has grown and developed and continues to provide fun and education for thousands of visitors each year. There are 2,500 animals on show in the park's 600 acres, and behind the scenes Whipsnade is at the forefront of wild animal welfare and conservation, specialising in the breeding of endangered species

such as cheetahs, rhinos and the scimitar-horned oryx. There are daily demonstrations - penguin feeding, sea lions, free-flying birds - and other attractions include a railway safari, Discovery Centre, Children's Farm and Adventure Playground. Feeding time for the animals is always a popular occasion, while humans who feel peckish can make tracks for the Café on the Lake or (in summer) the Lookout Café, or graze on ice cream and snacks from the many refreshment kiosks in the park.

DUNSTABLE

2 miles W of Luton on the A505

🏛 Church of St Peter   🐾 Dunstable Downs

Dunstable is a bustling town that grew up at the junction of two ancient roads, Icknield Way and Watling Street, and was an important centre in Roman Britain, when it was known as Durocobrivae. The town's finest building is undoubtedly the **Priory Church of St Peter**, all that remains of a Priory founded by Henry I in 1131; only the nave actually dates from that time. It was at the Priory that Archbishop

Priory Church of St Peter, Dunstable

🏛 historic building   🏛 museum   🏛 historic site   🐾 scenic attraction   🌳 flora and fauna

Cranmer's court sat in 1533 to annul the marriage of Henry VIII and Catherine of Aragon. On the B4541 Dunstable-Whipsnade road, **Dunstable Downs** commands some of the finest views over the Vale of Aylesbury. Designated a Site of Special Scientific Interest and a Scheduled Ancient Monument, it has much to attract the visitor, including a Countryside Centre with interpretive displays and gifts, circular walks and a picnic area; it's a popular spot with hang gliders and kite flyers, and a refreshment kiosk is open all year round. South of Dunstable Downs at the junction of the B4541 and B4540, Whipsnade Heath is a small area of woodland containing some unusual plants and fungi.

TOTTERNHOE
6 miles W of Luton off the A505

🌱 Tottenhoe Knolls

This attractive village is situated below **Totternhoe Knolls**, a steeply sloped spur of chalk that is now a nature reserve known nationally for its orchids and its butterflies. On the top of the spur are the remains of a motte and bailey castle dating from Norman times, with commanding views of the surrounding countryside.

BILLINGTON
8 miles W of Luton on the A4146

🌱 Mead Open Farm

Mead Open Farm is home to a variety of established farm animals and offers a particularly wide range of attractions for children, including an indoor play barn, activity house, sandpit, indoor pets corner and ride-on toys. There's also a tea room and shop and a number of daily activities and weekly events.

LEIGHTON BUZZARD
9 miles W of Luton on A505

🏛 All Souls Church   🥾 Greensand Ridge Walk

The town's interesting name tells a lot about its history: Leighton is Old English and refers to a centre for market gardening whilst the Buzzard is a reference not to the bird of prey but to a local clergyman, Theobald de Busar, the town's first Prebendary. The town's past prosperity as a market centre is reflected in the grandeur of its fine Market Cross, a 15th century pentagonal structure with an open base and statues under vaulted openings all topped off by pinnacles. The market is still held here every Tuesday and Saturday. The

WISHES DO COME TRUE

Market Square, Leighton Buzzard, Bedfordshire LU2 1EU
Tel: 01525 370107
e-mail: wishes@fsmail.net website: www.wishesdocometrue.org.uk

What began in a small way in the markets of Milton Keynes has developed into a thriving business here in Leighton Buzzard. **Wishes Do Come True** is the brainchild of Genine Orchard, and her delightful shop is filled with lovely things for the home and gifts for all occasions. Among the variety of items on display – this is a browser's paradise – are Fair Trade products from Africa, a full range of handmade bathtime products, award-winning gifts from British designers, candles, photo frames and collectables including Haynes giftware range. Gift sets can be made up, prettily packed and delivered to addresses in the Cotswolds.

🎬 stories and anecdotes   🐦 famous people   🎨 art and craft   🎭 entertainment and sport   🥾 walks

spire of **All Saints Church** is over 190 feet high and is a local landmark. This big ironstone church dates from 1277 and it contains a number of endearing features in the form of graffiti left by the medieval stonemasons: one shows a man and woman quarrelling over whether to boil or bake a simnel cake. Seriously damaged by fire in 1985, the church has been carefully restored to its medieval glory; the painstaking work included re-gilding the roof, which is particularly fine, with carved figures of angels.

Leighton Buzzard and its neighbour Linslade are on the Grand Union Canal and visitors can now take leisurely boat trips along this once busy commercial waterway on the *Leighton Lady*. Historic forms of transport seem to be the town's speciality as visitors can also take a steam train journey on the

Leighton Buzzard Railway, one of England's premier narrow gauge operations. It has the largest collection of narrow gauge locomotives in Britain. The return journey takes 70 minutes and the railway operates on Sundays and Bank Holiday weekends between March and October.

For life at a more leisurely pace than steam trains, the town lies at one end of the **Greensand Ridge Walk** which extends across Bedfordshire to finish some 40 miles away at Gamlingay, Cambridgeshire. The name Greensand comes from the geology of the area, a belt of greensand which stretches from Leighton Buzzard up to Sandy and beyond. The walk passes many attractions, including the Grand union Canal, Stockgrove Country Park, Woburn Abbey, Ampthill Park and Houghton House.

BARRINGTON'S RESTAURANT AND TEA ROOMS

44 b/d High Street, Leighton Buzzard, Bedfordshire LU7 1EA
Tel: 01525 854691 Fax: 01525 376157
e-mail: barringtons@pencilart.fsnet.co.uk
website: www.lbbiz.net

Toni Forestiero offers 'food with a difference' in her licensed café/restaurant and takeaway bar on the main street of Leighton Buzzard. Fresh produce gets the home-cooked treatment throughout the range, which runs from cakes and scones to warming soups and hot dishes such as lasagne and chicken provençale.

Barrington's, which has 30 seats inside (where paintings by local artists hang on the walls) and 40 outside, is open between 7am and 4pm Monday to Saturday. It also has a thriving business in outside catering, providing everything from novelty birthday cakes to full meals for business lunches and all other occasions.

🏚 historic building   🏛 museum   🏛 historic site   🌳 scenic attraction   🌿 flora and fauna

THE ANCHOR

Dunstable Road, Tilsworth, nr Leighton Buzzard,
Bedfordshire LU7 9PU
Tel: 01525 210289
website: www.anchorpub.co.uk

Mike and Anne Oliver welcome visitors to **The Anchor**, a family-friendly pub with a strong local following. Traditional pub games are played in the bar, where Greene King IPA and Abbot Ale head a long list of liquid refreshment. Mike prepares a fine selection of dishes using fresh local produce that can be enjoyed in the conservatory-style restaurant or outside in the spacious garden. The Anchor is located in the village of Tilsworth, just off the A5 and a short drive from Luton, Dunstable and Leighton Buzzard.

PUTTERIDGE

2 miles NE of Luton on the A505

🌱 Putteridge Bury

The University of Luton and the Hertfordshire Garden Trust have restored the gardens at **Putteridge Bury** to the original designs of Sir Edwin Lutyens and Gertrude Jekyll; one of the highlights is a superb rose garden.

Ampthill

🏛 Ampthill Park   🌿 Alameda

This historic town, situated on a rise and with fine views over the surrounding countryside, was a great favourite with Henry VIII. It was here that Katherine of Aragon stayed during the divorce proceedings conducted by Henry's court at Dunstable. At that time there was also a castle here, built by Sir John Cornwall for his bride, the sister of Henry IV. On the site now stands Katherine's Cross, erected in 1773, which bears the arms of Castile and Aragon. On land given to his family by Charles II, the 1st Lord Ashburnham built the castle's replacement, **Ampthill Park**, in

1694. The house was enlarged a century later and the 300-acre park was landscaped by the ubiquitous Capability Brown. Ampthill Park is famous for its old oak trees and visitors can also enjoy the views from the Greensand Ridge Walk, which runs through the grounds.

An attractive feature of the town is the **Alameda** (Spanish for a public walk), an avenue of lime trees 700 yards long, presented to the town in 1827 by Lord and Lady Holland.

Ampthill also boasts some fine Georgian and early-19th century buildings, especially in Church Street, Tudor almshouses and the large Church of St Andrew, which has a noble west tower. Inside can be found some 15th century brasses and a 17th century monument to Colonel Richard Nicholls that includes the cannon ball that killed him during the Battle of Sole Bay in 1672. Nicholls, who was born and lived most of his life in Ampthill, served the Stuart kings and was commander of the force that defeated the Dutch at New Amsterdam. He re-named it New York in honour of the Duke of York, later James II.

🎬 stories and anecdotes   🐦 famous people   🎨 art and craft   🎭 entertainment and sport   🚶 walks

Wrest Park, Silsoe

Around Ampthill

FLITTON
2 miles SE of Ampthill off the A507

🏛 de Grey Mausoleum

Next to the 15th century church is the **de Grey Mausoleum**, a series of rooms containing a remarkable collection of sculpted tombs and monuments to the de Grey family of Wrest Park.

SILSOE
3 miles SE of Ampthill off A6

🏛 Wrest Park

Although the manor of Wrest has been held by the de Grey family since the late 13th century, the house standing today dates from the 1830s. Built for the 1st Earl de Grey from the designs of a French architect, it follows faithfully the style of a French chateau of the previous century. Parts of the house at **Wrest Park** are open to the public but the real glory is the gardens. They are a living history of English gardening from 1700 to 1850 and are the work of Charles Bridgeman, with later adaptations by Capability Brown. The layout remains basically formal, with a full range of garden appointments in the grand manner - there is a Chinese bridge, an artificial lake, a classical temple, and a rustic ruin.

Two buildings of particular interest are the Baroque Banqueting House, designed by Thomas Archer, which forms a focus of the view from the house across the lake, and the Bowling Green House, dating from about 1740 and said to have been designed by Batty Langley, who was best known as a writer of

---

THE CROSS KEYS

Pullox Hill, nr Flitton, Bedfordshire MK45 5HB
Tel: 01525 712442
website: www.ukeventsandtents.co.uk

With 36 years' experience, Peter Meads is the Charles Wells Brewery's longest serving landlord. With his wife Sheila and their friendly, hardworking staff, he has made the 16th century **Cross Keys** one of the best-loved pubs in the region. Behind the Grade II listed frontage, the bar, with its beams, inglenook fireplace and flagstones, is a convivial spot for a drink, and a great place for a meal, with good home-cooked British dishes served every lunchtime and evening in the 50-seat restaurant. The fine food is complemented by an international wine list. The pub has a flower-decked patio and a pleasant rear garden that's a popular spot for the whole family.

🏛 historic building   📷 museum   🏛 historic site   � scenic attraction   🌿 flora and fauna

architectural books for country builders and built little himself. Immediately beside the house is an intricate French-style garden, with an orangery by the French architect Cléphane, flower beds, statues, and fountains. The village of Silsoe itself boasts more than 130 listed buildings.

TODDINGTON

5 miles S of Ampthill on A5120

🏛 Toddington Manor

Situated on a hill above the River Flitt, this village is often overlooked, particularly by those travelling the nearby M1 who think only of the service station of the same name. However, the village is an attractive place, with cottages and elegant houses grouped around the village green. Unfortunately all that remains of **Toddington Manor** (see panel below) is a small oblong building with a hipped roof which is believed to be the Elizabethan kitchen of the large quadrangular house that was built here in around 1570. Toddington is a place which makes much of its folklore and is host to Morris dancers in the summer and mummers who tour the

village providing traditional entertainment at Christmas. Local legend also has it that a witch lives under Conger Hill - which is actually a motte that would, at one time, have had a castle on top - and, on Shrove Tuesday, the children put their ears to the ground to listen to her frying pancakes.

RIDGMONT

4 miles W of Ampthill on the A507

Part of the Woburn Estate, this is a typical estate village where the owners of the land (in this case the Bedford family) provided the houses and other buildings. Here the workers lived in gabled, redbrick houses. The church, designed by George Gilbert Scott, was also built at the expense of the estate.

WOBURN

6 miles W of Ampthill on the A4012

🏛 Woburn Abbey 🦌 Wild Animal Kingdom

🌳 Aspley Woods

First recorded as a Saxon hamlet in the 10th century, and again mentioned in the Domesday Book, Woburn grew into a small market town after the founding of the

Toddington Manor Gardens

Park Road, Toddington, Bedfordshire LU5 6HJ
Tel: 01525 872576 Fax: 01525 874555
website: www.toddingtonmanor.co.uk

Toddington Manor Gardens have been developed, by the owners Sir Neville and Lady Bowman-Shaw, into one of the most attractive in the county. Amid the six acres of gardens and 20 acres of woods are a lovely lime avenue leading into a cherry walk, a walled garden with beds of delphiniums and peonies, a fine herb garden, old-fashioned roses and a very impressive double herbaceous border. There's also a wild garden and three small ponds with nets and buckets available for children to go dipping. Other attractions include rare breeds of livestock, plants for sale, picnic area and a magnificent collection of over 100 vintage tractors. Open noon to 5pm 1st May to 31st August; closed Sunday.

📖 stories and anecdotes   🐦 famous people   🎨 art and craft   🎭 entertainment and sport   🚶 walks

Woburn Safari Park

Woburn Park, Bedfordshire MK17 9QN
Tel: 01525 290407
e-mail: info@woburnsafari.co.uk website: www.woburnsafari.co.uk

Woburn Safari Park is a great day out for groups of all ages. Combine the excitement of the Safari Drive with the fun of the Wild World Leisure Area. Meet the animals in Animal Encounters, the Australian Walkabout and Rainbow Landing. Enjoy the many demonstrations, keeper talks and feeding times. Children can let off steam in the indoor and outdoor playgrounds, on the Swan Boats and take a ride on the Railway Train. All the attractions are included in the entry price.

You may tour the Safari Reserves as often as you wish during the day, with different animal encounters every time. See eye to eye with the tigers or enjoy the Barbary Apes, Colobus, Vervets and Patas monkeying around in the Jungle.

Your party can interact with the animals in the Wild World Leisure area as well as enjoying the busy programme of keeper talks and demonstrations. Visit Rainbow Landing where you may purchase a cup of nectar to feed to the colourful and noisy rainbow lorikeets. Enjoy the speed and antics of the penguins as they are fed – you can watch it from the underwater viewing area. Don't miss the Elephant Encounter, Damini and Chandrika, two of the Asian elephants, are excellent ambassadors for their critically endangered species.

Take to the walkways and walk amongst the lemurs, our most primitive of primate ancestors! Related to the monkeys and extremely agile, the three species of lemur here are all endangered. Don't miss a face to face encounter with them or with the inquisitive squirrel monkeys at the popular Monkey Business. The outdoor pool has underwater viewing. Visitors can marvel at the sea lions at their most natural – swimming and playing under the water.

One of the most popular attractions is the giant indoor playground, The Adventure Ark. It has a drop slide, ball pools and soft play equipment. For the adventurous, the outdoor Tree Top Action Trail provides the thrill of an army assault course. The younger children can bounce along the Tiny Tots Safari Tail and have fun in the outdoor playground, Badger Valley. The last entry into the Safari Reserves is 5pm or dusk, whichever is earlier. By bringing your group to Woburn, you are helping to support the upkeep of the animals, many of which, such as the Rothschild giraffe and Siberian tiger, are critically endangered in the wild. Every visitor is important in making the conservation work possible.

🏛 historic building   🏛 museum   🏛 historic site   🝆 scenic attraction   🌿 flora and fauna

Cistercian Abbey here in 1145. All but destroyed by fire in 1720, this pretty village has retained many of the pleasant Georgian houses that were built subsequently and the attractive shop fronts give the place a cheerful air. Situated at a major crossroads, between London and the north and Cambridge and Oxford, Woburn also saw prosperity during the stagecoach era and by 1851 there were 32 inns here.

THE BLACK HORSE AT WOBURN

1 Bedford Street, Woburn, Bedfordshire MK17 9QB
Tel: 01525 290210
e-mail: Blackhorse@peachpubs.com
website: www.blackhorsewoburn.co.uk

On the main street of Woburn, the **Black Horse** has an appealing bow-windowed Georgian frontage with a central doorway. Inside, there's an attractive mix of traditional and more contemporary fittings, while alongside the pub is a courtyard garden with plenty of chairs and tables. Greene King provides the resident real ales, and the interesting menu includes deli boards of cheese, ploughman's, fish and cold meats – ideal as a starter, snack or to share. A wide-ranging à la carte menu is served lunchtime and evening, and afternoon teas from 11am to 6pm. The pub has a good wine list – by glass or bottle.

FLYING DUCHESS PAVILION COFFEE SHOP

Woburn Abbey, Woburn, Bedfordshire MK17 9WA
Tel/Fax: 01525 290839
e-mail: liz@thegaires.com

Woburn Abbey is a place of many attractions, and to make a visit complete the **Flying Duchess Pavilion Coffee Shop** beckons with an excellent selection of traditional home-cooked food prepared fresh on the premises every day. Set in the grounds of the Abbey, it's a striking glass-sided building with an unusual cantilevered ceiling and plenty of seats both inside and out.

The coffee shop is open from 9am to 5pm from the end of March to the end of September for morning coffee, lunches, all-day snacks, afternoon teas and hot and cold drinks. Its name remembers the wife of the 11th Duke of Bedford, a lady with a passion for flying.

Elizabeth Gaire, who runs the pavilion under licence from the Bedford Estates, also has an outside catering business, Special Occasions (Tel: 01582 422546), providing everything from a finger buffet to a full à la carte service for all occasions. And with her husband she runs the Silver Cup at 5 St Albans Road, Harpenden, Herts, a 4 Diamond AA rated 17th century coaching inn refurbished and sensitively updated to provide exceptional cuisine and excellent b&b accommodation in six en suite rooms – singles, doubles and twins (Tel: 01582 713095).

Around Woburn

Distance: *5.5 miles (8.8 kilometres)*
Typical time: *150 mins*
Height gain: *37 metres*
Map: *Explorer 192*
Walk: *www.walkingworld.com ID:1122*
Contributor: *Tony Brotherton*

Park in free village car park in Park Street.

The deer park boasts nine species of deer, including the rare Pere David's.

A gentle walk from the attractive village of Woburn, traversing the 3,000-acre Bedford Estate and deer park and visiting Woburn Abbey.

Hills or Fells, Lake/Loch, Pub, Toilets, Play Area, Church, Stately Home, Wildlife, Birds, Flowers, Great Views, Butterflies, Food Shop

1|From Woburn Village car park opposite the Church of St Mary the Virgin, turn right down Park Street to reach cattle grid at lodge.

2|Take footpath signed right immediately after lodge, soon to pass lake on left. Continue as far as drive at Park Farm. Go up drive and to left of further buildings, over staggered cross-paths, to reach long narrow strip of water.

3|Skirt the water to left and proceed half-left across open parkland. Make for lone tree near the top of small rise, to meet road at the vehicle entrance to Woburn Abbey at crest of rise. Continue downhill alongside road to reach estate gates before buildings at Froxfield.

4|The footpath signed to left leads towards safari park. Our route lies to right on road leading to Milton Bryan, as far as cottages at Hills End and footpath signed to left.

5|Take path and enter field by stile, then cross on obvious path to reach orange-topped waymark post. Keep ahead through scrub and at next such post turn to right to reach a footbridge.

6|Cross footbridge and choose footpath leading straight ahead in next field. Enter via stile, gravel drive leading to lane. Here go left, past Helford House, to footpath off to right. Take footpath along left-hand edge of field and enter hedged path. Follow hedge boundary to right in next field. After next waymark post, path joins crossing track - Greensand Ridge Walk, which we follow back to Woburn.

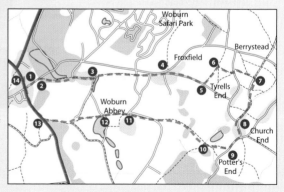

7 | Turn right along Greensand Ridge Walk, which emerges onto road at Church End, Eversholt.

8 | Opposite church of St John the Baptist is Green Man public house, your handy halfway hostelry. Continue through village and at T-junction turn right on road. Just before bend, divert right through gate at Greensand Ridge Walk sign.

9 | Follow path diagonally across field, cross stream at double stile and pass lake to right, to reach cross-paths and signpost.

10 | Now keep ahead, shortly to re-cross stream twice more, to arrive at stile. Follow path across field and pass through narrow belt of trees, then proceed uphill through young plantation. Greensand Ridge Walk continues uphill and into deer park, then descends to path junction after car park and entrance to Abbey.

11 | Keep ahead, soon to see large pond at left, with two smaller ponds on right.

12 | At crossing track, look back for fine view of frontage of Woburn Abbey. Continue ahead to pass between ponds on narrow causeway and cross parkland on route delineated by occasional small posts. Leave deer park via gate at corner of woods to enter fenced path, leading to exit at A4012 road.

13 | Now turn right to return to Woburn Village. At crossroads turn right into Park Street to finish walk at car park.

14 | Alternatively, continue along main street to tourist information office housed in redundant church.

Woburn Abbey, ancestral home of the Dukes of Bedford, is renowned for its art treasures, its deer park and its antiques centre. The estate was given to the 1st Earl of Bedford in the will of Henry VIII but the original building was partially destroyed by fire and the present stately home dates mainly from the 1700s. Its extraordinary stock of treasures includes paintings by Van Dyck, Gainsborough, Reynolds and the famous Armada portrait of Elizabeth I by George Gower. The Venetian Room showcases 21 views of Venice by Canaletto while other rooms display outstanding collections of English and French furniture, porcelain and antique statuary. Another attraction on site is the Woburn Abbey Antiques Centre with more than 50 dealers housed in a reconstruction of city streets of bygone days that includes genuine 18th century shop facades rescued from demolition.

A short distance north of the Abbey is the **Wild Animal Kingdom and Leisure Park**, (see panel on page 12) home to a vast range of animals including eland, zebra, hippos, rhinos, lions, tigers, elephants and sea lions.

There are fine views of Woburn Abbey and of Milton Keynes from **Aspley Woods**, one of the largest areas of woodland in Bedfordshire, set between Woburn and Woburn Sands. The woods offer peace, tranquillity and miles of tracks for walking.

MARSTON MORETAINE
3 miles NW of Ampthill off the A421.

Forest Centre

Forest Centre & Millennium Country Park offers a splendid day out in the countryside for all the family. The 600 acres of wetland and woodland are home to a wide variety of wildlife, and the park provides excellent walking and cycling; bikes can be hired from the Forest Centre, which also has an interactive Discover the Forest exhibition, café bar, art gallery, gift shop, free parking and children's play area.

Biggleswade

On the banks of the River Ivel, which was once navigable through to the sea, Biggleswade was an important stop on the Great North Road stage coach routes and several old inns have survived from that period. The town also has another link with transport as the home of Dan Albone (1860-1906), the inventor of the modern bicycle. He produced a number of variants, including a tandem and a ladies cycle with a low crossbar

and a skirt guard, but is best known for his racing cycle, which in 1888 set speed and endurance records with the intrepid CP Mills in the saddle. Dan Albone's inventiveness was not confined to bicycles, as he also developed the Ivel Agricultural Tractor, the forerunner of the modern tractor.

Around Biggleswade

SANDY
3 miles N of Biggleswade on A1

🌿 **The Lodge**

The sandy soil that gave the town its name helped it rise to fame as a market gardening centre in the 16th century. The 14th century Church of St Swithun contains an interesting

---

FOUR SEASONS

14 High Street, Sandy, Bedfordshire
Tel: 01767 680259
website: www.fourseasonsofsandy.co.uk

Easy to spot with its green-painted exterior and big window display on Sandy's High Street, **Four Seasons** first opened its doors 24 years ago. In that time much has changed, including a new owner in Sue Pelletier. She bought the business in 2005 after working there for five years, and she takes justifiable pride in the quality and range of the womens' fashions on display and offers exceptional standards of friendly, personal service. The ever-changing stock caters for sizes from 10 to 20 and for all occasions from leisure through everyday to evening and parties.

Four Seasons are stockists of Condici, Fisser, Finn Karelia, Presen, Gollehaug, Catherina Hepfer, Pola, Jomhoy, Libra, Lewis Henry, Michele, Olsen, Michael H, Sommermann, Gerry Weber and many others. Also shoes by Cheshire and Lotus, hats by Nigel Rayment and Failsworth and jewellery by Danté. Customers enjoy the very best of one-to-one attention and in the Mother of the Bride and the Mother of the Groom showroom they can complete the look for the special occasion with matching hats, shoes, bags and jewellery. Opening hours are 9.30am to 5.30pm Monday to Friday, 9.30am to 5pm Saturday.

🏛 historic building   🏛 museum   🏛 historic site   🌊 scenic attraction   🌿 flora and fauna

statue of Captain Sir William Peel, third son of Sir Robert Peel, famous Prime Minister and founder of the Police Force, who was awarded one of the first Victoria crosses for heroic action in the Crimean War.

The Greensand Ridge Walk runs through the town, and a little way southeast of the town, at **Sandy Lodge**, are the national headquarters of the Royal Society for the Protection of Birds and a nature reserve set in over 350 acres of open heath and woodland. As well as offering a great deal to those interested in birds, the formal gardens surrounding the mansion house were first created in the 1870s and were restored in the 1930s by Sir Malcolm Stewart and are well worth visiting in their own right. Also on the site is a newly developed wildlife garden.

MOGGERHANGER
3 miles W of Biggleswade off the A603

🏛 Moggerhanger Park

Grade I listed **Moggerhanger Park** was designed by Sir John Soane, architect of London's Bank of England, and is set amidst gardens and parkland designed by Humphry Repton.

BLUNHAM
5 miles N of Biggleswade off the A1

This quiet rural village was the home of the poet John Donne while he was rector here from 1622 until his death in 1632, a post he held while also Dean of St Paul's in London. While he was convalescing here after a serious illness in 1623 he wrote *Devotions* which contains the immortal lines *No man is an island, entire of itself*, and *Never send to know for whom the bell tolls; it tolls for thee*. Donne divided his time between London and Blunham, where he stayed in the house opposite the parish church. Inside can be seen some fine Norman work,

interesting bosses and the chalice Donne presented to the church in 1626.

Another building of interest is the Old Vicarage of 1874, constructed of startling yellow and orange bricks.

OLD WARDEN
3 miles W of Biggleswade off B658

🏛 Shuttleworth Collection   🌿 Swiss Garden

🦅 Bird of Prey Centre

This charming village of thatched cottages along a single street has developed its unique character as a result of the influence of two local families. In the early 18th century, Sir Samuel Ongley, a London merchant, ship-owner, and former director of the South Sea Company, bought this country seat for himself and his family, who stayed here for over 200 years. In 1776 Robert Henley Ongley was awarded an Irish peerage for his services to Parliament, and it was his grandson, also called Robert, who created Old Warden as it is seen today. Taking the original estate cottages, and also building new ones, Sir Robert developed this rustic village and also embellished the 12th century church with some interesting Belgian woodwork.

However, Sir Robert's most famous piece of work is the **Swiss Garden**, laid out in the early 19th century. Within its 10 acres are ornate bridges, winding ponds, a breathtaking fernery and a number of tiny follies. In season, the early bulbs, primroses, rhododendrons and the old-fashioned roses make wonderful displays.

In 1872, his fortune depleted by the extensive building and remodelling programme, Sir Robert sold the estate to Joseph Shuttleworth. A partner in a firm of iron founders, it was Joseph who led the way to the development of the steam traction

🎭 stories and anecdotes   🐦 famous people   🎨 art and craft   🎪 entertainment and sport   🚶 walks

engine and also built the Jacobean-style mansion house that can still be seen today. Another attraction on the estate is the **English Bird of Prey Centre & Owl Sanctuary**. 300 birds of various species are on public display and in addition to training and flying birds of prey from around the world, the centre is firmly committed to conservation and education, working with schools to create displays and informative workshops. Regular flying demonstration times are 11.30am for the Owl Experience, 1.30pm for Birds of the World and 3pm for Out of Africa featuring vultures, secretary birds, eagles, owls and falcons. The centre also features a children's adventure play ground, a picnic site, a restaurant and a gift shop.

Also at Old Warden is the famous **Shuttleworth Collection** of historic aircraft. In 1923, the 23-year-old Richard Ormonde Shuttleworth, who had inherited the estate, bought his first aircraft, a de Havilland Moth. Over the years he added further planes to his collection. At the outbreak of World War II he naturally joined the RAF but was sadly killed in a flying accident in 1940. After the war his mother put his collection on display and over the years other aircraft have been added. Housed in eight hangars, the collection now comprises some 40 airworthy craft, dating from 1909 (a Blériot) to 1955. Throughout the year there are a number of flying days when these grand old planes take to the skies. Many of them have been featured in films such as *Reach for the Sky*, *The Battle of Britain* and *Pearl Harbour*. The planes are complemented by a number of vintage cars, motorcycles and bicycles.

A short drive north of Old Warden are two

Maypole at Ickwell, near Old Warden

delightful villages, Ickwell and Northill. The former, which has a Maypole standing permanently on the green, is the birthplace of the great clock-maker Thomas Tompion. The 14th century Church of St Mary, which dominates the village of Northill, is noted for some fine 17th century glass and a one-handed clock built, it is thought, by Tompion's father. Some of the clocks could run for a year without rewinding and the Tompions also made barometers and sundials, including pieces for King William III.

STEWARTBY
10 miles W of Biggleswade off the A421

Stewartby takes its name from Sir Malcolm Stewart, founder of the London Brick

Company. He had the village built in 1926 to house employees at the nearby brickworks, which were thought to be the largest in the world and at their peak turned out 650 million bricks a year. The kiln took over a year to reheat after World War II.

HOUGHTON CONQUEST
9 miles W of Biggleswade off the B530

🏛 Houghton House

That this village is home to Bedfordshire's largest parish church seems fitting, as Houghton Conquest also has links with the county's most famous son, John Bunyan. On a hilltop a little way south of the village stands **Houghton House**, reputedly the inspiration for the House Beautiful in *The Pilgrim's Progress*. Built in 1615 for Mary, Countess of Pembroke, the house was visited by Bunyan in his days as an itinerant tinker. The property later came into the hands of the Dukes of Bedford, one of whom had it partially demolished, and the ruins are now in the care of English Heritage.

SHEFFORD
5 miles SW of Biggleswade on the A507

🌀 Hoo Hill Maze

The small town of Shefford grew up, as the name suggests, around a sheep ford across the Rivers Hitt and Flitt and enjoyed a brief status as an inland port on the Ivel Navigation. This waterway was built primarily to bring coal from Kings Lynn by way of the River Ouse. In North Bridge Street a wall plaque marks the house of the pastoral poet Robert Bloomfield, a poor farm labourer and shoemaker who found fame when he published *The Farmer's Boy* in 1800. The poet, who died, as he had lived, in extreme poverty, is buried in the churchyard at nearby Campton.

In Hitchin Road is the **Hoo Hill Maze,** constructed with hedges more than 6ft high. It stands in an orchard with a picnic site and plenty of space for children to romp.

Shefford is also the starting point of the 21-mile-long cycle route, the Jubilee Way, a circular route that passes through undulating landscape and picturesque villages.

LOWER STONDON
6 miles S of Biggleswade off the A600

🏛 Transport Museum

Lower Stondon attracts visitors from near and far to its renowned **Transport Museum** and garden centre. The museum, on the A600 next to Mount Pleasant golf course, contains a marvellous collection of several hundred exhibits covering all forms of transport – from motorcycles to helicopters, from a Jowett Javelin and a Bedford Dormobile to a London bus – and covers the period from the early 1900s to the recent past. The centrepiece of the collection is a full size replica of Captain Cook's barque, *Endeavour*, in which he undertook one of his most important journeys in 1768. The replica was built using the original plans. Guided tours of the museum are available and there's a café selling light refreshments.

Bedford

🏛 Church of St Peter de Merton	🏛 Castle Mound
🏛 Church of St Paul	🎨 Creative Arts Gallery
🏛 Bunyan Museum	🏛 Bedford Museum
🌿 Priory Country Park	🎨 Cecil Higgins gallery

This lively cosmopolitan town owes its origins and development to the River Great Ouse which remains one of the most important and attractive features of the town. Bedford was

---

🏛 stories and anecdotes   🦜 famous people   🎨 art and craft   🖉 entertainment and sport   🥾 walks

PINEWOOD STUDIOS

St Cuthberts Street, Bedford MK40 3JG
Tel: 01234 355344
website: www.pinewoodstudios.co.uk

Wilma Jassall and her family and staff have earned an enviable reputation for the quality that their customers always find at **Pinewood Studios**. The Jassalls produce top-class, durable pine furniture in the workshops on the premises for any room in the house, individual pieces from worktops, tables, dressers and wardrobes to bespoke kitchens. The natural pine pieces can be commissioned in any size in a wide range of finishes and colours, and all offer particularly good value for money. Customers can visit the showrooms any day between 9.30a, and 5pm.

already a thriving market place before the Norman Conquest and its market is still held on Wednesday and Saturday each week. There's also a farmer's market once a month and, in the summer months, a gourmet and speciality food market on Thursdays, a flower and garden market on Fridays, and an antiques and collectors' market on Sundays.

River Great Ouse, Bedford

The town's oldest visible structure is **Castle Mound,** all that remains of a fortress built here shortly after the battle of Hastings but destroyed in 1224. A regeneration project is currently under way to provide landscaped gardens here.

The **Church of St Peter de Merton,** Saxon in origin, boasts a fine Norman south doorway that was not actually intended for this building but was brought here from the Church of St Peter in Dunstable. St Peter's is not Bedford's main church: this is **St Paul's Church** in the centre of St Paul's Square, a mainly 14th and 15th century building, with some interesting monuments and brasses and a stone pulpit from which John Wesley preached in 1758. Outside the church is a statue of one of the best-known sons of Bedford, John Howard, an 18th century nonconformist landowner who denounced the appalling conditions in jails and prison ships. His name lives on in the Howard League for Penal Reform.

Bedford's most famous son, Bunyan was born just south of the town, in Elstow, but lived – and was twice imprisoned – in Bedford in the 1660s and 1670s. The son of a tinsmith, Bunyan followed the same trade as his father and so was able to travel the countryside more than most people of that time. In the 1650s, Bunyan met John Gifford, the then pastor of the Independent Congregation which held its meetings at St John's Church. It was their lengthy discussions that led to Bunyan's conversion and he was baptised shortly afterwards by Gifford in a backwater that leads off the Great Ouse. In 1660 Bunyan was arrested for preaching without a licence. He was to spend 12 years in goal, time he put to good use by writing *Grace Abounding*, his spiritual autobiography. But it was during a second imprisonment, in 1676, that he began writing his most famous work, *The Pilgrim's Progress*. This inspired allegory of the way to salvation still entrances even non-believers with the beauty and simplicity of its language. Following his release from prison in 1672, Bunyan was elected pastor of the Independent Congregation. The church seen today was constructed in 1849 and the magnificent bronze doors, with illustrations from *Pilgrim's Progress*, were given to the church by the Duke of Bedford in 1676. Within the church is also the **Bunyan Museum**, which tells graphically the story of the man as well as the times through which he lived. Among the many displays are the jug in which his daughter Mary brought him soup whilst in prison, his chair, his tinker's anvil, and the violin and flute which he made in prison. Another tribute to Bunyan in the town is Bunyan's Statue, which was presented to the town in 1874 by the Duke of Bedford. Made of bronze, the statue is the work of Sir JE Boehm; around the pedestal of the 9ft figure, which weighs more than three tons, are three bronze panels depicting scenes from *Pilgrim's Progress*.

Beside the river and running through the heart of the town are the Bedford Embankment Gardens, which provide a year-round display of plants. Close by is also the **Priory Country Park**, an area of 206 acres with a diverse habitat, which represents the flood meadows, reed beds and woodland that once surrounded the town. In Park Road North, Hill Rise Wildlife Area is a site for nature conservation specialising in butterflies, amphibians and small mammals.

For an insight into the history of the town and surrounding area the **Bedford Museum** is well worth a visit. Among the many interesting displays is a piece of wall which shows the construction of the wattle walls that were an essential building technique in the 14th century.

Housed within the unlikely combination of

Cecil Higgins Art Gallery

Castle Lane, Bedford,
Bedfordshire MK40 3RP
Tel: 01234 211222 Fax: 01234 327149
website: www.cecilhigginsartgallery.org

The Cecil Higgins Art Gallery is situated in pleasant gardens leading down to the river embankment and is a recreation of an 1880s home, with superb examples of 19th century decorative arts. Room settings include items from the Handley-Read collection and the famous Gothic bedroom containing works by William Burges.

In an adjoining gallery are housed renowned collections of watercolours, prints and drawings (exhibitions changed regularly – ring for details), and there are also ceramics, glass and the Thomas Lester Lace Collection.

A self-service coffee bar is on hand for refreshments and the gallery shop sells a range of souvenirs. Tours can be arranged for groups if booked in advance and there is a programme of lunchtime lectures & demonstrations (call for details).

Open: Tues – Sat 11am – 5pm (last admission 4.45pm). Sun & BH Mon 2-5pm

Closed Mons, Good Fri, 25/26th Dec & 1st Jan

The Gallery can be found from J13 of the M1, in the centre of Bedford just off The Embankment – it is signposted. There are public car parks adjacent and the town centre is a short walking distance. Free Admission.

🏛 historic building 🏛 museum 🏛 historic site 🍃 scenic attraction 🌿 flora and fauna

a Victorian mansion and an adjoining modern gallery, the **Cecil Higgins Art Gallery** (see panel opposite) was started in 1949 by a wealthy Bedford brewery family. It contains an internationally renowned collection of watercolours, prints, and drawings as well as some fine glass, ceramics, and furniture. The gallery hosts several important exhibitions each year. The permanent display includes works by Turner, Gainsborough, Picasso and Matisse and a needle panel entitled 'Bunyan's Dream'. This was designed by Edward Bawden in 1977 to commemorate the tercentenary of the publication of *Pilgrim's Progress*, the 350th anniversary of John Bunyan's birth and the Queen's Silver Jubilee. Other contemporary work can be seen at the **Bedford Creative Arts Gallery** which showcases the visual arts, including film, photography and animation.

A building with more modern connections is the Corn Exchange in St Paul's Square, from where Colonel Glenn Miller frequently broadcast during World War II. A bust of the bandleader who gave the world *In the Mood* and *Moonlight Serenade* stands outside the Exchange, and in 1994 a plaque was unveiled on the 50th anniversary of his mysterious disappearance over the English Channel. East of Bedford, Clapham Twinwood Control Tower is the last place where Miller was seen alive. A small museum is open at weekends and Bank Holidays in the summer.

Around Bedford

ELSTOW
1 mile S of Bedford off the A6

🏛 Abbey Church

John Bunyan connections are everywhere in the picturesque village of Elstow. The cottage where he was born in 1628 no longer stands, but its site is marked by a stone erected in

Moot Hall, Elstow

📷 stories and anecdotes 🐦 famous people 🎨 art and craft 🖊 entertainment and sport 🚶 walks

Festival of Britain Year, 1951. The **Abbey Church of St Helena and St Mary** has two renowned stained glass windows, one depicting scenes from *Pilgrim's Progress*, the other scenes from the Holy War. Here, too, are the font where Bunyan was christened in 1628 and the Communion Table used when he attended service. Bunyan's mother, father and sister are buried in the churchyard. The church also tells the story of the ill-fated R101 airship (see under Cardington), and there's a handsome memorial in the churchyard.

Elstow's notable buildings include a charming row of Tudor cottages and **Moot Hall** which was built in the 15th century. It served as a place for hearing disputes and as a store for equipment for the village fair. Restored by Bedfordshire County Council, it

is now a museum depicting life in 17th century England with particular reference to Bunyan.

CARDINGTON
1 mile E of Bedford off the A603

🏛 Hangars

The Whitbread brewing family is closely connected with Cardington. The first Samuel Whitbread was born in the village in 1720, and it was another Whitbread, also Samuel, who restored the church and endowed the red-brick almshouses of 1787 overlooking the green.

But Cardington is best known for the two giant **Hangars** that dominate the skyline. Built in 1917 and 1927 to construct and

---

COTTAGE FARM NURSERIES

312 Cople Road, Cardington, Bedford,
Bedfordshire MK44 3GH
Tel/Fax: 01234 838383
e-mail: cfplants@aol.com
website: www.cottagefarmplants.co.uk

The Cooper family established **Cottage Farm Nurseries** in 1971 and continue to attract customers with their specialist supplies of plants and garden accessories. The owners and their helpful, friendly staff offer everything from a single plant or a simple hanging basket to a complete landscape advice and supply service for retail and wholesale, schools, sports centres, local authorities, hotels, pubs, restaurants and others.

The range of plants includes ornamental and fruit trees; an extensive range of shrubs and climbers; hardy exotics such as windmill palms, phormium and bamboo; hanging baskets made up by a fully trained florist (or customers can bring their own baskets and have them filled with plants of their choice); and a fantastic range of bedding plants including many unusual plants for spring and autumn sales. Eighty percent of the plants sold are grown on site. Among the garden accessories are terracotta and glazed pots from around the world, statues, bird baths and sundials. Opening hours are 9 to 5 Monday to Saturday, 10 to 4.30 on Sunday.

🏛 historic building   🏛 museum   🏛 historic site   ⌖ scenic attraction   🌱 flora and fauna

DENBY POTTERY AT TREE GARTH B&B

Church End, Ravensden, nr Bedford,
Bedfordshire MK44 2RP

Tree Garth Tel/Fax: 01234 771745
Denby Pottery Tel: 01234 772955

e-mail: treegarth@ukonline.co.uk
website: www.treegarth.co.uk

Tree Garth is a large detached house built in the 1960s, set in attractive wooded gardens. Owners Sue and Bruce Edwards, a warm and hospitable couple, offer guests a very quiet, comfortable stay in the three letting bedrooms – a double, a twin and a single – all with handbasins and sharing a bathroom with power shower. Home baking is one of Sue's many talents, and guests are treated to tea with her cakes on arrival.

The tariff includes an excellent English or Continental breakfast that also features the home baking. Children of 12 and over are welcome, with younger ages by arrangement. No pets; no smoking. Sue and Bruce are experts in **Denby Pottery** and offer a matching service for Denby users and collectors. The extensive stocks runs from the 1950s and includes discontinued lines; they also give lectures on the history of Denby pottery.

house the airships that were once thought to be the future of flying, they are best known as the birthplace of the R100 and the R101. The R101 first took off from Cardington in October 1929 with 52 people on board for a five-hour flight over the southeast. The passengers enjoyed a four-course lunch in the luxurious dining saloon and were amazed at the airship's quietness - they could hear the sounds of traffic and trains below. In July 1930 the R101 started her maiden flight across the Atlantic and tied up in Montreal after an uneventful flight of 77 hours. In October of that year the world's biggest airship left the hangars at Cardington for her first trip to India. Disaster struck not long into the journey when the R101 crashed into a hillside near Beauvais in France. Forty-four

people, including the Air Secretary Lord Thomson of Cardington, died in the crash, which was believed to have been caused at least in part by lashing rain that made the ship dip suddenly. The Church of St Mary contains memorials to both Samuel Whitbreads, and in the churchyard extension is the tomb of those who perished in the R101 disaster.

WILDEN

4 miles NE of Bedford off the A421

🦋 Butterfly Park

Bedford Butterfly Park has quickly become one of the county's leading family attractions. It stands in 10 acres of land untouched by modern farming practices and specially selected by its founder Andrew Green. Some

Stevington Holy Well

village is the **Post Mill**, the only one of the county's 12 remaining windmills that still retains its sails. Dating from the 1770s, the mill continued to operate commercially until 1936, having been rebuilt in 1921. Extensively restored in the 1950s, it is in full working order today. Though milling was an important part of village life here for many years, lace making too was a thriving industry and mat makers also settled here, taking advantage of the rushes growing on the banks of the nearby River Ouse.

BROMHAM
2 miles W of Bedford off A428

🏚 Bromham Mill

This quiet residential village has a splendid ancient bridge with no fewer than 26 arches. Close to the river is a watermill that dates back to the 17th century. Now fully restored and in working order, **Bromham Mill** is also home to displays of natural history, a gallery with regularly changing exhibitions of contemporary craftwork and fine art, and a tea room overlooking the river where, if you're lucky, you can watch kingfishers diving from the bank.

Charles I is known to have stayed at Bromham Hall, the home of Royalist Sir Lewis Dyve, who made his escape from the house during the Civil War by swimming the river.

60 varieties of wildflowers flourish here, an irresistible attraction for 60 species of butterfly. The Wondrous World exhibit displays the variety of life found in rain forests and other attractions include an adventure playground, tea room and gift shop.

STEVINGTON
4 miles NW of Bedford off A428

🏚 Post Mill

This is a typical English village with a church that was certainly here at the time of the Domesday survey, a village cross decorated with capitals and a large finial, and a **Holy Well** that attracted visitors in the Middle Ages. However, the most important building in the

HARROLD
7 miles NW of Bedford off the A428

🌿 Harrold-Odell Country Park

A typical country village with an old bridge and causeway, an octagonal market house and an old circular lock-up that was last used in the 19th century. Close by is the **Harrold-Odell Country Park**, which covers 144 acres of landscaped lakes, river banks and water meadows that are home to a wealth of plant, animal and bird life.

HINWICK
10 miles NW of Bedford off the A6

Built between 1709 and 1714, Hinwick House is a charming Queen Anne building that is still home to the descendants of the Orlebar family for whom it was constructed. Occasionally open to visitors, this delightful brownstone house with details picked out in lighter coloured stone has a particularly pleasing entrance hall and an interesting collection of furniture and paintings.

YIELDEN
10 miles N of Bedford off the A6

A village on the River Til, guarded by the earthworks of a long ruined castle. Mentioned in the Domesday Book, Yielden Castle, of which only an oblong motte, two large baileys and stone foundations can be seen, is reputed to have been built on the site of the battle between the Romans and the Iceni in which the warrior queen Boadicea (Boudicca) was killed. On one Christmas Day John Bunyan came to the village to preach in the church, as a result of which the incumbent vicar, William Bell, was removed from his post for allowing Bunyan this freedom.

LOCATOR MAP

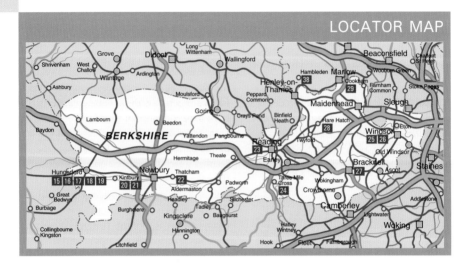

ADVERTISERS AND PLACES OF INTEREST

🏛 historic building   🏛 museum   🏛 historic site   ⌘ scenic attraction   🌱 flora and fauna

2| Berkshire

The county of Berkshire extends over some 485 square miles in the valley of the middle Thames and is divided into six main districts. The western area of the county is important for racing and the training of racehorses, with a top-class course at Newbury and the training centres of Lambourn and East Ilsley.

Another feature of West Berkshire is the number of communication routes that flow across the region linking London with the West Country, dominated today by the M4 motorway. The ancient Ridgeway Path, England's oldest road, follows the county border with Oxfordshire, and the Kennet and Avon Canal, completed in 1810, crosses southern England from Bristol to join the River Thames at Reading. Entering the county at Hungerford, this major waterway passes through a charming rural landscape as it winds through villages and market towns. The canal prospered until the arrival of the Great Western Railway in 1841, after which it inevitably declined; by the 1950s it was largely unnavigable. After a full clearing and restoration programme the canal can now once again be travelled its full length, providing a wide variety of leisure activities for thousands of visitors each year.

The central region of Berkshire is dominated by Reading, a thriving commuter town with excellent links to both London and the West Country. Though seeming to be very much a product of the last two centuries, it has a long and interesting history.

The Thames, forming the northern county border with Oxfordshire, has, especially along its southern banks, many delightful villages which became fashionable thanks to the Victorian and Edwardian passion for boating and remain fashionable to this day. The most important landmark in the east of the county is the 900-year-old Windsor Castle, one of three official residences of the Queen and a major tourist attraction.

Across Windsor Great Park, the remains of a royal hunting forest, lies Ascot racecourse, founded in 1711 by Queen Anne. Five days in June see the worlds of fashion and horseracing meet at the highest level at the Royal Ascot meeting, but the course stages many meetings throughout the year.

The Savill Gardens, Windsor Great Park

Lambourn

🏛 **Church of St Michael**   🏛 **Seven Barrows**

🖉 **Lambourn Trainers' Association**

Lying up on the Berkshire Downs, in the extreme west of the county, this village, which has the feel of a small town, is best known as a major centre for the training of racehorses. Over 1,200 horses are trained here, there are more than 100 miles of gallops, and the **Lambourn Trainers' Association** organises guided tours of the stables and trips to the gallops to view the horses going through their paces. Lambourn has been home to some of the greatest trainers in the history of the racing game, including Fred Winter and Fulke Walwyn over the jumps and Barry Hills and Peter Walwyn on the flat.

Lambourn's medieval **Church of St Michael** is one of the finest parish churches in Berkshire. Originally Norman and constructed on the cruciform plan, it has been greatly altered and extended, though the west end still has its Norman doorway, complete with zigzag ornamentation. The lychgate was dedicated to the memory of William Jousiffe, who brought horses from Newmarket to Lambourn in the 1870s and thus established a still-flourishing industry.

To the north of the village are **Lambourn Seven Barrows**, one of the most impressive Bronze Age burial sites in the country and actually comprising no fewer than 32 barrows.

Around Lambourn

EAST ILSLEY
10 miles E of Lambourn off the A34

This attractive downland village has managed to retain several interesting features and in particular the winding mechanism of the now long disused village well by the pond. It was because of sheep that the village chiefly prospered – from the early 1600s East Ilsley held fortnightly sheep fairs that were second only in size to Smithfield, London. At their peak in the 19th century, permanent pens were erected in the main street to contain the animals and, on one day, it was recorded that 80,000 sheep were penned. During the 19th century the station in the nearby village of **Compton** became an important centre for the passage of sheep to and from the great East Ilsley sheep market, but the decline in the sheep trade resulted in the closure of the station. About a mile south of Compton lie the remains of an Iron Age fort, Perborough Castle, while to the northeast, just above the Ridgeway, is

Lambourn Seven Barrows

🏛 historic building   📷 museum   🏛 historic site   💧 scenic attraction   🌱 flora and fauna

Lowbury Hill, where traces of a Roman temple and a Roman military outpost can be seen.

Today, along with its neighbour West Ilsley, the village is associated with racehorses which use the gallops on the downs as their training grounds.

Newbury

🏛 Church of St Nicholas   🛶 Kennet & Avon Canal

🏛 West Berkshire Museum   🛶 Racecourse

This crossroads town has, for many years, dominated the rural area of West Berkshire. Prospering during the Middle Ages, and afterwards, on the importance of the woollen industry, the town became famous as the Cloth Town. Among the various characters who made their money out of the weaving of the wool the best known is John Smallwood, always known as Jack of Newbury and the "richest clothier England ever beheld". Asked to raise two horsemen and two footmen for Henry VIII's campaign against the Scots, Jack raised 50 of each and led them himself. However, they only got as far as Stony Stratford in Buckinghamshire before news of the victory of Flodden reached them and they turned for home.

Evidence of the town's wealth can be seen in the splendid 'wool' **Church of St Nicholas**, which was constructed between 1500 and 1532. Built on the site of a Norman church, no expense was spared and Jack of Newbury gave the money for the magnificent five-bayed nave. The church has seen much restoration work, particularly during the Victorian age, but the fine pulpit and elaborately decorated nave roof have survived.

After the Civil War, the town's clothing industry declined. However, the 18th century saw the construction of turnpike roads and Newbury became a busy coaching stop on the road from London to Bath. The town further opened up to travellers and the needs of carriers with the completion of the **Kennet and Avon Canal** in 1810. Newbury Lock, built in 1796, was the first lock to be built along the canal and it is also the only one to have lever-operated ground paddles (the sluices that let in the water) which are known as 'Jack Cloughs'.

Back in the centre of the town, in the Market Square is the **West Berkshire Museum**, housed in two of the town's most historic buildings, the 17th century cloth hall and the adjacent 18th century granary, a store once used by traders travelling the canal. The history of the canal is explained, and other exhibits include crafts and industries, the two Battles of Newbury (1643 and 1644) during the Civil War, Greenham Common and local archaeology.

Those arriving in Newbury from the south will pass the Falkland Memorial, which has nothing to do with the 1980s conflict in the South Atlantic. It is in fact a memorial to Lord Falkland, who was killed at the first battle of Newbury. To the east of the town lies **Newbury Racecourse**, which stages top-quality flat and National Hunt racing throughout the year.

Around Newbury

HAMPSTEAD NORREYS
6 miles NE of Newbury on the B4009

🌱 Wyld Court Rainforest

Just to the north of the village lies **Wyld**

🎬 stories and anecdotes   🐦 famous people   🎨 art and craft   🛶 entertainment and sport   🚶 walks

Court Rainforest, an education and conservation charity devoted to the raising of awareness about the world's rain forests. Here, at the indoor rainforest, where the temperature never falls below 70°F, visitors can walk through the humid and shadowy jungles of the lowland tropical forests, the cool, orchid-festooned and ferny cloudforests, and the Amazon with its amazing flowers and wonderful bromeliads. There is also a unique collection of spectacular and rare plants, tranquil pools, the sounds of the tropics, and rainforest animals including a pair of Goeldi's monkeys, marmosets, tree frogs, iguanas, and Courtney the dwarf crocodile. Also on site are a shop selling plants and gifts, and a tea shop.

DONNINGTON
1 mile N of Newbury on the B4494

🏛 Castle

Donnington Castle

Despite being so close to the town of Newbury, Donnington has managed to retain its village identity and atmosphere. To the west of the village, and visible from the road, is Donnington Grove House. Built in 1759 and designed by the architect John Chute, this was the home, in the late 18th century, of the Brummell family; Beau Brummell, the instigator of the Bath Society, lived here as a child. However, most visitors to the village come to see **Donnington Castle** (English Heritage), a late-14th century defence that was built by Sir Richard Abberbury. Once a magnificent structure, only the twin-towered gatehouse survives amidst the impressive earthworks. The castle had its most eventful period during the Civil War when it was the scene of one of the longest sieges of the conflict. Charles I's troops were held here for 20 months and it was during this period that most of the castle was destroyed.

WINTERBOURNE
3 miles N of Newbury off the B4494

🌿 Snelsmore Common Country Park

Just south of the village lies **Snelsmore Common Country Park**, a heathland site surrounded by woodland. The common comprises several different habitats, including woodland, heathland and bog, and it supports a correspondingly wide variety of plant and animal life. It is a particularly important area for ground-nesting birds such as the nightjar and woodlark. The site has many footpaths and tracks and an area set aside for picnics.

WICKHAM
6 miles NW of Newbury on the B4000

🏛 Church of St Swithin

This ancient village with its typical Berkshire mix of brick and flint, thatch and tile is most

🏛 historic building   🏛 museum   🏛 historic site   🌣 scenic attraction   🌿 flora and fauna

notable for its **Church of St Swithin** that stands atop a hill with grand views across the Kennet valley. It has a Saxon tower – unique in the county – but it is the interior that is truly remarkable because of its elephants. Made of papier-mâché and gilded they were purchased at the Paris Exhibition of 1862 and intended for the rectory. They were too large however so they now appear to support the spectacular wooden roof of the church.

HUNGERFORD
9 miles W of Newbury on the A4

🏛 Bear Hotel 🏛 Tutti Day

Although not mentioned in the Domesday Book, by the Middle Ages this old market town was well established, and the manor of Hungerford had some distinguished lords including Simon de Montfort and John of Gaunt. Hungerford's heyday came in the 18th century when the turnpike road from London to Bath was built, passing through the town. By 1840, the town had eight coaching inns serving the needs of travellers and the prosperity continued with the opening of the Kennet and Avon Canal. The building of the railway took much of that trade away and the town reverted to its early, gentle lifestyle. However, several of the old coaching inns have survived, notably **The Bear Hotel**. Although it has an impressive Georgian frontage, the building actually dates back to 1494, making it one of the oldest buildings in the town. An event of great historical importance occurred in December 1688 when William of Orange arrived to stay at The Bear

THE TUTTI POLE
3 High Street, Hungerford,
Berkshire RG17 0DN
Tel: 01488 682515

August 2006 saw the 25th anniversary of **The Tutti Pole**, a delightful traditional tea shop and restaurant on Hungerford's High Street. The same family has owned and run the tea shop from the start, and their chef has been with them for 24 of the 25 years. Freshly prepared food is served throughout the day, from 9am to 5.30pm Monday to Friday and 9am to 6pm on Saturday and Sunday.

The oldest parts of the bow window fronted building date from the 15th century, and there's plenty of room here and in the more modern extension, as well as seats for 50 outside.

Owners and staff are warm and friendly, and a visit here is always a real pleasure. The unique name of The Tutti Pole refers to the annual ceremony of Hocktide, celebrated on the second Tuesday after Easter. Tutti Poles are still carried by the Tithingmen around the town on this day. Tutti means nosegay, the flowers which in this case are adorning a pole.

SUSAN PINK CO LTD

Unit 6, The Courtyard, off 24 High Street, Hungerford,
Berkshire RG17 0NF
Tel/Fax: 01488 684996
e-mail: emma@susanpink.co.uk

Whenever a really special occasion comes along, be it
Royal Ascot, Henley or a family celebration, a lady simply
must have a new outfit, so she probably goes to her
favourite clothes shop. But the clothes tell only half the
story, and to complete the ensemble the accessories are
every bit as important. And that's where **Susan Pink Co
Ltd** comes in. Emma Johnson, young, keen and dedicated
to providing the best for her clientele, runs this exclusive
boutique, where she welcomes customers of all ages. The
bulk of the stock concentrates on shoes and handbags:
leading brands of shoemakers include Baltarini, Victoria
Fox, Gabriella Castro and Pump & Circumstance, while
among the makers of handbags are Ripani and Kalivalson.

Susan Pink also stocks an exciting range of jewellery,
including pieces by local makers. The shop, in a handsome redbrick building in a pretty courtyard
that's full of character, is a delight to visit – light, airy, roomy and relaxing, with some
impressive old beams. The courtyard is set back from Hungerford's High Street, a five minute
walk from the railway station and a short drive from the A4 and M4.

THE CLOCKMAKER

Wessex Place, 127 High Street, Hungerford,
Berkshire RG17 0DL
Tel: 01488 682277
e-mail: theclockmaker@btconnect.com
website: www.clockmaker.info

In a Victorian brick building on Hungerford's High
Street, **The Clockmaker** is dedicated to the creation
and care of handcrafted clocks to the highest
standards of workmanship.

Founder and owner Chris Bessent started making
and repairing clocks as an apprentice in a Rolex
agency jewellers in Wiltshire, and he ran workshops
in various parts of the country before starting his
own business producing handmade clocks of the
highest quality, each one an individual work of art.

The Clockmaker also restores a range of clocks,
from simple mantel clocks to complex multi-
functioning mechanisms. Chris and his staff work
with master cabinetmakers, conservators of fine art
and decorative art specialists, ensuring that every
aspect of the work receives the closest attention.

🏠 historic building   🏛 museum   🏚 historic site   ⚜ scenic attraction   🌱 flora and fauna

ANNE'S B&B

59 Priory Avenue, Hungerford, Berkshire RG17 0AS
Tel: 01488 682290
e-mail: anne@hungerfordberks.co.uk
website: www.hungerfordberks.co.uk

Anne MacWilliam offers quiet, comfortable bed & breakfast accommodation in her spacious modern home. **Anne's B&B** comprises five rooms: one twin has en-suite facilities, while another twin, a double and two singles share two shower rooms. All the rooms have central heating, TV and tea/coffee facilities, and some rooms are on the ground floor – an advantage for less mobile guests. A full English breakfast is included in the tariff, and the house has off-road parking and a safe lock-up for bicycles. Guests' pets are welcome – Anne has two cats of her own.

to negotiate with the Commissioners of King James II concerning the future of the monarchy. The result was the Glorious Revolution of 1689, generally accepted as the beginning of true Parliamentary democracy as Willam and his wife Mary were invited to take the throne by a Protestant Parliament.

As well as still holding a weekly market, the town also continues the ancient tradition known as the Hocktide Festival or **Tutti Day** (tutti meaning a bunch of flowers). Held every year on the second Tuesday after Easter, the

CROWN NEEDLEWORK

115 High Street, Hungerford, Berkshire RG17 0LU
Tel: 01488 684011 Fax: 01488 686416

Crown Needlework is a specialist needlework shop located halfway along Hungerford's High Street, opposite the Town Hall and next to the Three Swans Inn.

The comprehensive thread stock includes full ranges of embroidery threads including Appletons, Paterna, Anchor, DMC, Madeira, Kreinik and Caron. Materials range from six count canvas to 36 count linen, and include Aida, Evenweave, Hardanger and Binca. All materials can be cut to customers' individual requirements. There is a large selection of printed canvases, charts, publications and kits for (amongst others) cross stitch, tapestry, trammed, bargello, hardanger, blackwork, and embroidery. Other items include magnifiers, simulated daylight lamps, frames and hoops, aperture cards, ribbons, braids, shisha mirrors, beads (including full Mill Hill range), bell pull ends, sewing baskets, boxes and organisers; plus many more too numerous to mention. It's definitely not a five-minute store - more an Aladdin's Cave.

The Bossom family and staff are very experienced in many aspects of embroidery and stitching, and are always willing to offer help and advice. Crown Needlework is open from 10am to 5pm Tuesday to Saturday (also by appointment Sunday and Monday). Postal service also available, most credit and debit cards accepted.

KENNET HOUSE

Kennet House, Kintbury, Berkshire RG17 9UT
Tel: 01488 608529
e-mail: amandaturner4@btinternet.com
website: www.berkshirebreaks.co.uk

Kennet House is an upmarket bed & breakfast establishment located in the heart of the village. The Grade II listed house is a handsome hydrangea-clad, tile-roofed brick building with lovely gardens and ample parking for guests' cars. The accommodation, all non-smoking, comprises a double room with a large bathroom, a twin with a shower room and a single. All three are bright, fresh and very comfortable, with little extras like bottled water, biscuits and fine toiletries. Breakfast, which can be served in the garden in the summer, includes porridge, croissants, an assortment of breads, pancakes, organic fruit yoghurts and scrambled farm eggs with smoked salmon.

festival was originally used as a means of collecting an early form of council tax. During the colourful event, two men carrying a six-foot pole decorated with ribbons and flowers go around each household collecting the tax.

To ease the burden of their visit, the men share a drink with the man of the house, give him an orange, and kiss his wife before collecting their penny payment. Today, however, though the visits are still made, no

BENCHMARK FURNITURE

BENCHMARK FURNITURE

Bath Road, Kintbury, nr Hungerford, Berkshire RG17 9SA
Tel: 01488 608020   Fax: 01488 608030
e-mail: info@benchmark-furniture.com
website: www.benchmark-furniture.com

Terence Conran and Sean Sutcliffe established Benchmark Furniture in 2004. It developed from Benchmark Woodworking, a design-led maker of bespoke furniture and joinery, which they founded 20 years ago. Benchmark's first workshop was in a converted stable building, making small quantities of furniture for commercial and retail customers; other buildings were converted into workshops as the business expanded, and it now employs over 45 craftsmen and designers and has an acclaimed apprentice training scheme.

The collection is exclusive to Benchmark Furniture with designs by well-known designers including Shin and Tomoko Azumi, Terence Conran, Russell Pinch and Thomas Heatherwick as well as Benchmark's in-house design team. Traditional quality and modern technology combine to produce a range of handmade contemporary furniture for the home all made in the workshops. It is sold direct to the public at workshop prices from an adjacent showroom and includes furniture for the dining room, sitting room, bedroom, home office and a number of outdoor pieces.

Visitors are welcome to tour the workshop and visit the showroom six days a week. Opening hours are 10am – 6pm Monday to Friday and 10am – 5pm on Saturdays. We are closed on public holidays.

🏛 historic building   🏛 museum   🏛 historic site   ⚘ scenic attraction   🌱 flora and fauna

money is collected but the kisses are still required.

Hungerford lies at the centre of the North Wessex Area of Outstanding Natural Beauty, designated as such in 1972. It stretches from the River Thames in the east to Devizes in the west, Wantage in the north and Andover in the south.

COMBE
7 miles SW of Newbury off the A338

🏃 Walbury Hill

The isolated hamlet of Combe is overlooked by **Walbury Hill**, which at 974 feet is the highest point in Berkshire and the highest chalk hill in England. A popular place for walking and hang-gliding, the hill offers terrific views and the bonus of an Iron Age fort on its summit. Close to the hill stands Combe Gibbet, one of the last public hanging places in the country. This gibbet was first

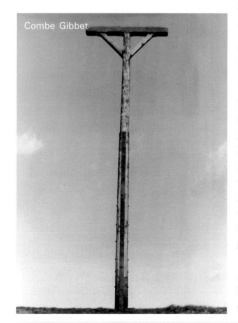
Combe Gibbet

used in 1676 to hang a pair of adulterous murderers, George Broomham and Dorothy Newman, and has a crossbar with a 'his' side and a 'hers' side.

GREENHAM
1½ miles SE of Newbury off the A34

🌿 Greenham Common and Crookham Common

Greenham Common and the adjacent **Crookham Common** make up the largest area of lowland heathland in Berkshire. In 1941 the common land was taken over by the Air Ministry and became an important military base, first for British squadrons and then for the US Air Force. In 1981 nuclear-armed Cruise missiles arrived at Greenham and the site became notorious for the anti-nuclear demonstrations. The airbase is gradually being returned to nature and the site is once again open to the public. Designated a Site of Special Scientific Interest (SSSI), it is home to many rare and endangered plants and animals.

THATCHAM
3 miles E of Newbury on the A4

🌿 Thatcham Moor

🌿 Thatcham Nature Discovery Centre

Believed to be the oldest village in Britain, it is hard to imagine that this now large suburb of Newbury was once a small place. **Thatcham Moor** is one of the largest areas of inland freshwater reed beds in the country and, as well as the reeds which can grow up to six feet in height, the area supports numerous species of marshland and aquatic plants. Birds also abound here and it is an important breeding ground for reed and sedge warblers.

Thatcham Nature Discovery Centre, situated close to the Thatcham Moors Local Nature Reserve, is a multi-activity based centre where visitors are encouraged to look,

Upper Woolhampton

Distance: *5.0 miles (8.0 kilometres)*

Typical time: *140 mins*

Height gain: *50 metres*

Map: *Explorer 159*

Walk: *www.walkingworld.com ID:683*

Contributor: *Liz and David Fishlock*

ACCESS INFORMATION:

From M4 (Junction 12) take A4 towards Theale/Newbury and stay on this road for about six miles until you reach Woolhampton, where you should turn right just after the Falmouth Arms into Woolhampton Hill. The walk starts from the main entrance to Elstree School which you will see on your right. Park considerately along this road.

DESCRIPTION:

An undemanding ramble through typical Berkshire countryside which takes the walker along quiet country lanes, through woodland and across open farmland. However, if you are in need of a short break, the Six Bells in the lovely village of Beenham is a little over halfway on this circular walk. The Elstree

School from where the walk starts was founded over 150 years ago and moved to its present location from Elstree in 1939. The Benedictine Douai Abbey which can be seen in the distance at various points of the walk has a car park and is open to the public.

FEATURES:

Pub, Play Area, Church, Birds, Flowers, Great Views, Butterflies, Food Shop, Woodland

WALK DIRECTIONS:

1 | Standing with your back to the lodge gate entrance of Elstree School, turn left along the road and after about 20 metres look out for and take signposted footpath on your right. The broad grassy track runs between fields and you will pass two ponds on your left. Go ahead over farm track to enter copse. Cross 2 stiles.

2 | After second stile turn sharp right in the direction of the footpath sign, now to keep to right-hand field perimeter. Carry on ahead, passing footpath sign, until you reach further footpath sign where you should turn right to enter woodland. Follow clear path through woodland until you reach crossing track.

3 | Turn right along broad track and shortly after bear right to enter field and then left, to follow left-hand field perimeter. At field corner turn right, still keeping field perimeter on your left. You will shortly be able to see Douai Abbey in the distance on your right. At field corner follow direction of footpath sign by turning left onto track to reach road.

4 | Turn right along road. Where road bends right, ignore footpath off to your left to carry on for a further 75 metres to stile on your left.

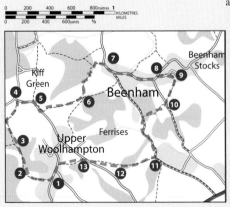

5|Cross stile into field and keep close to right-hand field perimeter, until you reach stile at field corner.. Cross and turn left along broad track to enter field with field boundary on your left. At field corner continue ahead (field boundary will now be on your right).

6|At junction of paths in field corner turn left, keeping field boundary on your right and follow path as it bears sharp right before woodland. Stay on this path as it skirts the edge of the wood with fields on your right. At edge of Greyfield Wood ignore path off to left to carry on ahead, passing substation on your left. Stay on gravel track to reach road.

7|Turn right along road which you will follow for almost 1km through the lovely village of Beenham, passing the Six Bells public house and the children's playground until you reach the primary school on your left.

8|Walk past the school, cross the main road and pick up the footpath on the other side along Stoneyfield (small residential development). Turn right into Church View. Carry on ahead through metal barriers and along road until about 25 metres before road junction.

9|Turn sharp right into Wickens Corner and where the drive goes off to the left, carry on ahead along enclosed path which first descends and then rises. Follow path, eventually to reach the road.

10|Turn left along road and then enter churchyard on opposite side through lychgate. Follow path to the left of the church to exit across stile in corner. Keep to right-hand field fence to cross further stile and enter woodland. Follow clear path through woodland which initially descends steeply. Leave woodland across stile and turn left along gravel track. Stay on this track for about 600 metres and where it climbs you should look out for a large wooden building on your left.

11|Immediately after the wooden building, turn sharp right to enter field. Initially walk between fences and then across open field making for left-hand edge of wood ahead. At field corner cross into next field, keeping edge of wood on your right. There are far-reaching views to your left across the Kennet Valley (and Aldermaston). In field corner cross stile to enter wood. After twenty metres or so, where path forks, take left fork (following direction of faint arrow on tree ahead). The winding path through this narrow strip of woodland is fairly clear. However, to assist, it should take you no more than a minute or so to follow the path through the wood and exit it on your right to arrive at the next waymark.

12|At wood edge go over crossing track (permitted bridleway) to go through V-stile and cross field, making for V-stile in left-hand field boundary. Cross into next field and bear diagonally right to cut off field corner and go through V-stile onto driveway. Go through two more V-stiles, maintaining same direction (going under power lines) to reach field corner and stile to road.

13|Turn right along road for about 25 metres and then take path on your left through trees to cross private driveway and enter playing fields through gap between wooden fence and holly bushes. Initially keep to left-hand side of playing fields until church spire comes into view and head towards it and gate into churchyard. Follow path through churchyard to main road. Turn left along road to return to start.

FLUTTERBY CRAFTS LTD

*Units 4-5 The Barns, Lower Hanwick Farm,
Turnpike Road, Thatcham, Berkshire RG18 3AP
Tel: 01635 860900 Fax: 01635 860130
e-mail: lynn@flutterbycrafts.co.uk
website: www.flutterbycrafts.co.uk*

Flutterby Crafts is a specialist supplier of quality goods to the discerning cardmaker and scrapbooker. Managing Director Lynn Courteney, who established the shop in 2004, turned a hobby and a passion into a thriving business, making it the leading papercraft specialist in the region. Awards include runner-up in Craft Retailer of the Year for the South of England. The shop is stocked with an amazing variety of materials, ideas and inspirations with a range of products to suit all needs.

Lynn and her helpful, friendly staff are experts in crafts and fully involved in the papercrafting business. It's something they all have a passion for, and like many practitioners they find it both practical and relaxing. Customer satisfaction is further guaranteed by the knowledge that all the items on sale and tried and tested. The shop also holds demonstrations and courses in papercraft secrets for the young and the not so young, beginners and more experienced, catering for up to 12 or 14 participants at a time. Flutterby Crafts is located in a converted granary building between Thatcham and Newbury, easily reached from the A4 and M4.

listen, touch and learn through an exciting range of interactive exhibits. In Discovery Hall they can find out what lives beneath the lake, get a birds-eye view of the world, or watch the wildlife from the comfort of the lakeside observation area.

WOOLHAMPTON

6 miles E of Newbury on the A4

This tranquil village on the banks of the Kennet and Avon Canal had a watermill at the time of the Domesday Survey of 1086 and was mentioned again in 1351, when the manor and mill were owned by the Knights Hospitallers. The present mill, built in 1820 and extended in 1875, was powered by a brook which runs into the Kennet and was last used in 1930. It has since been turned into offices.

BEENHAM

7 miles E of Newbury off the A4

🐾 UK Wolf Conservation Trust

Set in 6,000 acres of beautiful woodlands, the **UK Wolf Conservation Trust** proves that wolves are not the big, bad, dangerous animals of nursery rhymes and legend. There are wolves here you can actually stroke and which are taken to schools, shows and seminars. The European wolves are the first to be successfully bred in England for 500 years and the Trust also cares for packs of North American wolves. The site is open all year round, by appointment.

🏛 historic building 🖼 museum 🏛 historic site 💠 scenic attraction 🐾 flora and fauna

Reading

🏛 Abbey   🏛 Gaol   🏛 Museum

🏛 Museum of English Rural Life

This thriving commuter town, which took its name from the Saxon chief Reada, is a delightful combination of over a 1,000 years of history and a vibrant and modern city. There are Victorian brick buildings nestling beside beautiful medieval churches, famous coaching inns opposite high tech offices and some of the best shopping in the area. However, Reading began as a Saxon settlement between the Rivers Thames and Kennet and as a defensible was used by the Danes as a base for their attack on Wessex in the 9th century. The town grew up around its **Abbey**, which was founded in 1121 by Henry I, the youngest son of William the Conqueror, and it was consecrated by Thomas à Becket in 1164. The abbey went on to become one of the most important religious houses – its relics included a piece of Jesus' sandal, the tooth of St Luke, and a slice of Moses' rod. Henry, its great benefactor, was buried in front of the High Altar in 1136.

The atmospheric abbey ruins stand in

Forbury Gardens on the banks of the River Kennet; these gardens are also home to the Maiwand Lion, a magnificent statue of a lion which commemorates the men of the Berkshire Regiment who died in the Afghan War of 1879.

Reading boasts several other pieces of distinguished public art, including the Robed Figure by Dame Elizabeth Frink and the Soane Obelisk designed by Sir John Soane, architect of the Bank of England. Adjacent to the abbey ruins is another of Reading's famous buildings – **Reading Gaol** where Oscar Wilde was imprisoned and where he wrote *De Profundis*. His confinement here also inspired the writer to compose the epic *Ballad of Reading Gaol* whilst staying in Paris in 1898.

Though the town developed during the Middle Ages as a result of a flourishing woollen industry, it was during the 18th century with the coming of both the turnpike roads and the opening of the Kennet and Avon Canal that saw the town boom. By the 19th century, Reading was known for its three Bs: beer, bulbs, and biscuits. As the trade of the canal and River Thames increased, the movement of corn and malt explains the growth of the brewing trade, and the leaders in the bulb trade were Sutton Seeds, founded here in 1806 but now just a memory. The world renowned biscuit-making firm of Huntley & Palmer began life here in 1826, when Joseph Huntley founded the firm, to be joined, in 1841, by George Palmer, inventor of the stamping machine.

The Story of Reading, a permanent exhibition at the **Museum of Reading**, is the

Abbey Ruins, Reading

🎬 stories and anecdotes   🐦 famous people   🎨 art and craft   🖋 entertainment and sport   🚶 walks

ideal place to gain a full understanding of the history of the town, from the earliest times to the present day. Here, too, can be seen the world's only full size replica of the Bayeux Tapestry, made in the 19th century and featuring Edward the Confessor, once Lord of the Royal Manor in Reading, as a central figure. As a contrast to the museum's displays depicting the life of the town in the 20th century, The Silchester Gallery is devoted to the describing day to day life at Calleva Atrebatum, the Roman town of Silchester,

using Roman artefacts unearthed there during early excavations. This museum, one of the most go-ahead in the country, has special events and changing exhibitions throughout the year, so every visit will reveal something new and exciting to see.

Situated on the banks of the River Kennet, the former turbine house shows a little of the river in Reading. The buildings themselves are also of interest and are superb examples of Victorian industrial architecture combined with decorative Reading brickwork.

The Rural History Centre

University of Reading, Whiteknights, PO Box 229, Reading RG6 6AG
Tel: 0118 931 8660 Fax: 0118 975 1264
e-mail: rhc@reading.ac.uk
website: www.ruralhistory.org

The Rural History Centre at the University of Reading is the English national centre for the history of food, farming and the countryside. With artefact, library and archive collections of international importance, the Centre tells the story of farming and the countryside in England over the past 300 years.

Discover an amazing range of country crafts, find out about Victorian farmhouse kitchens and explore England's largest collection of vintage ploughs, wagons and machinery, including a steam-powered threshing machine. There are captivating displays for visitors of all ages, as well as quizzes and trails for children and families plus an interactive computer area.

The Object Collections is one of the country's finest collections of objects related to daily life and work in the countryside. The Library has over 50,000 books and periodicals. The Archive includes the business records of major agricultural engineering firms, archives of national countryside organisations and a large collection of individual farm records. The Archive of Photographs and Illustrations has over 750,000 images of farming and rural life.

Gallery opening times: Tuesday – Saturday, 10am – 1pm and 2pm – 4.30pm. Admission to Museum: £1 (OAPs 75p, children free). The reference collections are open Monday – Friday 9.30am – 4.45pm. Both are closed Bank Holidays, Easter Weekend and from Christmas to New Year. Visitors wishing to consult the reference collection are asked to make an appointment in advance.

🏚 historic building   🏛 museum   🏛 historic site   🏞 scenic attraction   🌱 flora and fauna

In 1925 Reading Extension College became a university in its own right. Lying to the south of the town centre in Redlands Road, the **Museum of English Rural Life** (see panel opposite) is the national centre for the history of food, farming and the countryside. The centre has one of the country's finest collections of artefacts relating to daily life and work in the countryside, an extensive library and archives and over 750,000 photographic images of rural life.

Around Reading

SONNING
3 miles NE of Reading off the A4

This pretty little village leading down to the Thames is a popular spot to visit, especially on summer weekends. In 1399, after he had been deposed, Richard II brought his young bride Isabella here to be looked after in the palace of the Bishops of Salisbury. Her ghost is said to appear on the paths beside the

river. On Grove Street stands Turpin's, a house which belonged to the aunt of Dick Turpin and provided occasional refuge for the notorious highwayman. Behind the wall of the old bishop's palace is Deanery Gardens, a house built in 1901 to the design of Sir Edwin Lutyens.

WOODLEY
3 miles E of Reading off the A329

🏛 Museum of Berkshire Aviation

At Woodley Airfield the **Museum of Berkshire Aviation** celebrates the contribution the county has made to the history of aviation. The exhibits include Spitfires and reconstructed Miles & Handley Page aircraft which are shown along with fascinating pictorial records and archives.

HURST
4½ miles E of Reading off the A321

🌳 Dinton Pastures Country Park

This attractive, scattered village is home to a Norman church, well endowed with monuments, and a row of fine 17th century almshouses. The village bowling green is said to have been made for Charles II.

Just to the south lies **Dinton Pastures Country Park**, a large area of lakes, rivers, hedgerows and meadows rich in wildlife. Until the 1970s, this area was excavated for sand and gravel, but the former pits are now attractive lakes and ponds; one of them has been stocked for coarse fishing and the largest is set aside for canoeing and windsurfing.

Sonning

🗟 stories and anecdotes   🐦 famous people   🎨 art and craft   🎭 entertainment and sport   🚶 walks

THE SWAN

Three Mile Cross, Nr Reading,
Berkshire RG7 1AT
Tel: 0118 988 3674

On the A33 three miles south of Reading and just seconds from Exit 11 of the M4, the **Swan** has established itself as one of the very best pubs in the whole region. It stands near the Madejski Stadium, and if Reading football team has proved itself in a different class from its rivals, the same can be said of the Swan in the competitive pub league. Its success is the reward for the hard work and dedication shown by owners Vic and Jenny Harrison, who have been at the helm for almost a quarter of a century. Their regular customers come from many miles around, and they are making new friends all the time.

The attractions of the Swan begin outside with the wonderful flower displays that have won many awards, including Best in Show Wokingham District Council Colour & Cheer 2005 and Best Pub Frontage 2004 and 2006. There are seats inside for 50, and outside for almost as many on a partly covered sun patio. Up to half a dozen real ales are available at any one time, with Young's Bitter, Wadworths 6X, London Pride and Bass all regularly featuring, and they serve food at the Swan every lunchtime and every evening. The menu sticks mainly to tried-and-tested favourites, and it's a formula that definitely works, as mealtimes are so busy that booking is always best to be sure of a table.

The Swan started life in the early 17th century as three timber-framed workers' cottages; 50 years on two of them became an ale house called the Globe Inn and in 1760 the premises were sold for £24 10s and acquired a new name, the Three Sugar Loaves. It became a well-known changing station for horses on the London-Portsmouth staging route. From Globe to Loaves to Swan, it's more popular than ever, and is a meeting place for several clubs and societies as well as a favourite destination for lovers of real ale and real food. Apart from the owners, it has another distinguished resident in Jumbo, the famous Irish wolfhound who is the official mascot of the London Irish Rugby Football Club. He has been seen at the head of many processions up and down the land, including the Mayor of London's Annual St Patrick's Day Parade.

🏤 historic building 🏛 museum 🏛 historic site 🔾 scenic attraction 🐦 flora and fauna

WOKINGHAM
6 miles SE of Reading on the A329

This largely residential town has, at its centre, an old triangular market place with a matching triangular Town Hall built in 1860. In the mainly Victorian town centre is a sprinkling of attractive Georgian houses and shops, and the medieval parish church of All Saints. The most attractive building however is Lucas Hospital, built of mellow red brick and rather like a miniature Chelsea Hospital. It was originally built in 1666 as almshouses and a chapel, by Henry Lucas, a mathematician and MP for Cambridge University. Today, the hospital still cares for the elderly though now in the style of a retirement home. It can be visited by appointment with the resident matron.

ARBORFIELD
4 miles S of Reading on the A327

🌱 California Country Park

Arborfield Garrison is the home base of REME, the Royal Electrical and Mechanical Engineers, and the site of their museum. To the south is **California Country Park**, a wooded beauty spot where the woods support 34 different species of tree and the bogland provides a range of habitats for the many animals, birds and plants that are found here.

SWALLOWFIELD
5 miles S of Reading off the A33

🏛 Swallowfield Park

The manor house here, **Swallowfield Park**, has been associated with both royalty and other notables. The present house (unfortunately now a shell) was built in 1678 by Wren's assistant William Talman for the 2nd Earl of Clarendon, who acquired the estate upon marrying the heiress. In 1719,

the park was purchased by Thomas Pitt, a former Governor of Madras, who used the proceeds of the sale of a large diamond he bought while in India. The diamond can now be seen in the Louvre Museum, Paris. The story of Pitt and his diamond provided the inspiration for the novel, *The Moonstone*, by Wilkie Collins, who visited the house in 1860. The Italian Doorway, by Talman, is probably the house's most outstanding remaining feature and it marks the entrance to the walled garden. Here can be found a dog's graveyard where lies one of Charles Dickens' dogs. The novelist had bequeathed the pet to his friend and owner of the house, Sir Charles Russell.

FINCHAMPSTEAD
8 miles S of Reading off the A327

🚶 Finchampstead Ridges

To the east of the village lie **Finchampstead Ridges**, a popular spot for walkers that offers wonderful views across the Blackwater Valley. Simon's Wood has a varied mixture of conifers and broad-leaved trees, and in the wood and on the heath are siskin and flycatchers, dragonflies, damselflies and a wide range of invertebrates and lichens.

ALDERMASTON
9 miles SW of Reading on the A340

🏛 St Mary's Church 🚶 Aldermaston Wharf

🌿 Kennet & Avon Canal Visitor Centre

It was in this tranquil village, in 1840, that the William pear was first propagated by John Staid, the then village schoolmaster. First known as the Aldermaston pear, a cutting of the plant is believed to have been taken to Australia where is it now called the Bartlett pear.

🎭 stories and anecdotes   🐦 famous people   🎨 art and craft   🌿 entertainment and sport   🚶 walks

Still retaining much of its original 12th century structure and with a splendid Norman door, the lovely **St Mary's Church** provides the setting for the York Mystery Cycle, nativity plays dating from the 14th century, which are performed here each year. Using beautiful period costumes and contemporary music, including a piece written by William Byrd, the cycle lasts a week and the plays attract visitors from far and wide. Another old custom still continued in the village is the auctioning of the grazing rights of Church Acres every three years. Using the ancient method of a candle auction, a pin, in this case a horseshoe nail, is inserted into the tallow of a candle one inch from the wick. The candle is lit while bidding takes place and the grazing rights go to the highest bidder as the pin drops out of the candle.

Outside under a yew tree in the churchyard lies the grave of Maria Hale, formerly known as the Aldermaston witch. She was said to turn herself into a large brown hare and although the hare was never caught or killed, at one time a local keeper wounded it in the leg and from then on it was observed that Maria Hale had become lame.

Close to the village is a delightful walk along the Kennet & Avon Canal to **Aldermaston Wharf**. A Grade II-listed structure of beautifully restored 18th century scalloped brickwork, the wharf houses the **Aldermaston Visitor Centre**, where the canalman's cottage contains an exhibition on the canal and information on its leisure facilities.

PANGBOURNE
6 miles NW of Reading on the A417

🐦 Church Cottage   📺 Whitchurch Lock

Situated at the confluence of the River Pang and the River Thames, the town grew up in the late 19th and early 20th centuries as a fashionable place to live. As a result there are several attractive Victorian and Edwardian villas to be seen including a row of ornate Victorian houses known as the Seven Deadly Sins. It was here that the author Kenneth Grahame retired, living at **Church Cottage** opposite the church. Grahame married late in life and it was whilst living here that he wrote for his son *The Wind in the Willows*.

Visitors to the town who cross the elegant iron bridge to neighbouring **Whitchurch** must still pay a toll, though now very small. The right to exact the toll has existed since 1792 and it is one of the very few surviving privately owned toll bridges. It was at **Whitchurch Lock** that the characters in Jerome K Jerome's *Three Men in a Boat* abandoned their craft, after a series of mishaps, and returned to London.

BASILDON
8 miles NW of Reading on the A417

🏛 Basildon Park   🐦 Beale Park

This small village is the last resting place of the inventor and agricultural engineer, Jethro Tull, and his grave can be seen in the churchyard. Outside the churchyard is a classic pavilion built in memory of his parents by the late Mr Childe-Beale which is, today, the focal point of **Beale Park**. Covering some 300 acres of ancient water meadow, the park is home to a wide range of birds and animals. There are small herds of unusual farm animals, including rare breeds of sheep and goats, Highland cattle, deer, and South American llama, more than 120 species of birds living in their natural habitat, and a pets' corner for smaller children. However, the park's work is not confined to the keeping of animals. As well as planting a Community Woodland, an ancient reed bed has been restored. The park's other main attraction housed in the pavilion is the Model Boat Collection, which is one of the finest of its kind.

However, the village's main feature is **Basildon Park** (National Trust), an elegant, classical house designed in the 18th century by Carr of York and undoubtedly Berkshire's foremost mansion. Built between 1776 and 1783 for Francis Sykes, an official of the East India Company, the house has the unusual addition of an Anglo-Indian room. The interior, finished by JB Papworth and restored to its original splendour after World War II, is rich in fine plaster work, pictures, and furniture and the rooms open to the public include the Octagon Room and a decorative Shell Room. If the name Basildon seems familiar it is probably as a result of the notepaper: the head of the papermaking firm of Dickinson visited the house and decided to use the name for the high quality paper.

ALDWORTH
11 miles NW of Reading on the B4009

🏛 Aldworth Giants

The parish Church of St Mary is famous for housing the **Aldworth Giants** - the larger

than life effigies of the de la Beche family which date back to the 14th century. The head of the family, Sir Philip, who lies here with eight other members of his family, was the Sheriff of Berkshire and valet to Edward II. Though now somewhat defaced the effigies were so legendary that the church was visited by Elizabeth I. Outside, in the churchyard, are the remains of a once magnificent 1,000-year-old yew tree that was sadly damaged in a storm.

Nearby, at **Little Aldworth**, the grave of the poet Laurence Binyon, who wrote the famous lines '*At the going down of the sun and in the morning, we shall remember them*' can be seen in the churchyard. Opposite the Bell Inn is one of the deepest wells in the country. Topped by great beams, heavy cogs, and wheels, it is some 327 feet deep.

Windsor

🏛 Castle 🏛 Guildhall 🏛 St George's Chapel
🏛 Frogmore House 🌿 Savil's Garden
🎭 Racecourse 🎭 Smith's Lawn 🎭 Legoland
🚶 Windsor Great Park 🚶 Long Walk

This old town grew up beneath the walls of the castle in a compact group of streets leading from the main entrance. Charming and full of character, this is a place of delightful timber-framed and Georgian houses and shop fronts, with riverside walks beside the Thames, and a wonderful racecourse. The elegant **Guildhall**, partly built by Wren in the 17th century, has an open ground floor for market stalls, while the council chambers are

Windsor

🎭 stories and anecdotes   🐦 famous people   🎨 art and craft   🎭 entertainment and sport   🚶 walks

on the first floor. Concerned that they might fall through the floor onto the stalls below, the council members requested that Wren put in supporting pillars in the middle of the market hall. As his reassurances that the building was sound fell on deaf ears, Wren complied with their wishes but the pillars he built did not quite meet the ceiling - thereby proving his point!

The grand central station, in the heart of the town, was rebuilt in 1897 to commemorate Queen Victoria's Diamond Jubilee.

In a pleasant setting close to the River Thames, **Royal Windsor Racecourse** is one of the most attractive in the country. Though less grand than neighbouring Ascot, its Monday evening meetings always bring a good crowd, but many regret the decision to give up the jumping fixtures.

The greatest attraction hereabouts is of course **Windsor Castle**, one of three official residences of the Queen (the others are Buckingham Palace and Holyrood House in Edinburgh). The largest castle in the country and a royal residence for over 900 years, it was begun in the late 11th century by William the Conqueror as one in a chain of such defences which stood on the approaches to London. Over the years its role changed from a fortification to a royal palace; various monarchs added to the original typical Norman castle, the most notable additions being made by Henry VIII, Charles II and George IV. Various parts of the castle are open to the public, in particular the state apartments with their remarkable collection of furniture, porcelain and armour. Carvings

COCOA BEAN

20 St Leonard's Road, Windsor, Berkshire SL4 3BU
Tel: 01753 831 500
e-mail: info@cocoabeanuk.com website: www.cocoa-bean.co.uk
Open seven days a week.

Located near the bottom end of Windsor's historic High Street, **Cocoa Bean** brings a beautiful and stylish range of gifts and home accessories to the Royal borough. Founded by Sarah Lock in 2004, the name Cocoa Bean was inspired by her family who used to make cocoa for chocolate in the old family plantation house in St. Lucia.

Over the years Sarah's keen sense of style and knack for collecting unique items led to the creation of a range which can only be described as eclectic . The shop, which is situated in a restored 19th century building, is an inspiration to anyone who walks through the doors. Everything from French roof tile candle sconces and handmade children's toys to luxury tableware from Copenhagen and gifts for gardener's can be found throughout the seasons. There is an indulgent variety of bath accessories, exqusite local pottery and almost everything in the shop is for sale including the hand carved display tables and light fixtures.

Sarah's discerning taste for quality was recognised by the trade when the shop was nominated for Best Independent Gift Retailer in the South in 2006. This achievement is echoed by the regular coverage in local and national press including being featured on *Country Living's* Emporium page.

🏠 historic building   🏛 museum   🏛 historic site   🍃 scenic attraction   🌿 flora and fauna

by Grinling Gibbons are to be seen everywhere and the walls are adorned with a plethora of masterpieces, including paintings by Van Dyck and Rembrandt. The Gallery shows changing displays from the Royal Library, including works by Leonardo, Michelangelo and Holbein. On a somewhat smaller scale, but nonetheless impressive, is Queen Mary's Dolls' House. Designed by Sir Edwin Lutyens for Queen Mary, this is a perfect miniature palace, complete with working lifts and lights and running water. Built on a 1 to 12 scale, it took three years to complete, and 1,500 craftsmen were employed to ensure that every last detail was correct; the house was presented to the queen in 1924.

In November 1992, a massive fire swept through the northeast corner of the castle and no-one in the country at the time will forget the incredible pictures of the great tower alight. Following five years of restoration, the damaged areas were re-opened to the public.

Within the castle walls is the magnificent **St George's Chapel**. Started by Edward IV in 1478, and taking some 50 years to finish, the chapel is not only one of the country's greatest religious buildings but also a wonderful example of the Perpendicular Gothic style. It is the last resting place of 10 monarchs, from Edward IV himself to Henry VIII with his favourite wife Jane Seymour, Charles I, George V with Queen Mary, and George VI, beside whom the ashes of his beloved daughter Princess Margaret were laid in February 2002. It is also the Chapel of the Most Noble Order of the Garter, Britain's highest order of chivalry.

Frogmore House (see panel below), a modest early-18th century manor house in Home Park, has over the years acted as a second, more relaxed royal residence than the nearby castle. It was bought in 1792 for Queen Charlotte, consort of George III, and later became a favourite retreat of Queen Victoria, who remarked that "all is peace and quiet and you only hear the hum of the bees, the singing of the birds". She and Prince Albert built a mausoleum in the grounds to house the remains of the Queen's mother, the Duchess of Kent, and their own - both Victoria and Albert are at rest here. The former library now contains furniture and paintings from the Royal Yacht *Britannia*. The house is surrounded by 30 acres of picturesque gardens containing masses of spring bulbs and some fine specimen trees.

To the south of the town lies the 4,800-acre **Windsor Great Park**, a remnant of the once

Frogmore House

Home Park, Windsor Castle, Windsor, Berkshire
Tel: 020 7766 7305
e-mail: information@royalcollection.org.uk
website: www.royalcollection.org.uk

Frogmore House has been a royal retreat since the 18th century and is today used by the Royal Family for private entertaining. It is especially linked with Queen Charlotte, the wife of George III, and her daughters, whose love of botany and art is reflected throughout the house. Many works by other royal artists are on display at Frogmore. Queen Victoria loved Frogmore so much that she broke with royal tradition and chose to build a mausoleum for herself and Prince Albert there.

🎭 stories and anecdotes   🐦 famous people   🎨 art and craft   🎭 entertainment and sport   🚶 walks

extensive Royal Hunting Forest, and a unique area of open parkland, woodland, and impressive views. Within the park, at Englefield Green, is the **Savill Garden**, created by Sir Eric Savill when he was Deputy Ranger and one of the finest woodland gardens to be seen anywhere. A garden for all seasons, its attractions include colourful flower beds, secret glades, alpine meadows and a unique temperate house. The **Long Walk** stretches from the Castle to Snow Hill, some three miles away, on top of which stands a huge bronze of George III on horseback erected there in 1831. The three-mile ride to nearby Ascot racecourse was created by Queen Anne in the early 1700s. On the park's southern side lies **Smith's Lawn**, where polo matches are played most summer weekends. Windsor Great Park is also the setting for the Cartier International competition, polo's highlight event held every July, and the National Carriage Driving Championships.

To the southwest, set in 150 acres of parkland, is **Legoland Windsor**, where a whole range of amazing Lego models is on display, made from over 20 million bricks. Designed for children aged two to 12 – and their families – the site also offers more than 50 rides, shows and attractions including the Jungle Coaster with twists and turns at 60km.

Around Windsor

ASCOT
6 miles SW of Windsor on the A329

  🐎 Racecourse　🌱 Englemere Pond

A small village until 1711 when Queen Anne moved the Windsor race meeting to here and founded the world famous **Ascot Racecourse**. Its future was secured when the Duke of

Cumberland established a stud at Windsor in the 1750s, and by the end of the century the meetings were being attended by royalty on a regular basis. Today, Royal Ascot, held every June, is an international occasion of fashion and style with pageantry and tradition and the very best flat racing spread over five days. To the west of the town lies **Englemere Pond**, a Site of Special Scientific Interest and also a local nature reserve. Once part of the royal hunting ground which surrounded Windsor Castle and still owned by the Crown Estate, the main feature is the shallow acidic lake which offers a wide range of habitats from open water to marsh, for the many species of plants, birds, and animals, and insects found here.

BRACKNELL
7 miles SW of Windsor on the A329

  🌳 Windsor Forest　🌳 Lookout Discovery Park

Designated a new town in 1948, Bracknell has developed quickly from a small village in poor sandy heathland, with some 3,000 inhabitants, into a large modern town of around 60,000 residents. It boasts one of the first purpose built shopping centres in the country - opened in the 1960s. As well as being home to a number of high tech companies, Bracknell is also the home of the Meteorological Office.

Seen from many parts of the town and a very prominent landmark is the centrally located Bill Hill. At the top of the hill can be seen a circular mound of earth, hollowed out at the centre, which is all that remains of a Bronze Age round barrow. Used throughout that period, these burial mounds, which may cover either individuals or groups, are the most common prehistoric monuments in the country.

What remains of the great royal hunting ground, **Windsor Forest** (also called

Look Out Discovery Centre

Nine Mile Ride, Bracknell, Berkshire RG12 7QW
Tel: 01344 354400 Fax: 01344 354422
e-mail: thelookout@bracknell-forest.gov.uk
website: www.bracknell-forest.gov.uk/lookout

The Look Out Discovery Centre in Bracknell is a great day out for all ages. The main attraction is an exciting hands on, interactive science and nature exhibition. Budding scientists will spend many hours exploring and discovering over 70 bright, fun-filled exhibits within five themed zones.

In the exhibition there is The Look Out tower. Climb the 88 steps and see over the Centre towards Bracknell and beyond. In the surrounding 2,600 acres of Crown Estate woodland, visitors can enjoy nature walks, a picnic area, child's play area. In the Coffee Shop you can relax over a cup of tea or take a break and have a hot lunch. The Gift Shop offers a wonderful range of gifts for every occasion or weird and wacky presents, ideal for birthday party bags at the right price. The Look Out is open daily from 10am - 5pm.

Bracknell Forest) lies to the south of the town and has over 30 parks and nature reserves and some 45 miles of footpaths and bridleways. Of particular interest in the area is the **Look Out Discovery Park** (see panel above), an interactive science centre that brings to life the mysteries of both science and nature. In the surrounding 2,600 acres of Crown Estate woodland there are nature trails and walks to points of interest as well as the inappropriately named Caesar's Camp. Not a Roman fort, this camp is an Iron Age hill fort built over 2,000 years ago but, close by, lies the Roman link road between London and Silchester. Known locally as the Devil's Highway, it is said to have acquired the name because the local inhabitants thought that only the Devil could have undertaken such a prodigious feat of engineering.

TWYFORD
10 miles W of Windsor on the A4

At Twyford, the River Loddon divides into two separate streams from which the town takes its name – 'double ford'. With its watery location it's not surprising that there have been several mills here. A miller is mentioned in a document of 1163 although the first mill is dated 1363. There was a silk mill here until 1845 and a flour mill until 1976 when it was destroyed by fire. The replacement modern mill lacks the traditional appeal but it does continue the milling tradition in the town.

BINFIELD
8 miles SW of Windsor on the B3034

🐿 Pope's Wood

Binfield is famous as the boyhood home of the poet Alexander Pope. The family moved here after his father had amassed a fortune as a linen draper, and the boy Pope sang in the local choir and gained a local following for his poems about the Windsor Forest and the River Loddon. To the south of the village lies **Pope's Wood**, where the poet is said to have sought inspiration. Other connections include the artist John Constable, who sketched the parish church while here on his honeymoon, and Norah Wilmot, who was one of the first lady racehorse trainers to be allowed to hold a

---

🎬 stories and anecdotes   🐿 famous people   ✍ art and craft   🎭 entertainment and sport   🚶 walks

SHEEPLANDS FARM SHOP

Wyevale Garden Centre, Bath Road, Hare Hatch,
Twyford, Berkshire RG10 9SW
Tel: 0118 940 4399
website: www.sheeplandsfarmshop.co.uk

A cow and her calf graze the forecourt of **Sheeplands Farm Shop** – actually they are models advertising the fresh milk available inside, just one element in an extraordinary range of top-quality produce. Owner Andrew Cardy draws on more than 100 suppliers to stock the 3,000 square feet of space in the shop. Sheeplands was established by Andrew's family 1981. Cheese-lovers will find a choice of more than 80 English and Continental varieties, and there's more Continental flavour in the popular patisserie with its croissants, pains au chocolat, pains aux raisins and other sweet treats. There are frozen fruits, vegetables and bakery items, and the Cooks range of ready meals in 1, 2 or 4-portion sizes.

Sheeplands also offers an extensive selection of free-range and organic meats (frozen), vegetarian, diabetic or gluten-free produce and tasty Thai, Chinese and Indian food. Bring your own fish here and they'll smoke it for you. The baguette bar offers a huge variety of fillings in baguettes freshly baked in store. They also specialise in seasonal produce for Easter, Hallowe'en and Christmas, including speciality free-range Bronze turkeys.

licence in her own name, having been forced to train for years in the name of her head lad. The Jockey Club abandoned this archaic ruling as recently as 1966.

WARGRAVE
10 miles W of Windsor on the A321

🏛 Hannen Mausoleum   🏛 Druid's Temple

This charming village developed as a settlement in the 10th century at the confluence of the Rivers Thames and Loddon on an area of flat land in a wooded valley. The peace that generally prevails here was disturbed in 1914 when suffragettes burnt down the church in protest at the vicar's refusal to remove the word 'obey' from the marriage service. In the churchyard, undisturbed by the riot or anything since,

stands the **Hannen Mausoleum**, a splendid monument that was designed for the Hannen family by Sir Edwin Lutyens in 1906.

Another interesting sight can be found on the outskirts of the village, at Park Place. In 1788 the estate was owned by General Henry Conway, Governor of Jersey. In recognition of his services, the people of the island gave the general a complete **Druids' Temple**. The massive stones were transported from St Helier to the estate and erected in a 25-foot circle in the gardens of his mansion. In 1870, Park Place was destroyed by fire and the estate broken up but today the temple stands in the garden of Temple Combe, close to a house designed by the famed American architect, Frank Lloyd Wright. The only house of his in this country, it was built in 1958 to an

🏛 historic building   🏛 museum   🏛 historic site   🏛 scenic attraction   🌱 flora and fauna

elaborate U-shaped design; its many unusual features include suede-panelled interior walls.

SANDHURST
11 miles SW of Windsor on the A3095

🏛 Royal Military Academy Staff College Museum

🌿 Trilakes

The town is famous as being the home of the **Royal Military Academy**, the training place for army officers since it was established in 1907. The academy's **Staff College Museum** tells the history of officer training from its inception to the present day. Close by is **Trilakes**, a picturesque country park set in 18 acres with, of course, some lakes. This is a wonderful place to visit with children as there are a wide assortment of pets and farm animals which they can get to know, including miniature horses, pygmy goats, donkeys, aviary birds, pot-bellied pigs and Soay sheep.

DORNEY
2 miles NW of Windsor off the A308

🏛 Dorney Court   🏛 Church of St Mary Magdalene

One of the finest Tudor manor houses in England, **Dorney Court**, just a short walk from the River Thames, has been the home of the Palmer family since 1530. Built in about 1440, it is an enchanting building which also houses some real treasures, including early 15th and 16th century oak furniture, beautiful 17th century lacquer furniture, and 400 years of family portraits. It is here that the first pineapple in England was grown in 1665.

On **Dorney Common** is the village of **Boveney**, which served as a wharf in the 13th century when timber was being transported from Windsor Forest. The flint and clapboard church of **St Mary Magdalene**, down by the riverside, was the setting for several scenes in Kevin Costner's film *Robin Hood Prince of Thieves*.

MAIDENHEAD
6 miles NW of Windsor on the A4130

🏛 Brunel's Rail Bridge

🌿 Maidenhead Commons and Cock Marsh

Transport has played a major role down the years in the history of Maidenhead, first with Thames traffic, then as a stop on the London-Bath coaching route, and finally with the coming of the railway, which helped to turn the town into a fashionable Victorian resort. The **Maidenhead Rail Bridge** was built by Isambard Kingdom Brunel in 1839 to carry his Great Western Railway over the Thames. The bridge, which comprises the widest, flattest brick arches in the world, was hailed at the time as the pinnacle of engineering achievement and has been immortalised in Turner's incredibly exciting and atmospheric painting *Rain, Steam and Speed*.

Boulter's Lock, one of the biggest on the Thames, takes its name from an old word for a miller. A flour mill has stood on Boulter's Island since Roman times. The island was also the home of Richard Dimbleby, the eminent broadcaster and father of the famous

Maidenhead Rail Bridge

🎬 stories and anecdotes   🦅 famous people   🎨 art and craft   🖊 entertainment and sport   🚶 walks

broadcasters David and Jonathan. To the north and west of the town, **Maidenhead Commons** and **Cock Marsh** contain a variety of habitats, including woodland, scrub thickets, grassland, ponds and riverside. Both are popular with walkers and nature-lovers: Cock Marsh is an important site for breeding waders, and both sites are rich in flora and invertebrate fauna.

COOKHAM
6 miles NW of Windsor on the A4094

🏃 Cookham Woods 🐦 Stanley Spencer Gallery

This pretty, small town, on the banks of the

River Thames, has been fortunate in being protected by **Cookham Woods** (National Trust) from becoming a suburb of Maidenhead and still has a distinctive character of its own. The town was made famous by the artist Sir Stanley Spencer, who used Cookham as the setting for many of his paintings. He was born here in 1891 and was buried here on his death in 1959. The town's tribute to its most renowned resident is the **Stanley Spencer Gallery** (see panel below), a permanent exhibition of his work which is housed in the converted Victorian chapel Stanley visited as a child. His painting,

The Stanley Spencer Gallery

The Kings Hall, High Street, Cookham, Berkshire
Tel: *01628-471885*
e-mail: *info@stanleyspencer.org.uk*

The Stanley Spencer Gallery is unique as the only gallery in Britain devoted exclusively to an artist in the village where he was born and spent much of his life. To Spencer (1891-1959), Cookham and its surrounding area were the scenes of heavenly visitations. Set in the heart of the village he immortalised, the gallery occupies the former Victorian Methodist Chapel where Spencer was taken to worship as a child. It contains a permanent collection of his work, together with letters, documents, memorabilia, and the pram in which Spencer wheeled his equipment when painting landscapes. It also displays important works on long-term loan, and mounts a winter and summer exhibition each year. Over 1,000 works have been shown since the gallery opened in 1962.

FERN LEA the artist's birthplace is in Cookham High Street. The village remained a source of inspiration throughout his life and formed the setting for numerous biblical and figure paintings, as well as landscapes. The parish church, the High Street, Cookham Moor and the river are all recognisable from his pictures. THE COLLECTION contains the gallery's important works which includes a fine group of early religious paintings: 'The Betrayal' 1914, 'The Last Supper' 1920, 'St. Veronica Unmasking Christ' 1921 and 'Christ Overturning the Money Changers' Table' 1921. The gallery also owns figure paintings from the 1930s, such as the 'Beatitudes of Love: Contemplation' 1937, portraits and later works. A major bequest of paintings and drawings from Barbara Karmel includes 'Sarah Tubb and the Heavenly Visitors' 1933, a self-portrait 1923, 'Neighbours' 1936 and a landscape 'Beacon Hill' 1927. A recent acquisition is 'View from Cookham Bridge' 1936.

🏛 historic building 🏛 museum 🏛 historic site ⚜ scenic attraction � flora and fauna

Resurrection, which depicts recognisable locals emerging from the graves in Cookham churchyard, caused some residents to protest when it was first exhibited in the 1930s.

ETON
1 mile N of Windsor on the A355

🏛 Eton College

Just across the River Thames from Windsor, this town has grown up around **Eton College**, the famous public school that was founded in 1440 by Henry VI. Originally intended for 70 poor and worthy scholars and to educate students for the newly created King's College, at Cambridge University, the college has been added to greatly over the years. Of the original school buildings, only the College Hall and the kitchen have survived; the great gatehouse and Lupton's Tower were added in the 16th century and the Upper School dates from around 1690. However, the school has kept many ancient traditions over the years including the black tail mourning coats that were originally worn on the death of George III in 1820 and which are still worn today. For centuries the college has educated the great and the good, among them William Pitt the Elder, Harold Macmillan, Thomas Gray (author of *Elegy Written in a Country Churchyard*), Henry Fielding, Shelley, George Orwell and Ian Fleming. Eton has also been famous in the past for its strict discipline, personified in 1832 by a master who told the pupils when they rebelled:

"Boys, you must be pure of heart, for if not, I will thrash you until you are."

SLOUGH
3 miles N of Windsor on the A355

🏛 Church of St Mary   🏛 Museum

A small settlement until the creation of a trading estate in 1920, Slough then grew rapidly from around 7,000 to 100,000. The area does have a long history, however, and a visit to **Slough Museum** makes for an interesting hour or two delving into the past. Slough has a lovely surprise in the shape of one of the most splendid churches in the county. The **Church of St Mary** is a real gem, notable particularly for the private family pew of the Kedermisters, totally screened from the main part of the church, and a library filled with painted panels.

DATCHET
2 miles E of Windsor on the B470

Just across the river from Windsor Castle's Home Park, Datchet has a spacious green and some attractive riverside houses. The town featured in Shakespeare's *Merry Wives of Windsor* when Falstaff, concealed in a laundry basket, is brought here for his 'Datchet mead' – i.e. a ducking in the river.

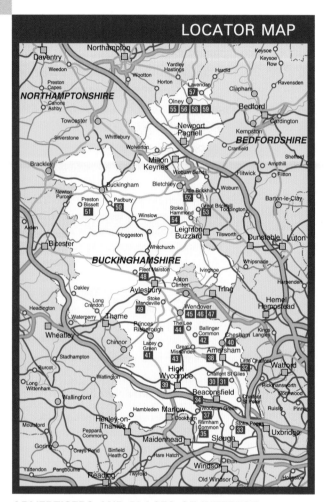

ADVERTISERS AND PLACES OF INTEREST

Accommodation, Food and Drink

30 | Chiltern Cottages & Flexmore House Traditional Farm,
Chalfont St Giles   *pg 58*

31 | The Ivy House, Chalfont St Giles   *pg 59*

37 | The Red Cow, Wooburn Green   *pg 67*

40 | The Drawingroom Art Gallery & Café, Chesham   *pg 71*

41 | The Whip Inn, Lacey Green   *pg 71*

42 | Hatters Bar & Restaurant, Ballinger Common   *pg 72*

44 | Cock and Rabbit Inn & Graziemille Restaurant,
The Lee   *pg 74*

46 | Rumsey's Chocolaterie, Wendover   *pg 75*

51 | The White Hart, Preston Bissett   *pg 83*

54 | The Three Locks, Stoke Hammond   *pg 87*

Antiques and Restoration

47 | Sally Turner Antiques & Jewellery, Wendover   *pg 76*

Arts & Crafts

32 | Chalfont Art & Framing, Little Chalfont   *pg 60*

40 | The Drawingroom Art Gallery & Café, Chesham   *pg 71*

55 | The New Studio, Olney   *pg 88*

Fashions

45 | Well Heeled of Wendover, Wendover   *pg 75*

🏠 historic building   🏛 museum   🏛 historic site   ⚜ scenic attraction   🌱 flora and fauna

3 | Buckinghamshire

The south of the county, with the River Thames as its southern boundary, lies almost entirely within the chalk range of the Chiltern Hills, most of which is classed as an Area of Outstanding Natural Beauty. The county town since the 18th century has been Aylesbury, the market centre for the attractive Vale of Aylesbury, which runs from the Chilterns in the south to Buckingham in the north. Here, the visitor will discover a rural patchwork of secluded countryside,

Pitstone Windmill

woodland and valleys, waterways, charming villages and busy market towns. A thousand miles of footpaths include the ancient Ridgeway, and the quiet country lanes and gentle undulations make cycling a real pleasure; the Vale is at the heart of the new National Cycle Network. The area around the former county town of Buckingham is perhaps the least discovered part of the county, still chiefly rural, with a wealth of attractive villages and a number of fine houses, including Ascott House, a former Rothschild residence; Claydon House, where Florence Nightingale was a frequent visitor; Winslow Hall, designed by Wren; and Stowe, where the deer park is being restored to its former glory. In this area are also two outstanding churches, the Saxon Church of All Saints at Wing and St Michael's Church at Stewkley, one of the finest Norman churches in the whole country. The northern region of the county is dominated by the new town of Milton Keynes, developed in the 1960s but incorporating many much older villages.

📖 stories and anecdotes   🐦 famous people   🎨 art and craft   🎭 entertainment and sport   🚶 walks

CHILTERN COTTAGES & FLEXMORE HOUSE TRADITIONAL FARM

Flexmore House, Hill Farm Lane,
Chalfont St Giles,
Buckinghamshire HP8 4NT
Tel: 07973 737107
Fax: 01494 872421
e-mail: bookings@chilterncottages.org.uk
website: www.chilterncottages.org.uk

The first property offered for letting by Stephen and Victoria Hinds at their **Chiltern Cottages** enterprise is a three-storey 15th century former farmhouse and coaching inn standing on the High Street of Old Amersham. The Old House is a beautifully furnished self-catering base with three bedrooms, lounge, kitchen and dining room with historic 16th century wall paintings. One of the bedrooms is on the first floor, where the sleeping arrangements can be four singles or two singles and a super-kingsize double.

On the second floor the master bedroom has an en-suite shower room and a handsome four-poster bed, and the third bedroom can be configurated as either a super kingsize double or two singles. The living room, on the first floor, is equipped with radio, CD and DVD player, TV, board games, books and jigsaw puzzles. The ground-floor kitchen is also splendidly appointed, with a cooker, hob, microwave, fridge, freezer, dishwasher, washing machine, iron and basic supplies. The highlight of the whole place has to be the magnificent wall paintings in the dining room. They are believed to have been painted either in the 1550s or to celebrate the first visit of Queen Elizabeth I to Amersham in 1592. Outside is a private garden with a terraced area.

Children and most pets are welcome at The Old House, which is a non-smoking establishment. A daily maid can sometimes be arranged. There are many historic houses and places of interest in the surrounding area, and the house is just over a mile from Amersham station (Underground and British Rail), with fast access to London.

The owners have prepared a second property on Old Amersham High Street for letting – a medieval cottage sleeping up to four guests – and by the end of 2006 they propose to bring a Georgian cottage for four on stream. Their home is a working farm in Chalfont St Giles, producing dairy and meat products. The livestock includes water buffalo as well as more familiar farm animals, and the shop on the farm sells a variety of meat including local rare breed produce.

🏠 historic building 🏛 museum 🏚 historic site 🌾 scenic attraction 🌿 flora and fauna

Chalfont St Giles

🏛 Chiltern Open Air Museum 🪶 Milton's Cottage

Among the various ancient buildings of interest in this archetypal English village there is an Elizabethan mansion, The Vache, which was the home of friends of Captain Cook, and in the grounds is a monument to the famous seafarer. However, by far the most famous building in Chalfont St Giles, with an equally famous resident, is **Milton's Cottage**. John Milton moved to this 16th century cottage, found for him by his former pupil Thomas Ellwood, in 1665 to escape the plague in London. Though Milton moved back to London in 1666, he wrote *Paradise Lost* and began work on its sequel, *Paradise Regained*, while taking refuge in the village. The only house lived in by the poet to have survived, the cottage and its garden have been preserved as they were at the time Milton was resident. The building is now home to a museum which includes collections of important first editions of Milton's works and a portrait of the poet by Sir Godfrey Kneller.

Another fascinating and unusual place to visit in the village is the **Chiltern Open Air Museum**, which rescues buildings of historic or architectural importance due to be demolished from across the Chilterns region and re-erects them on its 45-acre site. The buildings rescued by the museum are used to house and display artefacts and implements that are appropriate to the building's original use and history. Also on the museum site is a series of fields farmed using medieval methods

THE IVY HOUSE

London Road (A413), Chalfont St Giles, Buckinghamshire
Tel: 01494 872184 Fax: 01494 872870
e-mail: enquiries@theivyhouse-bucks.co.uk
website: www.theivyhouse-bucks.co.uk

Morning Advertiser Freehouse of the Year 2006 Award is just one of many accolades accorded to the **Ivy House**, which is situated in the beautiful Chiltern Vale, on the A413 between Old Amersham and Chalfont St Giles. The bar in the 250-year-old brick and flint building, with its beams, fires, brass, pictures and armchairs, is a delightful spot for a drink, with Cask Marque beers and wines available by the glass and bottle, and the Ivy House is also a great place to seek out for a meal, whether it's a romantic dinner for two or a small party or business meeting. The constantly changing menu includes both traditional favourites and more exotic offerings, and at the weekend the cream teas are always popular.

The restaurant is open lunchtime and evening, and all day at the weekend. Hosts Anthony and Jane Mears also offer excellent b&b guest accommodation in individually appointed bedrooms (no smoking) with very comfortable beds, en-suite shower, TV, drinks tray and work desk. The Ivy House has a lovely garden and two patios, one decorated with vines.

🎭 stories and anecdotes 🪶 famous people 🎨 art and craft 🎟 entertainment and sport 🚶 walks

where, among the historic crops, organic woad is grown, from which indigo dye is extracted for use in dyeing demonstrations. Madame Tussaud, famous for her exhibitions in London, started her waxworks here in the village, and another well-known resident was Bertram Mills of circus fame. His tomb stands beside the war memorial in the churchyard of St Giles.

Mayflower Barn, Jordans

Around Chalfont St Giles

JORDANS

1 mile S of Chalfont St Giles off the A40

This secluded village reached down a quiet country lane is famous as the burial place of William Penn, Quaker and founder of

Pennsylvania. He and members of his family are buried in the graveyard outside the Quaker meeting house that is among the earliest to be found in the country. In the grounds of nearby Old Jordans Farm is the Mayflower Barn, said to have been constructed from the

---

CHALFONT ART & FRAMING

7 Nightingales Corner, Little Chalfont, Buckinghamshire HP7 9PZ
Tel: 01494 766220
e-mail: info@chalfontartandframing.co.uk
website: www.chalfontartandframing.co.uk

Chalfont Art & Framing is located at Little Chalfont on the main A404, equidistant between Junction 18 (Rickmansworth) of the M25 and the town of Amersham. Founded and run by Ian Morris, this independent gallery stocks a wide range of artwork by both local and nationally and internationally acclaimed artists. Ranging from landscape to abstract and figurative to contemporary to cater for most tastes.

Chalfont Art & Framing has a dedicated viewing area for the works of the immensely popular Jack Vettriano. Here you can view his more traditional and familiar romantic beach scenes together with his more edgier and risque images. The gallery carries a wide selection of his limited edition works and the staff are extremely knowledgeable about the artist. Raymond Leech, Todd White, Pino, Gillian McDonald and Rolf Harris are among other well-known artists featured in the gallery. A recent coup is the acquisition of a new collection of work by Fred Beckett, a local and very well respected artist who is a member of the Royal Institute of Oil Painters (he was its president between 1995 and 1997). Chalfont Art & Framing has a Fine Art Trade guild approved framing service on site. Winner of the Design & Innovation Award of Merit 2006, the gallery opens daily 10am to 5pm. Browsers are welcome both in the gallery and on the excellent website.

🏛 historic building   🏛 museum   🏛 historic site   🄌 scenic attraction   🌱 flora and fauna

timbers of the ship that took the Pilgrim Fathers to America.

CHALFONT ST PETER
2 miles S of Chalfont St Giles on the A413

🌿 Hawk & Owl Trust

Now a commuter town, Chalfont St Peter dates back to the 7th century and, as its name means 'the spring where the calves come to drink', there is a long history here of raising cattle in the surrounding lush meadows. First mentioned in 1133, the parish Church of St Peter was all but destroyed when its steeple collapsed in 1708. The building seen today dates from that time as it was rebuilt immediately after the disaster.

Housed in a barn at Skippings Farm is the **Hawk and Owl Trust's National Education and Exhibition Centre**.

Dedicated to conserving wild birds of prey in their natural habitats, the Trust concerns itself with practical research, creative conservation and imaginative educational programmes.

STOKE POGES
6 miles S of Chalfont St Giles off the A355

🐿 Gray Monument

The ploughman homeward plods his weary way
And leaves the world to darkness and to me.

It was in the churchyard of this surprisingly still rural village that Thomas Gray was inspired to pen his *Elegy Written in a Country Churchyard*. He often visited Stoke Poges to see his mother and aunt who lived in a large late-Georgian house built for the grandson of the famous Quaker, William Penn. Gray lies buried with his mother in the church, and, to

---

PINEWOOD NURSERIES

Wexham Street, Stoke Poges, Buckinghamshire SL3 6NB
Tel/Fax: 01753 663443
e-mail: frankpinewood@onetel.com

Pinewood Nurseries is owned and run by the Franke family – Adrian and Patricia, daughters Marie and Liz, and her partner Tom. They are well known throughout the area for their vast range of summer bedding plants, potted plants, hanging baskets and perennials which are all home grown and of the highest quality. They produce 12,000 summer hanging baskets which are sold to the public as well as supplying them to many local garden centres and London wholesale markets. It is one of the largest working plant nurseries which is open to the public in the country. The two-acre glass house is open to the public all year round, enabling them to witness the whole process of producing the plants. For the winter season the greenhouse produces 50,000 poinsettias where customers can pick their own plant or have arrangements made up. They also sell cyclamen, winter bedding plants and Christmas trees. On the third weekend before Christmas they offer free mulled wine and mince pies to celebrate the festive season.

The family and their staff are courteous, helpful and always ready to advise new or inexperienced gardeners, and they also offer a personalised gift service. An adjoining farm shop is due to open around Christmas 2006, selling fresh meat and other organic produce.

COX & COX INTERIOR DESIGN

3 London End, Beaconsfield Old Town,
Buckinghamshire HP9 2HN
Tel: 01494 675494   Fax: 01494 675512
e-mail: info@coxandcox.biz
website: www.coxandcoxhome.com

Located in Beaconsfield for more than 20 years, Nick
and Pam Cox are the inspiration behind **Cox & Cox
Interiors Ltd**, specialists in top-to-bottom home decor
and furnishings. Six rooms on two floors of the
showroom display an impressive range of fabrics –
Ralph Lauren, Pierre Frey, Ian Sanderson, Mulberry,
Abbot & Boyd, Nina Campbell, Colefax & Fowler,
Manuel Canovas, Brunswig & Fils and many others;
also to be found Lexington & Ralph Lauren linen,
fabulous antique Swedish and French furniture and
decorative items, lamps, lighting, garden furniture,
tissue box covers and door stops.

Handmade
upholstered chairs and
sofas, curtains, blinds
and loose covers are
made in their own
workshops. Framed
photographic collections
include Classic, Black &
White, St Tropez and
Classic Motor Sports.

the east, is the imposing **Gray Monument**, designed by James Wyatt and erected in 1799. The Church of St Giles itself is very handsome and dates from the 13th century but perhaps its most interesting feature is the unusual medieval bicycle depicted in one of the stained glass windows. Behind the church is an Elizabethan manor house where Elizabeth I was entertained and Charles I was imprisoned.

BEACONSFIELD
3 miles SW of Chalfont St Giles on the A40

🏛 Beckonscot 🌿 Odds Farm Park

This is very much a town in two parts: the old town, dating back to medieval times and, to the north, the new town which grew up following the construction of the Metropolitan line into central London and consisting chiefly of between the wars housing. The old town is best known for its wealth of literary connections. The poet and orator Edmund Waller was born in the nearby village of Coleshill in 1606 and had his family home just outside Beaconsfield. His best-known lines are perhaps the patriotic *Others may use the ocean as their road / Only the English make it their abode*. Waller's tomb in the churchyard of St Mary and All Saints is marked by a very tall, sharply pointed obelisk with a tribute from fellow poet John Dryden. The church itself is one of the finest in the county and also contains the grave of the statesman and political theorist Edmund Burke (1729-1797). Beaconsfield was also the home of the writer of the *Father Brown* books GK Chesterton (his grave is in the nearby Catholic church), the poet Robert Frost and the much loved children's author Enid Blyton.

For a unique step back in time to the 1930s, or for anyone wanting to feel like Gulliver in Lilliput, a trip to the model village of **Bekonscot** is a must. The oldest model village in the world, Bekonscot was begun in the 1920s by Roland Callingham, a London accountant, who started by building models in his garden. As the number of buildings and models grew, Callingham purchased more land and, with the aid of a friend from Ascot who added a model railway, created the village seen today. When the model village first opened, people started throwing coins into buckets for charity and, even today, all surplus profits go to charity. Enid Blyton's house Green Hedges is depicted in Bekonscot, and she wrote a story about two children who visit the model village.

South of Beaconsfield, on the other side of the M40 at **Wooburn Common**, an entertaining day out is guaranteed at **Odds Farm Park**, home to many rare and interesting animals. The park was created particularly with children in mind and the regular events include pigs' tea time, pat-a-pet, bottle-feeding lambs and goat milking. As one of 20 approved rare breed centres in the country, the farm combines the family attractions with the breeding and conservation of many of Britain's rarest farm animals.

BURNHAM BEECHES
5 miles SW of Chalfont St Giles off the A355

A stretch of land bought in 1880 by the Corporation of the City of London for use in perpetuity by the public, and since then a favourite place for Londoners to relax. Burnham Beeches was designated a National Nature Reserve in 1993 and this extensive area of ancient woodland and heathland includes an important collection of old beeches and pollarded oaks.

TAPLOW

8 miles SW of Chalfont St Giles off the A4

🏛 Cliveden   🏛 Octagonal Temple

The name is of Taplow is derived from Taeppa, a Saxon warrior whose grand burial site high above the Thames was excavated in 1883. Nothing is known of Taeppa himself, but the items discovered at the site are on display in the British Museum. To the north of the village lies the country house of **Cliveden**, once the home of Lady Nancy Astor, the first woman to take her seat as a Member of Parliament. The first house on the site was built in 1666 for the Duke of Buckingham, but the present magnificent mansion, most of which is now a hotel, dates from the 19th century. The splendid grounds include a great formal parterre with fountains,

temples and statuary, a water garden and a wonderful rose garden. Some of the great names in architecture and garden design had a hand in the Cliveden of today: the house and terrace are the work of Sir Charles Barry, the rose garden was designed by Sir Geoffrey Jellicoe, and the renowned Italian country house architect Giacomo Leoni was responsible for the **Octagonal Temple**, now a chapel, where the American-born millionaire William Waldorf Astor, his son Waldorf and the ashes of Waldorf's wife Nancy are buried.

PENN

4 miles NW of Chalfont St Giles on the B474

A centre of the tiling industry after the Norman Conquest, Penn provided the flooring for Windsor Castle, the Palace of

IVORY WHITE

5 The Broadway, Farnham Common,
Buckinghamshire SL2 3PQ
Tel: 01753 644925
e-mail: info@ivory-white.co.uk
website: www.ivory-white.co.uk

Ivory White is a beautiful shop full of beautiful things – for personal treats, to give as special presents or to enhance the home. The light, all-white interior is the perfect setting for displaying the ever-changing mix of home accessories, furniture and lighting, glassware, jewellery, handbags, tableware and gifts. Owner Karen Lièvre has had a lifelong passion for interiors and lovely things, and each year she makes two trips through Europe looking for interesting and unusual pieces and one-off items of artwork as well as antique and contemporary French furniture.

Some of the display cabinets in the shop were specially designed and made for Karen. The glassware includes mirrors with hand-carved frames, Murano glass, Italian glass jewellery and hand-blown pieces by English artists. The handbag range runs from the very popular beaded bags to bags in luxurious leather. Contemporary artwork can be commissioned on request, and other services offered by Karen include interior design and gift wrapping. Ivory White, which stands on the A355 at Farnham Common, is open from 9.30am to 5.30pm Tuesday to Saturday.

🏛 historic building   🏛 museum   🏛 historic site   🔍 scenic attraction   🌿 flora and fauna

Village Pond, Penn

Donald Maclean, who died in Moscow in 1983. His ashes, contained in an urn decorated with a hammer and sickle, were brought back to England by his brother and buried in the family grave.

AMERSHAM
3 miles N of Chalfont St Giles on the A413

🏛 Museum

Another town with a split personality. Top Amersham is a thriving commercial centre; Old Amersham is a popular tourist spot with a wide sweeping High Street, half-timbered buildings and picturesque period cottages. Set beside the River Misbourne, the Old Town boasts many fine old buildings, including Sir William Drake's Market Hall of 1682 and the Church of St Mary with some fine stained glass and monuments to the Drake family. The Old Town is well-known for its shopping – there's a wide selection of antique and craft shops, designer boutiques, and an impressive range of

Westminster and many churches. But the village is best known as the ancestral home of William Penn, the Quaker and American pioneer, and in the village church are several memorials to the family. In the churchyard of Holy Trinity is the grave of the diplomat spy

Amersham Museum

49 High Street, Amersham, Bucks HP7 0DP
Tel: 01494 723700
website: www.AmershamMuseum.org.uk

The low doorway at 49 High Street in Old Amersham leads directly into an original timber-framed, Tudor Hall House built over 500 years ago, the home of Amersham Museum. This fascinating museum tells the story of the town of Amersham from early times, with Roman artefacts from the villa at Mantles Green, through to the coming of the railway and the establishment of Amersham on the Hill, WW2 activities and 20th century industries. The new displays on the ground floor of the museum illustrate everyday life in the town from what people wore to the job they did and how they enjoyed their leisure time.

Upstairs there are displays about the traditional local crafts of lacemaking, straw plait for hats, chairmaking and farming. This family friendly museum has interactive exhibits, traditional toys to try out and special bags of things to do for all ages from pre-school children to teens. The garden that runs down to the bank of the River Misbourne, hidden away behind the house, is full of culinary herbs and medicinal plants that our ancestors would have grown. The shop stocks a wide range of photgraphs taken by local photographer George Ward before 1930, books, postcards and toys linked to Amersham and famous visitors including Beatrix Potter.

🎞 stories and anecdotes   🐦 famous people   🎨 art and craft   ✒ entertainment and sport   🚶 walks

restaurants, snack bars and coaching inns.

The Romans were farming around Amersham in the 3rd and 4th centuries, the Saxons called it Agmodesham and to the Normans it was Elmondesham. So the town has plenty of history, much of which is told in the **Amersham Museum** (see panel on page 65).

The town was an important staging post in coaching days, and the Crown Hotel, one of the many coaching inns here, was featured in the film *Four Weddings and a Funeral*. Close to the town is Gore Hill, the site of a battle between the Danes and the Saxons in 921. It is recorded that in 1666 the Great Fire of London could be seen raging from the hill.

CHENIES
3 miles E of Amersham off the A404

🏛 Chenies Manor

This picturesque village, with a pretty green surrounded by an old school, a chapel and a 15th century parish church, is also home to **Chenies Manor**, a fascinating 15th century manor house. Originally the home of the Earls (later Dukes) of Bedford, before they moved to Woburn, this attractive building has stepped gables and elaborately patterned high brick chimneys. Built by the architect who enlarged Hampton Court for Henry VIII, the house played host not only to the king but also to his daughter Elizabeth I, whose favourite oak tree still stands in the garden. Naturally, there is a ghost here, that of none other than Henry, whose footsteps can be heard as he drags his ulcerated leg around the manor house in an attempt to catch Catherine Howard in the act of adultery with one of his entourage, Tom Culpeper. The house has much to offer, not just from the exterior but also inside where there are tapestries, furniture

and a collection of antique dolls, but the elaborate gardens should not be overlooked. Among the delights are a Tudor style sunken garden, some fine topiary, a turf maze, a kitchen garden and a physic garden with a variety of herbs that were used for both medicinal and culinary purposes.

High Wycombe

🏛 Little Market House   🏛 Museum

The largest town in Buckinghamshire, High Wycombe is traditionally known for the manufacture of chairs and, in particular, the famous Windsor design. It is still a centre of furniture manufacture today as well as being a pleasant town in which to live for those commuting to London. Originally an old Chilterns gap market town, High Wycombe still has several old buildings of note. The **Little Market House** was designed by Robert Adams in 1761 and is of a rather curious octagonal shape, while the 18th century Guildhall is the annual venue for a traditional ceremony showing a healthy scepticism for politicians when the mayor and councillors are publicly weighed - to see if they have become fat at the expense of the citizens.

Located in an 18th century house with a flint facade, the **Wycombe Museum** has displays which give the visitor an excellent idea of the work and crafts of the local people over the years. There is, of course, a superb collection of chairs, including the famous Windsor chair. Several skills and several woods were involved in the making of this classic chair: bodgers used the ubiquitous beech for the legs; benders shaped ash for the bowed backs; and bottomers made use of the sturdy elm for the seats.

In the landscaped grounds of the museum is a medieval motte which would normally indicate that a castle once stood here but, in this case, the structure was probably little more than a wooden tower. The oldest standing building in the town is All Saints Church, a large, fine building dating from the 11th century.

Around High Wycombe

MARLOW
4 miles S of High Wycombe on the A4155

An attractive commuter town on the banks of the Thames, Marlow is famous for its suspension bridge built in 1832 to the design of Tierney Clarke, who built a similar bridge linking Buda and Pest across the Danube. The High Street is lined with elegant houses, and Marlow has a good supply of riverside pubs; in one of them, the Two Brewers, Jerome K Jerome wrote his masterpiece *Three Men in a Boat*. Other literary connections abound: Mary Shelley completed *Frankenstein* while living here after her marriage to the poet Percy Bysshe Shelley and TS Eliot lived for a while in West Street, as did the author Thomas Love Peacock while writing *Nightmare Abbey*.

Marlow hosts an annual regatta and is one of the places the Swan Uppers visit each year counting and marking the swans belonging to the Queen and to two London Livery Companies.

BOURNE END
4 miles SE of High Wycombe on the A4155

A prosperous commuter town on the banks of the Thames; it began to expand in the late 19th century as the Victorians developed a passion for boating on the river. It was once the home of the writer Edgar Wallace, who died in Hollywood during work on the screenplay for *King Kong*. He is buried in the village cemetery at nearby Little Marlow.

HAMBLEDEN
6 miles SW of High Wycombe off the A4155

🏛 Church of St Mary

This much filmed village was given to the National Trust by the family of the bookseller WH Smith - who later became Viscount Hambleden. He lived close by at Greenlands, on the banks of the River Thames and is buried in the village churchyard. The unusually large **Church of St Mary**, known as the Cathedral of the Chilterns, dates from the 14th century and, though it has been altered

---

THE RED COW

The Green, Wooburn Green, Buckinghamshire HP10 0EF
Tel: 01628 531344 Fax: 01628 850377

Overlooking the huge green in a village just off the M40 (J3), the **Red Cow** is a 400-year-old pub with bags of character and atmosphere. In the bar with its beams, wooden floor and log fire, or out in the secluded beer garden, patrons can enjoy the excellent hospitality provided by keen golfer and cricketer John Randall and his partner Caitlin. Two real ales head the list of drinks, and a daily changing selection of home-cooked dishes is served from 12 noon to 2pm Monday to Friday, from 12 noon to 4pm on Saturday and from 12 noon to 3pm on Sunday. Booking is strongly recommended for the Sunday roasts.

📽 stories and anecdotes   🦜 famous people   🎨 art and craft   ✏ entertainment and sport   🚶 walks

THE CHILTERN VALLEY WINERY & BREWERY

Old Luxters Farm, Hambleden,
nr Henley-on-Thames, Buckinghamshire RG9 6JW
Tel: 01491 638330 Fax: 01491 638645
e-mail: david@chilternvalley.co.uk
website: www.chilternvalley.co.uk

Set in a designated Area of Outstanding Natural Beauty, Old Luxters is home to the **Chiltern Valley Winery & Brewery**. Wines have been produced here for more than 20 years, and with over 70 trophies, awards and commendations they have gained an enviable and far-reaching reputation for quality, a reputation being enhanced by David Ealand and his family. The first vines were planted in 1982 here on the slopes of the Chilterns, surrounded by beech woodland and overlooking the beautiful Hambleden Valley. The modern production, bottling and labelling facilities, the wine vats and the cellar shop are all housed in traditional farm buildings.

Old Luxters also produces superb cask and bottle conditioned ales, reviving the tradition of farm-brewed, full-mash real ales. In the gift shop, visitors can taste not only the wines and the beers, but the liqueurs and fortified drinks produced on the premises. Chiltern Valley also specialises in providing an in-house 'own' label service for individuals, shops and restaurants.

over the years, it still dominates the area with its size and beauty. Inside the building's 18th century tower is a fascinating 16th century panel which is believed to have been the bedhead of Cardinal Wolsey - it certainly bears the cardinal's hat and the Wolsey arms.

The village's other building of interest, Hambledon Mill, can be found by the River Thames and is reached by a road that was first used by the Romans.

WEST WYCOMBE
2 miles NW of High Wycombe on the A40

🏚 West Wycombe Park & Caves

🏚 Church of St Lawrence

🐿 Dashwood Mausoleum

This charming estate village, where many of the houses are owned by the National Trust,

has a main street displaying architecture from the 15th through to the 19th century. Close by is **West Wycombe Park** (National Trust), the home of local landowners the Dashwood family until the 1930s. Of the various members of the family, it was Sir Francis Dashwood who had most influence on both the house and the village. West Wycombe house was originally built in the early 1700s but Sir Francis boldly remodelled it several years later as well as having the grounds and park landscaped by Thomas Cook, a pupil of Capability Brown. Very much a classical landscape, the grounds contain temples and an artificial lake shaped like a swan, and the house has a good collection of tapestries, furniture and paintings.

Hewn out of a nearby hillside are **West Wycombe Caves** (see panel oppposite) which were created, possibly from some existing caverns, by Sir Francis as part of a programme of public works. After a series of failed harvests, which created great poverty and distress amongst the estate workers and tenant farmers, Sir Francis employed the men to extract chalk from the hillside to be used in the construction of the new road between the village and High Wycombe.

The village **Church of St Lawrence** is yet another example of Sir Francis' enthusiasm for remodelling old buildings. Situated within the remnants of an Iron Age fort, the church was originally constructed in the 13th century. Its isolated position, however, was not intentional as the church was originally the church of the village of Haveringdon, which has long since disappeared. Dashwood remodelled the interior in the 18th century in

West Wycombe

the style of an Egyptian hall and also heightened the tower, adding on the top a great golden ball where six people could meet

The Hell-Fire Caves

West Wycombe Caves Ltd. High Wycombe, Bucks HP14 3AJ
Tel: 01494 533739
website: www.hellfirecaves.co.uk

The **Hell-Fire Caves** at West Wycombe offer a totally unique experience. The Caves are owned by Sir Edward Dashwood, a direct descendent of Sir Francis Dashwood, who originally excavated them in the 1750s on the site of an ancient quarry. Throughout the 1700s and 1800s, the caves, which are quarter of a mile underground, were reputed to have hosted the Hell-Fire Club whose membership included some of Britain's most senior aristocrats and statesmen.

Today, the caves are a popular tourist attraction and a wonderful insight into our history. A tour of the caves includes a long winding passage that leads past various small chambers to the Banqueting Hall, down over the River Styx to the Inner Temple, which is about 300 feet beneath the church at the top of the hill. The Caves are scattered with statues in costume and a commentary with sound effects is included throughout the tour.

For a great family day out, with a little twist, visit the Hell-Fire Caves for a memorable experience that you are unlikely to forget. Open daily Apr – Oct, Weekends Nov – Mar, 11am – 5.30pm.

stories and anecdotes   famous people   art and craft   entertainment and sport   walks

in comfort and seclusion. The **Dashwood Mausoleum** near the church was built in 1765; a vast hexagonal building without a roof, it is the resting place of Sir Francis and other members of the Dashwood family. Sir Francis had a racier side to his character. As well as being remembered as a great traveller and a successful politician, he was the founder of the Hell-Fire Club. This group of rakes, who were also known as the Brotherhood of Sir Francis or Dashwood's Apostles, met a couple of times a years to engage in highly colourful activities. Though their exploits were legendary and probably loosely based on fact, they no doubt consumed large quantities of alcohol and enjoyed the company of women. Traditionally, the group meetings were held in the caves, or possibly the church tower, though between 1750 and 1774, their meeting place was nearby Medmenham Abbey.

HUGHENDEN

2 miles N of High Wycombe off the A4128

🏛 Hughenden Manor   🌲 Bradenham Woods

This village is famous for being the home of the Queen Victoria's favourite Prime Minister Benjamin Disraeli; he lived here from 1848 until his death in 1881. He bought **Hughenden Manor** (National Trust) shortly after the publication of his novel *Tancred*. Though not a wealthy man, Disraeli felt that a leading Conservative politician should have a stately home of his own. In order to finance the purchase, his supporters lent him the money so that he could have this essential characteristic of an English gentleman. The interior is an excellent example of the Victorian Gothic style and contains an interesting collection of memorabilia of Disraeli's life as well as his library, pictures and much of his furniture. The garden is based on the designs

of Disraeli's wife Mary Anne; the surrounding park and woodland offer some beautiful walks. Disraeli, who was MP for Buckinghamshire from 1847 to 1876 and Prime Minister in 1868 and from 1874 to 1880, is buried in the churchyard of St Michael. In the chancel of the church is a marble memorial erected in his memory by Queen Victoria. Disraeli was the son of a writer and literary critic, Isaac d'Israeli, who lived for a time in the village of Bradenham on the other side of High Wycombe. The Bradenham Estate, also owned by the National Trust, includes **Bradenham Woods**, an area of ancient beech that is among the finest in the whole Chilterns region. Although beech predominates, other trees, including oak, whitebeam, ash and wild cherry are being encouraged.

Chesham

A successful combination of a commuter town, industrial centre and country community, Chesham's growth from a sleepy market town was due mainly to its Metropolitan underground railway link with central London. Chesham was the birthplace of Arthur Liberty, the son of a haberdasher and draper, who went on to found the world famous Liberty's department store in London's Regent Street in 1875. Another resident of note was Roger Crabbe who, having suffered head injuries during the Civil War, was sentenced to death by Cromwell. After receiving a pardon, Crabbe opened a hat shop in the town where he is reputed to have worn sackcloth, eaten turnip tops and given his income to the poor. Perhaps not surprisingly, Crabbe was used by Lewis Carroll as the model for the Mad Hatter in *Alice in Wonderland*.

THE DRAWINGROOM ART GALLERY & CAFÉ

Francis Yard, Chesham,
Buckinghamshire HP5 1BG
Tel: 01494 791691
e-mail: info@the-drawingroom.co.uk
website: www.the-drawingroom.co.uk

FAIRTRADE
Guarantees
a **better deal**
for Third World
Producers

The Drawingroom Art Gallery & Café has
what is surely a unique appeal, combining
a café and live music venue with a gallery
exhibiting over 400 original sensuous works of art. The
building dates back to around 1600, and Richard Elkington
and Amy Deane have filled the rooms with paintings in
pastels, watercolours, oils, charcoal and pencil, and
sculpture in marble, Portland stone, solid bronze and cold
cast. They have selected the work from UK artists who
capture and celebrate beauty through their skills and their
use of light and form.

Home cooking is an equal attraction, to be enjoyed
inside or out in the cobbled yard. All the cakes are made
locally by Jill Glover, and savoury choices run from
organic scrambled eggs and toasties topped with five cheeses and sun-dried tomatoes to
fisherman's broth, super salads and lamb casserole. Lots of teas, Fair Trade coffees, wonderful
hot chocolate, cold drinks. All the food and drink are also available to take away.

Around Chesham

LACEY GREEN

8 miles W of Chesham off the A4010

🏠 Smock Mill 🐴 Home of Rest for Horses

Lacey Green is home to another of the
county's preserved windmills, this one a

Smock Mill, in which only the cap carrying
the sails rotates to meet the wind. As a result,
the body of the mill where the machinery is
housed can be bigger, heavier and stronger.
This example was built in the mid-1600s and
moved from Chesham to this site in 1821.
Lacey Green is the village where the young
poet Rupert Brooke used to spend his

THE WHIP INN

Pink Road, Lacey Green, nr Princes Risborough,
Buckinghamshire HP27 0PG
Tel: 01844 344060 website: www.whipinn.co.uk

The Whip Inn stands on the Chiltern Way just south of Princes
Risborough and the promise of the black and white exterior is
more than fulfilled within, where open fires, oak beams and
friendly staff all contribute to the cosy, relaxed ambience for enjoying a drink or a meal. When
the sun shines, the scene shifts to the glorious garden that overlooks the oldest working smock
mill in the country. Nick Smith's Whip Inn is renowned for its amazing, ever-changing selection
of real ales (up to 400 a year, and a beer festival every October) and a choice of food that runs
from lunchtime snacks and Sunday roasts to a full menu of traditional English dishes.

📖 stories and anecdotes 🐦 famous people 🎨 art and craft 🎭 entertainment and sport 🚶 walks

HATTERS BAR & RESTAURANT

The Pheasant, Ballinger Common, Great Missenden,
Buckinghamshire HP16 9LF
Tel: 01494 837236   e-mail: hats@janeking.co.uk
website: www.thepheasantballingercommon.com

The Pheasant Inn at Ballinger Common is wearing a new hat since it was acquired by former milliner Jane King. Jane has revitalised the whole place and opened **Hatters Bar & Restaurant**, creating a relaxed, friendly atmosphere in which to enjoy a drink or a meal or both. The residents of Ballinger Common still have their much-loved local, and with Jane and her chef Aaron at the helm they are steadily building a clientele who come here from near and far for the excellent food.

The bar menu has old favourites like fish & chips as well as more exotic offerings such as rare roast beef with Thai spices, and the platters to share – fish, cheese, Mediterranean, Italian meats – are proving very popular. Typical dishes on the main restaurant menu might include gnocchi with wild mushrooms, grilled sea bass with lime leaves and chilli, and slow-roasted belly of pork with garlic and sage. The excellent wine list includes several champagnes. Hatters enjoys a lovely setting opposite the village cricket green, and has the benefit of all year round al fresco dining on the heated decking which overlooks the rear garden . Food is served lunchtime and evening, and all day on Sunday. Booking is recommended to avoid disappointment.

THE PLANT SPECIALIST

Whitefield Lane, Great Missenden,
Buckinghamshire HP16 0BH
Tel/Fax: 01494 866650
e-mail: enquire@theplantspecialist.co.uk
website: www.theplantspecialist.co.uk

Established in April 2002, **The Plant Specialist** is a nursery growing a wide range of new and interesting herbaceous perennials and grasses that also make good, reliable garden plants. New plants are constantly coming to the owners' notice, and those that are successfully trialled are added to the impressive catalogue. They also sell a range of container-grown bulbs that bring added colour and interest early in the season. Everything is grown on site in a specially mixed loam-based potting mixture that makes for stronger plants that can best stand up to transplanting. The displays are carefully laid out to give customers the best idea of how the plantings would work in their own gardens.

The owners and staff take great pride in their detailed knowledge, which enables them to help and advise customers in their choice and care of plants. The nursery is located off Great Missenden High Street in Whitefield Lane, opposite the entrance to Missenden Abbey. Opening hours are 10am to 6pm Thursday, Friday and Saturday from April to October.

weekends in the company of friends at a local pub. The son of a master at Rugby School and a student at Cambridge University, Brooke began writing poetry as a boy and travelled widely in the years leading up to World War I. Early on in the war his poetry showed a boyish patriotism, but his later works were full of bitter disillusion. He died in 1915 while on his way to the attempted landings at the Dardanelles in Turkey. Close to the village lies Speen Farm and the **Home of Rest for Horses**, whose most famous patient was Sefton, the cavalry horse injured in the Hyde Park bomb blast of the early 1980s.

GREAT MISSENDEN
3 miles W of Chesham off the A413

🏛 Old Court House

Home to the only other court house in the Chiltern Hundreds (the other is at Long Crendon), Great Missenden's **Old Court House** dates from the early 1400s. Also in this village is an attractive flint and stone church and the site of Missenden Abbey, which was founded in 1133 by the Augustinian order. A daughter community of St Nicholas's Abbey in Normandy, the abbey has long since gone and in its place stands a fashionable Gothic mansion dating from 1810.

Great Missenden is probably best known as being the home of Roald Dahl, the internationally recognised author particularly loved for his children's books. He lived here for 30 years and is buried on the hillside opposite his home, Gipsy House, in the churchyard of St Peter and St Paul. His daughter Olivia, who died at the age of seven, is buried at Little Missenden in a plot that was intended for Dahl himself and his first wife, the actress Patricia Neal. But this plan was changed when Dahl and Neal were divorced in 1983, seven years before

his death. The gardens of his home are open to the public once a year.

PRINCES RISBOROUGH
9 miles W of Chesham on the A4010

🏛 Manor House

A busy little town with many 16th century cottages, 17th and 18th century houses and, at its centre, a brick Market House of 1824. The ground floor is an empty space providing shelter for market stalls, while in the room above the Town Council meets.

The Prince in the name of this Chilterns Gap market town is the Black Prince, the eldest son of Edward III, who held land and had a palace here. The town stands on the Icknield Way and during the stage coach era was a major stopping place. It is said that the last regular stage-coach service to run in England ended its journey from London here in 1898.

Off the market square, opposite the church, the **Princes Risborough Manor House** (National Trust) is a 17th century redbrick house with a handsome Jacobean staircase.

WENDOVER
6 miles NW of Chesham on the A413

🚶 Wendover Woods   🚶 Coombe Hill

This delightful old market town is situated in a gap on the northern escarpment of the Chiltern Hills, in the Metropolitan Green Belt and the Chilterns Area of Outstanding Natural Beauty. It has an attractive main street of half-timbered, thatched houses and cottages of which the best examples are Anne Boleyn's Cottages. A picturesque place, often seen as the gateway to the Chilterns, Wendover has a fine selection of antique and craft shops, tea rooms and bookshops. In 1300 the town was granted the right to send two representatives to Parliament; these have

🎬 stories and anecdotes   🦅 famous people   🎨 art and craft   🚲 entertainment and sport   🚶 walks

COCK AND RABBIT INN & GRAZIEMILLE RESTAURANT

The Lee, Nr. Great Missenden,
Buckinghamshire HP16 9LZ
Tel: 01494 837540
Fax: 01494 837512
e-mail: info@gianfranco.demon.co.uk
website: www.graziemille.co.uk

Hidden in the heart of the Chiltern Hills you can discover the delightful village of The Lee, familiar to many visitors as a filming location for a number of TV programmes, such as *Midsommer Murders, Treasure Hunt* and *Pie in the Sky*, to mention but a few. But who would have thought that in this quaint village, you would find a splendid Italian restaurant and pub? **The Cock & Rabbit Inn and Cafe Graziemille**, owned and run by Gianfranco Parola with his wife Victoria, is the perfect place for a relaxing lunch or elegant dinner. Surrounded by a lovely garden and sun terrace, this pub is an absolute delight. It has the appearance of a quintessential English country house, which of course it was when originally built, and Gianfranco arrived here in 1985 and renovated and restored it to what you see today.

Inside you will find two bar areas both with open fires, which add to the welcoming atmosphere and relaxed ambiance. The pub has become a popular destination and stop off point for walkers, ramblers and tourists exploring the local countryside. Open every lunchtime and evening, food is served at each session, with Gianfranco being responsible for the superb menu inspired by dishes from the Piedmont region of Italy where he was born. His specialities, many of which use the local wild garlic, include beef carpaccio, sautéed mushrooms and toasted goat's cheese to start, followed by pasta Graziemille, chicken contessa rosa or salmon Graziemille in dill, cream and champagne sauce. To finish there is, of course, that most famous of Italian desserts, tiramisu, made to Gianfranco's family recipe. Meals can be enjoyed in the delightful Garden Restaurant or in the bars.

Cafe Graziemille is dedicated to catering for weddings and other functions and to providing a delightful location and intimate setting to dine with friends. Any event can be specially catered in a distinctive Italian style. Simply let Gianfranco, Victoria and their friendly, efficient staff do all the hard work while you enjoy yourself.

🏚 historic building   🏛 museum   🏛 historic site   ⊕ scenic attraction   ⍦ flora and fauna

WELL HEELED OF WENDOVER

5 High Street, Wendover,
Buckinghamshire HP22 6DU
Tel: 01296 622186

If visitors to Wendover notice that the townspeople are particularly well shod, it's probably because they've bought their shoes at **Well Heeled of Wendover**. Owned and run by Kate and Ron Camans, the High Street shop sells a wide range of quality shoes in all styles.

Ladies' shoes include Gabor, Ava, Vandal, Ecco, H B Cappolini and Rohde and, among the men's brands, are Loake, Barker, Ecco, Camel Active and Rockport. The shop also stocks a range of accessories, including leather goods, handbags, silk ties and costume jewellery.

included John Hampden, George Canning and Edmund Burke, and the right was only extinguished by the Reform Act of 1832. The town is twinned with Liffre in Brittany, and the Twinning Stones outside the library are permanent reminders of the close ties.

The town also offers visitors an opportunity of seeing the glorious countryside through the medium of **Wendover Woods**. Created for recreational pursuits - there's a mountain bike course at Aston Hill - as well as for conservation and timber production, these Forestry Commission woods offer visitors numerous trails through the coniferous and broadleaved woodland. It is one of the best sites in the country to spot the tiny firecrest, a

RUMSEY'S CHOCOLATERIE

The Old Bank, 26 High Street, Wendover,
Buckinghamshire HP22 6EA
Tel: 01296 625060
e-mail: rumsey@btconnect.com
website: www.rumseys.co.uk

Stepping inside **Rumsey's Chocolaterie** on the high Street of Wendover you are greeted by the alluring smell of hot chocolate and freshly ground coffee. The interior of the chocolaterie is modelled on the marvellous film *Chocolat* and it's a perfect place to relax and take a break from the bustle of the world outside. Nigel Rumsey is a true master of his trade, and his chocolates – 'individually made for the individual' – have won numerous awards. They are made in more than 40 flavours, and with new flavours being added all the time, they really do provide a wonderful choice for chocolate lovers.

While Nigel is producing his enticing collections, Mary serves chocolates and a range of hot drinks, delicious cakes and pastries, and light savoury meals. If you sit at a table on the ground floor you can place your order with the friendly staff and watch the chocolate-making process through a glass wall. The upper floor is an ideal place to have a quiet lunch. Rumsey's, which is licensed for beer and wine, is open from 8.30am to 6.30pm Monday to Saturday and from 10am to 6pm on Sunday.

SALLY TURNER ANTIQUES & JEWELLERY

Hogarth House, High Street, Wendover,
Buckinghamshire HP22 6DU
Tel/Fax: 01296 624402

Sally Turner Antiques & Jewellery is in the attractive main street of Wendover, a pleasant market town with many fine old buildings. Sally is the third generation of a family business that started in Chelsea in the 1970s.

The services Sally and her staff offer include all types of repair work, and a master goldsmith is on site to carry out expert gold repairs. Quality and reliability are watchwords, and a same day service is available on certain items.

Sally buys and sells antique jewellery, and among other items held in her shop are 18th and 19th century furniture, clocks, new designer jewellery and fine pieces of silver and glass. Handmade commissions are another speciality, and the shop also undertakes valuations on pieces of jewellery. Shop hours are 10.30am to 5.30pm; closed Wednesday and Sunday.

bird that is becoming increasingly rare.

Off the B4010 a short drive west of Wendover, **Coombe Hill** is the highest point in the Chilterns and affords superb views across the Vale of Aylesbury, the Berkshire Downs and the Cotswolds. On the summit is a monument dedicated to the men who died in the Boer War. The National Trust has introduced a flock of sheep on to the hill to control the invasion of scrub and to encourage the grass.

Aylesbury

🏛 County Museum 🦉 Roald Dahl's Children's Gallery

Founded in Saxon times and the county town

HUNTERS FARM & COUNTRY SHOP

Fleet Marston, Bicester Road (A41), Aylesbury,
Buckinghamshire HP18 0PZ
Tel: 01296 651314

In a rural setting on the A41 northwest of Aylesbury, **Hunters Farm & Country Shop** is housed in a converted tithe barn and stables. The shop offers plenty to attract the visitor with a fine selection of goods to attract the eye and the palate. On the

food side, the shop sells a tempting choice of casseroles, cakes and desserts, all made on the premises or locally, along with jams and honeys, curds and chutneys, free-range eggs, fruit, vegetables and English wines. Also on display are toys and games, quality clothing from brands such as Slimma, Double Two and Tulcan, lovely textiles, mugs, trays, exquisite jewellery and unique gifts and cards. Open 9am to 5.30pm Monday to Saturday.

🏛 historic building 🏛 museum 🏛 historic site 🦆 scenic attraction 🌱 flora and fauna

since the reign of Henry VIII, Aylesbury lies in rich pastureland in the shelter of the Chilterns. Post-war development took away much of the town's character, but some parts, particularly around the market square, are protected by a conservation order. At various times in the Civil War, Aylesbury was a base for both Cromwell and the King, and this period of history is covered in the splendidly refurbished **County Museum & Art Gallery**. The museum, housed in a splendid Georgian building, also has an exhibit on Louis XVIII of France, who lived in exile at nearby Hartwell House. Also within the museum is the award-winning **Roald Dahl Children's Gallery**, an exciting hands-on gallery for children that uses Dahl's characters to introduce and explain the museum's treasures.

Around Aylesbury

MENTMORE
6 miles NE of Aylesbury off the B488

🏠 Mentmore Towers

The village is home to the first of the Rothschild mansions, **Mentmore Towers**, which was built for Baron Meyer Amschel de Rothschild between 1852 and 1855. A splendid building in the Elizabethan style it was designed by Sir Joseph Paxton, the designer of Crystal Palace, and is a superb example of grandiose Victorian extravagance. However, the lavish decoration hides several technologically advanced details for those times, such as central heating, and, as might be expected from Paxton, there are large sheets of glass and a glass roof in the design. In the late 19th century the house became the home of Lord Rosebery and the magnificent turreted building was the scene of many glittering parties and gatherings of

the most wealthy and influential people in the country. However, in the 1970s the house was put up for auction and, while the furniture and works of art were sold to the four corners of the world, the building was bought by the Maharishi Mahesh Yogi and it is now the headquarters of his University of Natural Law. Mentmore Towers is occasionally open to the public.

IVINGHOE
7 miles E of Aylesbury on the B488

🏠 Ford End Watermill   ⛰ Ivinghoe Beacon

🚶 Ridgeway National Trail

As the large village church would suggest, Ivinghoe was once a market town of some importance in the surrounding area. In this now quiet village can be found **Ford End Watermill**, a listed building that, though probably much older, was first recorded in 1767. The only working watermill, with its original machinery, left in Buckinghamshire, the farm in which it is set has also managed to retain the atmosphere of an 18th century farm.

To the east lies the National Trust's **Ivinghoe Beacon**, a wonderful viewpoint on the edge of the Chiltern Hills. The site of an Iron Age hill fort, the beacon was also the inspiration for Sir Walter Scott's *Ivanhoe*. The Beacon is at one end of Britain's oldest road, the **Ridgeway National Trail**. The other end is the World Heritage Site of Avebury in Wiltshire, and the 85-mile length of the Ridgeway still follows the same route over the high ground used since prehistoric times. Walkers can use the whole length of the trail (April to November is the best time) and horseriders and cyclists can ride on much of the western part.

📖 stories and anecdotes   🐦 famous people   🎨 art and craft   ✏ entertainment and sport   🚶 walks

PITSTONE
7 miles E of Aylesbury off the B489

🏛 Pitstone Windmill   🏛 Farm Museum

Though the exact age of **Pitstone Windmill** (National Trust) is not known, it is certainly one of the oldest post mills in Britain. The earliest documentary reference to its existence was made in 1624. It is open to the public on a limited basis. Also in the village is a **Farm Museum**, where all manner of farm and barn machinery, along with domestic bygones, are on display. A delightful hour or two can be spent cruising from Pitstone Wharf along a lovely stretch of the Grand Union Canal.

Pitstone Windmill

vegetables from the Farm Shop. Also here are the famous Aylesbury ducks and other poultry, pigs, small pet animals and donkeys, facilities for children, shops and a café.

STOKE MANDEVILLE
2 miles S of Aylesbury on the A4010

🐐 Bucks Goat Centre

The village is best known for its hospital, which specialises in the treatment of spinal injuries and burns. Just south of Stoke, on Old Risborough Road, **Bucks Goat Centre** (see panel below) has the most comprehensive collection of goat breeds in the country. Visitors can groom, cuddle and feed them with

GREAT KIMBLE
5 miles S of Aylesbury on the A4010

🏛 Chequers

Though the village is home to a church with an interesting series of 14th century wall paintings, its real claim to fame is the nearby 16th century mansion, **Chequers**, the country residence of the British Prime Minister. Originally built by William Hawtrey in 1565, but much altered and enlarged in the 18th and

The Bucks Goat Centre

Layby Farm, Stoke Mandeville, Buckinghamshire HP22 5XJ
Tel: 01296 612983
e-mail: info@bucksgoatcentre.co.uk
website: www.bucksgoatcentre.co.uk

The Bucks Goat Centre is a small, open farm, featuring every breed of domestic goat found in Britain. Other farm and pet animals to be seen include pigs, poultry, rabbits, guinea pigs, chinchillas, reptiles, donkeys and llamas. Visitors are invited to feed the goats with freshly prepared vegetables from the farm shop. There is good access to the attraction for the disabled visitors. Other facilities and attractions include safe, on-site parking, a souvenir shop, cafe, picnic lawn, a toddlers' play room and a children's play area with trampoline, swings and slides. Children's birthday parties are also catered for. Please contact for details.

🏛 historic building   🏛 museum   🏛 historic site   ♧ scenic attraction   🐐 flora and fauna

19th centuries, the house was restored to its original form by Arthur Lee in 1912. Later, in 1920, as Lord Lee of Fareham, he gave the house and estate to the nation to be used as the prime minister's country home. The first Prime Minister to make use of Chequers was Lloyd George, and many who came to know the house later moved to the area: Ramsay MacDonald's daughter lived at nearby Speen; Harold Wilson bought a house in Great Missenden; and Nye Bevan owned a farm in the Chilterns.

WOTTON UNDERWOOD
8 miles W of Aylesbury off the A41

🏠 Wotton House

In this secluded village stands the privately owned **Wotton House**, a charming early-18th century building said to be practically identical to the original Buckingham Palace. The gardens, which feature more than a dozen follies, were laid out between 1757 and 1760 by Capability Brown.

BOARSTALL
12 miles W of Aylesbury off the B4011

🏠 Boarstall Tower   🦆 Duck Decoy

A curious feature here is the 17th century **Duck Decoy** set on the edge of a lake to catch birds for the table. The site, run by the National Trust, contains a nature trail and exhibition hall. The National Trust is also responsible for **Boarstall Tower**, the 14th century stone gatehouse of a long demolished fortified house.

WADDESDON
4 miles NW of Aylesbury on the A41

🏠 Waddesdon Manor

The village is home to another of the county's magnificent country houses, in this case

Waddesdon Manor (National Trust). Built between 1874 and 1889 for Baron Ferdinand de Rothschild, in the style of a French Renaissance château, the house is set in rolling English countryside and borrows elements from several different French châteaux, surrounded by formal gardens and landscaped grounds. These contain, among many treasures, a French-style aviary in a part of the gardens designed by the popular 20th century American landscape artist Lanning Roper, hundreds of trees both native and foreign, a fabulous parterre, Italian, French and Dutch statuary, and a huge pheasant named Ferdinand made from 15,000 bedding plants on a steel frame. The French influence even extended to the carthorses used on the site - powerful Percheron mares that were imported from Normandy. The house contains one of the best collections of 18th century French decorative arts in the world, including Sèvres porcelain, Beauvais tapestries and fine furniture. There are also paintings by Gainsborough, Reynolds and 17th century Dutch and Flemish masters.

QUAINTON
5 miles NW of Aylesbury off the A41

🏠 Tower Mill   🚂 Buckinghamshire Railway Centre

A pleasant village with the remains of an ancient cross on the green, a number of fine Georgian houses and a row of almshouses built in 1687. Here, too, is another of the county's windmills, **Quainton Tower Mill**, built in the 1830s and 100ft high. Quite early in its life it was fitted with a steam engine, but despite this innovation the mill's working life extended barely 50 years. Just south of the village, at Quainton Railway Station, is the **Buckinghamshire Railway Centre**, a working steam museum where visitors can

📖 stories and anecdotes   🗣 famous people   🎨 art and craft   🎭 entertainment and sport   🚶 walks

Ludgershall

Distance: *5.2 miles (8.3 kilometres)*

Typical time: *180 mins*

Height gain: *85 metres*

Map: *Explorer 180*

Walk: *www.walkingworld.com ID:1234*

Contributor: *Ron and Jenny Glynn*

ACCESS INFORMATION:

Take the A4100 between Bicester and Aylesbury, turning right at sign for Ludgershall. There is ample parking on roadside in village.

DESCRIPTION:

This little walk in Buckinghamshire is a mixture of footpaths, bridleways and quiet country roads. It starts from near the church in the attractive village of Ludgershall and takes a minor road to another part of the parish, before leaving it on footpaths in lovely countryside.

The small setting of Wotton Underwood is approached on a hard-laid path which passes the magnificent Wotton House in its wonderful surroundings. The estate is quite extensive and includes a cluster of charming cottages and a large area of beautiful parkland. There follows a lengthy stretch on a country road that runs between dense and peaceful woodland and eventually returns to Ludgershall.

The architecture in these parts is of red brick, very appealing and individual. There are no great heights to contend with, just a gradual incline on Windmill Hill, just before Wotton, so this walk is suitable for those not wanting too strenuous an exercise in the great outdoors.

FEATURES:

Lake/Loch, Church, Stately Home, Wildlife, Birds, Flowers, Great Views, Butterflies, Woodland

WALK DIRECTIONS:

1 | Take the minor road signed to Wotton, just before the church at Peartree Farm, to walk along to junction.

2 | Walk over to narrow path at Wotton End and follow hedge-line to cross a brook. Take the right-hand fork over common ground across to an opening.

3 | Walk on, past stile on left where a network of paths lead off and continue with hedge on left, in ridge and furrow meadowland. Climb stile and continue over middle of next field and then another, in same direction and with Tittershall Wood over to the left.

4 | Take double stile and footbridge to turn right on bridleway, with hedge on right. Enter walkers' gate ahead and continue through another gate, to cross road to another stile. Walk on over large field, with farm buildings on right, gradually climbing uphill.

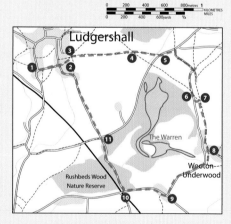

5 | Head slightly right over two stiles, aiming for the right of Middle Farm ahead. Take stile in corner of field onto hard track.

6 | Walk over to white gate of farmhouse and take stile on the left of it; follow edge of small field to metal kissing-gate.

7 | Turn right through wooden gate and pass back of farmhouse, to walk on a hard-laid path passing through a wildflower meadow. Cross over a miniature railway track, where you might be lucky enough to see a small-gauge locomotive being driven along. Pass a beautifully styled redbrick house, then turn right through gate to walk by Wotton House, a very large and imposing setting of three huge buildings standing behind high wrought-iron gates. The path runs downhill with the copper spire of Wotton Church in view.

8 | Walk ahead over large green to join road and follow it along between trees and hedgerows. Pass pretty half-timbered estate cottages and notice a large deer herd on the right, on the way to junction.

9 | Turn right to pass Lower Lawn Farm and cottages, with undulating countryside ahead.

10 | Turn right towards Ludgershall and Kingswood on narrow road running through woodland. A glimpse of the rear of Wotton House can be seen across parkland where there is a clearing. Continue again through woodland to meet junction.

11 | Walk on towards Ludgershall on a quiet country lane, hedged and tree-lined. Pass a row of houses on the edge of village and Brooklands Farm a bit further on. The road bends and passes other individually styled and interesting dwellings. Turn left into Church Lane and retrace steps to start, getting a better view from this direction of St Mary the Virgin Church, with its squat tower.

Quainton Tower Mill

relive the golden age of steam. The centre boasts one of the largest collections of preserved steam and diesel locomotives in the country, including engines from South Africa, the USA and Egypt as well as from Britain. Visitors can ride behind full-sized steam locos and on the extensive miniature railway. The beautifully restored Rowley Road Station (1851), moved here from Oxford, also serves as the main visitor centre.

Buckingham

🏛 Chantry Chapel 🏛 Old Gaol Museum

This pleasant town, the centre of which is contained in a loop of the River Ouse, dates back to Saxon times and was granted a charter by Alfred the Great. Although it became the

The Old Gaol, Buckingham

county town in AD 888, when Alfred divided the shires, from an early date many of the functions of a county town were performed by the more centrally located Aylesbury.

Thanks to a disastrous fire in 1725, this lively little market town is characterised by a fine array of Georgian buildings, including Castle House in West Street, the impressive Old Gaol, one of the first purpose-built county gaols in England, and the Town Hall, located at either end of the Market Square. The **Old Gaol Museum** not only illustrates the building's history but also has displays on the town's past and the county's military

exploits. A high-tech glass roof was added in 2000, spanning the original prisoners' exercise yard to create a new light-filled area for special exhibits and an educational resource centre. One building that did survive the devastating fire of 1725 is the **Buckingham Chantry Chapel** (National Trust). The chapel was constructed in 1475 on the site of a Norman building whose doorway has been retained. Well worth a visit, the chapel was restored by George Gilbert Scott in 1875.

A much more recent addition to this delightful country market town is the University of Buckingham, which was granted its charter in 1983.

Around Buckingham

WINSLOW
5 miles SE of Buckingham on the A413

A small country town of ancient origin, where Offa, the King of Mercia, stayed in AD752.

PADBURY MEATS

Main Street, Padbury, nr Buckingham,
Buckinghamshire MK18 2AY
Tel: 01280 823366

Local sources supply most of the top-quality meat that has won **Padbury Meats** a reputation that extends over a wide area. Friendly personal service and consistent high quality bring the customers here for the farm-reared meats in various cuts and joints, boned or bone-in, the excellent poultry and the seasonal game both furred and feathered. Sausages in a variety of great flavours, beef, lamb and venison burgers and turkey kebabs are good at any time of year and ideal for summer barbecues. The shop also sells cooked meats, salamis, Parma ham, pâtés and terrines, sauces and preserves and English cheeses. Opening hours are 10am to 5pm Monday to Saturday, 11am to 5pm Sunday.

🏛 historic building   🏛 museum   🏚 historic site   🗺 scenic attraction   🌱 flora and fauna

The village's most prominent building is Winslow Hall, a delightful Wren house set in beautiful gardens. House and gardens are open for visits by appointment only.

STEWKLEY
10 miles SE of Buckingham on the B4032

🏛 Church of St Michael

Stewkley, renowned as being the longest village in England, is even better known for its wonderful **Church of St Michael**, one of the finest Norman churches in the land, with spectacular zigzag patterns and a massive tower. Built between 1150-1180, this mighty building has remained virtually unaltered.

WING
12 miles SE of Buckingham on the A418

🏛 All Saints Church   🏛 Ascott

Another village famous for its church. **All Saints Church,** standing on a rise above the Vale of Aylesbury, retains most of its original Saxon features, including the nave, aisles, west wall, crypt and apse. The roof is covered in medieval figures, many of them playing musical instruments. This remarkable church also contains numerous brasses and monuments, notably to the Dormer family

who came to Ascott Hall in the 1520s. Just east of the village, **Ascott** was bought in 1874 by Leopold Rothschild who virtually rebuilt the original farmhouse round its timber-framed core. Now in the care of the National Trust, the house contains a superb collection of fine paintings, Oriental porcelain and English and French furniture. The grounds are magnificent too, with specimen trees and shrubs, a herbaceous walk, lily pond, Dutch garden, an evergreen topiary sundial and two fountains, one in bronze, the other in marble, sculpted by the American artist Thomas Waldo Story.

MIDDLE CLAYDON
5 miles S of Buckingham off the A413

🏛 Claydon House

The village is home to **Claydon House** (National Trust), a Jacobean manor house that was remodelled in the 1750s at a time of great enthusiasm for all things Oriental. The home of the Verney family for over 350 years, the house contains a number of state rooms with magnificent carved wood and plaster decorations on an Oriental theme. What makes the house particularly interesting is its associations with Florence Nightingale.

THE WHITE HART
Pound Lane, Preston Bissett, nr Buckingham, Buckinghamshire MK18 4LX
Tel: 01280 847969

Sarah and Roland Jones run the **White Hart**, a thatched pub full of atmosphere in a pretty village off the A421 southwest of Buckingham. The convivial atmosphere, the well-kept real ales (Timothy Taylor Landlord, Hook Norton and summer guests) and the excellent food have made this a very popular place for both local residents and visitors to the area. The choices range from lunchtime ciabattas to pasta and meat, fish and vegetarian dishes, many with an Italian inspiration. The traditional bar has a servery on both sides, one serving the 24-seat dining area. The county town of Buckingham is close by, and another local place of interest is the National Trust's Claydon House, a Jacobean manor house closely linked with Florence Nightingale.

📖 stories and anecdotes   🐿 famous people   🎨 art and craft   ✒ entertainment and sport   🚶 walks

Florence's sister married into the Verney family and the pioneer of modern hospital care spent long periods at the house, especially during her old age. Her bedroom in the house and a museum of her life and experiences during the Crimean War can be seen here. Florence died in 1910 after a long career which embraced concerns of public health as well as the training of nurses; she was the first woman to be awarded the Order of Merit.

Thornborough Medieval Bridge

THORNBOROUGH
3 miles E of Buckingham off the A422

This lively and attractive village is home to Buckinghamshire's only surviving medieval bridge. Built in the 14th century, the six-arched structure spans Claydon Brook. Close by are two large mounds which were opened in 1839 and revealed a wealth of Roman objects many of which are on display at the Old Gaol Musuem. Though it was known that there was a Roman temple here its location has not been found.

STOWE
3 miles N of Buckingham off the A422

🏛 Stowe School & Gardens

Stowe School is a leading public school which occupies an 18th century mansion that was once the home of the Dukes of Buckingham. Worked upon by two wealthy owners who both had a great sense of vision, the magnificent mansion house, which was finally completed in 1774, is open to the public during school holidays. Between 1715

and 1749, the owner, Viscount Cobham, hired various well known landscape designers to lay out the fantastic **Stowe Landscape Gardens** (National Trust) that can still be seen around the house. Taking over the house in 1750, Earl Temple, along with his nephew, expanded the grounds and today they remain one of the most original and finest landscape gardens in Europe. Temples, alcoves and rotundas are scattered around the landscape, strategically placed to evoke in the onlooker a romantic and poetic frame of mind. It is one of the more intriguing quirks of fate that Lancelot Brown, always known as Capability Brown because he told his clients that their parks had capabilities, was head gardener at Stowe for 10 years. He arrived here in 1741 and began to work out his own style, a more natural style of landscape gardening which was to take over where gardens like the ones at Stowe left off.

SILVERSTONE
5 miles N of Buckingham off the A43

The home of British motor racing, Silverstone is best known as the venue for the British Formula I Grand Prix. But it hosts many varied motorsport events throughout the year, including the Silverstone Historic Festival, British F3, GT, Touring Car and Superbike championships. It is also the place of dreams for boy racers, who can try their hand at driving a wide range of cars round the circuit, including single-seaters, rally cars, 4X4s, E-type Jaguars, Lotus Elises and Porsche 911 Carrera Supercars.

Milton Keynes

🏛 Christ Church 🏛 Museum

Most people's perception of this modern town is of a concrete jungle but the reality of Milton Keynes could not be more different. The development corporation that was charged, in 1967, with organising the new town has provided a place of tree-lined boulevards, uncongested roads, spacious surroundings, and acres of parkland. It is too, of course, a modern town, with new housing, high-tech industries, modern leisure facilities, and a large covered shopping centre. One of the town's most notable buildings is **Christ Church**, built in the style of Christopher Wren; the first purpose-built ecumenical city church in Britain, it was opened in March 1992 by the Queen. While Milton Keynes is certainly a place of the late 20th century, it has not altogether forgotten the rural past of the villages, which are now incorporated into the suburbs of the town. **Milton Keynes Museum**, run by a large and active group of volunteers, has a large collection of industrial, domestic and agricultural bygones that illustrates the lives of the people who lived in the area in the 200 years leading up to the creation of the new town. A Victorian house features a working kitchen and laundry, and among other eye-catching exhibits are a local tramcar and an impressive collection of working telephones.

Around Milton Keynes

BLETCHLEY
2 miles S of Milton Keynes on the A421

🏛 Bletchley Park

Now effectively a suburb of Milton Keynes, Bletchley is famous for **Bletchley Park**, the Victorian mansion which housed the wartime codebreakers who beat odds of 150 million million million to 1 and cracked the Nazi Enigma cypher, the crucial key to German military and intelligence communications. Along with a display of military vehicles and a wealth of World War II memorabilia, there

MOSELEY'S FARM SHOP
George Farm, Little Brickhill, Milton Keynes MK17 9LT
Tel: 01525 261642

Close to the A5 south of Milton Keynes and very near the Woburn Estate, **Moseley's Farm Shop** stands in the yard of a 20-acre farm. 2006 sees the 30th anniversary of the shop, which is now owned and run by Dean North. His many years as a butcher have ensured that he sources the very best meat, traditionally reared without antibiotic growth promoters, hormones or meat and bone meal feed. This means that his sausages and burgers are the best around, and other meats in the well-stocked freezers and chilled cabinets include home-cured bacon and game from the Woburn estate.

🎞 stories and anecdotes 🦜 famous people 🎨 art and craft 🎟 entertainment and sport 🚶 walks

is a Cryptology Trail that allows visitors to follow the path of a coded message from its interception through decoding to interpretation. At the height of the war, more than 12,000 people worked at Bletchley Park.

Volunteers have recently reconstructed one of the vast electro-mechanical decoders that broke the Enigma code. The first of these machines were installed in 1940 and by 1945 more than 200 were at work. The reconstructed machine, which weighs more than a ton, is due to go on public exhibition in 2007. Though Bletchley is now all but merged with its larger neighbour, it still retains a distinctive air. The original village here dates back to Roman times and was first recorded as a town in 1108.

STONY STRATFORD

3 miles NW of Milton Keynes off the A5

Often considered to be the jewel in the crown of the villages around Milton Keynes, Stony Stratford was a popular staging post on the old Roman road, Watling Street. Richard III, as the Duke of Gloucester, came in 1483 to detain the uncrowned Prince Edward before committing him to the Tower of London, and other notable visitors include Charles Dickens, Samuel Johnson and John Wesley, who preached under the tree that still stands in the market place.

GAYHURST

4 miles N of Milton Keynes off the B526

Built during the reign of Elizabeth I, Gayhurst House was given to Sir Francis

---

BEST BUTCHERS LTD

Unit 5, Lower Rectory Farm, Great Brickhill, nr Milton Keynes, Buckinghamshire MK17 9AF
Tel: 01908 375275
e-mail: bestbutchers@btconnect.com
website: www.thebestbutchers.co.uk

Quality, variety and personal service are watchwords at the **Best Butchers Ltd**, a retail shop specialising in locally sourced meat. Simon Boddy trained as a master butcher and followed his trade working for others for some years before opening his own shop in 1994 in these premises on a working organic farm. Besides the joints and cuts of beef, lamb and pork and the poultry, the shop is renowned for its pork, beef and lamb sausages, all made on the premises, for its bacon, dry-cured and smoked over beech, and the wonderful Brickhill ham. This is Simon's adaptation of Parma ham, air-dried and smoked. Best Butchers also sells fresh fish from

Billingsgate on Fridays and Saturdays, and a fine selection of English and Continental cheeses.

The shop is bright, modern and spotless, a winner every year of the Clean food Award. Shop hours are 8am to 5.30pm Monday to Friday, 8am to 4pm Saturday.

🏛 historic building   🏛 museum   🏛 historic site   🌳 scenic attraction   🌿 flora and fauna

THE THREE LOCKS

Leighton Road,
Stoke Hammond,
Bucks, MK17 9DD
Tel: 01525 270592
website: www.romaniinns.co.uk

Situated just outside the pretty Buckinghamshire village of Stoke Hammond and just 10 minutes drive from the bustling new city of Milton Keynes, The Three Locks is a traditional country pub and restaurant set on the Grand Union Canal.

This well-known canalside pub, built in the 19th century, takes it name from the flight of three locks directly outside the front of the pub, guaranteeing you a slice of canal life as you sip your pint or enjoy your meal. A relaxing walk or cycle along the canal or a round at the nearby golf course are among the local attractions.

The Three Locks comprises a large bar area, with outside seating area and a separate restaurant. The bar serves freshly prepared, wholesome meals and snacks as well as offering traditional ales, a pool table and darts. The restaurant is open seven days a week and is locally renowned for its superb Sunday carvery and for the extensive choice of vegetarian options available on its menu.

With an excellent local reputation for great live music on Friday and Saturday nights, and as a much sought after wedding reception venue, the Three Locks has much to offer the discerning visitor.

Drake in recognition of his circumnavigation of the world, though the building seen today was not the one that Drake lived in. It was later occupied by Sir Everard Digby, one of the conspirators behind the Gunpowder Plot of 1605.

OLNEY

8 miles N of Milton Keynes on the A509

🏛 Church of St Peter & St Paul

🜎 Emberton Country Park

🏛 Cowper and Newton Museum ⌖ Pancake Race

Variety's the spice of life;
Monarch of all I survey;
God made the country and
man made the town…

All these familiar phrases are now embedded in the language but how many could name the

writer? In fact, they all came from the pen of the 18th century poet William Cowper who spent the last 20 years of his life in the elegant market town of Olney.

He came to the town to be near his friend the Reverend John Newton, a former slave trader who had repented and become 'a man of gloomy piety'. The two men collaborated on a book of religious verse, the Olney Hymns, in which Cowper's contributions included such perennial favourites as

Oh! for a closer walk with God;
Hark, my soul! It is the Lord;
and God moves in a mysterious way.

The house in which Cowper lived from 1768 to 1786 is now the **Cowper and Newton Museum**, an interesting place that not only concentrates on Cowper's life and

---

🎭 stories and anecdotes   ⛴ famous people   🎨 art and craft   ⌖ entertainment and sport   🜎 walks

THE NEW STUDIO

Rose Court, Olney,
Buckinghamshire MK46 4BY
Tel: 01234 711994
e-mail: keren@thenewstudio.co.uk
website: www.thenewstudio.co.uk

The New Studio, opened in 1997 by Keren Monnickendam, is located in a 18th century building in a courtyard just off the main square in Olney. 1,600 square feet on two floors are given over to showcasing the work of talented British artists and craftspeople. The gallery supports their work at individual and group level, and it has, ever since opening, been one of the most comprehensive outlets for contemporary artists. Downstairs is light and airy, with cream-washed walls framing an abundance of colour and energy, and several jewellery cases are full of interesting and unusual pieces. Upstairs is a cool, calm and relaxed space for browsing among the unique artwork on display in the ever-changing exhibitions. The separate Glass Gallery exhibits changing collections of modern and antique glass. The scope of the studio covers painting, sculpture, metalwork, furniture, glassware, woodwork, ceramics, jewellery and textiles. More than 600 artists and craftspeople have shown their work here over the years, and over 80 currently show, each one described in detail, with examples of their work, on the studio's outstanding website. The New Studio holds major exhibitions in June and December, and others throughout the year. Exhibitions in 2006 have included the Chiltern & Decorum Potters Guild, work by the artist Rachelle Roberts, individual textile and furniture makers and the Annual Artists of Buckinghamshire Exhibition.

The Studio, which stands a few steps from the market place and public car park, is open from 10am to 4.30pm Monday to Saturday, 12 noon to 4.30pm Sunday.

A few of the current featured artists:

Furniture: Jonathan Knight and Paul Weatherup
Ceramics: Ralph Jandrell and Annie Peaker
Wood: Richard Forgan and Peter Lloyd
Paintings: Justin Tew and Ben Catt
Glass: Stuart Ackroyd and Emma Dicks
Textiles: Samantha Holmes and Boo & Peek
Jewellery: Carol Clift and David Weinberger
Sculpture: Jeni Clarke
Metal: Rob Mulholland

work but also has some exhibits and collections concerned with the times in which he lived and the life of Olney. Each of the rooms of the large early-18th century town house has been specially themed and there are numerous displays of Cowper's work, including the *Olney Hymns*. As we went to press, the museum was about to acquire the most important collection of Cowper-related material ever to come on the market – 170 letters, 24 books from Cowper's library, two miniatures by William Blake and many objects connected with his life (for details see www.cowperjohnson.org.uk). Cowper was also a keen gardener and the summer house, where he wrote many of his poems, can still be seen out in the rear

garden. Here he experimented with plants that were new to 18th century England. Also at the museum is the nationally important Lace Collection and items particular to the shoemaking industry which was another busy local trade in the 19th and early 20th century.

When Cowper died in 1800 he was buried at East Dereham in Norfolk but his associate, the reformed slave-trader, is interred in the churchyard of **St Peter and St Paul**, where he had been the curate. This church is a spacious building dating from the mid-14th century and its spire rises some 185 feet to dominate the skyline of Olney.

For more than 300 years Olney was a centre of lace-making by hand, using wooden or bone bobbins. When lace was at its most

OLNEY FURNITURE & COLLECTABLES

6 The Galleries, Market Place,
Olney, Buckinghamshire MK46 4EA
Tel: 01234 713338 Fax: 01234 713376
e-mail: enquiries@olneyfurniture.com
website: www.olneyfurniture.com

New proprietors Sandra & Bob Wingerath transformed this furniture shop in the Galleries off the High Street by the Market Square when they re-opened **Olney Furniture & Collectables** early in 2006.

Specialising in top quality traditional and contemporary furniture, principally manufactured within the UK they pride themselves in offering excellent personal service and products not to be found in city centre stores. "We aim to assist our customers, whatever their budget, to bring individuality into every room of their homes and we will take the time to source items and fabrics so that they may stamp their own identity on the end result."

Sumptuous upholstered sofas and chairs, crafted dining, bedroom and occasional furniture sit alongside a wide selection of lighting, mirrors and art. An area devoted to fabrics covers all tastes – Linwood, Monkwell/Crowson, Osborne & Little, Liberty and Nina Campbell to name a few. Look on the website to uncover the up to date range of stylists – Royal Oak, John Sankey/Henderson Russell, Whitehead, Winsor, Nina Campbell and Artistic furniture, Rochamp and Franklite lighting, Emily Readett-Bayley accessories and the more esoteric Lampe Berger, the unique way to fragrance and kill germs within the home – see the attractive burners and pick from the wide range of perfumes in stock.

The shop is able to offer a fully bespoke service on most of its glass, wooden or upholstered furniture so if you want something special and original for your home Olney Furniture & Collectables will be able to help. Normal opening hours are 9.30am – 5.30pm Monday to Saturday and 12 noon – 3.30pm on Sunday and at other times by prior arrangement.

TUSTING LUGGAGE & FURNITURE

The Tannery Warehouse, Lavendon,
nr Olney, Buckinghamshire MK46 4EU
Tel: 01234 712266 Fax: 01234 713545
e-mail: info@tusting.co.uk
website: www.tusting.co.uk

The name of **Tusting** has been associated with fine English leather goods for over 130 years. For five generations the Tusting family have been at the heart of the English leather trade – tanning, grading and trading the world's finest leather. The current factory lies in the heart of the English countryside on the Buckinghamshire-Northamptonshire border, close to the original factory founded in 1875 by the present owner's great' great grandfather. The firm was a major supplier of leather to the shoe trade, but with that trade diminishing with the rapid growth of imported footwear Tusting diversified into luggage and furniture.

The workshop produces a superb range of leather brief cases and business bags, travel luggage, ladies' bags and specialist country products. The expert knowledge is the secret ingredient in the selection of the perfect leather for each piece made in the factory. The workshop combines the precious heritage with staff highly skilled in the full range of leatherworking techniques; thoughtful and responsive design; meticulously chosen materials; and advanced production methods. The result is a bag or other piece to satisfy the demands of the modern lifestyle and still retain the classic and very distinctive Tusting look. When appropriate, the hides are coloured using aniline drum drying, which enhances the intensity of colour and guarantees longevity.

The canvas used in some of the items is tough 24oz cotton for heavy duty wear, specially woven and dyed for Tusting. The fittings are also of the very finest quality – zips and brass or nickel fittings are made by the Swiss company RiRi. For business people, the choice runs from discreet locking briefcases through computer-carrying flapovers to the largest zip-top pilot bags. For travel, the options include soft, part-framed or wheeled luggage in all-leather or leather and canvas. The Country range in strong bridle leather or leather and the strongest, includes gunslips, backpacks, saddle bags, cartridge bags and shoulder bags. Tusting has also built up a fine reputation for traditional English sofas and chairs built for looks and durability. Tusting supplies some of the top London stores and has a thriving export business, notably to the USA and Japan.

Olney

fall in prices and a sharp decline in Olney lace. A revival of the trade was tried by Harry Armstrong when he opened the Lace Factory in 1928 but, although handmade lace is still produced locally, the factory only lasted until Armstrong's death in 1943.

Amongst the town's present day claims to fame is the annual **Pancake Race**. Legend has it that the first 'race' was run in the 15th century when a local housewife heard the Shriving Service bell ringing and ran to church complete with her frying pan and pancake.

expensive, in the 1700s, only the well-to-do could afford to buy it, but the rise in machine-made lace from Nottingham saw a

Nearby **Emberton Country Park**, located

COOL & COLLECTABLE

35 High Street South, Olney,
Buckinghamshire MK46 4AA
Tel: 01234 711922
e-mail: info@coolandcollectable.co.uk
website: www.coolandcollectable.co.uk

The well-named **Cool & Collectable** is packed full of stylish and unusual gift ideas for the home. Among

the many desirable items on display are LSA vases, dicroic glass coasters, wall hangings and
jewellery by contemporary Cornish designer Jo Downs and luxurious L'Occitane toiletries from Provence. They also stock beautifully crafted German pens by Yoropen and Usus and hand made and fair traded leather journals from India. You will find a wide range of individual and original items, including photograph frames made from wood, hand stitched leather, mother of pearl and even slate! A newer addition to the shop is Burts Bees - a selection of natural toiletries, which includes the well known "Baby Bee" range. From wine racks made of solid slate to banana bark mirrors, if you're looking for that unique finishing touch for your home, this aladins cave is the shop for you. You will also find a selection of products available to view and buy on their superb website.

📖 stories and anecdotes 🦜 famous people 🎨 art and craft 🎭 entertainment and sport 🚶 walks

MUCH ADO DELICATESSEN

Stanley Court, Olney, Buckinghamshire
Tel: *01234 714006*
website: *www.muchadocatering.co.uk*

Shakespeare's *Much Ado* was about nothing, but Matt Prosky's **Much Ado** is about sourcing and selling the very best foodstuffs from around the world. New Yorker Matt is passionate about his food and personally selects everything he sells. The range is amazing, from fresh fish from Billingsgate and crabs from Scarborough to home-cooked ham and turkey, charcuterie, pâtés and terrines, Gloucester Old Spot pork pies, cheeses from Neal's Yard and beyond, quiches, prepared salads, specialist breads, rice and pasts, pickles and preserves, local eggs and milk, fruit and vegetables from New Covent Garden, stuffing mixes, fresh herbs, fruit juices, yoghurts, nuts, cakes and biscuits, chocolates and nougat. Much Ado is open seven days a week.

Outside catering is an important side of the business, offering an efficient, reliable service to many clients both private and commercial in and around Olney and Milton Keynes. The delicatessen is located in a modern brick building in a courtyard set back from the High Street close to the shoe factory.

on the site of former gravel pits, is an ideal place to relax. Not only are there four lakes and a stretch of the River Ouse within the park's boundaries but facilities here include fishing, sailing, and nature trails.

NEWPORT PAGNELL
3 miles NE of Milton Keynes on the A422

🏛 Police Museum

Modern development hides a long history at Newport Pagnell, which local archaeological finds indicate was settled in the Iron Age and during the Roman occupation. It was an important administrative centre, and in the 10th century the Royal Mint was established here. Lacemaking was once an important industry, and the town is also associated with the car-maker Aston Martin which started life in the 1820s as a maker of coaches for the nobility.

In the distinctive red, white and black Victorian police station visitors are invited every Tuesday to look round the **Police Museum**, where the exhibits include more than 600 models of police cars, truncheons, handcuffs and a 1903 hand-drawn ambulance. *The Blue Lamp* and *Dixon of Dock Green* are remembered in the nostalgic Jack Warner Corner.

CHICHELEY
5 miles NE of Milton Keynes on the A422

🏛 Chicheley Hall

This attractive village is home of **Chicheley Hall**, a beautiful baroque house that was built in the early 1700s for Sir John Chester and which remains today one of the finest such houses in the country. Down the years it was used by the military and as a school, but in

1952 it was bought by the 2nd Earl Beatty and restored to its former state of grace. The earl's father, the 1st Earl, was a particularly courageous naval commander and, as well as receiving the DSO at the age of just 25, he was also a commander in the decisive battle of Jutland in 1916.

WILLEN
1 mile NE of Milton Keynes on the A509

The village Church of St Mary Magdalene, built in the late 17th century, is an elegant building in the style of Sir Christopher Wren, but Willen is also home to another house of prayer, the Peace Pagoda and Buddhist Temple, opened in 1980. It was built by the monks and nuns of the Nipponsan Myohoji, and it was the first peace pagoda in the western hemisphere. In this place of great tranquillity and beauty, 1,000 cherry trees and cedars, donated by the ancient Japanese town of Yoshino, have been planted on the hill surrounding the pagoda, in memory of the victims of all wars.

GREAT LINFORD
2 miles NE of Milton Keynes on the A422

🏛 Stone Circle

Situated on the banks of the Grand Union Canal, this village, which is now more or less a suburb of Milton Keynes, has a 13th century church set in parkland, a 17th century manor house, and a **Stone Circle**, one of only a few such prehistoric monuments in the county. Despite the encroachment of its much larger neighbour, the village has retained a distinctive air that is all its own.

The central block of the present manor house was built in 1678 by Sir William Pritchard, Lord Mayor of London. As well as making Great Linford his country seat, Pritchard also provided a boys' school and almshouses for six unmarried poor of the parish. The manor house was extended in the 18th century by the Uthwatt family, relatives of the Lord Mayor, and they used various tricks to give an impressive and elegant appearance to the building. The Grand Union Canal cuts through the estate, whose grounds are now a public park.

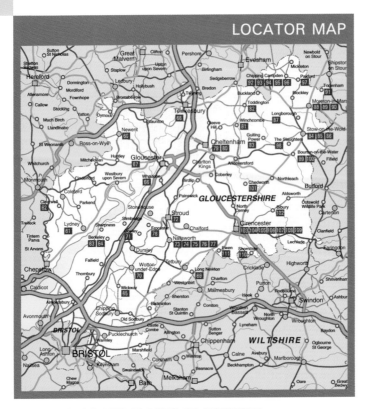

ADVERTISERS AND PLACES OF INTEREST

🏛 historic building   🏛 museum   🏛 historic site   🗘 scenic attraction   🌱 flora and fauna

4 | Gloucestershire

For many, Gloucestershire *is* the Cotswolds, the delightful limestone hills that sweep across the county from Dyrham in the south to Chipping Campden in the north. As well as providing some of the most glorious scenery and the prettiest villages in the country, the county is also home to the historic towns of Cirencester and Cheltenham. "The most English and the least spoiled of all our countryside." So wrote J B Priestley in 1933 in his *English Journey*, and more than 70 years later his verdict would surely have been the same.

Chavenage House, Tetbury

However, Gloucestershire is not all about the Cotswolds. To the west, on the River Severn, is the ancient city of Gloucester, while further down river is the Vale of Berkeley, and historic Berkeley Castle. On the opposite bank of the river lies the Forest of Dean. Wild woodland, royal hunting ground, naval timber reserve, important mining and industrial region: the Forest has been all these, and today its rich and varied landscape provides endless interest for walkers, nature-lovers and historians. Bounded by the Rivers Severn and Wye, the area has been effectively isolated from the rest of England and Wales and so has developed a character all its own.

🎭 stories and anecdotes   🦜 famous people   🎨 art and craft   🎭 entertainment and sport   🥾 walks

Newent

🏠 Market House   🏠 Chapel of St Mary

🏛 Shambles Museum   🦜 Bird of Prey Centre

🏞 Castle Hill Farm

Capital of the area of northwest Gloucestershire known as the Ryelands, and the most important town in the Vale of Leadon, Newent stands in the broad triangle of land called Daffodil Crescent. The rich Leadon Valley soil was traditionally used for growing rye and raising the renowned Ryelands sheep, an ancient breed famed for the quality of its wool. The town was one of the county's principal wool-trading centres, and the wealth produced from that trade accounts for the large number of grand merchants' houses to be seen here. The most distinctive building in Newent is the splendid timber-framed **Market House**, built as a butter market in the middle of the 16th century, its upper floors supported on 16 oak pillars that form an open colonnade. The medieval **Church of St Mary** has many outstanding features, including the shaft of a 9th century Saxon cross, the 11th century 'Newent Stone' and the 17th century nave. Royalist troops had removed the lead from the roof to make bullets, an act which caused the roof to collapse during a snowstorm in 1674. A new nave was started after Charles II agreed to donate 60 tons of timber from the Forest of Dean. The 150ft spire is a landmark for miles around.

The Shambles Museum of Victorian

JILLINGS ANTIQUE CLOCKS

Croft House, 17 Church Street, Newent, Gloucestershire GL18 1PU
Tel: 01531 822100
e-mail: clocks@jillings.com website: www.jillings.com

Antique clocks are bought, sold, repaired and restored by John and Doco Jillings at **Jillings Antique Clocks**. They started their business in 1985 in premises near Hampton Court Palace; they later moved to a smart gallery in London's Belgravia and set up here in Newent in 1999. The firm specialises in 18th and 19th century English and Continental clocks and takes great pride in the quality of itsr restoration work

and in the friendly personal service given to clients from all over the world. Jillings also undertakes top-quality repair work on fine antique longcase, mantel and bracket clocks. They provide free estimates and local collection and delivery, and of course all work is guaranteed.

The business is open from 10am to 6pm on Thursday, Friday and Saturday, or by appointment. Visitors should phone before setting out on a journey in case the owners are away exhibiting at a fair. The stock is shown on their excellent website. John is acknowledged as one of the UK's leading experts on antique clocks and has appeared with a restored clock on *The Antiques Roadshow*.

🏠 historic building   🏛 museum   🏚 historic site   🏞 scenic attraction   🦜 flora and fauna

Life is virtually a little Victorian town, a cleverly laid out jumble of cobbled streets, alleyways and squares, with shops and trades tucked away in all corners, and even a mission chapel and a Victorian conservatory.

There aren't too many windmills in Gloucestershire, but at **Castle Hill Farm** just outside town is a working wooden mill with great views from a balcony at the top.

A mile south of Newent is the **National Bird of Prey Centre** housing one of the largest and best collections of birds of prey in the world. Over 110 aviaries are home to eagles, falcons, owls, vultures, kites, hawks and buzzards. Between 20 and 40 birds are flown daily at the Centre, which is open every day from February to November.

On the road north towards Dymock, set in 65 acres of rolling countryside, the Three Choirs Vineyard is the country's largest wine producer.

Around Newent

DYMOCK
3 miles N of Newent on the B4216

 Dymock Poets

Dymock boasts some fine old brick buildings, including the White House and the Old Rectory near the church, and outside the village, the Old Grange, which incorporates the remains of the Cistercian Flaxley Abbey.

At the heart of the village is the early Norman Church of St Mary, whose unusual features include a tympanum depicting the Tree of Life, a 13th century stone coffin lid, stained glass by Kempe – and the last ticket issued at Dymock station, in 1959. A corner of the church is dedicated to the memory of the **Dymock Poets**, a group who based themselves in Dymock from before World War I. The group, which comprised Lascelles Abercrombie (the first to arrive), Rupert Brooke, John Drinkwater, Wilfred Gibson, Edward Thomas and Robert Frost, sent out its *New Numbers* poetry magazine from Dymock's tiny post office; it was also from here that Brooke published his *War Sonnets*, including *The Soldier* (*'If I should die, think only this of me: That there's some corner of a foreign field that is forever England...'*). Brooke and Thomas died in the war, which led to the dissolution of the group. Two circular walks from Dymock take in places

Dymock

associated with the poets.

Many other literary figures are associated with the Forest. Dennis Potter, born at Coleford in 1935 the eldest son of a Forest coal-miner, is renowned for writing the screenplays for some of TV's most memorable programmes, including *Pennies From Heaven* and *The Singing Detective*. But he also wrote with passion about the Forest in *The Glittering Coffin* and *The Changing Forest: Life in the Forest of Dean Today*. Mary Howitt, born in Coleford in 1799, is known as a translator, poet and author of children's books. It was as a translator that she met a Danish story-teller called Hans Christian Andersen who asked Mary to translate his stories into English.

UPLEADON

2 miles N of Newent off the B4215

🏠 Church of St Mary the Virgin

The **Church of St Mary the Virgin** features some fine Norman and Tudor work but is best known for its unique tower, half-timbered from bottom to top; even the mullion windows are of wood. The church has a great treasure in its Bible, an early example of the Authorised Version printed by the King's printer Robert Barker. This was the unfortunate who later issued an edition with a small but rather important word missing. The so-called Wicked Bible of 1631 renders Exodus 20.14 as "Thou shalt commit adultery".

KEMPLEY

3 miles NW of Newent on a minor road

🏠 Church of St Mary   🌲 Dymock Woods

A village famous for its cider and also for having two churches, of very different age and significance. The little **Church of St Mary**, easily the most popular church in the area,

Church of St Mary the Virgin, Upleadon

dates from the end of the 11th century and would be a gem even without its greatest treasure. That treasure, in the chancel, is an almost complete set of 12th century frescoes, the most renowned in the region and among the finest in the land, protected by Reformation whitewash and Victorian varnish. Their subjects include St Peter and the Apostles, Christ with his feet resting on a globe, and the de Lacy family, to whom William the Conqueror granted the manor. The red sandstone Church of St Edward the Confessor was built in 1903 by the 7th Earl Beauchamp in the style of the Arts and Crafts Movement using exclusively local materials.

This is the area of **Dymock Woods**, an area of Forestry Commission woodland famous for its daffodils.

🏠 historic building   🏛 museum   🏚 historic site   🌳 scenic attraction   🌿 flora and fauna

Longhope

Harts Barn & Craft Centre

Another good starting point for a tour in and around the Forest of Dean is Longhope, a pleasant settlement south of the A40 Gloucester to Ross-on-Wye road.

Longhope is the location of the **Harts Barn Crafts Centre**, situated in a hunting lodge built by William Duke of Normandy and housing an array of working crafts including jewellery, pine furniture, art gallery, handmade gifts, glassware, dried flowers and picture framing.

Around Longhope

MITCHELDEAN
2 miles W of Longhope on the A4136

St Anthony's Well

A peaceful community on the northern fringe of the forest. A mile or so south of the village is **St Anthony's Well**, one of many throughout the land said to have magical curative powers. The water at this well is invariably icy cold and bathing in it is said to provide a cure for skin disease (St Anthony's Fire was the medieval name for a rampant itching disease). The monks at nearby Flaxley Abbey swore by it.

DRYBROOK
5 miles SW of Longhope off the A4136

Mechanical Organ Museum

Hidden away at Hawthorns Cross on the edge of the Forest is the **Mechanical Organ Museum** with a vast collection of mechanical music spanning 150 years. The museum is open at Easter and on Tuesday and Thursday afternoons in April, May, July and August.

RUARDEAN
6 miles SW of Longhope on the A4136

Church of St John the Baptist   Ruardean Hill

A lovely old village whose **Church of St John the Baptist**, one of many on the fringe of the forest, has many interesting features. A tympanum depicting St George and the Dragon is a great rarity, and on a stone plaque in the nave is a curious carving of two fishes. These are thought to have been carved by craftsmen from the Herefordshire School of Norman Architecture during the Romanesque period around 1150. It is part of a frieze removed with rubble when the south porch was being built in the 13th century. The frieze was considered lost until 1985, when an inspection of a bread oven in a cottage at nearby Turner's Tump revealed the two fish set into its lining. They were rescued and returned to their rightful place in the church. Ruardean was the birthplace in the 1840s of James and William Horlick, later to be become famous with their Horlicks formula. Their patent for 'malted milk' was registered in 1883 and the granary where the original experiments were carried out still remains in the village.

Ruardean Hill is 951 feet above sea level and on a clear day Herefordshire, the Black Mountains and the Brecon Beacons can all be seen.

Newnham-on-Severn

One of the gateways to the Forest, and formerly a port, Newnham lies on a great bend in the river. Its heyday was at the beginning of the 19th century, when a quay was built and an old tramway tunnel converted into what was perhaps the world's first railway tunnel. The village has many interesting buildings which can be visited by following the Millennium Heritage Walk plaques installed by the parish council with funds provided by an open-air jazz concert.

Around Newnham-on-Severn

WESTBURY-ON-SEVERN
3 miles NE of Newnham on the A48

🐾 Severn Bore   🌿 Westbury Court Garden

The village, bounded on three sides by the river, is best known for the National Trust's **Westbury Court Garden**, a formal Dutch water garden laid out between 1696 and 1705. Historic varieties of apple, pear and plum, along with many other species introduced to England before 1700, make this a must for any enthusiastic gardener. The house was long ago demolished, and the only building to survive is an elegant two-storey redbrick pavilion with a tower and weather vane. Also worth a visit in Westbury is the Church of Saints Peter, Paul and Mary with its detached tower and wooden spire. Walmore Common is winter home to thousands of swans as well as many wading birds and unusual flora.

Westbury is an excellent spot to watch the famous **Severn Bore**. This is a tidal wave that several times a month makes its way along the river. The bore travels at an average speed of about 10 miles an hour and has been known to reach a height of 6.5ft. The Severn Estuary experiences the second highest tide anywhere in the world, and the difference between the lowest and highest tide in any one day can be

more than 14.5 metres. These high, or spring tides, occur on several days in each lunar cycle throughout the year.

LITTLEDEAN
2 miles NW of Newnham off the A4151

🏛 Littledean Hall

Places of interest here include the 13th century church, the 18th century prison and, just south of the village, **Littledean Hall**, reputedly the oldest inhabited house in England. The house has Saxon and Celtic remains in the cellars and is thought to have originated in the 6th century; it became a Royalist garrison during the Civil War. Highlights in the grounds, from which balloon flights launch, include a Roman temple site, a Victorian walled garden and a number of ancient chestnut trees.

CINDERFORD
3 miles NW of Newnham on the A4151

🏛 Church of St Andrew   🎋 Dean Heritage Centre

A former coal-mining community with evidence of the mines visible among the trees.

At Camp Hill in the nearby hamlet of Soudley is the **Dean Heritage Centre**, where four galleries tell the story of the Forest and its people. It is a perfect setting for a family day out with woodland walks, café, adventure playground and children's activity room, museum and crafts shops, farm animals and woodland crafts, including charcoal burning and woodturning. A level trail runs round Soudley Ponds, a designated Site of Special Scientific Interest.

At nearby **Awre**, an ancient crossing place of the Severn, the **Church of St Andrew** has changed little in its 700 years. Its most notable possession is a massive mortuary chest carved from a single piece of wood and used as a laying out place for bodies recovered from the Severn. In the churchyard are examples of headstones featuring the local speciality - cherubs.

Lydney

🏛 Dean Forest Railway & Norchard Railway Centre

🏛 Forest Model Village & Gardens

🏛 Roman Temple Site

🌿 Lydney Park Spring Gardens

The harbour and the canal at Lydney, once an important centre of the iron and coal industries and the largest settlement between Chepstow and Gloucester, are well worth exploring, and no visit to the town should end without a trip on the **Dean Forest Railway**. A regular service of steam and diesel trains operates between Lydney Junction, St Mary's Halt and Norchard. At **Norchard Railway Centre**, headquarters of the line, are a railway museum, souvenir shop and details of restoration projects, including the extension

of the line to Parkend. Popular events throughout the year include Days Out with Thomas, Santa Specials and Steam Footplate Experience Courses.

A popular family tourist attraction is the **Forest Model Village & Gardens**, which features more than 50 detailed miniatures of local landmarks and buildings in five landscaped garden zones.

One of the chief attractions in the vicinity is **Lydney Park Spring Gardens and Roman Temple Site**. The gardens, which lie beside the A48 on the western outskirts, are a riot of colour, particularly in May and June, and the grounds also contain the site of an Iron Age hill fort and the remains of a late-Roman temple excavated by Sir Mortimer Wheeler in the 1920s. The nearby museum houses a number of Roman artefacts from the site, including the famous 'Lydney Dog', and a number of interesting items brought back from New Zealand in the 1930s by the first Viscount Bledisloe after his term there as Governor General. Also in the park are traces

---

HIGHBURY COACH HOUSE

Highbury House, Lydney,
Gloucestershire GL15 5JH
Tel: 01594 842339
e-mail: midgleya1@aol.com

Anthony and Inez Midgley welcome guests to the three spacious and comfortable flats in the coach house of Highbury House, on the southern edge of the Royal Forest of Dean. **Highbury Coach House** is a listed building dating back to 1850, and the three self-contained flats, sleeping 2, 4 and 5, are fully equipped with all the usual cooking facilities and baths and showers. Shared amenities include a games room, with snooker table, guest laundry, a lock-up for bicycles and a lovely two acre garden commanding glorious views. The Coach House is graded 3 star by The English Tourist Authority.

🎭 stories and anecdotes   🐦 famous people   🎨 art and craft   🎟 entertainment and sport   🚶 walks

of Roman iron-mine workings and Roman earth workings.

Around Lydney

ALVINGTON
2 miles SW of Lydney on the A48

🌳 Wintour's Leap

In the churchyard at Alvington are the graves of the illustrious Wintour family, leading figures in the defeat of the Spanish Armada. Half a century after that event came Sir John Wintour's remarkable escape from Cromwell's men at what is now known as **Wintour's Leap**. Sir John was an adventurer, Keeper of the Forest of Dean and sometime secretary to Queen Maria Henrietta of the Netherlands. In 1644 he was at the head of a Royalist force defeated at Blockley, near Chepstow, by Parliamentary troops. Wintour is said to have

escaped from the battlefield by riding up by the Wye and hurling himself and his horse into the river from the cliffs.

Coleford

🏛 GWR Museum   🌳 Puzzle Wood

A former mining centre which received its royal charter from Charles I in the 17th century in recognition of its loyalty to the Crown. It was by then already an important iron processing centre, partly because of the availability of local ore deposits and partly because of the ready local supply of timber for converting into charcoal for use in the smelting process. It was in Coleford that the Mushet family helped to revolutionise the iron and steel industry. Robert Forester Mushet, a freeminer, discovered how spiegeleisen, an alloy of iron, manganese, silicon and carbon,

Roman Temple Site, Lydney

🏛 historic building   🏛 museum   🏛 historic site   🌳 scenic attraction   🌱 flora and fauna

could be used in the reprocessing of 'burnt iron' and went on to develop a system for turning molten pig iron directly into steel, a process which predated the more familiar one developed by Bessemer.

Coleford, still regarded as the capital of the Royal Forest of Dean, is a busy commercial centre with an interesting church and a number of notable industrial relics. The Forestry Commission is housed at Bank House and has information on all aspects of the Forest. There are miles of way-marked walks and cycle trails in the forest, and the famous Sculpture Trail starts at Beechenhurst Lodge.

Coleford is also home to the **Great Western Railway Museum**, housed in an 1883 GWR goods station next to the central car park. Another treat for railway fans is the Perrygrove Railway, where a narrow gauge steam train takes a 1.5 mile trip through farmland and woods. Nearby is another visitor attraction, also on the B4228 just south of town. This is **Puzzle Wood**, where 14 acres of open-cast ore mines have been redesigned as a family attraction, with paths forming an unusual maze, breathtaking scenery, wooden bridges, passageways through moss-covered rocks and lots of dead ends and circles.

Around Coleford

STAUNTON
3 miles NW of Coleford on the A4136

🏛 Buck Stone and Suck Stone

Lots to see here, including a Norman church with two stone fonts and an unusual corkscrew staircase leading up past the pulpit to the belfry door. Not far from the village are several enormous mystical stones, notably the **Buck Stone** and the **Suck Stone**. The former, looking like some great monster, used to buck, or rock, on its base but is now firmly fixed in place. The Suck Stone is a real giant, weighing in at many thousands of tons. There are several other stones in the vicinity, including the Near Harkening and Far Harkening down among the trees, and the Long Stone by the A4136 at Marion's Cross.

CANNOP
4 miles E of Coleford on the B4226

🏛 Hopewell Colliery 🌲 Cannop Valley

Cannop Valley has many forest trails and picnic sites; one of the sites is at Cannop Ponds, picturesque ponds created in the 1820s to provide a regular supply of water for the local iron-smelting works. Nearby is **Hopewell Colliery**, a true Forest of Dean free mine where summer visitors can see old mine workings and some of the old tools of the trade, then relax with a snack from the café.

PARKEND
3 miles SE of Coleford off the B4234

🌱 Nagshead Nature Reserve

A community once based, like so many others in the area, on the extraction of minerals. In the early years of the 19th century, before steam engines arrived and horses did all the donkey work, Parkend became a tramroad centre and laden trams ran from coalpits, iron mines, quarries, furnaces and forges to river-borne outlets at Lydbrook and Lydney. New Fancy Colliery is now a delightful picnic area, with a nearby hill affording breathtaking views over the forestscape. Off the B4431, just west of Parkend, is the RSPB's **Nagshead Nature Reserve**, with hundreds of nest boxes in a woodland site with footpaths, way-marked trails and a summer information centre.

CLEARWELL CAVES

Nr Coleford, Royal Forest of Dean, Gloucestershire GL16 8JR
Tel: 01594 832535   Fax: 01594 833362
e-mail: jw@clearwellcaves.com
website: www.clearwellcaves.com

Clearwell Caves are set in an Area of Special Landscape Value on the outskirts of the historic village of Clearwell. The caves are part of the last remaining working iron mine in the Forest of Dean and the last ochre mine in the UK. They are part of a natural cave system that became filled with iron ore around 180 million years ago.

Mining in the Forest of Dean is now believed to have begun over 7,000 years ago during the Mesolithic period (Middle Stone Age) as people migrated back into the area after the last Ice Age (10,000 years ago).

People were collecting ochre pigments, particularly red ochre which was very highly prized and had important decorative and ritual uses. Once the use of iron as a metal was established and certainly by the 1st century AD, there was a thriving iron industry here.

Large scale iron ore mining continued until 1945 and in its last year as a large scale mine it produced over 3,000 tons of ore. Today production of minerals rarely exceeds four tons per annum. Small scale ochre mining carries on, using traditional techniques which would often be familiar to even the earliest miners.

Visitors to the caves are offered a wide range of activities, from a leisurely and fascinating self-guided underground walk, descending for more than 100ft, to a more strenuous adventure caving trip – or even a Natural Paint workshop. The cave shop is a treat in itself with unusual gift ideas, books, souvenirs and a wide range of spectacular minerals and crystals from around the world. And of course you can buy the ochre mined here.

Don't forget to pay a visit to the tearoom. Here you'll find a good selection of freshly prepared lunches and refreshments, along with some very interesting mining artefacts displayed around the ceiling and walls. An unusual day out for all ages and a great underground experience. Clearwell Caves are open from 10am to 5pm, daily, from 14th February until 31st October. Visitors are still welcome during November but the caves are then being prepared for the Christmas Fantasy (open 1st - 24th December) so normal displays are interrupted.

CLEARWELL

1.5 miles S of Coleford off the A466

🏛 Clearwell Caves

Clearwell Caves (see paenl opposite) are part of the only remaining working iron mine in the Forest of Dean. This natural cave system became filled with iron ore around 180 million years ago and has been mined for at least 4,000 years. As a result, the cave complex now consists of many miles of passageways and hundreds of caverns. Visitors can take their own self-guided tour or take part in a more strenuous adventure caving trip. Other amenities on site include a gift shop and tea room. A memorable visit can be completed by wandering down to Clearwell village with its lovely French Gothic-style church and the pretty surrounding countryside.

St Briavels Castle

ST BRIAVELS

5 miles S of Coleford on minor roads

🏰 Castle

On the edge of a limestone plateau high above the Wye Valley, this historic village is named after a 5th century Welsh bishop whose name appears in various forms throughout Celtic Wales, Cornwall and Brittany, but nowhere else in England. In the Middle Ages St Briavels was an important administrative centre for the royal hunting forest and also a leading manufacturer of armaments, supplying weapons and ammunition to the Crown.

The ample Church of St Mary the Virgin,

Norman in origin, enlarged in the 12th and 13th centuries and remodelled by the Victorians, is the scene of a curious and very English annual custom, the St Briavels Bread and Cheese Ceremony. After evensong a local forester stands on the Pound Wall and throws small pieces of bread and cheese to the villagers, accompanied by the chant, "St Briavels water and Whyrl's wheat are the best bread and water King John can ever eat". This ceremony is thought to have originated more than 700 years ago when the villagers successfully defended their rights of estover (collecting wood from common land) in nearby Hudnalls Wood. In gratitude each villager paid one penny to the church warden to help feed the poor, and that act led to the founding of the ceremony. Small pieces of bread and cheese were considered to bring good luck, and the Dean Forest miners would keep the pieces in order to ward off harm.

St Briavels Castle, which stands in an almost impregnable position on a high promontory, was founded by Henry I and enlarged by King John, who used it as a

Clearwell

Distance: *5.0 miles (8.0 kilometres)*

Typical time: *180 mins*

Height gain: *280 metres*

Map: *Explorer OL 14*

Walk: *www.walkingworld.com ID:1729*

Contributor: *Pat Roberts*

ACCESS INFORMATION:

Parking is at the car park for Clearwell Caves, signed from Clearwell which is near Newland.

ADDITIONAL INFORMATION:

Anyone interested in caving, and the underground passages should make inquiries at Clearwell caves, where trips are arranged. In the woodland are fine examples of scowles left by ancient iron miners as long ago as pre-Roman times. **Pingry Lane** tradition says that at the time of the civil war this lane was running with blood and was known as "Bloody Lane". The red pigment was more likely to be red ochre from the iron ore.

DESCRIPTION:

The area around here was once rich in iron mines, and the woods contain old workings, which are rich in ferns and other plant life, resulting in a fairy-glen appearance as you walk through. Lovely views over to the Welsh mountains, and Newland Church. The Cathedral of the Forest, is well worth a visit.

FEATURES:

Hills or Fells, Church, Wildlife, Birds, Flowers, Great Views, Cafe, Woodland

WALK DIRECTIONS:

1 | From the car park, walk back down the approach track to the road, walk up to the right and pass the entrance to Clearwell Farm on the left side of the road, and walk 20 metres further on.

2 | 20 metres past the entrance to the farm, cross the stile on the left side of the road and follow the fence on your left. After 50 metres there is a large tree with a fence round it on the left, below which see the entrance to a system of underground passages reaching to Coleford. Within 30 metres cross a stile leading further into the wood. The path keeps to a northwesterly direction, but divides in places, to emerge at the edge of a field near the buildings of Clearwell Farm.

3 | Over the stile, walk diagonally across the field to a stile/gate on the edge of a small wood. Walk with the fence on your left and the trees on your right, to reach another stile.

4 | The view here is outstanding, over to the Black Mountains and the Sugar Loaf. There are two yellow arrows, take the one to the right. Follow the hedge on the right down the field, enjoying the view. Over another stile in the bottom corner to follow the right hedge down to a stile in the corner. (Can be very muddy at the bottom.) Over the stile onto Pingry Lane turn left. Walk as far as a wall on the left with a ruined barn behind it.

5 | Go through this gate on the right. The sign points left, but walk to the left of the pond but ahead through a gap between the trees, then to the right BEHIND the trees and left up the field towards a gate with an arrow on it. The arrow points up the next field, but walk diagonally left across the field, below Breckness Court seen at the top of the field.

Head for a point about 50 metres below the large house, and a gate in the hedge just below some trees. Once through the gate walk in a northerly direction the length of the field.

6|Over this stile into Galders Wood. Keep on the bottom of the wood to reach another stile into a field. Maintain direction to come down to a minor road by a house. Left past the house to a junction, here go straight ahead and pass under a bridge, and pass a ruin of a bridge which once carried the old mineral railway between Coleford and Newland. Ignore a turning off on the left into the wood to reach where the road bends right.

7|Here on the bend the sign says "Old Burial Route". This was used to carry the coffins from Coleford and the scowls to the church at Newland. Left here and arrive at a stile into a field. Good views ahead. DO NOT CROSS THE STILE, but bear left with the track and eventually reach a metal road down into Newland, next to the Ostrich Pub. Left through Newland, pass over Valley Brook and pass the entrance to Rookery Farm. Just after the road starts to gain height and bend right, look for a stile on the left.

8|The stile and footpath sign are in the hedge. Over it walk in the direction of the arrow to another stile, then in the same direction head for Millend Farm. There, left over a stile and a footbridge. At the end of the footbridge right with a fence on your left, cross the lawn to the drive, turn right and up to the road. Here turn left for 40 metres.

9|Take this bridle path up to the right. It is quite a pull in the beginning but soon levels out and drops down to Pingry Lane, turn right. This lane will bring you out to the main road through Clearwell, turn left up through the village. Opposite the Post Office a small detour follows a stream to a spring inscribed "He sendeth the Springs into the Valleys which run among the Hills". Continue on up the road to a junction.

10|At this junction, with the monument in the centre, take the left road up and signed "Clearwell Caves". Good footpath on the right side of the road.

11|Where the pavement runs out, see a track up on the right bank. Follow this, pass the Cafe and Visitor Centre for Clearwell Caves to return to the carpark.

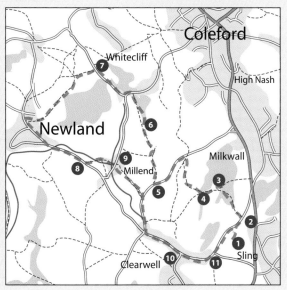

hunting lodge. Two sturdy gatehouses are among the parts that survive and they, like some of the actual castle buildings, are now in use as a youth hostel.

NEWLAND
1 mile SW of Coleford off the A466

🏛 Cathedral of the Forest

Frampton Manor

Newland's Church of All Saints is often known as the **Cathedral of the Forest** because of its impressive size. Its aisle is almost as wide as its nave and its huge pinnacled tower is supported by flying buttresses. Like many churches in the county, it was built during the 13th and 14th centuries and remodelled by the Victorians. Inside, it has a number of interesting effigies, including an unusual brass relief of a medieval miner with a pick and hod in his hand and a candlestick in his mouth. Other effigies depict a forester in 15th century hunting gear with a hunting horn, a sword and knife; and, from the 17th century, an archer with wide-brimmed hat, bow, horn and dagger.

South Gloucestershire and the Vale of Berkeley

Frampton-on-Severn

🏛 Frampton Court and Frampton Manor

🦌 Cotswold Canals 🦌 Arlingham Peninsula

The 22-acre Rosamund Green, incorporating a cricket ground and three ponds, is one of the largest village greens in England, formed when the marshy ground outside the gates of **Frampton Court** was drained in the 18th century. The court is an outstanding example of a Georgian country house, built in the Palladian style in the 1730s and the seat of the Clifford family ever since. Fine porcelain, furniture and paintings grace the interior, and in the peacock-strutted grounds an ornamental canal reflects a superb Orangery in Dutch-influenced Strawberry Hill gothic. A unique octagonal tower was built in the 17th century as a dovecote.

On the other side of the green is **Frampton Manor**, the Clifford family's former home, built between the 12th and 16th centuries. This handsome timber-framed house is thought to be the birthplace of Jane Clifford, who was the mistress of Henry II and bore him two children. The manor, which has a lovely old walled garden with some rare plants, is open by written appointment. At the southern edge of the village stands the restored 14th century Church of St Mary with its rare Norman lead font. The church stands beside the Sharpness Canal, which was built to allow ships to travel up the Severn Valley as

🏛 historic building   📷 museum   🏛 historic site   💧 scenic attraction   🌱 flora and fauna

far as Gloucester without being at the mercy of the estuary tides. The canal has several swing bridges and at some of these, as at Splatt Bridge and Saul Bridge at Frampton, there are splendid little bridge-keeper's cottages with Doric columns.

To the west of Frampton, on a great bend in the river, is the **Arlingham Peninsula**, part of the Severn Way Shepperdine-Tewkesbury long-distance walk. The trail passes close to Wick Court, a 13th century moated manor house. The land on which the village of **Arlingham** stands once belonged to the monks of St Augustine's Abbey in Bristol who believed it to be the point where St Augustine crossed the Severn on his way to converting the heathen Welsh tribes.

The Severn naturally dominated life hereabouts and at **Saul**, a small village on the peninsula, the inhabitants decorated their houses with carvings of sailors, some of which, in bright, cheerful colours, can be seen today. The village lies at the point where two canals cross. Two separate waterways, the Stroudwater Navigation and the Thames & Severn Canal, once linked the Severn and the Thames, a route of 37 miles. The canals, known collectively as the **Cotswold Canals**, were abandoned in 1933 and 1954 respectively but most of the route is intact and since 1972 the Cotswold Canals Trust has worked in partnership with local authorities on restoration work. Continuing round the bend in the river, **Epney** is the point from which thousands of baby eels are exported each year to the Netherlands and elsewhere to replenish their own stocks.

SLIMBRIDGE
4 miles S of Frampton on the A38

🦆 Wildfowl and Wetlands Centre

The **Wildfowl and Wetlands Centre** was

founded as a trust on the banks of the Severn in 1946 by the distinguished naturalist, artist, sailor and broadcaster Peter (later Sir Peter) Scott. He believed in bringing wildlife and people together for the benefit of both, and the Trust's work continues with the same aims. Slimbridge has the world's largest collection of ducks, geese and swans, and spectacular flamingoes among the exotic wildfowl. Also at the centre are a tropical house, pond zone, children's play area, wildlife art gallery, restaurant and gift shop, and there are magnificent views from the observation tower. Sir Peter died in 1989 and his ashes were scattered at Slimbridge, where he had lived for many years. A memorial to him stands at the entrance to the Centre.

BERKELEY
6 miles S of Frampton off the A38

🏰 Berekley Castle 🏛 Jenner Museum

🦋 Butterfly House & Plant Centre

⚓ Gloucester & Sharpness Canal

The fertile strip that is the Vale of Berkeley, bounded on the north by the Severn and on the south by the M5, takes its name from the small town of Berkeley, whose largely Georgian centre is dominated by the Norman **Berkeley Castle**. Said to be the oldest inhabited castle in Britain, with the same family resident from the start, this wonderful gem in pink sandstone was built between 1117 and 1153 on the site of a Saxon fort. It was here that the barons of the West met before making the journey to Runnymede to witness the signing of Magna Carta by King John in 1215. Edward II was imprisoned here for several months after losing his throne to his wife and her lover. He eventually met a painful death in the dungeons in the year 1327. Three centuries later the castle was besieged by

The Jenner Museum

Church Lane, Berkeley, Gloucestershire GL13 9BH
Tel: 01453 810631 Fax: 01453 811690
e-mail: manager@jennermuseum.com
website: www.jennermuseum.com

Born in Berkeley in 1749, Edward Jenner returned here after completing his medical training and his house, The Chantry, is now home the **Jenner Museum** where this pioneering doctor and immunologist's life and work is explored. Intrigued by the country lore that said that milkmaids who caught the mild cowpox could not catch smallpox, one of the most feared diseases of all time, Jenner set about developing a means of vaccinating against smallpox, which he successfully did in 1798. In 1967, the World Health Organisation masterminded a final global plan to eradicate the disease and, in 1980, smallpox was declared dead.

Not only did Jenner develop the first vaccination but his discovery has now been developed into one of the most important parts of modern medicine – immunology. Along with his work on smallpox, Jenner also made several other important contributions to medicine: he was probably the first to link angina with hardening of the arteries, he described rheumatic heart disease and he purified important medicines. Both Jenner's medical work and also his work as a naturalist and geologist are described here through numerous displays and exhibits.

Cromwell's troops and played an important part in the history of the Civil War. It stands very close to the Severn and once incorporated the waters of the river in its defences so that it could, in an emergency, flood its lands. Visitors passing into the castle by way of a bridge over a moat will find a wealth of treasures in the Great Hall, the circular keep, the state apartments with their fine tapestries and period furniture, the medieval kitchens and the dungeons.

The Berkeley family have filled the place with objects from around the world, including painted glassware from Damascus, ebony chairs from India and a cypress chest that reputedly belonged to Sir Francis Drake. Security was always extremely important, and two remarkable signs of this are a four-poster

bed with a solid wooden top and a set of bells once worn by the castle's dray horses and now hanging in the dairy. The castle is surrounded by sweeping lawns and Elizabethan terraced gardens. Special features include a deer park, Queen Elizabeth I's bowling green, a beautiful lily pond and the **Butterfly House & Plant Centre**. Denizens of the Butterfly House include the world's largest moth, and the Plant Centre is stocked with unusual varieties from the Castle grounds. The 6,500-acre Berkeley Estate incorporates farms, the WWT Slimbridge Wetlands Centre and part of the River Severn itself.

The parish church of St Mary, which contains several memorials to the Berkeley family, has a fine Norman doorway, a detached tower and a striking east window depicting

---

🏛 historic building   📷 museum   🏛 historic site   🝊 scenic attraction   🌿 flora and fauna

PUDDLEDITCH FARM SHOP

Berkeley Heath, Berkeley,
Gloucestershire GL13 9EU
Tel: 01453 810816
website: www.puddleditchfarmshop.co.uk

Lindsey Morgan owns and runs the **Puddleditch Farm Shop**. It is situated on her husband's dairy farm which stands by the A38, with easy access from the M5 (J13 or 14), and close to the River Severn. The shop specialities are homemade cakes, local and English cheeses, local clotted cream and meat products sourced from animals raised within a few miles radius. It also stocks seasonal fruit and vegetables, sauces, oils, mayonnaise and fruit juices.

Christ healing the sick. A curious piece of carving in the nave shows two old gossips with a giant toad sitting on their heads. Next to the castle and church is the **Jenner Museum** (see panel opposite) once the home of Edward Jenner, the doctor and immunologist who is best known as the man who discovered a vaccine against smallpox. The son of a local parson, Jenner was apprenticed to a surgeon in Chipping Sodbury in 1763 at the tender age of 14. His work over several decades led to the first vaccination against smallpox, a disease which had killed many thousands every year. His beautiful Georgian house in Church Lane has a state-of-the-art display showing the importance of the science of immunology. In the grounds of the house is a rustic thatched hut where Jenner used to vaccinate the poor free of charge and which he called the Temple of Vaccinia. The east window of the church is a memorial to Jenner, who is buried in the churchyard.

At **Sharpness**, a mile or so west of Berkeley, the world's first nuclear power station operated between 1962 and 1989. It marks the entrance to the **Gloucester & Sharpness Canal**, opened in 1827 to bypass the tricky waters of the lower Severn. Sixteen miles in length, it has a lock from the tidal River Severn at Sharpness and a lock back into the River Severn at the head of Gloucester Docks, from which the River Severn Navigation runs 43 miles north to Stourport. There are several interesting villages in the vicinity, including Breadstone, which has a church built entirely of tin.

Thornbury

🏰 Castle

The woollen industry was important here in late medieval times, and the church, set away from the centre near the site of the old manor house, reflects the prosperity of those days. The side chapel is dedicated to the Stafford family, the local lords of the manor, whose emblem, the Staffordshire knot, is much in evidence. Edward Stafford, 3rd Duke of Buckingham, was responsible for starting work on **Thornbury Castle** in 1511 but did not live to see its completion. Charged with high treason by Henry VIII, he was beheaded on Tower Hill in London in 1522. The building was competed by Anthony Salvin in the 1850s.

Around Thornbury

TORTWORTH
4 miles NE of Thornbury off the B4509

 Tortworth Chestnut

Overlooking the village green stands the Church of St Leonard, which contains some fine 15th century stained glass and a pair of canopied tombs of the Throckmorton family, former owners of the Tortworth Park estate. In a field over the church wall are several interesting trees, including an American hickory, a huge silver-leafed linden and two Locust trees. Nearby, and the most famous of all, is the famous **Tortworth Chestnut**, a massive Spanish chestnut which the diarist John Evelyn called 'the great chestnut of King Stephen's time'. Certainly it was well established by Stephen's time (the 1130s), and a fence was

Tortworth Chestnut

put up to protect it in 1800. At that time a brass plaque was put up with this inscription:

> *'May man still guard thy venerable form*
> *From the rude blasts and tempestuous storm.*
> *Still mayest thou flourish through succeeding time*
> *And last, long last, the wonder of the clime.'*

And last it has; its lower branches have bent to the ground and rooted in the soil, giving the impression of a small copse rather than a single tree.

ALMONDSBURY
6 miles S of Thornbury on the A38

The Church of St Mary has some fine windows, including a memorial to Charles Richardson, the 19th century engineer who designed the original Severn Tunnel. A curious event took place in 1817 at nearby Knole Park when a young woman arrived at the door of the local squire saying that she was an Oriental princess who had been kidnapped and taken on board a ship, from which she had escaped by jumping overboard. The squire believed the story and 'adopted' Princess Caraboo, who soon became the toast of Bath. Her fame spread far enough to come to the attention of her former Bristol landlady, who identified the fake princess as a certain Mary Baker, a penniless woman from Devon. The embarrassed squire raised the money to send the impostor to Philadelphia. She returned some years later to Bristol, where she died in 1865.

Chipping Sodbury

🏛 Dodington House

This pleasant market town was one of the earliest examples of post-Roman town planning, its settlement being arranged in strips on either side of the main street in the 12th century. The town once enjoyed prosperity as a market and weaving centre, and it was during that period that the large parish church was built.

A mile or so to the east, on a loop off the A432, is **Old Sodbury**, whose part-Norman church contains some exceptional tombs and monuments. One of these is a carved stone effigy of a 13th century knight whose shield is a very rare wooden carving of a knight. Also in the church is the tomb of David Harley, the Georgian diplomat who negotiated the treaty which ended the American War of Independence. A tower just to the east of the church marks a vertical shaft, one of a series sunk to ventilate the long tunnel that carried the London-South Wales railway through the Cotswold escarpment. Opened in 1903, the 2.5 mile tunnel required its own brickworks and took five years to complete.

A lane leads south from Old Sodbury to **Dodington House**, built between 1796 and 1816 where previously an Elizabethan house stood. It was designed in lavish neo-Roman style by the classical architect James Wyatt, who was killed in a carriage accident before seeing his work completed. The house, whose interior is even more ornate than the facade, is open daily in the summer. Connected to the house by an elegant conservatory is the private Church of St Mary, also designed by Wyatt, in the shape of a Greek cross.

Around Chipping Sodbury

DYRHAM
4 miles S of Chipping Sodbury on the A46

🏛 Dyrham Park

The National Trust-owned **Dyrham Park**

stands on the slope of the Cotswold ridge, a little way south of the site of a famous 6th century battle between Britons and Saxons. This striking baroque mansion, used as a location for the filming of *Remains of the Day*, houses a wonderful collection of artefacts accumulated by the original owner William Blathwayt during diplomatic tours of duty in Holland and North America (he later became Secretary of State to William III). Among the most notable are several Dutch paintings and some magnificent Delft porcelain. The west front of the house looks out across a terrace to lawns laid out in formal Dutch style. Much of the estate is a deer park, which perhaps it was originally, as the word Dyrham means 'deer enclosure' in Saxon. A charming little church in the grounds has a Norman font, a fine 15th century memorial brass and several memorials to the Winter and Blathwayt families.

MARSHFIELD
8 miles SE of Chipping Sodbury on the A420

This old market town was once the fourth wealthiest town in Gloucestershire, after Bristol, Gloucester and Cirencester, its prosperity based on the malt and wool industries. Its long main street has many handsome buildings dating from the good old days of the 17th and 18th centuries, but not many of the coaching inns remain that were here in abundance when the town was an important stop on the London-Bristol run.

Among the many notable buildings are the Tolzey Market Hall and the imposing Church of St Mary, which boasts a fine Jacobean pulpit and several impressive monuments from the 17th and 18th centuries. Each Boxing Day brings out the Marshfield Mummers, who take to the streets to perform a number of time-honoured set pieces wearing costumes made from newspapers and accompanied by a town crier. On the northern edge of town is a folk museum at Castle Farm.

A lane leads south through a pretty valley to the delightful hamlet of **St Catherine's**, whose church contains a splendid 15th century stained-glass window with four lights depicting the Virgin Mary, the Crucifixion, St John and St Peter.

BADMINTON
4 miles E of Chipping Sodbury off the B4040

🏛 Badminton Park

The **Badminton Park** estate was founded by Edward Somerset, the son of the Marquis of Worcester, whose 25-foot monument stands in the little church next to the main house. The central section of the house dates from the 1680s and contains some marvellous carvings in lime wood by Grinling Gibbons. The rest of the house, along with the grounds and the many follies and gateways, is the work of the mid-18th century architect William Kent. The house contains an important collection of Italian, English and Dutch paintings.

The game of badminton is said to have started here during a weekend party in the 1860s. The Duke of Beaufort and his guests wanted to play tennis in the entrance hall but were worried about damaging the paintings; someone came up with the bright idea of using a cork studded with feathers instead of a ball. In such a moment of inspiration was the game born, and it was one of the guests at that weekend bash who later took the game to Pakistan, where the first rules were formalised.

Many of the buildings on the estate,

including the parish church and the estate villages of Great and Little Badminton, were designed in an ornate castellated style by Thomas Wright. The park is perhaps best known as the venue of the Badminton Horse Trials, which annually attract the best of the international riders, and spectators in their thousands.

HORTON
3 miles N of Chipping Sodbury off the A46

🏛 Horton Court

On high ground northeast of the long, narrow village stands the National Trust's **Horton Court**, a part-Norman manor house rebuilt for William Knight, the man given the task of presenting Henry VIII's case to the Pope when the King was trying to divorce Catherine of Aragon. Among the many interesting features is a covered walkway resembling a Roman cloister. The 12th century Great Hall survives from the earlier building.

WICKWAR
5 miles N of Chipping Sodbury on the B4060

🔱 Hawkesbury Monument

A market town of some importance in days gone by, Wickwar had its own mayor and corporation and two breweries; in the 1890s it became the first town in the west to install electric street lighting. Wickwar boasts a number of handsome Georgian buildings, notably the town hall with its distinctive bell tower and arches. A round tower close to the church marks a vertical shaft sunk in 1841 to ventilate the railway tunnel that runs below. To the east, across South Moon Ridings and up on to the ridge, stands the **Hawkesbury Monument**, designed in Chinese style and erected in 1846 as a memorial to Lord Robert

---

🏛 historic building   📷 museum   🏛 historic site   🔱 scenic attraction   🌿 flora and fauna

THE BUTHAY INN

High Street, Wickwar, Gloucestershire GL12 8NE
Tel/Fax: 01454 294386
website: www.buthay.co.uk

Wickwar locals, Andy and Alison Mears, are the friendly hosts at the **Buthay Inn**, which has long been the social hub of the village. The cosy bar is a convivial spot for enjoying real ales from the nearby Wickwar Brewery (tours available), and in the dining area visitors can sample an excellent selection of lunchtime snacks and an evening à la carte menu, both with the emphasis on English fare prepared from fresh local produce. Outside, the pub has a pleasant garden with picnic benches under parasols and patio heaters for cooler evenings. For guests staying overnight in this handsome market town, the Buthay has five comfortably appointed en suite bedrooms.

Somerset of Badminton, a general at the Battle of Waterloo. It has 145 steps, and the reward for climbing to the top is great views along the Cotswold escarpment and across the Severn to the Welsh mountains.

DIDMARTON

8 miles NE of Chipping Sodbury on the A433

ſſ St Lawrence's Well

Plenty of interest here, notably the medieval Church of St Lawrence, left alone by the serial remodellers of Victorian times and retaining its original three-storey pulpit and antique box pews. Across the road a semicircle of stones marks the site of **St Lawrence's Well**, which the saint himself, after a personal visit, promised would never run dry. In the centre of the village, Kingsmead House has two oddities in its garden: an octagonal gazebo from which the owner could get the first view of the stagecoaches arriving from Bath, and a Gothic hermit's house made of yew.

WESTONBIRT

9 miles NE of Chipping Sodbury on the A433

🌱 National Arboretum

Westonbirt - The National Arboretum, three miles south of Tetbury, contains one of the finest collections of trees and shrubs in the world - 18,000 of them spread over 600 acres of glorious Cotswold countryside. Wealthy landowner Robert Stayner Holford

National Arboretum, Westonbirt

🎭 stories and anecdotes   🐦 famous people   🎨 art and craft   🎭 entertainment and sport   🥾 walks

founded this tree wonderland by planting trees for his own interest and pleasure. His son, Sir George Holford, was equally enthusiastic about trees and continued his father's work until his death in 1926, when he was succeeded by his nephew, the 4th Earl of Morley. Opened to the public in 1956 and now managed by the Forestry Commission, the arboretum has something to offer all year round: a crisp white wonderland after winter snows, flowering shrubs and rhododendrons in spring, tranquil glades in summer, glorious reds, oranges and golds in the autumn. The grounds provide endless delightful walks, including 17 miles of footpaths, and there's a visitor centre, plant centre, café and picnic areas.

Gloucester

🏛 Cathedral 🏛 Maverdine House

🏛 Llanthony Priory 🏠 Museum & Art Gallery

🏠 National Waterways Museum

🏠 Folk Museum 🏠 Transport Museum 🏚 Docks

🗔 House of the Tailor of Gloucester

The capital city of Gloucestershire first gained prominence under the Romans, who in the 1st century AD established a fort to guard what was then the lowest crossing point on the Severn. A much larger fortress soon followed, and the settlement of Colonia Glevum became one of the most important military bases, crucial in confining the rowdy Celts to Wales. William the Conqueror held a

---

POUND FARM SHOP & PLANT CENTRE

Stroud Road, Whaddon, Gloucestershire GL4 0UG
Tel: 01452 523936 Fax: 01452 308150

Gerald and Jenny Hyett own and run **Pound Farm Shop & Plant Centre**, which stands a short drive south of Gloucester. The family has farmed here for more than 100 years, and the Farm Shop was started some 40 years ago. They expanded it in 1978 and created a new shop in 2005. Local produce takes pride of place among the wide range of foodstuffs on display, which include fresh fruit and vegetables, sausages, bacon, eggs, butter, cream, preserves and chutneys, cordials and fruit juices, cakes and bread baked daily on the premises.

There's a particularly tempting selection of locally produced cheeses, including the famous Stinking Bishop and the superb Wick Court Double and Single Gloucesters. Also on site is an excellent Plant Centre selling bedding and hanging plants, perennials, alpines, climbers, seeds, fertilisers and plant care products, pots and garden accessories.

Christmas parliament and commissioned the Domesday Book in Gloucester, and also ordered the rebuilding of the abbey, an undertaking which included the building of a magnificent church that was the forerunner of the superb Norman Cathedral. The elaborate carved tomb of Edward II, murdered at Berkeley Castle, is just one of many historic monuments in **Gloucester Cathedral**; another, the work of the Wedgwood designer John Flaxman, remembers one Sarah Morley, who died at sea in 1784. She is shown being delivered from the waves by angels. The ashes of the educationalist Dorothea Beale, who founded St Hilda's College, Oxford, are buried in a vault in the Lady Chapel.

The exquisite fan tracery in the cloisters is the earliest and among the finest in existence, and the great east window, 72ft by 38ft, is the largest surviving stained-glass window in the country. It was built to celebrate the English victory at the Battle of Crécy in 1346 and depicts the coronation of the Virgin surrounded by assorted kings, popes and saints. The young King Henry III was crowned here, with a bracelet on his little head rather than a crown.

The old area of the city around Gloucester Cross boasts some very fine early buildings, including St John's Church and the Church of St Mary de Crypt. Just behind the latter, near the house where Robert Raikes of Sunday School fame lived, stands an odd-looking tower built in the 1860s to honour Hannah, the wife of Thomas Fenn Addison, a successful solicitor. The tower was also a memorial to Raikes.

Three great inns were built in the 14th and 15th centuries to accommodate the scores of pilgrims who came to visit Edward II's tomb. Two of them survive. The galleried New Inn,

Gloucester Cathedral

founded by a monk around 1450, doubled as a theatre and still retains the cobbled courtyard. It was from this inn that Lady Jane Grey was proclaimed Queen. Equally old is the Fleece Hotel in Westgate Street, which has a 12th century stone-vaulted undercroft. In the same street is **Maverdine House**, a four-storey mansion reached by a very narrow passage. This was the residence and headquarters of Colonel Massey, Cromwell's commander, during the Civil War siege of 1643. Most of the region was in Royalist hands, but Massey survived a month-long assault by a force led by the king himself and thus turned the tide of war.

Gloucester Docks were once the gateway for waterborne traffic heading into the Midlands, and the handsome Victorian warehouses are always in demand as location sites for period films. The docks are now home to several award-winning museums. The

National Waterways Museum (see panel below), occupying three floors of a splendid Victorian warehouse, is entered by a lock chamber with running water and tells the fascinating 300-year story of Britain's canals and inland waterways with films, hands-on displays and floating historic boats. Soldiers of Gloucestershire uses archive film, photographs and life-size reconstructions to tell the history of the county's regiments.

Elsewhere in the city **Gloucester City Museum and Art Gallery** houses treasures from all over the county to reveal its history, from dinosaur bones and Roman remains to antique furniture and the decorative arts. Among the highlights are the amazing Birdlip Mirror, made in bronze for a Celtic chief just before the Roman conquest, two Roman tombstones and a section of the Roman city wall revealed under the cut-away gallery floor. English landscape painting is represented by Turner, Gainsborough and Richard Wilson.

Timber-framed Tudor buildings house **Gloucester Folk Museum**, where the exhibits include farming, fishing on the Severn, the port of Gloucester, the Civil War, a Victorian schoolroom, a dairy, an ironmongery and a wheelwright's workshop. **Gloucester Transport Museum** has a small collection of well-preserved vehicles and baby carriages housed in a 1913 former fire station. The **House of the Tailor of Gloucester**, in College Court, is the house sketched by Beatrix Potter in 1897 and used in her tale

The National Waterways Museum

Llanthony Warehouse, Gloucester Docks,
Gloucester, Gloucestershire GL1 2EH
Tel: 01452 318200 Fax: 01452 318202
website: www.nwm.org.uk

There's so much to see and do for all ages at the award-winning **National Waterways Museum** located in a splendid Victorian warehouse in historic Gloucester Docks. The Museum charts the fascinating 300-year story of Britain's inland waterways through interactive displays, touch-screen computers, working models and historic boats. Visitors can find out what made the waterways possible, from the business brains and design genius to the hard work and sweat of the navvies, and try their hand at designing and painting a narrow boat, building a canal and navigating a boat through a lock.

The Museum has a working blacksmith's forge, a floor of displays dedicated to waterway trade and cargoes, a marvellous interactive gallery and family room where weights and pulleys, water playareas, period costume, large jigsaw puzzles and brass rubbings bring history to life in a way that is both instructive and entertaining. The museum shop sells unusual gifts and souvenirs and refreshment is provided in the café. There are computerised information points throughout the Museum and visitors can even take to the water themselves on a 45-minute boat trip running along the adjacent Gloucester & Sharpness Canal between Easter and October. The National Waterways Museum is owned by the Waterways Trust, which preserves, protects and promotes our waterway heritage while giving new life to their future.

The Tailor of Gloucester. It now brings that story to life, complete with Simpkin the Cat and an army of helpful mice.

In the south-western suburbs of Gloucester are the ruins of **Llanthony Priory**. The explanation of its Welsh name is an interesting one. The priory of Llanthony was originally founded in the Black Mountains of Wales at the beginning of the 12th century, but the inmates were so frightened of the local Welsh that they begged the Bishop of Hereford to find them a safer place. The Bishop passed their plea to Milo, Earl of Hereford, who granted this plot of land for a second priory bearing the same name as the first. Llanthony Secunda was consecrated in 1136. On a nearby hill the monks built St Ann's Well, whose water is believed to cure eye problems.

Around Gloucester

TWIGWORTH
2 miles N of Gloucester off the A38

🏛 Nature in Art

Twigworth is the home of **Nature in Art**, a renowned museum of wildlife art housed in 18th century Wallsworth Hall.

PAUNTLEY
8 miles N of Gloucester on the A417

🦅 Pauntley Court

The penniless orphan boy who in the pantomime fable was attracted by the gold-paved streets of London and who became its Lord Mayor was born at **Pauntley Court**. Richard Whittington, neither penniless nor an orphan, was born here about 1350, one of three sons of landowner Sir William de Whittington and Dame Joan. He became a mercer in London, then an important

financier and was three times Mayor (not Lord Mayor - that title had not been invented). He married Alice Fitzwarren, the daughter of a wealthy landowner from Dorset. The origin of the cat connection is unclear, but an event which could have contributed to the myth was the discovery in 1862 of the carved figure of a boy holding a cat in the foundations of a house in Gloucester. The carving can be seen in Gloucester Museum.

HARTPURY
5 miles NW of Gloucester on the A417

🏛 Tithe Barn

There are two very interesting listed buildings here: a rare medieval set of bee hives in a building known as a bee bole, and, in the churchyard, a Soper stone tomb with a shrouded body on top. At nearby **Ashleworth** is a magnificent 14th century tithe barn with a stone-tiled roof, projecting porches and elaborate interlocking roof timbers.

REDMARLEY D'ABITOT
9 miles NW of Gloucester on the A417

This hilltop village, built on the red marle (clay) from which it takes its name and once the property of the French d'Abitot family, was for a time the home of the actress Lily Langtry, mistress of the Prince of Wales, later King Edward VII. The link with the actress is remembered in two streets in the village - Drury Lane and Hyde Park Corner.

Tewkesbury

🏛 Abbey 🏛 John Moore Countryside Museum

🏛 Battle of Tewkesbury

A town of historic and strategic importance close to the confluence of the Severn and

🎭 stories and anecdotes 🦅 famous people 🎨 art and craft 🚲 entertainment and sport 🦶 walks

Avon rivers. Those rivers also served to restrict the lateral expansion of the town, which accounts for the unusual number of tall buildings. Its early prosperity was based on the wool and mustard trades, and the movement of corn by river also contributed to its wealth. Tewkesbury's main thoroughfares, High Street, Church Street and Barton Street, form a Y shape, and the area between is a marvellous maze of narrow alleyways and small courtyards hiding many grand old pubs and medieval cottages. At the centre of it all is **Tewkesbury Abbey**, the cathedral-sized parish church of St Mary. One of the largest and grandest parish churches in the country, it was founded in the 8th century and completely rebuilt in the 11th. It was once the church of the Benedictine Abbey and was among the last to be dissolved by Henry VIII. In 1540, it was saved from destruction by the townspeople, who raised £453 to buy it from the Crown. Many of its features are on a grand scale - the colossal double row of Norman pillars; the six-fold arch in the west front; and the vast main tower, 132ft in height and 46ft square, the tallest surviving Norman main tower in the world. The choir windows have stained glass dating from the 1300s, and the abbey has more medieval monuments than

Site of the Battle of Tewkesbury

any besides Westminster. A chantry chapel was endowed by the Beauchamps, an influential family that married into another, that of Richard Neville, Warwick the Kingmaker.

Three museums tell the story of the town and its environs: the Little Museum, laid out like a typical old merchant's house;

MYCRAFT STUDIO

7 Carrant Road, Tewkesbury, Gloucestershire GL20 8AA
Tel: 01684 293623
e-mail: info@mycraftstudio.co.uk
website: www.mycraftstudio.co.uk

Debbie Wilson, mother of four, works from home and from her Tewkesbury workshop with her husband Simon. The inspiration for the ideas behind **Mycraft Studio** come from Debbie's life and family, and the keepsake tins and boxes for which the

studio has become known are designed to enable children and adults to keep treasured memories of their own lives. The studio also sells everything needed for customers to personalise their own tins, boxes or books, along with instruction sheets. Opening hours are 10am to 6pm Monday to Friday, 10am topm 4 Saturday, or shoppers can order online via the website.

🏛 historic building   📷 museum   🏚 historic site   🐟 scenic attraction   🌱 flora and fauna

Tewkesbury Museum, with displays on the social history and archaeology of the area; and the **John Moore Countryside Museum**, a natural history collection displayed in a 15th century timber-framed house. The museum commemorates the work of John Moore, a well-known writer, broadcaster and naturalist, who was born in Tewkesbury in 1907.

The **Battle of Tewkesbury** was one of the fiercest in the Wars of the Roses. It took place in 1471 in a field south of the town which has ever since been known as Bloody Meadow. Following the Lancastrian defeat, those who had not been slaughtered in the battle fled to the Abbey, where the killing began again. Abbot Strensham intervened to stop the massacre, but the survivors, who included the Duke of Somerset, were handed over to King Edward IV and executed at Market Cross. The 17-year-old son of Henry VI, Edward Prince of Wales, was killed in the conflict and a plaque marking his final resting place can be seen in the Abbey. One of the victors of the battle was the Duke of Gloucester, later Richard III. Tewkesbury was again the scene of military action almost two centuries later during the Civil War. The town changed hands several times during this period and on one occasion Charles I began his siege of Gloucester by requisitioning every pick, mattock, spade and shovel in Tewkesbury.

Around Tewkesbury

BREDON
4 miles NE of Tewkesbury on the B4080

🏠 Bredon Barn

Bredon Barn is a 14th century barn built of Cotswold stone, with a splendid aisled interior and unusual stone chimney cowling.

DEERHURST
3 miles S of Tewkesbury off the A38

🏠 Odda's Chapel

On the eastern bank of the Severn, a village whose current size and status belies a distinguished past. The church, with a distinct Celtic feel, is one of the oldest in England, with parts dating back to the 7th century, and its treasures include a unique double east window, a 9th century carved font, a Saxon carving of the Virgin and Child and some fine brasses dating from the 14th and 15th centuries. One depicts the Cassey family, local landowners, and their dog Terri.

Another Saxon treasure, 200 yards from the church, is **Odda's Chapel**, dedicated in 1056 and lost for many centuries before being gradually rediscovered after 1885 under a half-timbered house. The connection was then made with a stone inscribed with the date of consecration discovered in 1675 and now on view in the Ashmolean in Oxford.

FORTHAMPTON
3 miles W of Tewkesbury off the A438

🏠 Forthampton Court

This unspoilt Severn Vale village is dominated by the ancient Church of St Mary and by **Forthampton Court**, sometime home to the abbots of Tewkesbury and still retaining its fine 14th century banqueting hall, chapel and a medieval wood-based picture of Edward the Confessor. Near the churchyard can be seen relics of harsher times - a set of stocks and a whipping post complete with manacles.

Tetbury

🏠 Chavenage House   🏛 Police Museum

A really charming Elizabethan market town,

another to have prospered from the wool trade. Its most famous building is the stone-pillared 17th century Market House in the heart of town, but a visit should also take in the ancient Chipping Steps connecting the market house to the old trading centre, and the Church of St Mary, an 18th century period piece with high-backed pews, huge windows made from recovered medieval glass and slender timber columns hiding sturdy iron uprights. **Tetbury Police Museum**, housed in the original cells of the old police station, has a fascinating collection of artefacts, memorabilia and uniforms from the Gloucestershire Constabulary.

Two miles northwest of Tetbury, west of the B4014, stands **Chavenage House**, a beautiful Elizabethan mansion built of grey Cotswold stone on earlier monastic foundations in the characteristic E shape of the period. The elegant front aspect has remained virtually unchanged down the years, and the present owners, the Lowsley-Williams family, can trace their lineage back to the original owners. Two rooms are covered with rare 17th century tapestries, and the house contains many relics from the Cromwellian period. Cromwell is known to have stayed at the house, and during the Civil War he persuaded the owner, Colonel Nathaniel Stephens, a relative by marriage, to vote for the King's impeachment. According to the Legend of Chavenage the owner died after being cursed by his daughter and was taken away in a black coach driven by a headless horseman. The present owner, who conducts tours round the property, welcomes visitors to

---

SHIPTON MILL

Long Newton, Tetbury, Gloucestershire, GL8 8RP
Tel: 01666 505050 website: www.shipton-mill.com

When the Mill at Long Newnton was discovered by the current owners in 1981 it was a derelict, though impressive, Cotswold stone building at the end of a rutted track. A tributary of the River Avon wound round the site but the mill race was choked and the mill wheel was all but rusted away.

The machinery to clean the corn and drive the traditional French Burr Stone Millwheels has been lovingly restored. Stoneground flour of the highest quality is once again being milled by dedicated and highly skilled Shipton Millers. There has been a mill here for over 900 years, as recorded in the Domesday book and even in those days much of the grain would have come from the surrounding fields as it does today.

In nearby Malmesbury, site of a Benedictine monastery, the High Street is partially paved in Shipton Mill millstones, seized by the Abbot in a quarrel with the miller over who owned the mill stream fishing rights. Closer to the mill, its current layout was created during the Napoleonic wars. Nowadays the mill and its associated waterways are home to a thriving and diverse ecosystem from the bats in the mill eaves to the trout and crayfish in the crystal pure stream waters fed by springs. It is said that otters pass by and the striking blue flashes of the Kingfishers are an almost hourly occurrence.

Whilst not open for casual tours, organised tours can be booked in advance – **01666 505050**. In addition flours from the 40 strong range of speciality flours can be bought from the office during normal working hours and on Saturday by special arrangements. There is also an online shop.

🏛 historic building   📷 museum   🏛 historic site   🌣 scenic attraction   🌿 flora and fauna

'Gloucestershire's second most haunted house' (Berkeley Castle is the most haunted!). In 1970 an astonishing find was made in the attic - a portfolio of watercolours by George IV of plans for the restoration of Windsor Castle.

Around Tetbury

BEVERSTON
2 miles W of Tetbury on the A4135

The same Robert Stayner Holford who started the Westonbirt Arboretum built the model village of Beverston in conjunction with the architect Lewis Vulliamy. Their aim was to combine rural practicality with improved standards of accommodation, and the limestone terraces and model farms can be seen from the main road. The village also had a castle, once occupied by Earl Godwin, father of King Harold, and the earthworks are still visible.

WOTTON-UNDER-EDGE
10 miles W of Tetbury on the B4508

🏛 Heritage Centre

A hillside former wool town with a number of interesting buildings: Berkeley House with its stone Jacobean front; the terraced house that was the family home of Isaac Pitman and where he devised his renowned method of shorthand; the Perry and Dawes almshouses; and the Church of St Mary with memorials to Lord Berkeley and his wife Margaret. The **Wotton-under-Edge Heritage Centre**, housed in a former fire station, provides an excellent introduction to the town and the surrounding Area of Outstanding Natural Beauty.

OZLEWORTH
11 miles W of Tetbury on minor roads

🏛 Newark Park 🏛 Nan Tow's Tump

🕏 Midger Wood Nature Reserve

A secluded hamlet with a very unusual circular churchyard, one of only two in England. The church itself has a rare feature in a six-sided Norman tower. Also at Ozleworth is the National Trust's **Newark Park**, built as a hunting lodge by the Poyntz family in Elizabethan times. James Wyatt later converted it into a castellated country house. It stands on the edge of a 40ft cliff with superb views across to the Mendips. Attractions include a 14-acre woodland garden, countryside walks across the estate

🎭 stories and anecdotes 🎐 famous people 🎨 art and craft 🎣 entertainment and sport 🕏 walks

GRANARY COTTAGES

Silver Street, Coaley, nr Dursley, Gloucestershire GL11 5AX
Tel: 01453 860728
e-mail: thegranary@fsmail.net
website: www.granaryholidaycottages.co.uk

In a pleasant semi-rural location a few minutes from the A38 and M5, **Granary Cottages** provide a quiet, civilised base for a self-catering holiday. Owners David and Sarah Randall have made an excellent job of converting Cotswold stone farm buildings into two superbly appointed non-smoking holiday cottages. Stables has a double bedroom and a double sofa bed, while Carthorse has one twin and one double bedroom. Both provide central heating, a comfortable living area and a fully fitted kitchen, and guests have the use of a pleasant garden and patio area. Book well ahead, particularly in high season.

and, for 2006, two new waymarked woodland walks connected to the Cotswold Way.

This is great walking country, and one of the finest walks takes in the **Midger Wood Nature Reserve** on its way up to **Nan Tow's Tump**, a huge round barrow whose tomb is said to contain the remains of Nan Tow, a local witch.

Dursley

🏛 Cam Long Down

One of the most notable buildings in this former centre of the cloth-making trade is the 18th century market hall standing on 12 pillars at a busy town-centre junction. It has a bell turret on its roof and a statue of Queen Anne facing the fine parish church. William Shakespeare reputedly spent some time in Dursley after being spotted poaching, and there is a reference to a bailiff from the town in *Henry IV*. Cloth is still produced in the mill at Cam on the northern edge of Dursley, continuing a tradition started in the 16th century. Local legend is rich in stories about **Cam Long Down**, a small, isolated peak that is sometimes claimed as the scene of King Arthur's last battle. One story concerns the

Devil, who decided one day to cart away the Cotswolds and dam the Severn. On setting out with his first cartload he met a cobbler and asked him how far it was to the river. The cobbler showed him one of the shoes he was taking home to mend and replied, 'Do you see this sole? Well, I've worn it out walking from the Severn.' This persuaded the Devil, who was obviously a lazy devil, to abandon his task; he tipped out his load, creating the hill that can be seen today.

Around Dursley

STINCHCOMBE
3 miles W of Dursley off the A4135

Stancombe Park, on the southern edge of Stinchcombe, is a handsome country house built in 1880 on the site of a Roman villa, whose mosaic floor can be seen in Gloucester Museum. The gardens at Stancombe are occasionally open to the public.

NORTH NIBLEY
2 miles SW of Dursley on the B4060

🏛 Tyndale Monument

This village was the birthplace, around 1494,

🏛 historic building   🏛 museum   🏛 historic site   ⚘ scenic attraction   🌱 flora and fauna of William Tyndale, the first man to translate and print the Old and New Testaments. He used the original sources instead of the approved Latin, for which heresy he was burnt at the stake in Belgium in 1536. Three-and-a-half centuries later the imposing **Tyndale Monument**, paid for by public subscription, was erected on the ridge above the village to commemorate his life and work. Standing 111 feet high on the escarpment, it is one of the most prominent landmarks on the Cotswold Way and offers superb views. North Nibley is also the site of the last 'private' battle in England, which took place in 1471 between rival barons William Lord Berkeley and Viscount de Lisle.

ULEY
11 miles NE of Chipping Sodbury on the B4066

🏛 Owlpen Manor 🏛 Uley Bury ⛰ Coaley Peak
🏛 Hetty Pegler's Tump 🏛 Nympsfield Long Barrow

Even in this part of the Cotswolds where almost every prospect pleases, Owlpen is uniquely lovely – "a breathtaking ensemble of truly English beauty" enthused one visitor; Prince Charles called it "the epitome of the English village". Manor house, church, mill and cottages of pearl-grey stone are framed by a natural amphitheatre of steep, wooded hills, a timeless setting for "the epitome of the English village".

The jewel in the crown of this enchanting village is **Owlpen Manor,** a romantic Tudor building built between 1450 and 1616 and set in formal Queen Anne terraced yew gardens. Inside, contrasting with the ancient polished flagstones and the putty-coloured plaster, are fine pieces of William Morris-inspired Arts and Crafts furniture; there's also a rare beadwork collection and some unique 17th century painted cloth wall hangings. Within the grounds are a Courthouse of 1620, an 18th century Mill and a licensed restaurant in a medieval Cyder House complete with a massive cider press.

The village lies in the shadow of **Uley Bury**, a massive Iron Age hill fort which has thrown up evidence of habitation by a prosperous community of warrior farmers during the 1st century BC. Another prehistoric site, a mile along the ridge, is Uley Long Barrow, known locally as **Hetty Pegler's Tump**. This chambered long barrow, 180 feet in length, takes its name from Hester Pegler, who came from a family of local landowners. Adventurous spirits can crawl into this Neolithic tomb on all fours, braving the dark and the dank smell to reach the burial chambers, where they will no longer be scared by the skeletons that terrified earlier visitors. The walls and ceilings of the chamber are made of huge stone slabs infilled with drystone material.

Owlpen Manor

🎭 stories and anecdotes 🐦 famous people 🎨 art and craft ⚽ entertainment and sport 🚶 walks

A little further north, at the popular picnic site of **Coaley Peak** with its adjoining National Trust nature reserve, is another spectacular chambered tomb, **Nympsfield Long Barrow**.

Stroud

📷 Museum in the Park 🌲 Stratford Park

The capital of the Cotswold woollen industry, Stroud stands on the River Frome at a point where five valleys converge. The surrounding hill farms provided a constant supply of wool, and the Cotswold streams supplied the water-power. By the 1820s there were over 150 textile mills in the vicinity. Six survive, one of them specialising in green baize for snooker tables; another, Snow Mill, has cornered a niche market producing more than 160 types of snowflake for films and other entertainments. A stroll round the centre of town reveals some interesting buildings, notably the Old Town Hall dating from 1594 and the Subscription Rooms in neo-classical style. An easy walk from the centre is **Stratford Park**, a large park containing dozens of trees both ordinary and exotic, and with lots of ducks on the pond. The **Museum in the Park** is a family-friendly place with innovative and colourful displays that include dinosaur remains, a Roman temple – and the world's first lawn-mower, invented by local entrepreneur Edwin Buddings.

Around Stroud

BISLEY
4 miles E of Stroud on minor roads

🏛 All Saints Church

Country roads lead across from Stroud or up from Oakridge Lynch to the delightful village of Bisley, which stands 780 feet above sea level and is known as 'Bisley-God-Help-Us' because of the winter winds which sweep across the hillside. Bisley's impressive **All Saints Church** dates from the 13th century and was restored in the early 19th by Thomas Keble, after whose poet and theologian brother John, Keble College in Oxford was named. The font has two carved fish inside the bowl and a shepherd and sheep on the base. In the churchyard is the Poor Souls' Light, a stone wellhead beneath a spire dating from the 13th century. It was used to hold candles lit for souls in purgatory. Below the church are the **Seven Wells of Bisley** (also restored by Thomas Keble), which are blessed

---

THE BUTCHERS ARMS

Oakridge, Stroud, Gloucestershire GL6 7NZ
Tel: 01285 760371

The **Butchers Arms** is a friendly, unpretentious pub standing north of the A419 Stroud-Gloucester road. Experienced tenants Mark and Rose provide a warm welcome at this Wadworth pub at the head of the Stroud Valley. The stone-walled bar – cool in summer, cosy in winter – is a delightful spot to meet (or make) friends over a drink and, here or in the separate restaurant, Mark produces a good choice of freshly prepared English dishes. In fine weather tables are set out on the lawn, offering alfresco supping with beautiful views over the valley. For guests touring this lovely part of the world, the pub has a self-catering cottage sleeping up to four.

🏛 historic building   📷 museum   🏛 historic site   🏞 scenic attraction   🌿 flora and fauna

and decorated with flowers each year on Ascension Day. At the top of the village is a double lock-up built in 1824, with two cells beneath an ogee gable.

The Seven Wells of Bisley

The village's main claim to fame is the story of the Bisley Boy. When Bisley was a rich wool town it had a royal manor, Over Court, where the young Princess Elizabeth (later Queen Elizabeth I) often stayed. The story goes that during one of those visits the princess, then aged 10, caught a fever and died. Fearing the wrath of her father Henry VIII, her hosts looked for a substitute and found a local child with red hair and remarkably similar physical characteristics except for the rather important fact that the child was a boy called John Neville. Could this explain the Virgin Queen's reluctance to marry, her problem with hair loss and her 'heart that beats like a man's', or was the story made up to fit those facts?

MINCHINHAMPTON
4 miles SE of Stroud off the A419

🦌 Minchinhampton and Rodborough Commons

A scattered community on a ridge between two picturesque valleys, Minchinhampton acquired its market charter as far back as 1213. The area is good for walking and exploring, with the old stone quarries at Ball's Green and the National Trust woodland and grassland at **Minchinhampton and Rodborough Commons**. The majority of the commons are open to walkers and riders, and nature-lovers might spot rare butterflies such as the Chalkhill Blue, the tiny Green Hairstreak and

the Duke of Burgundy Fritillary. The Commons are also famous for their grassland species, including the lovely Pasque flower, whose resurgence has been assisted by the introduction of a small herd of Belted Galloways to help manage the rich grassland areas of the lower slopes.

SELSLEY
2 miles S of Stroud off the A46

🏛 All Saints Church

All Saints Church, built in the 1860s by wealthy mill-owner Sir Samuel Marling, is notable chiefly for its exceptional stained glass. This was commissioned from William Morris and Company and features designs by many of the Morris partnership, including Philip Webb, Burne-Jones, Ford Madox Brown, Dante Gabriel Rossetti and Morris himself.

WOODCHESTER
2 miles S of Stroud off the A46

🏛 Woodchester Park Mansion

Woodchester Park Mansion is one of Britain's most intriguing Victorian country

🎭 stories and anecdotes　🦢 famous people　🎨 art and craft　🎶 entertainment and sport　🦌 walks

OLD MOTHER HUBBARD HOME INTERIORS

Old Market, Nailsworth,
Gloucestershire GL6 0BL
Tel: 01453 835679
e-mail: anne@oldmotherhubbardglos.co.uk
website: www.oldmotherhubbardglos.co.uk

Anne Russell owns and runs three separate
establishments in and around Nailsworth, each with
its own appeal and each reflecting the care and taste
of its owner. **Old Mother Hubbard Interiors**, which she established in 1998, occupies the ground
floor of the yard area of a converted 18th century mill. Nine areas set out as rooms contain a
selection of original pine dressers, tables and cupboards, and a range of reclaimed,
reconditioned, repaired or repainted furniture. There are mirrors of all shapes and sizes, a
profusion of table lamps from around the world, bed covers, quilts, throws and cushions, and a
choice of decorative gift items. In an outdoor area Anne stocks old and new garden artefacts,
pergolas, arches, benches, pots and pot holders, and the conservatory is a showcase for iron
and wire furniture, marble table tops, lanterns, baskets, palms and other tropical plants. The
French influence is strong throughout, and Anne sources many items from the South of France.

MY FAIR LADY

5b Fountain Street, Nailsworth,
Gloucestershire GL6 0BL
Tel: 01453 839243

My Fair Lady is a lovely shop on one of the main
streets in the middle of Nailsworth specialising in
ladies wear for special occasions. The shop is stocked
with a constantly changing range of beautiful gowns,
suits, dresses and tops, with top names such as Ann
Balon (Italian) and Brax (German) supported by hats
galore to buy or hire, jewellery and other accessories.
Friendly staff are always on hand with help and
advice at the shop, which is open from 9.30am to 5pm Monday to Saturday.

HIGHLANDS B&B

Shortwood, Nailsworth, Gloucestershire GL6 0SJ
Tel: 01453 832591 Fax: 01453 833590

In her home along one of the pretty valleys around
Nailsworth, Anne offers quiet, comfortable B&B guest
accommodation in a hillside village. The four
bedrooms – two en suite, the others with private
bathrooms – are very well appointed and beautifully
furnished. Guests can relax in a lovely conservatory,
and the day starts with an excellent breakfast. The
rooms are also available for most of the year for
letting by the week on a self-catering basis.

houses. Building started in 1854 and was halted abruptly in 1868, three-quarters finished, with the scaffolding in place and the workmen's tools abandoned. What stands now, as in 1868, is a vast shell with gargoyles and flying buttresses on the Gothic facade, and all the props and stays and tools inside. The mansion is now used as a training ground for stonemasons.

NAILSWORTH

4 miles S of Stroud on the A46

🏛 Stokescroft ℘ Ruskin Mill

This small residential and commercial town was once, like so many of its neighbours, a centre of the wool trade. Several of the old mills have been modernised, some playing new roles, others plying their original trades. **Ruskin Mill** is a thriving arts and crafts centre; **Stokescroft** an unusual 17th century building on Cossack Square. During restoration work in 1972 scribblings found on an attic wall suggested that soldiers had been billeted there in 1812 and 1815. Perhaps this is why it is known locally as 'the Barracks'. It is thought to have housed Russian prisoners during the Crimean War, which accounts for the name of the square.

About half a mile north of the town, the Dunkirk Mill Centre contains a fulling mill which lays on demonstrations of the finishing of fine woollen cloth.

PAINT-A-POT

5 Cossack Square, Nailsworth, nr Stroud, Gloucestershire GL6 0DB
Tel: 01453 835043
website: www.paint-a-pot.co.uk

The name sounds fun, and fun is what the children and families of Nailsworth and the surrounding area can look forward to when they visit **Paint-a-Pot**. Owners Deborah Pearson and her daughter Pollyanna ensure that there's always something for all the family to paint, and the range includes kitchen and dining plates, dishes, bowls, jugs, vases, pots, teapots and ornaments. Customers can create their own masterpieces on the premises or choose a piece, paint it at home and bring it back for glazing. Many customers commission pieces to celebrate a christening, a birthday or any other special occasion. Children's workshops and parties by arrangement.

POPPIES INTERIORS

28, Fountain Street, Nailsworth,
Gloucestershire GL6 0BL
Tel: 01453 833633
e-mail: carolvickery@ukf.net

Carol Vickery, the talented daughter of a talented mother, owns and runs **Poppies Interiors**. She is a designer and seamstress of outstanding ability, and she designs and makes bespoke curtains, blinds, cushions, loose covers, bedding, screens and headboards. Customers can browse through a number of pattern books, and with the help of Carol they can make sure that every room in the house is coordinated.

🎭 stories and anecdotes 🐦 famous people ℘ art and craft ✍ entertainment and sport 🚶 walks

STONEHOUSE
3 miles W of Stroud on the A419

The Domesday Book recorded a vineyard at Stonehouse in 1086; Elizabeth I spent a night here in what is now, appropriately, a luxury hotel.

FROCESTER
4 miles SW of Stroud off the A419

🏛 Tithe Barn

In the grounds of the village-centre chapel stands the wonderful **Frocester Tithe Barn**, a massive 186 feet in length and looking much as it did when built on the instructions of Abbot John de Gamages between 1284 and 1306.

Vale of Gloucester and the Central Cotswolds

SLAD
2 miles N of Stroud on the B4070

Immortalised by Laurie Lee in his autobiographical *Cider With Rosie*, the sprawling village of Slad in the valley of the same name was for centuries a centre for milling and the production of fruit. Cider gave way to champagne on March 13th, 2002 after a Polish-bred horse called Galileo, trained by Tom George at Slad, was successful in one of the big novice hurdles at the Cheltenham Festival. A Roman villa was found in the Valley, and the votive tablets discovered at the

FROCESTER FAYRE FARM SHOP

Church Farm, Frocester, nr Stroud, Gloucestershire GL10 3TJ
Tel: 01453 822054   Fax: 01453 791290

The Hawkins family run **Frocester Fayre Farm Shop**, which since opening its doors in 2000 has become well known throughout the region for fine foods. All pork and beef comes from animals raised on the farm, and lamb comes from neighbouring farms.

The selection ranges from individual chops and steaks to all types of joints and half-pigs and half-lambs for the freezer. The prepared meat products are equally outstanding and include the very best bacon, a dozen varieties of sausages, burgers (beef, lamb, pork and chicken), pork pies and ready-to-eat meals such as faggots in gravy, lamb and beef casseroles, beef stroganoff and chilli con carne. The fruit pies and puddings are superb, too, and the shop also stocks

delicious jams, preserves and honey. Opening hours are 8am to 5pm Monday to Friday and 9am to 12.30pm on Saturday. Closed Sunday.

🏛 historic building   🏛 museum   🏛 historic site   🏞 scenic attraction   🌿 flora and fauna

Slad

site are now in Gloucester Museum.

PAINSWICK
4 miles N of Stroud on the A46

🏛 St Mary's Church 🏛 Prinknash Abbey Park

🌱 Painswick Rococo Garden

🎨 Gloucestershire Guild of Craftsmen Gallery

This beautiful little town, known as the 'Queen of the Cotswolds', prospered with the wool trade, which had its peak in the second half of the 18th century. At that time 30 mills provided power within the parish, and the number of fine houses and farms in and around the town are witness to those days. Many of them are built of the pale grey limestone that was quarried at Painswick Hill.

St Mary's Church, which dates from around 1380, was the site of one of many local skirmishes in the Civil War when a party of Parliamentary soldiers came under cannon fire, which did considerable damage to the building. A later fire, a lightning strike, Victorian 'restoration' and more recent modernisation have left little of note inside

the church apart from a fine 18th century reredos and some 300 modern kneelers depicting biblical scenes, views of the town, animals, birds and memorials to local people. The project involved around 60 people and took four years to complete.

But if St Mary's interior is generally disappointing, its churchyard is one of the must-see sights of the county. In the 1790s local people planted 99 yews – it was said that whenever a 100th was planted it would wither away - and these now stand sentinel over the graveyard's other extraordinary feature, the 33 richly carved table tombs all dating from the wool trade's boom years in the 17th and 18th centuries. The craftsman who created these striking rhapsodies in stone, John Bryan, is himself buried here beneath a pyramidal tomb.

Other buildings of interest include Court House, where King Charles I spent a night in 1643 before setting off for the siege of Gloucester, and the Post Office, dating back to the 1400s and the only surviving wooden-framed house in the town. In Bisley Street, the **Gloucestershire Guild of Craftsmen Gallery** provides a showcase for pieces made by members of the guild which is one of the oldest in the country. This feast of creative design includes jewellery, glass, velvet and silk, turned woods, greeting cards and more.

In the grounds of early-18th century Painswick House, on the B4073 at the northern edge of town, **Painswick Rococo**

Garden, hidden away in magnificent Cotswold countryside, is a unique restored 18th century garden with plants from around the world and a maze planted in 1999 with a path structure in the shape of '250' to commemorate the garden's 250th anniversary. Other attractions are carpets of snowdrops in early spring, a kitchen garden, a children's nature trail, a gift shop and a restaurant.

A little further north, at Cranham, **Prinknash Abbey Park** (pronounce it 'Prinnage') comprises an active monastery, chapel, replica of a Roman mosaic, gift shop and tearoom. The Benedictine monks of Caldey Island moved here in 1928 when the old house was made over to them by the 20th Earl of Rothes in accordance with the wishes of his grandfather. They no longer occupy the old house, having moved into the impressive new monastery in 1972. The abbey chapel is open daily for solitude and contemplation. Part of the abbey gardens are given over to the **Prinknash Bird & Deer Park**, where visitors can feed and stroke the fallow deer and see the waterfowl, the peacocks and the African pygmy goats. By the lake is a charming two-storey Wendy House.

EDGE
4 miles N of Stroud on the A473

🌿 Scottsquarr Common

Straddling a hilltop across the Spoonbed Valley, Edge has two delightful village greens and the mid-19th century Church of St John the Baptist with an ornate spire. To the west of the village lies **Scottsquarr Common**, an Area of Special Scientific Interest with an abundance of wild flowers and butterflies and spectacular views.

MISERDEN
5 miles NE of Stroud off the B40470 or A417

🌿 Miserden Park Gardens

Miserden Park Gardens, with views over the lovely Golden Valley, were created in the 17th century and are known for their spectacular spring bulbs, perennial borders, roses, topiary and an avenue of Turkish hazels.

Cheltenham

🖼 Art Gallery & Museum   🪶 Holst Museum

🏛 Pittville Pump Room   🏇 Racecourse

Smart, fashionable Cheltenham: a small,

ROSABLUE

215 Bath Road, Cheltenham, Gloucestershire GL53 7NA
Tel: 01242 521234 Fax: 01242 704695
website: www.rosablue.com

Luca and Penelope Menato own and run **Rosablue**, a great place to visit for its range of arts, crafts, fashion items and giftware. Among the prominent items in stock are cotton and linen in three different weights, gingham linings and backings for bags and cushions, heart garlands, cloth dolls, canvas slings for deck chairs and directors' chairs, mugs, vases and silver and costume jewellery. Customers can supply their own photographs to be printed on tote bags, satchels, boxes, cushions and purses, and they can view the article online prior to committing to purchase.

🏚 historic building   🖼 museum   🏛 historic site   🌳 scenic attraction   🌿 flora and fauna

insignificant village until a mineral spring was accidentally discovered in 1716. According to tradition, the first medicinal waters were discovered when locals saw pigeons pecking at salty deposits which had formed around a spring. A local man, William Mason, built a pump room and began Cheltenham's transformation into one of Europe's leading Regency spa towns. Mason's son-in-law was the astute Captain Henry Skillicorne, who added a meeting room, a ballroom and a network of walks and carriageways, and called it a spa. A number of other springs were soon discovered, including one in the High Street around which the first Assembly Rooms were built. In 1788 the Royal seal of approval came in the shape of King George III, who spent five weeks taking the waters with his family

and made Cheltenham a highly fashionable resort. An entirely new town was planned based on the best features of neoclassical Regency architecture, and as a result very few buildings of any antiquity still stand. One of these is the Church of St Mary, with parts going back to the 12th century and some very fine stained glass.

Skillicorne's walks and rides are now the tree-lined Promenade, one of the most beautiful boulevards in the country, its crowning glory the wonderful Neptune's Fountain modelled on the Fontana di Trevi in Rome and erected in 1893. Housed in Pittville Park, overlooking picturesque gardens and ornamental lakes north of the town centre, is the magnificent **Pittville Pump Room**. Concerts and special exhibitions are held

LA SCALA DELI CAFÉ

24 Regent Street, Cheltenham,
Gloucestershire GL50 1HN
Tel: 01242 580800
e-mail: enquiries@lascaladeli.com
website: www.lascaladeli.com

Owner and manager Dejan, who has nearly 20 years experience in the industry, runs the fully licensed **La Scala Deli Café**. With seating for up to 50, it is a super place for a snack, a meal or a takeaway and, from the start, a great addition to the many eating options in Cheltenham.

There's a Mediterranean theme to many of the dishes, typified by Neapolitan sausages, pasta with chicken and fresh colourful salads. Panini and gourmet sandwiches are popular choices for a quick, satisfying and very tasty lunch or snack, and those with a sweeter tooth will find that the cakes and pastries are equally delicious.

Grocery items include superb oils and vinegars. Quality is the keynote throughout this café-deli-sandwich bar-wine cellar, and along with that go service, choice and value for money. La Scala is open from 9am to 6pm (11am to 4pm on Sunday). Good parking is available above Regent Arcade next to the café.

🎞 stories and anecdotes   🐟 famous people   𝒫 art and craft   𝄐 entertainment and sport   🎿 walks

throughout the year. **Cheltenham Art Gallery and Museum** has an acclaimed collection of furniture and silver, much of it made by Cotswold craftsmen and inspired by William Morris' Arts and Crafts Movements, as well as some fine paintings, Oriental porcelain and English ceramics.

Gustav Holst was born in 1874 in a terraced Regency house in Clarence Road which is now the **Holst Birthplace Museum and Period House**. The original piano of the composer of *The Planets* is the centrepiece of the story of the man and his works, and there's a working kitchen, a Regency drawing room and a nursery.

Two remarkable modern pieces of public art take the eye in the centre of town. The Wishing Fish Clock in the Regent Arcade is a work in metal by the famous artist and craftsman Kit Williams: below the clock, from which a mouse pops out when disturbed by the arrival of an egg laid by a duck on high, is suspended a 12ft-long fish which celebrates the hour by swishing its tail and blowing bubbles, to the delight and fascination of shoppers below. The mechanical parts of the clock are the work of the renowned local clockmaker Michael Harding.

Off the High Street are the Elephant Murals, which portray an event that occurred in 1934 when three elephants from a travelling circus escaped and raided a provision shop stocked with corn - an incident which older locals with long memories still recall. **Cheltenham Racecourse**, two miles north of town, is the home of National Hunt Racing, staging numerous top-quality races highlighted by the March Festival when the Gold Cup and the Champion Hurdle find the year's best steeplechaser and best hurdler. Several other festivals have their home in Cheltenham, including the International Jazz Festival (April), the International Festival of Music (July), the International Festival of Literature (April) and the Cheltenham Festival of Science (June).

Around Cheltenham

PRESTBURY
1 mile NE of Cheltenham on the A46

🐎 Prestbury Park

Racing at Cheltenham started at Cleve Hill but moved to land belonging to **Prestbury Park** in 1819, since when all the great names in steeplechasing and hurdling have graced the Prestbury turf. But Prestbury's greatest son was not a jump jockey but the amazing Fred Archer, undisputed champion of flat race jockeys, born in the village in 1857. In the King's Arms hangs a plaque with this inscription:

Cleve Hill

🏛 historic building   🏛 museum   🏛 historic site   🌄 scenic attraction   🌿 flora and fauna

'At this Prestbury inn lived
FRED ARCHER the jockey
Who trained upon toast,
Cheltenham water & coffee.

The shoe of his pony
hangs in the bar
Where they drink to his prowess
from near and from far

But the man in the street
passes by without knowledge
That 'twas here Archer
swallowed his earliest porridge.'

CLEEVE HILL
3 miles NE of Cheltenham on the B4632

🏛 Belas Knap ⛰ Cleeve Cloud

The Cotswolds rise to their highest point, over 1,000 feet above sea level, at **Cleeve Cloud** above Prestbury and a mile from the village of Cleeve Hill. The views from here are magnificent, and also worth the climb is a massive Neolithic long barrow known as **Belas Knap**, where excavations have revealed the bones of more than 30 people. It is very unusual in having a false entrance at the north end, apparently leading to no chambers.

GOTHERINGTON
5 miles NE of Cheltenham on the A435

🏁 Prescott Hill Climb 🏛 Bugatti Trust

This is the location of the famous **Prescott Hill Climb**, scene of hill climb championships and classic car meetings as well as the location of the **Bugatti Trust**. The whole fascinating story of the Bugatti family and its cars can be seen here: the little museum contains an amazing collection of drawings, documents, photographs and artefacts, including a few Bugatti cars.

WINCHCOMBE
6 miles NE of Cheltenham on the B4632

🏰 Sudeley Castle 🏛 Folk & Police Museum
🏛 Railway Museum 🏛 Hailes Abbey

The Saxon capital of Mercia, where in medieval times the shrine of St Kenelm, martyred here by his jealous sister in the 8th century, was second only to that of Thomas à Becket as a destination for pilgrims. Winchcombe grew in importance into a walled town with an abbot who presided over a Saxon parliament. The abbey was destroyed in 1539 after the Dissolution of the

LILIAN MIDDLETON'S ANTIQUE DOLLS SHOP & DOLL AND TEDDY BEAR HOSPITAL

7 North Street, Winchcombe, Gloucestershire GL54 5LH
Tel: 01243 603302

Doll and teddy bear collectors come from near and far to **Lilian Middleton's Antique Dolls Shop & Doll and Teddy Bear Hospital** in the historic town that was the Saxon capital of Mercia. Septuagenarian Lilian has built up a loyal clientele of collectors – and of patients, as over 200 dolls are cared for here as well as numerous teddy bears. The stock includes both antique and modern bisque dolls (most of them arrayed in splendid hand-sewn clothes), teddy bears in and out of uniform, dolls' prams, dolls' houses and contents, soft toys and miniatures. The shop is open every day except Wednesday and Sunday.

🎭 stories and anecdotes 🐦 famous people 🎨 art and craft 🎪 entertainment and sport 🚶 walks

Sudeley Castle

Monasteries and all that remains today is a section of a gallery that is part of the George Inn. As well as pilgrims, the abbey gave rise to a flourishing trade in wool and sheep.

One of the most famous townsmen of the time was Jack Smallwood, the Jack o' Newbury who sponsored 300 men to fight at Flodden Field in 1513 and was a leading producer of woollen goods. Silk and paper were also produced, and for a few decades tobacco was grown locally - a fact remembered in place names such as Tobacco Close and Tobacco Field. This activity ceased in 1670 when a law was passed banning home-produced tobacco in favour of imports from the struggling colony of Virginia.

The decline that followed had the effect of stopping the town's development, so many of the old buildings have survived largely unaltered. These include St Peter's Church,

built in the 1460s and known particularly for its 40 grotesques and gargoyles, the so-called Winchcombe Worthies. **Winchcombe Folk & Police Museum**, in the Tudor-style Town Hall by the Tourist Information Centre, tells the history of the town from neolithic times to the present day and also keeps a collection of British and international police uniforms and equipment.

A narrow passageway by an ordinary-looking house leads to **Winchcombe Railway Museum and Garden**, a wonderland full of things to do: the railway museum contains one of the largest collections of railway equipment in the country, and visitors can work signals and clip tickets and generally get misty-eyed about the age of steam. The Cotswold garden is full of old and rare plants. Winchcombe Pottery was established in 1926 on the site of an old

🏠 historic building   🏛 museum   🏚 historic site   ⚘ scenic attraction   🌱 flora and fauna

country potter dating back to the early 1800s. Visitors can see the potters at work.

A mile or so north of Winchcombe stand the ruins of **Hailes Abbey**, founded in 1246 by Richard, Earl of Cornwall. Richard, caught in a storm at sea, vowed that he would found a religious house if he survived, and in 1245 his brother Henry III gave him the manor at Hailes to do it. It was built on such an ambitious scale that the Cistercian monks were hard pressed to maintain it, but after Richard's son, Edmund, donated a phial said to contain the blood of Christ (later proved to be a fake) the abbey soon became an important place of pilgrimage and was even mentioned in Chaucer's *Canterbury Tales*. The closure of the abbey in 1539 brought great distress to the town: merchants lost the custom of the pilgrims and the poor no longer received their 'doles' from the monks.

The abbey fell into disrepair and today shattered walls and arches are all that remain of this mighty Cistercian foundation, yet the atmosphere of a 13th century monastery lingers most powerfully. Some of the many artefacts found at the site, including medieval sculptures and decorated floor tiles, are on display in the abbey's museum. Some of the medieval glass from the abbey is now in the church at Stanton.

One mile south of Winchcombe and set against the beautiful backdrop of the Cotswold Hills, is **Sudeley Castle** which has royal connections going back 1,000 years. This magnificent palace was the last home of Catherine Parr, sixth and last wife of Henry VIII. King Charles I stayed at the castle, and his nephew, Prince Rupert, established his garrison headquarters here during the Civil War. The interior of the castle, restored by the owning Dent family in sumptuous

Victorian style, is a treasure house of old masters (Turner, Rubens, Van Dyck), tapestries, period furniture, costumes and toys, and the beautiful grounds include a lake, formal gardens and a 15ft double yew hedge. Among the many other attractions are an exhibition on the evolution of the gardens, 'The Lace and Times of Emma Dent', a gift shop, plant centre, restaurant and adventure playground.

TODDINGTON
8 miles NE of Cheltenham on the B4632/B4077

Gloucestershire Warwickshire Railway

Toddington Station is the northern terminus of the restored **Gloucestershire Warwickshire Railway** (see panel on page 138), from where steam or diesel trains run a scenic round trip of 20 miles through delightful countryside by way of Winchcombe and Gotherington to Cheltenham racecourse. The line is open all year and there is a programme of special events and gala days.

STANWAY
9 miles NE of Cheltenham on the B4077

Stanway House

A charming village clustered round Jacobean **Stanway House** which is surely one of the most perfect of Cotswold mansions. Built using the warm, honey-coloured local stone, surrounded by gardens and landscaped grounds, Stanway is a dwelling-place at peace with the world and with itself. Its towering bay window looks across a scene where for centuries the only changes have been those ordained by the passing of the seasons.

Nearby stands an immense Tithe Barn which was built in 1370 when the Manor of Stanway was a small satellite of Tewkesbury

Gloucestershire Warwickshire Railway

A journey on the GWR

The railway offers a 20-mile round trip between Toddington and Cheltenham Race Course through some of the most spectacular scenery in the Cotswolds.

As you leave Toddington, once a major fruit distribution centre the train passes the workshops where the steam and diesel locomotives are maintained and restored. The journey then takes you past the village of Didbrook and the site of Hayles Abbey Halt, which served the nearby Abbey (English Heritage). Good views of the Cotswolds can be seen from both sides of the train, before arriving at Winchcombe station, which is actually at Greet, about a mile from the town.

The station building at Winchcombe once stood at Monmouth Troy and was painstakingly dismantled, moved and rebuilt by volunteers. This is also the headquarters of the carriage and wagon department. Shortly after leaving Winchcombe the train enters Greet tunnel which, at 693 yards, is the second longest on a preserved railway. Emerging on to an embankment offering splendid views over the Vale of Evesham to the distant Malverns, the train passes the village of Gretton and hamlets of Stanley Pontlarge and Far Stanley.

After a long straight through Dixton cutting the train reaches Gotherington. The original station (closed 1955) is now a private home, but the owner has a number of interesting railway artefacts in his grounds, including the award-winning 'Gotherington West' – an original 'pagoda' Great Western iron-built halt (no public access). Leaving Gotherington, you may get a glimpse of Tewkesbury Abbey in the distance with the distinctive Malvern Hills beyond. Now the train descends over the extension completed in 2003 to Bishops Cleeve – mature Scots Pine trees mark where the station once stood (closed 1960). Here, the train runs over what is believed to be the only continuously-welded section of line on a heritage railway.

As the line approaches Cheltenham Race Course, views of Cleeve Hill (the highest point of the Cotswolds) open up. Passing under Southam Lane, the racecourse comes into view before entering the station, which was opened by HRH The Princess Royal in April 2003. There is a new platform level building here with toilet facilities (including facilities for disabled visitors). The original and unique Swindon-built pre-fabricated station building, reached by a ramp, is perched high above the track at road level. The station once again fulfils its original purpose – bringing race-goers for important meetings such as the Cheltenham Gold Cup.

🏛 historic building   🏛 museum   🏛 historic site   🌄 scenic attraction   🌿 flora and fauna

Abbey. Four monks dedicated themselves in prayer for the souls of the two Saxon nobles who had presented the land to the abbot in 715AD.

The present house was built in the 1580s with the Great Hall at its heart, a glorious room whose function changed by the hour – from business room to manorial court to dining room. The raised dais on which the Lord of the Manor and his family took their meals is still in place as is a 23-feet-long 16th century shuffleboard carved from a single piece of oak. The house's other treasures include fine paintings, two superb Broadwood pianos, and a Chippendale exercising chair on which keep-fit enthusiasts of the time would bounce for half an hour a day.

The grounds are equally interesting, with a water mill, ice house, brewery, dogs' cemetery and a pyramid erected in honour of John Tracy from the owning family. Another resident was Thomas Dover, the sea captain who rescued Alexander Selkirk from a desert island, an event which gave Daniel Defoe the inspiration for *Robinson Crusoe*. Also of note in Stanway is a thatched cricket pavilion resting on mushroom-shaped stones. The pavilion was a gift from JM Barrie, the author of *Peter Pan*, who was a regular visitor to the village.

Stanway's water gardens are regarded as the finest in England and their beauty has recently been enhanced with the installation of a 165ft high fountain – Britain's highest fountain and the tallest gravity fountain in the world.

STANTON
10 miles NE of Cheltenham on the B4632

🏠 Stanton Court   🏠 Snowshill Manor

One of the prettiest spots in the Cotswolds, an attractive village of steeply-gabled limestone cottages dating mainly from the 16th and 17th centuries. The whole village was restored by the architect Sir Philip Scott in the years before World War I; his home between 1906 and 1937 was **Stanton Court**, an elegant Jacobean residence built by Queen Elizabeth I's Chamberlain. The village church, dedicated to St Michael and All Angels, has many interesting features, including some stained glass from Hailes Abbey and a number of medieval pews with scarred ends caused perhaps by the leashes of dogs belonging to local shepherds. Most of the glass is the much more modern work of Sir Ninian Comper (1864-1960), the Aberdeen-born architect and prolific designer of church fittings and furnishings; stained glass was one of his specialities. John Wesley is said to have preached in the church. Beyond Stanton, on the road to Broadway, the National Trust-owned **Snowshill Manor** is an elegant manor house dating from Tudor times; once the home of Catherine Parr, it contains a fascinating collection of crafts and artefacts assembled by the last private owner, Charles Paget Wade.

GUITING POWER
8 miles E of Cheltenham off the A4436

🐑 Cotswold Farm Park

A neat collection of Cotswold stone cottages round a triangular green. Noteworthy features include the part-Norman St Michael's Church and a World War I memorial cross. Close by is **Cotswold Farm Park** which was the first Rare Breeds Farm in England when it opened in 1971 and is now home to more than 50 flocks and herds of British farm animals. Using the hand-held audio guide, visitors can discover the animals' tales of survival. Among the many other attractions are shearing and spinning demonstrations, fleece sales, safari

GUITING GUEST HOUSE

Post Office Lane, Guiting Power, Gloucestershire GL54 5TZ
Tel: 01451 850470
e-mail: info@guitingguesthouse.com
website: www.guitingguesthouse.com

VisitBritain - 5 Diamonds, AA - 5 Diamonds Silver Award. Also featured in *Which*, *Good Housekeeping*, *Britains Best Bed & Breakfast Guide*, *Marks & Spencer B&B Guide* and *The Michelin Guide Great Britain & Ireland 2007*.

Barbara and Rob Millar guarantee a warm welcome for visitors to Guiting Guest House, a beautifully restored 16th century Cotswold stone farmhouse. Everywhere there are exposed beams, inglenook fireplaces and polished wooden floors of elm from the Wychwood Forest. The seven tastefully decorated bedrooms are warm and comfortable, have en suite or adjacent bathrooms and very attractive individual furnishings. Some have four-poster beds, and all are supplied with TV, hairdryer and many thoughtful little

extras including different types of tea and coffee, fresh fruit and biscuits on the hospitality trays, fresh flowers and the obligatory teddy bear which is available to adopt!

The dining room is an informal place to meet other guests over breakfast, or take the opportunity of enjoying a relaxed four-course evening meal made from fresh seasonal produce, sourced from local suppliers wherever possible. Prior notice is required, normally 48 hours.

Popular for walking, there are numerous walks and bridle paths which run from the village and it is within easy driving distance of many of the gems of the Cotswolds and beyond such as Blenheim Palace, Warwick Castle and Stratford-upon-Avon. All leisure facilities are catered for within a short drive including golf, fishing and horseriding.

A spacious and well-equipped self-catering cottage is also available.

---

rides, an indoor tractor school, adventure playground, pets corner, woodland walk and a host of other activities guaranteed to keep children happy for hours.

Stow-on-the-Wold

🏛 Toy & Collectors Museum

At 800ft above sea level, this is the highest town in the Cotswolds, and the winds sometimes prove it. The town's main source of wealth in earlier times was wool; twice-yearly sheep fairs were held on the Market Square, and at one such fair Daniel Defoe records that over 20,000 sheep were sold. Those days are remembered today in Sheep Street and Shepherds Way. The square holds

another reminder of the past in the town stocks, used to punish minor offenders. The sheep fairs continued until they were replaced by an annual horse fair, which was held until 1985.

The Battle of Stow, in 1646, was the final conflict of the Civil War, and after it some of the defeated Royalist forces retreated to St Edward's Church, while others were cut down in the Market Square. The church, which suffered considerable damage at this time, has been restored many times down the centuries, not always to its advantage, but one undoubted treasure is a painting of the crucifixion in the south aisle, thought to be the work of the 17th century Flemish artist Gaspard de Craeyer. The church is dedicated

---

🏛 historic building   🏛 museum   🏛 historic site   🍃 scenic attraction   🌿 flora and fauna

HERRING SHOES

4 Park Street Stow-on-the-Wold
Gloucestershire GL54 1AQ
Tel 01451 832244
website: www.herringshoes.co.uk

Set in the heart of the Cotswolds, **Herring Shoes** is a family business specialising in men's and women's quality footwear with service to match. The Stow branch offers a unique range of footwear from brands including Barker, Church's, Gabor, Gant, Ecco, Rockport, Timberland, Sioux & Van Dal.

Having built close relationships with many of the Northampton manufactures over the last 40 years they launched a range of handmade footwear made for them by Barkers, Cheaney, Loakes & Sargents. In recent years their own range of Herring Shoes have become very popular, made to the exact needs of their customers and by working direct with the factories to achieve unique styles and value for money. The Herring Brand is now being sold worldwide alongside brands such as Church, Barker & Loakes which are also available on the Herring website.

Adrian Herring says: "Our aim is to educate people just how important good shoes are in life.This is not just my business, it's my passion."

MABYS FOOD AND WINE

Digbeth Street, Stow-on-the-Wold, Gloucestershire GL54 1BN
Tel: 01451 870071

Maby's Food and Wine is widely considered to be the top delicatessen in the Cotswolds. For 20 years this outstanding shop has been serving the community, whether it's the large and loyal band of individual shoppers , local events, weddings, opera nights and the Hay Festival. The deli section includes a fantastic cheese selection (from the region, from the UK and from overseas), pies and quiches and pâtés, cooked meats and salami, olives, preserves and pickles, oils and vinegars, stuffed peppers, artichokes, anchovies and sardines.

There are super breads, cakes and pastries, ice creams, dairy products, teas and coffees, juices and wines mainly from France and Spain. Mabys also sells a range of chilled and frozen ready meals prepared by the resident chefs. Hampers can be ordered for any occasion, and the shop also sells other items that contribute to good living, including champagne, brandy and hand-rolled Havana cigars. Tom Maby has recently opened a second Mabys outlet in Bishops Walk, Cirencester.

to King Edward the
Martyr, who was
murdered at Corfe
Castle by his stepmother
Elfrida. Other buildings
of note in the town are
the 15th century
Crooked House and the
16th century Masonic
Hall. On Digbeth Street
stands the Royalist
Hotel, said to be the
oldest inn in England;
an inn has certainly
stood on the site since
947. In Park Street is the
Toy and Collectors Museum, housing a
charming display of toys, trains, teddy bears
and dolls, games and books, along with textiles
and lace, porcelain and pottery.

Stow-on-the-Wold

🏛 historic building   🏛 museum   🏛 historic site   🍃 scenic attraction   🌱 flora and fauna

Around Stow-on-the-Wold

UPPER & LOWER SWELL
1 mile W of Stow on the B4077 & B4068

A couple of Swells, neighbouring villages on the banks of the River Dikler. Lower Swell's focal point is the triangular village green, while the large mill pond is one of Upper Swell's many delights. Nearby, in Condicote Lane, is Donnington Trout Farm with a hatchery, smokery, farm shop and a lake for fly fishing.

MORETON-IN-MARSH
4 miles N of Stow on the A429

🏛 Wellington Aviation Museum   🌳 Batsford Park

🌳 Cotswold Falconry Centre

Moreton-in-the-Marsh is the scene, every Tuesday, of the biggest open-air street market in the Cotswolds. This attractive old town stands at the junction of the A44 and the A429 Fosse Way, and was once an important stop on the coaching route between London and the West Midlands. Its broad main street is lined with handsome 17th and 18th century buildings, while from earlier days are the old town gaol, the White Hart, where Charles I

LONGBOROUGH FARM SHOP

*Longborough, nr Stow-on-the-Wold,
Gloucestershire GL56 0QZ
Tel: 01451 830469 Fax: 01451 830413
e-mail: mail@longboroughfarmshop.com
website: www.longboroughfarmshop.com*

**Cotswold Life Winner Best Speciality
Food Shop 2004
Runner-up NFU Southwest Region Best
Farm Retailer 2003**

On the A424 two miles north of Stow-on-the-Wold, Katharine Assheton's multi-award winning **Longborough Farm Shop** is a foodie paradise, an absolute must for anyone driving or touring in the area. Under the beams of the stone-walled shop there's an amazing, mouthwatering display of specialist packaged foods along with bread, cakes baked by local women, cider, mead and fruit wines, and an assortment of food-related gifts, table accessories and paintings by local artists. From the fruit farm comes a variety of soft fruits and orchard fruits, and asparagus in its short but sensational season. Most of the vegetables are from local producers, with the emphasis, as with everything here, on quality and seasonality. The cheeses, mostly British, are kept in superb condition, but perhaps pride of place goes to the superb meats, including local Dexter beef, Jacob lamb pork from Old Spot Gloucester pigs, Dorset bacon and sausages and seasonal game. This marvellous place is open every day, closed only on Sunday from January to Easter.

🎭 stories and anecdotes   🐦 famous people   🎨 art and craft   ✒ entertainment and sport   🚶 walks

took refuge during the Civil War, and the Curfew Tower with its clock and bell dated 1633.

In Bourton Road, the **Wellington Aviation** Museum has a collection of World War II aircraft paintings, prints and models and a detailed history of the Wellington bomber.

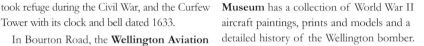

TOP MARKS FOR FASHION

23 High Street, Moreton-in-Marsh,
Gloucestershire GL56 0AF
Tel: 01608 651272

On the main street of one of the most attractive of all Cotswolds towns, **Top Marks for Fashion** is owned and run by Maria Drinkwater. Choice and value for money have always been watchwords. There is a frequently changing range of clothes for all ages and all the family, and accessories including hats, socks, belts, bags and jewellery. One of the less usual features is a range of quality seconds and end-of-line clothes from some of the leading high-street chain stores, such as Per Una from Marks & Spencer.

THE COTSWOLD CHEESE COMPANY

5 High Street, Moreton-in-Marsh, Gloucestershire GL56 0AH
Tel: 01608 652862   Fax: 01608 652925
e-mail: sales@cotswoldcheesecompany.co.uk
website: www.cotswoldhcheesecompany.co.uk

On the main street of Moreton-in-Marsh, Jon Gleeson's **Cotswold Cheese Company** has quickly become a place of pilgrimage for food-lovers in the area. Cheese rightly holds pride of place, with a fine selection of British and Continental varieties, but there's plenty more to entice the customer, including Mediterranean delicacies, Asian spices and pulses, fresh bread delivered daily from Broadway, locally grown fruit and vegetables, free-range eggs, cooked meats, pies and pastries, filled baguettes and takeaway snacks, juices, jams, chutneys, chocolates, teas and coffees, hampers and all the accessories for a perfect picnic.

WOLD GALLERIES

The Old Saddlery, 3a Oxford Street,
Moreton-in-Marsh, Gloucestershire GL56 0LA
Tel: 01608 650727
e-mail: sales@woldgalleries.com website:
www.woldgalleries.com

Kit & Ella Havelock-Davies own and run the long established Wold Galleries which is situated just off Moreton High Street, (the A429 Fosse Way) and within an easy walk of the mainline train station. The gallery features the work of 25 to 30 contemporary artists, whose talents spread across the media of oil, watercolour, pastel, acrylic, glass and ceramic. Many of the artists are local but the gallery also showcases work by Russian and Spanish painters. The gallery offers a bespoke picture framing service and can provide cleaning and restoration as well as a facility for reprinting and enlarging photographs on to canvas. Open 10am to 5pm every day except Tuesday, also closed on Sunday from January to March.

🏛 historic building   🏛 museum   🏛 historic site   🏞 scenic attraction   🌱 flora and fauna

One of the town's most popular amenities is **Batsford Park** which offers a variety of attractions. There's an arboretum set in 55 acres of typical Cotswold countryside and contains more than 1,500 species and varieties of trees, shrubs, bamboos and wild flowers. Visitors can wander along meandering paths and discover surprises at every turn – a Japanese Rest House, a hermit's cave or a number of magnificent bronze statues from the far east. Also within the park is the **Cotswold Falconry Centre** which is home to a large collection of falcons, hawks, owls, kites and vultures which are flown at regular intervals during the day. Other attractions in the park include a gift shop, tea room and garden centre.

A mile east of town on the A44 stands the Four Shires Stone marking the original spot where the counties of Gloucestershire, Oxfordshire, Warwickshire and Worcestershire met.

BLOCKLEY
7 miles N of Stow off the A44/A429

 Mill Dene Garden

Silk-spinning was the main industry here, and six mills created the main source of employment until the 1880s. As far back as the Domesday book water mills were recorded here, and the village also once boasted an iron foundry and factories making soap, collars and pianos. The mills have now been turned into private residences and

---

SIMPLE SUPPERS FARM SHOP
Ditchford Mill, Todenham, nr Moreton-in-Marsh, Gloucestershire
Tel: 01608 650399 Fax: 01608 650560
e-mail: office@simplesuppers.co.uk
website: www.simplesuppers.co.uk

The Graham family have been farming at Ditchford Mill Farm for nearly 30 years, and in 2004 they opened **Simple Suppers** here just off the A429 Fosseway north of Moreton-in-Marsh. They gained their reputation as producers of quality-assured pigs, and pork and pork products remain the star of the show, many winning gold awards. The pigs from their farm are slaughtered locally and butchered on the premises, the basis of the superb cuts and joints, hams and gammons, sausages (pork & mustard, hot & spicy Spanish, Cotswold herb and 95% meat Yeomans are just some of the wonderful varieties), dry-cured, smoked and unsmoked bacon, burgers, pork pies and ready meals such as pork & coconut curry or prune-stuffed tenderloin.

The butchery also prepares beef and lamb from local farms for sale as fresh meat and as ingredients in a wide range of dishes, from classics such as cottage pie to contemporary items like beef in madeira with wild mushrooms. Simple Suppers also produces delicious nursery and teatime favourites such as bread & butter pudding, coffee cake and Victoria sponge, sumptuous chocolate and lemon tarts and superb seasonal fruit pies. There's cheese from the region, butter, cream, seasonal vegetables, fruit and fruit juices, icecream, jams and honeys.......and everything is of the very finest quality.

Blockley is a quieter place. One of the chief attractions for visitors is **Mill Dene Garden**, set around a mill in a steep-sided valley. The garden has hidden paths winding up from the mill pool, and at the top there are lovely views over the Cotswolds. Also featured are a grotto, a potager, a trompe l'oeil and dye plants.

CHIPPING CAMPDEN
10 miles N of Stow on the B4081

🏛 Market Hall 🦋 Cotswold Olimpicks

The 'Jewel of the Cotswolds', full of beautifully restored buildings in golden Cotswold stone. It was a regional capital of the wool trade

---

MIRA

High Street, Chipping Campden, Gloucestershire GL55 6AT
Tel: 01386 840727

On the attractive main street of Chipping Campden, **Mira** is a lovely little shop in a Cotswold stone building, stocked with a well-chosen selection of stylish fashion wear, jewellery, fragrances and gifts. Anne Inston's shop stocks a range of smart clothes for women along with bags and belts, scarves, jewellery and other accessories. Among the gift items are glazed ceramic chickens, jugs and vases and plates from Italy, and useful things like pens and screwdrivers. The Di Palomo range of fragrances includes soaps, gels, oils, lotions and candles incorporating olive oil and orange blossom.

CHAUSALLE

High Street, Chipping Campden,
Gloucestershire GL55
Tel/Fax: 01386 841717
e-mail: sally.cahill@btopenworld.com
website: www.chausalle.co.uk

Chausalle is a pretty womens' shoe and fashion boutique located a few steps down from street level on Chipping Campden's High Street. The setting is archetypical old-world English, but the stock comes from Spain, France, Italy and Australia as well as England. Sally Cahill, who opened her shop in 2004, personally selects all the clothes and accessories, and she has built up a loyal clientele that comes from a wide area.

The shoe range encompasses both everyday and evening wear. Accessories include tops and skirts for summer, suede and leather coats and skirts for the cooler months, gilets, belts, Wolford hosiery, pashminas, cashmere and fabulous handbags and jewellery. Among the brands to be found are Jaime Mascaró, Rotta, Rebeca Sanver, Audley, Paco Gil, Arche, Radley and Spencer & Rutherford. Shop hours are 10am to 5pm Monday to Saturday.

🏛 historic building   🏛 museum   🏛 historic site   🌀 scenic attraction   🌿 flora and fauna

between the 13th and 16th centuries and many of the fine buildings date from that period of prosperity. In the centre of town is the Jacobean **Market Hall**, built in 1627 and one of many buildings financed by the wealthy fabric merchant and financier Sir Baptist Hicks. He also endowed a group of almshouses and built Old Campden House, at the time the largest residence in the town; it was burnt down by Royalists to prevent it falling into the hands of the enemy, and all that survives are two gatehouses, the old stable block and the

WOOLSTAPLERS HALL GUEST HOUSE

High Street, Chipping Campden, Gloucestershire GL55 6HB
Tel/Fax: 01386 849399
e-mail: woolstaplers@btinternet.com
website: www.woolstaplershall.com

Thought to be the original wool exchange and merchants' hall, the 14th century **Woolstaplers Hall** provides the most atmospheric of settings for a bed & breakfast break. In the heart of Chipping Campden, it was once the home of C R Ashbee, one of the founders of the Arts & Crafts Movement, and it contains a wealth of stunning Arts & Crafts features as well as many earlier points of interest, both inside and out. Sumptuous accommodation is offered in superbly equipped bedrooms in comfortable Cotswold style, with rich fabrics and soft furnishings. The day starts with a splendid breakfast cooked on a 1930s Aga and served on Wedgwood china in the medieval dining hall.

LAPSTONE

Westington Hill, Chipping Campden,
Gloucestershire GL55 6UR
Tel: 01386 841611 Fax: 01386 840455
e-mail: info@lapstone.net website: www.lapstone.net

For anyone looking for something to put the finishing touches to a home or garden, or to buy a unique present for a friend or relative, a visit to **Lapstone** will provide the perfect answer. Standing in the North Cotswolds on the B4081 between Chipping Campden and the A44, this outstanding establishment showcases the best in modern design along with traditional classics, and among the many eye-catching ranges on display are French furniture, Scandinavian tableware and linen, and Italian stoneware and fragrances. The owners source their stock from all over the UK and Europe, and many of the items for sale are exclusive to Lapstone. Typical of these are natural Italian room diffusers, Scottish chocolates, Belgian glassware, Irish go-karts and a wonderful model Land Rover for children.

Lapstone is also *the* place to visit for the very best in outdoor living, and prominent among the pieces on show are the cast aluminium metal furniture from Oxley – rust and rot proof and unaffected by wind, rain and sun. The site has plenty of free parking, and browsers can take a break in the café, where local seasonal produce features strongly on the menu. Lapstone is open 12noon to 5pm Monday, 9am to 5pm Tuesday to Saturday and 10am to 5pm Sunday. Closed Mondays between January and March.

THE CHURCHILL ARMS

Paxford, nr Chipping Campden, Gloucestershire GL55 6XH
Tel: 01386 594000
e-mail: info@thechurchillarms.co.
website: www.thechurchillarms.com

In a pretty village between Chipping Campden and Moreton-in-Marsh, **The Churchill Arms** has a reputation for fine food that few pubs in the county can match. The oldest part dates from the 17th century, and the timbered ceilings, the flagstoned or oak floors and the inglenook fireplaces assist in creating a wonderfully relaxed and inviting ambience. Leo Brooke-Little and his wife Sonya Kidney took over the pub in 1997, and Sonya's super cooking brings food-lovers from all over the country. She puts the finets fresh produce to excellent use in her dishes, and the day's menu, chalked up on a blackboard, makes mouthwatering reading. Nothing is over elaborate but everything is beautifully devised and faultlessly prepared. Typical dishes could include guinea fowl confit with a warm salad of chorizo, mushrooms and smoked bacon; cod fillet with a potato pancake, pine nut gremolata and a mustard sauce; and, to finish in style, a polenta and almond cake with morello cherries.

The Churchill is also a very pleasant place to stay, with four quiet, well-appointed en suite bedrooms, and fulfils an important role as a village local – there's always a great choice of beers, including real ales from local breweries.

banqueting halls. The 15th century Church of St James was built on a grand scale and contains several impressive monumental brasses, the most impressive being one of William Grevel measuring a mighty eight feet by four feet.

Dover's Hill, a natural amphitheatre above the town, is the scene of the **Cotswold Olimpicks,** founded in the 17th century by Captain Robert Dover, who lived at Stanway House. The Games followed the traditions of ancient Greece and added some more down-to-earth activities such as shin-kicking and bare-knuckle boxing. The lawlessness and hooliganism that accompanied the games led to their being closed down in 1852 but they were revived in a modern form in 1951 and are still a popular annual attraction on the Friday following the spring bank holiday. In 1990 a group of local people formed the Guild of Handicraft Trust and in 1998 it was offered the chance to take over Court Barn and to turn into a museum of local craftsmanship and design. The centre is due to open in the summer of 2007.

BROADWAY
10 miles NW of Stow on the A44

🌳 Broadway Tower   🌿 Snowshill Manor Garden

Just over the border into Worcestershire, where the Cotswolds join the Vale of Evesham, Broadway is one of the glories of the Cotswolds, a showpiece village with an abundance of scenic and historic attractions. The renowned Lygon Arms entertained both King Charles and Oliver Cromwell, and **Broadway Tower** at the top of Fish Hill affords spectacular views over the Severn Vale.

A couple of miles southwest of Broadway, **Snowshill Manor Garden**

(National Trust) is an Arts & Crafts garden designed to complement a handsome Cotswold manor house. Laid out by Charles Paget Wade as a series of outdoor 'rooms' with terraces and ponds, the garden is now run on organic principles.

HIDCOTE BARTRIM
3 miles NE of Chipping Campden off the B4632

🌿 Hidcote Manor Garden

Hidcote Manor Garden is one of the most famous in the country, a masterpiece created in the first years of the 20th century by the eminent horticulturist Major Lawrence Johnston. A series of small gardens, each with a different character and appeal, Hidcote is renowned for its rare shrubs and trees, herbaceous borders and unusual plant species from all parts of the globe. Visitors can refresh themselves in the tea bar or licensed restaurant.

UPPER AND LOWER SLAUGHTER
2 miles SW of Stow off the A429/B4068

The Slaughters (the name means nothing more sinister than 'muddy place') are archetypal Cotswold villages set a mile apart on the little River Eye. Both are much visited by tourists, much explored and much

Upper Slaughter

🎞 stories and anecdotes   🐦 famous people   🎨 art and craft   ✒ entertainment and sport   🥾 walks

The Slaughters

Distance: *5.5 miles (8.8 kilometres)*

Typical time: *180 mins*

Height gain: *65 metres*

Map: *Outdoor Leisure 45*

Walk: *www.walkingworld.com ID:1629*

Contributor: *Ron and Jenny Glynn*

ACCESS INFORMATION:

On the A429 between Moreton-in-Marsh and Cirencester.

ADDITIONAL INFORMATION:

Car park in Station Road. Charge is £3 for up to five hours. It is advisable to park here as the streets are narrow, often with double yellow lines.

DESCRIPTION:

Referred to as the Venice of the Cotswolds, Bourton-on-the-Water sits on the River Windrush, enhanced by its presence and character. Visitors to the village relax and take refreshment beside the waterside teashops, cafes and restaurants, and walk over the fine old stone footbridges that cross the river at various points. The village of Lower Slaughter is but a short distance, and although very small, presents a big impact to the visitor, its beautiful character and Cotswold stone construction, unforgettable.

Upper Slaughter is another wonderful setting, with a cluster of stone dwellings and a pretty church that is open to visitors; a photographer's paradise. The countryside is marvellous, natural and unspoilt; a pleasure to behold. The bustling centre of Bourton-on-the Water is approached on the return journey along a lengthy street with attractive residences on one side, and the River Windrush on the other. The little shops and stores are delightfully varied, selling quality goods to tourists all the year round, one of the many attractions that draw visitors to this quiet, restful setting.

FEATURES:

Hills or Fells, River, Pub, Toilets, Museum, Play Area, Church, Stately Home, Wildlife, Birds, Flowers, Great Views, Butterflies, Food Shop, Good for Kids, Tea Shop, Woodland

WALK DIRECTIONS:

1 | Leave car park from the main entrance and turn left onto Station Road. Walk past Moor Lane and a supermarket further on, then past The Cotswold School. Continue, to reach the main road.

2 | Go right up the road for a short distance. Cross road and turn left on signed path just before Coach & Horses PH. Follow path through wide open meadows to reach a gate.

3 | Continue on enclosed section to walk into Lower Slaughter.

4 | Turn left on Wardens Way beside running water. Turn right past St Mary's Church and follow dry stone wall to pass a Gloucestershire Way marker, then walk on along village street.

5 | Turn left on footpath from bend in road and enter two gates to walk beside fencing and trees. Take kissing gate and large metal gate to walk over meadow to another small gate in view. Maintain direction on well trodden path in meadowland, trees all around. The next gate leads into sheep pastures with a lake below and the Manor House to the side of it. Cross River Eye on narrow stone bridge and continue on tree lined path to reach road.

6|Turn left and follow road past Lords Of The Manor Hotel & Restaurant in Upper Slaughter. Walk on to pass village hall and small enclosed green, and notice church on right. Carry on to leave the village.

7|Take gate ahead on footpath that runs uphill beside allotments, then between open fields. Look back on fabulous views over glorious Cotswold countryside. Take gate on right and turn left.

8|Take the gate immediately on left and walk downhill beside dry stone wall and hedges.

9|Turn right on narrow road, hedge and treelined on an incline to reach another road.

10|Turn left towards Bourton-on-the-Water, views on either side far and distant.

11|Take right fork onto bridleway track, taking two metal gates, then along beside fields, and on to another gate to walk beneath archway of trees on enclosed section.

12|Turn right past stables and follow track past a very handsome and large mill called Little Aston. Continue on track uphill then turn left opposite entrance to Aston Farm.

13|Take footpath on left and walk uphill to follow it along between fields. Leave hedge to walk on over large field area. Cross track and climb stile following stone wall then fenceline on right. At end of field go on below a bank, the River Windrush running below. Climb stile out into clearing and maintain direction in uneven meadowland between thick tree growth. Reach a gate and stile at far corner and continue on narrow enclosed path to reach main road. Cross over and turn left on pavement.

14|Turn right over river bridge on Lansdowne Road and walk beside River Windrush. Pass Mousetrap Inn and attractive stone dwellings on the way to centre of Bourton-on-the-Water. St Lawrence Church stands on the left, plain and stark with a domed tower. The shops are all very individual and appealing, and the little riverside cafes are very popular with the many visitors.

15|Pass model railway exhibition and turn left by the Chestnut Gallery. Walk beside large hotel along a narrow alley alongside stone wall, turning left then right into car park of start of walk.

COTSWOLD BRIE CHEESE
BY SIMON WEAVER ORGANIC

Kirkham Farm, The Slaughters, Stow-on-the-Wold,
Gloucestershire GL54 2TS
Tel: 01451 870852 Fax: 01451 831753
e-mail: info@turnstonefarming.co.uk website: www.simonweaver.net

Milk has been produced at Kirkham Farm for generations, but Simon Weaver has recently put the place on the map with the outstanding cheese made here. The milk from the Friesian cows travels all of five metres from the milking shed to the creamery to be turned into the superb **Cotswold Brie Cheese**, which in its first year of production earned two Taste of the West Awards. Simon and his team are following up that success with a rich-tasting Blue Cotswold Brie and a Cotswold Herb Brie using a subtle mix of organically gown herbs. Customers can buy direct from the creamery or from many local shops.

photographed; they are also much as they have always been, since virtually no building work has been carried out since 1904. Francis Edward Witts, author of the *Diary of a Cotswold Parson*, was the rector here between 1808 and 1854.

At Lower Slaughter, the Old Mill, with its tall chimney and giant waterwheel, is a prominent feature by the river. This restored 19th century flour mill is open for visits and has a tearoom and organic ice cream parlour.

BOURTON-ON-THE-WATER
4 miles S of Stow on the A429

🏛 Miniature World   🏛 Model Village

🏛 Perfumery Factory   🐦 Birdland Park & Gardens

🐦 Cotswold Farm Park   🏛 Motoring Museum

Probably the most popular of all the

Cotswold villages. The willow-fringed River Windrush flows through the centre, crossed by several delightful low-arched pedestrian bridges, two of which date from the late 18th century. The golden stone cottages are pretty as a picture, and among the notable larger buildings are St Lawrence's Church, with its 14th century chancel and rare domed Georgian tower, and a manor house with a 16th century dovecote. In the High Street, **Miniature World - The Museum of Miniatures** is a unique exhibition of miniature scenes and models that took the country's leading master miniature makers three-and-a-half years to complete. It is accessible through another marvel of miniatures, the famous **Model Village,** complete with music in the church and the 'model of the model', and Bourton Model

🏛 historic building   🏛 museum   🏛 historic site   🝔 scenic attraction   🐦 flora and fauna

THE LIVING GREEN CENTRE & GARDENS

High Street, Bourton-on-the-Water, Gloucestershire
Tel: 01451 820942
e-mail: people@living-green.co.uk
website: www.living-green.co.uk

A few hours spent at the **Living Green Centre** and its gardens will provide a fascinating and educational insight into eco-friendly, environmentally aware living. Opened by owner Diana Ray late in 2005, Living Green's shop is filled with green gifts and essentials, sustainable lifestyle choices and planet-friendly ideas. Upwards of 1,000 products are on display. Find lovely gifts made in England and delicious very local preserves and soft drinks, interesting eco-gizmos like water-powered clocks and wind-up radios and stylish Fair Trade products. The show home on the premises really gets the conversations flowing - lots of tips for our 21st century living.

Relax in the organically run show garden, an oasis of serenity with glorious plantings, ponds and a host of ideas. Peat-free and organically grown plants on sale too. Bourton-on-the-Water is the most popular of all Cotswold villages, with stone cottages and grand buildings, museums and low-arched bridges across the River Windrush. The links with the past are many and varied, but the Living Green Centre provides an eye-opening glimpse into what the present can achieve and what the future holds.

Railway with over 40 British and Continental trains running on three main displays in OO, HO and N gauge. The **Cotswold Motoring Museum and Toy Collection**, in an 18th century water mill, has a fascinating collection of antique toys, a display of historic advertising signs and 30 or so (full-size!) cars and motorcycles. Bourton is also known for its **Cotswolds Perfumery Factory**, where a guided tour includes the Perfume Garden, the Perfume Laboratory, the Compounding Room mixing raw materials to make the concentrate

OXLEIGH COTTAGES

12 Moore Road, Bourton-on-the-Water, Gloucestershire GL54 2AZ
Tel: 07773 474108
e-mail: cdsmith.annexe@fsmail.net

In her attractive Cotswold stone house Barbara Smith has created two charming cottages each providing self-catering accommodation for up to six guests. Both cottages have well-appointed bedrooms, a comfortable living area, dining room, well equipped kitchens and hold a 4 star rating from VisitBritain. Outside is a private patio and a quiet lawned garden. Bourton-on-the-Water, sometimes described as the Venice of the Cotswolds, stands on the gentle shallow River Windrush. Bourton is midway between Oxford and Cheltenham. Walking, fishing and riding are just some of the many local attractions.

COTSWOLD FARM FAYRE & COFFEE SHOP

Denfurlong Farm, Chedworth, nr Cirencester, Gloucestershire GL54 4NQ
Tel: 01285 720265

March 2006 saw the opening of the **Cotswold Farm Fayre & Coffee Shop** just seconds off the A429 Fosseway, six miles north of Cirencester on the approach to Chedworth village. Rosanne Dickenson, the third generation of the Finch family who have lived and farmed in Chedworth since the 1920s, set up the enterprise with her sisters and father in a series of farm buildings that include the old milking parlour. Their aim was to provide the village with a much needed shop and to help support local farming communities.

They source everything they can from the Cotswolds – which helps the farmers and helps the environment by reducing transport levels. Andy and Russell run the on-site butchery, where the beef comes from the family farm at the other end of the village. The lamb is from a local farm, the pork comes from Moreton-in-Marsh, the poultry from Malmesbury. Customers can order their chickens boned and stuffed, and the sausages and burgers are naturally of the very best quality; the butchers offer barbecue deals with burgers, sausages and kebabs including vegetarian varieties.

Pamela runs the farm shop, which is stocked with a wide variety of top-quality produce. There are fresh and frozen fruit and vegetables, cows' and goats' cheese from the Cotswolds, ready-to-cook dishes, deli items such as rice and pasta salads and cured and dried hams, butter and oils, chutneys, honey and jams and apple juices. Bread is baked daily in their own ovens. Rosanne uses milk from their farm to make an amazing range of the most delicious ice creams which are sold in tubs – customers can order their own favourite flavours for parties.

The village store stocks a selection of household goods and everyday necessities. Cotswold Farm Fayre enjoys a rural setting with open fields and lovely views, and one of the waymarked farm walks goes to Stony Furlong railway cutting, a designated Site of Special Scientific Interest that's rich in wildlife. After a walk round the trail customers can relax with a cake or a snack in the Coffee Shop, which is managed by Mandy with help from Julie, Brenda, Kerry, Lynne, Helen, Amanda, Sophie and Hayley. Daily changing menus cater for all appetites, and among the dishes (all made on the premises) are steak & ale pie, smoked salmon & watercress frittata, roasts, mega pavlova and huge profiteroles with the delightful name of Camel's Knees. Cotswold Farm Fayre and the Coffee Shop are open daily.

and the Factory, where the processes comprise filtering, bottling, labelling, coding, cartooning and despatch.

A five-minute walk from the town centre brings visitors to **Birdland Park & Gardens** set in seven acres of woodland, water and gardens. The natural setting is home to more than 500 birds, including flamingos, pelicans, cranes, storks and waterfowl; there are over 50 aviaries of parrots, falcons, pheasants, hornbills, toucans, touracos and many others, and tropical, temperate and desert houses are home to the more delicate species. Open all year, Birdland has a café and facilities for children, including a play area, pets' corner and penguin feeding time.

Cotswold Farm Park is the home of rare breed conservation. Voted Farm Park of the Year 2003, it is both interactive and educational, providing the opportunity to see unusual species of farm animals. Rabbit handling and bottle feeding of lambs and calves makes it ideal for children.

NORTHLEACH
10 miles S of Stow on the A429

- 🏛 Church of St Peter & St Paul
- 🏛 Chedworth Roman Villa
- 🎖 Keith Harding's World of Mechanical Music

A traditional market town with some truly magnificent buildings. It was once a major wool-trading centre that rivalled Cirencester in importance and as a consequence possesses what now seems a disproportionately large church. The **Church of St Peter and St Paul**, known as the 'Cathedral of the Cotswolds', is a fine example of Cotswold Perpendicular, built in the 15th century with pinnacled buttresses, high windows and a massive square castellated tower. Treasures inside include an ornately carved font and some rare

monumental brasses of which rubbings can be made (permits obtainable from the Post Office).

The town's most popular attraction is **Keith Harding's World of Mechanical Music**, which occupies a handsome period house in the main street. Keith's love of mechanical music goes back some 40 years and he has accumulated the finest collection of automata, both antique and modern, to be found anywhere. It includes a tiny singing bird concealed in a snuff box to a mighty Welte Steinway reproducing piano of 1907. The instruments are introduced and played by the guides in the form of a live musical entertainment show and the tours include demonstrations of restored barrel organs, barrel pianos, musical boxes, polyphons, gramophones and antique clocks.

Close to the pretty village of **Chedworth**, a couple of miles west of Northleach, is what must be the region's oldest stately home, the National Trust's **Chedworth Roman Villa**, a large, well-preserved Romano-British villa discovered by chance in 1864 and subsequently excavated to reveal more than 30 rooms and buildings, including a bath house and hypocaust. Some wonderful mosaics are on display, one depicting the four seasons, another showing nymphs and satyrs. The villa lies in a beautiful wooded combe overlooking the valley of the Colne. A natural spring rises at the head of the combe – probably the main reason for choosing this site.

BIBURY
15 miles S of Stow on the B4425

- 🏛 Arlington Row
- 🎖 Arlington Mill

William Morris, founder of the Arts & Crafts Movement, described Bibury as "the most beautiful village in England" and, apart from the tourists, not a lot has changed since he made the claim. The Church of St Mary, with Saxon, Norman and medieval parts, is well worth a visit, but the most visited and most photographed buildings in Bibury are **Arlington Row**, a superb terrace of medieval stone cottages built as a wool store in the 14th century and converted three centuries later into weavers' cottages and workshops. Fabric produced here was supplied to nearby **Arlington Mill** for fulling, a process in which the material was cleaned in water and beaten with mechanically-operated hammers. Today the mill, which stands on

Bibury

BIBURY TROUT FARM

Bibury, Gloucestershire GL7 5NL
Tel: 01285 740215   Fax: 01285 740392
e-mail: biburytroutfarm@btconnect.com
website: www.biburytroutfarm.co.uk

Bibury Trout Farm occupies 18 acres alongside the River Coln in the middle of a village described by William Morris, founder of the Arts & Crafts Movement, as 'the most beautiful in England'. Primarily a working farm, it rears over 250,000 trout annually to restock fisheries across the country as well as up to six million eggs and a million fry. Visitors can learn all about rainbow and brown trout while wandering in the lovely surroundings, seeing the main processes including grading and feeding. The 'Catch Your own' fishing area allows visitors to do just that (open weekends March to October and local school holidays), and the farm shop sells delicious fresh and smoked trout and pâtés, as well as preserves, ciders, plants, cards, books and gifts.

The Terrace Café is a popular spot to pause for a drink and a snack, and the play area is guaranteed to keep the little ones busy and happy for hours. The Farm stands on the B4425 between Cirencester and Burford. Bibury is a place of many attractions, including Arlington Row and Mill and the Church of St Mary. Opening hours of Bibury Trout Farm are 9am to 6pm (Sunday 10am to 6pm) in summer and 10am to 4pm daily in winter.

🏠 historic building   🏛 museum   🏛 historic site   🍃 scenic attraction   🌱 flora and fauna

the site of a corn mill mentioned in the Domesday Book, is a museum with a collection of industrial artefacts, crafts and furniture, including pieces made in the William Morris workshops.

Cirencester

🏛 Corinium Museum   🏛 Church of St John Baptist

🎨 Brewery Arts House   🏊 Open Air Swimming Pool

The 'Capital of the Cotswolds', a lively market town with a long and fascinating history. As Corinium Dobonnorum it was the second largest Roman town in Britain (Londinium was the largest). Few signs remain of the Roman occupation, but the award-winning **Corinium Museum** features one of the

finest collections of antiquities from Roman Britain, and reconstructions of a Roman dining room and garden give a fascinating and instructive insight into life in Cirencester of almost 2,000 years ago.

The main legacy of the town's medieval wealth is the magnificent **Church of St John Baptist**, perhaps the grandest of all the Cotswold 'wool churches', its 120ft tower dominating the town. Its greatest treasure is the Anne Boleyn Cup, a silver and gilt cup made for Henry VIII's second wife in 1535, the year before she was executed for adultery. Her personal insignia - a rose tree and a falcon holding a sceptre - is on the lid of the cup, which was given to the church by Richard Master, physician to Queen Elizabeth I. The church has a unique three-storey porch which

---

OIL & VINEGAR

3 Market Place, Cirencester, Gloucestershire GL7 2PE
Tel: 01285 651751
e-mail: Cirencester@oilvinegar.co.uk
website: www.oilvinegar.co.uk

There can surely be no better place to get to know all about the best oils and vinegars than the shop that carries their name. **Oil & Vinegar** is a culinary gift shop with an exciting range of high-quality food and non-food products.

Pride of place naturally goes to the range of fantastic oils and vinegars, more than 30 of which can be tasted and bought on tap. They also sell bottled olive oils and vinegars and a wide and exciting range of culinary products sourced from small independent suppliers throughout the Mediterranean and from as far away as South Africa and Australia, including pasta, pesto, brilliant dips, marinades, mustards and antipasti.

The stock also includes non-food products such as hand-crafted ceramics from Portugal and Italy, olive spoons and picks, oil and vinegar bottles and bottle pourers, candles and speciality cook books. Oil & Vinegar really is a very special place, and the knowledgeable, helpful and friendly staff add to the delight of a visit.

📖 stories and anecdotes   🐦 famous people   🎨 art and craft   🎭 entertainment and sport   🚶 walks

MABYS CAFE AND FOOD SHOP

Unit 4, Bishop's Walk, Brewery Court, Cirencester,
Gloucestershire GL7 1JH
Tel: 01285 650165

Maby's began life as a catering company, set up by the Maby family over 20 years ago in Long Compton. A shop in Stow-on-the-Wold followed, and now the family firm is continuing to expand, having just opened a café and food shop in Cirencester.

'It's very much about local produce, on a very English theme,' explains director Tom Maby. 'We want to give people a relaxed place they can come for delicious food that's reasonably priced.'

Whether having 'boiled eggs and marmite soldiers' or the 'full maby' for breakfast, a 'deli-board' or the 'Maby's thyme burger' for lunch or simply popping in for a coffee and slice of the most amazing homemade cake, Maby's café is comfortable, relaxed and friendly with outstanding quality throughout.

Along side the café, the food shop is filled with fantastic chef-prepared food and inspiring meal ideas. With a superb choice of starters, mains, desserts, cheese, chocolates and more, the perfect meal couldn't be simpler. 'the idea is that people come in for a coffee and cake or to have lunch with friends and leave with a basket full of food to take-away' says Tom 'not only is everything natural, seasonal and delicious but all the cooking is done for you. It couldn't be easier'

JUST MAUDE

11 Dyer Street, Cirencester, Gloucestershire GL7 2PP
Tel: 01285 885456
e-mail: anne@justmaude.co.uk

'Chic and Unique' is vivacious owner Annie Lait's apt description of her shop **Just Maude**. Annie studied fashion and design at St Martin's College in London, and since February 2005 has run this stylish little womens' fashion shop in an atmospheric old stone building.

Her style and unerring taste are evident throughout the range of clothes on display, which are notable for their wonderful colours and fine fabrics and are complemented by an equally well-chosen selection of accessories, including shoes, hats, bags and jewellery.

Aiming mainly at the 20 to 50 age group, Annie seeks out one-off original designs sourced from near and far, and her experienced eye for beautiful clothes brings regular customers from as far afield as London. The clothes cover all occasions from smart stylish to evening and party wear; the stock includes some vintage clothes and many garments made by Annie herself.

LUCIA'S CAFÉ

36 Dyer Street, Cirencester,
Gloucestershire GL7 2PF
Tel: 01285 641570

Lucia's is a stylish and friendly café, with an outside area. The menu includes sandwiches, baguettes and paninis all freshly made to order. Lucia's other homemade specialities are cakes, hot daily roast as well other hot meals. With great coffees, and a choice of wines, beers and soft drinks, Lucia's also offers take-away as well as outside catering for buffets. Open from 8am Monday to Saturday the team at Lucia's look forward to serving customers old and new.

was used as the Town Hall until 1897.

Cirencester today has a thriving crafts scene, with workshops in the **Brewery Arts** House, a converted Victorian brewery. Sixteen resident craftworkers include a basket maker, jeweller, textile weaver, ceramicist and stained glass artist. A shop in the centre sells the best in British work, and there are galleries, a coffee house, arts and crafts classes and workshops.

Cirencester Open Air Swimming Pool, next to the park, was built in 1869 and is one of the oldest in the country. Both the main

CARRIAGES AT THREE LTD

3 The Wool Market, Cirencester, Gloucestershire GL7 2PR
Tel: 01285 651760
e-mail: sales@carriagesatthree.co.uk
website: www.carriagesatthree.co.uk

In a courtyard setting close to the town centre and market square, **Carriages at Three** specialises in womens' evening wear. One of the leading fashion retailers in the Cotswolds, the shop has two spectacular window displays that provide a beguiling sample of the vast choice within. More than 1,500 ball gowns, cocktail dresses, prom dresses, cruise wear, wedding wear and formal evening wear come in a stunning variety, from a simple classic black dress to a head turning one-off creation guaranteeing a grand and glamorous entrance.

Designers featured include Consortium, Bernshaw, Catwalk Collection, Amanda Wakeley, John Charles, Joseph Ribkoff and Attire. New owners Suzi Black and Ruth Small are already introducing ranges from new and up and coming labels such as Jaego, Tortoise and Avantgarde. Dresses come in a wide range of sizes, and the shop also offers a made-to-measure service for plus sizes and an in house bespoke alteration service.

A full range of accessories, from shoes, bags and shawls to costume jewellery, is available to complete the ensemble. The staff at this unique place are among the best in the business and a chat with the customer will enable them to make sound suggestions on what will be most suitable for each individual. Carriages at Three is a place for the special occasion, and one that fully deserves the boast that this is 'where the best evenings begin'.

🎞 stories and anecdotes   🐦 famous people   🎨 art and craft   🎭 entertainment and sport   🏃 walks

BREEZE CLOTHING

No 3 The Exchange, Brewery Court, Cirencester,
Gloucestershire GL7 1JZ
Tel: 01285 644942

In a convenient town centre site, with easy parking nearby, **Breeze Clothing** is a family-owned and run enterprise selling a wide range of informal and outdoor wear for men, women and children. Among the many leading brands in a constantly changing stock are Crew leisure clothing, Quba sailing wear, Musto leisure wear for women, Joules tops and skirts, and R M Williams shoes and boots. The owners have another Breeze Clothing outlet in Cirencester, in Regent Arcade.

ORIGINALS BY ALEXIA

The Stable Yard, 14 Black Jack Street, Cirencester,
Gloucestershire GL7 2AA
Tel: 01285 651717 e-mail: originalsbyalexia@hotmail.com
website: www.originalsbyalexia.co.uk

Always passionate about textiles and design, Alexia Durtnell began customising cardigans and making bags while at college in Cirencester, and in March 2006 she opened her own shop **Originals by Alexia**. Bags of all kinds – shopping, make-up, travel, beach with co-ordinating towels – come in a wonderful variety of contemporary styles and colours, all hand-crafted to unique one-off designs. Her creations are sold to customers all over the world, many of whom commission their own designs. Alexia also sells jewellery and other accessories that complement her range of bags. Her shop is located in an old stable yard off Black Jack Street.

pool and the paddling pool use water from a private well. Other sites of interest include St Thomas' Hospital – 15th century almshouses for destitute weavers – the Barracks of 1857, and a Yew Hedge which was planted in 1720. It now stands 40ft high and is reputed to be the loftiest in Europe. It can be found in Cirencester Park, a 3,000-acre expanse which was designed by the poet Alexander Pope.

Cirencester certainly lives up to its reputation as a market town with street markets on Monday and Friday; a craft market in the Corn Hall on Saturdays, and regular antiques markets on Fridays.

Around Cirencester

SHORNCOTE
3 miles S of Cirencester off the A419

🌿 Cotswold Water Park 🌿 Keynes Country Park

Two areas of flooded gravel workings form the **Cotswold Water Park** (see panel opposite), an increasingly important wetland area with a greater expanse of water than the Norfolk Broads. The area, which includes **Keynes Country Park**, is a centre for water sports, fishing, bird watching, walking and cycling.

🏛 historic building 🏛 museum 🏛 historic site 🌀 scenic attraction 🌿 flora and fauna

Cotswold Water Park

Keynes Country Park, Shorncote, Cirencester GL7 6DF
Tel: 01285 861459 Fax: 01285 860186
e-mail: info@waterpark.org website: www.waterpark.org

The Cotswold Water Park is Britain's largest water park, 50% larger than the Norfolk Broads consisting of 132 lakes covering 30 square miles set in outstanding countryside. There are two country parks open all year which are managed by The Cotswold Water Park Society, a not for profit environmental body with charitable status. The Society has for two years running been awarded the Civic Trusts Green Flag award for it's management of Keynes Country Park.

Keynes Park has a lot to offer the family including a children's beach which is the only inland site in Britain to have been awarded the European Blue Flag for it's high water quality. The park also has nature reserves, adventure playgrounds, boat and cycle hire, BBQ and picnic sites, angling, lakeside walks, a seasonal cafe and the Millennium visitor centre for which the Society was awarded the Queens award for sustainable development in 2000. Inside the centre you will find a gift shop, an exhibition of Jurassic fossils found within the Cotswold Water Park, a winter cafe and a hall which is hired out for corporate events and private parties. The Society also manages Neighbridge, which has a lakeside walk and adventure playground.

The Water Park is nationally recognised for its wildlife and nature reserves. Throughout the Water Park there are ten lakes and six meadows which are designated as SSSI's. There are also a network of footpaths, cycleways and bridleways. The Severn and Thames canal and a disused railway line also both run through the park. The park has water sports and activities for everyone from the novice to the expert. Water sports include sailing, windsurfing, kayaking, canoeing, waterskiing and jet skiing.

KEMBLE

4 miles SW of Cirencester on the A429

🏛 Bristol Aero Collection

Located close to the source of the River Thames, Kemble is best known for the **Bristol Aero Collection** at Kemble Airfield.

The Bristol Company's most prestigious aircraft was Concorde – at Kemble visitors can walk through the furnished passenger cabin and look down on the droop nose and the powerful Olympus engine. Other exhibits include Bristol helicopters, the only Britannia in working condition, Bloodhound guided

📕 stories and anecdotes   🐦 famous people   🎨 art and craft   🎭 entertainment and sport   🚶 walks

THE WILD DUCK INN

Drakes Island, Ewen, nr Cirencester,
Gloucestershire GL7 6BY
Tel: 01285 770310   Fax: 01285 770924
e-mail: wduckinn@aol.com
website: www.johansens.com/wildduck

The **Wild Duck** is a pretty-as-a-picture country inn, built of mellow Cotswold stone in the 15th century, at a time when many inns were being built up and down the land. It stands in the secluded village of Ewen, an easy drive from the M4 (J17) and very close to Cirencester. Ewen, signposted from the A429, is the first community of any size on the River Thames, which rises just two miles away at Coates. For many years Dino and Tina Mussell have run this outstanding inn, which is equally delightful inside and out. Behind the part-creeper-clad frontage the main bar is a cosy spot for relaxing with a drink, with portraits and trophies hanging on rich burgundy-coloured walls, lofty beams and large, inviting armchairs. The oak-panelled lounge is no less appealing, and the sheltered garden is a pleasant spot for sipping alfresco.

Five or six real ales, most of them from local breweries, are always on tap, and the inn has a top-class list of wines from around the world, with a large number available by the glass. Fine bar snacks are served at lunchtime, and the main printed menu, supplemented by daily specials, provides a wide choice of British and modern European dishes, with classics such as Caesar salad, seasonal game and fish delivered overnight from Brixham. This is a delightful place to tarry awhile, and for guests staying overnight or longer there are 12 individually decorated en-suite bedrooms, some on the ground floor and 11 with four-potser beds.

missiles, aero engines, a full scale Giotto satellite, scale models of various military aircraft – and a collection of Bristol buses.

FAIRFORD

9 miles E of Cirencester on the A417

🏠 Church of St Mary   🌿 Air Tattoo

A welcoming little town in the valley of the River Coln, with many fine buildings of the 17th and 18th centuries and an abundance of inns as evidence that this was an important stop on the London-Gloucester coaching run.

John and Edmund Tame, wealthy wool merchants, built the superb late-Perpendicular **Church of St Mary**, whose greatest glory is a set of 28 medieval stained glass windows depicting the Christian faith in picture-book style. John Tame's memorial stone, along with those of his wife and son, are set into the floor of the church.

In mid-July, nearby RAF Fairford hosts the annual **Royal International Air Tattoo,** the world's largest military air show which attracts thousands of visitors.

LECHLADE-ON-THAMES
12 miles E of Cirencester on the A417

Now part of the Cotswold Water Park, Lechlade is the highest navigable point on the Thames and head of the Thames towpath walk. In and around the town visitors can hire rowing boats, go sailing or wind-surfing, and enjoy lake and river fishing.

A statue of Old Father Thames, originally created for the Great Exhibition of 1851, overlooks St John's Lock, where barges loaded with building stone bound for Oxford and London have given way to pleasure craft. This bustling market town surrounded by green meadows boasts a fine 15th century church with a slender spire and a structure that has remained unaltered since the early 1500s. In its lovely churchyard, in 1815, the poet Shelley was inspired to write his *Stanzas in a Summer Evening Churchyard*. The verses are inscribed on a stone at the churchyard entrance.

Another interesting building is the Halfpenny Bridge, built in 1792, which crosses the Thames in the town centre and has a tollhouse at its eastern end.

INGLESHAM
1 mile S of Lechlade off the A361

🏛 Church of St John the Baptist

The splendidly unspoilt **Church of St John the Baptist** dates mainly from the 13th century, with some notable later additions. The chief features are important wall paintings, 15th century screens, 17th and 18th century pulpit and box pews and, perhaps its greatest treasure, a Saxon carving of the Virgin and Child blessed by the Hand of God. This is one of many churches in the care of the Churches Conservation Trust, formerly known as the Redundant Churches Fund. The trust was established to preserve churches which though no longer needed for regular worship are of historic or architectural importance.

LOCATOR MAP

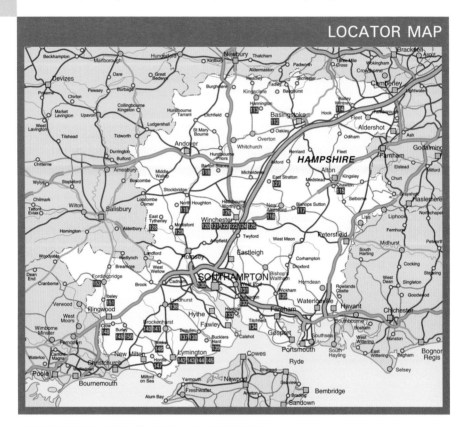

ADVERTISERS AND PLACES OF INTEREST

🏛 historic building 🏛 museum 🏚 historic site 🔱 scenic attraction 🌱 flora and fauna

5| Hampshire & The New Forest

You only have to travel a dozen or so miles from the M25 near Staines before you cross the county boundary into Hampshire. So it's not surprising that this corner of the county is quite heavily populated, dotted with prosperous, sprawling towns such as Farnborough, Farnham and Basingstoke. What *is* surprising is that once you turn off the busy main roads, you can find yourself driving along narrow country lanes with very little traffic.

This area forms part of the North Downs. Honouring the perverse tradition of English place-names, the Downs are actually uplands, softly rolling, wooded hills in whose folds lie scores of picturesque villages. As the crow flies, central London is little more than 30 miles away; for many of the north-eastern Hampshire villages, even today, the metropolis might just as well be 300 miles distant.

There are few grand houses in the area, although The Vyne near Basingstoke and the Duke of Wellington's home, Stratfield Saye House, are both very imposing. Two smaller dwellings, however, attract hundreds of thousands of visitors to this corner of the county: Jane Austen's House at Chawton, near Alton, and a few miles to the south in the village of Selborne, The Wakes, home of the celebrated naturalist, Gilbert White. Lovers of steam railways can combine a visit to these two houses with a ride on the Watercress Line which runs between Alton and Alresford.

The New Forest has been a Royal Forest for over 900 years. It acquired its name after William the Conqueror proclaimed it as his hunting ground and began a programme of planting thousands of trees. The area is famous for its wildlife, in particular the ponies, and is now a National Park, a status that will protect its 222 square miles from 'inappropriate development' in the future.

📖 stories and anecdotes   👤 famous people   🎨 art and craft   🎭 entertainment and sport   🚶 walks

Basingstoke

🏛 Basing House 🏛 The Vyne 🏛 Milestones
🏛 Willis Museum 🏛 Southview Cemetery
🏛 Chapel of the Holy Ghost 🏛 Viables Craft Centre

A vibrant, modern town whose name goes back to Saxon times when a farmer with a name something like Base, along with his extended family, or 'ing', established a 'stok', (stock or farmhouse) beside the River Lodden.

It comes as something of a surprise to discover that this busy, prosperous town with its soaring multi-storey buildings can boast no fewer than 25 parks and open spaces. A useful leaflet available from the Tourist Information Centre gives details of them all, ranging from the 16-hectare War Memorial Park, an 18th century park complete with bandstand, aviary and sports facilities, to **Southview Cemetery**, a site with a fascinating history. Some 800 years ago, during the reign of King John, England languished under an interdict pronounced by the Pope. Throughout the six years from 1208 to 1214, any baby christened, or dead person buried, lacked the official

blessing of Mother Church. At Basingstoke during those years, the deceased were interred in a graveyard known as the Liten and when the interdict was finally lifted, the ground was consecrated and a chapel built, the **Chapel of the Holy Ghost**. Today, it's a striking ruin surrounded by a well-managed site which provides a peaceful refuge from the bustling town.

As befits such a thriving place, Basingstoke offers visitors a wide choice of attractions: theatre, cinema, a vast Leisure Park and Festival Place, whose one million square feet of shopping and leisure contains some 165 shops, 26 bars, restaurants and cafés, and a 10-screen cinema.

The 'Old Town' area offers a lively cosmopolitan mix of bars, theme pubs and restaurants. Here, too, housed in the old Town Hall of 1832, is the excellent **Willis Museum**, which charts the town's history with lively displays featuring characters such as Fred, a Roman skeleton, and Pickaxe, a 19th century farm worker 'forced to scrape a living from the streets of Basingstoke as a scavenger'. The museum is named after George Willis, a local clockmaker and former mayor of Basingstoke who established the collection in 1931. Naturally, locally made grandfather clocks feature prominently in the displays.

A more recent attraction is **Milestones** (see

Chapel of the Holy Ghost, Basingstoke

panel opposite), a living history museum with reconstructed shops, factories, cobbled streets and staff in period costume. Highlights include the Tasker and Thorneycroft collections of agricultural and commercial vehicles and the fascinating AA collection. At the nearby **Viables Craft Centre**, visitors can watch craftspeople at work.

Just to the east of Basingstoke, **Basing House** was once one of the grandest residences in the realm. Built during the reign of Henry VIII, it rivalled even the king's extravagant mansions. Less than 100 years later, during the Civil War, Cromwell's troops besieged the house for an incredible three years, one of them reporting that the mansion was "as large as the Tower of London". When Basing House was finally captured the victorious New Army burnt it to the ground, but a magnificent 16th century barn survived, its timber roof a marvel of the carpenter's craft.

The Vyne (National Trust), four miles north of Basingstoke, has enjoyed a much happier history. Built in the early 1500s for Lord Sandys, Lord Chamberlain to Henry VIII, the house enjoys an idyllic setting with lawns sweeping down to a shimmering lake. A classical portico was added in 1654, the first of its kind in England. The Vyne's treasures include a fascinating Tudor chapel with Renaissance glass, a Palladian staircase, and a wealth of linenfold panelling and fine furniture.

Around Basingstoke

STEVENTON
6 miles SW of Basingstoke, off the B3400

At Steventon Rectory on December 16th 1775, Cassandra Austen presented her husband, George, with their seventh child, Jane. George was the rector of Steventon and Jane was to spend the first 25 years of her short life in the village. There is now very little evidence of her time here. The rectory was later demolished but there are memorials to the Austen family in the church where George Austen served for 44 years. It was at Steventon that Jane wrote *Pride and Prejudice*, *Sense and Sensibility* and *Northanger Abbey*. When the Revd George retired in 1800, the family moved to Bath. After her father's death, five

Milestones
Leisure Park, Churchill Way West, Basingstoke, Hampshire RG21 6YR
Tel: 01256 477766   Fax: 01256 477784
website: milestones-museum.com

Opened in November 2000, this is Hampshire's living history museum, where the county's heritage comes to life in cobbled streets with shops, factories, interactive areas, staff in period costume and superb exhibits relating to industrial and everyday life. Among the many highlights are the Tasker and Thorneycroft collections of agricultural and commercial vehicles, and the renowned AA collection. Disabled access and audio guides are available and there is a gift shop for souvenirs. A café serves teas, coffees and light snacks and there is a Victorian public house.

▥ stories and anecdotes   🐦 famous people   ✎ art and craft   ▨ entertainment and sport   𝑘 walks

years later, Jane and her mother took the house in Chawton that is now the Jane Austen Museum.

OVERTON

8 miles W of Basingstoke, on the B3400

🌿 Watership Down

A large village near the source of the River Test, Overton has a broad main street lined with handsome houses. During the stage coach era, it was an important staging post on the London to Winchester route and the annual sheep fair was one of the largest in the county selling at its peak up to 150,000 lambs and sheep. The fair flourished for centuries only coming to an end in the early 1930s.

To the north of the village, set high on a ridge, is **Watership Down,** immortalised in

Richard Adams' book of the same name. It is now a nature reserve. The down lies on the long distance footpath, the Wayfarer's Walk, which runs from Inkpen Beacon (just over the border in Berkshire) to Emsworth on the Hampshire coast.

KINGSCLERE

8 miles NW of Basingstoke, on the A339

Collectors of curiosities might like to make a short excursion to the little town of Kingsclere where the weather-vane on top of the parish church has baffled many visitors. With its six outstretched legs and squat body, the figure on the vane has been compared to a skate-boarding terrapin. Local historians, however, assert that it actually represents a bed bug and was placed here by the command

COVER UP DESIGNS LTD

The Barn, Hannington Farm, Hannington,
Nr Kingsclere, Hampshire RG26 5TZ
Tel: 01635 297981 Fax: 01635 298363
e-mail: info@coverupdesigns.co.uk
website: www.coverupdesigns.co.uk

Spacious premises in the centre of Hannington are home to **Cover Up Designs**, which offers a full range of interior design services. Started in Kingsclere in 1979, the company specialises in soft furnishings and provides a complete design and making-up service, from selecting and supplying the fabrics to professional upholstery and curtain-making. Cover Up also offers a unique range of fabric-covered and upholstered furniture, including bedside tables, dining tables, dressing tables, stools, padded mirrors, ottomans, wall units, screens, headboards and TV and computer cabinets. With its own workshop on site, each job can be undertaken to each customer's individual requirements.

Soft furnishings comprise cushions and bolsters, eiderdowns, bedspreads and valances. The premises include a light and airy design studio containing samples from more than 200 suppliers and over 1,000 of the latest books. Customers can therefore source fabrics, wallpaper, trimmings and all other aspects of interior design, all under one roof, with expert help on hand if required.

🏠 historic building   🏛 museum   🏛 historic site   🌄 scenic attraction   🌿 flora and fauna

of King John. The king had been hunting in the area when a thick fog descended and he was forced to spend the night at the Crown Hotel in Kingsclere. Apparently, he slept badly, his slumber continually disturbed by the attentions of a bed bug. The next morning, he ordered that the townspeople should forever be reminded of his restless night in Kingsclere by erecting this curious memorial to his tormentor.

SILCHESTER
7 miles N of Basingstoke, off the A340

Calleva Atrebatum   Church of St Mary

Excavation of the town which the Romans called **Calleva Atrebatum** took place at the turn of the 19th/20th centuries and revealed some remarkable treasures, most of which are now on display at Reading Museum. The dig also revealed the most complete plan of any Roman town in the country but, rather oddly, the site was 're-buried' and now only the 1.5 mile city wall is visible – the best-preserved

Roman town wall in Britain. Also impressive is the recently restored 1st century amphitheatre which lay just beyond the town walls.

Tucked in next to part of the Roman wall is the pretty **Church of St Mary** which dates from the 1100s. It boasts a superb 16th century screen with a frieze of angels and some unusual bench-ends from 1909 executed in Art Nouveau style.

PAMBER HEATH
7 miles N of Basingstoke, on minor road off the A340

Priory Church

There are three 'Pambers' set in the countryside along the A340. At Pamber End stand the picturesque ruins of a once-magnificent 12th/13th century **Priory Church**, idyllically sited in sylvan surroundings. Set apart from the village, they invite repose and meditation. Pamber Green, as you might expect, is a leafy enclave; but for anyone in search of a good country pub, the Pamber to make for is Pamber Heath. Lots of pubs have a few pots scattered around, but the collection at The Pelican in Pamber Heath is something else. There are hundreds of them hanging from the ceiling beams, in every imaginable shape and colour, some pewter and some ceramic.

Calleva Atrebatum, Silchester

stories and anecdotes   famous people   art and craft   entertainment and sport   walks

HARTLEY WINTNEY
9 miles NE of Basingstoke, on the A30

 West Green House    Old Church

Riding through Hartley Wintney in 1821, William Cobbett, the author of *Rural Rides* and a conservationist long before anyone had thought of such a creature, was delighted to see young oaks being planted on the large village green. They were the gift of Hartley Wintney's lady of the manor, Lady Mildmay, and were originally intended to provide timber for shipbuilding. Fortunately, by the time they matured they were no longer needed for that purpose and today the Mildmay Oaks provide the village centre with a uniquely sylvan setting of majestic oak trees.

Anyone with an interest in horticulture should also visit the magnificent gardens of **West Green House,** about a mile to the west of Hartley Wintney. Owned by the National Trust, this pretty early-18th century house is surrounded by lovely gardens planted with a dazzling variety of trees, shrubs and plants. One of its interesting features is a stone column surmounted by an elaborate finial which was erected in 1976. It bears a Latin inscription which declares that a large sum of money was needed to put the column in place, money "which would otherwise have fallen, sooner or later, into the hands of the Inland Revenue".

While you are in Hartley Wintney a visit to the **Old Church**, south of the village, is well worth while. Parts of the building date back to medieval times, but the fascination of old St

Mary's lies in the fact that, after being completely renovated in 1834, it has remained almost totally unaltered ever since. High-sided box pews line the main aisle, there are elegant galleries for choir and congregation spanning the nave and both transepts, and colourful funeral hatchments add to St Mary's time-warp atmosphere.

EVERSLEY
10 miles NE of Basingstoke, on the A327

🏛 Stratfield Saye House

🎋 Wellington Country Park

Charles Kingsley, author of such immensely popular Victorian novels as *The Water Babies* and *Westward Ho!*, was Rector of the village for 33 years from 1842 until his death in 1875 and is buried in the churchyard here. The gates of the village school, erected in 1951 for the Festival of Britain, include a figure of a boy chimney-sweep, the main character of *The Water Babies*. Kingsley was an attractive character with a burning passion for social justice, but modern readers don't seem to share the Victorian enthusiasm for his works. It's a sad fate for a prolific man of letters, although perhaps not quite so dispiriting as that met by one of Kingsley's predecessors as preacher at Eversley. He was hanged as a highwayman.

About four miles west of Eversley, **Stratfield Saye House** was just one of many rewards a grateful nation showered on the Duke of Wellington after his decisive defeat of Napoleon at Waterloo. The Duke himself doesn't seem to have been reciprocally grateful: only lack of funds frustrated his plans to demolish the gracious 17th century house and replace it with an even more impressive mansion which he intended to call Waterloo Palace. Quite modest in scale, Stratfield Saye fascinates visitors with its

collection of the Duke's own furniture and personal items such as his spectacles, handkerchiefs and carpet slippers. More questionable are the priceless books in the library, many of them looted from Napoleon's own bibliotheque. A good number of the fine Spanish and Portuguese paintings on display share an equally dubious provenance, 'relieved' during the Duke's campaign in those countries as 'spoils of war'. That was accepted military practice at the time and, these quibbles apart, Stratfield Saye House is certainly one of the county's leading attractions.

Within the estate is the **Wellington Country Park** where there are numerous attractions, including walks and nature trails, a children's animal farm, an adventure playground and a miniature railway.

ODIHAM
7 miles E of Basingstoke, on the A327

🏛 Castle

Odiham Castle must have a very good claim to being one of the least picturesque ruins in the country. It looks like something rescued from a giant dentist's tray, with gaping window holes and jagged, crumbling towers. Back in 1215, though, Odiham Castle was a state-of-the-art royal residence. Great pomp and circumstance attended King John's stay at the castle, then just seven years old, the night before he set off to an important meeting. The following day, in a meadow beside the River Thames called Runnymede, John reluctantly subscribed his name to a bill of rights. That document, known as Magna Carta, proved to be the embryo of democracy in western Europe.

Odiham itself is one of the most attractive villages in the county, with a handsome High

Odiham Castle

Street and a 15th century church, the largest in Hampshire, in which collectors of curiosities will be pleased to find a rather rare item, a hudd. A portable wooden frame covered with cloth, the hudd provided Odiham's rector with graveside shelter when he was conducting burials in inclement weather. In a corner of the graveyard stands the Pest House, built around 1625 as an isolation ward for patients with infectious diseases. From 1780 until 1950, it served as an almshouse and is now open to visitors on most weekends.

ALDERSHOT

14 miles E of Basingstoke on the A331

🏛 Military Museum 🏛 Heroes Shrine

🏛 Army Medical Centre Museum

🏛 Parachute Regiment Museum

🏛 Army Physical Training Museum

Back in 1854, Aldershot was a village of some 800 inhabitants. Then the Army decided to build a major camp here and the population has grown steadily ever since to its present tally of around 60,000. The story of how

Aldershot became the home of the British Army is vividly recounted at the **Aldershot Military Museum**, which stands in the middle of the camp and is a must for anyone with an interest in military history. Housed in the last two surviving Victorian barrack blocks, its tiny appearance from the outside belies the wealth of fascinating displays contained inside. For example, there's a detailed cutaway model of a cavalry barracks showing how the soldiers' rooms were placed above the stables, an economic form of central heating described as "warm, but aromatic".

It was the army at Aldershot who became the first military aviators in Britain, using Farnborough Common for flying and building their aircraft sheds where the Royal Aircraft Establishment stands today. **The Parachute Regiment and Airborne Forces Museum**, (which will move to Duxford in Cambridgeshire at some stage), has many interesting exhibits illustrating the part these pioneers played during the early days of the 20th century and during two World Wars. There are two further military museums to be found here: the **Army Medical Services Museum,** telling the story of medical services from 1660 to the present day, and the **Army Physical Training Corps Museum** where the Corps history is recounted with the help of numerous exhibits, pictorial records – and some Victorian gymnastic equipment.

🏛 historic building 🏛 museum 🏛 historic site 🏛 scenic attraction 🏛 flora and fauna

In the town's Manor Park, the **Heroes Shrine** commemorates the dead of World War I, while a nearby walled and sunken garden, shaded by deodar trees, honours the fallen of World War II. Another celebrated military figure, the Duke of Wellington, is represented by an imposing bronze statue crowning Round Hill, just outside the town. The statue originally stood atop the Triumphal Arch at Hyde Park Corner in London but was moved to Aldershot in 1885.

FARNBOROUGH
14 miles E of Basingstoke on the A331

 Air Sciences Trust Museum

🏛 St Michael's Abbey

The town is best known for the Farnborough Air Show which is held every other year. The town's unique aviation heritage is explored at the **Farnborough Air Sciences Trust Museum** which holds an extensive collection of exhibits, records and artefacts.

Less well-known is **St Michael's Abbey,** now a Benedictine foundation but with a curious history. After the fall of Napoleon III, his wife the Empress Eugenie came to live at a large house called Farnborough Hill where she was later joined by her husband and her son, the Prince Imperial. Napoleon died at Chislehurst after an operation to remove bladder stones; her son was killed in the Zulu War. The heartbroken Empress commissioned the building of an ornate mausoleum for their tombs and a monastery in

the flamboyant French style. The first monks arrived in 1895 from Solesmes Abbey, France, and they still continue their regime of liturgy, study and manual work. The abbey is open to the public and has a small farm and apiary that supplies not only the monks but also the abbey shop. Guided tours are available on Saturday and Bank Holiday afternoons.

Alton

🏛 St Lawrence's Church   🏛 Curtis Museum

🖼 Grave of Fanny Adams   🎨 Allen Gallery

Surrounded by hop fields and some of Hampshire's loveliest countryside, Alton is an appealing market town with a history stretching back far beyond Roman times. (The name actually means "Old Town.") Its market, held every Tuesday, has a history of more than 1,000 years and was the most valuable market recorded in the *Domesday Book*.

Alton boasts a large number of old coaching inns, and the impressive, partly-Norman **St. Lawrence's Church** which was the setting for a dramatic episode during the Civil War. A large force of Roundheads drove

Farnborough Air Sciences Trust Museum

some 80 Royalists into the church where 60 of them were killed. The Royalist commander, Colonel Boles, made a last stand from the splendid Jacobean pulpit, firing repeatedly at his attackers before succumbing to their bullets. The church door and several of the Norman pillars are still pock-marked with bullet holes inflicted during this close-combat conflict. More cheerful are the comical carvings on these pillars of animals and birds, amongst them a wolf gnawing a bone and two donkeys kicking their heels in the air.

Allen Gallery, Alton

Nearby is the old cemetery and the well-tended **Grave of Fanny Adams.** The expression "Sweet Fanny Adams" arose from the revolting murder in 1867 of an eight-year-old girl in the town who was hacked into pieces by her assassin. With macabre humour, sailors used the phrase "Sweet Fanny Adams" to describe the recently-introduced tinned mutton for which they had a certain mistrust. Over the years, the saying became accepted as a contemptuous description for anything considered valueless: a poor way to remember an innocent girl.

There's a different sort of monument in Amery Street, a narrow lane leading off the market place. On a small brick house is a plaque commemorating the Elizabethan poet Edmund Spenser who came to Alton around 1590 to enjoy its "sweet delicate air".

Well worth a visit while you are in Alton is the **Allen Gallery** in Church Street, home to an outstanding collection of English, Continental and Far Eastern pottery, porcelain

and tiles. Housed in a group of attractive 16th and 18th century buildings the gallery's other attractions include the unique Elizabethan Tichborne Spoons, delightful watercolours and oil paintings by local artist William Herbert Allen, and a comfortable coffee lounge. Across the road, the **Curtis Museum** concentrates on exploring 100 million years of local history with displays devoted to the "shocking tale of Sweet Fanny Adams", other local celebrities such as Jane Austen, Lord Baden Powell, Montgomery of Alamein; and a colourful Gallery of Childhood with exhibits thoughtfully displayed in miniature cases at a suitable height for children.

On the western edge of the town lies The Butts, a pleasant open area of grassland that was once used for archery practice. Today it is the setting for events such as the annual Victorian Cricket Match.

A good time to visit the town is mid-July

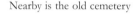
🏛 historic building   🖼 museum   🏚 historic site   🗺 scenic attraction   🌱 flora and fauna

when the Alton Show takes place. Established in 1840, this is one of southern England's most important agricultural gatherings with a wide range of events featuring such attractions as heavy horses, llamas, beagles, gun dogs and birds of prey.

Around Alton

SELBORNE
4 miles SE of Alton on the B3006

🐦 The Wakes and Oates Museum

🏛 Church of St Mary 🏺 Selborne Pottery

Like the neighbouring village of Chawton, Selborne also produced a great literary figure. **The Wakes** was the home of Gilbert White, a humble curate of the parish from 1784 until his death in 1793. He spent his spare hours meticulously recording observations on the weather, wildlife and geology of the area. Astonishingly, a percipient publisher to whom Gilbert submitted his notes recognised the appeal of his humdrum, day-to-day accounts of life in what was then a remote corner of England. *The Natural History and Antiquities of Selborne* was first published in 1788, has never been out of print, and still provides what is perhaps the most entertaining and direct access to late-18th century life, seen through the eyes of an intelligent, sceptical mind.

Visitors to The Wakes can see the original manuscript of his book along with other personal belongings, and the peaceful garden with its unusual old plant varieties.

The house also contains the **Oates Museum** which celebrates Francis Oates, the Victorian explorer, and his nephew

Capt. Lawrence 'Titus' Oates who was with Capt. Scott on his doomed expedition to the South Pole. Titus' last words – "I am just going outside. I may be some time" – are known around the world, as is Scott's diary entry describing Oates' selfless deed as "the act of a very gallant gentleman". The Wakes and the Oates Museum are open daily, and there's an excellent book and gift shop, and a tea room specialising in 18th century fare.

Gilbert White is buried in the graveyard of the pretty **Church of St Mary**, his final resting place marked by a stone bearing the austere inscription *GW 26th June 1793*. A fine stained glass window depicts St Francis preaching to the birds described in Gilbert's book. Outside in the churchyard, is the stump

Yew Tree Stump, Church of St Mary, Selborne

📖 stories and anecdotes 🐦 famous people 🎨 art and craft 🎡 entertainment and sport 🥾 walks

JANE AUSTEN'S HOUSE

Chawton, nr Alton, Hampshire GU34 1SD
Tel: 01420 83262
e-mail: enquiries@jahmusm.org.uk   website: www.jane-austens-house-museum.org.uk

Jane Austen's House at Chawton is where the writer spent the last eight years of her life, from 1809 to 1817. Now a museum, it contains a fascinating collection of items and memorabilia linked with Jane and her family. Her brother Edward had inherited the estate from the Knight family and was able to offer his mother and two sisters the use of the house for the rest of their lives. Settled in comfort, Jane was able to revise her earlier manuscripts of *Sense and Sensibility* and *Pride and Prejudice*, which were published in 1811 and 1813. In this extraordinarily productive phase of her life she wrote *Mansfield Park* (published 1814) and *Emma* (1816). She completed *Persuasion* and was working on *Sanditon* when she was overtaken by illness. In May 1817 Jane and her sister Cassandra left for Winchester to be near her doctor. She died in July 1817 and was buried in Winchester Cathedral.

The house is filled with treasures, which a recent Museum Enhancement Plan has reorganised to provide easier viewing for visitors. In the Drawing Room, with an elegant window overlooking the garden, is a Clementi square piano of 1810, similar to the one on which Jane practised every day. In the Vestibule are a bookcase housing a reference collection of books about Jane and her works; photocopies of some of her letters; and topaz crosses given to the sisters by their brother Charles bought with prize money awarded for the capture of a French vessel during the Napoleonic Wars. Here, too, is a portrait of Jane's brother Edward as a teenager. Highlights in the bedroom used by Jane and Cassandra include a copy of Cassandra's portrait of Jane, a landscape also by Cassandra and a copy of Jane's poem *Venta* written three days before she died.

Mrs Austen's bedroom contains showcases of books and family silver, while in the tiny Residences Room are drawings, paintings and photographs of places lived in or visited by Jane, and a showcase of textiles including some of Jane's needlework. Hugh Thompson's drawings for the 1894 edition of *Pride and Prejudice* are along the Corridor, where a lace collar sewn by Jane, a letter written by Cassandra on Jane's death and a copy of Jane's will may also be seen. One room is dedicated to Jane's brothers Francis and Charles, who both had distinguished

careers in the Royal Navy. Francis became Admiral of the Fleet and was knighted by King William IV, while Charles became a Rear Admiral. More mementoes are to be found in the kitchen, the bakehouse and the granary, and many of the plants in the garden are old varieties which might have been grown and tended by the Austens. The house is open daily from March to the end of November; Saturday and Sunday in winter.

🏛 historic building   🏛 museum   🏛 historic site   ❧ scenic attraction   ❧ flora and fauna

of a yew tree which was some 1,400 years old when it succumbed to the great storm of January 1990.

From the village centre there are several walks, one which leads to the 'Zig-Zag' path constructed by Gilbert and his brother in 1753. It winds its way up to the 'Hanger' (a wood on a steep hillside) that overlooks the village. The land at the summit is part of an area of meadow, woodland and common which is owned by the National Trust – the spot provides panoramic views across the South Downs.

Back in the village, the **Selborne Pottery** was established by Robert Goldsmith in 1985. Each piece of pottery made here is hand-thrown and turned, and the distinctive pots are not only functional but also decorative.

CHAWTON
2 miles SW of Alton, off the A31

🐦 Jane Austen's House

From the outside, the home (see panel opposite) in which Jane Austen spent the last eight years of her life and where she wrote three of her most popular novels *(Mansfield Park, Emma* and *Persuasion)*, is a rather disappointingly dull, blank-faced building. Chawton village itself is a delightful spot with old cottages and houses leading up to the village green outside Jane's house.

HINTON AMPNER
9 miles SW of Alton on the A272

🌾 Hinton Ampner Gardens

🎿 Itchen Way

The River Itchen, renowned for its trout and watercress beds, rises to the west of the village to begin its 25-mile journey to the sea at Southampton; the **Itchen Way** footpath follows the river throughout its course. Also to the west of the village are **Hinton Ampner Gardens** (National Trust), created by Ralph Dutton who inherited the house in 1936 and created a superb garden that combines formal and informal planting. The design produces some delightful walks with some unexpected vistas.

ALRESFORD
10 miles SW of Alton, off the A31

🏠 Manor House 🚂 Watercress Line

Pronounced *Allsford*, Alresford was created around 1200 by a Bishop of Winchester, Geoffrey de Lucy, as part of his grand plan to build a waterway from Winchester to Southampton. Where the river Arle flows into the Itchen, he constructed a huge reservoir covering 200 acres, its waters controlled to keep the Itchen navigable at all seasons. The Bishop's reservoir is now reduced to some 60 acres but it's still home to countless wildfowl

Alresford

and many otters. Known today as Old Alresford Pond, it's one of the most charming features of this dignified Georgian town. Alresford can also boast one of the county's most beautiful streets, historic Broad Street, lined with elegant, colour-washed Georgian houses interspersed with specialist shops and inviting hostelries.

Alresford's most famous son was Admiral Lord Rodney, a contemporary of Lord Nelson, who built the grand **Manor House** near the parish church, but the town can also boast two famous daughters. One was Mary Sumner, wife of the Rector of Alresford, who founded the Mother's Union here in 1876. The other was Mary Russell Mitford, author of the fascinating collection of sketches of 18th century life, *Our Village*, published in five

volumes between 1824-1832. Mary's prolific literary output was partly spurred on by the need to repay the debts of her spendthrift father. Dr Mitford managed to dissipate his own inherited fortune of many thousands of pounds. His wife's lavish dowry, which almost doubled that income, disappeared equally quickly, and when Mary at the age of 10 won the huge sum of £20,000 in a lottery, the good doctor squandered that as well. Mary's classic book tells the story.

One of Alresford's attractions that should not be missed is the **Watercress Line**, Hampshire's only preserved steam railway, so named because it was once used to transport watercress from the beds around Alresford to London and beyond. The line runs through 10 miles of beautiful countryside to Alton where

HÊTRE

39 West Street, Alresford, Hampshire SO24 9AB
Tel: 01962 733312

Listed in *Vogue* magazine's "100 Best Shoe Shops", **Hêtre** was opened in 1998 by Carol Walton who is a self-confessed "enthusiastic, obsessive shoe-aholic!" – so too are her staff. Over the years, Carol's collection has evolved to reflect current trends and what's new in fashion. It is always offering new labels and the shop stocks an enormous range of collections. Carol's selection of shoes includes designer names as well as quirky one-off pieces and is complemented by a fantastic selection of handbags and other accessories.

Hetre's dedicated staff will try and match outfits with shoes – and even telephone you with 'must-have' buys. The designer labels on offer include Paul Smith, Emma Hope, Anya Hindmarch, Lulu Guinness, Baccarolle by Jane Brown, Joseph Azagury and Boccaccini.

Hetre occupies a beautifully renovated Georgian house near the centre of this attractive town, noted for its many Georgian houses. The shop is known for its incredible eye-catching window displays and the interior is equally striking with its contemporary décor of wood, etched glass and Andrew Martin furniture.

KATE FORMAN FABRICS

Sutton Manor Farm, Bishops Sutton, Alresford, nr Hampshire SO24 0AA
Tel: 01962 732244 Fax: 01962 736644
e-mail: kate@kateforman.co.uk website: www.kateforman.co.uk

Kate Forman studied at the London School of Fashion and started her own interior design and antiques business in London in 1994. She moved to Bishops Sutton in 2003 and started **Kate Forman Fabrics**. In her showroom, in a beautifully converted courtyard building, Kate has assembled an array of lovely things for the home including French printed linen, cottons and accessories, lampshades, cushions, handbags, oil cloths, basket covers, lavender-filled linen hearts, teddy bears and many other delights. Kate offers her expertise to assist clients in their choice and also does a lot of business by mail order.

it links up with main line services to London. Vintage steam locomotives make the 35-minute journey up to eight times a day, and there are regular dining trains as well as frequent special events throughout the year. More details on 01962 733810.

TICHBORNE
12 miles SW of Alton off the A31

🎦 The Titchborne Dole and Titchborne Claimant

Two intriguing stories are associated with this lovely village of thatched and half-timbered cottages. The legend of the **Tichborne Dole** dates from the reign of Henry I. At that time the owner of Tichborne Park was the dastardly Sir Roger Tichborne. As his crippled wife, Mabella, lay dying, her last wish was to provide food for the poor. Sir Roger agreed – but only from an area she could crawl around. The brave woman managed to encircle an area of more than 20 acres of arable land, carrying a flaming torch as she did so. Ever since then the Park's owners have provided bags of flour every year to the villages of Tichborne and Cheriton. The field is still known as 'The Crawls'.

Equally notorious is the episode of the **Tichborne Claimant**. In 1871 a certain Arthur Orton, son of a Wapping butcher,

returned from Wagga Wagga, Australia, claiming to be the heir to the estate. Although he bore no resemblance to the rightful heir who had disappeared while sailing round the world, Arthur was 'recognised' by the widow as her son and supported in his claim. She, apparently, detested her late husband's family. Arthur's claim was rejected in a trial that lasted 100 days and he was put on trial for perjury. After a further 188 days he was found guilty and sentenced to 14 days in prison.

CHERITON
13 miles SW of Alton on the B3046

The pretty village of Cheriton has a church which is believed to stand over a prehistoric burial ground. In 1644, the Battle of Cheriton, fought near Cheriton Wood, resulted in the deaths of 2,000 men as the Roundheads defeated the Royalists.

Petersfield

🏛 Church of St Peter   🌿 Physic Garden

⛰ Butser Hill   🎨 Flora Twirt Gallery

🚶 Petersfield Heath

An appealing market town, Petersfield is dominated by the bulk of **Butser Hill**, 900

🎦 stories and anecdotes   🐦 famous people   🎨 art and craft   🎣 entertainment and sport   🚶 walks feet high and the highest point of the South Downs. It provides grand panoramic views over the town and even, on a clear day, to the spire of Salisbury Cathedral, some 40 miles distant. In the 1660s, Samuel Pepys noted his stay in Petersfield, at a hotel in which Charles II had slept before him. Another king is commemorated in The Square where William III sits on horseback, incongruously dressed in Roman costume. Unusually, the statue is made of lead.

Most of the elegant buildings around The Square are Georgian, but the **Church of St Peter** is much older, dating back to Norman times and with a fine north aisle to prove it. Just off the Square, the **Flora Twort Gallery** was once the home and studio of the accomplished artist of that name who moved to Petersfield at the end of World War I. Her delightful paintings and drawings capture life in the town over some 40 years – "reminders of some of the things we have lost" as she put it shortly before her death at the age of 91 in 1985.

From the gallery, a short walk along Sheep Street, (which has some striking timber-framed 16th century houses and Georgian cottages), brings you to The Spain, a pleasant green surrounded by some of the town's oldest houses. It apparently acquired its rather unusual name because dealers in Spanish wool used to hold markets there.

Visitors with an interest in gardening will want to visit the **Physic Garden** in the centre of the town. Set in an ancient walled plot, the garden has been planted in a style and with plants that would have been familiar to the distinguished 17th century botanist, John Goodyer, who lived in Petersfield.

Other attractions include the Dragon Gallery, providing a showcase for contemporary artists; the Petersfield Museum,

housed in the old Courthouse; and the Teddy Bear Museum, the first in the country to be dedicated to these cuddly comforters.

Just a short walk from the town centre is **Petersfield Heath,** an extensive recreational area with a cricket ground and a pond for boating and fishing. The town's annual Taro Fair is held here in October and the heath is also notable as the site of one of the most important groups of Bronze Age barrows, or burial mounds, in the country.

Around Petersfield

STEEP
1 mile N of Petersfield, off the A3

Appropriately, the village is reached by way of a steep hill. The village is famous as the home of the writer and nature poet Edward Thomas who moved here with his family in 1907. It was while living at 2 Yew Tree Cottages that he wrote most of his poems. In 1909 he and his wife Helen moved to the Red House (private) where his daughter Myfanwy was born in 1913. Many years later, in 1985, she unveiled a plaque on the house. Her former home featured in two of her father's poems, *The New House* and *Wind and Mist*. Thomas was killed in action in World War I. His death is commemorated by two engraved lancet windows installed in 1978 in All Saints Church, and by a memorial stone on Shoulder of Mutton Hill above the village.

It was at Steep in 1898 that the educational pioneer John Badley established Bedales, the first boarding school for both sexes in the country. His "preposterous experiment" proved highly successful. Members of staff and pupils at Bedales call each other by their first names and there is no formal school uniform. There is an absence of petty rules and, says the school brochure, "because the pupils are listened to, they learn to listen to each other".

Buriton

BURITON

2 miles S of Petersfield, on minor road off the A3

🏠 Uppark

An old church surrounded by trees and overlooking a tree-lined duck pond is flanked by an appealing early-18th century Manor House (private) built by the father of Edward Gibbon, the celebrated historian. The younger Gibbon wrote much of his magnum opus *Decline and Fall of the Roman Empire* in his study here. He was critical of the house's position, "at the end of the village and the bottom of the hill", but was highly appreciative of the view over the Downs: "the long hanging woods in sight of the house could not perhaps have been improved by art or expense".

About five miles south-east of Buriton, **Uppark** (National Trust), is a handsome Wren-style mansion built around 1690 and most notable for its interior. Uppark was completely redecorated and refurnished in the 1750s by the Fetherstonhaugh family and that work has remained almost entirely unchanged – not only the furniture but even some of the fabrics and wallpapers remain in excellent condition. The servants' rooms are as they were in 1874 when the mother of HG Wells was housekeeper here – the boy's recollections of life at Uppark with his mother are fondly recorded in his autobiography.

CHALTON

5 miles S of Petersfield off the A3

🏠 Butser Ancient Farm

Situated on a slope of chalk down, Chalton is home to **Butser Ancient Farm,** a reconstruction of an Iron Age farm that has received worldwide acclaim for its research methodology and results. There's a magnificent great roundhouse, prehistoric and Roman crops are grown, ancient breeds of cattle roam the hillside, and metal is worked according to ancient techniques. The latest project here is the construction of a replica Roman villa, complete with hypocaust, using the same methods as the Romans did. A wonderful living laboratory, the farm is open one weekend each month when there are themed events.

HAMBLEDON

8 miles SW of Petersfield, off the B2150

A village of red brick Georgian houses and well-known for its vineyard, Hambledon is

Hambledon

Distance: *6.8 miles (11.0 kilometres)*

Typical time: *150 mins*

Height gain: *189 metres*

Map: *Explorer 119*

Walk: *www.walkingworld.com ID:2139*

Contributor: *Sylvia Saunders*

ACCESS INFORMATION:

Hambledon is to be found nine miles south west of Petersfield and 10 miles north of Portsmouth. From the Petersfield to Portsmouth A3(T) / A3M take the turn off signposted to Clanfield, Chalton and Hambledon. Hambledon is well signposted from here but be careful not to miss the turn off to the right when leaving Clanfield. Park in the main road near to The Vine.

There is a No. 45 bus service from Portsmouth city centre to Hambledon run by First. Check out their website www.firstgroup.com for more information.

DESCRIPTION:

This circular walk is a must for those who are interested in cricket, lovers of good food and beer in idyllic country pubs, or those who just like a cracking good walk in the beautiful, gentle Hampshire countryside. The walk starts from The Vine in Hambledon. The route takes you along Windmill Down with far reaching views over Hampshire countryside and then past the current cricket ground at Ridge-Meadow. Then walking through a mixture of woodland and fields you arrive at The Bat and Ball Inn which is known as the first headquarters of English cricket. The original Hambledon cricket ground is on Broadhalfpenny Down and opposite the pub.

The return route takes you along well defined tracks and through farmland with some super views as far as the Isle of Wight on a clear day. There is a steep descent down a quiet lane back to Hambledon's West Street and The Vine. Dog owners may find it useful to know that my dog, a slim, fit Labrador who cannot jump, managed to get through all the stiles and fences.

FEATURES:

Hills or Fells, Pub, Wildlife, Birds, Flowers, Great Views, Butterflies, Public Transport, Restaurant, Tea Shop, Woodland

WALK DIRECTIONS:

1 | With The Vine on your left hand side walk along West Street until you reach a lane on the left marked "Unsuitable for HGVs". Turn left and walk up this lane. When the lane turns into a driveway, walk straight on and go over the stile into the field.

2 | Walk straight ahead with the flint wall on your right hand side. At the end of the wall you will find a metal kissing gate. Pass through this gate and again walk with the wall on your right with a field fence on your left. This path brings you out at the churchyard. Walk straight ahead through the churchyard and you will shortly emerge out onto a lane. Turn left on this lane for a few metres and you will see the school entrance on your right hand side.

3 | Turn right here and walk through the school entrance. When you reach the end of the buildings you are met with a choice of two footpaths. Turn left here and walk uphill past the back of the school building where you will see the entrance to a field on your right. Fork right across the field along the footpath. At the field corner walk straight across into the next field and continue uphill with the hedge

on your right hand side. Enjoy the panoramic view as you descend until you reach a lane.

4 | Turn right onto the lane. Ignore the left hand turn to Chidden, shortly after which you will pass Ridge - Meadow, the current home of Hambledon cricket club where they have played since 1782. Carry on along the road until you reach the crossroads.

5 | Turn left here. After you have passed the big house on this corner (Park House) you will see a track marked with a fingerpost. Turn left onto this track. After a short distance you will see a metal gate ahead. Pass through the gap on the right hand side of this gate and walk along the track on the right hand side of the field. Follow the track as it leaves the field and enters woodland. You will arrive at a sign which says "Wildlife Conservation Area, do not enter". Turn left here along the footpath and follow it into the field. Here you will see two footpaths, both crossing the field.

6 | Take the right hand path and walk diagonally across the field to the hedge and footpath post. If the path is unclear then head for the gap in the trees and as you get nearer to it you will spot a yellow marker.

7 | Turn right here and walk along the field edge with the hedge on your left hand side. Follow this route until you see a wooden post directing the footpath into

woodland. This post is about halfway between the previous post and the field corner. Turn left here into the woodland. Walk the narrow, winding path. There are a few animal routes going off it which may confuse you. If in doubt, take a route to the left rather than to the right. The woodland doesn't last for long - you soon emerge into a field. Turn right here walking along the field edge with the hedge / trees on your right hand side. Follow the footpath out to the road.

8 | Cross straight over to the metal gate opposite. There isn't a stile but you can open the gate by way of a chain on the right hand side. Follow the field edge on the left hand side to the stile ahead.

9 | Cross over the stile and turn right, walking with the fence on your right hand side. Continue in the same direction crossing several stiles until you reach the road.

Continued overleaf

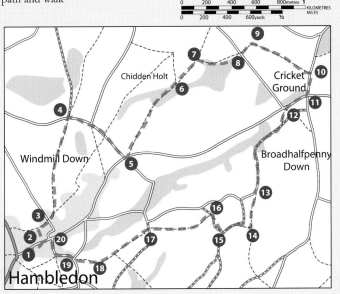

10 | Cross the stile and turn right along the road. You will soon arrive at The Bat and Ball Inn with the original Broadhalfpenny cricket ground opposite. Here you will see the monument marking the birthplace of cricket. Pass the pub and arrive at the crossroads.

11 | Turn right here along the road signposted to Hambledon, Fareham. Walk along the road until you see a road turning off to the right. Opposite this you will see a footpath and stile off to your left.

12 | Climb this stile and you will be met with a choice of two routes, neither of which is defined. Head for the stile which you can see up the hill and slightly to the right - at the end of the hedge line. Go over the stile and turn right along the track, but before you set off, pause to drink in the view. Continue along the track until you reach Scotland Cottage. Just past the cottage you will see a footpath off to the left. (The fingerpost here seems to get broken down quite frequently, so don't necessarily expect to see it. The footpath is between the large stone and the wooden pole. Don't be confused by the green arrow on the pole – this marks the metalled track which you are about to leave.)

13 | Turn left along this footpath and walk until you emerge out onto a track.

14 | Turn right along this track. In a short distance you will see a large tree ahead and a huge pile of manure! This manure heap has been here for years and I have every faith that it will have been renewed. Turn left here and you will soon arrive at a junction of tracks.

15 | Turn right here and continue walking until you reach a rather smelly pond and some farm buildings.

16 | Turn left here along the track just past the pond but before the buildings. When you reach the metal gate cross over the stile next to it. Follow the track up to another metal gate and stile, passing a barn on your left hand side. Go over this stile and continue walking straight ahead with the trees on your right hand side and you will arrive at another stile. Cross over and then follow the line of the telegraph poles until you reach another stile. Cross over this stile. This field was full of towering sweetcorn when I was last here and may well look entirely different now. Just follow the line of telegraph poles and you cannot go wrong. You will arrive at a stile. Go over this stile and cross straight over the track into the field.

17 | Again, follow the line of the telegraph poles across this field and you will arrive at a stile. Cross over this stile into the narrow field still following the telegraph poles. Ignore the footpath off to the left as the field narrows further. Continue along in the same direction, finally losing the telegraph poles and you will arrive at a stile next to a metal gate.

18 | Cross this stile and walk straight ahead between the horseboxes. In a few metres you will arrive at a driveway. Turn left along this driveway and you will soon arrive at several metal gates. Turn right along the footpath between the two metal gates on your right. This will bring you out upon a private driveway next to a house. Walk down the driveway and you will see two roads off to your right.

19 | Take the second right turn along the road walking down Speltham Hill until you arrive at the junction with West and East Street.

20 | Turn left here and walk back to The Vine.

most famous for its cricketing connections. It was at the Hambledon Cricket Club that the rules of the game were first formulated in 1774. The club's finest hour came in 1777 when the team, led by the landlord of the Bat and Ball Inn, beat an All England team by an innings and 168 runs! A granite monument stands on Broadhalfpenny Down where the early games were played.

Courthouse, East Meon

The village itself featured in the *Domesday Book* and, in the 13th century, was granted a licence to hold a market. About this time, the church was extensively rebuilt around the original Saxon church. Many of the village houses have their 16th century origins concealed by the striking Georgian facades.

EAST MEON

5 miles W of Petersfield, on minor road off the A3 or A272

🏠 Tournai Font

Tucked away in the lovely valley of the River Meon and surrounded by high downs, East Meon has been described as "the most unspoilt of Hampshire villages and the nicest". As if that weren't enough, the village also boasts one of the finest and most venerable churches in the county. The central tower, with walls four feet thick, dates back to the 12th century and is a stunning example of Norman architecture at its best. Inside, the church's greatest treasure is its remarkable 12th century **Tournai Font** of black marble, exquisitely carved with scenes depicting the

Creation and the fall of Adam and Eve. Only seven of these wonderful fonts are known to exist in England (four of them in Hampshire) and East Meon's is generally regarded as the most magnificent of them.

In the churchyard are buried Thomas Lord, founder of the cricket ground in London, and the mother of the spy Guy Burgess. Her son's ashes were sprinkled on her grave in a suitably clandestine night-time ceremony.

Just across the road is the 15th century Courthouse which also has walls four feet thick. It's a lovely medieval manor house where for generations the Bishops of Winchester, as Lords of the Manor, held their courts. It would have been a familiar sight to the "compleat angler" Izaac Walton who spent many happy hours fishing in the River Meon nearby.

Northwest Hampshire

Some of Hampshire's grandest scenery lies in this part of the county as the North Downs roll westwards towards Salisbury Plain. There's just one sizeable town, Andover, and

🎞 stories and anecdotes   🐦 famous people   🎨 art and craft   🎭 entertainment and sport   🚶 walks

one major city, Winchester: the rest of the region is quite sparsely populated (for southern England) with scattered villages bearing evocative names such as Hurstbourne Tarrant and Nether Wallop. Winchester is of course in a class of its own with its dazzling Cathedral, but there are many other attractions in this area, ranging in time from the Iron Age Danebury Hill Fort, through the Victorian extravaganza of Highclere Castle, to Stanley Spencer's extraordinary murals in the Sandham Memorial Chapel at Burghclere.

Andover

Andover

🏛 St Mary's Church　🏛 Museum

🏛 Heritage Trail　🏛 Museum of the Iron Age

🏛 Finkley Down Farm Park

Andover has expanded greatly since the 1960s when it was selected as a "spillover" town to relieve the pressure on London's crowded population. But the core of this ancient town, which was already important in Saxon times, retains much of interest. One outstanding landmark is **St Mary's Church**, completely rebuilt in the 1840s at the expense of a former headmaster of Winchester College. The interior is said to have been modelled on Salisbury Cathedral and if it doesn't quite match up to that sublime building, St Mary's is still well worth a visit.

Equally striking is the Guildhall of 1825, built in classical style, which stands alone in the Market Place where markets are still held every Tuesday and Saturday. Andover has also managed to retain half a dozen of the 16

coaching inns that serviced 18th century travellers at a time when the fastest stage coaches took a mere nine hours to travel here from London. As many as 50 coaches a day stopped at these inns to change horses and allow the passengers to take refreshments.

For a fascinating insight into the town's long history, do pay a visit to the **Andover Museum** in Church Close. There are actually two museums here, both of them housed in buildings which began life as an elegant Georgian town house in 1750 and were later extended to serve as Andover's Grammar School from the 1840s to 1925. The Andover Museum traces the story of the town from Saxon times to the present day with a range of colourful exhibits which include a 19th century Period Room. There's also a fascinating display evoking Victorian Andover and a workhouse scandal of the time. The museum hosts an exciting programme of temporary exhibitions with subjects including art, craft, photography, history and much more. Former classrooms of the grammar school now house the **Museum of the Iron Age**, which tells the story of Danebury, an Iron Age hillfort that lies six miles southwest of Andover.

A good way of getting to know the town is to join one of the guided tours along the **Andover Heritage Trail**. Scheduled tours, lasting about 90 minutes, take place on Tuesday and Saturday afternoons but can also be arranged for groups at other times.

Two miles east of Andover, **Finkley Down Farm Park** provides a satisfying day out for families with young children. Youngsters can feed and handle the animals, groom a pony, ride on a mini-tractor, and expend any excess energy in the well-equipped playground. Romany caravans and farming bygones are on display and other attractions include a tea room, gift shop and picnic area with a sandpit.

PENTON MEWSEY

2 miles NW of Andover, on minor road off the A342 or A343

For those who enjoy deciphering the cryptic place-names of English villages, Penton Mewsey offers a satisfying challenge. The answer goes like this: Penton was a 'tun' (enclosure or farm) paying a 'pen' (penny) as annual rent. That's the Saxon part. Later, in the early 1200s, Penton was owned by Robert de Meisy so his surname provided the second part of the village's name.

The town of Andover has now expanded to Penton Mewsey's parish boundaries but the village itself remains more rural than urban, with a field at its centre.

APPLESHAW

4 miles NW of Andover, off the A342

The houses in the village of Appleshaw sit comfortably along both sides of its broad,

single street. Many of them are thatched and a useful, century-old clock in the middle of the street, placed here to celebrate Queen Victoria's Jubilee, adds to the time-defying atmosphere. The former Vicarage, built in Georgian times, is as gracious as you would expect of that era, and the neo-Gothic architecture of the parish church, rebuilt in 1830, is in entire harmony with its earlier neighbours.

TANGLEY

5 miles NW of Andover, on minor road off the A342 or A343

For the best views, approach Tangley from the east, along the country lane from Hurstbourne Tarrant. Its mostly Victorian church is notable for its rare font, one of only 38 in the whole country made of lead and the only one in Hampshire. Dating back to the early 1600s, it is decorated with Tudor roses, crowned thistles, and fleur-de-lys.

The old Roman road from Winchester to Cirencester, the Icknield Way, runs through the parish of Tangley. Most of this part of the county is designated an Area of Outstanding Natural Beauty and the scenery is enchanting.

FACCOMBE

12 miles N of Andover, on minor road off the A343

🏰 Highclere Castle

This appealing little village, which is owned by the Faccombe Estate, is tucked away in the Hampshire countryside close to the Berkshire border, set on chalk Downs some 750 feet above sea level, with the highest points of the North Downs, Pilot Hill and Inkpen Beacon, both nearby. An extra attraction for walkers is the Test Way, a long-distance footpath which runs from Inkpen Beacon to the south coast following the track of the disused 'Sprat & Winkle' railway.

About five miles west of Faccombe, **Highclere Castle** is a wondrous example of Victorian neo-Gothic architecture at its most exuberant. If the central tower reminds you of another well-known building, that may be because the castle was designed by Sir Charles Barry, architect of the Houses of Parliament. It stands on the site of a former palace of the Bishops of Winchester, overlooking an incomparably lovely park, one of Capability Brown's greatest creations. Highclere is the family home of the 8th Earl and Countess of Carnavon. It was the 5th Earl who was with Howard Carter in 1922 at the opening of Tutankhamun's tomb. A small museum in the basement of the castle recalls that breathtaking moment. Another display reflects the family's love and success in the racing and breeding of horses. In addition to the superb parkland, there's also a walled garden planted entirely with white blooms, a gift shop, restaurant and tea rooms.

View Towards Watership Down from Highclere

BURGHCLERE
11 miles NE of Andover, off the A34

🎨 Sandham Memorial Chapel

A couple of miles northeast of Highclere Castle, at Burghclere, the **Sandham Memorial Chapel** (National Trust) is, from the outside, a rather unappealing construction, erected in 1926 by Mr and Mrs JL Behrend in memory of a relation, Lieutenant Sandham, who died in World War I. Their building may

be uninspired but the Behrends can't be faulted on their choice of artist to cover the walls with a series of 19 murals. Stanley Spencer had served during the war as a hospital orderly and 18 of his murals represent the day-to-day life of a British Tommy in wartime. The 19th, covering the east wall of the Chapel, depicts the Day of Resurrection with the fallen men and their horses rising up. The foreground is dominated by a pile of white wooden crosses the soldiers have cast aside. The whole series is enormously moving, undoubtedly one of the masterpieces of 20th century British art.

WHITCHURCH
6 miles E of Andover on the B3400

🏛 Silk Mill

This small market town was once an important coach stop on the London to Exeter route. The coaching inns have gone but the town still boasts a unique attraction – the **Whitchurch Silk Mill**, the last such working mill in the south of England. Located on Frog Island in the River Test, the mill's waterwheel has been fully restored although today's power is provided by electricity. The

---

🏛 historic building 🏛 museum 🏛 historic site 🌊 scenic attraction 🌿 flora and fauna

mill now functions as a museum making silks for interiors and costume dramas such as the BBC's acclaimed production of *Pride and Prejudice*. Visitors can see the working waterwheel, watch the late-19th century looms weave the silk, view the costume exhibition and enjoy the riverside garden. There's also a tea room and gift shop.

To the east of Whitchurch is Bere Mill, a weather-boarded construction where a French man, Henri Portal, set up a paper-making business in the early 18th century. By 1742 Portal's mill had won the contract to supply bank note paper to the Bank of England and he moved his operation upstream to Laverstoke. Now in Overton, the business continues to make paper for bank notes and supplies it to more than 100 countries.

LONGPARISH
6 miles E of Andover, on the B3048

Living up to its name, Longparish village straggles alongside the River Test for more than two miles. This stretch of the river is famously full of trout but no one has yet beaten the record catch of Col. Peter Hawker who lived at Longparish House in the early 1800s. According to his diary for 1818, in that year this dedicated angler relieved the river of no less than one ton's weight of the succulent fish. A previous owner of the colonel's house had actually captured double that haul in one year, but the bounder had cheated by dragging the river.

Longparish Upper Mill, in a lovely location on the river, is a large flour mill with a

CHURCH FARM

Barton Stacey, Winchester,
Hampshire SO21 3RR
Tel/Fax: 01962 760268

Set in beautiful countryside within easy reach of both Winchester and Salisbury, Oxford and Stonehenge, **Church Farm** was originally a 15th century tithe barn. It was extended in Georgian times but the Tudor Hall still has its original flagstone floor. James and Jean Talbot have lived in this lovely old property since 1934, its attractively furnished rooms full of much loved furniture, huge sofas and even a baby grand piano. Arriving guests are welcomed with tea and biscuits, cakes or a drink before being shown to one of the three immaculate rooms, each of which enjoys enchanting views. Guests have the use of a spacious sitting room with large latticed windows overlooking the beautifully maintained gardens where daffodils bloom in profusion in early spring.

Within the grounds there's also an unheated swimming pool, a croquet lawn, tennis court – and a secret tree house "for children and squirrels"! Evening meals are available on request and the price includes pre-dinner drinks and wine. In addition to the three rooms in the main house, accommodation is also available in the adjacent recently converted coach house which is particularly suitable for families. Smoking restrictions apply in both properties; Mastercard and Visa are accepted.

DAIRY BARN FARM SHOP

North Houghton, nr Stockbridge,
Hampshire SO20 6LF
Tel: 01264 811405
e-mail: shop@dairybarn.co.uk
website: www.dairybarn.co.uk
Opening times: Mon-Fri 9.30am-6pm,
Sat 9.30am-5pm, Closed Sun.

Sue Gotting and her family had farmed here for many years when they opened the **Dairy Barn Farm Shop** in 1999. This was largely in response to requests from friends and relatives who had enjoyed the unique flavour of rare and minority breed meat from the farm. Their aim at Dairy Barn is to sell environmentally aware products with taste, freshness and quality guaranteed.

The conservation-grade animals are husbanded to the highest welfare standards and the kitchen staff produce the finest in Hampshire cuisine. Only the very finest meat comes from the farm's Dexter and Galloway beef, lamb from Manx Loghtan, Hampshire and Ryeland breeds and pork from Gloucester Old Spot, Tamworth and Saddleback pigs. Water buffalo meat, known for its low cholesterol content, is a tasty alternative for those keeping an eye out for low-cholesterol food.

The poultry sold at the farm is equally outstanding, free-range and raised without hormones or additives. As well as the meat, cut into joints and steaks as required, the farm sells superb gluten-free gourmet sausages, pasties and pies (the pork & apple pie is sensational), cakes and ready meals, all made on the premises from home-raised meat and locally sourced organic fruit and vegetables. Cooked hams, salamis, olives and pesto complement a range of British cheeses; organic vegetables and free-range eggs are sold in the vegetable shed, along with ice creams and sorbets from the freezer cabinet, while outside, fresh-cut flowers and potted plants are available.

The shop also sells an extensive range of groceries and dry goods, from organic milk and bread to butter, yoghurts, fruit juices, honey and jams, flour, cakes and puddings, biscuits and luxury chocolates. The shop is open every day except Sunday, and the produce of the farm can also be bought at the Winchester and Andover farmers' markets. To promote awareness of their aims and methods, Dairy Barn offers one-day rare breed livestock courses to provide a memorable day out while learning more about the animals and how they are raised. They also offer basic butchery courses.

🏚 historic building   🏛 museum   🏛 historic site   ⌘ scenic attraction   🌱 flora and fauna

working waterwheel. Visitors can see the restoration work in progress.

STOCKBRIDGE
7 miles S of Andover on the A3057/A30

🌱 Houghton Lodge Gardens

The trout-rich River Test flows through, under and alongside Stockbridge's broad main street which reflects the street's earlier role as part of a drover's road. The town attracts many visitors for its famous antique shops, art galleries and charming tea rooms. Two exclusive clubs strictly control fishing on the River Test at this point but visitors may be lucky enough to catch glimpses of the fish from the bridge on the High Street.

Just to the south of Stockbridge are **Houghton Lodge Gardens**, the spacious gardens of an 18th century 'cottage orné' which have the tranquil beauty of the River Test as their border. Chalk cob walls shelter a kitchen garden with ancient espaliered fruit trees, glasshouses and herb garden, whilst in the hydroponicum greenhouse plants are grown "without soil, toil or chemical pesticides".

NETHER WALLOP
8 miles SW of Andover, on minor road off the A343

🏛 St Andrew's Church

The names of the three Wallops, (Over, Middle and Nether), have provided a good deal of amusement to visitors over the centuries, so it's slightly disappointing to discover that Wallop is just a corruption of the Old English word *waell-hop*, meaning a valley with a stream. At Nether Wallop the stream is picturesquely lined with willow trees, while the village itself is equally attractive with many thatched or timbered houses. The most

notable building in Nether Wallop is **St Andrew's Church,** partly because of its Norman features and handsome West Tower of 1704, but also because of its striking medieval wall paintings which provide an interesting contrast with Stanley Spencer's at Burghclere. Some 500 years old, these lay hidden for generations under layers of plaster and were only rediscovered in the 1950s. The most impressive of them shows St George slaying the dragon. Outside St Andrew's stands an item of great interest for collectors of churchyard oddities. It's a dark grey stone pyramid, 15ft high, with red stone flames rising from its tip. This daunting monument was erected at his own expense and in memory of himself by Francis Douce, 'Doctor of Physick', who died in 1760. Dr Douce also left an endowment to build a village school on condition that the parishioners would properly maintain the pyramid.

MIDDLE WALLOP
7 miles SW of Andover on the A343

🏛 Museum of Army Flying 🏛 Danebury Ring

The village of Middle Wallop became famous during the Battle of Britain when the nearby airfield was the base for squadrons of Spitfires and Hurricanes. Many of the old buildings have been incorporated into the **Museum of Army Flying** which traces the development of Army Flying from the balloons and kites of pre-World War I years, through various imaginative dioramas, to a helicopter flight simulator in which visitors can test their own skills of 'hand and eye' co-ordination. The Museum has over 35 fixed-wing and rotary aircraft on display, and other attractions include a museum shop, licensed café & restaurant, and a grassed picnic area.

In the 1990s, Middle Wallop, with its picturesque timber-framed thatched buildings became familiar to television viewers when it provided the main location for the *Miss Marple* mysteries.

Situated about a mile to the east of the village, Danebury Vineyards welcomes groups of visitors by arrangement for a guided tour of the six acres of vines and winery. Tastings and dinners can also be arranged. The vineyard was planted in 1988 on south facing slopes of free draining chalk, an excellent siting for the varieties of grape grown here. The British climate generally results in a late-ripening crop producing grapes which are most suitable for the white wines with which Danebury Vineyards has made its name.

About three miles east of Middle Wallop, **Danebury Ring** is Hampshire's largest Iron Age hill fort. Intensively occupied from about 550 BC until the arrival of the Romans, the site has been meticulously excavated over the last 30 years and the finds are now displayed at the Museum of the Iron Age in Andover. Visitors can wander the 13-acre site and with the help of explanatory boards reconstruct the once-bustling community with its clearly defined roads, shops, houses and what were probably temples.

WEYHILL
3 miles W of Andover on the A342

🌱 Hawk Conservancy

In its day the October Weyhill Fair was an event of some importance. In Thomas Hardy's *Mayor of Casterbridge* it appears as the Weydon Priors Market where the future mayor sells his wife and child.

A good family day out can be enjoyed at **The Hawk Conservancy** where there are more than 200 birds of prey to see in 22 acres

of grounds. The Hawk Conservancy is one of the largest collections of raptors in the world. Flying demonstrations take place three times daily and include species such as owls, eagles, vultures and condors, falcons, kites, hawks and secretary birds. The grounds here are also home to Shire horses, Sika deer, Hampshire Down sheep and red squirrels that have been given their own aerial runway.

THRUXTON
4 miles W of Andover off the A303

🌿 Motor Racing Circuit

This large village with many thatched cottages is well known for its **Motor Racing Circuit** which is built on a World War II airfield. Its annual calendar of events takes in many aspects of sport including Formula Three, Touring Cars, British Super Bikes, Trucks and Karts.

Winchester

🏛 Cathedral   🏛 College   🏛 The Great Hall

🏛 Wolvesey Castle   🪶 Jane Austen's House

🖼 The Brooks Experience   🏛 Hospital of St Cross

🌱 Marwell Zoological Park   🪶 Keats' Walk

One of the country's most historic cities, Winchester was adopted by King Alfred as the capital of his kingdom of Wessex, a realm which then included most of southern England. There had been a settlement here since the Iron Age and in Roman times, as Venta Belgarum, it became an important military base. **The Brooks Experience**, located within the modern Brooks Shopping Centre, has displays based on excavated Roman remains with its star exhibit a reconstructed room from an early-4th century town-house.

When the Imperial Legions returned to

Rome, the town declined until it was refounded by Alfred in the late 800s. His street plan still provides the basic outline of the city centre. A Saxon cathedral had been built in the 7th century but the present magnificent **Cathedral** (see panel below), easily the most imposing and interesting building in Hampshire, dates back to 1079. It's impossible in a few words to do justice to this glorious building and its countless treasures such as the famous Winchester Bible, a 12th century illuminated manuscript that took more than 15 years to complete using pure gold and lapis lazuli from Afghanistan. Winchester Cathedral boasts the longest nave in Europe, a dazzling 14th century masterpiece in the Perpendicular style, a wealth of fine wooden carvings, and gems within a gem such as the richly decorated Bishop Waynflete's Chantry of 1486. Sumptuous medieval monuments, like the

effigy of William of Wykeham, founder of Winchester College, provide a striking contrast to the simple black stone floorslabs which separately mark the graves of Izaak Walton and Jane Austen. One of the memorials is to William Walker, a diver who spent seven years, from 1906, laboriously removing the logs that had supported the cathedral for 800 years and replacing those rotting foundations with cement.

Just south of the cathedral, on College Street, are two other buildings of outstanding interest. 8 College Street, a rather austere Georgian house with a first-floor bay window, is **Jane Austen's House** in which she spent the last six weeks of her life in 1817. The house is private but a slate plaque above the front door records her residence here. Right next door stands **Winchester College,** the oldest school in England, founded in 1382 by Bishop William of Wykeham to provide

Winchester Cathedral

1, The Close, Winchester, Hampshire, SO23 9LS
Tel: 01962 857200
e-mail: cathedral.office@winchester-cathedral.org.uk
website: www.winchetser-cathedral.org.uk

The Cathedral is now over 900 years old, a priceless jewel in a scarcely less precious setting. See the tombs of Jane Austen and Izaak Walton, the Chantry Chapels and hear how the diver saved the Cathedral in 1906.

In The Close you can discover Pilgrims' Hall, dating from 1308, picturesque Cheyney Court and the Deanery, which has been in continuous occupation since the 13th century.

The Visitors' Centre was opened in 1993 by Queen Elizabeth II, it houses the Cathedral Shop and the Cathedral Refectory. Many innovative and exclusive mementoes are available whilst the Refectory is a tranquil setting for morning coffee, lunch or cream tea.

A comprehensive range of guided tours is available. Contact the information desk in the Cathedral or the Education Centre, 10a The Close, Winchester, Hampshire, SO23 9LA (01962) 857225.

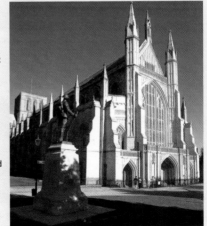

CADOGAN AND COMPANY

30-31 The Square, Winchester,
Hampshire SO23 9EZ
Tel: 01962 877399
website:
www.cadoganandcompany.co.uk

In a superb city centre location, with parking adjacent, **Cadogan and Company** has built up an enviable reputation for style and quality in womens' and men's fashion and accessories. Owner Alexander Edwards, who has spent all his working life in the retail trade, came to this address 10 years ago and turned what was effectively an empty shell into one of the city's leading private retailers.

Housed in a prestigious modern development, the shop is on three levels of open-plan display areas, all subtly lit and professionally laid out on stands and consoles, racks and shelves. Alexander travels the world seeking out what he knows will appeal to his discerning clientele, including elegant leather fashion garments and accessories from Italy.

Quality is the keynote throughout the range of goods on display, from indoor and outdoor fashion wear to boots and shoes, hats, nightwear, woollens, scarves and ties. Among the accessories are top-of-the-range suitcases, travel bags and accessories for the journey, umbrellas, the best leather briefcases and desk supplies, haberdashery, gold and silverware and a selection of lovely gifts, from glass and china ornaments to diaries, barometers and hip flasks.

Highly professional management and staff are on hand to attend to every need of customers at this superb shop, which is open from 9.30am to 5.30pm Monday to Saturday. Within walking distance of the shop are most of the major places of interest in the city, including the wonderful Cathedral, the City Museum and the College, the oldest public school in England. Tradition and modern amenities stand side by side in Winchester, and Cadogan and Company fully deserves its place right in the heart of the city.

education for 70 'poor and needy scholars'. Substantial parts of the 14th century buildings still stand, including the beautiful Chapel. The Chapel is always open to visitors and there are guided tours around the other parts of the college from April to September. If you can time your visit during the school holidays, more of the college is available to view.

Two years after Jane Austen was buried in the cathedral, the poet John Keats stayed in Winchester and it was here that he wrote his timeless *Ode to Autumn – Season of mists and mellow fruitfulness*. His inspiration was a daily walk past the cathedral and college and through the Water Meadows beside the River Itchen. A detailed step-by-step guide to

Keats' Walk is available from the Tourist Information Centre.

The city's other attractions are so numerous one can only mention a few of the most important. **The Great Hall**, off the High Street, is the only surviving part of the medieval castle rebuilt by Henry III between 1222 and 1236. Nikolaus Pevsner considered it "the finest medieval hall in England after Westminster Hall". Located within the castle grounds are no fewer than six military museums, including the Gurkha Museum, the King's Royal Hussars Museum whose displays include an exhibit on the famous Charge of the Light Brigade, and the Royal Green Jackets Museum which contains a

THE CLOCK-WORK-SHOP

6a Parchment Street, Winchester,
Hampshire SO23 8AT
Tel: 01962 842331 Mobile: 07885 954302
website: www.clock-work-shop.co.uk

Everyone visiting the historic city of Winchester should take time to look in at the **Clock-Work-Shop**, which occupies two floors of an old building in a side street just off the main street. Owned by Peter Ponsford-Jones and run by him and his partners Kevin Hurd and Richard Scorey, the shop specialises in the sale, purchase, repair, restoration, after care and valuation of antique clocks, mostly English and mostly from the period from the 17th century to the First World War. Around 100 clocks are usually on display, including carriage clocks, wall clocks, mantel clocks and long case clocks, and the shop also deals in fine antique barometers and has a small stock of pocket watches.

The shop hours are 9am to 5pm Monday to Saturday, when all the clocks are available to view, but customers can 'visit' the shop at any time of the day or night by accessing the splendid website, which includes comprehensive details, including photographs and prices, of the full stock. A typical entry from the long case clock catalogue: 'A very handsome 8 day longcase of super quality. The silvered dial is particularly beautiful - a real work of the engraver's art! The oak case has excellent colour, finish and proportions. A most original clock. Circa 1780. Local delivery and set-up.' With notes as interesting and tempting as these, a browse through the website could easily result in a real-life visit to the shop. All sales and repairs carry a three-year guarantee.

CADOGAN & JAMES

*31a The Square, Winchester,
Hampshire SO23 9EZ
Tel: 01962 840805
Fax: 01962 850571
e-mail:
cadoganandjames@ecosse.net*

A sea-blue awning shades the pavement tables outside **Cadogan & James** and, as you enter this outstanding delicatessen/café, you are engulfed with a medley of different aromas from the fresh bread, herbs and spices.

Enjoying a picturesque setting in the city's famous Square, the shop is a veritable Aladdin's Cave for gourmets, selling a vast range of products from around the world.

The interior reflects a mixture of traditional Italian-inspired designs. The rustic *trompe l'oeil* ceiling is complemented by garlands of hops surmounting the shelves deeply filled with a huge variety of products from pastas to preserves, truffles to speciality teas, cheeses of every kind to freshly-made sandwiches and cakes.

Manager Gail Collier and her friendly staff are exceptionally helpful and with their vast knowledge and enthusiasm encourage customers to sample the exciting gourmet products on offer. This must be one of the best delicatessens in the country – an absolute must for all food lovers.

Cadogan & James is also perfectly placed for tourist attractions, right next to Winchester Cathedral, close to the Guildhall, King Alfred's statue, the City Museum, Winchester College, the West Gate and the Great Hall where King Arthur's Round Table can be found.

superb diorama of the Battle of Waterloo.

Other buildings of interest include the early-14th century Pilgrim Hall, part of the Pilgrim School, and originally used as lodgings for pilgrims to the shrine of St Swithun, and **Wolvesey Castle** (English Heritage), the residence of the Bishops of Winchester since 963. The present palace is a gracious, classical building erected in the 1680s, flanked by the imposing ruins of its 14th century predecessor which was one of the grandest buildings in medieval England. It was here, in 1554, that Queen Mary first met Philip of Spain and where the wedding banquet was held the next day. Also well worth a visit is the 15th century **Hospital of St Cross,** England's oldest almshouse. Founded in 1132 by Henri du Blois, grandson of William the Conqueror, it was extended in 1446 by Cardinal Beaufort, son of John of Gaunt. It is still home to 25 Brothers and maintains its long tradition of hospitality by dispensing the traditional Wayfarer's Dole to any traveller who requests it.

About two miles east of the city, at Colden Common, **Marwell Zoological Park** is home to more than 200 species of animals, from meercats and red pandas to snow leopards and rhinos. Set in a 100-acre park, Marwell has the largest collection of hoofed animals in the UK, nine species of cat and many endangered species.

Just to the west of the city is a very modern attraction, Intech, which explores the technologies that shape our lives today – how light can be bent, for example, and how humans produce electricity. There are more than 100 exhibits, all of which have been

THE WESTGATE INN

2 Romsey Road, Winchester, Hampshire SO23 8TP
Tel/Fax: 01962 820222

Helen and Guy Carpenter have been licensees in Winchester for almost 20 years and throughout that time have always been energetic in promoting local food and drink. The **Westgate Inn**, which dates from the 18th century, stands at the top end of Winchester's main shopping street opposite the medieval West Gate and the historic Great Hall. The pub has a traditional wooden bar where a glass or two of real ale can be enjoyed while enjoying a chat and the views from the windows. Ringwood Best, Pride of Romsey and Young's Best are the regular brews, to quench a thirst or to accompany the excellent food served here.

The star of the show is the Tiffin Club, where the menu uses local produce of the highest quality in an eclectic selection of innovative Indian dishes, many of them not to be found anywhere else. A few dishes are familiar, but most will be new to first-time visitors: slow-cooked buffalo in a thick sauce with black cardamom; stuffed baby squid with a tangy tamarind sauce; chicken Anjali with lemon grass and lime; asparagus with roasted sesame seeds. For traditional palates the pub offers a small choice of English dishes and fish specials. The Westgate also provides a very comfortable and convenient base for exploring the many attractions of Winchester and the surrounding area. The accommodation comprises eight well-appointed rooms for bed & breakfast guests – six en-suite, the other two with private bathrooms.

GIOIA JEWELLERY

G i o i A

Studio House, 9 St Clement Street, Winchester,
Hampshire SO23 9HH Tel/Fax: 01962 850695
e-mail: sales@gioiajewellery.com website: www.gioiajewellery.com

What makes Gioia special? Could it be the joy and passion that goes into every handcrafted piece? Could it be the unique styling that the wearers of the jewellery love? Could it be the Italian inspiration reflected in the variety of textures and finishes of each of the designs? The answer to all those questions is yes - and yet Gioia is so much more.

In her "Classic" and "Individual" Collections, Lisa Sanders has designed jewellery that stands out from the crowd yet retains an air of style and sophistication. Her use of precious metals and diamonds, lovingly crafted, compliments the designs and are chosen with the individual in mind.

Aided by Jake Sanders who specialises in designing the "mens" collection and making the Gioia "Wedding" range, Lisa says, *"I want people who wear my designs to feel special, confident and beautiful - day or night, casual or formal"*.

Classic looks, contemporary styling and passion all combine to create Gioia - *dare to be different.*

15% discount for all online orders. Please enter code: CLS15.

GOODLIFE HOME & GARDEN CENTRE

Springvale Road, Headbourne Worthy, nr Winchester,
Hampshire SO23 7LD
Tel: 01962 889000 Fax: 01962 889400
e-mail: enquiries@goodlifegardencentre.co.uk

Choosing from the wide selection of healthy plants and shrubs is just one reason for visiting the **Goodlife Home & Garden Centre**. The Centre is partly sited on reclaimed watercress beds, which makes a perfect environment for maintaining plants in prime condition, and stocks are available throughout the season. The centre also keeps a fine collection of pots and ornamental wrought-iron garden furniture. In the Food Halls, visitors will find a wonderful range of food from around the world, including fresh seasonal fruit and vegetables, free-range eggs, olives and olive oils, French terrines, local and Continental cheeses, hand-made chocolates, cakes and ice creams.

The Gift Shop is filled with elegant and unusual ornaments and homeware, from scented candles and fragrant French toiletries to silk cushions and throws, hand-painted ceramics and tableware, glassware, hand-crafted jewellery and a super selection of cards (many locally made) for every occasion. On the run-up to Christmas, the shop is filled with table decorations, soft toys and stocking fillers. Visitors can take a break from browsing with a snack or light meal in the homely café-restaurant, where much of the menu is home-made. Goodlife is a stockist of several ranges of traditional and rustic kitchen, living and dining furniture in solid French oak or natural and painted pine.

🏛 historic building   🏛 museum   🏛 historic site   🜨 scenic attraction   🌱 flora and fauna

designed to provide a genuine hands-on experience. Intech is open daily all year round.

Around Winchester

CRAWLEY
5 miles NW of Winchester, on minor road off the B3049

Crawley is a possibly unique example of an early-20th century model village. The estate was bought in 1900 by the Philippi family who then enthusiastically set about adding to the village's store of genuine traditional cottages a number of faithful fakes built in the same style. (They also provided their tenants with a state-of-the-art bath house and a roller skating rink). Sensitive to tradition and history, they did nothing to blemish the partly Norman church, leaving its unusual interior intact. Instead of stone pillars, St Mary's has mighty wooden columns supporting its roof, still effective more than 500 years after they were first hoisted into place.

SUTTON SCOTNEY
6 miles N of Winchester, on the A34

Standing at a crossroads, Sutton Scotney was once a busy little place. Today, it is by-passed by the A34 so visitors can peacefully explore its picturesque side streets lined with thatched cottages and Georgian houses. Unusually, the village has no church but the clock tower of the Jubilee Hall, erected in 1897, has a distinctly ecclesiastical air about it.

ROMSEY
10 miles SE of Winchester, on the A27/A3090

🏛 Abbey 🏛 Broadlands 🏛 King John's House

🏛 Moody Museum 🏛 Romsey Signal Box

'Music in stone', and 'the second finest Norman building in England' are just two responses to **Romsey Abbey**, a majestic building containing some of the best 12th and 13th century architecture to have survived. Built between 1120 and 1230, the Abbey is remarkably complete. Unlike so many monastic buildings which were destroyed or fell into ruin after the Dissolution, the Abbey was fortunate in being bought by the town in 1544 for £100 – the bill of sale, signed and sealed by Henry VIII, is displayed in the south choir aisle. Subsequent generations of townspeople have carefully maintained their bargain purchase. The abbey's most spectacular feature is the soaring nave which rises more than 70ft and extends for more

---

THE NORTHBROOK ARMS

East Stratton, nr Winchester, Hampshire SO21 3DU
Tel: 01962 774150   e-mail: infonorthbrookarms@aol.com
Fax: 01962 774180   website: www.northbrookarms.co.uk

The **Northbrook Arms** is a free house, built in 1848 and located opposite the village green, which doubles as a beer garden. Inside, the look is delightfully traditional, with open fireplaces and a quarry-tiled floor, and the décor includes photographs of England rugby teams – landlord David Sheaff is a big rugby fan – and caricatures of locals. A decent selection of real ales, including Gales HSB, Otter and Hogsback, accompanies a choice of freshly cooked favourite pub dishes; the half-price steaks on Wednesday and the Sunday roasts are particularly popular. For guests staying overnight, the pub has five twin or double rooms – three above the bar, the other two alongside.

🎞 stories and anecdotes   🦋 famous people   🎨 art and craft   🖊 entertainment and sport   🚶 walks

than 76ft. Amongst the abbey's many treasures is the 16th century Romsey Rood which shows Christ on the cross with the hand of God descending from the clouds.

Just across from the Abbey, in Church Court, stands the town's oldest dwelling, **King John's House**, built around 1240 for a merchant. It has served as a royal residence but not, curiously, for King John who died some 14 years before it was built. He may though have had a hunting lodge on the site. The house is now a museum and centre for cultural activities; the garden has been renovated and replanted with pre-18th century plants.

The **Moody Museum** occupies the Victorian home of the Moody family who were cutlers in Romsey from the 18th century up until the 1970s. Visitors are greeted by (models of) William Moody and his sister Mary in a reconstruction of the family parlour and the exhibits include fixtures and fittings from the family's gun shop.

Train enthusiasts will want to seek out the curious exhibit located behind the infants' school in Winchester Road. **Romsey Signal Box** is a preserved vintage signal box in working order, complete with signals, track and other artefacts.

Romsey's most famous son was undoubtedly the flamboyant politician Lord Palmerston, three times Prime Minister during the 1850s and 1860s. Palmerston lived at Broadlands, just south of the town, and is commemorated by a bronze statue in the town's small triangular Market Place.

Broadlands is a gracious Palladian mansion

THE STAR INN

East Tytherley, nr Romsey, Hampshire SO51 0LW
Tel: 01794 340225
e-mail: info@starinn-uk.com
website: www.starinn-uk.com

The Star Inn enjoys a fine location by the village cricket green in the picturesque Test Valley, making it a perfect place to enjoy a drink, a meal or a stay. Dating back to the 16th century, it's very much a family affair, with Lesley Newitt front of house and her son Justin head of the kitchen. Using fresh seasonal produce, sourced locally as far as possible, his menus change every day, offering a choice of dishes that combine classical skills and contemporary flair and imagination. Typical dishes run from seared scallops with lentils, cumin cream and coriander oil to pork tenderloin with mustard mash, cod with squid ink pasta, homemade ices and sorbets and glazed lemon tart with a raspberry coulis. British cheeses make up an exceptional cheeseboard.

Patrons can enjoy real ales and fine wines in the cosy bar and comfortable lounge, and the pretty courtyard garden is the ideal spot for sipping a summer drink. For visitors looking for a touring base, cottages in the grounds provide excellent accommodation in en-suite rooms with double beds or twin beds; all rooms have TV and hospitality trays, with mineral water and fresh fruit on arrival. Romsey, just five miles away, is one of many interesting places to visit, and there are several locations for fishing very close to the inn.

🏛 historic building   🏛 museum   🏛 historic site   ☘ scenic attraction   🌿 flora and fauna

TWYFORD
3 miles S of Winchester, on the B3335

🏛 Waterworks Museum

Hampshire churchyards are celebrated for their ancient yew trees, but the one at Twyford is exceptional. A visitor in 1819 described the clipped tree as resembling "the top of a considerable green hillock, elevated on a stump". The grand old yew is still in apparently good health and provides a dark green foil to the trim Victorian church of striped brick and flint which was designed by Alfred Waterhouse, architect of the Natural History Museum in London.

Three well-known historical figures have strong associations with the village. Benjamin Franklin wrote much of his autobiography while staying at Twyford House; Alexander Pope attended school here until he was expelled for writing a lampoon on the Master; and it was at the old Brambridge House that Mrs Fitzherbert was secretly married to the Prince Regent, later George IV, in 1785.

An interesting example of our industrial heritage is the **Twyford Waterworks Museum.** It is housed in Twyford Waterworks which opened in 1898 to supply water to the surrounding rural area. Between 1903 and 1969 the water was also softened which explains the lime kilns found on the site. The present steam engine dates from 1914; the electric pumps were installed in 1951. Despite being scheduled as an Ancient Monument, the waterworks still extract more than five million gallons of water from the wells every day. The museum concentrates on the evolution of water supply during the 20th century and is open every Sunday between May and October, and every other Sunday during the rest of the year.

Romsey Abbey

that was built by Lord Palmerston's father in the mid-1700s. The architect was Henry Holland, the landscape was modelled by the ubiquitous Capability Brown. The important collections of furniture, porcelain and sculpture were acquired by the 2nd Viscount Palmerston. The house passed to the Mountbatten family and it was Lord Louis Mountbatten who first opened Broadlands to the public shortly before he was killed in 1979. The present owner, Lord Romsey, has established the Mountbatten Exhibition in tribute to his grandfather's remarkable career as naval commander, diplomat, and last Viceroy of India. An audio-visual film provides an overall picture of the Earl's life and exhibits include his dazzling uniforms, the numerous decorations he was awarded, and an astonishing collection of trophies, mementoes and gifts he received in his many roles.

EAST WELLOW
12 miles SW of Winchester, off the A27

🏛 Church of St Margaret

The **Church of St Margaret** is the burial place of Florence Nightingale who lies beneath the family monument bearing the simple inscription: *FN 1820-1910*. The church itself has several interesting features, including 13th century wall paintings and Jacobean panelling. Close to the village is Headlands Farm Fishery where there are two lakes available for fishing for carp, tench, perch, roach, pike and trout. Other facilities include rod hire, flies for sale and hot drinks.

MOTTISFONT
10 miles W of Winchester, off the A3057

🏛 Abbey

Mottisfont's little Church of St Andrew boasts a wealth of 15th century stained glass, including a superb Crucifixion, and should not be overlooked on a visit to **Mottisfont Abbey** (National Trust - see panel below). Built as an Augustinian priory in the 12th century, the

abbey was converted into a country mansion after the Dissolution and was further modified in the 1700s. Some parts of the original priory have survived, amongst them the monks' cellarium – an undercroft with vast pillars – but the main attraction inside is the drawing room decorated with a Gothic *trompe l'oeil* fantasy by Rex Whistler. He was also commissioned to design the furniture but World War II intervened and he was killed in action.

The superb grounds contain the National Collection of Old Fashioned roses, established in 1972, a lovely pollarded lime walk designed by Sir Geoffrey Jellicoe, and some superb trees, including what is thought to be the largest plane tree in England.

Southeast Hampshire

With a population of 1.2 million, Hampshire is the 5th most populous county in England. A goodly proportion of those 1.2 million people live along the coastal crescent that stretches from Southampton through Fareham and

Mottisfont Abbey and Garden
Mottisfont, nr Romsey, Hampshire SO51 0LP
Tel: 01794 340757

Once a 12th century priory, Mottisfont Abbey is now a handsome house set in glorious grounds alongside the River Test. With its famous walled gardens, tranquil riverside walks and its unrivalled setting, Mottisfont is the perfect place for an idyllic day out.

There are 30 acres of glorious landscaped grounds with sweeping lawns and magnificent trees, and the extensive walled gardens house the world-famous National Collection of Old Fashioned Roses.

Inside the house you can see the famous drawing room decorated by Rex Whistler in *trompe l'oeil* fantasy style, as well as an interesting collection of 19th and 20th century pictures donated by the painter Derek Hill.

🏛 historic building   🏛 museum   🏛 historic site   🔧 scenic attraction   🌿 flora and fauna

Bargate, Southampton

Portsmouth to Havant. Inland, though, there are parts of the South Downs as peaceful and scenic as anywhere in the county.

Southampton boasts one of the finest natural harbours in the world and has been the leading British deep-sea port since the days of the Norman Conquest. Portsmouth did not develop as a port until the 16th century but makes up for its shorter history by its romantic associations with such legendary ships as *HMS Victory*, the *Mary Rose*, and *HMS Warrior*. Portsmouth is also a popular seaside resort providing, together with its neighbour, Hayling Island, some seven miles of sandy beaches. Southsea Castle and massive Portchester Castle have interesting historical associations, and the ruins of Netley Abbey and the Bishop's Palace at Bishop's Waltham are both outstandingly picturesque.

Like most major ports, Southampton and Portsmouth have something of a cosmopolitan air about them, providing an intriguing contrast with the rural charms of the inland villages.

Southampton

🏛 Medieval Merchant's House   🏛 Solent Sky

🏛 Maritime Museum   🏛 Tudor House Museum

From this historic port, Henry V's army set sail for Agincourt in 1415, the Pilgrim Fathers embarked on their perilous journey to the New World in 1620 and, on April 10th, 1912, the *Titanic* set off on its maiden voyage,

steaming majestically into the Solent. Of the 1,500 who lost their lives when the ship struck an iceberg in the freezing Atlantic in 1912, around 500 were Southampton-based crew members. The city's sea-faring heritage is vividly recalled at the excellent **Maritime Museum**, housed in the 14th century Wool House. The museum tells the story of the port from the age of sail to the heyday of the great ocean liners.

As a major sea port, Southampton was a prime target for air raids during World War II and suffered grievously. But the city can still boast a surprising number of ancient buildings. Substantial stretches of the medieval Town Walls have miraculously survived, its ramparts interspersed with fortifications such as the oddly-named 15th century Catchcold Tower and God's House Gate and Tower, which now houses the city's archaeological museum. Perhaps the most impressive feature of the walls is Bargate, one of the finest medieval city gates in the country. From its construction around 1200 until the 1930s, Bargate remained the principal entrance to the city. Its narrow archway is so

Southampton City Art Gallery

Civic Centre, Southampton, SO14 7LP
Tel. 023 8083 2743
e-mail. esta.mion-jones@southampton.gov.uk
website: www.southampton.gov.uk/art

Southampton City Art Gallery is one of the most outstanding galleries in the South of England and is internationally renowned for its impressive collection and temporary exhibitions programme. Housed within a beautiful example of 1930s municipal architecture, the Gallery is fortunate in possessing a rich and varied collection of fine art. It's located in the Civic Centre, adjacent to Watt's Park and within easy walking distance of the city's shopping area. The visitor facilities are excellent and it's fully wheelchair accessible, including the Gallery Shop. The shop stocks a wide range of greetings cards, stationery, wrapping paper, postcards and crafts. Entrance to the Gallery is free of charge.

Opening times: Tues – Sat 10am- 5pm and Sundays

low that Southampton Corporation's trams had to be specially modified for them to pass through. Inside the arch stands a statue of George III, cross-dressing as a Roman Emperor. Bargate now stands in its own pedestrianised area, its upper floor, the former Guildhall, now a museum of local history and folklore.

Another remarkable survivor is the **Medieval Merchant's House** (English Heritage) in French Street which has been expertly restored and authentically furnished, now appearing just as it was when it was built around 1290. One of the most popular visitor attractions in Southampton is the **Tudor House Museum & Garden**, a lovely 15th century house with an award-winning Tudor Garden complete with fountain, bee skeps (baskets) and 16th century herbs and flowers. The house is currently closed for major refurbishment.

Southampton City Art Gallery (see panel above) is a treasure house of works ranging over six centuries, while the John Hansard Gallery and the Mallais Gallery specialise in contemporary art. The painter Sir John Mallais was a native of Southampton as was Isaac Watts, the hymnologist whose many enduring hymns include *O God, Our Help In Ages Past*.

There's so much history to savour in the city, but Southampton has also proclaimed itself "A City for the New Millennium". Major developments include the flagship shopping area of West Quay, the enhancement of the city's impressive central parks, the superbly appointed Leisure World; the state-of-the-art Swimming & Diving Complex which incorporates separate championship, diving and fun pools, and Ocean Village, an imaginatively conceived waterfront complex with its own 450-berth marina, undercover shopping, excellent restaurants and a multi-screen cinema.

As you'd expect in a city with such a glorious maritime heritage, there's a huge choice of boat excursions, whether along the

🏚 historic building   🏛 museum   🏛 historic site   🔾 scenic attraction   🌿 flora and fauna

River Hamble, around the Solent, or over to the Isle of Wight. Blue Funnel Cruises operate from Ocean Village; Solent Cruises from Town Quay.

The city also occupies an important place in aviation history. A short step from Ocean Village, **Solent Sky** (formerly the Hall of Aviation) commemorates the pioneering work of the Spitfire's creator R J Mitchell. Mitchell lived and worked in Southampton in the 1930s and designed not only the Spitfire but also the S6 Seaplane which won the coveted Scheider Trophy. The centrepiece is the spectacular Sandringham Flying Boat which you can board to sample the luxury of air travel in the past – very different from the cattle class standards of today's mass travel.

Around Southampton

WEST END
2 miles NE of Southampton, on minor road off the A27

🌿 Itchen Valley Country Park

An ideal destination for a family outing is **Itchen Valley Country Park** (see panel below) on the outskirts of Southampton. Its 440 acres of water meadows, ancient woodland, conifer plantations and grazing pasture lie either side of the meandering River Itchen, famous for its clear waters and excellent fishing. The Park is managed by Eastleigh Borough Council's Countryside Service to provide informal recreation, enhance and conserve wildlife habitats and as an educational resource. The best place to begin your visit is the High Wood Barn Visitor Centre, an attractive timber structure built in the style of a 17th century Hampshire Aisle Barn. From the Visitor Centre, waymarked trails help you to discover the different areas of the Park and an informative leaflet reveals the history and wildlife of a landscape shaped by hundreds of years of traditional farming and woodland management. Children are well-provided for at the park. In High Hill Field there's an adventure play area for the under-12s that includes an aerial runway, and behind the Visitor Centre a play area for the under-5s has giant woodland animals designed by local school children and built by sculptor Andy Frost.

Itchen Valley Country Park

High Wood Barn, Allington Lane, West End, Southampton, Hampshire SO30 3HQ
Tel/Fax: 023 8046 6091
e-mail: ivcp@eastleigh.gov.uk

A superb family day out is guaranteed at **Itchen Valley Country Park**, whose 440 acres of water meadows, ancient woodland, conifer plantations and grazing pasture span the River Itchen between Eastleigh and Southampton. The various areas support a great variety of bird life, insect and plant life and there are trails, cycle routes, picnic sites and a host of children's activities. The High Wood Barn Visitor Centre, built in 17th century style from timber recovered from the great storm of 1987, contains information, interactive exhibits, a café and a shop.

📖 stories and anecdotes   🐦 famous people   🎨 art and craft   🌿 entertainment and sport   🚶 walks

EASTLEIGH
5 miles NE of Southampton on the A335

🏛 Museum ⚜ Point Dance & Arts Centre

🌿 Lakeside Country Park ⚜ Beatrice Royal Gallery

Eastleigh is first mentioned in a charter of 932AD but it wasn't until some 900 years later that it began to expand. That was when the Eastleigh Carriage and Engine Works was established in the town. At one time the works covered 60 acres and employed 3,600 people. The town's railway connection is commemorated by Jill Tweed's sculpture, The Railwayman, which stands in the town centre.

Nearby, in a former Salvation Army building, is the **Eastleigh Museum** whose exhibits concentrate on the town's railway heritage. Visiting heritage, art, craft and photography exhibitions are also held here. The **Point Dance and Arts Centre** stages a full programme of theatre, dance, cinema and music events, while the **Beatrice Royal Contemporary Art and Craft Gallery** offers exhibitions of art, sculpture, ceramics, jewellery and textiles.

Just outside the town is the **Lakeside Country Park,** home to a variety of wildlife and also a place for model boating, windsurfing and fishing. Here, too, is the Eastleigh Lakeside Railway, a miniature steam railway that provides trips around the park.

To the south of Eastleigh lies Southampton International Airport, the home of **Carill Aviation** where you can take off for a scenic flight over the Solent or sign up for a trial flying lesson.

BISHOP'S WALTHAM
10 miles NE of Southampton, on the B2177/ B3035

🏛 Palace 🏛 Jhansi Farm rare Breeds Centre

Bishop's Waltham is a charming and historic

small town. It was the country residence of the Bishops of Winchester for centuries and through the portals of their sumptuous **Palace** have passed at least 12 reigning monarchs. Amongst them were Richard the Lionheart returning from the Crusades, Henry V mustering his army before setting off for Agincourt, and Henry VIII entertaining Charles V of Spain (then the most powerful monarch in Europe) to a lavish banquet. The palace's days of glory came to a violent end during the Civil War when Cromwell's troops battered most of it to the ground. The last resident bishop was forced to flee, concealing himself beneath a load of manure.

Set within beautiful moated grounds the ruins remain impressive, especially the Great Hall with its three-storey tower and soaring windows. Also here are the remains of the bakehouse, kitchen, chapel and lodgings for visitors. The Palace is now in the care of English Heritage and entrance is free.

The town itself offers visitors a good choice of traditional and specialist shops, amongst them a renowned fishmonger, butcher, baker – even a candle-maker. And just north of the town you can visit one of the country's leading vineyards. Visitors to Northbrook Springs Vineyard are offered a tour of the vineyard which explains the complex, labour-intensive process of planting, growing, pruning and harvesting the vines, and a free tasting in the Vineyard Shop (open Tuesday to Sunday) of a selection of crisp, clear, flavourful wines.

South of Bishop's Waltham, at Waltham Chase, **Jhansi Farm Rare Breed Centre** is dedicated to the conservation of rare breed farm animals, some of them critically endangered. The Farm has a pets' corner housing a large variety of pure bred rabbits,

🏛 historic building 🏛 museum 🏛 historic site ⚜ scenic attraction 🌿 flora and fauna

guinea pigs, chipmunks and birds, a souvenir and pet shop, tearoom, picnic and play area, nursery and water gardens, with events such as sheep shearing and hand spinning taking place throughout the season.

BOTLEY

7 miles E of Southampton on the A334

Set beside the River Hamble, Botley is an attractive village of red brick houses which remains as pleasant now as when William Cobbett, the 19th century writer and political commentator, described it as "the most delightful village in the world….it has everything in a village I love and none of the things I hate". The latter included a workhouse, attorneys, justices of the peace – and barbers. The author of *Rural Rides* lived a very comfortable life in Botley between 1804 and 1817 and he is honoured by a memorial in the Market Square.

NETLEY

5 miles SE of Southampton, off the A3025

🏛 Netley Abbey 🏛 Netley Hospital

🦌 Royal Victoria Country Park

A Victorian town on the shores of the Solent, Netley was brought into prominence when a vast military hospital was built here after the Crimean War. The foundation stone of **Netley Hospital** was laid by Queen Victoria in 1856 and the hospital remained in use until after World War II. A disastrous fire in the 1960s caused most of the buildings to be demolished but the hospital's Chapel, with its distinctive 100ft tower, did survive and now houses an exhibition about the hospital from the time of Florence Nightingale. The rest of the site has been developed as the **Royal Victoria Country Park** offering woodland and coastal walks, waymarked themed and

nature trails, and trips around the park on a miniature steam railway.

Heritage of a different kind can be found at ruined **Netley Abbey** (English Heritage), a wonderfully serene spot surrounded by noble trees. "These are not the ruins of Netley," declared Horace Walpole in the mid-1700s, "but of Paradise." Jane Austen was equally entranced by the Abbey's romantic charm and she made many visits. Dating back to 1300, the extensive ruins provide a spectacular backdrop for open-air theatre performances during the summer.

BURSLEDON

6 miles SE of Southampton, off the A3024

🏛 Windmill 🏭 Brickworks

Anyone interested in England's industrial heritage should pay a visit to Bursledon. Ships have been built here since medieval times, the most famous being the *Elephant*, Nelson's flagship at the Battle of Copenhagen. The yard where it was built, now renamed the Elephant Boatyard, is still in business. On a rise to the north of the village stands **Bursledon Windmill**, the only working windmill in Hampshire. Built in 1814 at a cost of £800, its vanes ground to a halt during the great agricultural depression of the 1880s. Happily, all the machinery remained intact and after a lengthy restoration between 1976 and 1991, the sails are revolving once again whenever a good northerly or southerly wind is blowing. The mill produces stoneground flour for sale and is open to visitors at weekends, or whenever the sails are turning.

The village can boast another unique industrial site. When **Bursledon Brickworks** was established in 1897 the machinery installed was at the very forefront of brick-making technology. The works closed in 1974

PICKWELL FARM – PYO FRUIT & VEG

Grange Road, Bursledon, nr Southampton,
Hampshire SO31 8GD
Tel: 023 8040 4616   Fax: 023 8040 6782
e-mail: Andrew@pickwellfarm.co.uk
website: www.pickwellfarm.co.uk

Andrew Draper's grandfather started the business, and Andrew's brother Robert and their parents Douglas and May all play an active part in running the splendidly named **Pickwell Farm**. The farm's 52 acres include 10 acres of Pick Your Own crops and a plant nursery.

32 varieties of fruit and vegetables are available for picking at various times of the year, including runner beans and broad beans, peas, sweetcorn, strawberries, raspberries, gooseberries and blackcurrants. In the shop customers will find many other varieties grown on the farm, including leeks, cauliflowers and squash, free-range eggs, home-baked cakes, freezer cabinets filled with meat, fish and ready meals, flowers, cards, gifts and crafts. Behind the shop is a nursery where trees, shrubs, roses and bedding plants, all grown on site, are for sale.

BONNE BOUCHE – FINE FOOD AND CATERING

High Street, Hamble, nr Southampton,
Hampshire SO31 4HA
Tel: 023 8045 5771   e-mail: info@bonne-bouche.co.uk
website: www.bonne-bouche.co.uk

A passion for sailing brought Carol Hill to Hamble, and commitment to fine food led her to buy an existing sandwich shop. She opened **Bonne Bouche** in 2001 and developed the delicatessen and catering sides of the business. It remains best known for its superb sandwiches, with more than 50 fillings available in genuine French baguettes, in white or granary bread or in rolls. All the fillings are made on the premises from fresh ingredients free from artificial additives or preservatives. Breakfast is served until 11 in the morning, soup and jacket potatoes are winter warmers and in summer the zingy fresh salads are very popular.

From the deli counter come English cheeses, pasta, olives and olive oil, sauces, dressings, ready meals, local preserves, chocolates and juices, pastries and cakes. Deli bags in various sizes are perfect for taking on a day's sailing or sightseeing, and the Bonne Bouche outside catering service is available for office lunches, parties and functions.

PARK GATE
8 miles SE of Southampton, on the A27

Back in the days when strawberries still had real taste and texture, Park Gate was the main distribution centre for the produce of the extensive strawberry farms all around. During the season, scores of special trains were contracted to transport the succulent fruit to London, some 3,000 tons of it in 1913 alone. By the 1960s, housing had taken priority over fruit farms and today the M27 marks a very clear division between the built up areas to the south, and the unspoilt acres of countryside to the north.

Portsmouth

🏛 Mary Rose Museum   🏛 Royal Naval Museum

🏛 Royal Armouries   🏛 HMS Victory, HMS Warrior

🏛 Charles Dickens Birthplace Museum

🏛 D-Day Museum   🔱 Spinnaker Tower

🏯 Southsea Castle

Bursledon Windmill

but a charitable trust has now restored its gargantuan machines, thus preserving the last surviving example of a steam-driven brickworks in the country. Special events are held here from time to time but the works are only open on a limited basis.

HAMBLE
7 miles SE of Southampton, on the B3397

Famous throughout the world as a yachting centre, Hamble takes its name from the river, a mere 10 miles long, that flows past the village into Southampton Water. Some 3,000 vessels have berths in the Hamble Estuary so an incredible variety of boats throngs the river during the season, anything from vintage barges to the sleekest of modern craft.

Currently, any brochure promoting Portsmouth always adds the words "Flagship City". With good reason, since the port is home to the most famous flagship in British naval history, **HMS Victory.** From the outside it's a majestic, three-masted ship: inside it's creepily claustrophobic, except for the Admiral's and Captain's spacious, mahogany-panelled quarters. Visitors can pace the very same deck from which Nelson master-minded the decisive encounter with the French navy off Cape Trafalgar in 1805. Standing on this deck, ostentatiously arrayed in the gorgeous uniform of a British Admiral of the Fleet, Nelson presented a clear target to a sharp-sighted French sniper. The precise spot where Nelson fell and the place on the sheltered

Portsmouth Spinnaker Tower

doesn't possess the same historical glamour as the *Victory* or the *Mary Rose*, but **HMS Warrior** merits a visit because when this mighty craft was commissioned in 1860, she was the Navy's first ironclad warship. A great advance in technology, but the distinctions between the officers' and crew accommodation show little difference from those in Nelson's day.

Also within the dockyard area are the **Royal Naval Museum** which has a marvellous exhibition on the life and exploits of Nelson; and The Dockyard Apprentice where visitors can become a new apprentice for a day and learn the skills that helped construct the mighty Dreadnought battleships. A precious part of Portsmouth's history, the Cathedral is set in the heart of historic Old Portsmouth, close to the seafront and the Millennium Walkway. The most recent notable addition to the seafront buildings is the slim 170-metre **Spinnaker Tower**, where lifts take visitors to the viewing platforms.

orlop (lowest) deck where he died are both marked by plaques.

The death of Nelson was a tragedy softened by a halo of victory: the loss of the *Mary Rose*, some 260 years earlier was an unmitigated disaster. Henry VIII had ordered the ship, the second largest in his fleet, to be built. He was standing on Southsea Common above Portsmouth in 1545, watching the *Mary Rose* manoeuvre, when it suddenly heeled over and sank. All 700 men on board drowned. "And the King he screeched right out like any maid, 'Oh, my gentlemen! Oh, my gallant men!'" More than four centuries later, in 1982, the hulk of the *Mary Rose* was carefully raised from the seabed where it had lain for so long. The impressive remains are now housed in the timber-clad **Mary Rose Museum**.

Another ship you can see at Portsmouth

Like Southampton, Portsmouth suffered badly during World War II, losing most of its 17th and 18th century buildings. St George's Church, a handsome Georgian building of 1754 with large galleries, was damaged by a bomb but has been fully restored, and just to the north of the church, the barn-like Beneficial Boy's School, built in 1784, is another survivor.

One of the most interesting buildings is to be found in Southsea, the city's resort area. **Southsea Castle** was built in 1544 as one of Henry VIII's series of forts protecting the south coast from French attacks. It has been modified several times since then but the

🏛 historic building   🏛 museum   🏛 historic site   🏞 scenic attraction   🌿 flora and fauna

Southsea Castle

its rural character. Much of the foreshore is still open ground with wandering sand dunes stretching well back from the four-mile-long shingle beach. Bathing is safe here and West Beachlands even boasts a European Blue Flag which is only awarded to beaches meeting 26 environmental criteria. One of Hayling's more unusual beach facilities is the line of old-fashioned beach huts, all of which are available to rent.

A good way to explore the island is to follow the **Hayling Billy Leisure Trail,** once the Hayling Billy railway line, which provides a level footpath around most of the 14 miles of shoreline.

Hayling is something of a Mecca for board sailors. Not only does it provide the best sailing in the UK for beginners and experts alike, it is also the place where board-sailing was invented. Many places claim that honour but Peter Chilvers has a High Court ruling to prove it. In 1982 a judge decided that Mr Chilvers had indeed invented the sailboard at Hayling in 1958. As a boy of 10, he used a sheet of plywood, a tent fly-sheet, a pole and some curtain rings to sail up an island creek.

original Keep is still intact and there are good views across the Solent from the gun platforms.

Portsmouth also offers visitors a wealth of varied museums, three of which deserve special mention: the **Royal Armouries,** housed in the huge Victorian Fort Nelson, claims to be 'Britain's Loudest Museum', with live firings every day; the **Charles Dickens Birthplace Museum** at 393 Old Commercial Road, has been restored and furnished to show how the house looked when the great novelist was born here in 1812; and the **D-Day Museum** in Southsea which commemorates the Allied invasion of Europe in 1944 and is most notable for the 83-metre-long Overlord Tapestry, a 20th century equivalent of the Bayeux Tapestry.

Around Portsmouth

HAYLING ISLAND
4 miles E of Portsmouth on the A3023

🚶 Hayling Billy Leisure Trail

A traditional family resort for more than a century, Hayling Island manages to provide all the usual seaside facilities without losing

GOSPORT
2 miles W of Portsmouth on the A32

🏛 Fort Brockhurst 🏛 Holy Trinity Church

🏛 Royal Naval Submarine Museum 🏛 Explosion!

🏛 Gosport Museum & Gallery

Gosport is home to another of Palmerston's forts – the circular **Fort Brockhurst** (English Heritage) which is in almost mint condition and open to visitors on Sundays from the end of March to the end of October. At the **Royal Navy Submarine Museum**, located at HMS Dolphin, visitors can experience a century of submarines. Stories of undersea adventures and the heroism of the Royal Navy's submarine services are recounted and there are also guided tours around HMS Alliance, a late World War II submarine.

The town's connections with the Royal Navy are further explored at **Explosion! The Museum of Naval Firepower** which is dedicated to the people who prepared armaments used by the Navy from the Battle of Trafalgar to the Falklands War. As well as browsing through the unique collection of small arms, cannons, guns, mines and torpedoes, visitors can experience the pitch and roll of a moving gun-deck, help move barrels of gunpowder, and dodge mines on the seabed.

Away from the Navy's influence on the town, there is Gosport's splendid **Holy Trinity Church** which contains an organ that was played by George Frederick Handel when he was music master to the Duke of Chandos. The town bought the organ after the duke's death. Gosport also boasts one of the county's best local museums – **Gosport Museum & Gallery** – where the history of the area from prehistoric times is brought to life through a series of fascinating exhibits.

PORTCHESTER
3 miles NW of Portsmouth on the A27

🏰 Castle 🏰 Portchester Church

Standing at the head of Portsmouth Harbour, **Portchester Castle** is not only the grandest medieval castle in the county but also stands within the best-preserved site of a Roman fort in northern Europe. Sometime around 280 AD, the Romans enclosed eight acres of this

strategic headland and used it as a base for their ships clearing the Channel of pirates. The original walls of the fort were 20ft high and 10ft thick, their depth much reduced later by local people pillaging the stone for their own buildings.

The medieval castle dates back to 1120 although the most substantial ruins are those of the royal palace built for Richard II between 1396 and 1399. Richard was murdered in 1399 and never saw his magnificent castle. Also within the walls of the Roman enclosure is **Portchester Church**, a superb Norman construction built between 1133 and 1150 as part of an Augustinian Priory. For some reason, the Priors moved inland to Southwick, and the church remained disused for more than five-and-a-half centuries until Queen Anne personally donated £400 for its restoration. Apart from the east end, the church is entirely Norman and, remarkably, its 12th century font of wondrously carved Caen stone has also survived the centuries.

FAREHAM
6 miles NW of Portsmouth on the A27

🏛 Westbury Manor Museum

🏛 Royal Armouries at Fort Nelson

Fareham has expanded greatly since Thackeray described it as a "dear little Hampshire town". It still has considerable charm and the handsome houses on the High Street reflect its prosperous days as a ship-building centre. Many aspects of the town's history are featured in **Westbury Manor Museum** which occupies a large 17th century town house in the centre of Fareham. This old market town is also home to **The Royal Armouries at Fort Nelson** whose displays of artillery dating from the Middle Ages form one of the finest collections of its kind in the world. Among the 300 guns on show are a Roman catapult; a wrought-iron monster of 1450 that could fire a 60 kilogram granite ball almost a mile; Flemish guns captured at Waterloo, and parts of the notorious Iraqi 'Supergun'. Visitors can see some of the guns in action at daily firings and at special event days when the dramatic interpretations include accounts of the defence of Rorke's Drift, experiences under shellfire in the World War I trenches, and a Royalist account of the execution of Charles I.

TITCHFIELD
7 miles NW of Portsmouth on the A27

🏛 Abbey 🏛 Wriothesley Monument

Just to the north of the village are the ruins of the 13th century **Titchfield Abbey**, its presence reflecting the former prominence of Titchfield as an important market town and a thriving port on the River Meon. The parish church contains a notable treasure in the form of the **Wriothesley Monument** which was carved by a Flemish sculptor in the late 1500s. This remarkable and massive work is a triple tomb chest depicting Thomas Wriothesley, 1st Earl of Southampton, along with his wife and son. It was the 1st Earl who converted part of the now ruined abbey into a house and it was there that his grandson, the 3rd Earl, entertained William Shakespeare.

WICKHAM
8 miles NW of Portsmouth on the A334

This village was the home of William of Wykeham (1324-1404), Chancellor of England, Bishop of Winchester, founder of Winchester College and New College, Oxford.

The mill by the bridge over the River Meon

📖 stories and anecdotes   🦅 famous people   🎨 art and craft   🎭 entertainment and sport   🚶 walks

THE CHESAPEAKE MILL

Bridge Street, Wickham, Hampshire PO17 5JH
Tel: 01329 834078   Fax: 01329 834888
e-mail: info@chesapeakemill.co.uk
website: www.chesapeakemill.co.uk

The **Chesapeake Mill** is a Grade II-listed building dating from 1820 and built using floor timbers from the USS frigate *Chesapeake*, captured during the American War of 1812. The recently restored mill is home to some 40 traders, including antique dealers, furniture specialists, interior and soft furnishing designers, toy and gift dealers and many more. The mill is open every day except Monday and also includes a pleasant tearoom.

will be of interest to American visitors since it contains beams from the American frigate, *Chesapeake*, which was captured in 1813 off Boston by the British frigate *Shannon*.

To the northwest of the village is Wickham Vineyard which was established in the 1980s and has expanded over the years. The vineyard and modern winery are open to visitors who can take advantage of an audio tour, sample the wines and browse through the gift shop.

The New Forest

The New Forest, as is the way with many English place-names, is neither New nor a Forest, although much of it is attractively wooded. Some historians believe that 'forest' is a corruption of an ancient British word, *gores* or *gorest,* meaning waste or open ground. 'gorse' comes from the same root word. The term New Forest came into use after William the Conqueror proclaimed the area a royal hunting ground, seized some 15,000 acres that Saxon farmers had laboriously reclaimed from the heathland, and began a programme of planting thousands of trees. To preserve wildlife for his sport, (the deer especially), William adopted all the rigorous venery laws

of his Saxon royal predecessors and added some harsh measures of his own. Anyone who killed a deer would himself be killed. If he shot at the beast and missed, his hands were cut off. And, perhaps most ruthless of all, anyone who disturbed a deer during the breeding season had his eyes put out.

There are still plenty of wild deer roaming the 145 square miles of the Forest Park, confined within its boundaries by cattle grids, (known to Americans as Texas Gates). You are much more likely though to see the famous New Forest ponies, free-wandering creatures which nevertheless are all privately owned. They are also something of a hazard for drivers, so do take care, especially at night.

The largest wild area in lowland Britain, the Forest is ideal walking country with vast tracts virtually unpopulated but criss-crossed by a cat's cradle of footpaths and bridle-ways. The Forestry Commission has also established a network of waymarked cycle routes which make the most of the scenic attractions and are also designed to help protect the special nature of the Forest. A map detailing the cycle network is available, along with a vast amount of other information about the area, from the New Forest Museum and Visitor Centre in

Lyndhurst. Visitors can watch an audio visual show, see life-sized models of Forest characters, make use of its Resource Centre and Library, and explore a gift shop specialising in locally made Forest crafts. The only town of any size within the New Forest, Lyndhurst is generally regarded as its 'capital', a good place then to begin a tour of the area.

Lyndhurst

🏛 Church of St Michael 🐿 Grave of Alice Liddell

🏛 New Forest Museum & Visitor Centre

The most striking building in this compact village is the **Church of St Michael**, rebuilt in mid-Victorian times in what John Betjeman described as "the most fanciful, fantastic Gothic style that I ever have seen". The rebuilding co-incided with the heyday of the Pre-Raphaelite movement so the church contains some fine stained glass by Burne-Jones, produced by the firm of William Morris, as well as a splendidly lush painting by Lord Leighton of *The Wise and Foolish Virgins*.

In St Michael's churchyard is the **Grave of Alice Liddell** who, as a young girl, was the inspiration for Lewis Carroll's *Alice in Wonderland*. As Mrs Reginald Hargreaves, Alice lived all her married life in Lyndhurst and was very active in local affairs.

Next to the church is the Queen's House which rather confusingly is re-named the

SOFIKA'S

8 High Street, Lyndhurst, Hampshire SO43 7BD
Tel: 023 8028 4066
e-mail: sofikas@btconnect.com

The centre of Lyndhurst is noted for its interesting shops, many of them on the High Street, and one of the most interesting is the recently opened **Sofika's**. This clothes shop is the brainchild of the young, vivacious and widely travelled Sophie Draper, a trained dressmaker with a keen eye

for style and design. She was once a member of a team that produced dresses for Queen Elizabeth and the Queen Mother, and one of the creations for the Queen Mother can be seen in Madame Tussaud's.

Sophie's shop is filled with contemporary menswear and women's wear, from casual and everyday to special occasion and evening wear. The shop offers an alteration service for purchased items and also stocks a range of bags and other accessories. Among the brands to be seen on the shelves are

Weird Fish, Great Plains, French Connection, Rusty, Chilli Pepper, Duck & Cover, Fever, On Fire. Lingerie:- Gossard, Hustler and Legs Avenue.

📖 stories and anecdotes   🐿 famous people   🎨 art and craft   🎭 entertainment and sport   🥾 walks

King's House whenever the reigning sovereign is male. Originally built as a royal hunting lodge, its medieval and Tudor elements are still visible. Many kings and queens have lodged here and the last monarch to stay, George III, graciously allowed loyal villagers to watch through the window as he ate dinner. The House is now the headquarters of the Forestry Commission and is also home to the **Verderer's Court**, an institution dating back to Norman times which still deals with matters concerning the forest's ancient commoning rights. The verderers (forest officials) still sit in public 10 times a year and work closely with the Commission in managing the forest. They also appoint agisters, or stockmen, who are responsible for the day-to-day supervision of the 5,000 ponies and cattle roaming the forest.

At the **New Forest Museum and Visitor Centre**, in the heart of the town, visitors can learn about the history and the wide variety of plants and animal life that the forest supports. There's also a display on the mysterious death in 1100 of William Rufus, son of William the Conqueror, who was killed by an arrow whilst out hunting. It was officially described as an accident but some believe that it was murder.

This little town is noted for its variety of small shops, many of them located in the High Street, an attractive thoroughfare of mostly Edwardian buildings that slopes gently down the hill to Bolton's Bench, a tree-crowned knoll where grazing ponies can usually be found. The spot enjoys excellent views over Lyndhurst and the surrounding forest. At the other end of the town, Swan Green, surrounded by picturesque thatched cottages, provides a much-photographed setting where cricket matches are held in summer.

Around Lyndhurst

MINSTEAD
2 miles NW of Lyndhurst off the A337

🏛 Church of All Saints   🌿 Furzey Gardens

🏛 Rufus Stone

The village of Minstead offers two interesting attractions, one of which is the **Church of All Saints**. During the 18th century, the gentry and squirearchy of Minstead seem to have regarded church attendance as a necessary duty which, nevertheless, should be made as agreeable as possible. Three of the village's most affluent residents paid to have the church fabric altered so that they could each have their own entrance door leading to a private "parlour", complete with open fireplace and comfortable chairs. The squire of Minstead even installed a sofa on which he could doze during the sermon. It's easy to understand his concern since these sermons were normally expected to last for at least an hour; star preachers seem to have thought they were short-changing their flock if they didn't prate for at least twice that long. It was around this time that churches began introducing benches for the congregation.

Admirers of the creator of Sherlock Holmes, Sir Arthur Conan Doyle, will want to pay their respects at his grave in the churchyard here. A puzzle worthy of Sir Arthur's great detective is the idiosyncratic sign outside the Trusty Servant pub in the village. Instead of showing, as one might expect, a portrait of a dutiful domestic, the sign actually depicts a liveried figure with the feet of a stag and the face of a pig, its snout clamped by a padlock. A 10-line poem underneath this peculiar sign explains that the snout means the servant will eat any old scraps, the padlock that he will tell no tales about his master, and the stag's feet that he will be swift in carrying his master's messages.

Minstead's other main attraction is **Furzey Gardens**, eight acres of delightful, informal woodland gardens designed by Hew Dalrymple in the 1920s and enjoying extensive views over the New Forest towards the Isle of Wight. Beautiful banks of azaleas and rhododendrons, heathers and ferns surround an attractive water garden, and amongst the notable species growing here are incandescent Chilean Fire Trees and the strange 'Bottle Brush Tree'.

To the northwest of Minstead stands the **Rufus Stone** that is said to mark the spot where William Rufus was killed by an arrow while out hunting. William's body was carried on the cart of Purkis the charcoal burner to Winchester where William's brother had

Rufus Stone, Minstead

already arrived to proclaim himself king. William had not been a popular monarch and his funeral in the cathedral at Winchester was conducted with little ceremony and even less mourning.

ASHURST
2 miles NE of Lyndhurst on the A35

🐾 Otter, Owl & Wildlife Conservation Park

Just to the east of the village, in acres of ancient woodland, is the **New Forest Otter, Owl and Wildlife Conservation Park**. Conservation is the key word here. The park has an ongoing breeding programme for otters and barn owls, both of which are endangered species. Visitors can meander along woodland trails and encounter the otters and owls in their enclosures along with other native mammals such as deer, foxes and badgers.

MARCHWOOD
5 miles E of Lyndhurst off the A326

🏛 British Military Powerboat Trust

The military port at Marchwood was built in 1943 for the construction of the Mulberry harbours deployed in Normandy after the D-Day landings. Today, the port provides a base for ships of the Royal Fleet auxiliary. Close by, at Cracknore Head, is the **British Military Powerboat Trust** where a number of historic military craft are on display. Visitors can wander around the craft in the static exhibition area and also take boat trips on certain days.

HYTHE
8 miles SE of Lyndhurst off the A326

This is one of the very best places to watch the comings and goings of the big ships on Southampton Water, and no visit here is

NORRIS OF BEAULIEU

The Country Store, Home Farm, Palace Lane, Beaulieu, Hampshire SO42 7YG
Tel: 01590 612215 Fax: 01590 612978 (Saddlers 01590 612673)
e-mail: mrnorris@norrisofbeaulieu.co.uk
website: www.norrisofbeaulieu.co.uk

Frederick Norris is the head of a family business that started in 1876, where quality of product and service come first in providing the very best in country life. In the **Country Store**, more than 500 saddles, new and used, are on display, along with a vast array of all kinds of riding wear and country clothing, equestrian accessories, a specialist dressage department and a full range of animal feeds for horses, farm animals, dogs, cats and birds.

The saddles feature top-quality English and German leather, and the store also has a fully equipped leather workshop. Helpful, highly qualified staff are always on hand to help and advise at the store, which is open every day of the week.

A wide range of gifts, cards, candles, jewellery, body care products and soft furnishings is sold at the Norris family's **Gift Shop** on Beaulieu's High Street.
Tel: 01590 612005.
e-mail: mrsnorris@norrisofbeaulieu.co.uk

The three rooms of the bay-windowed brick cottage, with wooden floors and beamed ceilings, contain many top brands, including Bridgwater china, Suzy Smith bags, Cath Kitson designs and Crabtree & Evelyn fragrances and toiletries.

The third Norris family outlet, also in the High Street, is the **Country Clothing Store**.
Tel: 01590 612662.
e-mail: masternorris@norrisofbeaulieu.co.uk

Here shoppers will find a range of high-quality country clothing and footwear, including Le Chameau brand, polo shirts, Barbour jackets, hats, gloves, walking sticks, Dubarry boots, shooting clothing and footwear, bags and country-themed gifts. The store is located in an old forge and the warm country atmosphere makes browsing and buying a real delight. Open 10 to 5 every day.

complete without taking a ride up the pier on the quaint little electric train, the oldest electric pier train in the world; from the end of the pier a ferry plies the short route across to Southampton. Hythe is the birthplace of the Hovercraft – its inventor Sir Christopher Cockerell lived in the village. In the 1930s Hythe was the home of the British Powerboat Company and of T E Lawrence (Lawrence of Arabia) while he was testing the RAF 200 series powerboats.

BEAULIEU
7 miles SE of Lyndhurst, on the B3056

National Motor Museum

Palace House   Maritime Museum

The ruins of a 13th century Cistercian Abbey, a stately home which grew up around the abbey's imposing gatehouse, and the **National Motor Museum** sited in its grounds are three good reasons why the village of Beaulieu has become one of the county's major visitor attractions. When Lord Montagu of Beaulieu first opened his family home to the public in the 1950s, he organised a display of a few vintage motor vehicles in homage to his father who had been a pioneer of motoring in Britain. That modest clutch of cars has now expanded to include some 250 of the oldest, newest, slowest and fastest motor cars and bikes in British motoring history, plus some rare oddities. The motoring theme is continued in fun features such as Go Karts, Miniature Motors, and 'Fast Trax' which is promoted as the 'best in virtual racing simulators'.

HAZELCOPSE FARM SHOP
Beaulieu, Hampshire SO42 7WU
Tel: 01590 612696

Colin Hutchings brought long experience in the worlds of agriculture and farming when he acquired the **Hazelcopse Farm Shop**. He has already expanded and developed the business, and further expansion plans include wine and wine-related products. The displays in the converted barn run from beef, lamb and pork, most of it produced locally, to fruit and vegetables, jams and preserves and honey, pickles and chutneys, oils and vinegars, fruit juices and bread baked fresh daily in the bakery on the premises.

There are usually at least four varieties of potatoes marked up on the board (Marfona, Wilja, Desirée and Maris Peer were recently noted) and the fruit includes the pick of British classics like apples and pears and top-quality imports including grapes, oranges, kiwis, lemons, limes and bananas. The famous Motor Museum brings visitors in their thousands to Beaulieu, but lovers of fresh seasonal food should make tracks for this splendid farm shop on the Lymington road out of the village. Opening hours are 8.30am to 5pm Monday to Friday, 8.30am to 5.30pm Saturday and 10am to 4pm Sunday.

HAMPSHIRE & THE NEW FOREST

Montagu family treasures are on display in **Palace House**, formerly the gatehouse of the Abbey, and visitors can meet characters from Victorian days who will talk about their lives in service.

It was an ancestor of Lord Montagu, the 2nd Duke of Montagu, who created the picturesque riverside village of **Buckler's Hard** (see panel below) in the early 1700s. It was designed as an inland port to receive and refine sugar from the Duke's West Indian estates and His Grace planned his model village on a grand scale: the streets, for example, were to be 80ft wide. Unfortunately, the enterprise failed and only a single street was built. That 18th century street remains intact and unspoiled, and one of its buildings has been converted into a **Maritime Museum** reflecting the subsequent history of the village when it became a ship-building centre. More than 50 naval ships were built at Buckler's Hard, amongst them one of Nelson's favourite ships, the *Agamemnon*. Displays include models of ships, among them *Victory*, *Agamemnon* and the yacht *Bluebottle*, which Prince Philip raced with success. A special display recounts the exploits of Sir Francis Chichester, who sailed round the world in *Gypsy Moth* from his home port of Buckler's Hard.

A lovely riverside walk passes through Bailey's Hard, a former brickworks where the first naval vessel built on the river was completed in 1698. Henry Adams, the most distinguished of a family of shipbuilders, lived in the village in what is now the Master

Buckler's Hard

Beaulieu, Hampshire

On the banks of the Beaulieu River, in the heart of the New Forest, you will find the picturesque village of Buckler's Hard. With a beautiful setting, riverside walk and river cruises to enjoy, Buckler's Hard is one of the most attractive and unusual villages in England. Yet there is also much to see and do in this unique village where time has almost stood still since the days when wooden ships were built here for Nelson's fleet.

The Buckler's Hard Story reflects the history of the village, from its origins as a port for importing sugar cane from the West Indies, through its shipbuilding history covering the construction of more than 50 naval and merchant vessels that were built here. Displays include models of the ships that were built for Lord Nelson, featuring his favourite, *HMS Agamemnon*, and other items of memorabilia. Historic cottage displays portray life at Buckler's Hard in 1793 and residents of the time gossip about local matters in the re-constructed Village Inn. Recent history of the village is portrayed through the river's role in the D-Day landings during World War II.

At the bottom of the Village street take a cruise on the tranquil Beaulieu River in *Swiftsure* which runs between April and October. A lively commentary bringing the history of the Beaulieu River to life and some magnificent scenery makes for a lively and memorable trip, not to be missed. The delightful Riverside Walk takes you through woodland to the village of Beaulieu.

Refreshment opportunities are available both at the Captain's Cabin Cafeteria, near the main entrance, and at the Master Builder's House Hotel. A wide range of gifts is available at the gift shop and there is even a Village Store.

🏠 historic building   🏛 museum   🏛 historic site   🌄 scenic attraction   🌿 flora and fauna

Builders Hotel. In the summer, half-hour cruises on *Swiftsure* depart from the pier at Buckler's Hard.

FAWLEY
5 miles E of Beaulieu on the A326

Oil is king here, and the terminals and refineries of what is probably the largest oil plant in Europe create a science fiction landscape; standing bravely apart is the village church, a link with earlier days, looking out over Southampton Water. Fawley is where some islanders from Tristan da Cunha settled after fleeing a volcano that threatened their island in 1961; a model of one of the boats they used for their escape can be seen in the chapel. Also of note in Fawley is Cadland House, whose eight-acre garden overlooking the Solent was designed for the banker Robert Drummond by Capability Brown. It houses the National Collection of Leptospermums and also features a splendid kitchen garden and a modern walled garden. Beyond the refineries a road leads off the B3053 Calshot road to **Ashlett Creek** and another world, the natural, unrefined world of creeks, mud flats and bird-haunted marshland.

CALSHOT
14 miles SE of Lyndhurst on the B3053

🏰 Castle

The RAF was based in both world wars at Calshot, where seaplanes were prepared and tested for the Schneider Trophy races. The hangars once used by the RAF are now the Calshot Activity Centre, whose many activities include an artificial ski slope. At the very end of a shingle spit stands one of Henry VIII's coastal defence castles. This is **Calshot Castle**, which is now restored as a pre-World War I garrison. Visitors can admire the view from the roof of the keep, walk round the

barrack room that looks as it did before World War I and see the exhibition of the Schneider air races. A little way to the west is Lepe, one of the major embarkation points for the 1944 D-Day invasion. The area at the top of the cliffs at Lepe is now a country park, and there's safe swimming off the beach.

EXBURY
10 miles SE of Lyndhurst off the B3054

🏛 Church of St Catherine 🌿 Exbury Gardens

Created by Lionel de Rothschild in the 1920s and still run by members of the family, **Exbury Gardens** fully justify the reaction of one visitor, who described them as 'Heaven with the gates open'. 150 gardeners and workmen took 10 years to create the gardens, and Rothschild sent expeditions to the Himalayas to find the seeds he wanted. He himself bred hundreds of varieties of plants and the displays of rhododendrons, camellias and azaleas which he planted are renowned the world over. The 200-acre grounds are a delight to visit in spring, summer or autumn, with May perhaps the best time of all. A leisurely way of seeing the gardens is by taking a trip on the narrow-gauge steam railway. Many varieties of the Exbury specialities are on sale in the plant centre, where there's also a gift shop, tea room and restaurant – there is free entry to all of these.

Exbury's **Church of St Catherine** is best known for its moving, lifelike bronze memorial to two brothers who were killed in action in World War l. The work was commissioned by the brothers' parents and executed by Cecil Thomas, a gifted young sculptor who was a friend of the brothers. The area around Exbury and Lepe is featured in Nevil Shute's sad story *Requiem for a Wren*, which describes the preparations made in the New Forest for the D-Day landings. Shute

CLAIRE-ROSE INTERIORS

Brockley Road, Brockenhurst, Hampshire
Tel: 01590 623977 Fax: 01590 624060
e-mail: jan.goodall@virgin.net

Brockenhurst is a lovely place to visit and to shop, a jewel amid ancient woodland with many interesting specialist shops. Among these outlets **Claire-Rose Interiors** is outstanding. This is an interior design company with a large retail store selling furniture, accessories for the home and a wide range of glassware and gifts for the discerning shopper. The company has been owned and run for 21 years by Jan Stillwell-Goodall, who has made it known as *the* Interior Designers in the New Forest and Hampshire region. Jan is also able to travel to other locations in the UK and overseas to advise on projects. Claire-Rose stocks all the major designers of fabrics and wallpapers and provides a full design and making-up service together with facilities for upholstery, carpets, flooring, lighting, carpentry, decorating, blinds and shutters and a design and installation service for bathrooms and kitchens.

They are also specialists in paints, with paints mixed on the premises according to customers' requirements, and colour boards and illustrations are available. Paints are a growing side of the business, and brands in stock include **Fired Earth**, **Zoffany**, **Sanderson**, **Little Green Paint Company**, **Farrow & Ball** and **Earthborn Clay Paints**.

In Jan's words, 'creating memorable design means breaking with convention' and she is always ready to discuss projects both large and small with existing and prospective clients. Personal service has always been a keynote of Claire-Rose Interiors, which is open from 10 to 4 Monday to Friday, and from 10 to 2 Saturday; other times by appointment.

THATCHED COTTAGE

Gastronomic Restaurant with Rooms
16 Brookley Road, Brockenhurst, Hampshire SO42 7RR
Tel: 01590 623090 e-mail: sales@thatchedcottage.co.uk
Fax: 01590 623479 website: www.thatchedcottage.co.uk

The 400-year-old, timber-framed **Thatched Cottage Hotel & Restaurant** is situated in the picturesque village of Brockenhurst, in the heart of the New Forest, England's 'youngest' National Park. It provides the ideal opportunity to escape from the daily routine and enjoy comfort, hospitality, personal service and fine food and wine, all in a lovely relaxed ambience. The house is owned and run by the Matysik family, whose intimate involvement in all aspects of the enterprise has earned accolades in many leading hotel and restaurant guides. Martin Matysik, head chef/proprietor, creates delicious lunches or sumptuous evening meals, with his experience in international hospitality using only the freshest local produce. The guest accommodation comprise of five individually decorated rooms, with en-suite facilities, antique furniture, supremely comfortable beds, TV, mini-bar and complimentary tea/coffee tray.

All rooms are named after blends of single Estate Teas and an award-winning cream tea, quoted 'better than the Ritz' is served all year round. Other highlights are the elegant 'al fresco' area and speciality picnic hampers to take with you, to explore the magnificent surroundings of the enchanting New Forest.

himself was an aero-engineer as well as a writer, and for a time worked here on a top-secret pilotless plane.

BROCKENHURST

3 miles S of Lyndhurst on the A337

🏛 Church of St Nicholas

A large village in a lovely setting in the heart of the New Forest. Forest ponies are frequent visitors to the main street and the village green (they naturally have right of way!). The **Church of St Nicholas** has a vast graveyard with a yew tree that is probably the oldest tree in the whole region. In the graveyard lie many soldiers, many of them from New Zealand, who had died of their injuries in a nearby military hospital. But the best known grave is that of Harry Mills, known as Brusher Mills,

who brushed the New Forest cricket pitch and worked as a snake-catcher.

Lymington

🏛 St Barbe Museum

An ancient seaport and market town, Lymington was once a major manufacturer of salt, with hundreds of salt pans between the quay and the tip of the promontory at Hurst Castle. **St Barbe Museum**, in New Street, tells the story of the area between the New Forest and the Solent, with special reference to the salt industry (salt was made here beside the sea for hundreds of years), boatbuilding, smuggling and the area at war. There is also a changing exhibition of the work of artists both local and world-renowned – the gallery

BRITANNIA GUEST HOUSE

Mill Lane, Lymington,
Hampshire SO41 9AY
Tel: 01590 672091
website: www.britannia-house.com

On the corner of Mill Lane and Station Street, **Britannia Guest House** is an ideal base for discovering the sights of Lymington and for touring the region. The accommodation comprises six luxurious en-suite double bedrooms, and guests have the use of a lounge with stunning views over the harbour and marinas, and a leafy courtyard garden. A superb four-course breakfast is served in the cosy farmhouse kitchen.

Owner, and perfect host, Tobias Feilke bought this property in 2000 and has put it among the top guest houses in the area, with 5 Diamonds and the ETC Silver Award. Personal service is very much to the fore, and Tobias has generated a real home-from-home atmosphere in the house. Britannia, a non-smoking establishment, has its own parking spaces and a lockable bicycle shed. The house can be made available for rent as a self-catering base for up to 12 guests.

🎭 stories and anecdotes   🐦 famous people   🎨 art and craft   🎟 entertainment and sport   🚶 walks

JAEGER

Rashley Mews, High Street,
Lymington, SO41 9AR
Tel: 01590 678259 - 679913

JAEGER is known worldwide for its stylish clothing ranges for both men and women and you'll find all the latest fashions in their new premises in Rashley Mews opposite the post office. Drawing from their ancestry in the 19th century, Jaeger has sourced the finest natural fibres to create capsule wardrobes that epitomise the best in quality and craftsmanship. Classic and modern styling in coordinating tailoring from couture chic to businesswear or simple and elegant pieces which then blend with sumptuous cashmere, silk/linen and cotton elements designed for customers with a more relaxed lifestyle.

Finish the look with accessories such as scarves, gloves, bags, belts, cufflinks, umbrellas, wallets and jewellery designed exclusively for Jaeger and you definitely have collectors items! The staff of Jaeger Lymington are only too pleased to offer advice in how to create a new versatile wardrobe, or to add onto existing favourites, as well as caring for your purchases.
Enjoy the experience!

THE MILL AT GORDLETON

Silver Street, nr Lymington, Hampshire SO41 6DJ
Tel: 01590 682219 Fax: 01590 683073
e-mail: info@themillatgordleton.co.uk
website: www.themillatgordleton.co.uk

Two miles from Lymington and a short drive from the New Forest, **The Mill at Gordleton** is a delightful, privately owned restaurant with rooms, a real pleasure to visit whether for a meal or for a stay in the most pleasant and civilised surroundings. Cooking combines classical skills with contemporary influences on menus that provide a tempting choice for all tastes and appetites. Typical dishes from the lunchtime menu include seafood and sweetcorn chowder, Thai chicken and tiger prawn curry and devilled kidneys in a Dijon mustard and cayenne cream, while the evening menu tempts with delights such as twice-baked smoked salmon and dill soufflé, or fillet of Aberdeenshire beef with portabella mushrooms and stilton, garlic mash, roasted shallots and a balsamic vinegar jus. The desserts keep the enjoyment level sky high, and the food is complemented by a 50-strong wine list with many available by the glass.

The guest accommodation comprises seven lovely bedrooms, each with its own character; top of the range is a gorgeous suite with a beamed sitting room overlooking the river, with the millstream running below, king-size bed and corner jacuzzi bath. The river and the lovely gardens are a great bonus at The Mill, and on a lucky day guests might glimpse a heron or even a kingfisher.

🏛 historic building 🏛 museum 🏛 historic site 🦢 scenic attraction 🌿 flora and fauna

BASKING COD

15 Gosport Street, Lymington, Hampshire SO41 9BG
Tel: 01590 670164 e-mail: sales@baskingcod.co.uk
website: www.baskingcod.com

Welcome to the colourful land of Basking Cod, where the most interesting world of gifts has been stylishly displayed. Within this land there are two floors, ranging from the very kitsch to the more designer, catering for children to the more 'growed up'. Many of the items have a fresh, quirky and humerous angle. 'Cod' favorites include Alessi kitchenware, Rice homewares from Denmark, Disaster Designs retro gifts and Suck Uk British design products.

The range of mens and ladies clothing, cushions, childrens

has in the past hosted works by artists as diverse as David Hockney and Goya. The broad High Street leading up from the quay is a hive of activity on Saturday, when the market established in the 13th century is held.

The Isle of Wight ferry runs from Walhampton, just outside Lymington, where a notable building is the Neale Obelisk, a memorial to Admiral Neale erected in 1840.

Around Lymington

BOLDRE

2 miles N of Lymington, on the A337

"The village is here, there, and everywhere," wrote Arthur Mee in the 1930s, struggling to give some literary shape to an agglomeration of hamlets – Portmore, Pilley and Sandy Down,

WARBORNE ORGANIC FARM

Warborne Lane, Boldre, nr Lymington, Hampshire
Tel: 01590 688488
website: www.warbornefarm.co.uk
e-mail: boxscheme@warborne.fsnet.co.uk

Owner George Heathcote's grandfather started farming here, establishing the farm's reputation for quality. Everything produced at **Warborne Organic Farm** is the very finest, organic and totally traceable. Meat and poultry are produced from animals raised on the farm, and customers can have packs made to their individual requirements. The seasonal fruit, vegetables, herbs and flowers are also home-grown, and the pick of locally sourced supplies on sale at the farm are of the same high quality.

The 360 acres of deep sandy loam provide ideal growing conditions, and the local microclimate allows luxury fruits such as grapes and figs to thrive. An increasingly popular offering is an award-winning box scheme, where seasonal fruit and veg is delivered weekly to local households. Warborne Farm is much more than just a farm and farm shop: there are open days when visitors can learn about the methods and aims of organic farming, walks around the farm, and a monthly newsletter with the latest news and recipe ideas.

📖 stories and anecdotes   🐦 famous people   🎨 art and craft   ✐ entertainment and sport   🚶 walks

APPLE COURT NURSERY & GARDEN

Hordle Lane, Hordle,
Hampshire SO41 0HU
Tel: 01590 642130
Fax: 01590 644220
e-mail: applecourt@btinternet.com
website: www.applecourt.com

Angela and Charles Meads are the joint proprietors of **Apple Court Nursery and Garden**, which they have established as one of the finest in all Hampshire. The formal garden at Apple Court has been developed since 1988 in the abandoned walled kitchen garden of Yeatton House, situated in rich farmland between the New Forest and the Solent.

The garden was designed as a series of interlocking areas, each intended to create a distinct visual impression and to have a microclimate best suited to its particular plants. Different interests succeed each other throughout the year, starting with snowdrops and hellebores, followed by pulmonarias, roses and peonies. The Hosta Walks come into their own in April and are followed by the Daylily Garden; this holds centre stage until the grasses take over through August and into the winter. Among many other features in this unique spot is a new Japanese garden, complete with tea house and pond.

The nursery was originally the frameyard, where seeds were raised in frames and grown on before being set out in the garden. The nursery contains a delightful selection of rare and unusual plants, offering something for the dedicated plantsman as well as the amateur gardener. Of particular interest are some magnolia relatives growing against the south-facing walls and a number of new and rare grasses, sedges, ferns and hostas. The nursery reflects the owners' chief interests – hostas, daylilies, ferns, grasses, scented plants and plants coloured black or purple. Specimens of many of the plants they offer in the nursery shop can be seen growing in the steadily maturing garden.

Opening times are 10am to 5pm Friday, Saturday, Sunday and Bank Holiday Mondays March to end October. The garden, but not the nursery, is suitable for visitors in wheelchairs. Dogs are not admitted. The owners are happy to greet all guests, including photographers and artists. Group parties from flower clubs and horticultural societies are always welcome, and other visiting times can be arranged with notice.

A two-bedroom cottage attached to the main house provides a delightful base for a self-catering break in beautiful, tranquil surroundings.

which together make up the parish of Boldre. Mee approved of the medieval church, with its squat square tower, standing isolated on a hill-top, and also paid due tribute to its 18th century rector, the Revd William Gilpin, whose books describing travels around Britain achieved cult status during his lifetime and even received a mention in Jane Austen's novel, *Sense and Sensibility*. Summing up his view of the village, Mee declared that, "The quaint simplicity of Boldre is altogether charming". Some 70 years later, there's little reason to dispute his description.

In School Lane, Spinners is a charming, informal woodland garden with a national collection of trilliums.

SWAY
3 miles N of Lymington off the A337

🏛 Peterson's Tower 🎨 Artsway

This rural village and the surrounding countryside were the setting for much of Captain Marryatt's *Children of the New Forest*, an exciting tale set in the time of the Civil War and written a year before Marryatt died in 1848. In Station Road, **Artsway** is a visual arts centre that was originally a coach house; the site contains a garden and a gallery. South of the village is a famous 220ft folly called **Peterson's Tower**. This curiosity was built by a retired judge, Andrew Peterson, in honour of his late wife and as proof of the efficacy of concrete. The tower was originally topped by a light that could be seen for many miles, but it was removed on the orders of Trinity House as a potential source of confusion to shipping. The judge's ashes were buried at the base of his folly but were later moved to be next to his wife in the churchyard at Sway.

MILFORD-ON-SEA
4 miles SW of Lymington, on the B3058

🏛 Church of All Saints 🏛 Hurst Castle

This sizeable coastal village is most notable for its fine, remarkably well-preserved 13th century **Church of All Saints;** its grand views across the Solent to the Isle of Wight, and the odd-looking construction called **Hurst Castle.** At the centre of Hurst Castle is a squat fort built by Henry VIII to guard the Solent entrance against incursions by the French. Its tower is flanked by two long low wings added in the 1860s for gun emplacements, the square openings making them look rather like shopping arcades. The castle was used a garrison right up until World War II but is now in the care of English Heritage which has an on-site exhibition explaining its history.

Hurst Castle stands at the tip of a long gravel spit which stretches out across the Solent to within three quarters of a mile of the Isle of Wight coast. It can only be reached by a 1.5 mile walk along the shingle beach or, in the summer months, by ferries operating from Keyhaven Quay, one mile east of Milford-on-Sea. The excursion makes a pleasant day or half-day trip since in addition

Hurst Castle, Near Lymington

Keyhaven

Distance: *4.9 miles (7.8 kilometres)*

Typical time: *165 mins*

Height gain: *0 metres*

Map: *Outdoor Leisure 29 & 22*

Walk: *www.walkingworld.com ID:1327*

Contributor: *Graham Hollier*

ACCESS INFORMATION:

Take the A337 New Milton/Lymington road and take the B3058 to Milford-On Sea. At junction turn left and left again, signed to Keyhaven (Hurst Castle) one mile. Continue along this road for just under a mile until you arrive at the Gun Inn on your right. Just past the Gun Inn, on your left, is the car park used for the start of the walk (toilets available).

ADDITIONAL INFORMATION:

At the start or the end of the walk, an excursion can be made to Hurst Castle which you will see, together with a lighthouse at the end of a shingle spit. This castle, completed in 1544, was built by Henry VIII to defend the western approaches to Portsmouth. Charles 1st was imprisoned here in 1648 on his way to London and execution, from Carisbrooke Castle on the IoW. The castle was modernised during the Napoleonic Wars and modernised again in the 1860s when large armoured wings were built. It saw active service during WW2, being manned with searchlights and coastal guns to protect against invasion. It is well worth a visit and combined with the walk, makes an excellent day out.

DESCRIPTION:

This is an easy-going short walk with plenty to see. If you are interested in birdlife, the sea,

history, bracing air, then this walk is a must. Much of it is along the Solent Way. Pennington and Keyhaven Marshes were, from the middle ages until the mid-1800s, used for salt extraction. Before refrigeration, meat was salted as a preservative. One large consumer was the dockyard at Portsmouth, for naval ships. The name 'Keyhaven' is reputed to come from the Saxon word 'cy-haefenn' - roughly translated as meaning "the harbour where cows were shipped". If you have binoculars, do take them - they may be put to good use.

FEATURES:

Lake/Loch, Pub, Toilets, Castle, Wildlife, Birds, Great Views, Butterflies, Mostly Flat, Ancient Monument

WALK DIRECTIONS:

1 | From car park, take a lane almost opposite the Gun Inn heading 080, keeping Keyhaven Harbour to the right. Continue on lane walking past a signpost, 'no vehicles beyond 200 yards ahead'. Walk on past a five- barred gate, small access to the left without having to climb over.

2 | In about 100 yards is a large, rusty green gate. There is a broken stile to the left of this; go through on to pathway, Iley Lane. Continue on this lane, keeping the quarry/landfill workings to your right. This can be a bit smelly but attracts a number of birds. The walk goes through this area for about a mile but it is well worth it for the coastal walk to which it leads. The Isle of Wight is visible on the right. Continue until you reach a council amenity tip which is 0.9 miles from the start of the walk.

3 | Cross a stile in front of you, cross a roadway servicing the amenity tip and make

for a track directly opposite, heading 082 and keeping the landfill workings to your left. After 1.1 miles of quarry/landfill workings you arrive at a six-barred metal gate. Go past the gate and walk on on a metalled roadway. Here you are surrounded by pleasant fields and hedgerows. Continue to a green metal six-barred gate.

4 | There is a small gap at the right of the gate; pass through on to a road and turn left.

5 | In about 150 yards, there is a stile and a footpath leading through a hedge on your right (opposite some farm buildings on your left). Cross the stile, keeping the field edge on your right, until you arrive at a further stile. Cross this stile, making for some houses straight in front of you. About 150 yards before you reach the houses is a stile in the hedge on your right. Cross this stile and immediately turn left, making for a path which is situated to the left of the garden fence in front of you. Cross a stile and continue on to a further stile which is also crossed. Make for a metalled driveway , which shortly leads on to a road.

6 | At the road, turn left, passing (or stopping!) at the Chequers public house on your left. Just past the Chequers the road forks. Take the right fork and walk along Platoff Road. This point is 1.5 miles from the start

of the walk. In 300 yards is a bench on your right, with a road also leading off to your right. Take this road, signed 'Maiden Lane leading to Normandy Lane'.

7 | In 180 yards, at a fork in the road turn right into Maiden Lane.

8 | Follow road around to the right, through a yacht club yard and passing the clubhouse on the left. Continue on to join the Solent Way, where the walk now becomes an absolute delight. Continue on this path. Excellent views are available here of saltwater inlets, the IoW and an abundance of nature and wildlife. Take an unmade road to the left of the 'Salterns'. Path gives way to a delightful pathway, leading

Continued overleaf

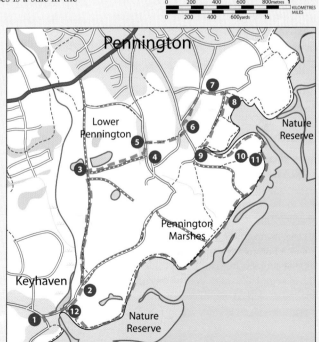

through a canopy of small trees and shrubs. Continue along this.

9 | Continue on this track until you arrive at a clearing with a farm building on your left and a house on your right. Walk past the front of the house. Immediately past the house, turn left over a stile to walk along a pathway, keeping the waterway on the left. Keep on this pathway until you reach a stile; cross and make for a pair of lock gates which are easily visible from this point.

10 | At the lock gates, continue along the sea defence wall (the sea is on the left all the way back to the start of the walk now) .

11 | In the background is the sea with the Lymington/Yarmouth ferry just visible on the right. The foreground shows an area of marshland/old salt extraction workings, prevalent now to the end of the walk. Birdlife is prolific here throughout the year. The relatively rare little egret (a small version of a grey heron), white with black legs and yellow feet, is normally to be seen. Continue on the sea defence wall for a stunning two-mile walk; take your time, there is plenty to see.

12 | If you have energy to spare, a trip can be taken to Hurst Castle. It can be reached by ferry which is just a short walk from the car park. Alternatively, you can walk/drive around to the start of the shingle spit and walk along this to the castle (hard work, walking on the shingle). Turn left when leaving the car park. If walking, go to sea wall and turn right until you reach the shingle spit. Alternatively if driving, turn left from the car park and follow the road for half a mile. Park on roadway in the spaces marked out, when you reach the shingle spit.

Milford-on-Sea

to the castle itself there's safe bathing north of the lighthouse, good fishing off the southern tip of the spit, and spectacular views of The Needles as well as of huge ships making their way up The Solent.

NEW MILTON
5 miles W of Lymington on the A337

🏰 Water Tower   🏍 Sammy Miller Museum

🎨 Forest Arts

If you were allowed to see only one visitor attraction in New Milton, you would have a difficult choice. One option is the town's splendid **Water Tower** of 1900. Late-Victorian providers of water services seem to have enjoyed pretending that their storage towers and sewage treatment plants were really castles of the Middle Ages. They built these mock-medieval structures all around the country, but the one at New Milton is particularly striking. Three storeys high, with a castellated parapet, the octagonal building has tall, narrow windows.

Devotees of vintage motorcycles will make for a very different attraction. The **Sammy Miller Museum,** to the west of the town, is widely regarded as one of the best motorcycle museums in the world. Sammy Miller is a legend in his own lifetime, still winning competitions almost half a century after his first racing victory. More than 300 rare and exotic motorcycles are on display here. Also within the museum complex are a craft shop, tea rooms and a children's play area.

If you are more interested in the arts, you'll be pleased to hear about **Forest Arts** in New Milton. Music of all kinds is on offer, from jazz, salsa and blues, to traditional and classical matinée concerts. Performances are conveniently timed so that you can arrive after picking up the kids from school. Other daytime events include slide talks by experts on a wide range of topics. Forest Arts also hosts some of the best contemporary dance companies around, ensembles who have

performed at The Place in London and indeed all over the world. And if you enjoy the buzz and excitement of seeing new, vibrant theatre, the type of theatre which is on offer at the Edinburgh Fringe Festival for example, Forest Arts provides that as well.

Ringwood

Meeting House   Monmouth House

Moors Valley Country Park

Wednesday morning is a good time to visit Ringwood since that is when its market square is filled with a notable variety of colourful stalls. The town has expanded greatly in recent years but its centre still boasts a large number of elegant Georgian houses, both large and small. **Ringwood Meeting House**, built in 1727 and now a museum, is an outstanding example of an

LIBERTY'S RAPTOR AND REPTILE CENTRE

Crow Lane, Crow, nr Ringwood, Hampshire BH24 3EA
Tel: 01425 476487
e-mail: libertyscentre@virgin.net
website: www.libertyscentre.co.uk

Just off the A31 five minutes from Ringwood, **Liberty's Raptor and Reptile Centre** gives visitors the opportunity of getting up close to a huge variety of birds and reptiles not normally encountered. The Centre is named after one of the stars of the show, Liberty, an American bald eagle, who is just one of dozens of birds housed here. Some 30 individual birds are flown in different sessions on a typical day, including eagles, hooded vultures and tawny owls.

There are regular falconry demonstrations and training courses, and the Centre also has a rescue centre for injured birds of prey. The reptiles include snakes, iguanas, lizards and an 11-stone Burmese python called Cuddles, and visitors can learn all about these creatures in the reptile lectures.

stories and anecdotes   famous people   art and craft   entertainment and sport   walks

THE MAGPIE'S NEST

Ringwood Road, Burley, Hampshire BH24 4BU
Tel: 01425 402404

Burley is a delightful village nestling in the heart of the New Forest where ponies and cattle roam freely amongst its many visitors. Right in the centre lies a little gem called the **Magpie's Nest**, a charming 100-year-old shop with an amazing selection of gold and silver gemstone jewellery. It also has a wonderful selection of unique gifts and antiques to suit all tastes and pockets. Some items to treasure both for now and the future, including Beswick, Wedgwood, Goebel and Portmeirion to name but a few.

Vanessa and her friendly staff will greet you with a warm welcome and assist you with choosing those all important gifts. Outside the famous Burley icecream parlour is a must, with a tantalising assortment of toppings and sauces. Don't leave without trying one.

RAINBOWS END

The Cross, Burley, nr Ringwood,
Hampshire BH24 4AB
Tel: 01425 402141 Fax: 01590 670510
e-mail: sales@rainbowsendgifts.co.uk

In the centre of Burley, in an area recently awarded National Park status, Rainbows End is a marvellous little shop filled with quality giftware for all occasions and things to enhance the home and garden.

Owner Caryl Kent has assembled a truly eclectic selection of items both traditional and contemporary, from pictures and plaques to ceramics and pots, jewellery from Zilver Designs, Compulsion pewter sculptures and wooden pieces from East of India.

Useful gifts for men include sporting memorabilia, wine box sets and desktop gadgets, and accessories large and small for the garden range from patio sets to tea lights, plant sticks and bird baths .Burley lies in great walking country between the A31 and A35, and visitors working up a thirst should know that this is also great cider country.

🏛 historic building   🏛 museum   🏛 historic site   ♧ scenic attraction   🌱 flora and fauna

early Nonconformist chapel, complete with the original, rather austere, fittings. **Monmouth House** is of about the same period and stands on the site of an earlier house in which the luckless Duke of Monmouth was confined after his unsuccessful uprising against James II. The duke had been discovered hiding in a ditch just outside the town and despite his abject pleas to the king to spare his life he was beheaded at Tower Hill a few days later.

Five miles west of the town stretch the great expanses of Ringwood Forest, which includes the **Moors Valley Country Park**. At the heart of the park stands an 18th century timber barn which is home to the Visitor Centre, where you will find a restaurant, a coffee shop, a gift shop and an exhibition area. A variety of other attractions including children's play areas, walks and cycle routes, and an 18-hole golf course can also be found here. Particularly popular are the Tree Top Trail which offers the opportunity to walk on a wooden walkway through the tops of the trees, and the Play Trail with its wooden structures, including 'Giant Ants' Nest', 'Snakes and Ladders' and 'Spiders Web'. Another popular attractions here is the Moors Valley Railway, a delightful narrow gauge steam railway with rails just 7¼ inches apart. The railway has 11 locomotives, all in different liveries, and 33 passenger vehicles. The signal box at Kingsmere, the main station, was purpose-built but all the equipment inside comes from old redundant signal boxes – the main signal lever frame for example came from the Becton Gas Works in East London. At Kingsmere Station, in addition to the Ticket Office and the Engine and Carriage Sheds, there's also a Railway Shop, Buffet and Model Railway Shop.

Around Ringwood

BURLEY
4 miles SE of Ringwood, on minor road off A31

At Burley, it's very clear that you are in the heart of the New Forest, with woodland running right through the village. A pleasant way to experience the peacefulness of the surrounding forest is to take a trip with Burley Wagonette Rides which run from the centre of the village. Rides in the open wagons last from 20 minutes to 1½ hours and are available from Easter to October. The village is also home to New Forest Cider where farmhouse cider is still made the old-fashioned way from local orchard apples and cider fruit. Visitors can taste and buy draught cider from barrels stored in the former cowshed. The centre is open most times throughout the year although ideally you should time your visit to coincide with pressing time, when the grand old cider press is in operation.

FORDINGBRIDGE
7 miles N of Ringwood, on the A338

🏠 Alderholt Mill

The painter Augustus John (1878-1961) loved Fordingbridge, a pleasant riverside town with a graceful medieval seven-arched bridge spanning the River Avon. He spent much of the last 30 years of his life at Fryern Court, a rather austere Georgian house just north of the town (not open to the public, but visible from the road). Scandalous stories of the Bohemian life-style he indulged in there circulated around the town but didn't deter the townspeople from erecting a strikingly vigorous statue to his memory in a park near the bridge.

ST MARTIN'S GALLERY

The Old Church, Mockbeggar Lane,
Ibsley, Hampshire BH24 3PP
Tel: 01425 489090 Fax: 01202 848188
e-mail: stmartins@ibsleyhants.freeserve.co.uk
website: www.stmartinsartandcrfatcentre.com
website: www.silkflowersbypost.com

St Martin's Gallery is located in the village of Ibsley, just off the A338 north of Ringwood. It is housed in the mid-17th century Church of St Martin, which was partially restored after a fire in 1832. Deconsecrated in 1986, it fell derelict before being bought by Pamela Denton and restored in 1998. She converted it into an art gallery while retaining the original altar, font and organ in the design. The gallery shows a wide and continually changing exhibition of local and international arts and crafts including many unique pieces, paintings and limited edition prints.

For many visitors the star of the show is the spectacular array of silk flowers and beautiful arrangements, and also featured are glassware, jewellery, pottery, ceramics, sculptures in wood and stone, furniture and some delightful bespoke teddies and gollies. The gallery is open for visits from 11am to 5pm Thursday to Sunday.

Branksome China Works is well worth a visit. Visitors can see how the firm, established in 1945, makes its fine porcelain tableware and famous animal studies.

On the edge of the town, there's a special treat for anyone who savours daft public notices. As a prime example of useless information, it would be hard to beat the trim little 18th century milepost which informs the traveller:

Fordingbridge: 0.

Two miles west of Fordingbridge off the B3078 - follow the signposts - is **Alderholt Mill**, a restored working water-powered corn mill standing on Ashford Water, a tributary of the Hampshire Avon. The site includes an arts and crafts shop and a place for the sale of refreshments and baking from the mill's own flour.

BREAMORE

3 miles N of Fordingbridge on the A338

🏛 Breamore House 🏛 Countryside Museum

🍃 Breamore Down

Breamore is a lovely and largely unspoilt 17th century village with a very interesting little church with Saxon windows and other artefacts. Most notable, in the south porch, is a

Mizmaze, Breamore Down

Rockbourne Roman Villa

Rockbourne, Fordingbridge, Hampshire SP6 3PG
Tel: 01725 518541

Rockbourne Roman Villa, the largest of its kind in the region, was discovered in 1942 when oyster shells and tiles were found by a farmer in the course of digging out a ferret. A local chartered surveyor and noted antiquarian, the late AT Morley Hewitt, recognised the significance of the finds and devoted 30 years of his life to the villa. Excavations of the site, which is set in idyllic countryside, have revealed superb mosaics, part of the amazing underfloor heating system and the outline of the great villa's 40 rooms. Many of the hundreds of objects unearthed are on display in the site's museum, and souvenirs are for sale in the well-stocked museum shop.

Saxon rood, or crucifixion scene. **Breamore House**, set above the village overlooking the Avon Valley, was built in 1583 and contains some fine paintings, including works of the 17th and 18th century Dutch School and a unique set of 14 Mexican ethnological paintings; superb period furniture in oak, walnut and mahogany; a very rare James I carpet and many other items of historical and family interest. The house has been the home of the Hulse family for well over 250 years, having been purchased in the early 18th century by Sir Edward Hulse, Physician in Ordinary at the Courts of Queen Anne, George I and George II. In the grounds of the house, the **Countryside Museum** is a reconstructed Tudor village with a wealth of rural implements and machinery, replicas of a farm worker's cottage, smithy, dairy, brewery, saddler's shop, cobbler's shop, general store, laundry and school. Amenities for visitors include a tea shop and a children's adventure play area. The Museum's Millennium Project was the restoration of an extremely rare Bavarian four-train turret clock of the 16th century. On **Breamore Down** is one of those oddities whose origins and purpose remain something of a mystery: this is a mizmaze, a

circular maze cut in the turf down as far as the chalk. Further north can be seen part of Grim's Ditch, built in late-Roman times as a defence against the Saxons.

ROCKBOURNE

3 miles NW of Fordingbridge off the B3078

🏛 Roman Villa

One of the prettiest villages in the region, Rockbourne lies by a gentle stream at the bottom of a valley. An attraction that brings in visitors by the thousand is **Rockbourne Roman Villa** (see panel above), the largest of its kind in the region. It was discovered in 1942 when oyster shells and tiles were found by a farmer as he was digging out a ferret. Excavations of the site, which is set in idyllic surroundings, have revealed superb mosaics, part of the amazing underfloor heating system and the outline of the great villa's 40 rooms. Many of the hundreds of objects unearthed are on display in the site's museum and souvenirs are on sale in the well-stocked museum shop.

A mile or so beyond the Roman Villa, looking out on to the downs, is the little village of **Whitsbury**, a major centre for the breeding and training of racehorses.

LOCATOR MAP

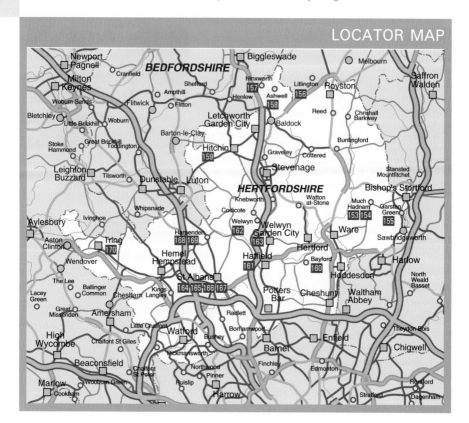

ADVERTISERS AND PLACES OF INTEREST

🏭 historic building   🏛 museum   🏚 historic site   🔍 scenic attraction   🌾 flora and fauna

6| Hertfordshire

The novelist EM Forster, who lived in the county, described Hertfordshire as "England at its quietest; England meditative". When he wrote that in the 1950s the county's population was just over 600,000; it has now topped one million. The more southerly towns expanded as residential areas for London commuters, and after World War II, with an acute housing shortage in the blitzed capital, New Towns such as Stevenage were created to cater for the thousands of Londoners who had lost their homes.

But the centre of the county is still largely agricultural and the southern edge lies within the precarious protection of the Metropolitan Green Belt. There is still some excellent walking and splendid scenery, most notably within the National Trust's Ashridge Estate, where the woodlands and downlands are home to a wide variety of wildlife, and the views from the highest points are magnificent.

The strongest historical ties in the county are to be found in the ancient city of St Albans, while Hatfield combines old and new elements: it was designated a New Town after World War II, but the old town survives, along with the magnificent Hatfield House and part of the medieval Royal Palace, which was the childhood home of the future Elizabeth I.

Close to Hatfield lies Welwyn Garden City, conceived by Ebenezer Howard and built in the 1920s with the aim of providing working people with a pleasant and attractive place to live, with easy access to the countryside. One of the best known monuments in Hertfordshire is the Eleanor Cross at Waltham Cross, one of 13 such crosses erected by Edward I to commemorate the resting places of the funeral cortege of his Queen, Eleanor of Castile.

Cottages at Much Hadham

Bishop's Stortford

🏛 St Michael's Church   📷 Museum

🌳 Rhodes Museum

The old Roman road from St Albans to Colchester forded the river here and some nine centuries later the Saxon king Edward the Elder built a castle to protect the crossing. His fortress has disappeared but the great mound on which it was built survives in the town's spacious Castle Gardens. In about 1060 the whole town was sold to the Bishops of London, hence its name. In medieval times Bishop's Stortford was a stopping place on the route between London and both Newmarket and Cambridge and became famous for its many hostelries. Even today, the town still boasts three inns dating back to the 15th and

16th centuries. In the 20th century, the building of Stansted Airport, just seven miles away, has brought the town within easy reach of Europe and beyond.

In the compact town centre markets are still held twice a week, on Thursdays and Saturdays, as they have been for centuries and, standing high on a hill, **St Michael's Church** dominates the surrounding countryside. Inside, a memorial commemorates the life of Cecil Rhodes, son of a former Rector. The great imperialist's exploits are also documented in his former home, Nettlewell House, now the **Rhodes Museum and Commonwealth Centre**.

The Rhodes Museum forms part of the **Bishop's Stortford Museum** which contains an exhibit celebrating another famous son – Sir Walter Gilbey who founded the famous gin firm when he was living at nearby Elsenham Hall in the 1860s.

Around Bishop's Stortford

MUCH HADHAM
4 miles W of Bishop's Stortford on B1004

📷 Forge Museum   🌳 Perry Green

A large and largely unspoilt village, which still retains many old timber-framed houses and cottages, the oldest of which dates back to the 15th century. The **Forge Museum and Victorian Cottage Garden** not only tells the story of the work of the blacksmith over the years but is also home to a delightful cottage garden. As well as displaying and growing plants that would have been familiar to a 19th century country gardener, the garden contains an unusual 19th century bee shelter.

Castle Mound, Bishop's Stortford

🏛 historic building   📷 museum   🏚 historic site   🍀 scenic attraction   🌿 flora and fauna

Nearby **Perry Green** became the home of Henry Moore. Following bomb damage to his Hampstead studio in 1941, the famous sculptor moved with his wife Irina to the peace and tranquillity of the village and he remained there for the rest of his life. The Henry Moore Foundation, which operates from Dane Tree House, Perry Green, and from the Henry Moore Institute in Leeds, was established in 1977 "to advance the education of the public by the promotion of their appreciation of the fine arts and in particular the works of Henry Moore". The Perry Green site comprises several studios and two

THE JOLLY WAGGONERS

Widford Road, Much Hadham, Hertfordshire SG10 6EZ
Tel: 01279 842102

Experienced hosts Simon and Jude Clarke took over the **Jolly Waggoners** in 2003, since when they have built up the reputation of the pub both as a friendly village local and as a place to seek out for an excellent meal. Local produce features strongly on the seasonal menus served in the comfortable 50-seat restaurant, where the specialities include Scottish beef and super fish dishes. The pub has a flower-decked patio at the side and a pleasant garden to the rear. In the next field, sheep and Vietnamese pigs are guaranteed to keep the children amused.

HOPLEYS PLANTS

High Street, Much Hadham,
Bishop's Stortford, Herts, SG10 6BU
Tel: 01279 842509 Fax: 01279 843784
e-mail: sales@hopleys.co.uk
website: www.hopleys.co.uk

A friendly family nursery, Hopleys Plants has been responsible for introducing numerous new plants to our gardens, from Potentilla Red Ace in the 70s to Abelia Hopleys - a superbly variegated free-flowering shrub deservedly becoming popular worldwide. Both feature in Hopleys catalogue along with 1,300 other perennials, shrubs, climbers and rock plants available for collection or by mail-order.

Situated in the picturesque village of Much Hadham, beside the nursery, Hopleys Garden displays four acres of fine specimens and several quirky water and garden features - entry is free. Lectures and a full garden design service are offered as well as helpful down-to-earth advice from knowledgeable staff whose talents have won gold medals at the Chelsea and Hampton Court Flower shows. Hopleys is also well-known for its Wavy Spade, an indispensable tool for general purpose digging as it slices easily through the ground - an ideal present perhaps. From individual plant lovers to coach parties, all enjoy a visit to the nursery and garden, but also to sample the self-service refreshments which include tea, coffee and outrageously delicious homemade cakes and ice cream. And reward your driver with a freshly-made buttonhole from the on-site florist.

Do visit, there's so much to see, buy and eat!

converted barns containing the Foundation's collection of Moore's work, as well as tapestries based on his drawings which were woven at West Dean College in Sussex. On the far side of the village green is a visitor centre selling books, posters, postcards and other Moore-themed merchandise along with a limited number of original prints. The estate contains many fine trees and hedgerows, much loved by Moore and to be seen in many of his works, and it was Irina who over the years created the garden areas in which the studios and sculptures are sited. The Foundation is open to the public from April to September by appointment (call: 01279 843333). Moore, who died in 1986, is buried in the village churchyard.

STANDON
6 miles W of Bishop's Stortford on A120

🏛 Balloon Stone

This old village, which once had a weekly market and two annual fairs, derived its importance from the families who held the manor and also from the Order of St John of Jerusalem. Though there is little evidence of it today, the order established a commandery, a hospice and a school which is believed to be the building now known as Knights' Court.

In a field to the west of the village lies the **Balloon Stone**, a giant sandstone boulder which marks the spot where, in 1784, Vincenzo Lunardi completed the first balloon flight in England. He began his flight in Finsbury, north London, and landed here some two hours later having first touched down briefly in a field at North Mimms.

Stevenage

🏛 Museum   🏛 Six Mills

Designated the first of Britain's New Towns in 1946, the town grew up along the Great North Road, and as traffic increased from the 13th century it developed round its parish church, the main road becoming its High Street. The idea of New Towns grew from the severe shortage of housing following the World War II air raids on London, and the first new houses in Stevenage were occupied in 1951; the new town centre was completed in 1958. Within the new town area, by a roundabout near the railway station, lie **Six Hills**, reputed to be Roman burial mounds. The history of the town, from the earliest days to the development of the New Town and the present day, is told in the **Stevenage Museum** in the undercroft of

---

LITTLE HALLINGBURY MILL RESTAURANT & ROOMS

Old Mill Lane, Gaston green, nr Bishops Stortford, Hertfordshire CM22 7QT
Tel: 01279 726554   e-mail: info@littlehallingburymill.net
website: www.littlehallingburymill.net

Little Hallingbury Mill is a lovely place to visit, whether it's for a drink, a meal or a stay in quiet, scenic surroundings. The historic four-storey mill is a great place for walking, enjoying the scenery and watching the boats on the navigation link to the River Lea. The food choice comprises the ground floor bistro/wine bar and the first floor restaurant, where the menu offers an evening selection of traditional English dishes with a hint of Italy. The non-smoking bedrooms, all with en-suite showers, are divided between second and third floor rooms in the mill and ground floor rooms in the annexe.

🏠 historic building   🏛 museum   🏛 historic site   🔱 scenic attraction   🌱 flora and fauna

St George's Church.

Stevenage became Hilton in the classic novel *Howards End* by E M Forster, who spent much of his childhood at Rooks Nest on the outskirts of town.

Around Stevenage

KNEBWORTH
3 miles S of Stevenage off A602

🏠 Knebworth House

🏠 Church of St Mary & St Thomas

Knebworth House has been the home of the Lytton family since 1490. The present magnificent Gothic mansion house was built in 1843 to the design of the Victorian statesman and novelist, Edward Bulwer-Lytton, who wrote *The Last Days of Pompeii*. However, fragments of the original Tudor house remain, including parts of the Great Hall, and there is also some superb 17th century panelling. Other members of the Lytton family of note include Constance, a leading figure in the suffragette movement, and Robert, Viceroy of India. The Raj Exhibition at the house brings to life the story of Lord Lytton's viceroyship and the Great Delhi Durbar of 1877. The house has also played host to such notable visitors as Elizabeth I, Benjamin Disraeli, Sir Winston Churchill and Charles Dickens, who is said to have taken part in amateur theatrical performances here. Dickens christened his 10th child Edward Bulwer Lytton Dickens

in honour of their great friendship. The grounds of Knebworth House are also well worth visiting and, as well as the beautiful formal gardens laid out by Lutyens, there is a wonderful herb garden established by Gertrude Jekyll, a lovely Victorian wilderness area, a maze that was replanted in 1995 and acres of grassland that are home to herds of red and sika deer. Children will enjoy the adventure playground, where they will find Fort Knebworth, a Dinosaur Trail, a monorail suspension slide and a bouncy castle among the amusements.

Also within the grounds is the **Church of St Mary and St Thomas** which contains some spectacular 17th and 18th century monuments to members of the Lytton family. Especially striking is the memorial to Sir William Lytton who died in 1705. A well-fed

Knebworth House

🎬 stories and anecdotes 🐦 famous people 🎨 art and craft 🎭 entertainment and sport 🚶 walks

figure with a marked double chin and dressed in the height of early-18th century fashion, Sir William reclines gracefully atop his tomb, his expression one of impermeable self-satisfaction.

BENINGTON
4 miles E of Stevenage off the B1037

One of the county's most attractive villages, Benington has a lovely green fringed by 16th century timber-and-plaster cottages. The village church dates from the 13th century, and next to it, on the site of a largely disappeared castle, is a large Georgian house known as Benington Lordship. The house is private but the superb grounds are open at

restricted times. The hilltop gardens include lakes, a Norman keep and moat (the remains of the castle), kitchen, rose and water gardens, a charming rockery, magnificent herbaceous borders and a splendid folly dating from 1832.

CROMER
4 miles NE of Stevenage on the B1037

🏚 Cromer Windmill

Half a mile east of the village, on the B1037 towards Hare Street, stands Hertfordshire's sole surviving post mill. **Cromer Windmill** was built on an artificial mound where windmills have stood for over 600 years. The present mill dates back at least to 1720, possibly as early as 1681. Blown over in a storm around 1860 and subsequently rebuilt, it was in use until the 1920s, by which time milling by wind had become uneconomic. The mill was basically left to deteriorate until an appeal by local people in 1967 saved its life. On completion of the first phase of restoration work the mill was presented to the current owners the Hertfordshire Building Preservation Trust. The first open days were held in 1991 and the mill was restored to full working order in 1998 with the help of grants from the Heritage Lottery Fund and English Heritage. The mill can be visited on Sundays, Bank Holiday Mondays and the second and fourth Saturdays from the second Sunday in May until the end of August.

ROYSTON
12 miles NE of Stevenage on A10

🏚 James I's Hunting Lodge

🏛 Museum 🏚 Royston Cave

This light industrial town grew up at the

Benington Castle

intersection of the Icknield Way and Ermine Street and is named after a wayside cross erected by Lady Roysia. A favourite hunting base for royalty, **James I's Hunting Lodge** can still be seen, though the only original features which remain are the two large chimneys.

Discovered in 1742 below the junction of the two ancient thoroughfares is the man-made **Royston Cave**. Bottle-shaped and cut out of the chalk, the cave is 28 feet deep and 17 feet across. Inside the chamber is a series of crude carvings on the walls, including St Christopher and the Crucifixion; the purpose of the cave and the date of the carvings have never been determined.

The **Royston Museum**, in the former Congregational Schoolroom building, houses the Royston and District Local History Society

collections, which relate to the history of this late medieval town and the surrounding area. Also here is a substantial collection of late-19th century ceramics and glass.

LETCHWORTH GARDEN CITY
6 miles N of Stevenage off the A1

🏛 1st Garden City Heritage Museum

🏛 Museum & Art Gallery

This attractive country town is proud to be the first Garden City, where the ideals of Ebenezer Howard were put into practice (see Welwyn Garden City). The site for Letchworth was purchased in 1903 and Barry Parker and Raymond Unwin were appointed architects. The residential cottages were designed and built by different architects for the 1905 Cheap Cottages Exhibition and, with

THE CROWN
Litlington, nr Royston, Hertfordshire SG8 0QB
Tel: 01763 853859

Debbie and David, Diane and Dave make a great team at **The Crown**, which lies on the Hertfordshire-Cambridgeshire border off the A1198 north of Royston. Hanging baskets make a colourful show on the smart white-painted exterior, and inside is equally delightful.

The public and lounge bars are convivial spots for enjoying a drink, and IPA and Speckled Hen are the real ales here. In the cosy little dining area the food choice runs from light snacks to a full menu that includes homemade daily specials and a good choice for vegetarians.

Petanque is played on a pitch next to the pub. The Crown was once a favourite local for two nearby American bases (Steeple Morden with a fighter squadron, Bassingbourne with bombers) and part of the bar is hung with photographs and other memorabilia.

The Crown is open Tuesday to Thursday 12 noon-3pm and 6pm-11pm, and all day Friday, Saturday and Sunday.

none costing more than £150, they each demonstrated new techniques and styles of building and living accommodation.

Housed in a beautiful thatched Arts and Crafts building of 1907 is the **First Garden City Heritage Museum**, a unique place which traces the history and development of this special town; among the many displays are the original plans and drawings of Letchworth. **Letchworth Museum and Art Gallery** is home to displays of local natural history and archaeology including finds of late Iron Age and Roman origin that were unearthed at Baldock.

On the outskirts of the town, Standalone Farm is a working farm which welcomes anyone who wants to learn more about farming and raising animals. A wide range of farm animals, including Shire horses, occupy the 170-acre site which also has a recently-planted arboretum containing more than 1,000 trees of 35 species, hides to view wildfowl, a natural history exhibition, a picnic area and café.

BALDOCK
7 miles N of Stevenage on the A505

🏛 Museum

A settlement of some size during the Iron Age and Roman times, the Baldock of today dates from the 13th century; it was founded by the Knights Templar and takes its name from the Old French for Baghdad. The Church of St Mary has an impressive 14th century tower and spike steeple, and the town boasts many handsome Georgian houses, both in the tree-lined main street and in the side streets.

FARROWBY FARM SHOP

New Inn Road, Hinxworth, nr Baldock, Hertfordshire SG7 5EY
Tel: 01462 733700 Fax: 01462 733302
e-mail: pigs@farrowbyfarm.co.uk
website: www.farrowbyfarm.co.uk

Beverley and Tim Burrows have built up their traditionally-run free-range farm into a reliable source of top-quality produce and a great place for a family outing. **Farrowby Farm Shop** sells the owners' own range of pork and pork products, including oak-smoked sweetcure back bacon and ham and super sausages. They also produce wonderful bronze turkeys (fresh for Christmas, frozen all year) and a fine selection of free-range and organic meats from other sources, jams and marmalade, chutneys and mustard and local craftware.

The tea room serves home-prepared snacks and light meals to be enjoyed inside or out on the lawn. Visitors can see the free-range pigs and poultry, wander round the farm and meet the goats and rabbits and birds. Under-fives can romp in an enclosed safe play area. Farrowby is open every day except Wednesday and Bank Holidays.

🏛 historic building   🏛 museum   🏛 historic site   🏛 scenic attraction   🌿 flora and fauna

Baldock is proud of this architectural heritage: it has more than 100 listed buildings. The local superstore has kept the historic façade of the old Kayser Bondor factory. **Baldock Museum** reflects the town's history and its connections with coaching, malting and brewing.

ASHWELL
9 miles N of Stevenage off the A505

🏠 Church of St Mary 🏛 Museum

An appealing village with a wealth of attractive old houses, Ashwell was one of the five boroughs of Hertfordshire in medieval times and took its name from the ash trees around the source of the River Rhee. The village later prospered through a malting industry that only ceased in the 1950s. The 14th century **Church of St Mary** has the highest tower in the county, at 176 feet, and

Ashwell Museum

ASHWELL GALLERY

Dixies Barns, High Street, Ashwell,
Hertfordshire SG7 5NT
Tel: 01462 743366
website: www.ashwellgallery.com

Ashwell Gallery is the culmination of many years browsing in and purchasing from other people's galleries by owner Mike Berry. Mike, a talented painter himself, has always been fascinated by art in all its many guises, and the art on show in his gallery highlights the talents of up and coming artists and sculptors. It is a mix of contemporary fine art, limited edition and a few open edition prints to suit all tastes.

Mike is able to provide a comprehensive framing service for pictures, prints, photographs and three-dimensional objects. He is happy to re-frame old or damaged pictures, and all work is done to conservation standard as defined by the Fine Arts Guild. The materials he uses are selected for the longevity and preservation of the works as well as the finished result. Browsers are very welcome, whether in the gallery or on the very informative website. The pictures change regularly, and Mike can help clients track down a favourite artist or a favourite style or medium. Some of the gallery's works are an ideal investment, but all of them fit the bill of providing a very special gift.

inside there are several inscriptions referring to the Black Death of 1349 and the plague and great storm of 1361. **Ashwell Museum**, in the restored Town House, affords a insight into the natural history, social history and archaeology of the town. It began in 1927 as the private collection of two schoolboys who displayed their treasures in a garden shed.

HITCHIN
4 miles NW of Stevenage on A600

🏛 St Mary's Church 🏛 The Biggin

🏛 The Priory 🏛 Museum

🏛 Museum of Hertfordshire Imperial Yeomanry

Pevsner considered that, after St Albans, Hitchin was "the most visually satisfying town in Hertfordshire". Situated on the banks of the River Hiz, this old town was, during medieval times, a vast market area where straw was purchased for the local cottage industry of straw plaiting and where the completed plaits were sold. As the trade in straw declined so the market at Hitchin reduced in size but there is still a small market place today, west of the parish church. Many of the town's older buildings have survived, if now surrounded by newer developments. The oldest parts of **St Mary's Church** date from the 12th century, though there was a minster church here at the time of the Domesday Survey. The low tower is the only part of the original building to have survived an earthquake of 1298. Rebuilt in the 14th

---

THE LORD LISTER HOTEL

1 Park Street, Hitchin, Hertfordshire SG4 9AH
Tel: 01462 432712 Fax: 01462 438506
website: www.lordlisterhotel.co.uk

Two minutes from Hitchin's historic town centre, the **Lord Lister Hotel** is an excellent base for both leisure and business guests. It's been run since 1998 by Josie and Nick Raviele, who generate a warm, friendly atmosphere throughout. The bed & breakfast accommodation comprises 20 recently renovated en-suite bedrooms, each with its own personality, and all with TV, telephone, hot drinks tray, bottle water and hairdryer. They include singles, doubles, twins and family rooms, and two rooms boast romantic four-posters.

The residents' lounge and the cosy bar that overlooks the garden are ideal spots to unwind with a drink and a chat, and the hotel has a boardroom for small conferences and a private car park. The late-18th century building was originally a woolcomber's house and later became a Quaker school specialising in science. The name commemorates its most famous pupil, Joseph Lister, a pupil in the 1840s who was to become known as the 'father of antiseptics'.

🏛 historic building 🏛 museum 🏛 historic site 🍀 scenic attraction 🌿 flora and fauna

century, the grandeur of the church reflects the prosperity which Hitchin once enjoyed. Standing on the site of a Gilbertine Priory is **The Biggin**, constructed in the early 17th century. For a while it was a private residence, then a school, before becoming, in 1723, an almshouse for 'poore, auncient or middle aged women', a function which it still performs today. Another building worthy of mention is **The Priory**, which takes in fragments of a Carmelite Priory founded in the 14th century. Built in 1770 by Robert Adams as the private residence of the Radcliffe family, it was extensively renovated in the 1980s after being disused for many years.

Finally, **Hitchin Museum**, home to the county's largest collection of period costumes, is an excellent place to visit. It shares a building with the **Museum of the Hertfordshire Imperial Yeomanry** - a band of men mustered to repel Napoleon's threatened invasion. As well as the numerous displays of local social history, part of the museum includes the Victorian Chemist Shop and Physic Garden. This re-creation of a chemist's shop uses much of the stock and fittings from Perks and Llewellyn, who ceased trading as a pharmacy in 1961; the original cabinets still contain the lavender toiletries for which the firm was world famous. To carry the connection further between the town and pharmacy, the medical pioneer Lord Lister had family ties with Hitchin and began his education here. The Physic Garden reflects the historical and modern importance of plants as a source of medicine.

Hertford

🏠 Church of St Leonard 🏠 Quaker Meeting House
📷 Museum 🏛 Castle ⚔ Cole Green Way
⚔ Nature Walk

Dating back to Saxon times, the town was founded at a ford across the River Lea, at that time the boundary between Saxon and Viking England. A once important waterway linking Hertford with London, the River Lea, which became the Lea (Lee) Navigation at Hertford, was used to transport flour and grain but today its traffic is leisure cruisers. The **Hertford Nature Walk** is situated in the meadows between the Rivers Lea and Beane, and takes in the canal basin, known as The Folly.

Hertford is very much a mix of the old and new, and among the interesting buildings are the particularly beautiful Norman **Church of St Leonard,** in the area known as Bengeo, and the **Quaker Meeting House**. Said to be the oldest purpose-built meeting house in the world that has been in constant use as a place of

Hertford Castle

worship, the meeting house dates from 1669 and stands behind a walled courtyard; it has a unique four-tiered platform for the ministers that is screened from the entrance. The collections at **Hertford Museum** were started in the 1890s and cover a wide variety of subjects relating to the town and the surrounding area. The Museum is located in a 17th century town house that is complemented by a reconstructed Jacobean garden. The Shire Hall was where Darcy first met Elizabeth in Jane Austen's *Pride and Prejudice*.

Little remains of the original **Hertford Castle**, which was built by King Alfred's son Prince Edward to guard the ford on the river and to protect London from the Danes. However, the 15th century gatehouse is still standing and, now modernised, is used as administrative offices for the town council. The site of the castle is now a public park and evidence of the castle's original motte and bailey can still be seen in the lie of the land. A short length of the massive Norman flint wall, complete with a 14th century postern gate, is also preserved in the park. The town centre incorporates Salisbury Square, which features a water sculpture depicting the four rivers that meet in Hertford – the Rib, Beane, Mimram and Lea (Lee).

To the south of the town lies **Cole Green Way**, a delightful nature trail that follows the route of the now disused Hertford and Welwyn Junction Railway. Passing through attractive meadowland, the trail runs from Hertford to Cole Green, where the former station provides a pleasant picnic spot.

THE BAKER ARMS

Ashendene Road, Bayford, nr Hertford,
Hertfordshire SG13 8PX
Tel: 01992 511235
e-mail: leesnook@hotmail.com

The Baker Arms in Bayford is a classic village pub offering excellent standards of hospitality, accommodation (wireless broadband available), food and drink. Lee and Joy's pub has plenty of space beyond the long brick exterior to meet friends and enjoy a glass or two of McMullens ale, and when the sun shines the picnic benches on the lawn are in demand. The restaurant, open every lunchtime and evening except Monday, serves a good and varied menu that includes outstanding fish specials such as herb-crusted cod and salmon, spicy king prawns and smoked haddock fish cakes. There's also a good choice for meat-eaters – beef Wellington, rack of lamb, gammon with egg and chips are typical specials – and always a main dish for vegetarians.

The area is popular with walkers, horse riders, golfers and anglers, and the pub's four comfortable bedrooms provide a convenient base. It's also well placed for anyone with business in the nearby towns of Hertford, Hatfield and Hoddesdon. The Baker Arms lies south of Hertford, a short drive from the A10.

🏠 historic building   🏛 museum   🏚 historic site   ᕯ scenic attraction   🌱 flora and fauna

Around Hertford

HODDESDON
2 miles S of Hertford on the A1010

🏛 Rye House Gatehouse 🏛 Lowewood Museum

The town grew up around the road along the Lea Valley that replaced the Roman Ermine Street in Saxon times. In Lea Valley Park stands the 15th century **Rye House Gatehouse**, a fascinating historic attraction which includes an exhibition where visitors can eavesdrop on the conspirators in the Rye House Plot. In 1683, Rye House was the scene of a plot to assassinate Charles II as he passed through the town on his way back from Newmarket to London. The plot failed and the conspirators, including Richard Rumbold, the then tenant of Rye House, were executed. **Lowewood Museum** in the High Street depicts past local life.

CHESHUNT
8 miles S of Hertford off the A10

🏛 Temple Bar

In 1564 Lord Burghley, Chief Minister to Elizabeth I, built his great house Theobalds here. Later, James I was so taken with the house that he persuaded Burghley's son Robert to exchange the house for his palace at Hatfield. Theobalds was all but destroyed in the aftermath of the Civil War, and what remains of the building stands in the public Cedars Park. Also in the park is **Temple Bar**, designed by Wren and originally erected at the Fleet Street entrance to the City of London after the Great Fire of 1666. By the 1870s London's traffic had increased to the extent that the gateway was causing an obstruction, so it was removed and rebuilt in the park.

WALTHAM CROSS
9 miles S of Hertford on the A1010

🏛 Eleanor Cross

The town takes its name from the cross built in the centre in 1291. It is an **Eleanor Cross**, one of three survivors of the 12 which Edward I erected to commemorate the resting places of the funeral cortege of his Queen, Eleanor of Castile. Eleanor died in Lincolnshire and the cortege took 13 days to travel to Westminster Abbey where she is buried. The building materials in the cross include Caen stone, Sussex and Purbeck marble and precious stones, and it is recorded that the total cost was £95.

The other surviving crosses are at Northampton and Geddington, and a Victorian replica stands in the forecourt of Charing Cross Station. In 1859 Anthony Trollope came to live in Waltham Cross. He kept pigs, tended his garden and wrote some of his best works while living here.

WARE
3 miles E of Hertford on the A1170

🏛 Place House 🏛 Museum 🏛 Scott's Grotto

Situated at the point where Ermine Street crosses the River Lea, Ware was the scene of a famous encounter between King Alfred and the Danes in 895 and, during the Middle Ages, it became a trading rival to Hertford. The construction of a viaduct in the 1970s to carry the A10 across the valley has removed much of the traffic from the town and, despite development over the years, Ware still retains many of its original buildings. Behind the east end of the High Street, there is access to Blue Coat Yard where, on the right, stands **Place House**, possibly one of Ware's two Domesday manor houses, which was rebuilt during the 13th century as a splendid aisled hall and in the 1680s was purchased by the governors of Christ's Hospital for use as a school for boys being fostered in Ware. Most of this building still remains and on the opposite side of the yard stand the cottages which were built in 1698 and provided accommodation for a foster mother and up to 14 boys.

The High Street crosses the River Lea at Bridgefoot, and here can still be seen some unique 18th century gazebos, many of which have been restored to their former glory. The riverside path leads on into an attractive public garden behind what was once a Franciscan Priory, of which only a few traces remain. Founded in 1338 as a friary, the priory became a private house in 1568 and remained so for several centuries. In 1920, the owner, Mrs Page-Croft, gave the house and gardens to the town and, fully restored in 1994, the building stands pristine surrounded by seven acres of parkland.

No trip to Ware would be complete without a visit to **Scott's Grotto**, built by the poet John Scott in the late 18th century and located off the A119 Hertford Road. The son of a wealthy Quaker family, Scott devised this elaborate series of six chambers linked by passageways and air tunnels during the 1760s; they are lined with flints, fossils, minerals and thousands of shells. On a hill above the grotto is an octagonal summerhouse approached by horseshoe-shaped steps. The grotto was described by Scott's friend Dr Johnson as "a fairy hall", adding that "none but a poet could have made such a garden". The grotto was extensively restored in 1990, and the replacement shells came from local donors and from as far afield as Japan. It is open every Saturday and Bank Holiday Monday from April to the end of September.

The history of Ware and its major role in the malting industry is explained in **Ware Museum** at Priory Lodge. The Great Bed of Ware, mentioned by Shakespeare, is in the Victoria & Albert Museum in London.

GREAT AMWELL
2 miles SE of Ware off the A10

🗠 New River

Between 1609 and 1613 the **New River** was created to carry fresh water from local springs by way of Hoddesdon and Cheshunt to the New River Head reservoir at Clerkenwell in London. Wooden pipes then carried the water to the houses and businesses of North London. This enterprise was the brainchild of Sir Hugh Myddelton, whose achievement is commemorated at Great Amwell by an island laid out by the architect of the New River Company in 1800. Just south of the village church lie the imposing buildings of Haileybury College, which was established in 1809 as a training school for the East India Company. The architect was William Wilkins, whose best-known work is the National Gallery in Trafalgar Square.

Hatfield

🏛 Church of St Etheldreda 🏛 Hatfield House

This historic town grew up around the gateway to the palace of the abbots and Bishop of Ely. Beside the palace gatehouse stands the **Church of St Etheldreda,** the East Anglian princess and first abbess of Ely in the 7th century. The church is notable for its magnificent memorials to the Cecil family of nearby Hatfield House, the Brocket family chapel from the Tudor era, and dazzling stained glass by Burne-Jones. Also buried here are the novelist Lady Caroline Lamb and her husband Henry William Lamb, 2nd Viscount Melbourne. The viscount, who was Prime Minister in 1834 and from 1835 to 1841, has a memorial in the church, but there is no mention of Lady Caroline, whose public infatuation with Lord Byron had brought about their separation in 1825.

Hatfield Old Palace Banqueting Hall

Elizabeth I spent her early life in the **Royal Palace of Hatfield**, of which only the Banqueting Hall remains. This can be seen in the delightful gardens of the spectacular Jacobean mansion, **Hatfield House** (see panel on page 252), which now stands on the site. It was built in the early 1600s for Robert Cecil (later 1st Earl of Salisbury), Chief Minister to both Elizabeth and James I. Designed with entertaining royalty in mind, no expense was spared to make Hatfield the most striking house of its time. The most impressive room is the superb Marble Hall, a richly-decorated version of the medieval Great Hall with a sumptuously carved Screen and Minstrel's Gallery, a specially made 30ft long refectory table and a black and white marble floor. Here hang the two most famous paintings of Elizabeth I – Nicholas Hilliard's *Ermine Portrait* and Isaac Oliver's deeply allegorical *Rainbow Portrait*. The Cecil family still live here, in the East Wing, and the present Marchioness has taken a special interest in restoring the superb gardens to their 17th century appearance, complete with herb and knot gardens, and a foot maze typical

of the period. Visitors to the Park can also enjoy the national collection of model soldiers, five miles of marked park trails, a picnic site, children's play area, gift shop, licensed restaurant and tea room.

Back in the centre of town lies the Eight Bells pub, which was frequented by Charles Dickens when, as a newspaper reporter for the *Morning Chronicle*, he visited Hatfield to report on the fire, which not only destroyed a substantial part of Hatfield House but also resulted in the death of the Dowager Lady Salisbury. The pub also features in Dickens' *Oliver Twist*, as following the murder of Nancy, Bill Sikes 'shaped his course' for Hatfield and, in the tap room of the Eight Bells, a fellow drinker saw the blood on Sikes' hat.

The idea of Hatfield New Town was nothing new in post World War II Britain as in 1848 proposals for a new town were advertised to coincide with the completion of the railway line in 1850. Though some development did take place, it was not until the 1950s that the rapid expansion began. However, the two areas remain separate, on

📖 stories and anecdotes 🐦 famous people ⚲ art and craft 🎭 entertainment and sport 🚶 walks

Hatfield House

Hatfield, Hertfordshire AL9 5NQ
Tel: 01707 287010
website: www.hatfield-house.co.uk

Hatfield House, where Elizabethan history began, is a superb redbrick Jacobean mansion built by Robert Cecil, 1st Earl of Shaftesbury and Chief Minister to King James I, in 1611. The house has been in the Cecil family ever since, and is the home of the Marquess of Salisbury. Superb examples of Jacobean craftsmanship can be seen throughout the house, notably in the Grand Staircase with its elaborately carved wood and in the stained-glass window in the private chapel. The state rooms are treasure houses of the finest furniture, world-renowned paintings, exquisite tapestries and historic armour; they include the fabulous Marble Hall, the Long Gallery and King James' Drawing Room.

The gardens at Hatfield House are a great attraction in their own right, laid out by John Tradescant the Elder and planted by him with many species never previously grown in England. The gardens, where restoration started in Victorian times and still continues, include herb, knot and wilderness areas which can be visited when the house is open to the public.

A variety of arts and crafts events are hosted throughout the season - see website for details.   **Open:** Easter Saturday to end September. **House:** 12 noon – 4pm, Wednesday to Sunday only. **Park, West Garden, Restaurant & Shop:** Daily, 11am - 5.30pm. **East Garden:** Open only on Thursdays (except during August).

either side of the railway line and, fortunately, much of the older part of the town has survived. Hatfield has strong links with the history of aviation and was the home of the Mosquito, Comet and Trident (see under London Colney).

Around Hatfield

BROOKMANS PARK
3 miles S of Hatfield on the A1000

🌂 Northaw Great Wood

A quiet residential area with a large commuting population. To the east lies

Northaw Great Wood, the remains of the forest that once covered a large part of Hertfordshire. It is now preserved with conservation in mind, and visitors can wander through the woodland and perhaps spot muntjac deer, badgers, foxes and some of the 60 or so species of birds that have been sighted here.

WELWYN
1 mile N of Hatfield on the A1(M)

🏛 Welwyn Roman Baths

This historic town has grown up along the route of the Great North Road, which became the High Street, but, since the construction of

🏠 historic building   🖼 museum   🏛 historic site   🌂 scenic attraction   🌱 flora and fauna

SUSU

21-25 High Street, Welwyn, Hertfordshire AL6 9EG
Tel: 01438 718161
e-mail: info@susustyle.co.uk
website: www.susustyle.co.uk

SuSu, in the heart of a vibrant village, is a positive Aladdins cave of womens fashion clothing, gifts and accessories.

The shop takes its name from two friends, Susan Bull and Susanne Stevens, who have combined their fashion experience to create a shop crammed with different labels, many that you won't see on the high street, and some that are exclusive to SuSu in the United Kingdom.

The emphasis of the shop is smart casual, clothes you might wear to a special occasion but can be transformed in different ways to other aspects of your life - having said that, much of the offer is clothing, bags, jewellery, hats, belts etc. that are more 'every day' wear. Much work goes into ensuring a wide price range to give a designer-wear look but at more affordable prices.

The friendly staff at SuSu are trained to give you as much or as little help as you need, and as the stock changes rapidly it is unlikely to be seen elsewhere - Susan and Susanne make it their policy to carry only a few of each item, making your purchase even more unique.

Shop hours are 9.30am to 5pm Monday to Saturday.

---

the A1(M) took the route away from the town centre, Welwyn is now relatively traffic-free. During the excavations for the new motorway, the famous **Welwyn Roman Baths** were uncovered. Part of a 3rd century villa or farm, the bath house is preserved in a steel vault within the motorway embankment.

WELWYN GARDEN CITY
2 miles N of Hatfield on the A1000

🏛 Mill Green Museum

As the name of this town would suggest, Welwyn is indeed a Garden City, one of two in Hertfordshire that followed the ideas and plans of Ebenezer Howard. After seeing the squalor in which people lived in the cities, particularly London, Howard conceived the idea of providing working people with an

opportunity to live in well- spaced housing with access to the clean air of the countryside and to the industrial areas close by. The land for Welwyn Garden City was first acquired in 1919 and the building began a year later, with the present station completed in 1926. Howard's ideas are still perhaps best seen here, as the railway line also acts as the demarcation line for the two areas of the town: industry to the east; the shopping and commercial areas to the west; and the residential areas, with extensive planting and many open spaces beyond.

Just to the south of the town lies **Mill Green Museum**, in the tiny hamlet of Mill Green. Housed in the workers' cottages for the adjoining watermill, this was, between 1911 and 1973, a private residence. There are

Ayot St Lawrence

Distance: *6.5 miles (10.4 kilometres)*

Typical time: *180 mins*

Height gain: *80 metres*

Map: *Explorer 182*

Walk: *www.walkingworld.com ID:353*

Contributor: *Les Weeks*

Difficult to access by public transport. Car parking is in the sports ground car park just north of the church off the B651in Kimpton. Follow the unmade track signposted 'Parkfield Sports Ground'. Please close the gate behind you.

ADDITIONAL INFORMATION:

At Ayot St Lawrence a very short detour allows a visit to Shaw's Corner (NT), the home of G B Shaw (summer months only).

DESCRIPTION:

Mainly on footpaths and farm tracks with a little road walking. There are some fine views across the Chilterns. Many farmland birds can be seen and sometimes kingfishers can be spotted along the Mimram. In the winter months and after a period of heavy rain, some of the paths can become muddy and boots would be recommended.

Pub food and snacks are available in Kimpton (White Horse and Boot pubs) and Ayot St Lawrence (The Brocket Arms); a phone call beforehand is recommended.

FEATURES:

Hills or Fells, River, Pub, Museum, Church, National Trust/NTS, Wildlife, Birds, Great Views

WALK DIRECTIONS:

1 | Opposite the track to the car park there is a private drive which is also a footpath. Walk along the drive until you reach a farmhouse. To your right is a stile.

2 | Cross the stile and follow the obvious track across the field (E) until it meets the NE corner of a small wood where there is a stile and field-gate. Cross the stile. Keep to the right of the trees close to the fence. If the stinging nettles and brambles are high and your trousers short, it is possible to walk to the left of the trees on the edge of the pasture. At the end of the wood is another stile. Cross this stile and remain on the path along the field edge with the fence/hedge now on your left. Pass through the field boundary and carry straight on to the end of the next field, where there is another stile. Cross this stile and follow the trodden track diagonally left, down past an old sweet chestnut to another stile which meets a made-up drive.

3 | Cross this stile and join the drive towards, and over, a folly bridge now in a state of disrepair. Do not take the footpath marked off to the right before the bridge. Follow the drive until it meets the main road.

4 | Where the drive meets the road, turn sharply to the right along a farm track signposted as a bridleway and part of the Hertfordshire Way. Continue along this track until you reach a farmhouse. At the farmhouse keep left (straight on). Continue until the track meets a minor road joining from the left. Join the road and keep right towards Kimpton Mill. Approx 60m before the mill is a track to the left marked as the Hertfordshire Way. This is our path. However a look at the mill might be of interest. Although now converted, the mill sits over the little River Mimram and is attractive.

5 | Take the signposted path. The path runs parallel to the Mimram. A short detour can be taken when a stile is reached down to the shaded riverbank -an ideal place for a short break, especially when the sun is shining. Keep your eyes open for kingfishers. Follow the path for some distance, until it forks. Where the path divides (signpost) we take the right-hand option and follow the brideway. Continue until the road is reached.

6 | When you reach the road turn right and walk 100m to the junction at Codicote Bottom Farm. Take care as this road can be busy - it is probably safest to walk on the left. At the junction take the road off to the left signposted Ayot St Lawrence. 50m along this road is a farm track leading off and up to the right.

7 | Pass through the gate and make your way up the steepish track. Continue until the track makes a turn to the right. At this point a marker on a gate-post opposite you shows that

the footpath continues straight ahead alongside a field fence. Keep this fence to your right and follow it until you reach a metal kissing-gate. Once again take the time to stop occasionally and look behind you at the views. Pass through the kissing gate and turn left onto the drive and then right along the quiet road towards Ayot St Lawrence, passing the Brocket Arms pub on your left. Walk past the derelict church until you reach a white house on your right.

8 | By the side of the white house there is a footpath that leads towards the Palladian church (built by order to replace the previous one). This is our path. However a small detour is possible here for the literati. Continue along the road a further 50m to Shaw's Corner, home of GBS and now run by the National Trust. Back on our path we follow through wooden kissing-gates and across a field, past the church and through a small metal kissing-gate.

9 | After passing through the gate cross the stile to your right and follow the trodden track towards the trees to your left. Pass to the left of the second pine tree. The path eventually comes against the fence under some oaks. The OS map wrongly shows the path inside the wood to your left. Approach a stile in the corner formed by the fencing. Cross this stile into Priors Wood and follow the obvious, signed, track. This track crosses other stiles into a more open area which has been cleared and replanted. The track goes down and then sharply up, to a gap in the wood leading to an open field. A path leads across this open field directly in front of you. This path is well-maintained by

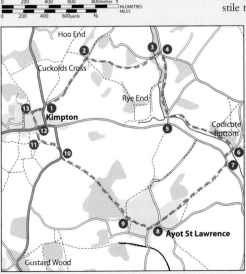

Continued overleaf

the farmer but if newly ploughed and indistinct, the path takes you to a footpath sign just to right of the solitary tree on the horizon. On reaching the post continue left along the farm track until you emerge onto the main road (B651). This road can be busy - take care!

10 | Carefully cross the road to the steep and sometimes slippery step through the hedge opposite, onto a path along the edge of the field. Turn right and follow the path beyond where it passes either side of a large oak, to where the field boundary bends to the right. Continue on until just before a sharp turn to the left, there is a break in the hedge leading onto the top of the recreation ground. (if you miss the gap, don't worry, there's another in 50m or so).

11 | Pass through the break with the bowling green to your right and chestnuts to the left. Go under the latter and move left along the top of the sports field until you join the track which leads down to a gate onto the High Street. Turn right along the road, cross and turn left into Church Lane.

12 | Walk along the lane until, just before a wall starts on the left, there is a gap leading onto an open green area - Garden Fields. The OS map does not show this as open ground. Pass through the gap and keep close along the wall to your right. The right of way stays hard against this wall and the back of the houses, through some apple trees and through an arch cut in some leylandii bushes. It may feel like someone's back garden, but it isn't. However, you can wander anywhere over the open green.

13 | Through and beyond the 'arch' pass through the first of two wooden gates. The car park is on your left.

two permanent galleries here where local items from Roman times to the present day are on display, including pottery, craft tools, underwear and school certificates. A further gallery is used for temporary exhibitions. The adjoining **Mill Green Mill** is a wonderful watermill restored to full working order. Standing on the site of one of the four such mills in Hertfordshire that featured in the Domesday Book, Mill Green Mill was originally owned by the Bishops of Ely. Reconstructed and altered many times, the mill finally ceased to grind corn at the beginning of the 20th century when the incumbent miller emigrated to Australia. Milling recommenced in 1986, after much careful restoration work by the Mill Green Water Mill Restoration Trust, and not only can it be seen working but freshly ground flour is on sale.

AYOT ST LAWRENCE
3 miles NW of Hatfield off the B653

🐦 Shaw's Corner 🚶 Ayot Greenway

The most famous resident of the village was the playwright George Bernard Shaw, who lived here from 1906 until his death in 1950. It seems that while on a visit to the area looking for a country home he saw a headstone in the churchyard with the inscription 'Her time was short'. The lady in question had in fact died at the age of 70, and Shaw thought that if 70 was considered a short span of years, this was the place for him. The house in which he lived, **Shaw's Corner**, has been preserved by the National Trust as it was in his lifetime and contains many literary and personal mementos of the great Irish writer. All the plants in the lovely garden are pre-1950, including phlomis, delphinium, agapanthus, allium, acanthus and aster. The ashes of Shaw and his wife

CHOICE CHINA CRYSTAL COLLECTABLES

27 Stonehills, Welwyn Garden City, Hertfordshire AL8 6NA
Tel/Fax: 01707 335014
e-mail: info@giftsatchoice.co.uk

One of the best shops in the county for china, crystal and glass. **Choice China** features some of the leading worldwide brands, including Lladro porcelain figurines. Choice also stocks Swarvoski

Crystals for figurines, fashion jewellery and accessories, a selection of fine jewellery by other makers, and lovely gifts for christenings, weddings and other special occasions.

China and porcelain are represented by Aynsley, Wedgwood, Spode, Royal Doulton and Royal Crown Derby; these include delightful Winnie the Pooh and much-loved Walt Disney characters for children to collect. Dartington, Waterford and Edinburgh Crystal are among the glass and

crystal collections stocked in the shop, which stands off Bridge Road, a short drive from the A1000 on the northern edge of the town.

Charlotte were scattered throughout the garden and around the 6ft square writing hut where GBS wrote most of his famous works. Close by, just south of Ayot St Peter, runs **Ayot Greenway**, an attractive footpath, rich in flora, that follows part of the route of the old Luton, Dunstable and Welwyn Junction Railway which hit the buffers under the Beeching axe in 1966.

St Albans

🏛 Clock Tower 🏛 Verulamium Museum
🏛 Verulamium 🏛 Museum of St Albans 🏛 Abbey
🏛 Organ Museum ⚒ Kingsbury Watermill

This historic cathedral city, whose skyline is dominated by the magnificent Norman abbey,

is a wonderful blend of the old and new. One of the major Roman cities in Britain, the remains of **Verulamium** (see panel on page 259) were excavated only quite recently, but there was already a settlement here before Julius Caesar's invasion in 54 BC. Attacked and ruined by Boadicea in the 1st century, the city was rebuilt and today the remains of the walls, Britain's only Roman theatre (as distinct from an amphitheatre) and a hypocaust can still be seen in Verulamium Park. Also in the park is the **Verulamium Museum**, where the story of everyday life in a Roman city is told; among the displays are ceramics, mosaic floors, personal possessions and room re-creations.

Designated as a cathedral in 1877, **St Albans Abbey** was built on the site where

---

🎬 stories and anecdotes 🦜 famous people 🎨 art and craft ✏ entertainment and sport 🚶 walks

STUDIOFABRICA GALLERY

10 Holywell Hill, St Albans, Hertfordshire AL1 1BZ
Tel: 01727 863000
e-mail: info@studiofabrica.com
website: www.studiofabrica.com

Studiofabrica Gallery is the creation of Jane Pritchard, a former graphic designer and a student and practitioner of ceramics. She opened the studio in November 2005 to give opportunities for new and established artists, designers and makers. For visitors, it provides the opportunity to browse at leisure in friendly, relaxed surroundings and to choose a unique piece to treasure now and for the future or to give as a very special present. Contemporary style and brilliant craftsmanship are the common thread throughout the studio.

As well as paintings and limited edition prints by local and national artists, the displays include studio and functional ceramics by Sophie Cook, Avril Farley, Emma Johnstone, Sarah Perry; lovely pieces of china from Repeat Repeat in Stoke; Innermost acrylic designs, handmade glass from Loco; handmade jewellery from Miranda Hughes, Emily Morgan and others; the Sophie Conran range of oven-to-tableware; Bath House fragrances and toiletries; textiles; photography; photo albums and notebooks; greetings cards and much, much more.

🏛 historic building   📷 museum   🏛 historic site   🌲 scenic attraction   🐾 flora and fauna

The Roman Theatre of Verulamium

Bluehouse Hill, St Albans,
Hertfordshire AL3 6AE
Tel: 01727 835035
e-mail: stalbans@struttandparker.co.uk

The Roman Theatre of Verulamium was built in 140 AD and is the only one of its kind in Britain. The current ruins were found in 1847 but were not fully excavated until 1930 – 5. Also on site are partial remains of a Roman Villa and undergound shrine and the Verulamium Museum is close by.

Open Daily; 10am – 5pm Summer, 10am – 4pm Winter. Closed Christmas Day and Boxing Day, New Years Day by appointment.

Alban, the first British martyr, was beheaded in 303 for sheltering a Christian priest. Dating from the 11th century and built from flint and bricks taken from the Roman remains, the cathedral has been added to and altered in

Clock Tower, St Albans

every century since. It was the premier Abbey of medieval England until its monastic life ended in 1539, when all but the Abbey Church and Gatehouse were destroyed. Among its many notable features, the medieval paintings, said to be unique in Britain, are the most interesting. In the nearby Church of St Michael are the tomb and life-size monument of Lord Chancellor Francis Bacon (1561-1626), 1st Baron Verulam and Viscount St Albans, who lived in St Albans for the last five years of his life. The shrine of St Alban is a beautiful structure of carved Purbeck marble made in 1308. It was restored in 1993. In 2002 a bone believed to be of St Alban was given to the Cathedral by the Church of St Pantaleon in Cologne.

In the town's central market place stands the **Clock Tower**, the only medieval town belfry in England, built between 1403 and 1412. Originally constructed as a political statement by the town, it asserted the citizens' freedom and wealth in the face of the powerful abbey as the town was allowed to sound its own hours and ring the curfew bell. The original 15th century bell, Gabriel, is still in place.

📖 stories and anecdotes   🦜 famous people   🎨 art and craft   🎭 entertainment and sport   🚶 walks

LAVENDERBLUE

22, London Road, St Albans, Hertfordshire
Tel: 01727 893222
website: lavenderblueshop.com

'Gorgeous things for you, your home and your friends'. That's what customers read on the sign above the door of **Lavenderblue**, and that's definitely certainly what they find inside. In her shop in the city centre, close to the Cathedral, Joanne Marks personally chooses the stock of things to enhance the home and garden, giftware and jewellery.

Among the items in the constantly changing displays for all ages and pockets are East of India gifts for weddings, christenings, birthdays and other special occasions; Two's Company Interiors; Roger Lascelles clocks; Neal's Yard remedies; Somerset candles; stylish mirrors; handmade jewellery; handmade greetings cards; and children's story books.

Browsers are always welcome, and very few of them leave without finding something special to treasure or to give as a present.
You can also buy on line at:- www.lavenderblueshop.com.

THE WAFFLE HOUSE & KINGSBURY WATER MILL MUSEUM

St Michael's Street, St Albans, Hertfordshire AL3 4SJ
Tel: 01727 853502

Waffles don't come any tastier than the ones served at **The Waffle House**, and the setting is another big plus. The 120-seat restaurant is located in a 16th century watermill on the River Ver, close to the Cathedral and Verulamium Park. Lots of organic ingredients go into the bases and the toppings, and the sweet and savoury versions are equally delicious.

The regular list is supplemented by mouthwatering daily specials such as garlicky field mushrooms with Brie and onion jam on rocket; organic beef with a tomato and paprika sauce, celery, peppers and soured cream (beef Espagnol); and banana split with a berry sauce, chocolate sauce, ice cream, cream and chopped hazelnuts. Excellent service completes the picture at the Waffle House, which is open from 10am to 6pm (to 5pm in winter) seven days a week.

The mill stands on the site of an earlier mill that was mentioned in the Domesday Book. The restored mill still turns, and visitors can see the milling machinery and a collection of agricultural implements in the museum.

Close to the peaceful and tranquil Verulamium Park, on the banks of the River Ver, is **Kingsbury Watermill**, a wonderful 16th century mill that is built on the site of an earlier mill that was mentioned in the Domesday Book. Beautifully restored, the waterwheel is still turned by the river and visitors can not only enjoy this idyllic setting but also see the working milling machinery and a collection of agricultural implements.

Two other museums in the town are very well worth a visit. The **Museum of St Albans** relates the fascinating history of the town from Roman times through to the present day and among the exhibits on show is the famous Salaman collection of trade and craft tools that is considered to be the finest in the country. In **St Albans Organ Museum** visitors can enjoy the stirring sounds of an amazing collection of working mechanical musical instruments, which include two theatre organs, musical boxes, the Mills self-playing violin and reproducing pianos, all of which have been lovingly restored. All the most famous manufacturers are represented, including Mortier, Decap, Bursens, Wurlitzer and Steinway.

Just to the north, in the tiny hamlet of Redbournbury, lies Redbournbury Mill, an 18th century watermill that stands on the site of a mill that was mentioned in the Domesday Book. Once owned by the abbey at St Albans, the mill was seized by the crown following the Dissolution of the Monasteries. In 1652 it was sold to an ancestor of the present Earl of Verulam and stayed in his family until 1931 when it once again became Crown property. Now back in private hands, this splendid mill, on the banks of the River Ver, has been restored to its former glory and is now in full working order, powered by a large 1935 Crossley oil engine. Open to the public on Sundays from March to October, and on other days for special events, the mill also sells its own stone-ground flour and bread.

Around St Albans

CHISWELL GREEN
2 miles SW of St Albans on A414

🌱 Gardens of the Rose

This village is home to probably one of the biggest attractions in Hertfordshire, the **Gardens of the Rose**, a site that contains one of the most important rose collections in the world. The Royal National Rose Gardens can boast some 30,000 rose trees and upwards of 1,700 varieties. It isn't necessary to be a horticultural enthusiast to appreciate the sheer natural beauty of gorgeous displays such as the President's Walk or the Queen Mother Rose Garden, named after the garden's patron, which contains some of the oldest varieties of rose, including Damask, Gallicas, Albas and Portland. With the model gardens, the miniature roses, and the breathtaking pergola, it would be difficult to exaggerate the beauty of this place, which really has to be visited to be appreciated.

LONDON COLNEY
3 miles SE of St Albans off the A414

🏛 Mosquito Aircraft Museum

Among the interesting old buildings in this pleasant village on the River Colne is the late-Victorian All Saints Convent, which stands within the former Colney Park. Begun in 1899 as an Anglican establishment, with a church added in the 1920s, it was bought by the Roman Catholic Church in 1973 as a pastoral centre. A mile south of London Colney, aircraft enthusiasts will be in their element at the **Mosquito Aircraft Museum**, which is

THREADS GIFTS

7 High Street, Harpenden, Hertfordshire AL5 2RT
Tel: 01582 766113
e-mail: admin@threadsgifts.co.uk
website: www.ThreadsGifts.co.uk

Threads: The Gift and Needlecraft Shop in Harpenden is a real find. It is the kind of truly unique, family run business that has all but disappeared from High Streets today.

The owners, mother and daughter team, Cheryl and Lara Wares along with their "fantastic loyal team" of 11 staff work really hard to ensure that the shop offers its customers a constantly changing range of wonderful gift ideas to suit all ages and occasions. The shop is quite literally a mini-department store. Baby gifts are a real speciality; with gorgeous outfits, soft toys, newborn gift-baskets and lovely ideas for christening gifts. Older children are also well catered for with creative kits, pocket money toys, games and a whole host of fluffy pink things guaranteed to delight little girls. For adults the variety is remarkable; to-die for jewellery and handbags, stylish silver and leather gifts for special occasions, a huge range of kitchenware from suppliers such as Emma Bridgewater and Sophie Conran, funny little novelties and many ranges of cards, toiletries, candles, stationery and homeware that you just don't see anywhere else.

Customers tell us that what they love about Threads is that there is always something new and exciting. At the time of publication, products 'just in' included funky walking sticks, Retro Sweet Hampers, marble sporting coasters "a very different present for a hard-to-buy-for man" and fair-trade, organic babygrows "lovely designs, very soft and really reasonably priced"

In fact, so many visitors to Harpenden have commented that they wish they had a shop like Threads where they live, that Cheryl and Lara have now launched the **website www.ThreadsGifts.co.uk**. The site allows customers to shop online, confident in the knowledge that they'll receive the same quality of service and products that Threads customers have enjoyed for the last 21 years. Like the shop, new and exciting product lines are added to the website every week, ensuring you can always find something a bit different and special.

Threads is a lovely shop to visit; you can comfortably while away an hour or two browsing the wonderful displays or, if you prefer, helpful staff are always on hand to help select the perfect gift.

The shop is open Monday – Saturday 9am–5.30pm alternatively visit the website at **www.ThreadsGifts.co.uk**

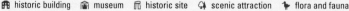

🏛 historic building   📷 museum   🏛 historic site   🏞 scenic attraction   🐾 flora and fauna

part of the de Havilland Aircraft Heritage Centre. It was here in 1940 that the first Mosquito aircraft was built and taken by road to the de Havilland airfield at Hatfield. In addition to the prototype Mosquito there is a collection of other de Havilland planes, plus various engines and displays of all kinds of aeronautical memorabilia. The museum is located within the grounds of moated Salisbury Hall (private). Built in the mid-1500s, the house was modernised a century later in order to provide a secluded but not too distant refuge for Charles II's mistress, Nell Gwynne.

SHENLEY
5 miles SE of St Albans on B5378

🏚 Lock-Up

A traditional country village with, at its centre, two inns, a pond, the site of a former pound for stray animals, and the village lock-up. One of several in Hertfordshire, this **Lock-Up** is a brick beehive-shaped construction where the village's drunks and petty criminals were locked up overnight before being put before the magistrate the next day. On either side of the door is the warning sign: 'Be sober, do well, fear not, be vigilant'.

The architect Nicholas Hawksmoor lived near Shenley and is buried in the churchyard of the neighbouring village of Shenleybury.

Here, too, is the grave of the dashing racing driver Graham Hill, who was killed in a flying accident at Arkley, three miles from Shenley.

ALDENHAM
6 miles S of St Albans on the B462

🌳 Country Park

The greatest feature of **Aldenham Country Park**, established in 1971 on what was formerly Aldenham Common, is a large reservoir that was dug by hand by French prisoners of war in the 1790s. Designed to maintain the levels of local rivers following the building of the Grand Union Canal, it is now used for recreational purposes and also supports a wealth of wildfowl and plant life. Coarse fishing is available by permit. The park has a lakeside nature trail and woodland walks and is home to several rare breeds of domestic animals, including Longhorn cattle. Families can have fun in Winnie the Pooh's '100 Aker Wood', where the homes of Pooh Bear, Christopher Robin, Piglet, Eyeore and Owl have been recreated in association with the Disney Corporation.

HARPENDEN
5 miles N of St Albans on A1081

🏛 Local History Centre 🏛 Railway Museum

The whole of the town centre is now a conservation area and, in particular, the High

---

JAYNE'S BRASSERIE & RESTAURANT

4 Harding Parade, Harpenden, Hertfordshire AL5 4SW
Tel: 01582 769034

Located in a modern block just a minute from the railway station, **Jayne's Brasserie** offers a bright, relaxing setting in which to enjoy breakfast, brunch, lunch or dinner. The main menu specialises in fish, bought on a daily basis from Billingsgate. On a typical day the choice might include chargrilled sardines, scallops and tiger prawns thermidor, sea bass with fennel and pernod, lemon sole, Nile perch, yellow snapper, halibut, skate, mussels and smoked haddock. Non-fishy options could include risottos, duck à l'orange and the ever-popular Sunday lunchtime roasts. Open 10am to 3pm and 6pm to 10pm (no food Sunday evening).

🎭 stories and anecdotes   🐦 famous people   🎨 art and craft   🎵 entertainment and sport   🚶 walks

Street is lined with many listed 17th and 18th century buildings. The **Harpenden Local History Centre** is an ideal place to find out more about this charming old agricultural community and, as well as the small permanent collection, there are regularly changing themed exhibitions. The **Harpenden Railway Museum**, a small private collection that was begun in 1963, contains several thousand items of railway memorabilia, many of which originate from the county. The ashes of the comedian Eric Morecambe were scattered in the garden of remembrance next to the Church of St Nicholas. Every summer, Harpenden hosts the Harpenden Highland Gathering, one of the largest outside Scotland.

MARKYATE
7 miles NW of St Albans off the A5

Markyate's narrow main street is part of the great Roman road, Watling Street, the route between London and Holyhead. A mansion in the village, built on the site of a medieval nunnery known as Markyate Cell, became famous as the home of Lady Katherine Ferrers, the notorious highwaywoman of Nomansland Common near Sandridge, just north of St Albans. Married as a teenager to a man she did not like, Katherine found escape and adventure by disguising herself as a highwayman and holding up the coaches that plied the busy Watling Street. She kept both her disguise and her booty in a secret room above the kitchen in the house. Famed and feared for her audacity, the 'Wicked Lady' always rode a jet black horse. In her last hold-up she was mortally wounded but managed to escape and reach her house, dying at the door of her room. She was buried quietly by her husband, who had her room sealed in the hope that her secret would die with her. It did not.

Hemel Hempstead

🏛 St Mary's Church   🏛 Charter Tower
🎞 Snook's Grave   ⚘ Gadebridge Park

This is a place with two distinct identities: the charming old town centred around the ancient Church of St Mary and tranquil Gadebridge Park; and the new town, one of the first to be built following World War II, planned as an integrated series of communities, each with its own individual centre.

Gadebridge Park is an extensive expanse of open parkland through which runs the River Gade. The park's attractive walled garden adjoins the High Street of the old town alongside the grounds of **St Mary's** which is an outstanding example of a large Norman parish church. Its interior has remained essentially unchanged since it was completed in 1180. St Mary's 200ft-high spire, made of oak and lead and added in 1340, is believed to be the loftiest in Europe.

Evidence of a settlement here long before the Norman Conquest can be found surprisingly close to the town's industrial area. Protected by a fenced enclosure and visible from the road lies the mound of a Bronze Age barrow.

The **Charter Tower**, just inside one of Gadebridge Park's entrances, is reputed to be the tower from whose upper window Henry VIII handed down Hemel Hempstead's royal charter, but the tower was in fact built long after the charter was given. On the road close to the railway station is a curious stone tablet known as **Snook's Grave**, marking the spot where James Snook, a notorious highwayman, was hanged and buried. Thought to be the last person in England to be taken back to the scene of his crime for the ultimate punishment, Snook was found guilty in 1802 of robbing a postboy and killing him in the process.

The village of **Bedmond**, three miles southeast of Hemel Hempstead, was the birthplace of Nicholas Breakspear, the only British Pope, who was crowned in office as Adrian IV in 1154.

Around Hemel Hempstead

KING'S LANGLEY
2 miles S of Hemel Hempstead on the A4251

The home of Ovaltine. A Swiss doctor called George Wander invented the drink in 1865 and his son Albert later took over the business. The King's Langley canal-side factory was built in 1912 and greatly expanded subsequently. Local farms produced eggs, barley, milk and malt for the popular drink, and the factory even had its own narrow boats on the Grand Union Canal. One of these boats has been renovated and bears the name *Albert*.

WATFORD
5 miles S of Hemel Hempstead on the A411

🏦 Bedford Almshouses   🏛 Museum

🌿 Cheslyn House

Originally a country market town, Watford was transformed in the 19th century by the arrival of the railway, which brought new industry and new building. Among the few earlier buildings to survive the rapid

St Mary's Church, Hemel Hempstead

development are the five-gabled **Bedford Almshouses**, which date back to 1580, and the early-18th century Fuller and Chilcott school. On the high street stands the splendid Mansion House, once the offices of the Benskin Brewery and now home to **Watford Museum**, where visitors can learn about the industrial and social history of the town. The local brewing and printing industries feature prominently, along with a tribute to Watford Football Club.

In the north of the town, off the A411 Hemel Hempstead road, Watford Council manages the gardens at **Cheslyn House**. The

3½-acre garden has woodland, lawns, a bog garden, rock garden, splendid herbaceous borders and an aviary and is open from dawn to dusk every day except Christmas.

Tring

Situated on the edge of the Chiltern Hills and on the banks of the Grand Union Canal, Tring is a bustling little market town whose character has been greatly influenced by the Rothschild family. However, the members of this rich and famous family are not the only people of note to be associated with the town. In **St Mary's Church** can be found the grave of the grandfather of the first US president, George Washington, while the 17th century **Mansion House**, designed by Sir Christopher Wren, was reputedly used by Nell Gwynne.

The town's narrow winding High Street, off which lead little alleyways and courtyards, contains many late-Victorian buildings, all designed by local architect William Huckvale. Of particular note is the Market House, built by public subscription in 1900 to commemorate, albeit a little late, Queen

Victoria's Diamond Jubilee. A fine example of the Arts and Crafts style, so popular at the turn of the century, the building was later converted into a fire station and today it serves as the town council chamber.

The old Silk Mill, first opened in 1824, once employed over 600 people, but towards the end of the 19th century the silk trade fell into decline and Lord Rothschild ran the mill at a loss to protect his employees rather than see them destitute. Unable to carry on in this fashion, the mill closed to the silk trade and, after losing some of its height, the building was converted into a generating station. From 1872 to the 1940s, the Rothschild family lived at Tring Park and from here they exercised their influence over the town. Perhaps their greatest lasting feature is the **Walter Rothschild Zoological Museum** (see panel below), which first opened in 1892 and, on Walter's death in 1937, became part of the Natural History Museum. An eccentric man with a great interest in natural history, Walter collected over 4,000 rare and extinct species of animals, birds and reptiles.

Tring's focal point is The Square, remodelled in 1991 and featuring an ingenious Pavement Maze in the form of a zebra's head

The Walter Rothschild Zoological Museum

Akeman Street, Tring, Herts, HP23 6AP
Tel: 020 7942 6171
e-mail: tring-enquiries@nhm.ac.uk
website: www.nhm.ac.uk/tring

The Walter Rothschild Zoological Museum in Tring became part of the Natural History Museum in 1937. It was once the private museum of Lionel Walter, the second Baron Rothschild. Visit the galleries and come face to face with a full sized gorilla, a huge anaconda, an extinct giant moa and 88 domestic dogs, including the famous greyhound Mick the Miller.

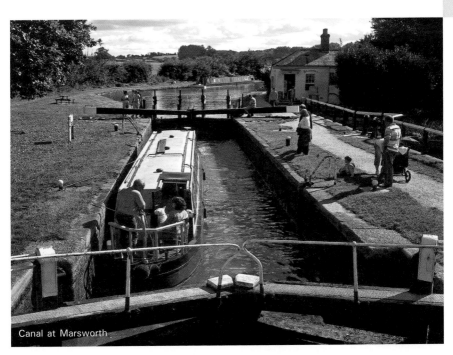
Canal at Marsworth

- a tribute to Walter's work. The town's war memorial, unveiled in 1919, stands in The Square, as does the flint and Totternhoe stone Church of St Peter and St Paul. Dating chiefly from the 15th century, this parish church contains some fine medieval carvings as well as 18th century memorials.

Extending south from close to the town centre, Tring Park provides 300 cares of excellent walking.

Around Tring

MARSWORTH
2 miles N of Tring off B489

🏃 Nature Reserve

Mentioned in the Domesday Book and situated on the banks of the Grand Union Canal, Marsworth was known as Mavvers to the canal people. The village is home to the **Tring Reservoirs National Nature Reserve**. The four reservoirs were built between 1802 and 1839 to store water for the then Grand Junction (now Grand Union) Canal, which reached its summit close by. Declared a nature reserve in 1955, this is a popular place for birdwatchers, and there is also a nature trail and a variety of trees and marshland flora.

ALDBURY
2 miles E of Tring off A4251

🌳 Ashridge Estate

🌳 Ashridge Management College

🏛 Bridgewater Monument

This picturesque village, with its green, pond, stocks, village shop, timber-framed houses and parish church, dates back to Saxon times and is often used as a film location. There was once a castle in the village that is said to have disappeared in a flash of light sometime during the 14th century. The story goes that the castle's owner Sir Guy de Gravade, in league with the Devil, raised the dead from their graves and from them learned the secret of turning base metals into pure gold. One night a servant, having seen his master at work, decided to experiment on his own; the results were disastrous, for the castle and all the residents within were engulfed in a flash of lightning.

The village lies on the western boundary of the **Ashridge Estate**, formerly part of the estate of Lord Brownlow and now owned by the National Trust. With grounds and woodland extending to some 4,000 acres on the Hertfordshire-Buckinghamshire border, this is a lovely place for walking and spotting the wealth of local flora and fauna. The focal point of the area is the **Bridgewater Monument**, an impressive tower that was erected in memory of the Duke of Bridgewater, who was famous for his pioneering work in the development of canals. Open on afternoons between April and October, the tower offers magnificent views across the countryside.

To the east of Aldbury, a mile south of Little Gaddesdon off the A4146, lie the 150 acres of **Ashridge Management College**, 90 acres of gardens and the rest woodland. Designed by Humphry Repton (he presented his Red Book to the 7th Earl of Bridgewater in 1813), the gardens were actually laid out by Sir Jeffrey Wyatville. Among the highlights are an Italian garden and fountain, a circular rosarie, a large oak planted by Princess (later Queen) Victoria, an avenue of Wellingtonias, a

Bible garden, a sunken garden once used as a skating pond and a grotto constructed from Hertfordshire pudding-stone.

NORTHCHURCH
3 miles SE of Tring on A4251

⚓ Grand Union Canal

On the south wall of the Church of St Mary is a memorial plaque to Peter the Wild Boy, who is buried close to the porch. Found living wild in a wood near Hanover, Germany, in 1725, he was brought to this country by the royal family and entrusted to the care of a farmer in this parish. He died in 1785 at an estimated age of 75.

Though the full length of the **Grand Union Canal** towpath in Hertfordshire can be walked, the section of canal from Northchurch to Tring has been developed with recreational use particularly in mind. As well as the attractive canal-side walk there are numerous maintenance and conservation projects to preserve this magnificent waterway and the wealth of wildlife and plant life found along its banks.

BERKHAMSTED
4 miles SE of Tring on the A4251

🏛 Castle   🏛 Dean John Incent's House

It was in this historic town - one of Hertfordshire's five boroughs at the time of the Domesday Survey - that William of Normandy, William the Conqueror, two months after the Battle of Hastings, accepted the British throne from the defeated Saxons. Shortly afterwards, William's half-brother Robert, Count of Mortain, commenced work on **Berkhamsted Castle**, which as a precaution against the low lie of the land was surrounded by a double moat. The castle entertained many distinguished visitors down the years: the Black

Prince on honeymoon with his bride Joan, the Fair Maid of Kent; King John's wife Isabel, besieged in 1216 by the Barons; Thomas à Becket when he was Lord Chancellor; Geoffrey Chaucer as Clerk of the Works. The castle was a place of considerable importance until at least the 15th century, although now all but ruined.

Berkhamsted Castle

One of the most interesting of the town's surviving ancient buildings is **Dean John Incent's House**, an impressive black-and-white timbered and jettied building in the main street opposite the 13th century Church of St Peter. A notable feature of this church is a window dedicated to the poet William Cowper, who was born at the local rectory in 1731. The town's cultural connections reach modern times through an annual festival to Graham Greene, son of Berkhamsted School's headmaster, and frequent visitor JM Barrie, creator of Peter Pan. Berkhamsted lies in the Chilterns Area of Outstanding Natural Beauty.

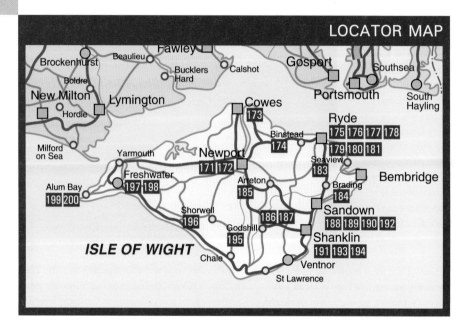

ADVERTISERS AND PLACES OF INTEREST

🏠 historic building   🏛 museum   🏛 historic site   🌊 scenic attraction   🌿 flora and fauna

7| The Isle of Wight

The Isle of Wight has adopted a motto which declares: "All this beauty is of God". It echoes the poet John Keats, "A thing of beauty is a joy for ever", the first line of his poem *Endymion* which he wrote while staying on the island in the hope that its crisp country air would improve his health.

Other distinguished visitors have described Wight as "The Garden Isle", and "England's Madeira" but it was quite late in the day before the island became popular as a resort. This was partly because for centuries, right up until the 1600s, the island was a first port of call for pestiferous French raiders who made the islanders' lives a misery with their constant incursions. These attacks ceased following the Napoleonic wars but the turning point came in the 1840s when Queen Victoria and Prince Albert bought an estate near East Cowes. They demolished the existing house and Albert designed and built an Italianate mansion he named Osborne House. A few years later, the Poet Laureate, Alfred, Lord Tennyson, bought Farringford on the eastern side of the island. Socially, the Isle of Wight had arrived.

Most of the island's 125,000 residents, (the mainland town of Peterborough outnumbers all of them by about 10,000), live in the northeast quadrant of the island, with its main resort towns of Sandown and Shanklin strung along the east coast. The rest of Wight is wonderfully peaceful with a quiet, unassertive charm all of its own.

We begin our tour of the island at its capital, Newport, and then make a clockwise circuit of the island starting at Cowes and ending up at Yarmouth.

The Needles Park, Alum Bay

Newport

🏛 Classic Boat Museum 🌱 Butterfly World

🏛 Isle of Wight Bus Museum 🏛 Roman Villa

🎨 Quay Arts Centre 🌲 Parkhurst Forest

Set around the River Medina, Newport has a history going back to Roman times. Excavations in 1926 uncovered the well-preserved remains of a **Roman Villa**, a 3rd century farmhouse in which one side of the building was given over entirely to baths. Visitors can follow the bather's progress through changing room, cold room, warm and hot rooms with underfloor heating systems, and integral cold and hot plunge baths. A Roman style garden has been re-created in the grounds and provides an interesting insight

into the wealth of new plants the Romans introduced into Britain.

Newport received its first charter back in 1190 but the growth of the small town received a severe setback in 1377 when it was completely burnt to the ground by the French. Recovery was slow and it wasn't until the 17th century that Newport really prospered again. Indirectly, the new prosperity was also due to the French since the island was heavily garrisoned during the Anglo-French wars of that period. Supplying the troops with provisions and goods brought great wealth to the town.

Some striking buildings have survived, amongst them God's Providence House, built in 1701 and now a tea room; John Nash's elegant Town Hall of 1816 which is now

---

THE FLOWER GARDEN

45 Upper St James Street, Newport, Isle of Wight PO30 1LG
Tel: 01983 524061

One of the most delightful places to visit in Newport, and indeed on the whole Island, the **Flower Garden** will enchant anyone with a genuine love of flowers. In the centre of town, with private off-road parking for customers, the shop was taken over as a going concern and expanded by Jayne Roberts, and Jayne and her staff take great pride in the beautiful, artistic displays on show throughout the year in the bright, open-plan premises.

There are garden flowers and shrubs, potted plants and hanging baskets, and lovely handmade bouquets and wreaths can be made to order for any occasion, from christenings and birthdays to weddings and funerals. The shop also sells a range of vases, pots and other accessories. The Flower Garden enjoys a high profile on the Island, and its many accolades include a Silver Award for excellence among the 2006 National Florist of the Year Awards.

🏛 historic building   🏛 museum   🏛 historic site   🏞 scenic attraction   🌱 flora and fauna

Roman Villa, Newport

Victoria's consort, Prince Albert. The church contains the tomb of the tragic Princess Elizabeth, daughter of Charles I, who died of a fever at the age of 14 while a prisoner at nearby Carisbrooke Castle.

There's also an 18th century brewer's warehouse near the harbour which now houses the **Quay Arts Centre**, incorporating a theatre, two galleries, a craft shop, café and bar; another old warehouse is home to the **Classic Boat Museum**. Among the highlights here are a 1910 river launch and Lady Penelope, a

occupied by the Museum of Island History, a charming Tudor **Old Grammar School,** and the parish Church of St Thomas whose foundation stone was laid in 1854 by Queen

THE MARKET BAKERY

Scarrots Lane, Newport, Isle of Wight PO30 1JD
Tel: 01983 521187 Fax: 01983 530819
e-mail: huw@marketbakery.co.uk

Baking the traditional way has made **The Market Bakery** an Island favourite for more than 25 years. Just off the main street of Newport, the shop is filled with lovely things to eat both sweet and savoury. As well as time-honoured delights such as jam tarts and sticky buns, Bob and the other bakers produce specialities like Isle of Wight dough cakes and Newport buns. On the savoury side they make sausage rolls and some terrific pies such as minced beef and onions or chicken curry, and the generously filled rolls are a morning mainstay of many a citizen of Newport. Opening hours are 7.30am to 5pm, closed Sunday.

fabulous speedboat once owned by the 1950s socialite Lady Docker. Other exhibits include beautifully restored sailing and power boats, along with engines, equipment and memorabilia, and a restoration project is a launch that belonged to the Beken family.

Next door to the Boat Museum is the **Isle of Wight Bus Museum**, which displays an impressive array of island buses and coaches and a former Ryde Pier tram. The buses include a 1920s Daimler and a Bristol Lodekka that completed a successful trip to Nepal.

Church Litten Park, on the site of an old churchyard whose Tudor gateway still remains, is a peaceful spot and interesting for its memorial to Valentine Gray, a nine-year-old chimney sweep whose death in 1822 as a result of ill-usage by his master caused a national outcry.

To the northwest of Newport, **Parkhurst Forest** offers miles of woodland walks.

Around Newport

CARISBROOKE
1 mile SW of Newport, on the B3323/B3401

🏛 Carisbrooke Castle

Another quote from John Keats: "I do not think I shall ever see a ruin to surpass **Carisbrooke Castle**." The castle is set dramatically on a sweeping ridge and it's quite a steep climb up from the picturesque village to the massive gatehouse. This was built in 1598 but the oldest parts of the castle date back to Norman times, most notably the mighty keep which, apart from Windsor Castle, is the most perfect specimen of Norman architecture in Britain. Archaeologists believe that the castle stands

on the site a Roman fort built some thousand years earlier.

During the season costumed guides, or 'storytellers' as English Heritage prefers to call them, conduct visitors around the noble ruins. The most poignant of their stories concern Charles I and his youngest daughter, Elizabeth. Charles was imprisoned here in the months before his trial and the guides will point out the mullioned window through which he unsuccessfully attempted to escape. After the King's execution, Cromwell's Council of State ordered that his daughter Elizabeth, "for her own safety", should also be incarcerated at Carisbrooke. The 14-year-old implored them not to send her to her father's former prison, but they were adamant. Elizabeth was a sickly child and less than a week after her arrival at the Castle she "was stricken by fever and passed away, a broken-hearted child of fourteen". The story touched the heart of Queen Victoria who set up a monument in St Thomas' Church in Newport where the Princess was buried. The effigy, in pure white Carrara marble, bears an inscription stating that it had been erected "as a token of respect for her virtues, and of sympathy for her misfortunes by Victoria R 1856".

More cheerful aspects of a visit to the Castle include the Donkey Centre. Donkeys walking a treadmill were once used to turn the huge 16th century wheel in the wellhouse to draw water from a well 161ft deep. A light at the bottom of the well gives some idea of its depth. Before donkeys were trained to raise the water, the task was performed by prisoners and nowadays visitors are invited to have a go at walking the treadmill themselves.

Also within the Castle grounds are a Coach House Exhibition and Victorian Island Exhibition, the Isle of Wight Museum and a tea room.

🏛 historic building   📷 museum   🏛 historic site   🦢 scenic attraction   🌿 flora and fauna

CALBOURNE
5 miles W of Newport off the B3401

🏚 Calbourne Mill

Calbourne Mill is a 17th century watermill in full working order, with an overshot wheel, millstones and an 1896 roller plant. Also on site are a World War and Rural Museum, gardens, a putting green, peacocks, waterfowl and punting on the millpond.

COWES
5 miles N of Newport, on the A3020

🏛 Cowes Maritime Museum 🐚 Cowes Week

🏛 Sir Max Aitken Museum 🏚 Osborne House

🚂 Model Railway Exhibition

Cowes' origins as the most famous yachting resort in the world go back to the early 1800s. It was then a rather shabby port whose main business was shipbuilding. In 1811, the Duke of Gloucester came to stay and as part of the rather limited entertainment on offer watched sailing matches between local fishermen. The Duke's patronage led to amateur gentlemen

running their own race and founding a club. The Prince Regent joined in 1817 and, on his accession as George IV, it was first re-christened the Royal Yacht Club, and then the Royal Yacht Squadron with its headquarters in one of Henry VIII's castles. Nowadays, **Cowes Week** has become the premier yachting event of the year and also a fixture in the aristocratic social calendar.

Shipbuilding was for centuries the main industry of East Cowes, making ships for the Royal Navy, lifeboats, flying boats and seaplanes. Many of the seaplanes took part in the Schneider Trophy races, which brought great excitement to the Solent in the inter-war years. Sir Donald Campbell's Bluebird was built here, and the hovercraft had its origins in what is now the home of Westland Aerospace. Westland's factory doors were painted with a giant Union Jack to mark the Queen's Jubilee in 1977 – a piece of patriotic paintwork that has been retained by popular demand. Two museums in Cowes have a nautical theme. The **Sir Max Aitken Museum** in an old sailmaker's loft in West Cowes High Street houses Sir

Osborne House

East Cowes, Isle of Wight PO32 6JY
Tel: 01983 200022

Queen Victoria's seaside home, Osborne House, gives an intriguing glimpse into the private life of the former Queen and her family. See the private rooms and Royal Apartments, including the recently refurbished Durbar Room with its new interactive display housing Queen Victoria's exquisite collection of Indian gifts. See the bedroom she shared with Prince Albert, the Nursery and take a glimpse below stairs in the Table Deckers Room. The Swiss Cottage, built for the royal children complete with miniature furniture, is entrancing. The extensive grounds with the Victorian Walled Garden and Terrace Garden overlooking the Solent will delight any garden enthusiast.

Open: 29th Mar-30th Sept 10am-6pm daily (last admission to house 4pm, house closes 5pm); 1st-31st Oct 10am-5pm daily (last admission 4pm, house closes 5pm). Call house for details of winter and spring openings and events.

📖 stories and anecdotes 🗣 famous people 🎨 art and craft 🎭 entertainment and sport 🚶 walks

Max's remarkable collection of nautical paintings, instruments and artefacts, while the **Cowes Maritime Museum** charts the island's maritime history and has a collection of racing yachts that includes the Uffa Fox pair Avenger and Coweslip. (Uffa Fox, perhaps the best known yachtsman of his day, is buried in the Church of St Mildred at Whippingham.) On the Parade, near the Royal Yacht Squadron, the **Isle of Wight Model Railways Exhibition** has for almost 20 years been one of the most admired attractions of its kind in the country. The displays include models spanning the whole history of railways, from the Rocket to Eurostar. Some are set in a British landscape, others against a stunning Rocky Mountains backdrop, and there is even a low-level layout which small children can operate and see without being lifted.

Across the River Medina, linked by a chain ferry, East Cowes is most famous for **Osborne House** (see panel on page 275), a clean-cut,

Italianate mansion designed and built by Prince Albert in 1846. Queen Victoria loved "dear beautiful Osborne" and so did her young children. They had their very own house in its grounds, a full-size Swiss Cottage, where they played at house-keeping, cooking meals for their parents, and tending its vegetable gardens using scaled-down gardening tools. In the main house itself, visitors can wander through both the State and private apartments which are crammed with paintings, furniture, ornaments, statuary and the random bric-à-brac that provided such an essential element in the decor of any upper-class Victorian home. Osborne House possessed a special place in the queen's affections. It had been built by the husband she adored with an almost adolescent infatuation: together they had spent many happy family days here. After Albert's premature death from typhoid in 1861, she often returned to Osborne. Her staff had instructions to lay out the Prince's clothes in his dressing-room each night, and the queen herself retired to bed with his nightshirt clasped in her arms. In 1901 she returned to Osborne for the last time, dying here on January 22nd in her 83rd year, her death co-incidentally signalling the beginning of the slow decline of the British Empire over which she had presided as Queen-Empress.

Osborne House and its grounds featured prominently in the film *Mrs Brown* (2001) starring Judi Dench and Billy Connolly, which explored the controversial relationship between the queen and her Scottish ghillie, John Brown.

Cowes

🏛 historic building   🖼 museum   🏚 historic site   🍃 scenic attraction   🌿 flora and fauna

WHIPPINGHAM

3 miles S of Cowes on the A3021

🏠 Barton Manor

Queen Victoria also acquired **Barton Manor** at nearby Whippingham, a peaceful retreat whose grounds are occasionally open to the public. Prince Albert had a hand in the design of the gardens and of the ornate Church of St Mildred, where the contractor and co-designer was AJ Humbert, who was also responsible for Sandringham. The royal family regularly worshipped at St Mildred's, which is predictably full of royal memorials, including a monument to Victoria's son-in-law Prince Henry of Battenberg, who succumbed to malaria in Africa at the age of 38. Alfred Gilbert's wonderful art nouveau screen in the chancel arcade is a unique work of art, and other notable pieces are a bronze angel and the font, both of them designed by Princess Louise, a daughter of the Queen, a memorial to Albert and a chair used by the Queen.

Quarr Old Abbey Barn

WOOTTON CREEK

3 miles W of Ryde, off the A3054

🌷 Butterfly World

Wootton is notable for its ancient bridge and mill-pond, and as the western terminus of the Isle of Wight Steam Railway, with an old wooden booking office and signal box moved from elsewhere on the island. It is also the home of **Butterfly World & Fountain World**. This complex comprises a sub-tropical indoor garden with hundreds of exotic butterflies flying free; a colourful Italian garden with computer-controlled fountains; a Japanese garden with Oriental buildings and a koi carp lake; and a five-acre garden centre.

FISHBOURNE

2 miles W of Ryde on the A3054

🏛 Quarr Abbey

Fishbourne is the port where the car ferry from the mainland docks. Nearby **Quarr Abbey** is a handsome redbrick Benedictine monastery built around 1910 near the ruins of a 12th century Cistercian Abbey. The old abbey, founded by a certain Baldwin de Redvers, enjoyed 400 years of prestige and influence, owning much of the land and many of the grand houses, before its destruction in 1536.

The stone for the original Quarr Abbey at Fishbourne came from the quarries at nearby Binstead, where a major family draw is Brickfields Horse Country (see page 122).

HAVENSTREET

3 miles SW of Ryde off the A3054

🏛 IOW Steam Railway 🌳 Parkwood Forest

Headquarters and nerve centre of the **Isle of**

BRICKFIELDS HORSECOUNTRY

*Newnham Road, Binstead,
nr Ryde, Isle of Wight PO33 3TH
Tel: 01983 566801
website: www.brickfield.net*

Brickfields Horsecountry is an all-weather family attraction, open all year round and a must for anyone with an interest in horses and the countryside. Owner Philip Legge, a farrier by trade, has made Brickfields one of the most popular places on the Island to visit, and with his two sons and hard-working staff is always looking for ways to expand the scope of the business.

The horse is naturally very much at the centre of life here, from the splendid gentle giants the Shire horses to the delightful Shetland ponies and donkeys. In high season pig racing draws in the crowds and a tractor and trailer ride takes visitors to meet the pigs, weigh up the form and get a ringside position for the races. There are farm animals to see, and a very interesting heritage collection of unique carriages in the museum. Demonstrations are held at the Blacksmith's Forge, which was one of the first buildings to be opened by Philip when he was developing the site at Brickfields. The Gift and Saddlery shop sells a large variety of accessories and gifts, many with a horsey theme, the saddlery department caters for all equestrian needs. The café and bar on site serves a selection of freshly prepared food throughout the day.

Brickfields has a BHS approved riding school on site, with indoor and outdoor schools, the riding school caters for all abilities from beginners through to experienced riders, for those wishing to have a lesson or a go trekking. Brickfields runs a club for regular riding clients and produces a monthly newsletter about special events and various topics.

For visitors wishing to have a holiday base, Brickfields offers bed & breakfast accommodation, with en-suite facilities, TV and tea/coffee tray. The site is close to many places of scenic and historic interest, and the 103 Wootton-Ryde bus passes the door. The whole Island is served by a comprehensive bus route.

Wight Steam Railway, Havenstreet has a small workshop and museum, gift shop and refreshment room. The locomotives working the line date back as far as 1876 and include a tiny A1 class engine acquired from the London, Brighton & South Coast Railway in 1913, and a W14, named Calbourne, which was built in 1891 and came to the island in 1925. The carriages and goods wagons are of a similar vintage.

The road south from Cowes to Newport (A3020) passes by the edge of **Parkwood Forest**, 1,000 acres of ancient royal hunting forest now managed by the Forestry Commission. From the car park and picnic area a waymarked trail leads through the forest, which is one of the few remaining 'safe houses' for the red squirrel.

RYDE
9 miles NE of Newport, on the A3054

🏛 St Mary's Church ✍ Appley Tower

🐾 Waltzing Waters 🐾 Puckpool Park

Ryde is the largest town on the island and its attractions include a huge expanse of sandy beach and a half-mile long pier, one of the first to be built in Britain. Passenger ferries from Portsmouth dock here, the hovercraft service settles nearby, and the car ferry from the mainland disgorges its cargo a couple of miles to the west. The town is essentially Victorian, a popular resort in those days for affluent middle-class families. Then, as now, visitors enjoyed strolling along the elegant Esplanade with its sea views across Spithead Sound to Portsmouth.

THE OLD FORGE

3 Albert Place, Ryde,
Isle of Wight PO33 2HP
Tel: 01983 563364

Richard Greenwood, a dealer in antiques for 35 years, rescued and restored a former blacksmith's forge and wheelwright's workshop. Dating from 1830, **The Old Forge** is one of the very few rural buildings in the centre of Ryde, and its interior is filled with antique English and Continental stripped pine, domestic antiques in copper and brass and a wide variety of curiosities and collectables. The opportunity to buy a little piece of history, perhaps decorative, perhaps practical, often both, whether it's an old copper kettle, a coal scuttle, a bed warmer, a storage box or a piece of furniture, brings customers from all over the Island and mainland.

There's always something fascinating that they didn't spot on the last visit – or, more likely it wasn't there, as the stock is constantly changing. A board outside announces some of the new arrivals – a typical day might announce a large Victorian chest of drawers, a dairy table, pine sideboards and a Victorian pine tool chest. Richard also undertakes renovation and restoration of original pine pieces.

MARTINDALE'S

108 High Street, Ryde, Isle of Wight PO33 2SZ
Tel: 01983 562382

All the meat sold at **Martindale's** is naturally reared and fed, with no artificial additives, so owner Des Jarvis can guarantee the quality of everything sold in his shop on Ryde's High Street. Des has been a butcher on the Island for more than 25 years, and the Victorian premises that house Martindale's has been selling meat for upwards of 130 years. Des seeks out the very best meat, including lamb and pork from Dorset, grass-fed Aberdeen Angus beef from accredited Scottish farms, chickens and turkeys from Norfolk and wild boar and venison from the New Forest.

Apart from the superb joints, cuts and steaks, Martindale's sells home-cooked hams and gammons, hand-raised pork pies, the very best bacon and a range of up to 20 superb home-made sausages in natural skins. On the run-up to Christmas, Des sells some 2,000 turkeys, and to complement the meats and poultry the shop sells the excellent stuffings and mixes produced by the Shropshire Spice Company, along with jars of apple sauce, mint sauce, cranberry sauce and other traditional accompaniments. The shop is open from 8.30am to 5pm Tuesday to Saturday.

IVAN BERRYMAN FINE ART

142 High Street, Ryde, Isle of Wight PO33 2RE
Tel: 01983 566662
e-mail: ivanberryman@aol.com
website: www.ivanberrymanoriginals.com

On the High Street of Ryde, **Ivan Berryman Fine Art** is a friendly, approachable gallery packed with interest. Ivan Berryman is one of the country's leading artists in the fields of aviation, marine, rail and motorsport art. His originals hang in private collections and galleries throughout the world, and more than 300 of his paintings have been published as both open and limited edition prints. Spitfires, Concorde, warships, railway scenes and Trafalgar prints are just a few of his subjects, which are sure to appeal to anyone with a nostalgic interest in land, sea and air transport.

The Isle of Wight Archive provides a fascinating insight into the history of the Island's transport, and original paintings can be commissioned from clients' photographs. The gallery also displays a collection of fairies, nudes and landscapes by Heller.

Ivan is always happy to meet visitors, and the gallery is open from 9am to 5pm Monday to Saturday; Fine Art also has an excellent website.

🏛 historic building   🏛 museum   🏛 historic site   🂾 scenic attraction   🌿 flora and fauna

Reminders of the town's Georgian and Victorian heyday are still there in abundance, among them a fine arcade in Union Street opened in 1837, the year of Queen Victoria's accession. The town has some important churches including All Saints, which was designed by Sir George Gilbert Scott and the Roman Catholic church of St Mary's which boasts a Pugin chapel.

On the beach by Appley Park stands **Appley Tower**, built as a Victorian folly and now open to the public as a centre for fossils, crystals, natural gems, oracles and rune readings. Another public space is **Puckpool**

FAIRYTALE

21 Cross Street, Ryde, Isle of Wight PO33 2AA
Tel: 01983 565565
website: www.fairytale-iow.co.uk

'Fairy tales can come true, it could happen to you, if you're young at heart.' **Fairytale** endorses the words of the song with a treasure trove of things to enchant all ages. Michael Green and wife Anne provide fun and nostalgia with hundreds of gift ideas ranging from pocket money toys to printed and audio books. From Matryoshka Russian dolls to Robert Opie Keyrings, fridge magnets and steel signs. From traditional wooden toys to marbles. From Circus skills toys to glove puppets. Browsing is encouraged, and with constantly changing stock, every visit provides a new and quirky selection of gifts for every occasion. Gift Tokens are available.

FIFTY-ONE

51 Union Street, Ryde, Isle of Wight PO33 2LF
Tel: 01983 563666
e-mail: barbarafiftyone@aol.com   website: www.home-interiors-51.co.uk

In a prime position on one of Ryde's main shopping streets, **Fifty-One** has been a favourite with shoppers ever since it opened in 2001. With a lifelong interest in all aspects of home furnishings and interior design, Barbara Hooper was fulfilling a long-held ambition when she opened the *Country Living*- style shop, which has established itself as the best of its kind on the Island.

Behind the large, attractive window displays, every inch of space is taken up with a vast range of things to enhance the home, from small ornaments and gifts for all occasions to kitchen and table ware, lamps, baskets and bags, fabrics and soft furnishings, the very finest bed linen, quilts and cushions, nightwear and children's clothes, Esteban toiletries – even some pieces of pretty country-style furniture from France. Fifty-One also offers a service for designing and making curtains and blinds.

ELIZABETH PACK

29-30 Cross Street, Ryde,
Isle of Wight PO33 2AA
Tel: 01983 812252
Fax: 01983 613900

A family concern with a history
going back to Victorian times,
Elizabeth Pack is known throughout
the Island and indeed way beyond
it as the leading womens' fashion
house on the Isle of Wight.
Occupying a handsome three-storey
building in a prime town-centre site,
the business has been run for more than 30 years by a remarkable lady, Elizabeth Barrow, who
has spent practically all her life in the worlds of drapery and fashion.

Elizabeth numbers local celebrities among her loyal clientele, who stay loyal in the certain
knowledge that the lady and the shop will never let them down; nothing is too much trouble, no
notice too short, and on more than one occasion her dresses have been sent across the world
by special express courier. She knows all the leading manufacturers and has access to many of
the major collections, enabling her to produce just the right garment or garments for any
occasion, from a dinner dress to a complete wardrobe. The bridal service is something of a
speciality, supplying everything from the bridal gown to top-to-toe outfitting for the bridesmaids
and ushers. The shop has plenty of space to show off the clothes to the best advantage, and
the stock includes a complete range of clothes, all accessories, shoes and jewellery.

Shoppers hesitating
before making a final
decision can relax with
a cup of coffee and a
snack in the Coffee
Bean café on the first
floor. Down the years
the Elizabeth Pack
trademarks of quality,
style and
professionalism have
won both local and
national recognition,
and the business has
rightly gained
international standing.
Ryde is a town of wide
and varied appeal, with
attractions as diverse
as ex-London
Underground trains and
a George Gilbert Scott
church, but there's only
one Elizabeth Barrow
and there's only one
Elizabeth Pack.

🏛 historic building   🏛 museum   🏛 historic site   ♧ scenic attraction   🌿 flora and fauna

LIBERTY'S

12 Union Street, Ryde,
Isle of Wight PO33 2DU
Tel: 01983 811007
e-mail: annie@libertyscafebar.co.uk
website: www.libertyscafebar.co.uk

On one of the main shopping streets in the largest town on the Island, **Liberty's Café Bar** has proved a hit from the moment it opened its doors in 2005. Equally popular with the residents of the Island and with the tourists who flock here throughout the year, it's the perfect place to relax with friends and enjoy great food, drinks and service in stylish contemporary surroundings. The switched-on staff have a warm welcome for everyone who passes through the doors, whether they've come for a drink, a snack or a full meal. In the informal main lounge and bar area customers can order food, either at the counter or by using the notepad and giving the order to one of the waiting staff.

The Café Bar offers an enticing range of wines and champagnes by the glass (regular or large) or bottle. The acclaimed Le Verre de Vin wine preservation system keeps the bottle, once opened, in perfect condition. The Stay a While deli menu provides plenty of choice, from bread and dips to soups, fish or meat antipasti platters (great for sharing), sandwiches, salads, pasta, frittata and some very tempting puddings, including lemon cheesecake, chocolate chip pancakes and the renowned Mr Minghella's ice creams, made on the Island and known far beyond. A Sunday brunch menu combines brunch classics with hangover favourites and seasonal specials. The Italian coffee is top-notch, and there's a good choice of teas, smoothies and milk shakes.

The upstairs dining room offers full table service and a menu that additionally includes main courses typified by sea bass on a bed of vegetables and noodles, roast duck with a compote of plum and stem ginger, sand ribeye steak topped with smoked bacon and blue cheese. There's always a choice for vegetarians. The kitchen team is made up of skilled professionals who are passionate about the preparation, cooking and presentation of the dishes, all of which are cooked to order. On the first Friday of most months Liberty's holds a wine tasting event in the cellars and vaults.

WIGHT LOCATIONS

The Old Post Office, Madeira Road, Seaview, Isle of Wight PO34 5BA
Tel: 0870 0802950 Fax: 01983 616900
e-mail: enquiries@wightlocations.co.uk
website: www.wightlocations.co.uk

Wight Locations are specialists in letting holiday properties and are passionate about providing their clients with the highest levels of service both in planning a holiday and during their stay on the Isle of Wight. Their self-catering holiday homes are ideal for everything from a romantic getaway to a family holiday or a base for discovering all that the Island has to offer the visitor. And that includes everything from a relaxing restful break to beautiful beaches, delightful countryside (much of the Island is designated an Area of Outstanding Natural Beauty), sports facilities, historic houses and unrivalled amenities for family entertainment.

The company is based in Seaview, a charming village with safe, sandy beaches, a famous yacht club and a mixture of little whitewashed cottages and grand Edwardian and Victorian houses. Wight Locations have many properties in Seaview, Bembridge and St Helens plus a growing selection across the island in both rural and coastal locations.

The choice of over 100 properties ranges from one-bedroom apartments and cosy cottages to large detached houses with up to six bedrooms.

Properties are available to rent throughout the year and out of season short breaks are very popular. Wight Locations offers a range of optional services including ferry crossings to the island, hiring cots and highchairs and recommending a range of "things to do and places to eat".

🏠 historic building 🏛 museum 🏛 historic site ♨ scenic attraction 🌿 flora and fauna

ATTRACTION

15 Cross Street, Ryde, Isle of Wight PO33 2AD
Tel: 01983 618811
website: www.attractionltd.co.uk

Ann Bullivant and her daughter Claire are the joint owners of **Attraction**, where customers can add the finishing touches to their home or choose a treat for themselves or a gift for a friend or relative. Ann and Claire take pride in providing a high standard of service and excellent value for money, and they take great care in building relations with their suppliers, who are all based in the UK.

Among the popular ranges are Female Attraction, with hair accessories, decorations for jeans and jackets, body care products and handmade jewellery; Minor Attraction, including hair decorations, children's plaques, clocks and money boxes; and Home Attraction, with perfumed candles, fridge magnets and a range of durable, hand-painted ceramic tiles from postcard size to foot square wall-mounted plaques.

Park, a leisure area behind the sea wall between Ryde and Seaview. It surrounds what was once a battery, built in the 19th century; its last gun was removed in 1927. At the Westridge Centre, just off the A3055 road to Brading, **Waltzing Waters** is an indoor water, light and music spectacular performed several times daily in a comfortable modern theatre.

SEAVIEW

2 miles SE of Ryde, on the B3330/B3340

🌷 Flamingo Park

To the east of Ryde, the aptly named resort of Seaview has a good beach with clean firm sand, ideal for making sandcastles. There are little rock pools where small children can play in safety while trying to catch the abundant crabs and shrimps. Lines of clinker-built wooden dinghies bob about on the waves, and

out to sea rise two of "Palmerston's Follies" – forts constructed in the 1850s as a warning signal to the French to keep away.

A short distance west of Seaview on the B3330 lies **Flamingo Park Waterfowl & Water Gardens**, whose colonies of flamingos, penguins, macaws and waterfowl are among the largest in the country. Visitors are encouraged to join in feeding the birds and also the giant carp and koi carp.

ST HELENS

4 miles SE of Ryde, on the B3330

📷 Sophie Dawes' Cottage

Famed for its picturesque harbour and magnificent village green, St Helen's straggles down the hillside above the mouth of the River Yar, a quiet spot beloved by yachtsmen. It must be the only English village to be named after a

---

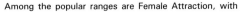

📷 stories and anecdotes 🐦 famous people 🎨 art and craft 🎵 entertainment and sport 🥾 walks

Roman Emperor's wife – the Helen who was the wife of Constantine and in whose honour a church was erected here in 704.

Another "royal" figure, the Queen of Chantilly was actually born in the village, and if the name is unfamiliar to you, seek out **Sophie Dawes' Cottage** which bears a wall plaque stating that "Sophie Dawes, Madame de Fouchères, Daughter of Richard Dawes, Fisherman and Smuggler, known as the Queen of Chantilly, was born here in 1792". As a young girl, Sophie left St Helens to seek her fortune in London where she worked (non-professionally) in a Piccadilly brothel for a while before ensnaring the exiled Duc de Bourbon and becoming his mistress. The duke paid for her education and when he was able to return to France, took her with him, marrying her off to a compliant Baron. Eventually, she married her duke, now Prince de Condé and having made sure that his will was in order, contrived his murder. Although she was tried for the crime, political considerations led to the case being quietly dropped. Sophie returned to England with her ill-gotten gains but in her last years she seems to have been stricken with remorse and gave lavishly to charity.

BEMBRIDGE
5 miles SE of Ryde, on the B3350

🏛 Windmill 🏛 Maritime Museum

🏛 Roy Baker Heritage Centre 🎨 Ruskin Gallery

The most easterly point of the island, this popular sailing centre was itself an island until the reclamation of the huge inland harbour of Brading Haven in the 1880s. The story of that major work is one of many aspects of the town's history that features in the **Shipwreck Centre & Maritime Museum** which also displays ship models, artefacts from shipwrecks, and diving equipment, as well as action videos of underwater footage and lifeboat rescues. The Shipwreck Centre has moved to Arreton Barns (see under Arreton). A fascinating exhibition of life in Bembridge, past and present, is portrayed in photographs and artefacts at the **Bembridge Roy Baker Heritage Centre** in Church Road. Art lovers should find time to visit the **Ruskin Gallery**, where an impressive collection of paintings and manuscripts of the 19th century artist are housed, and Bembridge Gallery in the High Street which features the work of island artists.

Also well worth a visit is the **Bembridge Windmill** (National Trust). Dating from around 1700, it is the only windmill to have survived on the island and much of its wooden machinery is still intact. There are spectacular views from the top floor.

BRADING
2 miles N of Sandown on the A3055

🏛 Nunwell House & Gardens 🏛 Morton Tower

🏛 Lilliput Museum 🏛 Roman Villa

🎨 Brading Experience

For what is little more than a large village, Brading is remarkably well-stocked with visitor attractions. Amongst them are a diminutive Town Hall with whipping post and stocks outside, and a fine church housing some striking tombs of the Oglander family. The most ancient of the village's sights is the **Brading Roman Villa** which in the 3rd century was the centre of a rich and prosperous farming estate. Discovered in 1880, the villa covers some 300 square feet and has fine mosaic floors with a representation of that master-musician, Orpheus, charming wild animals with his lyre.

The oldest surviving house on the island is

now home to the **Brading Experience**, an all-weather family attraction displaying scenes and characters from island history. Naturally, there's a Chamber of Horrors, as well as a World of Nature Exhibition, World of Wheels, Legends Gallery, Professor Copperthwaite's Extraordinary Exhibition of Oddities, some delightful gardens, and a shop. Close by, **The Lilliput Antique Doll & Toy Museum** (see panel below) exhibits more than 2,000 dolls and toys, ranging across the centuries from around 2000 BC to 1945. The collection also includes dolls' houses, tinplate toys, trains, rocking horses, and many unusual and rare playthings.

On the edge of the village stands **Morton Manor**, a lovely old house, dating back to 1249, largely rebuilt in 1680, and now set amidst one of the finest gardens in England. The landscaped grounds feature rose and Elizabethan sunken gardens, ponds and cascades, and many mature specimen trees including the largest London Plane you're ever likely to see. Other attractions include the Stable Shop, licensed tearooms, a safe children's play area with a traditional Elizabethan turf maze, and even a vineyard. In fact, Brading has two vineyards. The other is the well-known Adgestone Vineyard, planted in 1968 and the oldest on the island. Entry is free, as is the wine tasting, there are pony trap rides around the vineyard during the season, a gift shop and café.

A mile or so northwest of the village, **Nunwell House & Gardens** should definitely not be missed. The picturesque house has been a family home since 1522 and is of great historic and architectural interest. It was here that Sir John Oglander, an ancestor of the present owner, was host to Charles I on

Lilliput Museum of Antique Dolls & Toys

High Street, Brading, Isle of Wight. PO36 ODJ
Tel: 01983 407231

This cottage museum contains one of the finest collections of old and antique dolls and toys in the country with over 2,000 exhibits on display dating from c2000 BC to approximately 1945. There are examples of almost every seriously collectable doll together with a number of dolls' houses; rocking horses; tin plate toys; trains; bears; soft toys and many other unusual play things. Amongst the many exhibits can be found, for example, a wax doll made circa 1790 and dressed by a lady-in-waiting to Princess Caroline of Brunswick - the material used was a remnant of the Princess's wedding dress. Next to her is the modem equivalent, one of only two contemporary dolls in the Museum, this is a portrait doll of Diana Princess of Wales produced by a member of the British Doll Artists Association in 1981. Like the wax doll this exhibit is also dressed in a remnant of the original wedding gown.

Most of the dolls and toys have been acquired from the original owners or their descendants so there is a fund of stories about them. Adjoining the museum is a specialist shop stocking a variety of collectable dolls houses and furniture, china dolls, limited edition bears and traditional toys.

🎭 stories and anecdotes   🐦 famous people   🎨 art and craft   🎭 entertainment and sport   🎿 walks

Stocks and Whipping Post, Brading

his last night of freedom and modern day visitors can still see the Parlour Chamber in which they met. The house is beautifully furnished, there are exhibits recalling the family's military connections, and Nunwell is surrounded by five acres of tranquil gardens enjoying views across the Solent.

Some of the grandest views on the island can be enjoyed from **Brading Down**, just west of the village on the minor road that leads to Downend.

ARRETON
5 miles W of Sandown on the A3056

🏚 Arreton Manor   🏚 Haseley Manor

From Downend, it's less than a mile to **Arreton Manor**, which claims, with some justification, to be 'the most beautiful and intriguing house on the Isle of Wight'. There was a house on this site long before Alfred the Great mentioned Arreton in his will of 885 AD and the manor was owned by successive

Island Brass Rubbing Centre

The Coach House, St. George's Church, Arreton, Isle of Wight, England
Tel/Fax 01983 527553
e-mail: islandbrass@talktalk.net

Britain's age of chivalry – crowned kings, knights in armour, costumed ladies and heraldic beasts live on in Arreton on the beautiful Isle of Wight. Here in a restored coach house, adjacent to the medieval Church of St.George, discover the simple

craft of brass rubbing using metallic waxes and specialist papers. Learn about the craft of the medieval engraver and discover facts about costume and heraldry by listening to experts as they demonstrate the art of brass rubbing and teach the skills needed to make your own knight or lady – a unique gift to take home with you as a memento of a fascinating visit.

Specialists in Educational Visits, the centre welcomes many student groups and other groups and organisations. Contact the centre for a workpack or for more information about the service it provides – which can be tailored to your requirements.

🏚 historic building   📷 museum   🏛 historic site   ♧ scenic attraction   🌱 flora and fauna

monarchs from Henry VIII to Charles I. The present house was built during the reigns of Elizabeth and James I and it's a superb example of the architecture of that period, with mellow stone walls and Jacobean panelling complemented by furniture from the same era. Perhaps the most appealing aspect of Arreton is that indefinable atmosphere of a house that has been lived in for centuries. Other attractions here include a Museum of Childhood, Lace Museum, National Wireless Museum, gift shop, tea rooms and picnic area. Arreton Barns, a traditional working craft village, is the new home of the Shipwreck Centre, previously located in Bembridge (see under Bembridge).

A mile or so southwest of Arreton Manor stands another grand old house, **Haseley Manor**. In the mid-1970s, it was a deserted and decaying shell but in a heroic work of restoration has been saved by Raymond and Krystyna Young. They have furnished and decorated the rooms in period, adding audio-visual tableaux explaining the different eras. Visitors can also watch a film showing how the mammoth task of restoration was carried out. Inside the house, there's an indoor play area for small children, a working pottery where children can try their hand at the slippery craft, a tea-room and gift shop. Outside, the attractions include magnificent herb, flower and water gardens; a Children's Farm and Adventure Playground, and a picnic area.

NEWCHURCH

2 miles W of Sandown on the A3056

🐦 Amazon World

Amazon World is a popular family attraction that tells the story of the rain forest with the help of a large number of exotic animals and

MOLLY ATTRILL'S POTTERY

Mersley Lane, Newchurch,
Isle of Wight PO36 0NR
Tel: 01983 731116/862028

Born on the Island, Molly Attrill trained with Michael Leach in North Devon and West Surrey College of Art and Design, Farnham; she worked in studios in Canada and France before establishing her own pottery in 1982.

Working mostly in earthenware, she makes pots for the table and kitchen, and also hand-cut tiles and large commissioned panels. Many of the pieces feature beautiful representations of animals, birds, sea creatures and fruit. The freehand drawings which form the design are either scratched through slip (sgraffito) or painted in oxides or as a wax resist onto a tin glaze (majolica).

Molly has been a finalist in the *Country Living Magazine's* "Enterprising Rural Women Award" and her work is featured in a number of books and journals. **Opening hours for visitors 10.30am to 4pm, Monday to Saturday.**

🎞 stories and anecdotes   🐦 famous people   🎨 art and craft   🎭 entertainment and sport   🚶 walks

THE GARLIC FARM & MERSLEY FARM SELF-CATERING

Newchurch, Isle of Wight PO36 0NR
Tel: 01983 865378   Fax: 01983 862294
e-mail: colin@thegarlicfarm.co.uk
website: www.thegarlicfarm.co.uk

Garlic Farm is the UK's premier grower of garlic and source of all things connected with garlic. Colin Boswell has been the driving force behind the farm for more than 30 years, and his wife Jenny and their five children are all involved in various ways in the business. Intrigued by the ancient origins of garlic and its wide range of culinary, health and legendary properties, Colin has developed the business and has personally become the number one garlic expert in the UK, perhaps in Europe. The shop sells plain garlic, smoked garlic, garlic planting packs and garlic in dozens of products made on the farm. These include pickles and relishes, garlic mayonnaise, garlic-infused oils and vinegars, smoked garlic honey, mint sauce with a hint of garlic, sweet garlic cloves in oil, garlic and horseradish mustard, pesto, tapénade, oak-smoked garlic butter, garlic salsa, garlic bread.......the range grows each year. The relocated farm shop is open every day all year round, and in summer visitors can relax over coffee and croissants with the papers and jazz music.

The Garlic Festival that started here in 1983 has become one of the largest annual events on the Island, attracting some 25,000 visitors in an ambience that mixes all things garlic with a country fair and a pop festival.

A variety of excellent self-catering accommodation is available in converted barns and cottages on **Mersley Farm**.

Tel: 01983 865213. e-mail: web@mersleyfarm.co.uk

Little Mersley Farmhouse, sleeping 10, was built in 1672. It stands alone in its own grounds, a fine and little-altered example of an Island yeoman's house. The master bedroom is in on the ground floor, with en-suite toilet and shower. There's a separate sitting room and dining room off a well-appointed kitchen. The other bedrooms are on the first floor. The Milking Parlour, sleeping eight, is a large unit first built as a threshing barn and then used for milking cows. This attractive barn conversion features a spacious, comfortable sitting room and kitchen with a vaulted ceiling. There are four bedrooms – two with double beds, one twin-bedded and one bunk-bedded; with the option of extra accommodation on a sofa bed/Z bed in the living room. Adjoining the Milking Parlour is Paddock Cottage, sleeping two in a double bedroom (plus an optional single bed). French windows open from the living room on to a patio and paddock. Paddock Cottage and the Milking Parlour can be rented as one. The Barn Cottage, sleeping four, is an attractive conversion on one level with its own entrance, garden and barbecue areas with access to the farm grounds and tennis court.

Free Wi-Fi broadband internet access is available in all the properties.

🏛 historic building   🏛 museum   🏛 historic site   🐿 scenic attraction   🌱 flora and fauna

birds – conservation is the name of the game here. One of the Island's most renowned products is garlic, and the annual Garlic Festival, held in Newchurch on a weekend in August attracts many thousands of visitors. The village church and its steeple are clad in wood.

ALVERSTONE
2 miles NW of Sandown, off the A3055

A couple of miles west of Haseley Manor, the secluded and picturesque village of Alverstone sits beside the tiny River Yar. It has everything you expect of an English village – except for a pub. The deeds of the estate's owner, Lord Alverstone, specifically forbid the sale of intoxicating liquor within the village.

Sandown

🏛 Museum of Geology   🌴 Zoological Gardens

🌴 Dinosaur Isle

'A village by a sandy shore' was how a guide-book described Sandown in the 1870s. Since then, its superb position on sweeping Sandown Bay has transformed that village into the island's premier resort. Now a lively town, Sandown offers its visitors every kind of seaside attraction. There are miles of flat, safe sands where a Kidzone safety scheme operates during the season; a traditional pier complete with theatre; colourful gardens; a Sunday market; abundant sporting facilities, and even pleasure flights from the nearby airfield. On the edge of the town, the **Isle of Wight Zoological Gardens** specialises in breeding severely

ROYAL CLIFF HOLIDAY APARTMENTS

Roayl Cliff Estate, Private Drive off Grange Road, Sandown, Isle of Wight PO36 8NE
Tel: 01983 402138
website: www.royalcliff.co.uk

Positioned on a sweeping bay, Sandown is the Isle of Wight's premier resort, and for a relaxing break the **Royal Cliff Holiday Apartments** are the perfect choice. The large Mediterranean-style house provides everything for a carefree self-catering holiday in a superb setting on the cliff tops. There are seven apartments in all, and shared facilities include an outdoor swimming pool, south-facing gardens, a large private car park and glorious views.

Cheetah, on the ground floor can sleep four comfortably in two bedrooms, both en-suite. Dolphin, also on the ground floor can sleep up to four guests in large bunk beds and a sofa bed in the lounge. The ground-floor Eagle, the largest of the apartments, has a combined kitchen/diner/lounge with a sofa bed and a sliding patio door opening on to the pool area and can sleep up to nine in total. Fox, on the first floor can sleep four while Greyhound, which overlooks the pool and the sea, can sleep six.

The owners have a further two apartments without sea views – a one-bedroom and a two bedroom apartment, both en-suite. All apartments feature central heating, TV and excellent kitchen facilities. The cliff path down to the safe, sandy beach can be reached directly from the grounds, and all Sandown's many amenities are an easy walk away.

GLORY ART GLASS

Melville Street, Sandown,
Isle of Wight PO36 8HX
Tel: 01983 402515
e-mail: martin@gloryartglass.com
website: www.gloryartglass.com

Martin Evans, his wife Nicola and their sons Edward and Meredith are a family of very talented artists who all contribute to the success of **Glory Art Glass** - and eldest daughter Danielle is a successful glassmaker with her own studio in the USA. 2006 sees the **tenth anniversary** of the studio, where the family design and make unique pieces that form a dazzling display of innovative and dynamic art glass. Most of their work is sold from the studio gallery, but they also sell in a few selected galleries and on the internet through their excellent website. Their Romano series is sold at Brading Roman Villa and other historic sites.

Their principal interest is colour and light, and glass is the perfect conveyor of the beauty of those two elements. Opaque or transparent, textured or smooth, glass has the ability to reflect and refract light in a fascinating way. This is the closest you can get to painting in light, and when the sunlight streams into the gallery the whole place comes to life. The Hot glass work includes bowls, glasses, vases and sculpture with subjects including flowers, animals, birds, fish, trees and torsos. They have a selection of souvenirs, corporate gifts and presents for anniversaries and celebrations. Edward produces beautiful **Eternity paperweights**" holding the ashes of customers loved ones - a lasting special memory.

They also etch flat glass designs, completing a number of prestigious public commissions as well as designs for doors and screens in private houses.

Martin studied as a sculptor at Portsmouth University working in wood, metal and clay following 10 years as a Naval shipwright. All his life he has been a maker, working in many materials. He worked for 20 years as a glass maker before opening **Glory Art Glass** in 1996, in order to pursue his own ideas in glass. The family show their glass along with **paintings and sculptures** in the gallery, which is open from 9.30am to 5pm each day except Sunday,when they are making glass visitors are welcome to watch them at work and learn more about this fascinating art form. There is no charge to watch the glassmaking. If you are taking a day out or a short break don't miss this opportunity to visit the artists studio. and the opportunity to maybe buy your own unique and enduring work of glass art .

🏠 historic building   🏛 museum   🏛 historic site   ◔ scenic attraction   🌿 flora and fauna

endangered exotic species and is home to the UK's largest variety of Royal Bengal, Siberian and Chinese tigers. The zoo is also a World Health Organisation centre for venomous snakes, their venom extracted for use in antidotes for snake bites. You may well see TV "Snake Man" Jack Corney handling these lethal reptiles and children who are photographed with a small harmless snake are presented with a handling certificate to prove it. There are all-weather snake and parrot shows, a kiddies' play area and Pets' Corner, a seafront pub and café, the Zoofari Gift Shop, and a snack bar. A Road-Runner Train operates frequent services between the zoo and the town centre.

In Sandown's High Street, the **Museum of Isle of Wight Geology** is especially popular with children who love its life-sized dinosaurs – the Isle of Wight is renowned for the number and quality of the dinosaur remains that have been discovered here. The museum, "120 million years in the making", has excellent displays on all aspects of the island's geology. As part of its educational programme, museum staff will advise you on the best places to look for fossils and, when you return with your discoveries, will identify them for you. On Culver Parade, **Sandown Dinosaur isle** (see panel below) is Britain's first purpose-built

dinosaur attraction, where the life-size replicas include the animatronic Neovenator.

Throughout the season, the Sandown Bay area hosts a wide range of special events – from the Regatta in August to Sunday markets, from the Isle of Wight Power Boat Festival in May to the National Strong Man finals in September.

SHANKLIN
2 miles SW of Sandown, on the A3055

🐚 Shanklin Chine 🏛 Heritage Centre

Like Sandown, Shanklin was just a small village a century or so ago. The old village has survived intact, a charming little complex of thatched houses standing at the head of the **Shanklin Chine** (see panel on page 295). The famous Chine is a spectacular ravine some 300 feet deep, 180 feet wide, noted for its waterfalls and rare flora. There's a Nature Trail to follow or you can join a guided tour. The **Heritage Centre** contains an interesting exhibit on PLUTO (the Pipe Line Under The Ocean) secretively constructed during World War II to transport fuel from the island to the Continent during the D-Day landings. There's also a memorial to the soldiers of 40 Commando who trained in this area for the disastrous assault on Dieppe in 1942.

Dinosaur Isle

Culver Parade, Sandown, Isle of Wight PO36 8QA
Tel: 01983 404344
website: www.dinosaurisle.com

In a spectacular pterosaur shaped building watching over Sandown's blue flag beach is Britain's first purpose built dinosaur museum. Walk back through fossilised time to the period of the dinosaurs where you will find amongst the fossils many interactive displays. On a recreated landscape enhanced by sights, smells and sounds you will meet life sized dinosaurs including the animatronic Neovenator. Guided fossil hunts (which must be pre-booked) have proved to be a popular addition to a visit. For more information regarding opening times and admission prices, please call the museum.

📖 stories and anecdotes 🐦 famous people 🎨 art and craft 🖊 entertainment and sport 🚶 walks

THE ROCK SHOP

93 High Street, Shanklin, Isle of Wight PO37 6NR
Tel: 01983 862950 Fax: 01983 861460
e-mail: jennyrocks@tiscali.co.uk

Traditional sweet shops are few and far between these days, so the Isle of Wight is lucky in having two of the very best. Among the stars of the show at the **Rock Shop** in Shanklin are the traditional sticks of rock in a variety of flavours – classic minty pink is still the favourite. Shortbread is made on the premises in the shape of the Island by manager Jenny Bryant and fudge in many flavours is made specially for the shops. There is always a good selection of chocolates, old fashioned boiled sweets; also preserves, chutneys and an extensive range of sugarfree products. Shop hours are 9.30 to 5.30/6, till 10 in high season.

THE ROCK SHOP

1 High Street, Sandown, Isle of Wight PO36 8LX

The sister shop to the **Rock Shop** in Shanklin, both of them illustrating just how good a traditional sweet shop can be. The colourful exterior on a High Street corner site promises good things, and what's inside is guaranteed to delight customers of all ages who pass through the doors. Traditional sticks of rock are always best-sellers, along with shortbread shaped like the Island, fudge and Turkish delight in many flavours, and chocolates from the UK and Belgium. Shop hours are 9.30 to 5.30/6, till 10 in high season.

ST GEORGE'S HOUSE HOTEL

2 St George's Road, Shanklin, Isle of Wight PO37 6BA
Tel: 01983 863691
e-mail: info@stgeorgesiow.com
website: www.stgeorgesiow.com

St George's House Hotel enjoys a quiet location between the town centre and the cliff top, a short walk from the cliff lift, the shops, the splendid beaches, the old village and the Chine. Built in 1870 and a hotel for most of its life, the house retains many attractive original features while providing the up-to-date comfort and amenities expected by today's guests. The nine en-suite bedrooms – all doubles or twins – have individually controlled central heating, digital TV and radio and hospitality trays. Most of the rooms enjoy fine views.

Day rooms comprise a lounge with wide-screen TV, videos, music and games, a well-stocked cocktail bar and a bright dining room where breakfast and off season pre-ordered evening meals are served. Jan and Mick Dawson, with 30 years' experience in the Island's hotel industry, are the friendliest of hosts, and there's a cosy, welcoming feel throughout the hotel. Charles Darwin, Longfellow and Keats were all entranced by the charms of Shanklin, which are as alluring now as they were in their day.

🏚 historic building   🏛 museum   🏛 historic site   ⚘ scenic attraction   🌿 flora and fauna

Shanklin Chine

Shanklin Esplanade, Shanklin,
Isle of Wight PO37 6BW
Tel: 01983 866432
e-mail: jillshanklinchine1@msn.com
website: www.shanklinchine.co.uk

Part of our national heritage, this scenic gorge at Shanklin, Isle of Wight, is a magical world of unique beauty and a rich haven of rare plants, woodland, wildlife, including red squirrels and enchanting waterfalls. A path winds through the ravine with overhanging trees, ferns and other flora covering its steep sides. The Exhibition "The Island – Then And Now" is housed in the Heritage Centre and features "Flora of the Island", also PLUTO (Pipe Line Under The Ocean) which carried petrol to the Allied troops in Normandy, and local history displays.

The Memorial to 40 Royal Marine Commando, who trained here during the war in preparation for the Dieppe Raid of 1942, can be seen at the lower entrance. After dusk, during the main summer months, subtle illuminations create a different world. There is also a gift shop and tea room. On the beach below, Fisherman's Cottage, built by William Colenutt in 1817, offers a choice of excellent food and real ale, which can be enjoyed on the sun terrace.

Open 31 March - 29 October daily, illuminated 26 Mat - 10 Sept

The old village stands on a 150ft cliff from which the ground slopes gently down to the safe, sheltered beach, with its long, seafront esplanade. With its scenic setting, many public gardens, and healthy climate, Shanklin has appealed to many celebrities. Charles Darwin was particularly fond of the town, the American poet Longfellow fell in love with it, and John Keats was a familiar figure in Sandown throughout the summer of 1818. The grassy open space known as **Keats Green** commemorates his stay here during which he wrote some of his best-known poems.

GODSHILL

4 miles W of Shanklin on the A3020

🏛 Church of All Saints   🏚 Nostalgia Toy Museum
🏡 Model Village   🌱 Natural History Centre

A short drive inland from Shanklin leads to the charming village of Godshill, which with its stone-built thatched cottages and its medieval **Church of All Saints** is one of the most popular stops on the tourist trail. The double-naved church, whose 15th century pinnacled tower dominates the village, contains some notable treasures, including a 15th century wall painting of Christ crucified on a triple-branched lily, a painting of Daniel in the Lions' Den and many monuments to the Worsleys and the Leighs, two of the leading island families.

Godshill has much to entertain visitors, including the magical **Model Village** with its 1/10th scale stone houses, trains and boats, even a football match taking place on the green, and the **Natural History Centre** with its famed shell collection, minerals and aquarium. The miniature village was built with the help of model-makers from Elstree film studio and after two years' preparation was

🎭 stories and anecdotes   🦅 famous people   🎨 art and craft   🎟 entertainment and sport   🚶 walks

Church of All Saints, Godshill

opened to the public in 1952. The models are made of coloured cement and the detail is quite incredible. Real straw was prepared in the traditional way for thatching; the church on the hill took 600 hours of work before being assembled in its position; each house has its own tiny garden with miniature trees and shrubs. The airfield is in the style of small landing strips of the 1920s and 1930s, and the little railway is modelled on the older Island systems. Things get even smaller in the model garden of the model Old Vicarage, where there is another (1/100 scale) model village with yet another Old Vicarage, and within its garden another (1/1000 scale) model village – a model of a model of a model!

Also in Godshill is the **Nostalgia Toy Museum**, where 2,000 Dinky, Corgi and Matchbox toys and 1960s dolls bring back childhood memories.

SHEEPWASH FARM

Sheepwash Lane, Godshill, Isle of Wight PO38 3JP
Tel: 01983 840978 Fax: 01983 840035
e-mail: sue@brownriggonline.co.uk
website: www.brownriggonline.co.uk

On a 400-acre working poultry farm in wonderful walking country a mile from Godshill and Whitwell, Sue and Paul Brownrigg provide excellent self-catering accommodation in two separate properties. The larger letting building at **Sheepwash Farm** is Pilgrim Lodge, a 19th century Grade II listed house in a completely self-contained wing with its own drive, a secluded walled garden with furniture and barbecue, traditional furnishings and many original features. The house has two double bedrooms, a twin and a big room with twin beds and bunk beds. Beyond the flagstoned hall are a sitting room, and an open-plan kitchen with electric oven and hobs, microwave, dishwasher, fridge-freezer, washing machine and tumble dryer.

The pleasant dining area has a 'Captain's Table' that can seat 10 in comfort. Loves Cottage, which dates from the 17th century, retains many original features, including splendid beams in the kitchen. It offers excellent accommodation for 6 guests in a double room, a single room and a large room with three single beds. It, too, has a well-equipped kitchen, comfortable eating and sitting areas and a secluded fenced garden. Guests can buy fresh eggs from the farm, also chickens, ducks, seasonal game and Christmas turkeys.

🏛 historic building   🏛 museum   🏛 historic site   🐸 scenic attraction   🌿 flora and fauna

BONCHURCH

2 miles S of Shanklin on the A3055

The poet Algernon Swinburne spent some of his childhood in Bonchurch, and is buried in the churchyard of St Boniface. Charles Dickens wrote part of *David Copperfield* while staying in Bonchurch. His first impressions of the place were very favourable – "I think it is the prettiest place I ever saw". He seemed likely to make it his permanent home, but he soon grew to dislike the weather and the place and returned to his familiar Broadstairs.

Ventnor

VENTNOR

3 miles SW of Shanklin on the A3055

🏛 Heritage Museum   🏛 Smuggling Museum

🌱 Visitor Centre   🌱 Botanical Gardens

🌱 Coastal Visitor Centre   🜨 St Boniface Down

Along the south-eastern corner of the island stretches a six-mile length of ragged cliffs known as Undercliffe. Clinging to the slopes at its eastern end, Ventnor has been described as "an alpinist's town" and as "a steeply raked auditorium with the sea as the stage". Promoted as a spa town in the 1830s, its distinguished visitors have included a young Winston Churchill and an elderly Karl Marx.

Ventnor Heritage Museum houses a fascinating collection of old prints, photographs and working models relating to the town's history, while **Ventnor Botanical Gardens** shelters some 10,000 plants in 22 acres of grounds, amongst them many rare and exotic trees, shrubs, alpines, perennials, succulents and conifers. The gardens received a huge boost in the spring of 2000 with the opening of an exciting new **Visitor Centre** whose exhibits include an interactive display called The Green Planet – the Incredible Life of Plants. Many unusual varieties are for sale in the shop. There's a picnic area and children's playground, and during August the Gardens host open-air performances of Shakespearean plays. Also snuggling in the garden grounds is the **Smuggling Museum**, whose 300 exhibits illustrate 700 years of smuggling lore.

Back in town, the **Coastal Visitor Centre** provides a fascinating and educational insight into the island's coastal and marine environment, with special features on animal and plant life, coastal defences and living with landslides a problem very familiar to the island as well as to many parts of England's south coast.

Above the town, **St Boniface Down** (National Trust), at 785ft the highest point on

Blackgang

Distance: *5.0 miles (8.0 kilometres)*
Typical time: *140 mins*
Height gain: *165 metres*
Map: *Outdoor Leisure 29*
Walk: *www.walkingworld.com ID:546*
Contributor: *David L White*

ACCESS INFORMATION:

Large car park, nearest bus stop 'Blackgang'.
If travelling from the mainland best crossings:
Ryde/Portsmouth - Catamaran;
Ryde/Southsea - Hovercraft;
Fishbourne/Portsmouth - Car ferry

ADDITIONAL INFORMATION:

Seafaring history is evident here as may be
seen in the form of the three lighthouses all
built at different periods in history. The area
of Blackgang and Niton featured strongly in
the business of smuggling in earlier days.
During the warmer weather there is an
abundance of wildlife and flowering plants.
Should you wish to take a short diversion
from the Niton parish church further into the
village, shops and a local pub may be found
(the pub serves food). Opposite the church
are the public toilets.

DESCRIPTION:

A walk with fabulous views over the Isle of
Wight and English Channel taking in some of
the local history and landmarks.

FEATURES:

Hills or Fells, Sea, Pub, Toilets, Church,
Wildlife, Birds, Flowers, Great Views

WALK DIRECTIONS:

1 | A Heritage Coast information board in the
car park will tell you about the coastal area.
Climb steps on seaward side of car park -
follow path to cliff top. Turn left along cliff
top towards Niton. Follow path past radio
mast station on your left. After second stile
beyond radio station turn immediately left
over another stile heading inland.

2 | From this high vantage point looking
slightly South East St. Catherine's lighthouse
may be seen. It was built in 1840 to replace
the earlier lighthouses that were further
inland. This coastline was famous for its many
wrecks, one night it is said that there were as
many as 14.

3 | Keeping fence on your right walk across to
far end of field to stile. Head across small
meadow slightly to your left to stile, cross and
walk through a coppice path until you reach

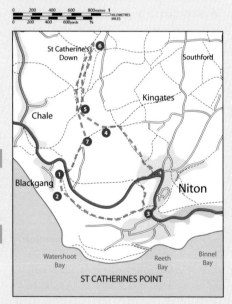

the main road. Follow road to right - until it bears left (marked through traffic) to church. At lychgate turn left and go up Pan Lane, which eventually turns into a bridle path. Follow path eventually turning left and you soon reach a metal gate. Follow blue arrow sign straight ahead.

4 | After passing through gate follow track indicated by blue waymark arrow, upon reaching metal gate at other end of the field (keeping radio mast on your left). After passing through this gate turn immediately left and climb to summit of the hill where the 'Old Oratory' stands. Here you will see fantastic views. If you do not wish to visit Hoy's Monument ignore waymarks 5 and 6, proceed to waymark 7.

5 | To visit Hoy's Monument, instead of turning left walk across the field bearing slightly to your right towards a visible signpost follow bridleway C6 to Hoy's monument.

6 | Hoy's Monument - top right corner of photo. Viewed from the Old Oratory (waymark 6). Return to waymark 5 by same path.

7 | The Oratory, known to locals as the 'Pepper-pot'. One of the original lighthouses built in 1314 and manned by a local duty monk. Also visible to the East from here is the 'Salt Pot', built later in history but before completion it was decided that due to mist and fog on the hills often obscuring the glow of the light the project would be abandoned in favour of a building closer to the coast and lower down (the present St. Catherine's). From Oratory, cross field heading towards the sea where you will see a stile. Standing on the stile and looking down slightly to your left you will see your starting point car park.

the island, provides some dizzying views across coast and countryside.

ST LAWRENCE
1 mile W of Ventnor on the A3055

Catherine's Point   Studio Glass

Blackgang Chine

Nestling in the heart of the Undercliff, the ancient village of St Lawrence has a 13th century church that once laid claim to being the smallest in Britain. It was extended in 1842 but remains diminutive, measuring just 20 feet by 12 feet.

Not far away, old farm buildings were converted into **Isle of Wight Studio Glass**, where skills old and new produce glass of the highest quality. Lord Jellicoe, hero of Jutland, lived for some years in St Lawrence and often swam in Orchard's Bay, a small cove where Turner sketched.

The coast road continues through the village of Niton to **St Catherine's Point**, the most southerly and the wildest part of the island, in an Area of Special Scientific Interest. Steps lead down to St Catherine's lighthouse and a path leads up to the summit of St Catherine's Hill, where the remains of a much older lighthouse, known as the Pepperpot, can be seen. Close by is the Hoy Monument erected in honour of a visit by Tsar Nicholas I.

Blackgang Chine, at the most southerly tip of the island, has been developed from an early Victorian scenic park into a modern fantasy park with dozens of attractions for children. Also inside the park are two heritage exhibitions centred on a water-powered sawmill and a quayside, with displays ranging from cooper's and wheelwright's workshops to a shipwreck collection, a huge whale skeleton and a 19th century beach scene complete with a bathing machine. The coastline here is

CHEVERTON FARM

Shorwell, nr Newport, Isle of Wight PO36 3JE
Tel/Fax: 01983 741017

Cheverton Farm, which lies just north of the village of Shorwell in the beautiful Bowcombe Valley, offers top-quality self-catering accommodation in two outstanding properties. They are located on a working beef, sheep and arable farm, with lots of animals and poultry for children to see. The larger of the two, **Brummell Barn**, is one of the original outbuildings to the farmhouse, a superb conversion of an old stone barn completed in 1998 and retaining many original and interesting stone and timber features. The accommodation caters for up to ten guests, plus two cots or a Z bed, and includes everything needed for a relaxing family holiday or for walking groups. On the ground floor is a large kitchen with a dishwasher, fridge-freezer, a second fridge, twin-oven electric range and microwave. There is a very spacious dining area with a television, radio and cassette/CD player. A utility room with a washing machine and tumble dryer opens on to a secure play area with a Wendy house, garden furniture and barbecue. On the lower ground floor level are three bedrooms – a double with shower en suite and two twin-bedded rooms, a bathroom with spa bath, bidet and WC and a separate WC. An impressive hallway with a lofty beamed ceiling leads to the first floor and two more bedrooms – a double with en suite shower and a twin. There's a bathroom with shower over the bath and a separate WC. On the upper first floor is a delightful galleried sitting room with beams, a wooden floor, television, VCR and a lovely south-facing view over the surrounding countryside. West-facing windows overlook the farm and the countryside beyond.

Cheverton Farm Cottage is a charming beamed cottage attached to the owners' 17th century farmhouse. It has three bedrooms: on the first floor is a spacious twin-bedded room with a washbasin, and stairs from the landing lead up to two attic rooms, a double with a 5' bed and a twin-bedded room with a cot. Also on the first floor are a cosy sitting room, a bathroom with bath, shower and WC and a second separate WC. On the ground floor is a traditionally furnished, comprehensively equipped kitchen and dining area. Outside is a large garden and patio with garden furniture and barbecue. The two properties, open all year round, share a play area with a trampoline, slide, swings and climbing frame, and a games room with table tennis, billiards/snooker table and darts, as well as a fitness centre, a billiards/snooker room with a full-size table (for adults) and a heated indoor swimming pool. There's access to 550 acres of farmland with several footpaths and bridleways, including the Worsley Trail running through the farm. Cheverton Farm is a perfect base for a family holiday, with ponies, goats, ducks, hens and dogs around the farmyard and lambing in April. The farm offers lovely views and walks on to downland. The picturesque village of Shorwell is a mile away, and it's only four miles to Newport and the nearest beach. All the many attractions of the Island are within an easy drive. Bookings are normally Saturday to Saturday; shorter breaks are available between end October and Easter. All linen and fuel are included in the tariff; well-behaved pets are welcome. For further details and prices ring 01983 741017.

🏛 historic building   🏛 museum   🏛 historic site   🗺 scenic attraction   🌿 flora and fauna

somewhat fragile, and a large slice of cliff has been lost to storms and gales in recent years.

WROXALL
2 miles N of Ventnor on the B3327

🏛 Appuldurcombe House

🦉 Owl & Falconry Centre   🦉 Donkey Sanctuary

Owls, falcons, vultures and donkeys all call Wroxall their home. **Appuldurcombe House**, once the grandest mansion on the whole island, with gardens laid out by Capability Brown, was badly bombed in 1943 and has never been lived in since. The building has been partly restored and visitors can stroll in the 11 acres of ornamental grounds landscaped by Capability Brown which provide an enchanting setting for picnics. The **Owl & Falconry Centre**, in what used to be the laundry and brewhouse, stages daily flying displays with birds of prey from around the world and holds courses in the centuries-old art of falconry.

Heaven for 200 donkeys and many other animals is the **Isle of Wight Donkey Sanctuary** at Lower Winstone Farm. The rescue centre is a registered charity relying entirely on donations, and visitors have several ways of helping, including the Adopt a Donkey scheme.

SHORWELL
7 miles SW of Newport, on the B3323

🏛 St Peter's Church   🦆 Yafford Mill

Pronounced 'Shorell' by Caulkheads, as Isle of Wight natives are known, this village of thatched stone cottages has no fewer than three venerable manor houses within its boundaries. West Court, Wolverton, and North Court were built respectively during the reigns of Henry VIII, Elizabeth I, and James I. They possess all the charm you would

expect from that glorious age of English architecture but sadly none of them is open to the public. However, you can visit **St Peter's Church** to gaze on its mesmerisingly beautiful 15th century wall-painting and admire its 500-year-old stone pulpit covered by an elaborate wooden canopy of 1620. The church also has a real oddity in a painting on wood of the Last Supper, brought from Iceland in 1898.

This small village boasts another attraction. **Yafford Mill** is an 18th century water mill in full working order. It's surrounded by ponds and streams where you'll find Sophie, the resident seal, and within the grounds there are paddocks which are home to rare cattle, sheep and pigs, a collection of antique farm machinery, a steam engine and narrow-gauge railway. There are also waymarked nature walks, a playground, picnic area, gift shop, tea gardens and a licensed bar.

BRIGHSTONE
8 miles S of Newport on the B3399

🏛 Dinosaur Farm Museum

🦉 Mottistone Manor Garden   🌲 Mottistone Common

One of the prettiest villages on the island, Brighstone was once notorious as the home of smugglers and wreckers. Today, the National Trust runs a shop in a picturesque row of thatched cottages, and there's a little museum depicting village life down the years.

The island has long been known for its fossil finds, especially relating to dinosaurs. On a clifftop near the village the bones of a completely new species of predatory dinosaur were unearthed. The 15ft carnivore, which lived in the cretaceous period about 120 million to 150 million years ago, has been named *cotyrannus lengi* after Gavin Leng, a local collector who found the first bone. On Military Road (A3055) near Brighstone, the

Dinosaur Farm Museum came into being following the unearthing in 1992 of the skeleton of a brachiosaurus, at that time the island's largest and most spectacular dinosaur discovery. This unique attraction follows the tale of this and other finds. Visitors are invited to bring their own fossils for identification, and the farm also organises guided fossil tours at various locations on the Island.

A mile or so west of Brighstone, the National Trust is also responsible for **Mottistone Manor Garden**, a charming hillside garden alongside an Elizabethan manor house. The garden is particularly well known for its herbaceous borders and terraces planted with fruit trees. The Mottistone Estate extends from Mottistone Down in the north

to the coast at Sudmoor. On **Mottistone Common**, where New Forest ponies graze, are the remains of a neolithic long barrow known as the Longstone.

FRESHWATER
11 miles W of Newport, on the A3055

🏛 Church of All Saints   🏛 Dimbola Lodge
🏛 Old Battery   ⛰ Tennyson Down   ⚲ Farringford
⚲ Tennyson Trail   ⛰ The Needles
🌿 Needles Pleasure Park

Freshwater and the surrounding area are inextricably linked with the memory of Alfred, Lord Tennyson. In 1850, he succeeded Wordsworth as Poet Laureate, married Emily Sellwood, and shortly afterwards moved to **Farringford,** just outside Freshwater. The

HILL FARM RIDING SCHOOL
Hill Lane, Freshwater, Isle of Wight PO40 9TQ
Tel: 01983 752502 /07748253899
website: www.hillfarmridingschool.co.uk

Queen Victoria adored the Isle of Wight, and the stables built to house her horses and coaches are now the main stables of the **Hill Farm Riding School**, open 364 days a year. Set in the grounds of the house occupied by Mr Lionel Osman and his family for the last 45 years, the business is run by three generations of this Island family and is the oldest and longest established stables on the Island. Enjoy the west Wight on horseback and see not only the beautiful island scenery and vast network of bridlepaths and downland, but also the mainland coast across the Solent.

There are hourly, and 1½ hourly hacks daily, catering for all abilities from the age of five years, on individually tailored rides. There are also private and group lessons in the sand manège daily from tots trots (age 4 and up) through to flatwork and jumping lessons for the more ambitious. The stables also boasts a 40 jump cross country course over picturesque countryside. Hill Farm Riding School is now a Pony Club Centre where members and non members can enjoy fun days such as 'own a pony' and gymkhana games day, during the school holidays. For more information check out the website. Hill Farm Riding School is situated on the A3054 Freshwater to Yarmouth road.

🏛 historic building   🏛 museum   🏛 historic site   ⛰ scenic attraction   🌿 flora and fauna

Dimbola Lodge

Terrace Lane, Freshwater Bay, Isle of Wight PO40 9QE
Tel: 01983756814 Fax: 01983755578
website: www.dimbola.co.uk

Owner: Julia Margaret Cameron Trust   Contact: Ron Smith

This historic house is the former home of internationally known 19th century photographer Julia Margaret Cameron, and contains a museum and galleries. There is a permanent display of Cameron's images and contemporary revolving photographic exhibitions, lectures, photographic courses and musical performances. The Lodge is also available for hire, book launches, etc.

Open: All year: Tues - Sun inclusive & BH Mons, 10am-5pm. Closed 24th,25th,26th Dec for Christmas, and 31st Dec, 1st Jan for New Year. Admission: Adult £3 (£3.50 after 31/1102), Child (under 16yrs) Free. Groups (10 or more) 10% discount.

house, set in 33 acres of parkland, is now a hotel where visitors can relax in the luxuriously appointed drawing room with its delightful terrace and views across the downs. Tennyson was an indefatigable walker and however foul the weather would pace along nearby High Down dramatically arrayed in a billowing cloak and a black, broad-brimmed sombrero. After his death, the area was re-named **Tennyson Down** and a cross erected high on the cliffs in his memory.

There are more remembrances of the great poet in the **Church of All Saints** in Freshwater town where Lady Tennyson is buried in the churchyard and a touching memorial inside commemorates their son Lionel, "an affectionate boy", who died at the age of 32 while returning from India. As Tennyson grew older, he became increasingly impatient with sightseers flocking to Farringford hoping to catch sight of the now-legendary figure. He moved to his other home at Blackdown in Sussex where he died in 1892.

About a mile south of the town, Freshwater Bay was once an inaccessible inlet, much favoured by smugglers. Today, the bay is the start point of the 15-mile **Tennyson Trail**, which ends at Carisbrooke and its scenic beauty attracts thousands of visitors every year. They also flock in their thousands to **Dimbola Lodge** (see panel above), one of the most important shrines in the history of early photography. It was the home of Julia Margaret Cameron (1815-1879) who bought it in 1860 to be close to her friend Tennyson. Three years later, she was given a camera and immediately devoted herself with her usual energy to mastering the technical and artistic aspects of what was then called the "Black Art". (Because handling the chemicals involved usually left the photographer's hands deeply stained).

The coal-house at Dimbola Lodge was turned into a dark room and within a year, Julia had been elected a member of the Photographic Society of London. She photographed most of the leading lights of the artistic community of the time including Thackeray, Darwin, GF Watts and his wife the actress Ellen Terry, who all at some time lived locally. Perhaps the most famous of her images is the classic portrait of Tennyson himself, a craggy, bearded figure with a visionary gaze. Dimbola Lodge was acquired by the Julia Margaret Cameron Trust in 1993 and it has been converted into a museum and galleries devoted to her photography. There's also a gift shop, antiquarian bookshop, and vegetarian restaurant.

From the bay itself, there are regular cruises around the island's most spectacular natural feature, the dreaded **Needles**. The boat trip takes you through the swirling waters around the lighthouse, and past the line of jagged slabs of gleaming chalk towering some 200ft high. The sea has gouged deep caves out of the cliffs. Two of them are known as Lord Holmes' Parlour and Kitchen, named after a 17th century Governor of the Island who once entertained his guests in the 'Parlour' and kept his wines cool in the 'Kitchen'.

The Needles are undoubtedly at their most impressive when viewed from the sea, but they are still a grand sight from the land.

FRENCHMAN'S COVE

WEBSITE: WWW.FRENCHMANSCOVE.CO.UK

Alum Bay Old Road, Totland Bay,
Isle of Wight PO39 0HZ
Tel: 01983 752227
e-mail: boatfield@frenchmanscove.co.uk

Not far from the famous Needles and Alum Bay, **Frenchman's Cove** nestles beneath Tennyson Down in a peaceful rural location. The surrounding countryside is ideal for walking with many well-signed footpaths with both country and sea views. Frenchman's Cove is the home of Sue and Chris Boatfield who spare no effort to make sure their guests feel at home. There are two lounges - one has a digital TV, library, board games and jigsaw puzzles, the other has bagatelle, shove-halfpenny and other games. They have been recipients of the Green Island Gold Award for Sustainable Tourism since 2003, with every effort being made to live a green life style and to encourage the local flora and fauna.

There is a choice of menu for breakfast. The accommodation comprises a mix of family and double/twin rooms, all with en-suite facilities, colour TV and hospitality tray, four of which are on the ground floor. Two double bedrooms have large bay windows and along with the two family suites enjoy magnificent views over the Solent. Also available is a self-contained apartment for a family, The Coach House, where guests can enjoy the freedom of a self-catering holiday while taking advantage of the guest house facilities.

WARREN FARM FARMHOUSE CREAM TEAS

Warren Farm, Alum Bay, Totland,
Isle of Wight PO39 0JB
Tel/Fax: 01983 753200
e-mail: lizosman@lycos.co.uk
website: www.farmhousecreamteas.co.uk

John Osman has farmed 160 acres here for almost 40 years on what is now National Trust land, and half those acres make up **Warren Farm**. In the 350-year-old farmhouse, Liz Osman started the **Farmhouse Cream Teas** enterprise in 2000, and they have gradually extended the opening hours and length of season. The current hours are 12noon to 5.30pm weekends only between Easter and the May Bank Holiday and Saturday to Thursday from May Day to the end of October.

Scrumptious homemade cakes, clotted cream teas with scones and light lunches can be enjoyed inside or out on the patio overlooking the National Trust's West High Down. They raise beef cattle on the farm, and in most years they grow wheat, barley, peas and beans. Kune kune pigs and a pygmy goat are kept as pets. The farm is located on the B3322, the main road into Alum Bay; it's also close to the Tennyson Trail and the coastal path, and is just off Route 1 Yarmouth Circular Cycleway.

There are some particularly striking vistas from the **Needles Old Battery** (National Trust), a Victorian coastal fort standing 250ft above the sea. Visitors pass through a 200ft long tunnel and emerge onto a platform with panoramic views.

Alternatively, **The Needles Pleasure Park** at Alum Bay also has good views and offers a wide range of family entertainments, a chairlift from the clifftop to the beach, boat trips to the lighthouse, a glass-making studio and many other attractions. . In the car park at Alum Bay is a monument to Marconi, who sent messages to a tug in Alum Bay and set up the first wireless station here in 1897. The first paid Marconigram was sent in the following year by Lord Kelvin.

YARMOUTH
10 miles W of Newport, on the A3054

🏰 Castle   🌿 Fort Victoria Country Park

A regular ferry links this picturesque little port to Lymington on the mainland. Yarmouth was once the principal port on the island which was why Henry VIII ordered the building of **Yarmouth Castle** (English Heritage) in the 1540s. It was garrisoned until 1885 but is now disused, though much remains. The town also boasts a quaint old Town Hall, a working pier, and a 13th century church rather unhappily restored in 1831. It's worth going inside to see the incongruous statue on the tomb of Sir Robert Holmes, Governor of the Island in the mid-17th century. During one of the endless

---

Yarmouth Castle

conflicts with the French, Sir Robert had captured a ship on board which was a French sculptor with an unfinished statue of Louis XIV. He was travelling to Versailles to model the King's head from life. Sir Robert decided that the elaborate statue of the King (in full French armour) would do nicely for his own tomb. The sculptor was ordered to replace the Royal head with Sir Robert's. No doubt deliberately, the artist made a poor fist of the job and the head is decidedly inferior to the rest of the statue.

One mile west of this appealing little town, **Fort Victoria Country Park**, owned by the Isle of Wight Council, is one of the major leisure complexes on the island and uses the area around one of Palmerston's forts. Set on the Solent coastline, the park offers an enormous range of attractions. There are unspoilt sandy beaches, woodland

walks, and Ranger-guided tours around the park highlighting the local and natural history of the area. Within the park you'll also find the largest model railway in Britain, a state-of-the-art Planetarium and Astronomy Resources Centre, a Marine Aquarium with some 80 different species of local and tropical fish, and a Maritime Heritage Exhibition. Speedboat trips are also available from the slipway next to the Boathouse Lunch & Tea Gardens.

NEWTOWN
5 miles E of Yarmouth off the A3054

🐾 Colemans Animal Farm

Founded in the 13th century by a Bishop of Winchester, Newtown once had a large, busy harbour, but silting led to its decline as a maritime centre and the harbour is now a nature reserve. At its height, the town was the most important on the island and regularly sent two MPs to Westminster; among them were John Churchill, later the 1st Duke of Marlborough, and Prime Minister George Canning. The town's most notable building is the Old Town Hall, erected in 1699 and now owned by the National Trust. A small, unassuming building of brick and stone, it contains many interesting documents and memorabilia. The records include the exploits of Ferguson's Gang, an anonymous group of benefactors who gave donations to save selected properties. It is not recorded why this building was chosen, but in 1934 one of the gang went into the National Trust offices and discreetly dropped £500 on the secretary's desk to save the town hall.

At Porchfield, two miles east of Newtown, fun in the country for the whole family is promised at **Colemans Animal Farm**, where visitors are encouraged to stroke and feed the animals. Children will also love the huge wooden play area, the sandpit, the straw maze and the mini-farm with pedal tractors.

LOCATOR MAP

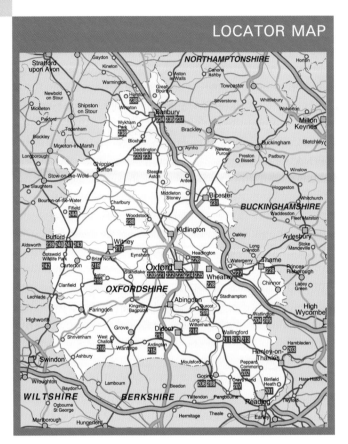

ADVERTISERS AND PLACES OF INTEREST

🏠 historic building   🏛 museum   🏚 historic site   🌀 scenic attraction   🌿 flora and fauna

8| Oxfordshire

Oxfordshire is a county covering about 1,000 square miles, contained largely within the Thames Basin. Between Henley and Wallingford lie the beginnings of the Chiltern Hills, while in the north are the most easterly hills of the Cotswolds as well as rich farmland based on the clay soil that stretches up from Oxford to the Midlands. In the east, Henley is one of many attractive Thames-side settlements, towards the west are Faringdon and Witney, and in the north Bicester, Chipping Norton and Banbury. The county is of course dominated by its capital, Oxford, which from the 12th century grew from a small and little known market town into one of the major seats of learning in the world. It also prospered as a central point of communication, first as a stopping point on coaching routes and later with the coming of the canals and the railways. Industry grew, too, and in the suburb of Cowley, Lord Nuffield's Morris car works were a major employer.

Fawley Court, Henley-on-Thames

Many palaeolithic, mesolithic and neolithic finds have been made in the county, but the most eyecatching early archaeological feature is the Uffington White Horse from the Iron Age. Dorchester and Alchester were the most important sites in Roman Oxfordshire, the Saxons built many settlements along the Thames, and the Danes overran the area in the 10th and 11th centuries. The county was heavily involved in the Civil War (1642-1651) and the towns of Oxford (for three years the Royalist headquarters), Banbury and Wallingford were all besieged by Parliamentary forces during the conflict.

🎞 stories and anecdotes   🍃 famous people   ✒ art and craft   ✎ entertainment and sport   🐾 walks

Henley-on-Thames

🏛 Greys Court 📷 River & Rowing Museum

📷 Fawley Court Museum 🌿 Regatta

Reputed to be the oldest settlement in Oxfordshire, this attractive riverside market town has over 300 listed buildings covering several periods. The Thames has always played an important role in its life; in 1829 the first varsity boat race, between Oxford and Cambridge, took place here on the river and, within a decade, the event was enjoying royal patronage. The **Henley Regatta**, held every year in the first week of July, is a marvellous and colourful event with teams competing on the mile long course from all over the world. Opened in 1998, the **River and Rowing Museum** is a fascinating place that traces the

rowing heritage of Henley, the river's changing role in the town's history, and even provides the opportunity to 'walk' the length of the River Thames, from source to sea, taking in all the locks. Housed in spacious, purpose-built premises designed by the award-winning architect, David Chipperfield, its exhibits include the boat in which the British duo, Steve Redgrave and Matthew Pinsent, won their gold medals at the 1996 Olympics. A major new attraction recreates Kenneth Grahame's much-loved tale *The Wind in the Willows*. In a spectacular walk-through exhibition visitors can meet all the familiar characters and places in the book, with E H Shepard's illustrations brilliantly brought to life.

Henley was the site of Rupert's Elm, where Prince Rupert is said to have hanged a

HOLMWOOD

Shiplake Row, Binfield Heath,
nr Henley-on-Thames, Oxfordshire RG9 4DP
Tel: 0118 947 8747 Fax: 0118 947 8637
e-mail: wendy.cook@freenet.co.uk
website: www.holmwoodbandb.co.uk

Holmwood is a large, secluded Georgian country house set within four acres of delightful gardens with lawns and colourful flower beds, banks of rhododendrons and many fine specimen trees. Beyond the gardens are a further 26 acres of paddocks and woods, and the south-facing aspect of the house commands extensive views across the Thames Valley. The Grade II listed building has been home to the Talfourd-Cook family for 25 years, and Wendy and Brian have opened up their home to bed & breakfast guests for the past 12 years. Beyond the inmposing entrance hall, guests will find an elegant drawing room with log fires and comfortable settees and armchairs that make it a perfect spot to relax, unwind and meet friends.

   The five large guest bedrooms – a single, two twins and two doubles – are individually furnished with mainly antique or period furniture. All are Silver rated, with en suite bathrooms with new power showers, TV and hot drinks facilities. Traditional breakfasts are served in the dining room. The location, six miles from Henley and within a 30-minute drive of Heathrow Airport, makes this an ideal choice for tourists and overseas visitors. Children over 12 are welcome. No pets.

Greys Court

Apart from the boating, which is available throughout the summer, and the pleasant walks along the riverbanks, there are lots of interesting shops, inns, and teashops in the town.

Just down river from the town centre lies **Fawley Court**, a wonderful private house that was designed by Christopher Wren and built in 1684 for a Colonel Freeman. Now owned by the Marian Fathers, the **Museum** it contains includes a library, documents relating to the Polish kings, and memorabilia of the Polish army. The house, gardens, and museum are open to the public from March to October.

To the northwest of Henley, at Rotherfield Greys, is another interesting house, **Greys Court** (National Trust), dating originally from the 14th century but much altered down the centuries; a beautiful courtyard and a tower survive from the earliest building. A Tudor wheelhouse is among the interesting outbuildings, and the gardens offer many delights, notably old-fashioned roses and wisterias, an ornamental vegetable garden, a ha-ha, an ice-house and the Archbishop's Maze, which was inspired, in 1980, by Archbishop Runcie's enthronement speech.

Roundhead spy. A portion of the tree is preserved in this museum. Also situated on the riverbank, beside the town's famous 18th century bridge decorated with the faces of Father Thames and the goddess Isis, is the Leander Club, the headquarters of the famous rowing club.

THE RED LION

Peppard Common, Henley-on-Thames, Oxfordshire RG9 5LB
Tel: 01491 628329

What do we all look for in the perfect country pub? Attractive location? Friendly, efficient staff? A warm welcome for all the family? Character and atmosphere? Well-kept beer? Interesting food? A garden? Off-road parking? The 500-year-old **Red Lion** has all these, which is why with William and Liza at the helm it is one of the most popular and best-loved pubs in the region. In the cooler months log fires keep things cosy in the bar and dining areas, while in the summer the place to be is the garden, where children can romp happily in their own play area. Brakspears ales are kept in top condition, and Liza's daily changing menu offers an interesting choice of freshly prepared dishes with British, European and American influences.

🎦 stories and anecdotes   🐦 famous people   🎨 art and craft   🖉 entertainment and sport   🚶 walks

Henley-on-Thames

Distance: *6.0 miles (9.6 kilometres)*

Typical time: *180 mins*

Height gain: *90 metres*

Map: *Chiltern Hills*

Walk: *www.walkingworld.com ID:5*

Contributor: *David and Chris Stewart*

Easily reached by train on the Paddington line from London. The station is just a few yards from the walk start. Traffic and parking in Henley can be difficult. The Henley River and Rowing Museum has its own parking, inclusive in the entrance ticket price.

The Henley River and Rowing Museum is new and well worth a visit. Henley-on-Thames is an affluent and attractive town, home of the well-known annual regatta, with galleries, old pubs, tea shops and more.

A short and pleasant walk taking in a famous stretch of the River Thames and the surrounding countryside, with a conveniently placed pub half way round.

River, Pub, Museum, Play Area, Great Views

1 | Start by the Henley River and Rowing Museum and take the riverside path back towards the town centre

2 | Cross the bridge to the south side of the river and turn left onto the tow path. The path starts by passing between some buildings but soon you are walking alongside the river. Continue along the path until you reach Hambledon lock.

3 | At the lock you may want to take a detour to cross the river above the weir. Continue the walk from the end of the lock where you join a track. A short distance from the lock bear right on the track, away from the river.

4 | Follow the track, ignoring the fork to the right, towards the Flowerpot Hotel. This is a

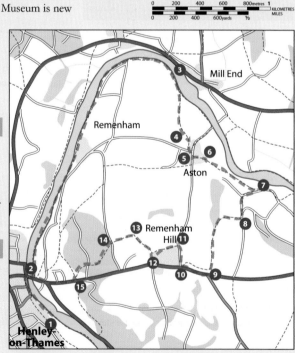

great place to stop for lunch or a quick drink. From the Hotel turn right up Aston Lane.

5 | Not far from the Hotel, turn left into this lane.

6 | The lane turns into a path crossing a field. The recently renovated Culham Court is on your right. Pass in front of the house.

7 | Crossing a field after Culham Court you come to a junction of paths. Take the path to the right, which switches back towards the lane leading to the House. At the entrance gate turn left up the lane (this is marked as a public footpath).

8 | Turn right at this point to cross the field. At the woods, bear left. Ignore the path leading into the woods. At the corner of the woods, cross through the hedge and continue down the side of the hedge towards the houses.

9 | Just before you reach the houses, turn right. The path passes along the end of the gardens. Finally you can bear left towards the junction of Aston Lane and the main road.

10 | At the junction, turn right down Aston Lane.

11 | After passing the last set of houses on the right, take the footpath on your left.

12 | You come to a driveway. Take the path into the woods, to the left of the white post in the middle of this picture.

13 | Turn left to cross the field. You can see a stile in the middle of the field. Keep in the same direction until you reach the road.

14 | Cross the road and take the path over the stile opposite. Follow the path down through the woods, following the white arrows on the trees.

15 | At the main road, turn right and walk the short distance back to the bridge in Henley-on-Thames.

Around Henley-on-Thames

SONNING COMMON
3½ miles SW of Henley on the B481

Sonning Common was originally part of the manor of Sonning-on-Thames with the livestock driven up from the flooded riverside pastures to winter on the higher ground.

Widmore Pond, on the edge of the village, is said to have been a Roman silver mine: according to a 17th century account, while the pond was emptied for cleaning out, upturned oak tree stumps were found in the bottom of the pond along with stag antlers and Roman coins.

MAPLEDURHAM
6½ miles SW of Henley off the A4074

🏚 Mapledurham House 🏚 Church of St Margaret

🏚 Watermill

A narrow winding lane leads to this famously picturesque village set beside the Thames. The cluster of brick and flint cottages and the church are overshadowed by the lovely Elizabethan mansion, **Mapledurham House.** It was built on the site of an older manor house by the Blount family and has remained with their descendants ever since. As well as viewing the great oak staircase and the fine collection of paintings housed here, visitors will find the house's literary connections are equally interesting: Alexander Pope was a frequent visitor in the 18th century; the final chapters of John Galsworthy's *The Forsyte Saga* were set here; and it was the fictional Toad Hall in *The Wind in the Willows*. The house has also featured in films such as *The Eagle has Landed* and the TV series *Inspector Morse*.

THE CHILTERN VALLEY WINERY & BREWERY

Old Luxters Farm, Hambleden,
nr Henley-on-Thames, Buckinghamshire RG9 6JW
Tel: 01491 638330 Fax: 01491 638645
e-mail: david@chilternvalley.co.uk
website: www.chilternvalley.co.uk

Set in a designated Area of Outstanding Beauty, Old Luxters is home to the **Chiltern Valley Winery & Brewery**. Wines have been produced here for more than 20 years, and with over 70 trophies, awards and commendations they have gained an enviable and far-reaching reputation for quality, a reputation being enhanced by David Ealand and his family. The first vines were planted in 1982 here on the slopes of the Chilterns, surrounded by Beech woodland and overlooking the beautiful Hambleden Valley. The modern production, bottling and labelling facilities, the wine vats and the cellar shop are all housed in traditional farm buildings.

Old Luxters also produces superb cask and bottle conditioned ales, reviving the tradition of farm-brewed, full-mash real ales. In the gift shop, visitors can taste not only the wines and the beers, but the liqueurs and fortified drinks produced on the premises. Chiltern Valley also specialise in providing an in-house 'own' label service for individuals, shops and restaurants.

THE GRANARY DELICATESSEN

30 High Street, Watlington,
Oxfordshire OX49 5PY
Tel: 01491 613585
e-mail: granarydeli@btinternet.com
website: www.granarydeli.co.uk

The residents of Watlington and the surrounding towns and villages have every reason to be grateful for the efforts of Robin and Francesca Holmes-Smith, who saved **The Granary Delicatessen** from closure in 2002.

Always a cheese shop at heart, it stocks an impressive selection of some 170 cheeses, mainly from the UK (many of them award winners), but with prime varieties also from France and Italy.

The shop hosts cheese tastings on Friday and Saturday. Cheese-related items such as knives and scoops are always available, and other produce includes preserves, olive oil and olives, pickles and chutneys, biscuits, breads from two local bakeries, coffees, organic wines and store cupboard basics. The Granary can make up hampers for any occasion.

Another attraction on the estate is the old riverside **Watermill**, a handsome late-15th century construction, which stands on the site of an earlier building that was mentioned in the Domesday Book. The mill remained in operation until 1947 and it was then the longest surviving working mill on the river. Now fully restored, the traditional machinery can be seen in action grinding wholemeal flour, which is then sold through the mill shop.

The **Church of St Margaret** has a number of notable features. It provided a major location for the film *The Eagle has Landed* and is believed to be the only church in the country to have had a king's son as vicar – Lord Augustus FitzClarence, one of William IV's 10 illegitimate children by the actress Mrs Jordan, was appointed to the living in 1829. Another curiosity here is that the south aisle is owned outright by the Blount family and partitioned off from the rest of the church. Major restoration was carried out in 1863 by the architect William Butterfield who made great use of coloured brickwork and also refaced the tower with a bold chequered pattern using flint and brick.

WATLINGTON
8 miles NW of Henley off the B480

🌱 Watlington Hill

There are superb views over the surrounding countryside from **Watlington Hill**, which rises 700ft above Watlington Park with its woods of beech and yew. Watlington Hill and its neighbour Pyrton Hill are designated a Site of Special Scientific Interest and are home to over 30 species of butterflies and a wide variety of chalk-loving plants.

TWO & SIX

26 High Street, Watlington, Oxfordshire OX49 5PY
Tel/Fax: 01491 614802

Andrea Tingey brought many years' experience in the retail business when she opened **Two & Six** on Watlington's High Street in 2003. She has stocked the shop with a fine array of decorative and practical gifts and products to enhance any room in the house.

Her love of ceramics is evident - you can find Moorland pottery, Burleigh, Susie Watson, Caroline Zoob and lots of Swedish linens too. There is lovely glassware, enamelled kitchenware, fine toiletries and a wide choice of Christmas decorations and trimmings.

Two & Six is definitely not a place to nip in and out, and browsers will find lots of new stock on every visit. The shop is genuinely welcoming, with a stylish interior and a variety of gentle music to set the relaxing tone. Watlington is located just 2 miles from J6 of the M40, and a trip to Two & Six is well worth the detour.

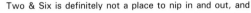

📖 stories and anecdotes　🦜 famous people　🎨 art and craft　✒ entertainment and sport　🚶 walks

THE MILLER OF MANSFIELD

High Street, Goring-on-Thames,
Oxfordshire RG8 9AW
Tel: 01491 872829 Fax: 01491 873100
e-mail: paul@wickedvarlet.com
website: www.millerofmansfield.com

On the main street of Goring-on-Thames, well connected for both motorists and rail users, **The Miller of Mansfield** scores on all fronts. It's a great place for a drink, a snack or a meal, and also provides excellent guest accommodation. The smartly refurbished building, part creeper-clad, combines traditional and contemporary elements in real harmony, and the oak-beamed bar is a convivial spot for enjoying real ales from the wood, mainly from local breweries. Head chef Gavin Young uses the best British produce in his imaginative modern European menus, and everything from the bread to the smoked meats, the chutneys, the chocolate and the cakes is made in house. Typical choices run from sea bream with a herb risotto and sauce vierge to super steaks with proper chips. A lighter bar menu with sandwiches, fish & chips, and pasta is also available.

The pub can cater for wedding receptions and other special occasions for up to 140 guests. The ten individually designed bedrooms and suites are superbly appointed, with Philippe Starck fittings, antique fireplaces, wooden floors, flat-screen televisions and marble bathrooms with stone resin baths and high-pressure showers. Owner Paul Suter's philosophy of offering the highest standards of service and quality extends to his other pub, the nearby White Lion at Crays Pond.

THE WHITE LION AT CRAYS POND

Goring Road, Crays Pond, Goring Heath,
Oxfordshire RG8 7SH
Tel: 01491 680471 Fax: 01491 684254
e-mail: chris@thewhitelioncrayspond.com
website: www.thewhitelioncrayspond.com

In a pleasant village setting at the junction of the B471 and B4526, **The White Lion at Crays Pond** is traditional country pub that is also a fine restaurant. The head chef's modern British and European cuisine covers a tempting daily changing selection of beautifully prepared dishes such as confit of duck with red cabbage and bubble & squeak, skate with caper butter, devilled lamb's kidneys with mushrooms on toast and, to round off a memorable meal, apple, rum & raisin filo with a baked custard tart and apple sorbet. Well-kept real ales and an excellent wine list complement the outstanding food. The White Lion is in the same ownership as The Miller of Mansfield on Goring's High Street.

🏛 historic building   🏛 museum   🏛 historic site   ⌘ scenic attraction   🌿 flora and fauna

GORING-ON-THAMES

9½ miles W of Henley on the B4009

This ancient small town lies across the River Thames from its equally ancient neighbour, Streatley, and, while today they are in different counties, they were once in different kingdoms. This is a particularly peaceful stretch of the river, with the bustle of Pangbourne and Henley-on-Thames lying downstream, and it is some distance to the towns of Abingdon and Oxford further upstream.

In the 19th century, after Isambard Kingdom Brunel had laid the tracks for the Great Western Railway through Goring Gap, the village began to grow as it was now accessible to the Thames-loving Victorians. Though there are many Victorian and Edwardian villas and houses here, the original older buildings have survived, adding an air of antiquity to this attractive place.

STONOR

4 miles N of Henley on the B480

🏛 Stonor

The village is the home of Lord and Lady Camoys and their house, **Stonor**, has been in the family for over 800 years. Set in the a wooded valley in the Chilterns and surrounded by a deer park, this idyllic house dates from the 12th century though the beautiful, uniform facade is Tudor and hides much of the earlier work. The interior of the house contains many rare items, including a mass of family portraits, and there is also a medieval Catholic Chapel here that was in continuous use right through the Reformation. In 1581, Edmund Campion sought refuge at the house and from a secret room in the roof supervised the printing of his book *Decem Rationes* – 'Ten Reasons for being a Catholic'. An exhibition features his life and work. The gardens too are well worth a visit

THE LEATHERNE BOTTEL RIVERSIDE RESTAURANT

Goring-on-Thames, Berkshire RG8 0HS
Tel: 01491 872667   e-mail: leathernebottel@aol.com
Fax: 01491 875308   website: www.leathernebottel.co.uk

'Fabulous food and so much more' is the well-earned boast of **The Leatherne Bottel**, a delightful restaurant in a lovely setting by a tranquil stretch of the River Thames. It's one of the best-loved and most highly regarded restaurants in the region, a winner of many awards and a real pleasure to visit at any time of the year. In summer, you can enjoy a drink or lunch on the terrace overlooking the river and the Berkshire Downs, in winter large open fires keep things cosy in the dining rooms, and a new orangery is planned for early 2007. Chef-Director Julia Storey proposes a modern European menu with a touch of the Pacific Rim (she spent many years working in New Zealand).

Freshness, colour and flavours are to the fore in her dishes; everything is made on the premises, and Julia grows her own herbs and salad leaves in a polytunnel in the garden. Fish comes fresh from Brixham, meat, poultry and game from top suppliers, fruit and vegetables from the best local sources. A few typical dishes: from the luncheon menu pan-fried squid with saffron risotto, roast boneless quail on potato rösti, with a herb salad and tomato salsa, and steak sandwich with rocket, cherry tomatoes and aioli; from the a la carte menu grilled fillet of red mullet with a prawn, cucumber and tarragon broth, Shiraz-glazed confit of duck leg with duck livers on braised Puy lentils, and Basil roulade with goat's cheese and a capsicum salsa. Fine wine and friendly, professional service complete the picture at this outstanding country restaurant.

📖 stories and anecdotes   🐦 famous people   🎨 art and craft   🎭 entertainment and sport   🚶 walks

with their lawns, orchard and lovely lavender hedges, and they offer splendid views over the rolling parkland.

Almshouses, Ewelme

EWELME
9 miles NW of Henley off the B4009

At the centre of this pretty village is a magnificent group of medieval buildings, including the church, almshouses and school, which were all founded in the 1430s by Alice Chaucer, grand-daughter of the poet Geoffrey, and her husband, the Duke of Suffolk. There is a wonderfully elegant alabaster carving of Alice inside the church and under this effigy is another rather macabre carving of a shrivelled cadaver. In the churchyard is the grave of Jerome K Jerome, author of *Three Men in a Boat*, who moved to the village following the success of his book.

CHALGROVE
10 miles NW of Henley on the B480

Chalgrove is the site of an English Heritage registered Battlefield, where in 1643 Prince Rupert defeated John Hampden. An information board at the site gives details of the battle, and there is also a monument to John Hampden, a local squire and sometime MP for Buckinghamshire who refused to pay Ship Money to the king. He was taken to court in 1638 and incarcerated in the Tower of London. He was a cousin of Oliver Cromwell and in the Civil War became a leading opponent of the king.

Abingdon

🏛 Church of St Helen   🏛 Museum   🏛 Abbey

This is an attractive town and one of the country's oldest, as it grew up around a Benedictine **Abbey** that was founded in 675. Sacked twice by the Danes for its gold and silver, the abbey was practically derelict by the 10th century but, under the guidance of Abbot Ethelwold, the architect of the great Benedictine reform, it once again prospered and was, in its heyday, larger than Westminster Abbey. At one time the abbot here was the largest landowner in Berkshire after the Crown. Unfortunately little remains today of this great religious house, but the Gatehouse, built in the late 15th century, is a splendid reminder.

The largest town in the Vale of the White Horse, Abingdon was also the county town of Berkshire between 1556 and 1869. The prosperity this brought enabled the townspeople to build the impressive and outsize County Hall of 1678 that dominates the Market Place. This outstanding example of English Renaissance architecture was designed by a pupil of Sir Christopher Wren. In its former Assize court is the **Abingdon Museum** which provides interesting insights into the town's history.

Another of Abingdon's pleasing buildings, set close to the lovely bridge over the

🏛 historic building   🏛 museum   🏛 historic site   🏛 scenic attraction   🏛 flora and fauna

THE CHEQUERS AT BURCOT

Abingdon Road, Burcot, Oxfordshire OX14 3DP
Tel: 01865 407771
e-mail: steve@thechequers-burcot.co.uk
website: www.thechequers-burcot.co.uk

Steven and Laura Sanderson have recently taken over
The Chequers at Burcot, overseeing a complete
refurbishment programme that has put the place in
excellent order. Parts of the inn are thought to date back
to the 15th century, and behind the smart black-and-
white frontage with thatched roof and hanging baskets, a
black-beamed ceiling tops the sensitively modernised
drinking and eating. There's plenty of comfortable
seating, with some upholstered pew benches, leather
settees and polished wooden chairs set at polished
wooden tables. When the weather is kind, the picnic
benches on the large lawn are popular spots for a drink
or a meal.

Hook Norton beers and seasonal guests from
Ridgeways are on tap to quench thirsts, but the main
reason for many visits is Steven's top-notch cooking.
Hand-cut sandwiches, jacket potatoes and old favourites such as ham, eggs & chips, burgers or
beer-battered cod are popular lunchtime orders, with 'small plates' (garlic and herb mushrooms,
sesame duck salad, salmon fishcakes) for lighter appetites. In the evening, those small plates
become starters, with ribeye steak, roast rump of lamb, monkfish & bacon kebabs and grilled
vegetable skewers among the main courses. A private room is available.

Thames, is the **Church of St Helen** whose
150ft-high steeple dominates the skyline
here. Originally built in the 14th century, the
church was remodelled in the 15th and 16th
centuries, when the town prospered from a
thriving wool trade, to provide an altogether
larger and more elaborate building. With its
five aisles it is now broader than it is long.
The main glory of the church, the painted
ceiling of the Lady Chapel, has been retained
from the 14th century. Beside the
churchyard, which contains a curious small
building that was the blowing chamber for
the church organ, are three sets of
almshouses. The oldest, Christ's Hospital,
was founded in 1446 while the other two,
Twitty's Almshouses and Brick Alley
Almshouses, date from the early 1700s.

Around Abingdon

DORCHESTER

5 miles SE of Abingdon off the A4074

🏛 Abbey Church 🏛 Abbey Museum

This charming little town, situated on the
River Thame just before it flows into the
River Thames, has been described as 'the most
historic spot in Oxfordshire', since it was here
that Christianity was established in the
southwest of England by St Birinus. Known
as the Apostle of the West Saxons, Birinus was
consecrated in Genoa, landed in Wessex in
634, and converted the King Cynegils of
Wessex in the following year. As a mark of his
devotion to the church, Cynegils gave
Dorchester to Birinus and the church he built

🎭 stories and anecdotes   🕊 famous people   🎨 art and craft   🎟 entertainment and sport   🐾 walks

here became the cathedral of Wessex.

The **Abbey Church of St Peter and St Paul** was built in 1170 on the site of that Saxon church and greatly extended during the next two centuries. Its chief glory is the 14th century choir and the huge Jesse window, showing the family tree of Jesus, which has retained its original stained glass. The story of the abbey, along with the history of settlement in the area going back to neolithic times, is told in the **Abbey Museum**, which is housed in a classroom of the former Grammar School, built in 1652.

The town itself has some attractive old houses with overhanging upper stories, a fine Georgian coaching inn, and there's a pleasant footpath that crosses fields to the bank of the Thames.

LITTLE WITTENHAM
5 miles SE of Abingdon off the A4130

🏛 Wittenham Clumps 🏠 Pendon Museum

This village, which has a number of pretty cottages, lies beneath the **Wittenham Clumps**, which for centuries formed an important defensive position overlooking the Thames. In the village church of St Peter are effigies of Sir William Dunch, a former MP for Wallingford, and his wife, who was the aunt of Oliver Cromwell. A little way northwest, towards the village of Long Wittenham, is the unique **Pendon Museum** (see panel below), whose main attraction is a model village built in tiny scale to resemble a typical 1930s village in the Vale of the White Horse. The model is the incredibly skilled and detailed work of Roye England, an

Pendon Museum Trust Ltd

Long Wittenham, Abingdon, Oxfordshire OX14 4QD
Tel: 01865 407365
website: www.pendonmuseum.com

Pendon Museum at Long Wittenham in Oxfordshire is a delightful museum devoted to portraying parts of rural England as they were in the 1920s and '30s - in particular, it reflects how life was influenced by the transport infrastructure of the period. It achieves this through the medium of modelling - accurate, authentic and carried out to the highest standard at a 1:76 scale; literally art in three dimensions. The museum is run, and the models it displays are built, almost entirely by a number of dedicated volunteers and it is open to the public at weekends, on bank holidays and on Wednesdays in school holidays. For anyone interested in rural social history, model railways, or simply appreciative of superb craftsmanship, Pendon is well worth a visit.

Australian who came to this country in 1925 to study. The model incorporates a model railway (Roye England's first passion) and, as a tribute to the master, who died in 1995, there's a tiny model of himself in the 1:76 scale of the whole model.

BLEWBURY
7 miles S of Abingdon on the A417

In the foothills of the Berkshire Downs, this pretty village was, and remains, a favoured spot for artists and writers. Among these was Kenneth Grahame, the author of *The Wind in the Willows*, who lived in a Tudor brick house in the village from 1910 to 1924. He wrote the book for his son, who tragically died while an undergraduate at Oxford. They are buried together in the churchyard of St Cross in Oxford. Mr Toad compares himself favourably with Oxford students in the book:

*'The clever men at Oxford
Know all that there is to be knowed
But they none know one half as much
As intelligent Mr Toad.'*

WALLINGFORD
8 miles SE of Abingdon on the A4130

A strategic crossing point of the Thames since ancient times. Alfred the Great first fortified the town, against the Danes, and the Saxon earth defences can still be seen. It was here that William the Conqueror crossed the river on his six-day march to London. Wallingford was also an important trading town; it received its charter in 1155 and for several centuries had its own mint. During the Civil War the town was a Royalist stronghold defending the southern approaches to Oxford, the site of the Royalist headquarters. It was besieged in 1646 by the Parliamentary forces

FIRST EDITION
9 Market Place, Wallingford, Oxfordshire OX10 0EG
Tel: 01491 837195

On the market square in Wallingford, **First Edition** specialises in ladies clothes and shoes featuring designer makes such as Ischiko, Save the Queen and Oska. The shoes are mainly Italian and are complemented by beautiful original jewellery, gorgeous belts and handbags with big personalities. Owners Lynn Dancer and Elaine Hornsby put the emphasis on style combined with value for money.

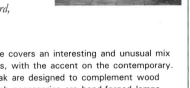

HORNSBYDUNMORE
6 St Mary's Street, Wallingford,
Oxfordshire OX10 0ES
Tel: 01491 825742

The stock in HornsbyDunmore covers an interesting and unusual mix of furniture, interiors and gifts, with the accent on the contemporary. Stand-alone pieces in oiled oak are designed to complement wood flooring, and among the stylish accessories are hand-forged lamps, polished steel tableware and sumptuous cushions. Smaller items include photo frames and vases. In one corner there is an Aladdin's Cave of toys both traditional and modern to delight any child.

CAMILLE'S AT PETTITS

46-50 St Mary's Street, Wallingford,
Oxfordshire OX10 0EY
Tel: 01491 835253 Fax: 01491 826009
e-mail: enquiries@pettitsofwallingford.co.uk

Located on the first floor of Pettits Department Store, **Camille's at Pettits Tea Room** is a bright, airy and inviting place, its walls adorned with attractive prints and owner Camille Scott's collection of unusual china teapots. Many of these were donated by regular customers who use the tea room as a meeting place. Camille's family has a long history in the catering trade and everything on her menu is home-made and freshly cooked to order. It includes an all-day breakfast, omelettes, salads (avocado with bacon is a great favourite), homemade soup and quiche of the day, sandwiches and jacket potatoes. Among the teatime treats are some wonderful homemade sponges, cakes and tray bakes. Customers can see their food prepared in the spotless open-plan modern kitchen.

Camille's is open from 9.30am to 4.30pm Monday to Saturday. Pettits is a fine old independent department store founded in 1856 and now owned and run as a family business. Managing Director Richard Rouse is proud of the fact that the store thrives on value for money and quality of service – two members of staff have each completed a remarkable 50 years of service.

under Sir Thomas Fairfax and its walls were breached after a 12-week siege; it was the last place to surrender to Parliament. The castle built by William the Conqueror was destroyed by Cromwell in 1652 but substantial earthworks can still be seen and the museum tells the story of the town from its earliest days.

SUTTON COURTENAY

2 miles S of Abingdon on the B4016

🏛 Church of All Saints

A pretty village that was mentioned in the Domesday Book with an abbey that was founded in 1350. The village **Church of All Saints**, which dates back to Norman times, contains some fine stone carvings and woodwork but the real interest lies in the churchyard. Here can be found the chest tomb of Herbert Asquith, the last Liberal Prime Minister (from 1908 to 1916) and his wife;

they lived by the Thames not far from the church. Also here is the grave of Eric Blair, better known as George Orwell, author of *1984* and *Animal Farm*; several yew trees are planted here in his memory.

DIDCOT

4½ miles S of Abingdon on the A4130

🏛 Railway Centre

The giant cooling towers of Didcot's power station dominate the skyline for miles around and there is little left of the old town. But the saving grace is the **Didcot Railway Centre** (see panel opposite), a shrine to the golden days of the steam engine and the Great Western Railway. Isambard Kingdom Brunel designed the Great Western Railway and its route through Didcot, from London to Bristol, was completed in 1841. Until 1892 its trains ran on their unique broad gauge tracks and the GWR retained its independence until the nationalisation of the railways in 1948. Based around the engine shed, where visitors can inspect the collection of steam locomotives, members of the Great Western Society have recreated the golden age of the railway at the centre which also includes a beautiful recreation of a country station, complete with level crossing. The locomotives on display include 4079 *Pendennis Castle*, repatriated from Australia in 2000, King class 6023 *King Edward II* and one of the streamlined and very distinctive Great Western diesel railcars, this one dating from 1940. The Firefly Trust has recently completed the building of a reproduction of the broad-gauge Firefly locomotive of 1840. Steam days are held throughout the year when locomotives once again take to the broad gauge track and visitors can also take in the Victorian signalling system and the centre's Relics Display.

Wantage

🏛 Church of St Peter & St Paul

🏛 Vale & Downland Museum

This thriving market town in the Vale of the White Horse was, in 849, the birthplace of Alfred the Great and remained a Royal Manor until the end of the 12th century. In the central market place, around which there are some fine Georgian and Victorian buildings, is a huge statue of the King of the West Saxons, who spent much of his life (he died in 899) defending his kingdom from the Danes in the north before becoming the overlord of England. An educated man (as a boy Alfred had visited Rome), he not only codified the laws of his kingdom but also revived the tradition of learning.

Unfortunately, only the **Church of St Peter and St Paul** has survived from medieval

Didcot Railway Centre

Didcot, Oxfordshire, OX11 7NJ
Tel: 01235 817200 Fax: 01235 510621
website: www.didcotrailwaycentre.org.uk

The Great Western Railway was incorporated in 1835 to build the railway from Bristol to London and it was designed and engineered by Isambard Kingdom Brunel to be the finest in the land.

Now, at Didcot, half way between Bristol and London, members of the Great Western Society have created a living museum of the Great Western Railway. It is based around the original engine shed and depot to which have been added a typical branch line with a country station and signalling demonstrations and a recreation of Brunel's original broad gauge trackwork on which a replica of the Fire Fly locomotive dating from 1840 operates on special occasions. There is a large collection of GWR steam locomotives, carriages and wagons.

On Steamdays the locomotives come to life and you can ride in the 1930s trains on one or both of the demonstration lines. Children under 12 must be accompanied by an adult; disabled visitors are advised that there is an awkward flight of steps at the entrance, with level access within the Centre (help can normally be given with prior advice). Phone for details of times and prices.

🎞 stories and anecdotes   🐦 famous people   🎨 art and craft   ✏ entertainment and sport   🚶 walks

SMITH'S BISTRO

High Street, Ardington,
Oxfordshire OX12 8PS
Tel: 01235 833237 Fax: 01235 833858
website: www.smithsatardington.co.uk

Lucky indeed are the citizens of Ardington and the surrounding towns and villages to have the versatile **Smith's Bistro** on their doorstep. Winners of *Country Living* magazine's 'Rural Newsagent of the Year 2004', Karen and Peter Smith have transformed the ailing shop that occupied these premises for more than 200 years into a thriving business combining Bistro, village store and Post Office. Since buying and renovating the shop, which stands on the estate created by Lord and Lady Wantage in the 1860s, they have added the Bistro and also offer various other services, including dry cleaning, shoe repair, photocopying and grocery deliveries.

The Bistro is open from 10am to 4pm seven days a week for morning coffee, lunch and afternoon tea, and also for monthly theme and gourmet evenings. They also offer outside catering for all occasions, from christenings to funerals and everything in between, and private dining any day of the week for parties of 15 or more.

The owners are lucky to live in an area with an abundance of producers and suppliers of top-quality ingredients, and their enthusiastic and talented chef Sean compiles his menu using as much local produce as possible, letting real flavour and freshness shine through his dishes. A full English breakfast, with lighter alternatives, is served until 11.45am, when the main menu takes over until 2.30pm: grilled mackerel with rocket and chive crème fraiche; croque monsieur; club and steak sandwiches; Caesar salad; burgers; tuna niçoise; mussels & frites; quiche; fish cakes; penne pasta.

Desserts could include bread & butter pudding, lemon posset and chocolate tart, and there's always an excellent selection of cakes (carrot, coffee, chocolate, ginger, banana), scones and tray bakes (flapjacks, marble crunch, grenola slice, shortbread). For takeaway customers the deli serves sandwiches and rolls, soup and snacks, fresh-baked bread, cakes from the local bakery and a selection of chilled and frozen food.

The Bistro has a lovely tiered garden with a patio area, lawns, flower beds, heather and rosemary. The Smiths set out to meet the needs of those who live and work in the local community and in this they have succeeded triumphantly, but their Bistro is also a super place to pause for people passing through or touring the area.

🏛 historic building 🏛 museum 🏛 historic site ⌖ scenic attraction 🌱 flora and fauna

first steam tramway operated, starting in 1873 and surviving until 1948.

Just to the east of the town lies Ardington House, a beautifully symmetrical, early-18th century building that is the home of the Baring family. Occasionally open to the public, the best feature here is the Imperial Staircase - where two flights come into one - of which this is a particularly fine example.

Fields Near Wantage

Around Wantage

KINGSTON BAGPUIZE
6 miles N of Wantage off the A420

🏠 Kingston Bagpuize House

times and, though it was heavily restored in 1857 by G E Street, various features have survived from the original 13th century structure. There's also a brass commemorating the life of Sir Ivo Fitzwarren, the father of Dick Whittington's wife, Alice.

Opposite the church is the **Vale and Downland Museum Centre**, which is located in another of the town's old buildings - a house dating from the 16th century - and a reconstructed barn. Dedicated to the geology, history, and archaeology of Wantage and the Vale of the White Horse, the displays cover the centuries from prehistoric times to the present day.

Built as the home of the Wantage Sisterhood, an Anglican Order, in the 19th century, three architects were involved in the construction of St Mary's Convent: GE Street; William Butterfield, architect of Keble College, Oxford; and John Pearson, architect of Truro Cathedral. It was in Wantage that the

The intriguing name of this straggling village goes back to Norman times when Ralf de Bachepuise, a contemporary of William the Conqueror, was given land in the area. The village grew to serve the needs of **Kingston Bagpuize House**, a fine mansion of 1660 with superb gardens. Notable features include a magnificent cantilevered staircase, panelled rooms with some good furniture and paintings, Chinese porcelain and hand-painted wallpaper. Within the mature parkland are many noble trees and a woodland garden – a detailed map is available giving the names and precise location of almost 300 plants. There's also a tea room and gift shop. Opening times are restricted: for details phone 01865 820259.

STEVENTON
5 miles NE of Wantage on the A4185

In Mill Street stand the National Trust's Priory Cottages, former monastic buildings now converted into two houses. South Cottage contains the priory's original Great Hall, which can be visited in the summer by written appointment.

LETCOMBE BASSETT
2 miles S of Wantage off the B4001

🏛 Segsbury Camp

This tiny village has a notable place in literary history: it is called Cresscombe in *Jude the Obscure*, which Thomas Hardy wrote while staying here. Earlier, Jonathan Swift spent the summer of 1714 at the village's rectory where he was visited by the poet Alexander Pope.

Just to the east of the village lies **Segsbury Camp**, which is sometimes also referred to as **Letcombe Castle**. Set on the edge of the Berkshire Downs, this massive Iron Age hill fort encloses some 26 acres of land.

KINGSTON LISLE
4½ miles W of Wantage off the B4507

🏛 The Blowing Stone

Just to the southwest of the attractive Norman Church of St John lies the **Blowing Stone** (or Sarsen Stone), a piece of glacial debris that is perforated with holes. When blown, the stone emits a fog-horn like sound and tradition has it that the stone was blown by King Alfred.

UFFINGTON
5½ miles W of Wantage off the B4507

🏛 Tom Brown's School Museum   🏛 White Horse
🏛 Uffington Castle & Dragon's Hill

This large village was, in 1822, the birthplace of Thomas Hughes, the son of the vicar. The

MANOR FARM

Silver Lane, West Challow, nr Wantage, Oxfordshire OX12 9TJ
Tel: 01235 763188
e-mail: enquiries@manorfarm-wantage.co.uk
website: www.manorfarm-wantage.co.uk

Manor Farm comprises 300 acres of arable land for growing crops and raising horses. The farm is owned and run by Robert Raines, who has lived here all his life, and his wife Sara, and it was Sara who started the bed & breakfast side in 2003. Their home, the centrepiece of the farm, is a striking Queen Anne building, Grade II listed, with wisteria-clad walls and roses and lavender growing all around. Lawns and shrubs at the front create a very attractive, secluded setting, and the six guest bedrooms provide a particularly peaceful and civilised base for discovering the many scenic and historic delights of the region.

The rooms include a family two-room suite and a room with a very handsome darkwood four-poster bed. A fine English breakfast is served in the traditionally appointed dining room with blue-painted walls, panelling and lovely blue-and-white china (both for use and on display). Guests have the use of an equally delightful drawing room where they can relax after the day's activities or plan the next day's outings. Sara will prepare an evening meal by arrangement, and wedding parties can be catered for.

🏛 historic building   🏛 museum   🏛 historic site   🌿 scenic attraction   🌾 flora and fauna

Blowing Stone, Kingston Lisle

871, but modern thinking now considers that it dates from about 100 BC.

Above the White Horse is the Iron Age camp known as **Uffington Castle**, and to one side is a knoll known as **Dragon's Hill** where legend has it that St George killed the dragon.

GREAT COXWELL
8 miles NW of Wantage off the A420

🏠 Great Barn

🏠 Church of St Giles

This village is best known for the magnificent **Great Barn** of a monastic grange (farm) of the Cistercian Abbey at Beaulieu in Hampshire, dating back to around 1300 and its 12th century **Church of St Giles**. A simple and elegant building, the church is often overlooked in favour of the barn, originally staffed by lay brethren who took vows of obedience, poverty and chastity but never became monks or priests. An impressive building that is some 152ft long, with Cotswold stone walls more than four feet thick, this huge barn was used to store the tithe - or taxes - received from the tenants of the church land. At the Dissolution it passed into private ownership and is now owned by the National Trust.

BUSCOT
11 miles NW of Wantage on the A417

🏠 Old Parsonage and Park

This small village, in the valley of the upper Thames, is home to two National Trust properties: **Buscot Old Parsonage** and

author of *Tom Brown's Schooldays*, Hughes incorporates many local landmarks, including the White Horse and Uffington Castle, in his well-known work. The **Tom Brown's School Museum** tells the story of Hughes' life and works.

However, the village is perhaps best known for the **Uffington White Horse.** This mysteriously abstract and very beautiful figure of a horse, some 400 feet long, has been created by removing the turf on the hillside to expose the gleaming white chalk beneath. It is a startling sight which can be seen from far and wide, and many a tantalising glimpse of it has been caught through the window of a train travelling through the valley below. Popular tradition links it with the victory of King Alfred over the Danes at the battle of Ashdown, which was fought somewhere on these downs in

Buscot Park. The parsonage is a lovely house with a small garden on the banks of the River Thames and was built of Cotswold stone in 1703. Buscot Park is a much grander affair, a classic example of a late Georgian house, built in 1780. It houses the magnificent Faringdon Art Collection which includes paintings by Rembrandt, Murillo and Reynolds; one room is decorated with a series of pictures painted by Edward Burne-Jones, the pre-Raphaelite artist who was a close friend of William Morris. Painted in 1890, they reflect Burne-Jones' interest in myths and legends and tell the story of the Sleeping Beauty. The grounds of Buscot Park were largely developed in the 20th century and include a canal garden by Harold Peto, a large kitchen garden and an Egyptian avenue created by Lord Faringdon in 1969 featuring sphinxes and statues based on originals in Hadrian's Villa outside Rome. Anyone interested in the work of Burne-Jones should also visit the village church, where a stained-glass window showing the Good Shepherd was designed by him in 1891, when he was working with William Morris's firm, Morris and Co. The church itself is very pleasantly situated by the river just outside the village.

Witney

🏛 St Mary's Church 🏛 Museum

🏛 Cogges Manor Farm Museum

Situated in rich sheep-farming land in the valley of the River Windrush, this old town's name is derived from Witta's Island and it was once of importance as the meeting place of the Wittan, the council of the Saxon kings.

From the Middle Ages onwards the town became much better known for its wool and even more so for its woollen blankets – the water of the River Windrush was said to contribute to their softness. The Witney Blanket Company was incorporated in 1710 but before that there were over 150 looms here working in the blanket trade employing more than 3,000 people. The Blanket Hall, in the High Street, has on it the arms of the Witney Company of Weavers; it was built for the weighing and measuring of blankets in an age before rigid standardisation. The story of the blanket trade and other local industries, including brewing and glove-making, is recounted at the **Witney and District Museum** (see panel below), located in a courtyard just off the High Street.

Witney & District Museum

Gloucester Court Mews, High Street, Witney, OxfordshireOX8 6LR
Tel: 01993 775915   website: www.witneymuseum.com

Opened in 1996, the Witney & District Museum is situated in a traditional Cotswold stone building at the northern end of Witney High Street. The ground floor gallery houses permanent displays reflecting the industrial, military and social history of Witney and the surrounding area, while the upper floor incorporates a large gallery which is used for art exhibitions and temporary displays. Other exhibits include a display of historic toys and a typical Witney domestic kitchen of circa 1953. The museum is open from April to October, Wednesdays to Saturdays 10 am - 4pm, and Sundays 2pm - 4pm. Admission is £1 for adults and free for children.

🏛 historic building   🏛 museum   🏛 historic site   🔾 scenic attraction   🌱 flora and fauna

St Mary's Church is notable for its soaring spire which is all the more striking set amidst the surrounding level fields. Built on the scale of a mini-cathedral, the church and spire are 13th century; as Witney's wool trade prospered in the 14th and 15th centuries, chapels and aisles were added; but the interior is marred by over-enthusiastic restoration in Victorian times.

By 1278, Witney had a weekly market and two annual fairs and in the centre of the market place still stands the Buttercross. Originally a shrine, the cross has a steep roof with rustic-looking stone columns; it dates from about 1600.

Just outside the town is the **Cogges Manor Farm Museum**, which stands on the site of a now deserted medieval village of which only the church, priory, and manor

house remain. The displays tell the story of the lives of those who worked the surrounding land down the centuries.

Around Witney

STANTON HARCOURT
4 miles SE of Witney off the B4449

🏛 Stanton Harcourt Manor

🏛 Church of St Michael 🕯 Pope's Tower

This beautiful village is noted for its historic manor house **Stanton Harcourt Manor**, which dates back to the 14th century. Famed for its well-preserved medieval kitchen, one of the most complete to survive in this country, the house is also renowned for its fine collection of antiques and the tranquil

ASTON POTTERY

Kingsway Farm, Aston, Nr Witney, Oxfordshire OX18 2BT
Tel: 01993 852031 Fax: 01993 851877
website: www.astonpottery.co.uk

On the edge of the Cotswolds, on the B4449 between Standlake and Bampton, lies Aston Pottery, which was opened 18 years ago by Jane and Stephen Baughan to develop a range of household ceramics that offer the combination of quality, style and durability. Today they employ 25 staff and supply over 200 shops. All the pottery is hand-decorated on to a range of 45 different shapes from teapots to jugs and bowls to huge oval platters.

The working pottery itself is a complex of period Cotswold farm buildings which have been extensively renovated to provide an efficient and modern working environment for staff and visitors. The pottery includes a large shop where any one of the 125 designs can be bought, all exquisitely decorated by hand in themes featuring British animals and birds; wild and garden flowers; farmyard

animals; English gardens and children's nursery sets. Visitors can look around the working pottery and see the wide variety of techniques employed to make and decorate teapots, mugs, jugs and plates. The pottery shop and tea room are open seven days a week. A mail-order catalogue is available. Please visit the website for more information.

📖 stories and anecdotes 🕊 famous people ✏ art and craft 🎭 entertainment and sport 🚶 walks

gardens. It was while staying here, from 1717 to 1718, that Alexander Pope translated Homer's great work, the *Iliad*. He worked in the tower, part of the original manor house and now referred to as **Pope's Tower**. While the manor house draws many people to the village, the splendid Norman **Church of St Michael** is also worthy of a visit. Naturally, the Harcourt chapel dominates but there are other features of interest, including an intricate 14th century shrine to St Edburg.

STANDLAKE
5 miles SE of Witney on the A415

🏛 Newbridge

A little way south of the village is the three-arched **Newbridge,** built in the 13th century and now the second oldest bridge across the

Thames. Newbridge saw conflict during the Civil War and the 'Rose Revived' pub was used by Cromwell as a refreshment stop.

BRIZE NORTON
3 miles SW of Witney off the A40

Best known for its RAF transport base, Brize Norton village lies to the north of the airfield. It's a long straggling village of old grey stone houses and a Norman church which is the only one in England dedicated to a little-known 5th century French bishop, St Brice.

RADCOT
7 miles SW of Witney on the A4095

🏛 Radcot Bridge

This tiny hamlet boasts the oldest bridge across the River Thames. Built in 1154,

CASWELL HOUSE
Brize Norton, Oxfordshire OX18 3NJ
Tel: 01993 701064 Fax: 01993 774901
e-mail: stay@caswell-house.co.uk
website: www.caswell-house.co.uk

Caswell House is a wonderful late-15th century Cotswold stone building reached up a sweeping drive. Well off the beaten track, but easy to find, it stands a mile out of Brize Norton on the Curbridge road just south of Witney. Richard and Amanda Matthews are the fourth generation to have lived on this 500-acre farm, which includes streams, ponds, gardens, orchards and lawns that reach down to the ancient moat. They offer a choice of bed & breakfast and self-catering accommodation, both high-spec and spacious. The B&B facility comprises en suite doubles and twins, with TV/DVD players and tea/coffee trays. An excellent Aga-cooked breakfast is served in the dining room, and guests have the use of a comfortable sitting room.

Self-catering guests have three holiday lets sleeping two, four and six respectively in the Coach House, the Granary and the Keepers Retreat, all providing additional sleeping accommodation, good living and eating space, very comfortable bedrooms and well-fitted kitchens. The area is rich in historic and scenic interest, but guests staying at Caswell House will find plenty to see and do without leaving the farm: the views, the gentle strolls, the nature trails, the full-size snooker table and much more.

🏛 historic building   🏛 museum   🏛 historic site   🝔 scenic attraction   🌱 flora and fauna

Radcot Bridge represents an important crossing place and, as a result, the hamlet has seen much conflict over the centuries. To the north of the bridge are the remains of a castle where, in 1141, King Stephen battled with the disenthroned Queen Matilda. In the following century King John fought his barons here before finally conceding and signing the Magna Carta.

FILKINS
8 miles SW of Witney off the A361

🏛 Cotswold Woollen Weavers

🏛 Swinford Museum

This tiny Cotswold village is now the home of a flourishing community of craft workers and artists, many of whom work in restored 18th century barns. One of these groups operates the **Cotswold Woollen Weavers**, a working weaving museum with an exhibition gallery and a mill shop. In the same village is the **Swinford Museum**, which concentrates on 19th century domestic and rural trade and craft tools.

KELMSCOTT
9 miles SW of Witney off the A4095

🏛 Kelmscott Manor

William Morris called the village of Kelmscott "a heaven on earth" and **Kelmscott Manor,** the exquisite Elizabethan manor house he leased jointly with Dante Gabriel Rosetti, "the loveliest haunt of ancient peace that can well be imagined". Located near the River Thames and dating from about 1570, the manor was Morris's country home from 1871 until his death in 1896. He loved the house dearly and it is the scene of the end of his utopian novel *News from Nowhere*, in which he writes of a world where work has become a sought after pleasure. The house, which along with the beautiful garden is open to visitors during the

Kelmscott Manor

🎭 stories and anecdotes　🦜 famous people　🎨 art and craft　🎭 entertainment and sport　🎿 walks summer, has examples of Morris's work; the four-poster in which he was born, and memorabilia of Dante Gabriel Rosetti. Rosetti is reputed to have found the village boring, so presumably the fact that he was in love with Morris's wife, Jane, drew him here. Rosetti's outstanding portrait of her, *The Blue Silk Dress*, hangs in the Panelled Room. Opening times at the manor are limited – more details on 01367 252486.

Morris is buried in the churchyard, under a tombstone designed by his associate Philip Webb on the lines of a Viking tomb house. The church itself is interesting, the oldest parts dating from the late 12th century, and the village includes some fine farmhouses from around the end of the 17th and beginning of the 18th centuries.

Oxford

🏛 The College   🏛 Church of St Mary

🏛 Martyrs Memorial   🏛 Radcliffe Camera

🏛 Bodleian Library   🏛 Bridge of Sighs

🏛 Sheldonian Theatre   🏛 Oxford Story

🏛 Ashmolean   🏛 Museum of Oxford

🏛 Museum of History of Science   🖉 Folly Bridge

🏛 University Museum   🏛 Pitt River Museum

🏛 Bate Collection of Historical Instruments

🌿 Botanic Garden   🌿 Harcourt Arboretum

🖉 Christ Church Picture Gallery   🌿 University Parks

The skyline of this wonderful city can be seen from many of the hilltops which surround it and the view is best described by the 19th century poet, Matthew Arnold:

SALTER'S STEAMERS

Folly Bridge, Oxford OX1 4LA
Tel: 01865 243421   Fax: 01865 248185
e-mail: info@salterssteamers.co.uk
website: www.salterssteamers.co.uk

Salters have a history of hospitality on the Thames dating back to 1858, when the brothers John and Stephen Salter founded a small boat building enterprise in Oxford. The firm was quick to flourish and they began operating passenger boats in the 1880s, when the company operated the famous Oxford to Kingston steamer service. Today, the company is still family-run and the firm continues to operate scheduled cruises from every major location on the non-tidal Thames between Oxford and Staines (including Abingdon, Wallingford, Goring, Reading, Henley, Marlow, Cookham, Maidenhead, Windsor and Runnymede). There are scheduled cruises to suit everyone, with a range of short scenic round trips as well as a number of longer "services" between a variety of locations.

Although they have since been converted to diesel the company still boasts one of the most exclusive collection of Edwardian craft on the river – amongst the most recognisable and much-loved boats on the waterway. These are available for all forms of private charter from wedding receptions and corporate hospitality to works parties and family celebrations. The finishing touches to any event can be provided by well-chosen wine, a choice of professional entertainment and a wide range of delicious menus to suit every palate. All details are entirely flexible in order to tailor each party to the individual needs of the client.

🏛 historic building   🏛 museum   🏛 historic site   🌊 scenic attraction   🌿 flora and fauna

'*that sweet city with her dreaming spires*'

George Bernard Shaw was rather less effusive when he wrote:

'*Very nice sort of place, Oxford, I should think, for people who like that sort of place*'.

Oxford is not all beautiful ancient buildings but a town of commerce and industry and around the academic centre there are suburbs and factories. A city which has been the centre of the country's intellectual, political, religious and architectural life for over 800 years, it is still an academic stronghold, housing some of the finest minds in some of the finest buildings in the country.

River Cherwell at Oxford

A walled town in Saxon times, Oxford grew on a ford where the River Thames meets the River Cherwell. The first students came here in the 12th century when they were forced out of Paris, at that time

THE HAT BOX

Avenue 3, The Covered Market, Oxford, OX1 3DY
Tel/Fax: 01865 200844 e-mail: gillian.hatbox@vodaphone.net

The Hat Box has been located in Oxford's Covered Market for 15 years. Its current owner, Gillian Senior-MacDonald, has long had a passion for hats, born from years working in the fashion industry.

The shop carries a full range of formal hats and cocktail fascinators, by the best of British designers, as well as many more casual hats for everyday wear and for every season. Oxford is a city where people wear hats, and many of them come from this little shop! They are seen at Buckingham Palace, Royal Ascot, Henley and beyond, Oxford graduations and garden parties.

Also available is a fast tailor-made service, in an exciting range of styles and materials, by one of the UK's leading milliners. Matching handbags are available, and the bespoke hats can even be made using customer's own material.

The shop also has a great range of men's hats, from bowlers to flat caps. A visit to the shop will leave you with a passion for hats as well!

🎬 stories and anecdotes 🦜 famous people 🎨 art and craft ✏️ entertainment and sport 👣 walks

Europe's leading academic centre. Intellectual pursuits then were chiefly religious, and, as the town already had an Augustinian Abbey, it soon became the country's leading seat of theological thinking. However, there was considerable tension between the townsfolk and the intellectuals and in the 13th century, in a bid to protect their students, the university began to build colleges - enclosed quadrangles with large, sturdy front doors. The first colleges, University (1249), Balliol (1263) and Merton (1264) were soon joined by others which to this day maintain their own individual style while all coming under the administration of the university.

Merton College was founded by Walter de Merton, Lord Chancellor of England, as a small community of scholars. The present

buildings mostly date from the 15th to 17th centuries, with Mob Quad as the university's oldest. The key feature of the college is its splendid medieval library where the ancient books are still chained to the desks. Once considered the poor relation to other, wealthier colleges, **Balliol College** was founded as an act of penance by John Balliol and for many years it was reserved for poor students only. Most of the college buildings now date from the 19th century when the college was instrumental in spearheading a move towards higher academic standards.

Thought by some to have been founded by Alfred the Great, **University College** was endowed in 1249 but the present college buildings are mostly 17th century. The poet Shelley was the college's most famous scholar though he was expelled in 1811 for writing a

SARAH WISEMAN GALLERY

40-41 South Parade, Summertown,
Oxford, OX2 7JL
Tel: 01865 515123
website: www.wisegal.com

Sarah Wiseman Gallery offers a wide range of original contemporary art within an affordable price range. It is the largest selling gallery in Oxford and alongside the exhibitions of paintings and prints there is a wide range of ceramics, glass and jewellery by leading designer makers.

The gallery hosts six formal exhibitions a year, working with both emerging and established contemporary artists; details of which can be found on the website www.wisegal.com.

In between exhibitions there are regular displays of new works by gallery artists, Kathryn Thomas, Allyson Austin, Mychael Barratt, Karolina Larusdottir and Trevor Price to name but a few, as well as the works of new artists. So throughout the year there is always something new and exciting to see and buy.

Over the past eight years Sarah Wiseman Gallery has worked hard to build a reputation for promoting contemporary art of quality and integrity.

🏛 historic building   🏛 museum   🏛 historic site   🐦 scenic attraction   🌷 flora and fauna

pamphlet on atheism. Shelley drowned at the age of 30 while in Italy, and his memorial can be seen in the Front Quad.

One of the most beautiful colleges in the city, **Christ Church**, was founded in 1525 as Cardinal College by Thomas Wolsey and re-founded as Christ Church in 1546 by Henry VIII after Wolsey had fallen from royal favour. The visitor entrance is at the garden gate, through the Memorial Gardens, and leads through the bottom of Tom Tower (designed by Christopher Wren and home of the Great Tom bell) into Tom Quad, the largest of the city's quadrangles. From here there is access to the rest of the college and also to the college's chapel. Christ Church Cathedral is the only college chapel in the world to be designated a cathedral and was founded in 1546 on the remains of a 12th century building.

Another splendid college well worth a visit is **Magdalen College**, which has extensive grounds that include a riverside walk, a deer park, three quadrangles and a series of glorious well-manicured lawns. It was founded in 1458 by William Waynflete, Bishop of Winchester, and its bell tower is one of the city's most famous landmarks.

Oxford was closely involved in the Civil War and was for three years the King's headquarters. Several of the colleges were pressed into service as part of the headquarters by the Royalists: Wadham and New College were both used as stores for arms and gunpowder; Magdalen was Prince Rupert's headquarters and the tower was used as Charles' lookout when the Earl of Essex laid siege to the city. The damage caused by Cromwell's men is dramatically illustrated by bullet holes in the statue of the Virgin in the wonderful **Church of St Mary**. It was in this church that the trial of the Protestant martyrs Hugh Latimer,

Nicholas Ridley and Thomas Cranmer was held. They were found guilty of heresy and burned to death in a ditch outside the city walls. The three are commemorated by the **Martyrs Memorial**, erected in 1841 in St Giles. If Oxford was the temporary home of countless luminaries (from Wolsey, Wesley and Wilde to 12 British Prime Ministers) it is also the permanent resting place of many others. In the churchyard of St Cross are buried Kenneth Grahame (*The Wind in the Willows*), Kenneth

Martyrs Memorial, Oxford

Tynan and the composer Sir John Stainer. William Laud, 17th century Archbishop of Canterbury, is buried in the chapel of St John's College; JRR Tolkien, Oxford professor and author of *The Lord of the Rings*, and the philosopher Sir Isiah Berlin lie in Wolvercote cemetery; and CS Lewis, critic and writer of the Nania series of books, is at rest in the churchyard of Holy Trinity, Headington.

Many of the colleges have lovely peaceful gardens, some of them open to the public at various times, and the **University Parks** are a perfect place for a stroll at any time. As well as the college buildings, Oxford has many interesting and magnificent places to explore. At the city's central crossroads, unusually named Carfax and probably derived from the Latin for four-forked, is a tower, Carfax Tower, which is all that remains of the 14th century Church of St Martin. A climb to the top of the tower offers magnificent views across the city. One of the most interesting buildings, the **Radcliffe Camera**, was built between 1737 and 1749 to a design by James Gibb. England's earliest example of a round reading room (camera means chamber, or room), this splendid domed building still serves this purpose for the **Bodleian Library**. Named after Sir Thomas Bodley, a diplomat and a fellow of Merton College, it contains over 5.5 million books and is one of the world's greatest libraries. The collection of early printed books and manuscripts is second only to the British Library in London and, though members of the University can request to see any book here, this is not a lending library and the books must be read and studied on the premises.

THE ISIS TAVERN

The Towing Path, Iffley Lock, Oxford, Oxfordshire, OX4 4EL
Tel: 01865 247006
website: www.romaniinns.co.uk

Built originally as a farmhouse in the 1800s, the Isis Tavern remains secluded, nestling in the Oxfordshire countryside on the bank of the River Thames. Iffley Lock itself was the location for the very first organised rowing races in Oxford. Bumping races used to take place during the summer months, with boats lining up in front of each other and having to catch and 'bump' the boat in front. Customers have to walk to this traditional country tavern, either along the river from the city centre, or park at Iffley Lock and cross the bridge to the towing path.

Beautifully restored, the Isis has kept much of its rich history with rowing memorabilia adorning the walls in the bar area. Popular with tourists and students alike, this peaceful tavern really harks back to a time gone by when messing about on the river was a much enjoyed part-time.

Today, the Isis Tavern offers a warm welcome with a wide range of traditional, satisfying bar meals and snacks, and a large beer garden in which to relax and enjoy a drink while watching the boats go by. Check out the website for more information on special events held at the Isis Tavern.

🏛 historic building   🏛 museum   🏛 historic site   🏞 scenic attraction   🌱 flora and fauna

Close by is the Clarendon Building, the former home of the Oxford University Press and now part of the Bodleian, and also in this part of the city is the **Bridge of Sighs**, part of Hertford College and a 19th century copy of the original bridge in Venice. In Oxford the bridge crosses a street rather than a canal. The magnificent **Sheldonian Theatre** was designed and built in the style of a Roman theatre by Christopher Wren between 1664 and 1668 while he was Professor of Astronomy at the University. It is still used today for its intended purpose, as a place for University occasions including matriculation, degree ceremonies, and the annual Encaenia, when honorary degrees are conferred on distinguished people. As well as the superb wooden interior, the ceiling has 32 canvas panels, depicting Truth descending on the Arts, which are the work of Robert Streeter, court painter to Charles II.

Naturally, the city has a wealth of museums and the best place to start is at the innovative **Oxford Story** (see panel below), which presents a lively review of the last 800 years of university life, from the Middle Ages to the

The Oxford Story

6 Broad Street, Oxford OX1 3AJ
Tel: 01865 728822
website: www.oxfordstory.co.uk

The key to unlock the door of Oxford University

The Oxford Story provides a unique and entertaining introduction to Oxford. Created in conjunction with the University and brought to you by the team that created the Jorvik Viking Centre in York, The Oxford Story brings to life the key events and characters that have shaped the history of one of the world's most renowned institutions.

Seated at moving school desks, visitors are taken on a journey through time, past a series of life-size tableaux depicting the important events and people that make up the University's formidable history, complete with the sights, sounds and even smells of the times. Visitors enjoy an entertaining and informative commentary from Magnus Magnusson via personal headsets attached to their desks. There is also a special commentary for children, narrated by Timmy Mallett.

After the ride through time, there is the opportunity to quiz University experts on current areas of research in the interactive "Innovate" exhibition. From GM foods and climate change to memory ageing, visitors can use computer touch-screens to discover the latest facts behind modern day research at Oxford University, bringing the story right up to date. From don to DNA, The Oxford Story lets visitors absorb the history and explore the future of the University in an enjoyable and educational experience for the entire family.

🎭 stories and anecdotes   🐦 famous people   🎨 art and craft   🎭 entertainment and sport   🚶 walks

The Pitt Rivers Museum

South Parks Road, Oxford OX1 3PP
Tel: 01865 270927

The Pitt Rivers Museum is one of Oxford's most popular attractions. Founded in 1884, it is now internationally celebrated for its outstanding collections, (over half a million artefacts and photographs), and its unique period atmosphere. Objects from many cultures around the world, past and present, are grouped by type rather than country of origin, providing a thought provoking and rewarding experience for visitors of all ages.

present day. The **Museum of Oxford**, with a different style, also covers the story of Oxford through a series of permanent displays showing various archaeological finds. First opened in 1683 and the oldest museum in the country, the **Ashmolean Museum** was originally established to house the collection of the John Tradescants, father and son. On display in this internationally renowned museum are archaeological collections from Britain, Europe, Egypt, and the Middle East; Italian, Dutch, Flemish, French, and English old masters; Far Eastern art, ceramics, and lacquer work and Chinese bronzes. The Ashmolean, named after the 17th century antiquary Elias Ashmole, also features many items from the Civil War, including Cromwell's death mask, his watch, King Charles' spurs and a collection of coins, among them the famous Oxford crown and a £3 coin minted by Charles. Here, too, is the **Museum of the History of Science**, a remarkable collection of early scientific instruments including Einstein's blackboard and a large silver microscope made for George III.

In a splendid high-Victorian building, near the University Science Area, is the **University Museum** where the remains of a dodo, extinct since around 1680, and a mass of fossilised dinosaur remains are on display. Also here is the **Pitt Rivers Museum** (see panel above), with its interesting collection taken from all over the world. Musicians will enjoy the **Bate Collection of Historical Instruments**, the most comprehensive collection in Britain of European woodwind, brass and percussion instruments and one of the top five in the country of harpsichords and clavichords. Those captivated by Old Masters should take time to visit the **Christ Church Picture Gallery**, with its collection of works by Tintoretto, Van Dyck, Leonardo da Vinci and Michelangelo. Another place worthy of a visit and a particularly peaceful haven in the city is **Oxford Botanic Garden**, down by the river opposite Magdalen College. Founded in 1621, when plants were practically the only source of medicines, this was a teaching garden where the plants grown here were studied for their medicinal and scientific use.

Today the garden contains 8,000 species of plants in its four-nad-a-half acres, including the National collection of Euphorbias. Outside the

🏛 historic building   🏛 museum   🏛 historic site   🍃 scenic attraction   🌿 flora and fauna

entrance is a rose garden commemorating the work of Oxford's scientists in the discovery and use of penicillin. In the same ownership as the Botanic Garden is the **Harcourt Arboretum** at Nuneham Courtenay, six miles south of Oxford off the A4074. As well as a magnificent collection of trees, the site includes a bluebell wood and a 22-acre meadow.

Oxford is also the place where the River Thames changes its name to the poetic Isis and, at **Folly Bridge**, there are punts for hire and river trips can be taken, both up and down stream, throughout the day and evening.

Around Oxford

HEADINGTON
2 miles E of Oxford on the A40

Now a popular residential suburb of Oxford, Headington pre-dates the city by several centuries. It was the centre of an Anglo-Saxon

royal domain with a palace where St Frideswide grew up and Henry I came to stay. From the nearby quarries came the stone for building many of the Oxford colleges. You can enjoy a grand view of them from South Park where Parliamentary troops camped during the Civil War.

WHEATLEY
4 miles E of Oxford on the A40

🌱 Waterperry Gardens

This former quarry village retains many old buildings, of which the most interesting is a curious conical lock-up. To the west, close to the M40 (junction 8), are the famous **Waterperry Gardens** of Waterperry House (the house is not open to the public). Established as a residential gardening school for women in the 1930s, Waterperry is now part pleasure garden and part commercial garden centre. The gardens are host each year

---

ANNIE SLOAN INTERIORS

117 London Road, Headington, nr Oxford, Oxfordshire OX3 9HZ
Tel: 01865 768666
e-mail: annie@anniesloan.com website: www.anniesloan.com

Annie Sloan is the author of 20 books on colour and decorative painting and has appeared on TV many times in both the UK and the USA. In **Annie Sloan Interiors**, her shop on the northern edge of Oxford, customers will find her own range of paints, painted and unpainted furniture and a range of colour-inspired fabrics – and, of course, the books. The business undertakes all aspects of interior design and decoration for residential and commercial properties, from planning and building work through to the finishing touches.

Their bespoke kitchen furniture is made completely of wood and is supplied unpainted. This means that clients can paint and decorate the pieces themselves or have the firm do it. For other blank furniture, from lamps and frames to dressers, tables, cupboards and shelves, customers can choose from the extensive range of chalk colours. Throughout the year, Annie runs day and half-day courses on how to gild furniture and frames, how to decorate a room and how to paint furniture, with never more than six students at a time.

📖 stories and anecdotes   🦜 famous people   🎨 art and craft   🎭 entertainment and sport   🥾 walks

COMMON LEYS FARM

Waterperry Common, Waterperry,
Oxfordshire OX33 1LQ
Tel: 01865 351266
e-mail: allie@commonleysfarm.com
website: www.commonleysfarm.com

Allie and Doug Cherry own and manage **Common Leys Farm**, which is open for guest accommodation and from 11 every morning for gourmet food and happy hours spent meeting the amazing collection of animals who have their home here. The heart of the farm is a Tudor house set in 38 acres of fine Oxfordshire countryside (look for Waterperry Common on the map) and guests will find a perfect base for a relaxing, stress-free break. The owners' proud claim that visitors arrive as guests and leave as friends is borne out by the large number of repeat bookings.

The main accommodation consists of four beautifully appointed, spacious Bed & Breakfast rooms, most of them under the eaves – Scenic Suite is a double/family, Forest Suite and Courtyard Suite are twins and all have en suite facilities. Aromatherapy massages and holistic treatments are available on site and the farm also has five self-contained, self-catering apartments within the courtyard. The recently opened campsite has electrical hook-ups, showers and laundry facilities.

Common Leys also has a top-class restaurant serving traditional English cuisine with some modern touches cooked by Allie – much of it on her beloved trusty Aga. As far as possible the Seasonal menus make excellent use of fresh local ingredients but soon the new market garden at the farm will be supplying fresh fruit and vegetables for the table. Guests can enjoy a drink in the lounge while pondering the enticing menu before moving into the dining room, where a woodburning stove keeps things cosy in the cooler months. Pub-style snacks and dishes are typified by cottage pie, scampi and an open steak sandwich, while the main menu tempts with such dishes as salmon fish cake with a sweet chilli sauce, creamy wild mushrooms, zingy fresh salads and daily specials like green Thai prawn curry, calves' liver and bacon and minted lamb steak.

But the unique attraction of Common Leys is an extraordinary collection of animals, many of them enchanting miniature varieties. The happy denizens include goats, a wallaby, cows, a cob horse, Shetland ponies, a mule, meerkats, chinchillas, rheas (mini-ostriches), black and white Jacob sheep, kune kune pigs, guinea pigs, Peruvian pot-bellied pigs, rabbits, doves, chickens and occasionally a selection of reptiles are on show to the public. Common Leys Farm can now provide corporate entertainment days including clay shooting, quad biking and hoovercrafting to name but a few. The farm is easily reached from the M40 (Junction 8) and Oxford, Thame and Wheatley are all within a short drive.

COUNTRY COLLECTIONS

47 High Street, Wheatley, Oxfordshire OX33 1XX
Tel: 01865 875701

Anita Desenclos started her antiques and collectables business, **Country Collections**, in 1996 and in 2001 moved one door along the High Street into these present, roomier premises. Anita trained as an accountant before deciding to embark on a more exciting career when her two young daughters started school.

Now she deals in an intriguing variety of attractive and interesting items. In addition to the antiques, sourced in the UK and France, Country Collections offers a range of small items of furniture, old pine, soft furnishings, glassware, china, ceramics, costume jewellery, Art Deco pieces and general gift ideas.

Her shop is located in the middle of peaceful Wheatley and comprises a spacious ground-floor showroom with lots of nooks and crannies, and a second smaller display area on the first floor. Anita's delightful shop is a great place to look for something to brighten the home or to find an unusual and distinctive present for almost any occasion.

to Art in Action, which brings together many of the world's finest craftspeople.

GARSINGTON

4 miles SE of Oxford off the B480

🏛 Garsington Manor   🏛 Church of St Mary

The most distinguished building hereabouts is **Garsington Manor**, built on a hilltop of mellow Cotswold stone in the 16th century. Between 1915 and 1927, this was the home of the socialite Lady Ottoline Morrell and her husband Philip who were hospitable to a whole generation of writers, artists, and intellectuals including Katherine Mansfield, Lytton Strachey, Clive Bell, Siegfried Sassoon, DH Lawrence, TS Eliot, Rupert Brooke, Bertrand Russell and Aldous Huxley. Huxley based an account of a country house party in his novel *Crome Yellow* on his experiences at

Garsington, thereby causing a rift with his hostess. She found his description all too recognisable and they were estranged for some time. It seems that Lady Ottoline was not very lucky in the artists on whom she lavished her attention and hospitality. DH Lawrence also quarrelled with her after drawing a less than flattering, but clearly recognisable, portrait of life at her house in *Women in Love*.

Garsington's other claim to literary fame is that Rider Haggard was sent to the school run by the Rev HJ Graham at the rectory in 1866. The present house is later, built in 1872, but across the road from the Church is a 16th century gateway from the rectory he would have known. While there Haggard became friendly with a local farmer named Quartermain whom he must have

🎞 stories and anecdotes   🐦 famous people   🎨 art and craft   🎭 entertainment and sport   🥾 walks

remembered with affection as he used the name for his hero, many years later, in his novel *King Solomon's Mines*.

The village **Church of St Mary** is a pleasant and cosy building with fine views to the south over the Chilterns from its hill top position, but it also looks over the industrial belt to the south of Oxford. Though the interior is chiefly Victorian, the church has retained its Norman tower and inside there is an elegant memorial to Lady Ottoline.

THAME
11 miles E of Oxford on the A418

🏛 Church of St Mary 🏛 Grammar School

🏛 Prebendal House

Founded in 635 as an administrative centre for the Bishop of Dorchester, Thame first became a market town in the 13th century and its importance as a commercial centre is evident by the wide main street it still has today. Lined with old inns and houses, some of which go back to the 15th century, this is a delightful place to visit.

The imposing **Church of St Mary**, tucked away at one end of the High Street, was built in the 13th century though the aisles were widened in the 14th century and the tower was heightened in the 15th century. In the centre of the chancel is a monument to Lord John Williams who was notorious for having helped burn Archbishop Thomas Cranmer in the 16th century. To the west of the church lies the **Prebendal House** which, in its oldest parts, dates from the 13th century. A prebend was an income granted to a priest by a cathedral or

MI CASA
3 Upper High Street, Thame, Oxon OX9 3ER
Tel: 01844 218730 Fax: 01844 218983

Anyone in search of ideas to brighten up their home décor should make their way to **Mi Casa** in the centre of Thame. From the outside it looks quite small but the display areas extend right through to the back of the property and the many cabinets, gondolas and wall-mounted displays are stacked with a huge variety of items. The owner of Mi Casa, Adrian Mills, used to work in the information technology industry but left that business in 2000 for the more congenial lifestyle of developing this fascinating shop.

His selection includes LSA glassware, Pecksniffs fine fragrances, Sophie Conran tableware, ceramics, artwork, candlewares, jewellery and much, much more. Everything is contemporary and chosen for its elegant design and value for money. And if you want to add a distinctive touch to your house, there's a varied selection of house name and number plates. Mi Casa also stocks a wonderful choice of contemporary gifts, gift wraps and cards – a great place to visit in the run-up to Christmas.

🏛 historic building 🖼 museum 🏛 historic site 🏞 scenic attraction 🌿 flora and fauna

collegiate church. At Thame the prebend was established in around 1140 by Lincoln Cathedral. A special residence for the holders of the office was first mentioned in 1234.

The town also has a famous **Grammar School**, housed in a Tudor building in Church Lane. The schoolmaster's house faces the road and over the doorway are the arms of Lord Williams, who founded the school in 1558. John Hampden, one of the Parliamentary leaders during the Civil War, was at school here and he also died at Thame. When the Civil War broke out he raised a regiment of infantry for the Parliamentary Army and fought with great bravery at Edgehill and Reading. He was wounded at the battle of Chalgrove Field in June 1643 and was carried back to Thame where he died some days later in an inn which stood on the High Street. A plaque on a wall denotes the site.

NUNEHAM COURTENAY
5 miles S of Oxford on the A4074

🏛 Nuneham Park

When the 1st Earl of Harcourt moved his family here from Stanton Harcourt in 1756 he built the splendid **Nuneham Park**, one of the grandest mansions in Oxfordshire. The earl commissioned Capability Brown to landscape the grounds and observing the completed work deemed it

> *"as advantageous and delicious as can be desired, surrounded by hills that form an amphitheatre and, at the foot, the River Thames."*

To achieve this idyllic result, the earl had the old village moved a mile away and out of sight. It's a charming model village of 18th century cottages facing each other in matched pairs on either side of the road. The mansion house is now a conference centre but its parkland forms the **Arboretum** of Oxford

University and is open to the public (see under Nuneham Courtenay).

ELSFIELD
2 miles N of Oxford off the A40

Elsfield was the home of the author and administrator John Buchan, 1st Baron Tweedsmuir, from 1919 until 1935 when he left to take up his appointment as Governor-General of Canada. During his time at Elsfield Manor House he wrote a number of books, including *Midwinter*, written in 1923 and partly set in the vicinity. His ashes are buried by the east wall of the churchyard of St Thomas of Canterbury. RD Blackmore, author of *Lorna Doone*, lived in Elsfield as a child while his father was the vicar.

NOKE
5 miles NE of Oxford off the B4027

The tiny hamlet of Noke stands at the end of a winding lane that peters out at the edge of Otmoor. It has a small medieval church with a notable Elizabethan brass that depicts Johan Bradshaw with her two husbands and eight children.

WOODSTOCK
8 miles NW of Oxford on the A44

🏛 Blenheim Palace

🏛 Oxfordshire County Museum   🌱 Secret Garden

Situated in the Glyme Valley, in an area of land that was originally part of the Wychwood Forest, the name of this elegant Georgian market town means a 'place in the woods'. To the north of the River Glyme is the old Saxon settlement, while on the opposite bank lies the town that was developed by Henry II in the 13th century to serve the Royal Park of Woodstock. There had been hunting lodges for the Kings of England here long before the

Blenheim Palace

Norman Invasion and it was Henry I who established the deer park around the manor of Woodstock. It was while at his palace here that Henry II first seduced Rosamund, whom he is said to have housed in a bower in the park. One story tells how Henry's wife, Queen Eleanor, managed to uncover the couple by following an unravelled ball of silk that had become attached to her husband's spur.

This long since disappeared medieval palace was also the birthplace of the Black Prince in 1330 and Princess Elizabeth was held prisoner here in 1558 during the reign of her sister, Queen Mary. On ascending the throne, a grateful Elizabeth I granted the town a second weekly market and two fairs for its loyalty. The palace was damaged during the Civil War, when it served as a Royalist garrison, and the last remains were demolished in 1710.

While the new town became an important coaching centre, many of the old inns survive to this day, and prospered as a result of the construction of the Oxford Canal and later the railway. The old town's trade was glove-making and traditionally a pair of new gloves is presented to a visiting monarch.

The town is also home to the **Oxfordshire County Museum**, which is housed in the wonderful and imposing 16th century Fletcher's House. As well as the permanent displays on the life of the county through the centuries, the museum hosts regular exhibitions and has a sculpture court and a peaceful garden at whose entrance stand the old town stocks.

It is the magnificent **Blenheim Palace**, one of only a handful of sites in the country to be included on the World Heritage List, which brings most people to Woodstock. The estate and the cost of building the palace was a gift from a grateful Queen Anne to the heroic John Churchill, 1st Duke of Marlborough, for his victory at the Battle of Blenheim during the Spanish War of

THE CRAFTSMEN'S GALLERY

1 Market Street, Woodstock,
Oxfordshire OX20 1SU
Tel: 01993 811995
e-mail: richard.marriott@btconnect.com
website: www.craftsmensgallery.co.uk

With over 20 years' experience in the trade, owner Richard Marriott has built up a strong customer base of artists and art-lovers at the **Craftsmen's Gallery**. They find a comprehensive range of artists' materials to meet every need, whether they are professionals, amateurs, students or enthusiastic youngsters. These items are all stocked on the ground floor, along with hand-crafted work by British craftspeople. There are ceramics from Poole Pottery, Cain Pottery, Isis, Paul Gooderham and Christine Cummings (Christine is famed for her ceramic pigs); glassware; jewellery by Ola Gorie and hand-painted military figures by Dino Lemonofides.

The gallery's extensive range also includes pieces in wood (Perry Lancaster), bronze, crystal and other materials. Both on the ground floor and in the basement, original works of art in watercolours and oils, pastels and etchings and prints by talented contemporary artists are displayed (Ken Messer is one of the featured artists). The Craftsmen's Gallery also provides a complete bespoke picture framing service, with a huge selection of styles to choose from. The gallery is located in the heart of historic Woodstock, a short walk from the entrance gate to Blenheim Palace.

Succession. However, the Queen's gratitude ran out before the building work was complete and the duke had to pay the remainder of the costs himself. As his architect, Marlborough chose Sir John Vanbrugh, whose life was even more colourful than that of his patron. He was at once both an architect (although at the time of his commission he was relatively unknown) and a playwright, and he also had the distinction of having been imprisoned in the Bastille in Paris. The result of his work was the Italianate palace (built between 1705 and 1722), which is now seen sitting in a very English park that was designed by Charles Bridgeman and Henry Wise and later landscaped by Capability Brown. Unfortunately, once completed, the new

house did not meet with universal approval: it was ridiculed by Jonathan Swift and Alexander Pope, and Marlborough's wife, Sarah, who seems to have held the family purse strings, delayed paying Vanbrugh as long as possible.

Blenheim is a marvellous, grand place with a mass of splendid paintings, furniture, porcelain, and silver on show. Visitors will also be interested in the more intimate memorabilia of Sir Winston Churchill. Born here in 1874, Churchill was a cousin of the 9th Duke and the family name remains Churchill.

The **Secret Garden** was opened in 2004, the 300th anniversary of the Battle of Blenheim. The garden was originally planted in the 1950s by the 10th duke but after his

North Leigh

Distance: *5.8 miles (9.3 kilometres)*

Typical time: *180 mins*

Height gain: *40 metres*

Map: *Explorer 180*

Walk: *www.walkingworld.com ID:2379*

Contributor: *Ron and Jenny Glynn*

North Leigh lies off the A4095 between Bicester and Witney. There is ample car parking by the village hall, opposite the church.

The beautiful west Oxfordshire village of North Leigh is the starting point for this super little walk to Stonesfield and East End. The

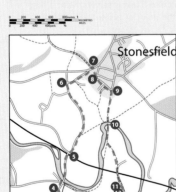

Cotswold stone buildings and dry stone walling are attractive features of this area, combining with the splendour of green and glorious landscape that make up the wonderful scenes encountered. The Roman Villa of North Leigh is a tremendously interesting and exciting spectacle, a valuable relic of the distant past, giving us a little insight into life in ancient Britain. The paths and bridleways that we tread today link us to our ancestors who trod the very same ones, a fact that is brought sharply into focus on this historical route.

River, Pub, Church, Wildlife, Birds, Flowers, Great Views, Woodland, Ancient Monument

1 | Starting from the church, turn left by The Old School and follow a hard track above open countryside.

2 | A short distance on, turn right through a metal gate, and walk downhill in a meadow to cross a stream. Continue through a gate with fence on right, passing a large pond and newly planted trees.

3 | Take metal gate and turn left on narrow road for few yards, then right on bridleway signed to Ashford Bridge. Pass Holly Farm in a lovely woodland setting, then stone barns and old stables before a cottage. Continue beside stream that runs below a high embankment, the path tree-lined and partly enclosed.

4 | Join a single track road and walk on over Ashford Bridge, crossing the River Evenlode, then uphill past Bridgefield Farm.

5 | Go on to walk over railway bridge and turn right with a spread of farmland and wooded areas in all directions. Pass a derelict barn and farm buildings and continue beside open fields for some distance.

6 | Turn right beside Spratts Farm and walk downhill into Stonesfield. Turn right out of Witney Lane passing quaint and pretty stone cottages.

7 | Turn right on the Oxfordshire Way on an uphill climb to reach the Wesleyan Chapel.

8 | Turn right along Churchfields passing handsome residences.

9 | Turn right into Brook Lane to leave village with lovely views over very picturesque landscape. Continue downhill to Stockey Bottom.

10 | Cross River Evenlode on a superb wooden footbridge and continue over large meadow and through gateway to meet hedge on left. Arrive at large wooden gate and go through walker's gate beside it to join a track. Cross railway track on large brick built bridge.

11 | Turn left to visit North Leigh Roman Villa remains, an English Heritage site. Much of it was excavated in 1815-16 by Henry Hakewell, and there is a wonderful mosaic floor housed in a little building for protection, at the side of the villa.

12 | Take stile to walk beside the villa and follow a defined path towards woodland. Climb a stile onto woodland path, and follow it to turn right up the steep bank and onto a path above, following it to leave Sturt Wood. Turn left along road to pass the handsome Sturt House, then a mix of dwellings in East End.

13 | Turn right over stile to walk between houses, then beside copse. Walk on between fields to another stile that is very walker friendly, and on past a new tree plantation. Go on between fields, then turn right on the Wychwood Way over a meadow, and onto a narrow path between hedgerows, then fencing.

14 | Join road and walk the short distance to North Leigh, the village church in view.

death became overgrown and virtually inaccessible. Now restored, this 'Four Seasons' garden with its many unusual trees, shrubs and flowers offers an enchanting mix of winding paths, soothing water features, bridges, fountains, ponds and streams.

First grown by George Kempster, a tailor from Old Woodstock, the Blenheim Orange apple took its name from the palace. Though the exact date of the first apple is unknown, Kempster himself died in 1773 and the original tree blew down in 1853. So famous did the spot where the tree stood become that it is said that London-bound coaches and horses used to slow down so that passengers might gaze upon it.

BLADON
1.5 miles S of Woodstock on the A4095

🕏 Churchyard

The village lies on the southern edge of the Blenheim estate and it was in the **Churchyard** here in 1965 that Sir Winston Churchill was laid to rest in a simple grave after a state funeral. Also interred here are his parents, his brother John, and his daughters. The ashes of his wife Clementine were buried in his grave in 1977.

LONG HANBOROUGH
2 miles S of Woodstock

🏛 Oxford Bus Museum

Located next to Long Hanborough railway station, the **Oxford Bus Museum** has some 40 vehicles on display, all of which were used at one time for public transport in and around Oxford. They range from early 19th century horse-trams to buses from the 1980s. Also on show is the double-decker bus used in the Spice Girls movie. The museum is open at weekends and daily throughout August.

NORTH LEIGH
4.5 miles SW of Woodstock off the A4095

🏛 Roman Villa

The Saxon-towered St Mary's Church is well worth a visit, and just to the north of the village lies the **Roman Villa** (English Heritage), one of several known to have existed in this area. Little remains apart from the foundations and some mosaic flooring, but this is enough to measure the scale of the place; it had over 60 rooms, two sets of baths and a sophisticated under-floor heating system, all built round a courtyard and clearly the home of a prosperous farming family.

FINSTOCK
5 miles W of Woodstock on the B4022

A charming village with two notable literary associations. It was in 1927, at the 19th century Holy Trinity Church, that TS Eliot was baptised at the age of 38 following his controversial conversion to Catholicism. The novelist and churchwoman Barbara Pym lived in retirement with her sister in a cottage in the village; she died in 1980 and is buried in the churchyard. A lectern in the church is dedicated to her memory.

CHARLBURY
5 miles NW of Woodstock on the B4026

🏛 Museum 🏛 Railway Station

🏛 Cornbury Park

Now very much a dormitory town for Oxford, Charlbury was once famous for its glove-making as well as being a centre of the Quaker Movement - the simple Friends' Meeting House dates from 1779 and there is also a Friends' cemetery. **Charlbury Museum**, close to the Meeting House, has displays on the traditional crafts and industries

North Leigh Roman Villa

of the town and the town's charters given by Henry III and King Stephen can also be seen. Well known for its olde-worlde **Railway Station**, built by Isambard Kingdom Brunel, complete with its fishpond and hanging baskets, the town also has two interesting great houses.

On the other bank of the River Evenlode is **Cornbury Park**, a large estate that was given to Robert Dudley by Elizabeth I. Although most of the house now dates from the 17th century, this was originally a hunting lodge in Wychwood Forest that had been used since the days of Henry I. Glimpses of the house can be seen from the walk around the estate.

Lying just to the west of the town is **Ditchley Park**, a restrained and classical house built in the 1720s by James Gibbs. The interiors are splendid, having been designed by William Kent and Henry Flitcroft, and Italian craftsmen worked on the stucco decorations of the great hall and the saloon;

the first treated to give an impression of rich solemnity, the second with a rather more exuberant effect. The house has associations with Sir Winston Churchill, who used it as a weekend headquarters during World War II. Appropriately enough, given that Sir Winston had an American mother, Ditchley Park is now used as an Anglo-American conference centre and is not open to the public.

Bicester

Though the name (which is pronounced Bister) suggests that this was a Roman settlement, the town was not, in fact, established until Saxon times and the Roman name comes as a result of the nearby and long since vanished Roman town of Alchester. By the time of the 12th century, the town was the home of both an Augustinian priory and a

Benedictine nunnery. Growing up around these religious houses and its market, the town suffered a disastrous fire in the early 18th century and most of the buildings seen here today date from that time onwards. Hunting and horse-racing played as much a part in the prosperity of Bicester as agriculture though industrialisation has been sporadic.

Around Bicester

DEDDINGTON
8 miles NW of Bicester off the A423

🏛 Deddington Castle & Castle House

Visitors to this old market town might recognise it as the place that was demolished by a runaway crane in the television adaptation of Tom Sharpe's *Blott on the Landscape*. The damage was, of course, cleverly faked and

ART-FILE GALLERY
Unit 2, The Courtyard, Home Farm, Bicester, Oxfordshire OX27 8TG
Tel: 01869 354753
e-mail: info@art-file.co.uk   website: www.art-file.co.uk

Alison Honour, graduate of Central St Martins School of Art & Design and Wimbledon School of Art, opened the **Art-File Gallery** in October 2004. Her aims were to introduce clients to the pleasure of buying and owning contempory art and helping them to personalise their living space and enhance their work environment. The art on display in the converted barn space covers the whole spectrum – abstract, figurative, still life, nature, landscapes, seascapes and cityscapes, sculpture, ceramics, glass, textiles, metals, jewellery and photography.

Alison, who personally selects all the work on display, offers a unique service in sourcing, promoting and selling the exciting and innovative work of artists and designer-makers both new and established to both private and corporate clients. She and her staff are friendly, motivated and knowledgeable, opening up the world of contemporary art in a relaxing, stress-free way. The gallery's superb website provides the option of buying online easily and painlessly.

🎭 stories and anecdotes   🐦 famous people   🎨 art and craft   🎟 entertainment and sport   🥾 walks

Deddington, which hovers between a small town and a large village, still retains all its medieval character. Surveyed in the Domesday Book at twice the value of Banbury, the town never developed in the same way as Banbury and Bicester, but it remains a prosperous agricultural centre with a still bustling market place. Little can now be seen of the 12th century **Deddington Castle**. This was destroyed in the 14th century and most of the building materials were put to good use in other areas of the town. However, excavations have revealed the remains of a curtain wall, a hall

Castle House, Deddington

and a small rectangular keep.

Close by is **Castle House**, where Pier Gaveston, Edward II's favourite, was held before his execution in 1312. The house's two towers were added later, in the 1650s, when

---

F EAGLES FRESH FOODS

The Market Place, Deddington,
nr Banbury, Oxfordshire OX15 0SE
Tel: 01869 338500
Fax: 01869 388588
e-mail: info@feaglesfreshfoods.co.uk
website: www.feaglesfreshfoods.co.uk

The name of Eagles has been among the high flyers in the fresh food business for more than 50 years. Paul Eagles and Sheila Adams, who run the business together, have ensured that **Eagles** remains synonymous with delicious, high-quality foods, and their food hall in Deddington is stocked with a fine selection of the very best produce. Paul is a butcher and Sheila has a farming background, the merging of their experience and expertise is one of the main reasons for the success of their enterprise, along with the guarantee of top quality allied to amazingly competitive prices.

The staff, all locally recruited, are as passionate as the owners about food, and their number includes highly trained chefs, experienced fishmonger and butchers. Award-winning meat and poultry, large variety of fish, a great choice of cheeses and a mouthwatering deli selection are among the highlights. Typical hot dishes include classics like fish pie, lasagne, moussaka, chicken with a variety of sauces, and there's a wonderful array of puddings - pies, tarts, steamed puddings, pancakes, panacotta, trifles, gateaux, parfaits, poached and prepared fruits. Catering is also available with menus for fabulous food for every occasion – finger, party, at-home buffets and a fine hot selection that all take the pain out of party giving.

🏛 historic building   🏛 museum   🏛 historic site   ⚜ scenic attraction   🌾 flora and fauna

OTTERS RESTAURANT

Market Place, Deddington, nr Banbury,
Oxfordshire OX15 0SA
Tel: 01869 338813
e-mail: ottersrestaurant@hotmail.co.uk

Deddington Castle and Deddington House are part of the town's interesting past, but one of the attractions very much of today is **Otters Restaurant**. Chef-patron Mike Whitley and his wife Mandy run this excellent restaurant located in a corner building on the Market Place. The light pine floors and lightwood furnishings create a relaxed, contemporary ambience assisted by fresh flowers and some eyecatching features, including a giant fish on one wall and a picture of an otter on another.

Mike seeks out the very best local produce for his menus, which put a modern slant on familiar dishes that range from top-notch soups to the day's pasta, seafood specials (typified by deep-fried whitebait with paprika salt and pepper mayonnaise, and salmon on a bed of julienne vegetables), succulent steaks and always a choice for vegetarians. Friendly, attentive service and a well-chosen wine list complete the pleasure of a meal at Otters, which is open lunchtimes and evenings Tuesday to Saturday and lunchtime Sunday.

the house was in the ownership of Thomas Appletree. A supporter of Cromwell, Appletree was ordered to destroy the property of Royalists and it was material from two local houses that he used in his building work.

LOWER HEYFORD

6 miles W of Bicester on the B4030

🏛 Rousham House

Situated at a ford across the River Cherwell, which was replaced in the 13th century by a stone bridge, the village lies on the opposite bank from its other half - Upper Heyford. To the south lies **Rousham House**, a fine mansion built in the mid-1600s for Sir Robert Dormer and set in magnificent gardens. The gardens as seen today were laid out by William Kent in 1738 and include many water features, sculptures and follies. Next to the house are very attractive pre-Kent walled gardens with a

parterre, herbaceous borders, a rose garden and a vegetable garden. The garden is open to the public all year round; the house has limited opening times.

Banbury

🏛 St Mary's Church 🏛 Banbury Cross

🏛 Museum & Tooley's Boatyard

Famous for its cross, cakes, and the nursery rhyme, this historic and thriving market town has managed to hang on to many of its old buildings as well as become home to Europe's largest livestock market.

The famous **Banbury Cross** can be found in Horsefair where it was erected, in 1859, replacing the previous one demolished by the Parliamentarians during the Civil War. It was built to commemorate the marriage of Queen Victoria's oldest daughter to the Prussian

🎭 stories and anecdotes   🦉 famous people   🎨 art and craft   ✒ entertainment and sport   🚶 walks

WHOOSH & BLAH

3-4 George Street, Banbury, Oxfordshire OX16 5BH
Tel/Fax: 01295 262677
e-mail: info@whooshandblah.co.uk
website: www.whooshandblah.co.uk

Since leaving the Royal College of Art in 1997, Catherine Roberts has worked for some of the top names in the world of entertainment. Her designs have been commissioned by some of the best-known performers, and her fashion work has graced the red carpets of many a première. Who better then to run a shop such as **Whoosh & Blah**, whose display areas are filled with gorgeous fashion accessories and creative gifts that run from stocking fillers and knick-knacks to design-led homeware, jewellery, photo boxes, key rings, cufflinks, watches and clocks and paintings?

Everything in the shop demonstrates that Catherine really puts the style into lifestyle, and her philosophy that lifestyle and fashion should be fun is very evident in her clothes. These extend from everyday wear to designs for weddings and other special occasions. This splendid shop, located just off the main street in the old part of Banbury, is open from 9.30 to 5.30 (Saturday from 9, Sunday 11.30 to 3.30). Customers can keep up to date with activities at Whoosh & Blah by joining the customer club – the Gorgeous Gang – and learning about the latest offers and products by mailing list.

LUMBERS JEWELLERY

90 High Street, Banbury,
Oxfordshire OX16 5JF
Tel: 01295 263807 Fax: 01295 273106
e-mail: lumbersbanbury@yahoo.co.uk

On Banbury's busy High Street, **Lumbers** is a specialist jeweller, silversmith and diamond merchant with a spacious display area behind its double-fronted, bay-windowed exterior. Owner Alex Pomerance, a qualified diamond mounter, has been in the business of designing and selling jewellery for 25 years, and he and his local staff are always ready with help and advice for their customers.

The range of jewellery includes in-house designs, the Bien collection of wedding rings and the Lady Heart diamond collection, and all the top names in watchmaking are represented.

Silverware includes trays, candlesticks and gifts for all occasions. Lumbers undertakes rapid and reliable repairs to all items of jewellery, engraving work and valuations. The shop also specialises in clock repairs – collecting from the customer, repairing and delivering and installing back in the customer's home.

Crown Prince, and the figures around the bottom of the cross, of Queen Victoria, Edward VII, and George V, were added in 1914.

The town's other legendary claim to fame is its cakes, made of spicy fruit pastry, which can still be bought. Banbury was also, at one time, famous for its cheeses, which were only about an inch thick. This gave rise to the expression 'thin as a Banbury cheese'.

On the east side of the Horsefair stands **St Mary's Church**, a classical building of warm-coloured stone and hefty pillars which are pleasantly eccentric touches. The original architect was SP Cockerell, though the tower and portico were completed between 1818 and 1822 by his son, CR Cockerell. The style reflects the strong influence on English architecture of Piranesi's *Views of Rome*, using massive shapes and giving stone the deliberately roughened appearance which comes from the technique known as rustication.

In **Banbury Museum** can be found the story of the town's development, from the days when it came under the influence of the bishops of Lincoln, through the woollen trade of the 16th century, to the present day. Adjoining the striking modern museum is **Tooley's Boatyard**, a scheduled ancient monument that can be visited as part of a guided tour. Established in 1790 and in continuous use ever since, Tooley's is the oldest working dry dock in the country. It was designed to build and repair canal barges and narrowboats.

WYKHAM PARK FARM SHOP

*Wykham Park Farm, Banbury,
Oxfordshire OX16 9UP
Tel: 01295 262235 Fax: 01295 252323
e-mail: jhncolegrave@clara.co.uk*

John and Julia Colegrave and their helpful, hardworking staff run the **Wykham Park Farm Shop**, which has acquired a large and loyal clientele since opening in 2000. Angus X and Longhorn beef as well as lamb is produced from animals raised on the farm and butchered on the premises. Local, welfare friendly pork, veal, poultry and seasonal game is also sold in the shop.

Many of the vegetables on display are also home-produced; these include potatoes and quite superb asparagus, which is particularly well suited to the soil on the farm and supplied to a number of local restaurants (also available by mail order). The Farm is proud to have accreditations from Les Routiers as well as LEAF, which links environment and farming.

Other food on sale at this outstanding farm shop includes cheeses (with the emphasis on British farmhouse varieties), cakes and pastries, jams and preserves, pickles and chutneys, all of the best quality and most of it from local sources. The owners welcome visitors not just to buy the excellent provisions but for educational sessions and farm walks; school parties are welcome with a little notice.

PICCANTE DELICATESSEN & CAFÉ

21 Parsons Street, Banbury,
Oxfordshire OX16 5LY
Tel: 01295 279559
e-mail: lphelps1@virgin.net

Piccante is a delicatessen and café located in a shopping area close to the town centre. Owner Louise Phelps has filled the premises with a wonderful range of top-quality food sourced from the UK and Europe. Among the stars of the show are the cheeses, with a least 40 varieties usually available, along with hams and salamis, pâtés and terrines, pastries and superb French breads, and a host of goodies in bottles, jars and tins.

Louise and her partner Frank are both qualified chefs, and quality is the keynote on the café menus – lunch is served every day, dinner (6pm to 8.45pm) on Wednesday, Thursday and Friday. For those eating on the premises there are seats both inside and out in a sheltered, wooden-floored patio area.

Piccante will prepare hampers for picnics and other occasions and offers a catering service for dinners, parties and functions.

THE DUN COW

West End, Hornton, nr Banbury,
Oxfordshire OX15 6DA
Tel: 01295 670524 Fax: 01295 678516
e-mail: gwynethgelling@hotmail.co.uk
website: www.drunkenmonk.co.uk

Martin and Gwyneth Gelling offer a warm welcome at the **Dun Cow**, an early-17th century thatched pub located off the A422 six miles northwest of Banbury. The two beamed and flag-floored bars are perfect spots to meet or make friends and enjoy a glass or two of real ale or sample some unusual bottled beers and ciders, country wines or mead.

The pub is renowned for its beer and holds beer festivals on the first weekend in February and at the end of July. Freshly prepared traditional English food is served weekends and evenings, with plenty of choice for all tastes.

Picnic benches are set out under parasols on the lawn in the summer, and children can romp happily and safely in the playground opposite. The pub is open weekday evenings and all day Saturday and Sunday. The Dun Cow is part of a small company, the Drunken Monk, supplying and manning beer tents and organising themed events at the pub or in the client's chosen venue; medieval banquets are a speciality.

Around Banbury

BROUGHTON

2½ miles SW of Banbury on the B4035

🏰 Broughton Castle

Arthur Mee considered **Broughton Castle** *"One of the most fascinating buildings in the county"*. As you cross the ancient bridge over a moat and approach the sturdy 14th century gatehouse, it becomes clear that it is indeed something special, the perfect picture of a great Tudor mansion. The house has been owned by the Broughton family since 1451 – Nathaniel Fiennes, 21st Lord Saye & Sele is the present occupant. Over the years, there have been several royal visitors including Queen Anne of Denmark, wife of James I. Both James I and Edward VII used the aptly named King's Chamber, with its hand-painted Chinese wall paper. The house also played a part in the Civil War as it has a secret room where leaders of the Parliamentary forces laid their plans. Arms and armour from that period are displayed in the castle's grandest room, the Great Hall, which is also notable for its dazzling plaster ceiling installed in 1599.

BLOXHAM

3½ miles SW of Banbury on the A361

🏛 Museum

Dominated by the 14th century St Mary's Church, whose spire is a highly visible local landmark and its Victorian public school, this large village is one of narrow lanes and fine gentlemen's houses. The old court house, to the south of the church, contains the **Bloxham Village Museum**, where there is a permanent collection of items on display which tell the life of the inhabitants of the village and surrounding area.

SOUTH NEWINGTON

6 miles SW of Banbury on the A361

⛪ Church of St Peter ad Vincula

This small village of ironstone dwellings is home to the **Church of St Peter ad Vincula**, which contains the best medieval wall paintings in the county. Detail and colouring are both superb in the depictions, which include the murders of Thomas à Becket and Thomas of Lancaster (a rebel against Edward II), St Margaret slaying a dragon and a wonderful Virgin and Child.

GREAT TEW

7 miles SW of Banbury off the B4022

One of the most picturesque villages in the county, Great Tew, a planned estate village, had fallen into such disrepair by the 1970s that it was declared a conservation area in order to save it from complete dereliction. Today, the

Village Stocks, Great Tew

🎭 stories and anecdotes 🦢 famous people 🎨 art and craft 🎶 entertainment and sport 🚶 walks

thatched cottages and houses from the 16th, 17th and 18th centuries nestle in a fold in the landscape of rolling countryside. The big house hereabouts is Great Tew Park, dating mainly from the 19th century. Only the garden walls remain of its 17th century predecessor, owned by Lucius Carey, Lord Falkland. It was a gathering place for some of the great writers and intellectuals of the day, including Edmund Waller and Ben Jonson. In the 17th century the 5th Viscount Falkland was Secretary to the Navy and gave his name to the Falkland Islands.

HOOK NORTON
7 miles SW of Banbury off the A361

This large village is best known for its brewery, which was set up by John Harris from his farmhouse in 1849. He started there as a maltster and after years of gaining expertise and learning from experiments he constructed a purpose-built brewery in 1872. The Brewery, which moved to its present premises in 1900, remains in the Harris family.

SWALCLIFFE
5 miles W of Banbury on the B4035

🏛 Church of St Peter and St Paul

🏛 15th Century Barn 🏛 Madmarston Hill

The village is dominated by the large **Church of St Peter and St Paul** which towers over all the other buildings here. Founded in Saxon times, the bulk of the building dates from the 12th, 13th and 14th centuries and it is the tracery in the east window which makes the church noteworthy. However, by far the most impressive building in Swalcliffe is the **Barn**, which has been acknowledged as one of the finest 15th century half-cruck barns in the country. Built as the manorial barn by New College, Oxford, between 1400 and 1409, it

was used to store produce from the manor and never to store tithes. Today, it is home to a collection of agricultural and trade vehicles.

To the northeast of the village, on **Madmarston Hill**, are the remains of an Iron Age hill fort which was occupied from the 2nd century BC to the 1st century AD.

WROXTON
3 miles NW of Banbury on the A422

🏛 Abbey

A charming village of brown stone cottages clustered round the village pond, from which a road leads to **Wroxton Abbey**. This impressive Jacobean mansion was built by Sir William Pope, Earl of Downe, and was the home of the North family for 300 years. The gardens and grounds of the Abbey, now restored as an 18th century park, are open to the public, but the house is not. All Saints Church contains several imposing monuments including those to Sir William and his wife, to Lord North who was Prime Minister from 1770 to 1782, and to the banker Thomas Coutts.

Burford

🏛 Church of St John the Baptist

🏛 Tolsey Museum 🌾 Cotswold Wildlife Park

Often referred to as The Gateway to the Cotswolds, Burford is an enchanting old market town of honey coloured Cotswold stone set on the banks of the River Windrush. It was the site of a battle between the armies of Wessex and Mercia in 752, and after the Norman Conquest the town was given to William I's brother, Bishop Odo of Bayeux. Lying on important trade routes, both north-south and east-west, the town prospered and its first market charter was granted in 1087. In the 16th century, the town was an important centre of the woollen trade and it was used as the setting for *The Woolpack*, in which the author Celia Harknett describes the medieval wool trade in Europe. After the decline in the wool trade, Burford became an important coaching centre and many of the old inns can still be seen today.

The **Church of St John the Baptist** was built on the wealth of the wool trade and this grand building has the atmosphere of a small cathedral. Originally Norman, the church has been added to over the centuries and there are several interesting

Burford

BURFORD WOODCRAFT

144 High Street, Burford, Oxon, OX18 4QU
Tel: 01993 823479
website: www.burford-woodcraft.co.uk

Historically people have been drawn to Burford for its beautiful Cotswold architecture and one of the top 20 churches in England. Less well known is the diversity of its unusual shops and independent galleries. One such gallery, **Burford Woodcraft** has an excellent reputation for a contemporary collection centred on wood that is innovative, value for money and fun. Since 1978 it has worked with many talented and inspired specialist woodworkers in promoting high quality handmade British woodwork. Jayne and Robert Lewin offer their customers carefully chosen pieces from new and established craftsmen in a welcoming, informal atmosphere.

All the designer makers understand and combine wood's natural beauty and tactile quality with individuality, versatility and a superb standard of craftsmanship to achieve the best possible results. Customers returning time and again are amazed by a continuously evolving selection. The extensive variety will tempt and delight; practical for the kitchen or office, boxes for jewellery or treasures, humorous pieces, unusual gifts and accessories; games and toys; decorative objects to be relished and those extra special unique or indulgent pieces - a real treat.

📖 stories and anecdotes   🐦 famous people   🎨 art and craft   🎭 entertainment and sport   🚶 walks

THE HOUSE OF SIMON

123 High Street, Burford,
Oxfordshire OX18 4RG
Tel: 01993 822281

Burford is an attractive old market town of honey-coloured Cotswold stone on the banks of the River Windrush.' There are many fine old buildings in the town, some of them on the High Street. **The House of Simon** is a timber-framed stone building dating from 1582 and bearing the name of the man who built it, wool merchant Simon Wisdom. Its role now is as a shop selling town and country wear for women, and everything in the stock, all personally chosen by owner Jackie Kekwick, has a timeless style and elegance.

Among the many notable names in stock are Ebony skirts and dresses from Kendal; Slenderella pure cotton lingerie and nightwear made in Derbyshire; Tanya British knitwear; Hodgson from Scotland; top-of-the-range alpaca knitwear; Poppy tops; Lampert jackets; Double Two blouses; Sportleigh trousers; Finnkarelia; GorRay skirts and Vedonis underwear. The shop comprises three spacious rooms, two changing rooms and plenty of seats; a wood-burning stove keeps the cold at bay, and the comfortable, relaxed ambience makes it a pleasure to shop here.

THE HIGHWAY HOTEL

117 High Street, Burford, Oxfordshire
OX18 4RG
Tel: 01993 823661
Fax: 01993 824740
e-mail: enquiries@thehighwayhotel.co.uk
website: www.thehighwayhotel.co.uk

The building occupied by the **Highway Hotel** has been a landmark on the High Street of Burford for at least 500 years. Entering the house is taking a step back in time, but sensitive updating has provided all the comfort and amenity expected by today's guests, making it a great base for touring the Cotswolds. The 10 en suite bedrooms are named after towns or villages in the area, and each has its own individual style and character. Breakfast (also available for non-residents) is definitely not to be missed, with freshly squeezed juices, home-made muesli, cereals or fruit preceding a full English plate or lighter dishes such as mushrooms on toast or smoked haddock.

The best seasonal produce, locally sourced as far as possible, makes its way into the kitchen to provide excellent meals on menus combining British and European cuisines in the atmospheric Cellar Restaurant. Hosts Tally and Scott Nelson have also maintained the status of the Highway as a favourite local meeting place, and the bar and snug are perfect spots to meet friends for a drink and a chat.

🏠 historic building   🏛 museum   🏛 historic site   🌣 scenic attraction   🌿 flora and fauna

monuments and plaques to be found. In the south wall of the tower stair is a carved panel, dated around 100 AD, which is thought to show the Celtic fertility goddess Epona, with two male supporters and a horse. In the nave north aisle a monument erected to Edmund Harman, the barber-surgeon to Henry VIII, shows North American natives - possibly the first representation of native Americans in the country. In the south porch is a small plaque which commemorates three Leveller mutineers who were imprisoned in the church by Cromwell's men and shot in the churchyard in 1649.

The Levellers were troops from Cromwell's army who mutinied against what they saw as the drift towards the authoritarian rule they had been fighting against. While they were encamped at Burford, the Levellers were taken by surprise by Cromwell's forces. After a brief fight, some 340 prisoners were taken and placed under guard in the church. The next day a court martial was held and three of the rebels were shot as an example to the rest, who were made to watch the executions. They were spared similar punishment when their leader recanted in a sermon.

The town's old court house, built in the 16th century with an open ground floor and a half-timbered first floor, is now home to the **Tolsey Museum**. An interesting building in its

COTSWOLD WILDLIFE PARK & GARDENS

Burford, Oxon OX18 4JW
Tel: 01993 823006 Fax: 01993 823807
website: www.cotswoldwildlifepark.co.uk

Cotswold Wildlife Park & Gardens is one of the leading attractions in the county and provides a perfect family day out. Children especially enjoy the Walled Garden which is home to penguins, tropical birds, monkeys, meerkats and otters – all of them available for adoption as are the many endangered species of animals. These include Asiatic lions, Amur leopards, Red Pandas, rhinos, camels, ostriches and giant tortoises. Other attractions within the Park include the Tropical House, Reptile Courtyard, Insect House and the Bat House with more than 100 Fruit Bats.

For gardeners there are formal plantings, the "Hot Bed", flamboyant borders, container planting and hanging baskets, while the 160 acres of beautiful parkland contain fine specimen trees including Giant Redwood, Wellingtonia, cedars and a huge 600-year-old oak. Snacks and hot meals are served in the Oak Tree Restaurant and amenities for children include a farmyard, adventure playground, brass rubbing centre and a narrow gauge railway. The Park is open

every day except Christmas Day from 10am; last admissions are at 4.30pm, March to September; 3pm, October to February. The Park is located on the A361, two miles south of its junction with the A40 at Burford.

🎬 stories and anecdotes   🦜 famous people   🎨 art and craft   🎭 entertainment and sport   🥾 walks

COUNTRY HOUSE GIFTS

51 High Street, Burford, Oxfordshire OX18 4QA
Tel/Fax: 01993 823172
e-mail: countryhousegifts@btconnect.com

Situated on the picturesque main street of the 'Gateway to the Cotswolds', **Country House Gifts** stocks an impressive selection of items for the home along with gifts for all occasions. Owners Tina and Malcolm Mustoe have put their personal seal of approval on an amazing emporium that ranges from Belgian chocolates to Royal Scot crystal; from Woods of Windsor , Norfolk Lavender and Claremont & May products to greetings cards and gift wrap. Other items include English cushions and china, a large selection of tapestries/wall hangings from England and Belgium, collectables from Robert Harrop.....and much, much more.

own right, the collection on display here covers the history of the town and the surrounding area. Other buildings worth seeking out include the 16th century Falkland Hall, the home of a local wool and cloth merchant Edmund Sylvester, and Symon Wysdom's Cottages, which were built in 1572 by another of the town's important merchants.

The 160 acres of park and garden which make up **The Cotswold Wildlife Park** (see panel on page 359) are home to a whole host of animals, many of whom roam free in the wooded estate. Rhinos, zebras, ostriches and tigers are just some of the animals in the spacious enclosures while tropical birds, monkeys, reptiles, and butterflies are all given the chance to enjoy the warmth of their natural habitat by staying indoors. With an adventure playground and a narrow-gauge railway, the park has something to offer all the family.

Around Burford

TAYNTON
1.5 miles NW of Burford off the A424

Up until the end of the 19th century Taynton was a quarrying village, with the limestone taken from the quarries used in the

construction of Blenheim Palace, Windsor Castle, St Paul's Cathedral as well as many Oxford colleges and local buildings.

CORNWELL
9 miles N of Burford off the A436

This village had the distinction of being renovated in the 1930s by Clough Williams Ellis, best known for creating the remarkable Italianate Welsh holiday village of Portmeirion.

CHASTLETON
10 miles N of Burford off the A44

🏛 Chastleton House

Chastleton is home to one of the best examples of Jacobean architecture in the country. In 1602, Robert Catesby, one of the Gunpowder Plot conspirators, sold his estate here to a prosperous wool merchant from Witney, Walter Jones. A couple of years later, Jones pulled the house down and built **Chastleton House,** a splendid Jacobean manor house with a dramatic five-gabled front and a garden where the original rules of croquet were established in 1865. Until it became a National Trust property, Chastleton had been inhabited by the same family for more than 400 years. One of the finest and most complete Jacobean houses in England, it is filled with a remarkable collection of furniture, textiles and items both rare and everyday. Visits by appointment only.

SWINBROOK

2 miles E of Burford off the A40

The Fettiplace family lived in a great manor house in this peaceful village in the valley of the Windrush. The manor has long gone, but the family is remembered in several impressive and highly distinctive monuments in the Church of St Mary. The family home of the Redesdales was also at Swinbrook, and in the churchyard are the graves of three of the six Mitford sisters, who were daughters of the 2nd Baron Redesdale. Nancy, Unity and Pamela are buried here.

MINSTER LOVELL

4.5 miles E of Burford off the B4047

🏛 Minster Lovell Hall

One of the prettiest villages along the banks of the River Windrush, Minster Lovell is home to the ruins of a once impressive 15th century manor house. **Minster Lovell Hall** was built in the 1430s and was, in its day, one of the great aristocratic houses of Oxfordshire, the home of the Lovell family. However, one of the family was a prominent Yorkist during the Wars of the Roses and, after the defeat of Richard III at Bosworth Field, he lost his lands to the Crown. The house was purchased by the Coke family in 1602, but around the middle of the 18th century the hall was dismantled by

THE MERRYMOUTH INN

Stow Road, Fifield, nr Burford,
Oxfordshire OX7 6HR
Tel: 01993 831652   Fax: 01993 830840
e-mail: tim@merrymouthinn.fsnet.co.uk
website: www.hotelinthecotswolds.co.uk

The **Merrymouth Inn** has a long and interesting history that goes back as far as the 13th century. It stands in the heart of the Cotswolds on the A424 between the antiques centres of Burford and Stow-on-the-Wold, and is ideally located for touring this beautiful part of the world. Excellent hospitality and service under the Flaherty family and their staff complement the fine food and comfortable accommodation for which the inn has become renowned. The comfortable L-shaped bar, with flagstones, beams, brasses and bottles, is a great place for a drink, and when the weather is kind tables on the terrace and in the garden are in demand.

Top-quality fresh seasonal ingredients, many of them sourced locally, are the basis of an excellent selection of food from a light snack to a full à la carte meal. Tim Flaherty is the driving force in the kitchen, and among his specialities are braden rost (hot-smoked salmon), fresh fish dishes, chicken with mushrooms, bacon, cheese and cream, and some unmissable desserts. The nine stylish double bedrooms, all with en-suite facilities, TV and tea/coffee trays, are located in attractively converted stables around a pretty courtyard garden. Breakfast includes sausages from the local butcher and free-range eggs from the neighbours' hens. The name of the inn is adapted from the Murimuth family, who once owned the village of Fifield.

Thomas Coke, Earl of Leicester, and the ruins became lowly farm buildings. They were rescued from complete disintegration by the Ministry of Works in the 1930s and are now in the care of English Heritage. What is left of the house is extremely picturesque, and it is hard to imagine a better setting than here, beside the River Windrush. One fascinating feature of the manor house which has survived is the medieval dovecote, complete with nesting boxes, which provided pigeons for the table in a way reminiscent of modern battery hen houses.

SHIPTON-UNDER-WYCHWOOD
4 miles NE of Burford on the A361

🏛 Shipton Court 🌲 Wychwood Forest

The suffix 'under-Wychwood' derives from the ancient royal hunting forest, **Wychwood Forest**, the remains of which lie to the east of the village. The name has nothing to do with witches - wych refers to the Hwicce, a Celtic tribe of whose territory the forest originally formed a part in the 7th century. Though cleared during the Middle Ages, it was still used as a royal hunting forest until the mid-1600s. By the late 1700s there was little good wood left and the clearing of the forest was rapid to provide arable land.

The forest was one of the alleged haunts of Matthew Arnold's scholar gypsy and in the poem, published in 1853, Arnold tells the legend of the brilliant but poor Oxford scholar who, despairing of ever making his way in the world, went to live with the gypsies to learn from their way of life.

The village itself is centred around its large green, which is dominated by the tall spire of 11th century St Mary's Church. Here, too, can be found The Shaven Crown, now a hotel, which was built in the 15th century as a guest house for visitors to the nearby (and now demolished) Bruern Abbey. Finally, there is the superb **Shipton Court**, built around 1603, which is one of the country's largest Jacobean houses.

CHIPPING NORTON
10 miles NE of Burford on the A44

🏛 Church of St Mary 🏛 Bliss Tweed Mill
🏛 Museum

The highest town in Oxfordshire, at 650 feet above sea level, Chipping Norton was once an important centre of the wool trade and King John granted the town a charter to hold a fair to sell wool. Later changed to a Mop Fair, the tradition continues to this day when the fair is held every September.

The town's medieval prosperity can be seen in the fine and spacious **Church of St Mary** which was built in 1485 with money given by John Ashfield, a wool merchant. The splendid east window came from the Abbey of Bruern, a few miles to the southwest, which was demolished in 1535 following the Dissolution of the Monasteries. In 1549, the minister here, the Rev Henry Joyce, was charged with high treason and hanged from the then tower because he refused to use the new prayer book introduced by Edward VI.

As with many buildings in the town, there has been substantial 19th century remodelling and the present church tower dates from 1823.

Still very much a market town today - the market is held on Wednesdays - Chipping Norton has been little affected by the influx of visitors who come to see this charming place. The **Chipping Norton Museum** is an excellent place to start any exploration and the permanent displays here cover local history from prehistoric and Roman times through to the present day.

Whispering Knights, Over Norton

Found just to the west of the town centre is **Bliss Tweed Mill**, an extraordinary sight in this area as it was designed by a Lancashire architect, George Woodhouse, in 1872 in the Versailles style. With a decorated parapet and a tall chimney which acts as a local landmark, this very northern looking mill only ceased operation in the 1980s.

OVER NORTON
11 miles N of Burford off the A3400

🏛 Rollright Stones

To the northwest of Over Norton are the

Rollright Stones - one of the most fascinating Bronze Age monuments in the country. These great gnarled slabs of stone stand on a ridge which offers fine views of the surrounding countryside. They all have nicknames: the **King's Men** form a circle; the **King Stone** is to the north of the circle; and, a quarter of a mile to the west, stand the **Whispering Knights**, which are, in fact, the remnants of a megalithic tomb. Naturally, there are many local legends connected with the stones and some say that they are the petrified figures of a forgotten king and his men that were turned to stone by a witch.

LOCATOR MAP

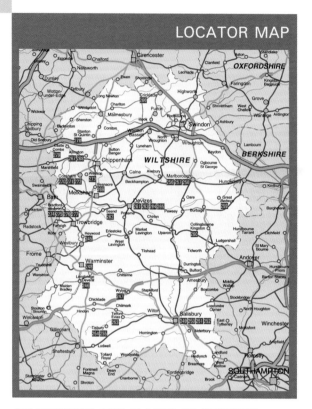

ADVERTISERS AND PLACES OF INTEREST

🏠 historic building   🏛 museum   🏛 historic site   ⛲ scenic attraction   🌿 flora and fauna

9| Wiltshire

Wiltshire is a county that is rich in the monuments of prehistoric man; it also boasts one of the highest concentrations of historic houses and gardens in the country. This makes it a great place for the tourist, and it's also a perfect choice for walkers, cyclists and lovers of nature, with wide open spaces, woodland and downland and a number of chalk streams that are home to a huge variety of wetland wildlife.

The industrial heritage is also strong, taking in Brunel's Great Western Railway and the railway town of Swindon, brewing at Devizes and carpet-making at Wilton. And the county has many surprises, from the white horses carved in hillsides and the mysterious crop circles to the ancient hill forts and the greatest mystery of them all, the stone circles of Stonehenge - how *did* those stones get from the Marlborough Downs and the mountains of Pembrokeshire and what *was* their use? Pepys didn't have the answer when writing in his Diary in June 1668: '.....*to Stonage, over the plain and some great hills, even to fright us. Come thither, and find them as prodigious as any tales I ever heard of them, and worth going this journey to see. God knows what their use was! They are hard to tell, but yet may be told.*' ....and we don't have the full answer yet.

The jewel in the crown of Wiltshire is the city of Salisbury, at the confluence of the rivers Avon, Wylye, Bourne and Nadder, with its glorious cathedral, a masterpiece of the Early English style, and many other fine buildings. The cathedral for the episcopal see stood originally at nearby Old Sarum, a flourishing town in medieval days that lost its status when a 12th century bishop moved flock, stock and barrel down the hill to the more amenable surroundings of Salisbury and began to build a new cathedral. Atmospheric ruins are all that remain of Old Sarum.

Westbury, at the western edge of the chalk downlands of Salisbury Plain, was an important centre of the medieval cloth and wool trades and still boasts some handsome buildings from its days of great prosperity. Like Old Sarum, Westbury was formerly a 'rotten borough', returning two MPs until the 1832 Reform Act stopped the cheating (Old Sarum was the more notorious, having two MPs at a time when it had no voters!). Stourhead, a beautiful Palladian mansion full of treasures, stands in magnificent grounds laid out by Henry Hoare, and another house filled with wonderful things is Longleat, whose grounds contain the famous safari park.

The National Trust village of Lacock, the market town of Devizes with its extraordinary flight of locks on the Kennet and Avon Canal, the historic abbey town of Malmesbury, the lovely Vale of Pewsey and the ancient 4,500-acre Savernake Forest, designated a Site of Special Scientific Interest, are other attractions that no visitor to this wonderful county should miss.

Westbury

🏰 White Horse   🎄 Woodland Park

🎄 Salisbury Plain

Westbury, at the western edge of the chalk downlands of **Salisbury Plain**, was a major player in the medieval cloth and wool trades, and still retains many fine buildings from the days of great prosperity, including some cloth works and mills. Westbury was formerly a 'rotten borough' and returned two MPs until 1832, when the Reform Bill put an end to the cheating. Scandal and corruption were rife, and the Old Town Hall in the market place is evidence of such goings-on, a gift from a grateful victorious candidate in 1815. This was Sir Manasseh Massey Lopes, a Portuguese financier and slave-trader who 'bought' the

borough to advance his political career.

All Saints Church, a 14th century building on much earlier foundations, has many unusual and interesting features, including a stone reredos, a copy of the Erasmus Bible and a clock with no face made by a local blacksmith in 1604. It also boasts the third heaviest peal of bells in the world.

On the southern edge of town is another church well worth a visit. Behind the simple, rustic exterior of St Mary's, Old Dilton, are a three-decker pulpit and panelled pew boxes with original fittings and individual fireplaces.

To the west of the town, at Brokerswood, is **Woodland Park and Heritage Centre**, 80 acres of ancient broadleaf woodland with a wide range of trees, plants and animals, nature trails, a lake with fishing, a picnic and

BRIDOON

Heywood Equestrian & Therapy Centre
Church Road, Heywood, nr Westbury,
Wiltshire BA13 4LP
Tel: 01373 864760
e-mail: sales@bridoon.co.uk
website: www.bridoon.co.uk

Bridoon is a modern, dynamic business established by Paula Alderman and located in a log cabin-style building with flower baskets and outside seats. Bridoon sells the complete range of equestrian products, riding apparel and dog products, all sourced from leading manufacturers; top brands include Equitector, Driza-Bone, William Funnell, Shires, Mark Todd, Cottage Craft, New, Aerborn, Rodney Powell, Pegasus, Puffa and Tuffa. Also in stock are books, gifts and novelty items with an equestrian theme.

Paula is an expert in the choosing and fitting of head and body protective wear, and among the services she offers at Bridoon are rug washing and repair, tack and saddle repair and blade sharpening. Broswers are welcome, and a warm welcome is guaranteed from Paula, her staff and Jester the shop's dog. Bridoon is located directly off the A350 between Westbury and Trowbridge.

🏰 historic building   🏛 museum   🏰 historic site   🌀 scenic attraction   🌿 flora and fauna

barbecue area, a tea room and gift shop, a museum, a play area and a narrow-gauge railway.

By far the best-known Westbury feature is the famous **Westbury White Horse**, a chalk carving measuring 182 feet in length and 108 feet in height. The present steed dates from 1778, replacing an earlier one carved to celebrate King Alfred's victory over the Danes at nearby Ethandun (Edington) in 878. The white horse is well looked after, the last major grooming carried out in 1996. Above the horse's head are the ruins of Bratton Castle, an Iron Age hill fort covering 25 acres.

Around Westbury

WARMINSTER
4 miles S of Westbury on the A350

🏛 Dewey Museum   ⛏ Cley Hill

🜨 Arn Hill Nature Reserve

Warminster is a historic wool, corn-trading and coaching town with many distinguished buildings, including a famous school with a door designed by Wren. In addition to the 18th and 19th century buildings, Warminster has a number of interesting monuments: the Obelisk with its feeding troughs and pineapple top erected in 1783 to mark the enclosure of the parish; the Morgan Memorial Fountain in the Lake Pleasure Grounds; and *Beyond*

Harvest, a statue in bronze by Colin Lambert of a girl sitting on sacks of corn. Warminster's finest building is the Church of St Denys, mainly 14th century but almost completely rebuilt in the 1880s to the design of Arthur Blomfield. The **Dewey Museum**, in the public library, displays a wide range of local history from Iron Age times to the present day, including the Victor Manley collection of geology. To the west of town is the 800ft **Cley Hill**, an Iron Age hill fort with two Bronze Age barrows. Formerly owned by the Marquess of Bath, the hill was given to the National Trust in the 1950s and is a renowned sighting place for UFOs. (The region is also noted for the appearance of crop circles and some have linked the two phenomena.)

On the northern edge of Warminster, **Arn Hill Nature Reserve** forms a circular walk of two miles along public footpaths through woodland and open downland.

CODFORD ST PETER & CODFORD ST MARY
8 miles SE of Westbury on the A36

Sister villages beneath the prehistoric remains

Cley Hill, Warminster

🎞 stories and anecdotes   🐦 famous people   🎨 art and craft   🎵 entertainment and sport   🜨 walks

PURELY ORGANIC TROUT FARM & SHOP

Deverill's Trout Farm,
Longbridge Deverill, Warminster,
Wiltshire BA12 7DZ
Tel: 01985 841093
e-mail: trout@purelyorganic.co.uk
website: www.purelyorganic.co.uk

Tony and Eleanor Free, owners of the **Purely Organic Trout Farm & Shop,** must be feeling really pleased with themselves. Leading chef Rick Stein named them amongst his Superheroes of Food; food writer and farmer Hugh Fearnley-Whittenstall declared their trout, "Better than any I have tasted"; the *Independent* newspaper placed them in the top ten Best British Fish or Meat Producers; in 2002 the farm won the National Small Food Producer of the Year award for its trout, smoked trout and pâté and it has been named Independent Food Producer of the Year for 2006. It also received the accolade of the Gold Prize for services to the environment in the 1999 Green Apple Awards.

This outstanding farm is located in the village of Longbridge Deverill on the A350 Warminster to Blandford road and attracts health-conscious and environmentally aware visitors from near and far with its range of organic Fair Trade products. Naturally, the best known of these are the trout which are among the best and most natural in the country. The spring water used is drawn at a constant temperature from 35 metres down and flows first through organic watercress beds which enrich it with natural freshwater shrimps, minnows, sticklebacks and the like which provide an excellent, nourishing base for the diet of the trout.

The fish grow from natural exercise rather than from additives in their food, making them firm and fibrous and totally unlike river or lake trout which can often be both earthy and mushy. Purely Organic sells the trout fresh, smoked, in pâté or fish cakes.

Other produce on sale in the well-stocked shop includes soups (the watercress is wonderful), fresh baked bread seven days a week, local honey, dairy products, meat, general groceries, hen and duck eggs, flour for bread, ice creams, soft drinks, sandwiches, organic plant seeds and the Green Things range of body products. The shop is open from 9am to 6pm, seven days a week.

of Codford Circle, an ancient hilltop meeting place which stands 617 feet up on Salisbury Plain. The church in Codford St Peter has one of Wiltshire's finest treasures in an exceptional 9th century Saxon stone carving of a man holding a branch and dancing. East of Malmpit Hill and visible from the A36 is a rising sun emblem carved by Australian soldiers during World War I. In the military cemetery at Codford St Mary are the graves of Anzac troops who were in camp here. Anzac graves may also be seen at Sutton Veny.

WYLYE
10 miles SE of Westbury off the A36

🏛 Yarnbury Castle

Peace came to Wylye in 1977, when a bypass diverted traffic from the busy main roads. It had long been an important junction and staging post on the London-Exeter coaching route. A statue near the bridge over the River Wylye (from which the village, Wilton and indeed Wiltshire get their names) commemorates a brave postboy who drowned here after rescuing several passengers from a stagecoach which had overturned during a flood.

Above the village is the little-known **Yarnbury Castle**, an Iron Age hill fort surrounded by two banks and an outer bank. To the west is a triangular enclosure from Roman times which could have held cattle or sheep. From the 18th century to World War I Yarnbury was the venue of an annual sheep fair.

Wylye Down

Wylye, Wiltshire
website: www.english-nature.org.uk

Wylye Down spans a dry valley running south to north and the predominantly east and west facing slopes are gently to moderately sloping. The downland flora is very rich throughout and more than 40 plant species have been recorded within an area one metre square. The reserve was purchased by English Nature in 1978 from the Barrett family who continue to use farm animals to graze the land on a traditional basis.

Wylye Down is of considerable archaeological importance for its 'Celtic fields' which used to cover the entire area. These fields, indicated by banks or lynchets, were in cultivation during the period of Roman occupation, but they possibly date back to the early Bronze Age. During the Roman era the encampment was at Bilbury Rings but the Down and Bilbury Rings were later cultivated in the mediaeval age.

Centuries of cultivation reduced soil fertility on the Down. The herb-rich grassland flora developed on the impoverished soils as the land was grazed from Roman times to the present day. The turf has been maintained by a suitable grazing regime coupled with a lack of ploughing, re-seeding and fertiliser application. Since the Barrett family took over the farm in 1946 the area has been grazed by Ayrshire cattle, and since the mid-1960s by cross-bred ewes as well.

The brown hare is one of the residents here and others include species of insect, spider, mollusc, other invertebrates and butterflies that include chalk-hill blue, marsh fritillary and meadow brown. Birds such as wheatears have been seen migrating over the down, whilst kestrels and wintering flocks of goldfinch have been seen feeding on the reserve.

📰 stories and anecdotes   🍴 famous people   🎨 art and craft   🎭 entertainment and sport   🚶 walks

IMBER

5 miles E of Westbury off the B3098

The part of Salisbury Plain containing the village of Imber was closed to the public in 1943 and has been used by the Army ever since for live firing. The evicted villagers were told that they could return to Imber after the war, but the promise was not kept and the village remains basically inaccessible. A well-marked 30-mile perimeter walk skirting the danger area takes in Warminster, Westbury, Tilshead in the east and Chitterne in the south.

LONGLEAT

6 miles SW of Westbury off the A362

🏛 Longleat House   🦌 Safari Park

2004 saw the 55th anniversary of the opening of **Longleat House** to the public. The magnificent home of the Marquess of Bath was built by an ancestor, Sir John Thynne, in a largely symmetrical style, in the 1570s. The inside is a treasure house of old masters, Flemish tapestries, beautiful furniture, rare books and Lord Bath's racy murals. The superb grounds of Longleat House were landscaped by Capability Brown and now

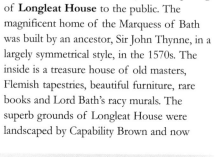

Longleat

Warminster, Wiltshire BA12 7NW
Tel: 01985 844400
e-mail: enquiries@longleat.co.uk
website: www.longleat.co.uk

The star of SSC's hugely popular *Animal Park* series, Longleat Safari Park, celebrates its 40th Anniversary this year. Discover some of the world's most magnificent animals in this first safari park outside of Africa ... see how you measure up to a giraffe, watch out for the zebras crossing and be enthralled by the majestic lions and tigers!

Continue your adventure aboard the Safari Boats for a sea lion-escorted cruise, find yourself going round in circles in the Longleat Hedge Maze, enjoy a fun-packed ride on the Longleat Railway before discovering the treasures and heirlooms within Longleat House ... your day at Longleat will never be long enough. The Longleat Passport Ticket offers once-only entry into each attraction but on any day during the season. See as many attractions as you like one day and then come back on any date before the close of season to see those attractions previously missed - the choice is yours.

Keepers at Longleat Safari Park are often kept busy during the summer with the birth of baby animals and have recently seen the arrival of wolf cubs, sea lion pups, ostrich chicks, lion cubs as well as baby girafes, Bactrian camels and tapirs. Visitors can see the young animals on display.

At birth the baby wolves measure just 15 cms in length and weigh around 500 grams. After spending the first weeks of life underground, the pups begin to emerge into the outside world. The cubs are just the latest in a string of breeding successes at the Wiltshire wildlife attraction.

As well as all the animal attractions, Longleat puts on special shows during the summer. Phone or visit the website for all details including prices and opening times.

contain one of the country's best known venues for a marvellous day out. In the famous **Safari Park** (see panel below) the Lions of Longleat, first introduced in 1966, have been followed by a veritable Noah's Ark of exotic creatures, including rhinos, zebras and white tigers. The park also features safari boat rides, a narrow-gauge railway, children's amusement area, garden centre and the largest hedge maze in the world.

STOURTON
9 miles SW of Westbury off the B3092

🏠 Stourhead

The beautiful National Trust village of Stourton lies at the bottom of a steep wooded valley and is a particularly glorious sight in the daffodil season. The main attraction is, of course, **Stourhead**, one of the most famous examples of the early-18th century English landscape movement. The lakes, the trees, the temples, a grotto and a classical bridge make the grounds, laid out by Henry Hoare, a paradise in the finest 18th century tradition, and the gardens are renowned for their striking vistas and woodland walks as well as a stunning selection of rare trees and specimen shrubs, including tulip trees, azaleas and rhododendrons. The house itself, a classical masterpiece built in the 1720s in Palladian style for a Bristol banker, contains a wealth of Grand Tour paintings and works of art, including furniture by Chippendale the Younger and wood carvings by Grinling Gibbons. On the very edge of the estate, some three miles by road from the house, the imposing King Alfred's Tower stands at the top of the 790ft Kingsettle Hill. This

160ft triangular redbrick folly was built in 1772 to commemorate the king, who reputedly raised his standard here against the Danes in 878.

MERE
12 miles SW of Westbury off the A303

🏠 Museum 🏛 Castle Hill

A small town nestling below the downs near the borders with Dorset and Somerset. The town is dominated by **Castle Hill**, on which Richard, Earl of Cornwall, son of King John, built a castle in 1253. Nothing of the castle remains, though many of the stones were used in building Mere's houses. The Church of St Michael the Archangel in High Gothic style features some fine medieval and Victorian stained glass, carved Jacobean pews, an unusual octagonal font and a 12th century statue of St Michael slaying a dragon. **Mere Museum**, in the public library in Barton Lane, is principally a local history collection with a good photographic archive. Displays are changed regularly but a permanent feature is a

Stourton

large, detailed map of Mere drawn in colour by a local artist. This is a great area for rambling, one of the best spots being the Whitesheet Hill Nature Trail with wonderful views and a wealth of plants and insects, including some rare chalk-loving butterflies.

EAST KNOYLE
14 miles S of Westbury on the A350

Two items of interest here. A simple stone monument marks the birthplace, in 1632, of Sir Christopher Wren, son of the village rector of the time. East Knoyle Windmill is a tower mill on a circular base, without sails and unused for over a century. It offers good views over Blackmoor Vale and has a large grassy area for picnics.

TOLLARD ROYAL
6 miles SE of Shaftesbury on the B3081

Tollard Royal is a historic village atop Zigzag Hill in the heart of Cranborne Chase. King John had a small estate here which he used on his hunting trips. King John's House is a part-stone, part-timber residence whose fine condition is largely due to the efforts of General Pitt Rivers, an eminent Victorian

archaeologist who inherited the estate and spent the last 20 years of his life unearthing Bronze Age remains. His collection is housed in the Salisbury and South Wiltshire Museum, where a gallery is named in his honour.

LUDWELL
2 miles E of Shaftesbury on the A30

🌿 Win Green Hill

Near the village is the National Trust-owned **Win Green Hill**, the highest point in Wiltshire, crowned by a copse of beech trees set around an ancient bowl barrow. From the summit there are wonderful views as far as the Quantock Hills to the northwest and the Isle of Wight to the southeast.

Salisbury

🏛 Cathedral   🏛 Medieval Hall   🖊 Boy Bishop

🏛 Mompesson House   🏛 Old Sarum

🏛 Salisbury and South Wiltshire Museum

🏛 Royal Gloucestershire, Berks & Wilts Museum

🏛 John Creasey Museum

℘ Edwin Young Collection

The glorious medieval city of Salisbury stands at the confluence of five rivers, the Avon, Wylye, Bourne, Ebble and Nadder. Originally called New Sarum, it grew around the present Cathedral, which was built between 1220 and 1258 in a sheltered

Old Sarum

🏛 historic building   🏛 museum   🏛 historic site   🌿 scenic attraction   🌿 flora and fauna

position two miles south of the site of its windswept Norman predecessor at Old Sarum. Over the years the townspeople followed the clergy into the new settlement, creating a flourishing religious and market centre whose two main aspects flourish to this day.

One of the most beautiful buildings in the world, **Salisbury Cathedral** is the only medieval cathedral in England to be built throughout in the Early English style - apart from the spire, the tallest in England, which was added some years later and rises to an awesome 404 feet. The Chapter House opens out of the cloisters and contains, among other treasures, one of the four surviving originals of Magna Carta. Six hundred thousand visitors a year come to marvel at this and other priceless treasures, including a number of magnificent tombs. The oldest working clock in Britain and possibly in the world is situated in the fan-vaulted north transept; it was built in 1386 to strike the hour and has no clock face. The cathedral is said to contain a door for each month, a window for each day and a column for each hour of the year. A small statue inside the west door is of Salisbury's 17th century **Boy Bishop**. It was a custom for choristers to elect one of their number to be bishop for a period in December lasting from St Nicholas Day to Holy Innocents Day. One year the boy bishop was apparently literally tickled to death by the other choristers; since he died in office, his statue shows him in full bishop's regalia.

The Close, the precinct of the ecclesiastical

THYME & SPACE

50 High Street, Salisbury, Wiltshire SP1 2NT
Tel: 01722 421350   Fax: 01722 417835
e-mail: info@thymeandspace.co.uk
website: www.thymeandspace.co.uk

Shoppers seeking the best in French style and elegance should put **Thyme & Space** at the top of their list. Owner Patsy Seddon started her business career in the fashion industry, building the clothes chain Phase Eight from one small shop to a total of 80 outlets throughout the country.

Patsy has a real passion for France and all things French, and at Thyme & Space, close to Cathedral Close on Salisbury's High Street, she offers customers the chance to buy products with the charm and simplicity of French and continental design.

The shades of blue in the shop's interior provide a subtle backdrop for the furniture, fabrics, pictures and objets d'art in stock. France is also the source, along with Denmark, Holland, Belgium and small local suppliers, of home goods that include linens, towels, bath mats, throws, napkins, candles, kitchenware and garden products. Opening hours are 9.30am to 5.30pm Monday to Saturday.

---

community serving the cathedral, is the largest in England and contains a number of museums and houses open to the public. **Salisbury and South Wiltshire Museum**, in the 17th century King's House, is the home of the award-winning redesigned Stonehenge Gallery and a designated archaeological collection of national importance. Displays include Early Man, the Romans and Saxons, Old Sarum with the Giant and Hob Nob, Romans and Saxons, the Pitt Rivers collection, pottery, ceramics, costume, lace, embroidery, a pre-NHS surgery and Turner watercolours.

A few doors away is **The Wardrobe Military Museum** housed in a 13th century building called the Wardrobe because it was originally used to store the bishop's clothes and documents. The museum tells the story of the Royal Berkshire Regiment, the Wiltshire Regiment and the Duke of Edinburgh's Royal regiment and the exhibits include Bobbie the Dog, the hero of Maiwand, and many artefacts from foreign campaigns. The house has a tea room and a riverside garden with views of the famous water meadows. The historic **Medieval Hall** is the atmospheric setting for a 30-minute history of Salisbury in sound and pictures.

Mompesson House, a National Trust property, is a perfect example of Queen Anne architecture notable for its plasterwork, an elegant carved oak staircase, fine period furniture and the important Turnbull collection of 18th century drinking glasses. In the Library are the **John Creasey Museum** and the **Creasey Collection of Contemporary Art**, a permanent collection of books, manuscripts,

THE POLLY TEA ROOMS

8 St Thomas's Square, Salisbury,
Wiltshire SP1 1BA
Tel: 01722 336037

A sister establishment to Polly's Tea Rooms in Marlborough, **The Polly Tea Rooms** in Salisbury maintains the same high standards as its elder sibling. Known as Snell's Tea Rooms until purchased by Sir Brian Mussell, Polly's in Salisbury opened in December 2003. Just a five minute walk from the city centre and next door to St Thomas's Church, which was originally built as a place of worship for the builders working on the cathedral, it has quickly established itself as *the* place to take tea in the city.

A light and airy building, it provides a welcoming, relaxed environment in which to enjoy breakfast, morning coffee, lunch or afternoon tea. In addition to its extensive choice of tea-time treats, Polly's also boasts its own chocolate factory on the first floor which produces an enticing selection of exquisite homemade chocolates.

🏠 historic building   🏛 museum   🏚 historic site   🌄 scenic attraction   🌿 flora and fauna

FISHERTONMILL

galleries • café • studios

108 Fisherton Street, Salisbury, Wiltshire SP2 7QY
Tel/Fax: 01722 415121
e-mail: thegallery@fishertonmill.co.uk
website: www.fishertonmill.co.uk

Built in 1880 as a grain mill, **Fisherton Mill** is the south of England's largest independent art gallery. Spread over two floors and a courtyard, the Gallery retains many of the Mill's original features, which makes for a very unique setting. The beamed ceilings, cast iron pillars and fine old pieces of machinery will add to your visit as you enjoy the wide range of art on display.

The Gallery continuously shows work in the exhibition spaces by leading artists, sculptors and furniture makers, whilst the Gallery shop stocks an array of accessories, both functional and decorative, including ceramics, textiles, glasswork, jewellery and unframed prints as well as cards and carefully selected gifts, which complement the art work.

The Gallery Cafe, situated within the ground floor Gallery, offers an atmospheric setting in which to enjoy a great selection of homemade cakes, freshly made smoothies and juices, teas and Fair Trade Organic coffee. Lunch is light and modern, using fresh produce prepared to order, and includes soups, salads, sandwiches and main dishes as well as healthy choices for children. (Lunch is from 12 noon - 2.30pm). The courtyard has seating for fine days.

The studio workshops around the courtyard display work by photographer Alan Hayward and work by sculptor Paul Wilson.

Fisherton Mill is easily accessible from Salisbury railway station, Market Square and Central Car Park, through the archway on Fisherton Street. Open Tuesday-Friday 10am-5pm. Saturday 9.30am-5.30pm.

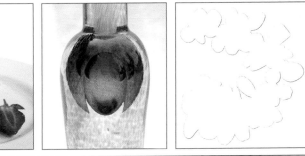

THE LEMON TREE

92 Crane Street, Salisbury, Wiltshire SP1 2QD
Tel: 01722 333471
e-mail: chris@thelemontree.co.uk
website: www.thelemontree.co.uk

In the heart of historic Salisbury, next to Cathedral Close, the **Lemon Tree** welcomes visitors for drinks and meals from 10 in the morning to 10 in the evening every day except Sunday. Chef-proprietor Chris Hayden has made his restaurant an equally popular spot with shoppers, local workers, residents and visitors to the city, and they all come here for morning coffee, lunch and evening meals. The interior is smartly contemporary, roomy and relaxed, with a conservatory leading out to a lovely garden that's perfect for summer dining.

Chris sets great store by fresh natural produce freshly cooked to order; typical dishes on the main menu range from filo-wrapped prawns and red onion tatin to the day's fish special, pork with apricots, main-course salads (chicken & bacon, hot duck & orange), chicken florentine and spinach & ricotta pancakes. The Lemon Tree is perfectly placed for taking a break while shopping or exploring the many attractions of this wonderful city.

objects and art, and the **Edwin Young Collection** of 19th and early 20th century water-colours, drawings and oil paintings of Salisbury and its surrounding landscape.

Salisbury racecourse, a short drive west of the city, stages flat racing during the summer months.

There are many other areas of Salisbury to explore on foot and a short drive takes visitors to the ruins of **Old Sarum**, abandoned when the bishopric moved into the city. Traces of the original cathedral and palace are visible on the huge uninhabited mound, which dates back to the Iron Age. Old Sarum became the most notorious of the 'rotten boroughs', returning two Members of Parliament, despite having no voters, until the 1832 Reform Act

stopped the practice. A plaque on the site commemorates Old Sarum's most illustrious MP, William Pitt the Elder.

Around Salisbury

BRITFORD
1 mile S of Salisbury on the A338

Lying within branches of the Wiltshire Avon, Britford has a moated country house and a fine Saxon church with some early stone carvings. An ornate tomb is thought to be that of the Duke of Buckingham, who was beheaded in Salisbury in 1483. Nearby **Longford Castle**, mainly 16th century, houses an interesting collection of paintings.

DOWNTON
5 miles S of Salisbury off the A338

🏛 **Moot House**

The Saxons established a meeting place, or moot, on an earlier earthwork fortification, and it was in commemoration of that ancient parliament that the present **Moot House** was built on the foundations of the old castle. The building and its garden stand opposite a small 18th century amphitheatre built to resemble the Saxon moot. In 1955, a Roman villa comprising seven rooms and a bath house was discovered nearby.

LOVER
6 miles SE of Salisbury off the A338

🔾 **Pepperbox Hill**

In the vicinity of this charmingly named village is the National Trust's **Pepperbox Hill** topped by an early 17th century octagonal tower known as **Eyre's Folly**. Great walking,

great views, and a great place for nature-lovers, with a variety of plant and bird life.

WILTON
3 miles W of Salisbury on the A30

🔾 **Carpet Factory** 🏛 **Wilton House**

The third oldest borough in England and once the capital of Saxon Wessex. It is best known for its carpets, and the **Wilton Carpet Factory** on the River Wylye continues to produce top-quality carpets, maintaining a worldwide reputation for quality that goes back 300 years. Wilton carpets as we know them today were created by a French carpet weaver who was brought to England by the Earl of Pembroke in the early 1700s to teach the local weavers his skills. In 1835 redundant handlooms were brought from the Axminster factory in Devon and set up in Wilton. Luxurious hand-knotted Axminsters, with each tuft individually tied by hand, were made alongside traditional Wiltons up to 1958. Alongside the factory is the Wilton Shopping Village offering high-quality factory shopping in a traditional rural setting.

Wilton House is the stately home of the Earls of Pembroke. When the original house was destroyed by fire in 1647, Inigo Jones was commissioned to build its replacement. He designed both the exterior and the interior, including the amazing Double Cube Room, and the house was further remodelled by James Wyatt. The art collection is one of the very finest, with works by Rembrandt, Van Dyke, Rubens and Tintoretto; the furniture includes pieces by Chippendale and Kent.

There's plenty to keep children busy and happy, including a treasure hunt quiz and a huge adventure playground. There's a Tudor kitchen, a Victorian laundry and 21 acres of landscaped grounds with parkland, cedar

Eyre's Folly, Lover

trees, water and rose gardens and an elegant Palladian bridge. It was used as an operations centre during World War II and is thought to be where the Normandy landings were planned.

The Church of St Mary and St Nicholas is a unique Italianate church built in the style of Lombardy by the Russian Countess of Pembroke in 1845. The interior is resplendent with marble, mosaics, richly carved woodwork and early French stained glass.

BROAD CHALKE
7 miles W of Salisbury off the A354

A Saxon village where the 17th century diarist John Aubrey had a small estate. A warden of the parish church, he was also a keen angler and wrote of his beloved River Ebble: *'There are not better trouts in the Kingdom of England than here'*. The designer and photographer Cecil Beaton spent his final years in Broad Chalke and is buried in the churchyard of All Saints.

TEFFONT EVIAS
9 miles W of Salisbury off the B3089

🐑 Farmer Giles Farmstead

Teffont Evias is a quiet little village with some handsome houses built with stone from the local Chilmark quarries. Close by, on the road that connects with the A303, is **Farmer Giles Farmstead**, a 175-acre working farm where a wide variety of farm animals can be seen at close quarters.

HOWARD'S HOUSE HOTEL

Teffont Evias, nr Salisbury, Wiltshire SP3 5RJ
Tel: 01726 716392   Fax: 01722 716820
e-mail: enq@howardshousehotel.com
website: www.howardshousehotel.com

Built as a farmhouse in 1623 and restored in 1989, **Howard's House Hotel** stands in a quintessential English garden of rolling lawns, ancient box hedges, a pond with a fountain and secret corners for daydreaming and quiet contemplation. In this most civilized of settings, nine luxurious bedrooms were created, each with its own bathroom, bathrobes, telephone, TV and hairdryer. Floral prints and pastel shades combine to enhance the feeling of informality and relaxation, and the sitting room offers abundant comfort and calm, with French windows open to the garden in summer and a log fire glowing warmly in winter.

In the beautifully appointed, non-smoking dining room tip-top produce is handled with skill and flair on outstanding table d'hôte and à la carte dinner and Sunday lunch menus. Typical choices might include pan-seared king scallops with oven-baked tomatoes and a saffron vinaigrette, Gressingham duck breast with wild muchroom risotto, roast root vegetables and a beetroot jus, and char-sealed fillet of Scotch beef with a rosemary galette, garlic confit, green beans and Madeira. Howard's House is a real gem of an hotel and an ideal place for a relaxing break, for country walks or for visiting the many places of historic interest in the area.

🏠 historic building   🏛 museum   🏚 historic site   🐚 scenic attraction   🐑 flora and fauna

FOVANT
8 miles W of Salisbury on the A30

☙ Fovant Badges

The **Fovant Badges** are badges carved in the chalk hillside by troops during the First World War. They include the Australian Imperial Force, the Devonshire Regiment, 6th City of London Regiment, the London Rifle Brigade, the Post Office Rifles, the Royal Corps of Signals, the Royal Wiltshire Yeomanry, the Wiltshire Regiment and the YMCA. The badges can be seen from the A30.

DINTON
9 miles W of Salisbury off the A30

There are two National Trust properties to visit near this lovely hillside village. Little Clarendon is a small but perfectly formed Tudor manor house with three oak-furnished rooms open to visitors; Philipps House is a handsome white-fronted neo-Grecian house with a great Ionic portico. Built by the early 19th century architect Jeffrey Wyattville for William Wyndham, it stands in the beautiful landscaped grounds of Dinton Park.

TISBURY
12 miles W of Salisbury off the A30

🏚 Tithe Barn   🏚 Old Wardour Castle

Tisbury is the most prominent of the villages strung along the River Nadder. It has a fine parish church that has a 15th century clerestory and used to have a lofty spire. This was hit by lightning in 1742, rebuilt, and then struck by lightning again 20 years later. At this point the parishioners gave up.

To the east of the village stands the magnificent gateway of Place Farm. It was built for the abbesses of Shaftesbury in the late-14th and early-15th centuries and gives a

---

AMORRIO

The Square, Tisbury, nr Salisbury, Wiltshire SP3 6JP
Tel: 01747 871920
e-mail: victoria.foulk@btinternet.com

Business partners Sharon Hollis and Vicky Foulk were responding to a definite gap in the market when they opened their fashion shop **Amorrio** in the autumn of 2005. And what a good idea that was! Behind the double frontage on the Square in Tisbury, the most prominent of the villages along the River Nadder, the shop is filled with an excellent selection of designer clothes, accessories and gifts, some sourced in England and many from overseas. Many of the shop's regular customers have their favourite brands, while others are happy to browse through the displays and perhaps find new favourites.

Among the brand names that will be familiar to many are Aura Bella, Johann Brun, Lesley George, Natural Magic, Balu, Stills, Passport, Turnover, Oui, Out of Xile, Jackpot, Speedway and Cut Loose. There are Hamilton Davis belts, lovely chunky knitwear, scarves, cushions and throws, Azuni and locally made jewellery, handbags for everyday and special occasion use, toilet bags, candles from Mandala and True Grace, cosmetics and essential oils from Kat Aromatherapy, cards from Tom Dickens fine art and gift vouchers.....all this and much more in one of the most delightful shops in the whole county.

---

clear idea of the splendour of the farm at that time. The only building that remains is the huge **Tithe Barn**, believed to be the largest in England. Built of local stone, it has a thatched roof that was originally covered by stone tiles.

Tithe Barn, Tisbury

Notable sons of the village include Thomas Mayhew, a prosperous mercer in the early 1600s who emigrated to New England where he acquired the off-shore islands of Martha's Vineyard and Nantucket. He and his family also helped establish the township of Tisbury.

In the churchyard of the Wiltshire Tisbury are buried John Lockwood and Alice Kipling, the parents of the author Rudyard Kipling. He often visited them at their home, The Gables in Hindon Lane, and wrote much of his novel *Kim* while staying in Tisbury.

To the south, **Old Wardour Castle** was the scene in 1643 of a bloody battle when

---

KATE GOOD POTTERY

High Street, Tisbury, nr Salisbury, Wiltshire SP3 6TD
Tel: 01747 870367

At the **Kate Good Pottery** visitors will find a selection of more than 150 items of fine household and decorative stoneware pottery. Kate Good studied at London's Central School of Arts and has lived in the Tisbury area for nearly 25 years. Everything in her repertoire is thoughtfully designed, expertly made and safe in ovens, microwaves, freezers and dishwashers. All the pieces are made and finished by hand using carefully selected clays and unique glazes. Most of the items in the range of practical cookware and tableware are available plain or decorated and besides the plates, dishes and bowls there are storage jars, table lamps, candlesticks and candle holders, plant pots, money pigs and cats, along with unusual items such as egg cups small enough for bantam eggs or large enough for goose eggs.

Anything can be made and decorated to special order with names and commemorative words incorporated into the design. Kate also produces a series of durable, colourful mosaic tiles that are suitable for indoor or outdoor use. Open 9.30am to 1.30pm and 2.30pm to 5.30pm (4.30pm on Saturday) Closed Sunday and Monday.

🏚 historic building 🏛 museum 🏚 historic site 🐾 scenic attraction 🌱 flora and fauna

Parliamentarian forces besieged the castle for several weeks, causing great loss of life and extensive damage to the building. The landscaped grounds in which the castle stands include an elaborate grotto.

WOODFORD VALLEY
6 miles N of Salisbury off the A345

🌿 Heale Garden & Plant Centre

A seven-mile stretch between Salisbury and Amesbury contains some of the prettiest and most peaceful villages in the county, among them **Great Durnford** with its Norman church and restored mill, **Lake**, with an imposing Tudor mansion, and **Middle Woodford**, where the internationally renowned **Heale Garden and Plant Centre** lies within the grounds of 16th century Heale House in an idyllic setting by a tributary of the Avon. Much of the garden was designed by Harold Peto (1854-1933), whose own garden at Iford Manor is in the Italianate style that he so favoured. Highlights at Heale include a superb collection of plants, shrubs and roses, a water garden and a Japanese bridge and teahouse made in 1910 with the help of four Japanese gardeners.

AMESBURY
8 miles N of Salisbury on the A345

🏛 Stonehenge 🏛 Woodhenge

Queen Elfrida founded an abbey here in 979 in atonement for her part in the murder of her son-in-law, Edward the Martyr, at Corfe Castle. Henry II rebuilt the abbey's great Church of St Mary and St Melor, whose tall central tower is the only structure to survive from the pre-Norman monastery. A mile to the north of Amesbury, the A345 passes along the eastern side of **Woodhenge**, a ceremonial monument even older than Stonehenge. It was

the first major prehistoric site to be discovered by aerial photography, its six concentric rings of post holes having been spotted as crop marks by Squadron Leader Insall in 1925. Like Stonehenge, it seems to have been used as an astronomical calendar. When major excavation was carried out in the 1920s, a number of neolithic tools and other artefacts were found, along with the skeleton of a three-year-old child whose fractured skull suggested some kind of ritual sacrifice.

Two miles west of Amesbury at the junction of the A303 and A344/A360 stands **Stonehenge** itself, perhaps the greatest mystery of the prehistoric world, one of the wonders of the world, and a monument of unique importance. The World Heritage Site is surrounded by the remains of ceremonial and domestic structures, many of them accessible by road or public footpath. The great stone blocks of the main ring are truly massive, and it seems certain that the stones in the outer rings - rare bluestones from the Preseli Hills of west Wales - had to be transported over 200 miles. Stonehenge's orientation on the rising and setting sun has always been one of its most remarkable features, leading to theories that the builders were from a sun-worshipping culture or that the whole structure is part of a huge astronomical calendar ...or both. The mystery remains, and will probably remain for ever.

STRATFORD-SUB-CASTLE
2 miles NE of Salisbury off the A343

🏛 Figbury Rings

Old Sarum is not the only impressive mound hereabouts, as three miles to the east is the Iron Age hill fort of **Figbury Rings**. Above it, the bleak expanse of Porton Down is a largely undisturbed conservation area where

THE KITCHENMONGER

Millies Yard, Marlborough, Wiltshire SN8 1BE
Tel/Fax: 01672 514588
e-mail: Marlborough@kitchenmonger.co.uk
website: www.kitchenmonger.co.uk

The Kitchenmonger is part of an independent chain of cookshops dedicated to providing the very best in stylish, practical products backed up by friendly, professional service. The shop is packed with stock on two floors, and the staff are all local people with a deep knowledge of their products and a real passion for cooking and baking. The various sections of the shop cover knives, cookware, oven-to-tableware, tableware, woodware, electrical gadgets, glassware, storage, cleaning, kitchen trolleys, tea and coffee, food preparation and bakeware, including specialist baking products and cake tin hire.

All the leading brands are stocked – the knives, for example, include Wusthof, Global, Henkel, I.O.Shen, Furi and Sabatier. The shop is open from 9am to 5pm (to 5.30pm Thursday to Sunday); closed Sunday. Orders can be places online through one of the most comprehensive websites of any retail outlet. The Kitchenmonger has other shops in Newbury, Hungerford and Wells.

THE CAT'S WHISKERS

45 Kingsbury Street, Marlborough, Wiltshire SN8 1JE
Tel: 01672 511577/01264 850801/07712 081543

Admire Marlborough's picturesque Town Hall at one end of the High Street, then take a few steps around the corner to the left into Kingsbury Street, where, on the right, you will find the delightful and intriguing **Cat's Whiskers**.

With a flair for design and long experience in the field of antiques, Sue Rumbold is the ideal person to run this well-stocked and charming shop, which is crammed with treasures behind its Dickensian frontage. Two floors burst with an amazing range of antiques and decorative items, including: vintage quilts, eiderdowns and textiles; silver and ethnic jewellery; garden furniture, planters, watering cans and accessories; Victorian and Edwardian china (including flow blue); bags, scarves and velvet jackets; kitchenalia; furniture; prints; and lots, lots more.

Sue, always friendly and helpful, works hard to source interesting, unusual, decorative and practical items from all over the world, to buy as gifts or to use in your own home, at surprisingly reasonable prices. Nobody should leave Marlborough without visiting The Cat's Whiskers, one of the most fascinating shops in town.

the great bustard has been making a comeback. This large, long-legged bird was once a common sight on Salisbury Plain and is incorporated in Wiltshire's coat of arms.

CHOLDERTON
9 miles NE of Salisbury on the A338

🌱 Cholderton Rare Breeds Farm Park

Close to this pleasant village is **Cholderton Rare Breeds Farm Park** set in beautiful countryside and a major family attraction since opening to the public in 1987. The park is home to many rare breeds of rabbits and poultry, and other rare breed animals are saved from extinction. At peak times the farm organises twice-daily pig races, sheep parade, calf and piglet walking and tractor-trailer rides. There are nature trails and guided tours, an adventure playground and a cafeteria.

Marlborough

🏛 Marlborough College

Famous for its public school and its wide high street – where markets are held every Wednesday and Saturday, Marlborough is situated in the rural eastern part of Wiltshire in the upland valley of the Kennet, which flows through the town. It was once an important staging post on the coaching run from London to Bath and Bristol, and the presence

of the A4 means that it still has easy links both east and west. Its main street, one of the finest in the country, is dignified by many Tudor houses and handsome Georgian colonnaded shops, behind which are back alleys waiting to be explored. St Mary's Church, austere behind a 15th century frontage, stands in Patten Alley, so named because pedestrians had to wear pattens (an overshoe with a metal sole) to negotiate the mud on rainy days. The porch of the church has a ledge where churchgoers would leave their pattens before entering. Other buildings of interest include those clustered round The Green (originally a Saxon village and the working-class quarter in the 18th and 19th centuries); the turn-of-the-century Town Hall looking down the broad High Street; and the ornate 17th century Merchant's House, now restored as a museum.

Marlborough College was founded in 1843 primarily for sons of the clergy. The Seymour family built a mansion near the site of the Norman castle. This mansion was replaced in the early-18th century by a building which became the Castle Inn and is

Merle Barrow, Marlborough

📖 stories and anecdotes 🐦 famous people 🎨 art and craft 🎭 entertainment and sport 🥾 walks

THE POLLY TEA ROOMS

26-27 High Street, Marlborough, Wiltshire SN8 1LW
Tel: 01672 512146
e-mail: info@thepolly.com
website: www.thepolly.com

Country Life magazine hailed **The Polly Tea Rooms** as "the finest tea room in England" and AA members also voted it amongst the Top 10 tea rooms in the country. Polly's was established way back in 1932 and after so many years no-one is quite sure where the name came from. Some cite the nursery rhyme *Polly, put the kettle on*, others claim that the two ladies who opened the tea room had a parrot of that name, but the most likely source is believed to be Polly Peacham, heroine of *The Beggar's Opera*. Whatever the origin of the name, this is an outstanding tea room and is today "a lovingly owned small group of tearooms" – a quote from the menu.

In addition to wonderful afternoon teas with homemade cakes, biscuits and breads, this also offers an extensive breakfast and lunch menu with the not very often found kedgeree amongst the former, and appetising dishes such as Polly's homemade fishcake on a leek and potato cream amongst the latter. There's a good selection of teas, coffees, soft drinks, beers and wine, a special children's menu, and a wide choice of speciality ice creams. And in the Polly Shop you'll find an enticing range of Polly's own handmade chocolates, fudge, marzipan fruits, homemade jams and marmalade, and honey from Polly's own hives. See separate entry for Polly Tea Rooms in Salisbury.

now C House, the oldest part of the College. A mound in the private grounds of the school is linked with King Arthur's personal magician Merlin. It was said that he was buried under this mound and gave the town its name '**Merle Barrow**' or Merlin's Tomb. Among the many notable pupils of the college were William Morris and John Betjeman.

Around Marlborough

SAVERNAKE FOREST
2 miles E of Marlborough off the A346

🌱 Savernake Forest

The ancient woodland of **Savernake Forest** is a magnificent 4,500-acre expanse of unbroken woodland, open glades and bridle paths. King Henry VIII hunted wild deer here and married Jane Seymour, whose family home was nearby. Designated a Site of Special Scientific Interest, the forest is home to abundant wildlife, including a small herd of deer and 25 species of butterfly. One day each winter the forest is closed to prevent rights of way being established.

GREAT BEDWYN
6 miles SE of Marlborough off the A4

🏛 Lloyds Stone Museum

In the chancel of the 11th century Church of St Mary the Virgin is the tomb of Sir John Seymour, the father of Henry VIII's third wife Jane. Nearby is **Lloyds Stone Museum**, a monument to the skills of the English stonemason. Among the items on display are

🏛 historic building   🏛 museum   🏛 historic site   🌱 scenic attraction   🍃 flora and fauna

an assortment of tombstones and a stone aeroplane with an 11ft wingspan.

CROFTON
6 miles SE of Marlborough off the A338

🏛 Crofton Beam Engines

The eastern end of the Vale of Pewsey carries the London-Penzance railway and the Kennet and Avon Canal, which reaches its highest point near Crofton. The site is marked by a handsome Georgian pumping station which houses the renowned **Crofton Beam Engines** (see panel below). These engines - the 1812 Boulton & Watt and the 1845 Harvey of Hayle - have been superbly restored under the guidance of the Canal trust. The 1812 engine is the oldest working beam engine in the world, still in its original building and still doing its original job of pumping water to the summit

level of the canal. Both engines are steamed from a hand-stoked, coal-fired Lancashire boiler. The brick chimney has also been restored, to its original height of 82 feet.

WILTON
8 miles SE of Marlborough off the A338

🏠 Windmill

A footpath of about a mile links the Crofton Beam Engines with Wilton. This is the smaller of the two Wiltshire Wiltons and is the site of the **Wilton Windmill**. This traditional working mill, the only one operating in the county, was built in 1821 after the Canal Company has taken the water out of the River Bedwyn for their canal, thereby depriving the water mills of the power to drive their mills. The mill worked until 1920, when the availability of steam power and electricity

Crofton Pumping Station

Gt Bedwyn, Marlborough, Wiltshire SN8 3DW
Tel: 01672 870300
website: croftonbeamengines.org
Situated in the delightful Wiltshire countryside this Grade 1 listed building houses two magnificent Cornish beam engines, one of which (the 1812 Boulton and Watt) is the oldest working beam engine in the world still in its original engine house and capable of actually doing the job for which it was installed.

Crofton Pumping Station was built in 1807 to provide water to the summit of the Kennet and Avon Canal. The first engine installed in the building in 1809 was a 36 inch bore Boulton and Watt and in 1812 a 42 inch bore Boulton and Watt engine was installed beside it. The first was replaced in 1846 by a Sims Combined Cylinders Engine constructed by Harvey of Hayle which was converted in 1903 to the Cornish Cycle. Both the 1812 Boulton and Watt, and the 1846 Harvey engine are in working condition, and are regularly steamed publicly through the summer months from a coal fired Lancashire boiler. When the Pumping Station is in steam, it actually carries out the job for which it was built, the electrically powered pumps that normally do the job being switched off.

When open, the visiting public have access to all parts of the station, whether in steam or not, and when in steam, can experience close up the smell and sounds of these wonderful relics of our past in operation. Refreshments and souvenirs are available in the shop, and there is plenty of room in the grounds for sitting and enjoying the splendid views. There is parking for visitors in the car park opposite the gate.

🎞 stories and anecdotes   🐦 famous people   🎨 art and craft   ✒ entertainment and sport   🚶 walks

literally took the wind out its sails. After standing derelict for 50 years the mill was restored at a cost of £25,000 and is now looked after by the Wilton Windmill Society. This superb old mill is floodlit from dusk until 10pm, making a wonderful sight on a chalk ridge 550 feet above sea level.

Wilton Windmill

CLENCH COMMON
2 miles S of Marlborough on the A345

This is a lovely part of the world for walking or cycling. The Forestry Commission's West Woods, particularly notable for bluebells in May, has a picnic site, and nearby is Martinsell Hill topped by an ancient fort.

WOOTTON RIVERS
4 miles S of Marlborough off the A345

An attractive village with a real curiosity in its highly unusual church clock. The Jack Sprat Clock was built by a local man from an assortment of scrap metal, including old bicycles, prams and farm tools, to mark the coronation of King George V in 1911. It has 24 different chimes and its face has letters instead of numbers.

PEWSEY
7 miles S of Marlborough on the A345

🏛 Heritage Centre   ⚜ White Horse

In the heart of the beautiful valley that bears its name, this is a charming village of half-timbered houses and thatched cottages. It was once the personal property of Alfred the Great, and a statue of the king stands at the crossroads in the centre. The parish church, built on a foundation of sarsen stones, has an unusual altar rail made from timbers taken from the *San Josef*, a ship captured by Nelson in 1797.

Attractions for the visitor include the old wharf area and the **Heritage Centre**, housed in an 1870 foundry building. It contains an interesting collection of old and unusual machine tools and farm machinery. The original **Pewsey White Horse**, south of the village on Pewsey Down, was cut in 1785, apparently including a rider, but was redesigned by a Mr George Marples and cut by the Pewsey Fire Brigade to celebrate the coronation of King George VI. Pewsey Carnival takes place each September, and the annual Devizes to Westminster canoe race passes through Pewsey Wharf.

A minor road runs past the White Horse across Pewsey Down to the isolated village of **Everleigh**, where the Church of St Peter is of unusual iron-framed construction. Rebuilt on a new site in 1813, it has a short chancel and narrow nave, an elegant west gallery and a neo-medieval hammerbeam roof.

THE BARLEYCORN INN

Collingbourne Kingston, nr Marlborough,
Wiltshire SN8 3SD
Tel/Fax: 01264 850368
e-mail: rking124@hotmail.com
website: www.barleycorninn.co.uk

Roy and Suzanne keep the welcome mat out for visitors to the **Barleycorn Inn**, a smartly kept village pub just off the A338 south of Burbage. Behind the substantial brick frontage, the 200-year-old inn has an appealing traditional look, with beams and a handsome brick inglenook fireplace. In fine weather, tables are set out under parasols in the lawned garden. Five real ales are always on tap, with many other draught and bottle beers, cider, wines, spirits and non-alcoholic drinks, and wide-ranging menus provide plenty of choice for patrons. Always in demand are the steaks, which cater for all appetites, from 8oz rump, sirloin, rib-eye and fillet to a daunting 48oz T-Bone. They can be served plain or with a choice of very tasty sauces.

Other dishes – the choice changes daily – might include super fish cakes, deep-fried Camembert with a sweet chilli sauce, sizzling chicken, mini-roast pork loin and chargrilled salmon with ginger, spring onion and cashew nuts. There are always plenty of vegetarian options and some hard-to-resist desserts such as apple pie or lemon meringue ice cream cake, and for those with less time to spare the ploughman's platters and the filled jacket potatoes are tasty alternatives. Plans for

ALTON BARNES AND ALTON PRIORS

6 miles SW of Marlborough off the A345

🌣 White Horse

The largest **White Horse** in Wiltshire can be seen on the hillside above Alton Barnes; cut in 1812, it is 54 metres high and 51 metres long and is visible from Old Sarum, 20 miles away. According to the local story the original contractor ran off with the £20 advance payment and the work was carried out by one Robert Pile, who owned the land. The runaway contractor was later arrested and hanged for a string of offences. Other notable Wiltshire White Horses in the locality are at Hackpen, just north of Marlborough (cut to commemorate Queen Victoria's coronation) and at Pewsey.

AVEBURY

6 miles W of Marlborough on the A4361

🏛 Stone Circles   🏠 Avebury Manor

🏛 Alexander Keiller Museum

An internationally renowned 28-acre World Heritage Site is the centre of the **Avebury Stone Circles**, the most remarkable ritual megalithic monuments in Europe. A massive bank and ditch enclose an outer circle and two inner circles of stones. The outer circle has almost 100 sarsen stones (made of sand and silica); the two inner rings have 40 stones still standing. Some of the individual stones weigh 40 tons and had to be dragged here from Marlborough Downs. They are in two basic shapes which have been equated with male and female, supporting the theory that the site

🏛 stories and anecdotes   🐦 famous people   🎨 art and craft   🎭 entertainment and sport   🚶 walks

Avebury

Distance: *5.3 miles (8.5 kilometres)*

Typical time: *180 mins*

Height gain: *60 metres*

Map: *Explorer 157*

Walk: *www.walkingworld.com ID:68*

Contributor: *David and Chris Stewart*

ACCESS INFORMATION:

Buses are available from Devizes, Marlborough and Swindon (Wiltshire Bus Line 0345 090899). By car: Avebury is half way between Marlborough and Calne on the A4. The National Trust provide a free car park just before.

ADDITIONAL INFORMATION:

This walk does involve crossing the busy A4 twice. The Avebury henge is part of the National Trust and a great deal of information is available from the Alexander Keiller Museum (01672 539 250).

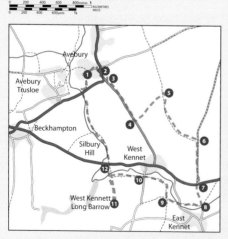

DESCRIPTION:

Starting at the Avebury stone circle the walk takes you along the stone Avenue and up to the Ridgeway with spectacular Wiltshire views of "hedgehogs" and curious burial mounds.

The route then takes you to visit the Sanctuary, yet another ancient site, and then through lush farmland to see the famous West Kennet Long Barrow. You then return to Avebury via the amazing man-made Silbury Hill (carbon dating suggests that Silbury Hill was built around 2500 BC, making it an extraordinary feat for its time).

FEATURES:

Pub, Museum, National Trust/NTS, Great Views

WALK DIRECTIONS:

1 | Leave the car park and follow the signs to Avebury village. When you reach the road turn right before the Henge shop and the post office. You are now inside the ring. Follow it round to the left towards the main road.

2 | Carefully cross the main road and go into the next part of the ring. Bear right and climb up onto the bank.

3 | Go down the other side towards a gate. Cross the road and enter the field. This is the beginning of The Avenue. Walk down The Avenue between the stones.

4 | When you reach the last stones of The Avenue you will find a gate. Cross the road and take the path on the opposite side. After a short distance you reach the one remaining stone of Falkner's Circle. Keeping on the same side of the hedge as the path you have just followed, cross into the next field. Follow the left hand edge of the field up a slight gradient to the next field boundary.

5 | Turn right onto the track leading towards the clumps of trees on the horizon (these are known as 'hedgehogs').

6 | Just past the 'hedgehogs' the path bears left. Then you can turn right onto the very last section of the Ridgeway path. Follow the Ridgeway down to the main road.

7 | Cross the road extremely carefully. Just on your right there is the Sanctuary, the site of an ancient wooden circle (later a stone one which was taken up in the 18th century). Having visited the Sanctuary, the path to take is the one signed 'Byway' directly opposite the end of the Ridgeway path. Follow this path down a gentle hill.

8 | Just before the path turns to the left and crosses a bridge, take the path going right. Follow this path alongside the river until you reach a small road. Turn left and cross the bridge. Turn right onto the track.

9 | This pathway is very easy to miss. It's just after where the track turns to the left. On the right there is a yellow sign which says 'Private Path' and an arrow to the left. Walk a few feet further on looking for a path on your right going down the middle of a hedgerow. There is a small arrow on a tree. Follow this path to a field and then keep along the lefthand edge of the field to reach a road.

10 | Cross the road and continue on the track. When you reach the path leading up to West Kennet longbarrow, turn left and walk up a gentle slope to the barrow.

11 | West Kennet longbarrow, where there is an informative sign about its origins and the opportunity to enter some of its chambers. After your visit retrace your steps down the path and continue straight on towards Silbury Hill.

12 | Cross the main road again very carefully and take the path directly opposite. This follows a small stream and there are magnificent views of Silbury Hill on your left (it is no longer possible to climb the hill). Follow the path all the way back to Avebury - it brings you out at the main car park.

was used in fertility rites. Archaeologists have also found the remains of a long-vanished avenue of stones leading south towards Beckhampton, a discovery that vindicated the theory of the 18th century antiquary, William Stukeley, who made drawings of the stone circles with this avenue marked.

Many of the archaeological finds from the site are displayed in Avebury's **Alexander Keiller Museum**, which also describes the restoration of the site by Keiller in the 1930s.

Keiller's home is the 16th century **Avebury Manor**, which stands on the site of a 12th century priory. The house and its four-acre walled garden, which features a wishing well, topiary, a rose garden and an Italian walk, are owned by the National Trust.

WEST OVERTON
3 miles W of Marlborough off the A4

🏛 Overton Hill   🌿 Fyfield Down

🏛 Devil's Den

The area between Marlborough and Avebury sees the biggest concentration of prehistoric remains in the country. The scattered community of West Overton stands at the foot of **Overton Hill**, the site of an early Bronze Age monument called **The Sanctuary**. Concrete markers have now replaced the giant standing stones at the southeastern end of West Kennet Avenue, an ancient pathway which once connected them to the main megalithic circles at Avebury. Overton Hill is also the start point of the Ridgeway long-distance path, which runs for 80 miles to the Chilterns. Just off this path is **Fyfield Down**, now a nature reserve, where quarries once provided many of the great stones that are such a feature of the area. **Devil's Den** long barrow lies within the reserve. The local legend that Satan

WINE STREET GALLERY

1 Wine Street, Devizes, Wiltshire SN10 1AP
Tel: 01380 728387/07866 698201   website:
www.winestreetgallery.com

Wine Street Gallery is located on the first floor of a Grade II*
listed Georgian building overlooking the historic market place
of Devizes. This elegant and well-lit display area is a
showcase for a selection of the best contemporary painting,
sculpture, ceramics and studio glass by artists drawn from the West Country and beyond.
Among the artists regularly represented in the Gallery are David Inshaw, John Wragg RA, David
Imms, Eric Stanford FRBS, Robin Tanner and Willliam Shakspeare. Regular exhibitions reflect the
diversity of contemporary art, and the Gallery also offers life-drawing classes.

Opening hours are 11 to 5 Thursday, Friday and Saturday and by appointment. Please note
these times are variable according to the exhibition schedule and season. It is advisable to
phone in advance.

A changing selection of artwork from the Wine Street Gallery is on display in Juliet Reid's
B&B establishment near Seend.

MALTHOUSE BARN B&B

The Malthouse Barn, Baldham, Seend, nr Melksham, Wiltshire SN12 6PW
Tel: 01380 828308   e-mail: julietreid7@aol.com
website: www.themalthousebarn.com

The **Malthouse Barn** is a charmingly converted former cow
byre in a delightful riverside rural setting. Since the spring of
2006, Juliet Reid, who owns the Wine Street Gallery in
Devizes, has been offering characterful self-contained Bed &
Breakfast accommodation in two well-appointed bedrooms –
a twin and a double, both with full en suite bathrooms,
galleried seating areas, tea/coffee trays and television and
audio systems. A selection of
paintings, sculpture and ceramics
from Juliet's gallery in Devizes is
displayed in the day rooms. A
delicious breakfast starts the day,
and when the weather is kind
guests can make the most of the
lovely location with a walk in the
garden, meeting the chickens and
ducks, the swans and the
moorhens. The Malthouse has
fishing rights on Semington Brook.
Day fishing available.

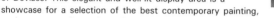
🏛 historic building   🏛 museum   🏛 historic site   🌿 scenic attraction   🌱 flora and fauna

sometimes appears here at midnight attempting to pull down the stones with a team of white oxen has not in recent times been corroborated.

EAST AND WEST KENNET

4 miles W of Marlborough on the A4

🏛 Long Barrow

West Kennet Long Barrow, one of Britain's largest neolithic burial tombs, is situated a gentle stroll away from the twin villages. The tomb is of impressive proportions – 330 feet long, 80 feet wide and 10 feet high - and is reached by squeezing past some massive stones in the semicircular forecourt.

The Sanctuary

SILBURY HILL

5 miles W of Marlborough on the A4

The largest man-made prehistoric mound in Europe, built around 2800BC, standing 130 feet high and covers five acres. Excavation in the late 1960s revealed some details of how it was constructed but shed little light on its purpose. Theories include a burial place for King Sil and his horse and a hiding place for a large gold statue built by the Devil on his way to Devizes. Scholarship generally favours the first.

Devizes

🏛 Wiltshire Heritage Museum 🏛 Canal Museum

🏛 Visitor Centre 🏛 Market Cross

🏃 Devizes Locks Trail

The central market town of Wiltshire, Devizes boasts no fewer than 500 listed buildings within a quarter square mile. Many of the town's finest buildings are situated in and around the old market place, including the Town Hall and the Corn Exchange. Also here is an unusual **Market Cross** inscribed with the story of Ruth Pierce, a market stall-holder who stood accused, on January 25th, 1753, of short-changing a customer. When an ugly crowd gathered round her, she stood and pleaded her innocence, adding, "May I be struck dead if I am lying". A rash move, as she fell to the ground and died forthwith. The missing money (three pence – 1.4p) was found clutched in her hand.

Devizes was founded in 1080 by Bishop Osmund, nephew of William the Conqueror. The bishop was responsible for building a timber castle between the lands of two powerful manors, and this act brought about the town's name, which is derived from the Latin *ad divisas*, or 'at the boundaries'. After the wooden structure burnt down, Roger, Bishop of Sarum, built a stone castle in 1138 that survived until the end of the Civil War, when it was demolished. Bishop Roger also built two fine churches in Devizes. Long Street is lined with elegant Georgian houses and also

THE EMPORIUM

6-7 St John's Street, Devizes,
Wiltshire SN10 1BD
Tel: 01380 721647
Fax: 01380 721476

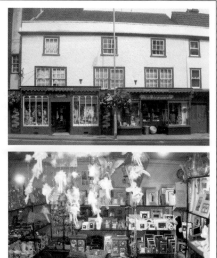

Teresa Garraud started her business life in Canada and had many years' experience in the world of arts and crafts before opening **The Emporium** in 1981. Behind its traditional shop front just off the market place, with large windows and an awning, the shop is an Aladdin's Cave of affordable clothes, jewellery, gifts and things for the home.

Everything has Teresa's seal of approval, from pocket-money toys and stocking fillers to handmade Indian crafts, books, scarves, throws, cushions and cushion covers, rugs, baskets, silk flowers, toys, novelties, candles, incense, jugs, mugs, vases, bowls, greetings cards and wrapping paper. Value for money, fun and fair trade are watchwords throughout.

The Emporium is open from 9.30am to 5.30pm Monday to Saturday.

THE HEALTHY LIFE, BISTRO & COOKERY SCHOOL

4-7 Little Brittox, Devizes, Wiltshire SN10 1AR
Tel: 01380 720043 Fax: 01380 727772
e-mail: health@thehealthylife.co.uk
website: www.thehealthylife.co.uk

Chef/patron Peter Vaughan, a member of The Academy of Culinary Arts, has mastered a naturally balanced cooking style. This incorporates using the best local produce, ethically traded and unrefined ingredients with close regard to ecological issues that help to sustain the planet as well as providing delicious 'body friendly' food. The light lunches are served 11.00 a.m. – 3.00p.m. and then from 7.00p.m The Bistro invites diners to experience a lively atmosphere and exciting tastes. Special diets are catered for.

The Cookery School classes are run in small groups providing hands-on experience and following the naturally balanced cooking style. Private cookery demonstrations are available also, details on request.

An impressive range of the ingredients used in The Bistro and Cookery school, plus many more interesting items are for sale in The Healthy Life natural food store. Vitamin and mineral supplements and herbal remedies are also available.

BLUESTONE GALLERY

8 Old Swan Yard, Devizes, Wiltshire SN10 1AT
Tel: 01380 729589
e-mail: info@bluestonegallery.com
website: www.bluestonegallery.com

Guy and Janice Perkins opened the Bluestone Gallery in May 2000. Guy has been a full time professional potter since 1977, and for 20 years lived and worked in the middle of Avebury Stone Circle. The Gallery takes its name from the inner ring of stones at nearby Stonehenge (the Bluestones brought from the Preseli Hills). The Gallery, in a listed building, is situated in a group of attractive independent shops and cafes.

With two floors of work there is an impressive amount on display, all carefully selected for quality and originality. Guy and Janice travel widely in the British Isles searching for the finest work from established and up-and-coming artists. The wide variety of work includes jewellery, ceramics, glass, wood, sculpture, automata, prints and original paintings. At any time you will find the work of over 70 artists on display. The range of jewellery has developed into one of the highlights of the Gallery.

An interest free loan scheme helps take the sting out of impulse buys. You will be made welcome in the peaceful and friendly atmosphere.

---

contains the **Wiltshire Heritage Museum,** which has a splendid collection of artefacts from the area, and an art gallery with a John Piper window and regularly changing exhibitions. Here, amongst other local industries, you can learn about the Wadworth Brewery, founded in 1875 and still a family business. The brewery continues to use Shire horses for local deliveries and they have become a familiar and much-loved part of the local scene. Their stables can be visited by prior arrangement.

Devizes Visitor Centre offers a unique insight into the town. The Centre is based on a 12th century castle and takes visitors back to medieval times, when Devizes was home to the finest castle in Europe and the scene

of anarchy and unrest during the struggles between Empress Matilda and King Stephen. An interactive exhibition shows how the town came to be at the centre of the 12th century Civil War and later thrived as a medieval town.

Devizes stands at a key point on the Kennet & Avon Canal, and the **Kennet and Avon Canal Museum** tells the complete story of the canal in fascinating detail. Many visitors combine a trip to the museum with a walk along the towpath, which is a public footpath. The route of the canal involved overcoming the rise of 237ft from the Avon Valley to Devizes. The engineer John Rennie devised the solution, which was to build one vast flight of locks, 29 in all of which 16

Devizes Locks

here and built the very grand **Parish Church** before they started work on the Cathedral. This church, dedicated to St Mary, has often been likened to the Cathedral and does indeed bear some resemblance, notably in its tall, tapering spire. This is Moonraker country, and according to legend a group of 17th century smugglers from Bishops Canning fooled excisemen when caught recovering dumped brandy kegs from a pond known as the Crammer. The smugglers pretended to be mad and claimed that the moon's reflection on the pond was actually a cheese, which they were trying to rake in. The ruse worked, so who were the real fools? A hollow in the downs west of the village was the scene of a bloody Civil War battle in 1643, when the Royalist forces under Prince Rupert's brother Maurice defeated the Parliamentarian forces at Roundway Down. According to a local legend the cries of the dead can be heard coming from a burial ditch on the anniversary of the battle (July 13).

were set very close together down Caen Hill. The **Devizes Locks Discovery Trail** descends from Devizes Wharf, through the town and to the bottom of the flight at Lower Foxhangers, returning by way of open countryside and the village of Rowde. Each July the Canalfest, a weekend of family fun designed to raise funds for the upkeep of the canal, is held at the Wharf, which is also the start point of the annual Devizes-Westminster canoe race held every year on Good Friday.

Around Devizes

BISHOP'S CANNINGS
4 miles NE of Devizes on the A361

🏛 Church of St Mary

The bishops of Salisbury once owned a manor

MARKET LAVINGTON
5 miles S of Devizes on the B3098

🏛 Museum

The 'Village under the Plain' is home to a little museum in the former schoolmaster's cottage behind the old village school. Displays at **Market Lavington Museum** include a Victorian kitchen and archive photographs.

Swindon

🏛 STEAM   🏛 National Monuments Record Centre
🏛 Museum & Art Gallery

Think Swindon, think the Great Western Railway. Think GWR, think Isambard Kingdom Brunel. The largest town in

🏛 historic building   🏛 museum   🏛 historic site   🔱 scenic attraction   🌿 flora and fauna

Wiltshire, lying in the northeast corner between the Cotswolds and the Marlborough Downs, Swindon was an insignificant agricultural community before the railway line between London and Bristol was completed in 1835. Swindon Station opened in that year, but it was some time later, in 1843, that Brunel, the GWR's principal engineer, decided that Swindon was the place to build his locomotive works. Within a few years it had grown to be one of the largest in the world, with as many as 12,000 on a 320-acre site that incorporated the Railway Village; this was a model development of 300 workmen's houses built of limestone extracted from the construction of Box Tunnel. This unique example of early-Victorian town planning is open to the public as the Railway Village Museum, with a restored Victorian railway worker's cottage. Lit by gas, the cottage, open only by appointment, contains many original fittings such as the range and copper in the kitchen.

STEAM, the Museum of the Great Western Railway provides both a great family day out and a tribute to one of the great railways of the world. The leading stars in its fascinating collection of locomotives are the *King George V*, heading *The Bristolian* in the station platform, and the Castle class *Caerphilly Castle*. As well as displaying railway memorabilia such as engine nameplates, signalling equipment and an exhibition of the life and achievements of Brunel, the centre also focuses on the human aspects of the industry, telling the story of the men and women who built and repaired the locomotives and carriages of the GWR (God's Wonderful Railway) for seven generations. The last locomotive to be built at the works was 92220 *Evening Star*, a

powerful 2-10-0 freight engine of a type that proved surprisingly versatile but was destined to have all too short a working life. Engineering work continued on the site until 1986, when the works finally closed. STEAM has a café and a shop with an impressive range of GWR and other railway gifts, books, souvenirs and pocket-money toys. It's family-friendly, and all areas are fully accessible to wheelchairs. The site now also contains the **National Monuments Record Centre** - the public archive of the Royal Commission on the Historical Monuments of England, with seven million photographs, documents and texts.

There's lots more to Swindon than the legacy of the GWR: it's a bustling and successful commercial town with excellent shopping and leisure facilities and plenty of open spaces. In an elegant early-19th century house on the Bath Road, **Swindon Museum & Art Gallery** contains a variety of displays on the history, archaeology and geology of the town and the surrounding area and also houses a fine collection of 20th century British art.

Around Swindon

CRICKLADE
6 miles N of Swindon off the A419

🏛 Museum 🌿 North Meadow

The only Wiltshire town on the Thames was an important post on the Roman Ermine Street and had its own mint in Saxon times. There are many buildings of interest, notably the Church of St Sampson, with its cathedral-like four-spired tower, where a festival of music takes place each September; the famous school founded by the London goldsmith

THE OLD BEAR INN

101 High Street, Cricklade, Wiltshire SN6 6AA
Tel: 01793 750005
e-mail: teresacleverly@aol.com

The **Old Bear Inn** enjoys a prominent position on the main street of the historic Saxon town of Cricklade, the only Wiltshire town on the River Thames. The pub is in the excellent care of Teresa and Steven Cleverly, who brought long experience in the licensed trade when they took it over in November 2005. They have the warmest of welcomes for their customers, whether they've popped in a for a quick drink, settled down to sample the traditional home cooking or to taking an overnight or longer break while touring the region.

The lounge and public bars are convivial spots for enjoying a glass of well-kept Arkell's or one of the guest ales, and there are seats out in the garden for taking a sip in the sun. Appetites are satisfied with a selection of home-cooked pub favourites, and for guests staying overnight the Old Bear has comfortable bed & breakfast accommodation in the converted stables. The pub probably got its name from a performing bear who was part of a touring Russian circus that used to visit Cricklade in the 18th century. The circus left town long, long ago but there's plenty to interest today's visitors, and those wanting to make the most of the local scenery, for it is the first town on the Thames Path Walk.

Robert Jenner in 1651; and the fancy Victorian clock tower. **Cricklade Museum** contains displays on social history, Roman occupation, Rotten Borough elections and an archive of 2,000 photographs. Nearby **North Meadow** is a National Nature Reserve where the rare snakeshead fritillary grows.

HIGHWORTH

5 miles NE of Swindon on the A361

  🌳 Highworth Hill

The name is appropriate, as the village stands at the top of a 400ft incline, and the view from **Highworth Hill** takes in the counties of Wiltshire, Gloucestershire and Oxfordshire. There are some very fine 17th and 18th century buildings round the old

square, and the parish church is of interest: built in the 15th century, it was fortified during the Civil War and was attacked soon after by Parliamentarian forces under Fairfax. One of the cannonballs which struck it, is on display outside. The church contains a memorial to Lieutenant Warneford, who was awarded the VC for destroying the first enemy Zeppelin in 1915.

WROUGHTON

3 miles S of Swindon on the A4361

  🏛 National Museum of Science and Industry

  🌿 Butterfly World   🌿 Clouts Wood Nature Reserve

  🏛 Barbury Castle

Wroughton Airfield, with its historic Second World War hangars, is home to the **National**

🏛 historic building   🏛 museum   🏛 historic site   🌳 scenic attraction   🌿 flora and fauna

Museum of Science and Industry's superb collections, including Air Transport and Aviation, Land Transport and Agriculture, Radar and Firefighting Equipment.

A popular attraction in Wroughton is **Butterfly World** at Studley Grange Garden & Leisure Park. Visitors can get close to some of the largest and most spectacular insects on the planet. They fly freely against a backdrop of tropical plants, skimming over fish-filled pools. The 'mini-beasts' house is home to a fascinating display of spiders, scorpions, mantis and other creepy crawlies.

Nearby **Clouts Wood Nature Reserve** is a lovely place for a ramble, and a short drive south, by the Ridgeway, is the site of **Barbury Castle**, one of the most spectacular Iron Age forts in southern England. The open hillside was the scene of a bloody battle between the Britons and the Saxons in the 6th century; the Britons lost and the Saxon kingdom of Wessex was established under King Cealwin. The area around the castle is a country park.

Barbury Castle, Wroughton

BROAD HINTON
5 miles S of Swindon off the A4361

In the church at Broad Hinton is a memorial to local bigwig Sir Thomas Wroughton, who returned home from hunting to find his wife reading the Bible instead of making his tea. He seized the Bible and flung it into the fire; his wife retrieved it but in doing so severely burnt her hands. As punishment for his blasphemy Sir Thomas's hands and those of his four children withered away (very hard on the children, surely). The monument shows the whole handless family and a Bible with a corner burnt off.

LYDIARD TREGOZE
2 miles W of Swindon off the A3102

🏛 Lydiard Park

On the western outskirts of Swindon, **Lydiard Park** is the ancestral home of the Viscounts Bolingbroke. The park is a delightful place to explore, and the house, one of Wiltshire's smaller stately homes, is a real gem, described by Sir Hugh Casson as "a gentle Georgian house, sunning itself as serenely as an old grey cat". Chief attractions inside include the little blue Dressing Room devoted to the 18th century society artist Lady Diana Spencer who became the 2nd Viscountess Bolingbroke. St Mary's Church, next to the house, contains many monuments to the St John family, who lived here from Elizabethan times. The most striking is the Golden Cavalier, a life-size gilded effigy of Edward St John in full battledress (he was killed at the second Battle of Newbury in 1645).

ALLINGTON FARM SHOP

Allington Bar Farm, Allington, nr Chippenham,
Wiltshire SN14 6LJ website: www.allingtonfarmshop.co.uk
Tel: 01249 658112 e-mail: tim@allingtonfarmshop.co.uk

A visit to this family-run farm shop, just on the outskirts of Chippenham, is a must. Established for over 25 years, the shop is run by the Reynolds Family, in parallel with their 400-acre farm and specialises in quality, home produced and locally sourced food.

With a large selection of products on sale you could spend a long time choosing your goodies, which range from; fresh meat produced on the farm and from the local area which has been traditionally butchered and hung; a large selection of homemade sausages and homemade burgers – a good place to visit if you are planning a barbeque; locally made honey, preserves, chutneys & pickles – which make great gifts and souvenirs; home cooked meats; Somerset organic Jersey milk, cream & butter; West Country cheeses and a selection of fine cheese biscuits; homemade cakes & pies produced in the farmhouse kitchen; a large range of locally produced ice cream; Prue's Meringues from nearby Marshfield; loose frozen and fresh fruit & vegetables and much, much more.

Allington Farm Shop is open 7 days a week 9am – 6pm Mon – Sat (incl. Bank Holidays) and 10am – 5pm on Sundays. The shop also stocks a range of convenience items, handy if you are self-catering or camping in the area.

GET AHEAD HATS

Rhyddian Roper
Allington Grange, Allington, nr Chippenham,
Wiltshire SN14 6LW
Tel: 01249 660863
e-mail: rhyddian@getaheadhats.co.uk
website: www.getaheadhats.co.uk

Visitors to **Get Ahead Hats** have access to an outstanding range of hats in all colours, shapes and styles, for all occasions and for all ages. Get Ahead Hats is a co-operative of farmers' wives networked throughout the UK. Rhyddian has a lovely showroom, with fitting area and she is on hand to help and advise. The exquisite designs run from demure and 'neat petite' to simple elegance, feathered flair and flamboyant extravagance. There's something for every occasion, from weddings and christenings to days at the races and any other chance to dress up.

Rhyddians' display features the latest designs from the UK's top millinery designers, offering exceptional quality and value for money. The collection changes each year to include the latest ideas and fashion trends. All the hats can be purchased or hired. There are also accessories including handbags and jewellery for sale.

Flexible opening hours including evenings. Please phone in advance.

WOOTTON BASSETT
3 miles W of Swindon off the A3102

A small town with a big history. Records go back to the 7th century, and in 1219 Henry III granted a market charter (the market is still held every Wednesday). The town boasts some fine Georgian buildings, a good range of family-run businesses – including a butcher, baker, greengrocer and ironmonger – and some good eating places. You can eat al fresco across from the striking Old Town Hall which stands on a series of stone pillars, leaving an open-sided ground-floor area that once served as a covered market. The museum above, open on Saturday mornings, contains a rare ducking stool, silver maces and a mayoral sword of office.

A section of the Wilts & Berks Canal has been restored at Templars Fir. In May 1998 about 50 boats of all kinds were launched on the canal and a day of festivities was enjoyed by all. The railway station, alas, has not been revived after falling to the Beeching axe in 1966.

Chippenham

🏛 Museum & Heritage Centre

🚶 Maud Heath's Causeway

A dynamic town with a population of around 40,000 whose major employer today is the Westinghouse Brake & Signal Co. established here in 1920.

Set on the banks of the Avon, Chippenham was founded around 600AD by the Saxon king Cyppa. It became an important administrative centre in King Alfred's time and later gained further prominence from the wool trade. It was a major stop on the London-Bristol coaching run and is served by the railway between the same two cities. Buildings of note include the Church of St Andrew (mainly 15th century) and the half-timbered Yelde Hall, once used by the burgesses and bailiffs of the Chippenham Hundred. This Grade I building houses the tourist information office.

The new **Chippenham Museum and Heritage Centre** in the Market Place tells the story of the town from the Jurassic period onwards, and the displays focus on Saxon Chippenham, Alfred the Great, Brunel's railway, the celebrated cheese market, Victorian living conditions and Chippenham curiosities. At Hardenhuish Hall on the edge of town, John Wood the Younger of Bath fame built the Church of St Nicholas; completed in 1779, it is notable for its domed steeple and elegant Venetian windows. Wealth from the wool trade built many fine houses using local stone and Bath stone, which led to Chippenham being called 'little Bath'.

In the flood plain to the east of Chippenham stands the 4.5 mile footpath known as **Maud Heath's Causeway**. This remarkable and ingenious walkway consisting of 64 brick and stone arches was built at the end of the 15th century at the bequest of Maud Heath, who spent most of her life as a market trader trudging her often muddy way between her village of Bremhill and Chippenham. She died a relatively wealthy woman, and the land and property she left in her will provided sufficient funds for the upkeep of the causeway, which is best seen near the hamlet of Kellaways. A statue of Maud, basket in hand, stands overlooking the flood plain at Wick Hill. Chippenham is twinned with La Flèche, on the banks of the Loire near Le Mans, and with Friedberg, 40 miles from Munich and the Bavarian Alps.

🎬 stories and anecdotes   🐦 famous people   🎨 art and craft   🎭 entertainment and sport   🚶 walks

Around Chippenham

CALNE
5 miles E of Chippenham on the A4

🏠 Bowood House 🏛 Atwell-Wilson Motor Museum

A former weaving centre in the valley of the River Marden; the prominent wool church reflects the prosperity of earlier times. One of the memorials in the church is to Dr Ingenhousz, who is widely credited with creating a smallpox vaccination before Jenner. Another remembers the King of the Gypsies, who died of smallpox in 1774.

A short distance from Calne, to the west, stands **Bowood House**, built in 1625 and now a treasury of Shelborne family heirlooms, paintings, books and furniture. In the Bowood Laboratory Dr Joseph Priestley, tutor to the 1st Marquess of Lansdowne's son, conducted experiments that resulted in the identification of oxygen. The house is set in lovely Capability Brown grounds with a lake and terraced garden. The mausoleum was commissioned in 1761 by the Dowager Countess of Shelborne as a memorial to her husband and was Robert Adam's first work for them. A separate woodland garden of 60 acres, with azaleas and rhododendrons, is open from late April to early June. Also within the grounds are an adventure playground for under-12s, a Soft Play Palace, a coffee shop and restaurant.

The **Atwell-Wilson Motor Museum**, on the A4 east of Calne, has a collection of over 125 vintage and classic cars and motorcycles from the years 1924 to the late 1980s. Most of them are still in running order.

LACKHAM
3 miles S of Chippenham on the A350

🏛 Museum of Agricultural and Rural Life

The **Lackham Museum of Agriculture &**

Rural Life offers a variety of displays set within a wonderful complex of historic Wiltshire farm buildings. With 18th century Lackham House (private) as a backdrop, the extensive themed gardens contain a walled garden, a large ornamental pond, bog garden, sensory garden, wartime kitchen garden and Lackham's famous giant lemons. For children there's a willow house, a maze and Rupert the Bear's House. Souvenirs and Lackham-grown produce are on sale in the walled garden shop.

LACOCK
4 miles S of Chippenham on the A350

🏠 Abbey 🏛 Fox Talbot Museum

The National Trust village of Lacock is one of the country's real treasures. The quadrangle of streets - East, High, West and Church - holds a delightful assortment of mellow stone buildings, and the period look (no intrusive power cables or other modern-day eyesores) keeps it in great demand as a film location. Every building is a well-restored, well-preserved gem, and overlooking everything is **Lacock Abbey**, founded in 1232 by Ela, Countess of Salisbury in memory of her husband William Longsword, stepbrother to Richard the Lionheart. In common with all monastic houses Lacock was dissolved by Henry VIII, but the original cloisters, chapter houses, sacristy and kitchens survive.

Much of the remainder of what we see today dates from the mid-16th century, when the abbey was acquired by Sir William Sharington. He added an impressive country house and the elegant octagonal tower that overlooks the Avon. The estate next passed into the hands of the Talbot family, who held it for 370 years before ceding it to the National Trust in 1944.

The most distinguished member of the Talbot family was the pioneering photographer William Henry Fox Talbot, who carried out his experiments in the 1830s, mainly at the Abbey. The **Fox Talbot Museum** commemorates the life and achievements of a man who was not just a photographer but a mathematician, physicist, classicist, philologist and transcriber of Syrian and Chaldean cuneiform. In 1839 William Henry Fox Talbot presented to the Royal Society "an account of the art of photogenic drawing or the process by which natural objects may be made to delineate themselves without the aid of the artist's pencil" - photography, in short. Louis Daguerre was at the same time demonstrating a similar technique in France, and it is not certain which of the two pioneers should be called the father of photography. But it was indisputably true that

Fox Talbot invented the positive/negative process that permitted multiple copies. The museum is located in an old barn at the entrance to the abbey and contains Fox Talbot memorabilia and a collection of early cameras. Fox Talbot also remodelled the south elevation of the abbey and added three new oriel windows. One of the world's earliest photographs shows a detail of a latticed oriel window of the abbey; the size of a postage stamp, it is the earliest known example of a photographic negative.

MELKSHAM
7 miles S of Chippenham on the A350

Once an important weaving centre, Melksham was also very briefly in vogue as a spa town. It didn't make much of a splash, being overshadowed by its near neighbour Bath, so

BEECHFIELD HOUSE HOTEL

Beanacre, nr Melksham, Wiltshire SN12 7PU
Tel: 01225 703700 e-mail: reception@beechfieldhouse.co.uk
Fax: 01225 790118 website: www.beechfieldhouse.co.uk

One of the most distinctive houses in the region was for many years one of the best and most civilised country house hotels. New owners Christopher and Felicity Whyte live on the premises and aim to provide again the highest standards of comfort and hospitality in a relaxed and informal atmosphere.

Beechfield House Hotel stands back from the A350 Chippenham road in eight acres of beautiful, secluded gardens and grounds. Behind the classical Bath Stone façade, the handsome interior is elegant and formal and at the same time warm and welcoming. Guests will feel instantly at ease in the day rooms – the Morning room, the Bar, and the Orangery. The 18 guest bedrooms, each named after a species of tree in the garden, are spacious and well appointed, providing every comfort for a memorable stay. All rooms are ensuite and are available as double, twin or for single occupancy, with ground floor rooms accessible for wheelchair users. Family rooms can sleep up to five with the addition of folding beds.

Fine dining will be the highlight of your stay, with the emphasis on locally produced ingredients. Much of the fruit, vegetables and herbs used in the kitchen will be grown in the hotel kitchen garden in 2007. Guests can be pampered in the Beauty Treatment Centre, play croquet, swim in the heated outdoor pool (May-Sept) or enjoy a leisurely walk down to the Avon. The hotel is ideally placed to explore the region: the unique National Trust village of Lacock is less than 2 miles away, it's 6 miles to Bradford-on-Avon and 9 to Bath. Junction 17 of the M4 is a mere 15 minute drive.

it turned to manufacturing and was given a boost when the Wiltshire & Berkshire Canal was opened. The canal, built between 1795 and 1810, linked the Kennet and Avon Canal with Abingdon, on the Thames. The Wilts & Berks was abandoned in 1914, but much of its path still exists in the form of lock and bridge remains, towpaths and embankments. Not far from Melksham is Great Chalfield Manor, a beautiful moated manor house with a tiny parish church in the grounds. Owned by the National Trust, it is open between April and October for guided tours.

TROWBRIDGE
13 miles S of Chippenham on the A350

🏛 Museum

The county town of Wiltshire, and another major weaving centre in its day. A large number of industrial buildings still stand, and the Town Council and Civic Society have

devised an interesting walk that takes in many of them. The **Trowbridge Museum**, located in the town's last working woollen mill, has a variety of interesting displays, including a reconstructed medieval castle and tableaux of a weaver's cottage and Taylor's drapery shop. It also features some working textile looms. The chancel of the parish church of St James, crowned by one of the finest spires in the county, contains the tomb of the poet and former rector George Crabbe, who wrote the work on which Benjamin Britten based his opera *Peter Grimes*. Trowbridge's most famous son was Isaac Pitman, the shorthand man, who was born in Nash Yard in 1813.

CORSHAM
3 miles SW of Chippenham off the A4

🏛 Corsham Court

A town made prosperous by wool and the quarrying of local Bath stone. Pevsner was

---

CINNAMON BISTRO

8 High Street, Corsham, Wiltshire SN13 0HB
Tel: 01249 701190
website: www.cinnamonbistro.co.uk

Tony and Sara Chivers own and run **Cinnamon Bistro**, a delightful 30-seat restaurant in a gabled building with leaded windows, beams, wooden floors and paintings and prints by local artists. Tony was chef at a local recording studio, and his cooking is sweet music to his many regular customers. During the day (9am to 4pm) this is a charming coffee shop serving teas and coffees (a fine selection of both), cakes, pastries and scones.

The lunchtime menu, available between 12 noon and 2pm, tempts with filled focaccia, baked jacket potatoes, terrific soups (tomato & lentil, mushroom & sage, spicy sweet potato & coconut) and daily specials such as quiche, steak sandwich, lamb tagine or vegetable-stuffed pancake. The full range of the kitchen's talents are shown in the evening à la carte, when typical dishes include the day's fish special or five-spice roast duck. To finish, perhaps chocolate truffle tart with raspberry coulis or a selection of homemade icecream.

The fine food is complemented by a well-chosen wine list. The bistro sells coffees and homemade fudge and vinaigrette to take away.

🏛 historic building　🏛 museum　🏛 historic site　🔱 scenic attraction　🌿 flora and fauna

COPPINS OF CORSHAM

1 Church Street, Corsham, Wiltshire SN13 0BY
Tel: 01249 715404   Fax: 01249 716163
e-mail: john.coppins@virgin.net
website: www.coppinsofcorsham.com

On a corner site in a fine old wool town, **Coppins of Corsham** is a family-run business specialising in bespoke rings and other top-quality jewellery. The family, which has been established in business in Corsham for 25 years, includes Daisy, an expert gemmologist, and John, who can be seen making jewellery for all occasions with two other craftsmen in the workshop. They have built up a great reputation for the quality of their work, which includes the most superb engagement and wedding rings.

Coppins also holds an extensive stock of rare and unusual gems and undertakes repairs and evaluations. Corsham is an attractive town, which no less an authority than Pevsner admired for its ' wealth of good houses', and visitors should find time to look at the exhibitions on the wool trade and the mining of Bath stone in the Tourist Information Centre. But for anyone looking for a unique piece of jewellery to make a special occasion even more special, Coppins is definitely the place to visit.

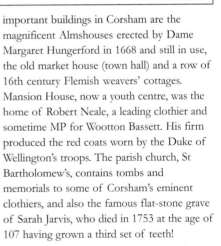

very much taken with Corsham, asserting that it had no match in Wiltshire "for wealth of good houses". The composer Sir Michael Tippett spent the 10 years between 1960 and 1970 living at Parkside on the High Street – he was attracted here by the peace of the town and its easy access to the countryside.

Corsham Court, based on an Elizabethan house of 1582, was bought by Paul Methuen in 1745 and later housed his inherited collection of paintings. The present house and grounds are chiefly the work of John Nash, Capability Brown, Thomas Bellamy and Humphry Repton, a top-pedigree setting for the treasures within, which include paintings by Caravaggio, Fra Filippo Lippi, Reynolds, Rubens and Van Dyck and furniture by Chippendale. The house has been used as the location for several films, including *Northanger Abbey* and *Remains of the Day*. Among other

important buildings in Corsham are the magnificent Almshouses erected by Dame Margaret Hungerford in 1668 and still in use, the old market house (town hall) and a row of 16th century Flemish weavers' cottages. Mansion House, now a youth centre, was the home of Robert Neale, a leading clothier and sometime MP for Wootton Bassett. His firm produced the red coats worn by the Duke of Wellington's troops. The parish church, St Bartholomew's, contains tombs and memorials to some of Corsham's eminent clothiers, and also the famous flat-stone grave of Sarah Jarvis, who died in 1753 at the age of 107 having grown a third set of teeth!

Corsham Tourist Information Centre has an ongoing exhibition about the wool trade and about the mining of Bath stone. It includes items used in the old stone mine, which was also used as an ammunition depot during

RED FORGE GALLERY

9a Station Road, Corsham, Wiltshire SN13 9EU
Tel: 01249 701110
e-mail: redforge@btinternet.com
website: www.redforgestudio.com

The ambition of four friends was the driving force behind the **Red Forge Gallery**, which occupies a handsome stone building a two minute walk from Corsham town centre. Bought in a semi-derelict condition, the building has been sensitively refurbished with wooden floors, beams and natural stone walls providing plenty of space for displaying the work of artists and craftspeople, many of whom work in the surrounding area.

The Red Forge Gallery's resident artist, Caroline Rudge, can be seen at work most days and specialises in portraits, both of people and pets. The portraits on show in her studio are well worth seeing if only to admire her undoubted technical expertise as a painter. From time to time other artists and craftspeople can also be seen working in the gallery.

The Red Forge Gallery is host to a regular programme of exhibitions and is open Wednesday to Saturday throughout the year.

PARK FARM BARN B&B

Westrop, Corsham, Wiltshire SN13 9QF
Tel: 01249 715911 Fax: 01249 701107
e-mail: parkfarmbarn@btinternet.com
website: www.parkfarmbarn.co.uk

Kate and Terry Waldron run **Park Farm Barn B&B** in a delightful setting a mile from Corsham. They converted the Tithe Barn from dereliction into a comfortable home in the early 1990s, and in 1998 the barn's outbuildings were turned into guest accommodation. The three bedrooms – two doubles and a twin – are decorated and furnished in keeping with the rural surroundings, and all have bath and shower en-suite, central heating, TV, radio-alarm, tea/coffee tray and hairdryer.

The tariff includes a choice of full English or Continental breakfast, and guests have the use of a lovely secluded garden. Park Farm Barn, a non-smoking establishment, is perfectly placed for touring a particularly interesting and attractive part of the world.

Corsham is a mile away, Lacock three, Chippenham three, Bradford-on-Avon and Bath ten, and with the A4, A350 and M4 (J17) within a short drive, access is easy in all directions.

World War II, and relates the story of Bath stone from rock face to architectural heritage.

BOX
6 miles SW of Chippenham on the A4

🏛 Box Tunnel

Bath stone is still quarried at this delightful spot, which is best known for one of the most remarkable engineering feats of its time, **Box Tunnel**. The 1.8 mile railway tunnel took five years to excavate and when completed in 1841 was the longest such tunnel in the world. According to local legend the sun shines through its entire length on only one occasion each year - sunrise on April 9th, the birthday of its genius creator, Isambard Kingdom Brunel. The tunnel is still in use; Box station, sadly, is not.

HOLT
9 miles SW of Chippenham on the B3107

🌱 The Courts

The village was once a small spa, and the old mineral well can still be seen in a factory in the village. Right at the heart of the village is **The Courts** (National Trust), an English country garden of mystery with beautiful

herbaceous borders divided by yew hedges and enriched by unusual topiary, ponds, water gardens and an arboretum. The garden is mainly the work of Sir George Hastings and was created in the reign of Edward VII. The house is not open to the public.

GREAT CHALFIELD
9 miles SW of Chippenham off the B3107/3109

🏛 Great Chalfield Manor

Great Chalfield Manor, completed in 1480, is a delightful moated manor house with an impressive great hall and a tiny parish church.

BRADFORD-ON-AVON
13 miles SW of Chippenham on the A363

🏛 Church of St Lawrence   🏛 Tithe Barn

🌱 Peto Garden   🏛 Westwood Manor

🦌 Barton Farm Country Park

A historic market town at a bridging point on the Avon, which it spans with a superb nine-arched bridge with a lock-up at one end. The town's oldest building is the **Church of St Lawrence**, believed to have been founded by St Aldhelm around 700. It 'disappeared' for over 1,000 years, when it was used variously as a school, a charnel house for storing the bones of the dead, and a residential dwelling. It was re-discovered by a keen-eyed clergyman who looked down from a hill and noticed the cruciform shape of a church. The surrounding buildings were gradually removed to reveal the little masterpiece we see today. Bradford's Norman church, restored in the 19th

Bradford-on-Avon

THE EARTH COLLECTION

5 Market Street, Bradford-on-Avon,
Wiltshire BA15 1LH
Tel: 01225 868876
website: www.theearthcollection.com

The **Earth Collection** is devoted to stylish, affordable, environmentally friendly clothing and accessories for all the family. Owner Pam Langton traded in her job as a district nurse when she discovered the Collection and was inspired to have her own shop selling these products.

Comfortable, easy to pack and ideal for leisure and holiday wear, the clothes are made from natural fibres: cotton, silk, hemp and ramie with respect for the environment. That respect extends to the buttons, which are made from coconut shells and bamboo, and even the hang tags, which come from recycled paper with water-based inks.

The accessories include bags, scarves and jewellery. The clothes and accessories are made in China, and much of the jewellery is produced in people's homes in the Philippines. Nobody in the chain is exploited or unfairly treated, from the artisans and factory workers to the retail customers.

THE GEORGIAN LODGE HOTEL & RESTAURANT

25 Bridge Street, Bradford-on-Avon, Wiltshire BA15 1BY
Tel: 01225 862268   Fax: 01225 862218
e-mail: georgianlodge@btinternet.com
website: www.georgianlodgehotel.co.uk

The **Georgian Lodge Hotel & Restaurant** enjoys what must surely the finest location in Bradford-on-Avon, right beside the town bridge over the river. Its position is a bonus in what is one of the very best and most characterful restaurants with rooms in the region. Proprietor Brian Howe, Head Chef Alex Stock and Restaurant Manager Mario Bonello head an excellent team who make every guest welcome, whether they've come here for a drink, a meal or an overnight or longer stay.

Alex seeks out the best produce for his menus, which offer classics from British and European cuisines such as poached soft roes, moules marinière, confit of duck, scallops with white wine and herbs, haddock fishcake and beef bourguignon. The daily specials are always in demand, and there are some tempting desserts (lemon soufflé, dark chocolate terrine, bread & butter pudding) to round things off in style.

The food is complemented by a good selection of wines available by glass or bottle. Light lunches, afternoon teas and evening cocktails can be enjoyed inside or out in the secluded courtyard garden. For guests touring the region or business people needing a quiet, comfortable base, the Georgian Lodge had ten well-appointed rooms situated round the courtyard.

THE BEECHES FARMHOUSE & PIGWIG SELF-CATERING COTTAGES

Holt Road, Bradford-on-Avon, Wiltshire BA15 1TS
Tel: 01225 865170
e-mail: beeches-farmhouse@netgates.co.uk
website: www.beeches-farmhouse.co.uk

Reached by a private drive off the B3107 Bradford-on-Avon to Melksham road, **The Beeches Farmhouse** provides luxurious accommodation. The 18th century farmhouse in mellow local stone has been beautifully restored, offering modern comfort and amenities while losing nothing of its rustic charm and ambience. Pauline Stanley and her mother Maureen offer a choice of b&b or self-catering accommodation. The former comprise double, twin and family rooms, all with en-suite bath and shower, TV, radio-alarm, tea/coffee tray, mineral water, fresh fruit and flowers. Guest Bed & Breakfast bedrooms are in converted farm buildings, each with its own patio and seating. Each room has its own door key allowing guests complete feedom to come and go as they please. Guests can also relax and unwind or plan their day in a

spacious, comfortable lounge. Breakfast is served in a delightful Victorian-style conservatory overlooking the stream and garden with free range hens and ducks.

In converted barns and farm buildings, the self-catering facility comprises three two-bedroom cottages in the grounds, with ample dining/living space and well-equipped kitchens. The cottages are available all year and throughout the winter, including Christmas and the New Year, and their open log fires will keep you warm and cosy.Two of the cottages can be linked for groups of up to 10 making this very much the place for the whole family, with a games room and an outside play area with a slide, ladder, climbing wall and football pitch.

century, has an interesting memorial to Lieutenant-General Henry Shrapnel, the army officer who, in 1785, invented and gave his name to the shrapnel shell. Another of the town's outstanding buildings is the mighty **Tithe Barn**, once used to store the grain from local farms for Shaftesbury Abbey, now housing a collection of antique farm implements and agricultural machinery. The centrepiece of the museum in Bridge Street is a pharmacy which has stood in the town for 120 years before being removed lock, stock and medicine bottles to its new site.

Off the A363, **Barton Farm Country Park** offers delightful walks in lovely countryside by the River Avon and the Kennet and Avon Canal. It was once a medieval farm serving Shaftesbury Abbey. Barton Bridge is the original packhorse bridge built to assist the transportation of grain from the farm to the tithe barn.

Half a mile south of town by the River Frome is the Italian-style **Peto Garden** (see panel on page 408) at Iford Manor. Famous for its romantic, tranquil beauty, its steps and terraces, statues, colonnades and ponds, the garden was laid out by the architect and landscape gardener Harold Ainsworth Peto between 1899 and 1933. He was inspired by the works of Lutyens and Jekyll to turn a difficult hillside site into 'a haunt of ancient peace'.

Outside Bradford, off the A366, the charming 15th century **Westwood Manor** (National Trust) has many interesting features, including Jacobean and Gothic windows, ornate plasterwork and a topiary garden.

The Peto Garden at Iford Manor

Bradford on Avon, Wiltshire BA15 2BA
Tel: 01225 863146
e-mail: info@ilfordmanor.co.uk   website: www.ilfordmanor.co.uk

Harold Peto (1854-1933) began his career by training as an architect and, in 1874, entered into parnership with Ernest George which was to last for 16 years. Among their assistants were the young Sir Edwin Lutyens, Guy Dawber and Herbert Baker. Peto became increasingly interested in garden design after the dissolution of the partnership in 1892 and, on finding himself out of sympathy with current trends in English architecture, his own taste inclined much more towards the style of the Italian Renaissance.

After several visits to Italy, Peto's attention was turned to the idea of designing house and garden together. He combined a knowledge of gardening with an architect's feel for the layout, and by the end of the century had become well known as a designer both in England and the South of France. It is in the Alpes Maritimes in France that the villas and gardens, for which he is most well known are found. There he was able to concentrate on designing Italianate villas in a garden setting for his clients – wealthy expatriate Americans, for the most part – as well as collecting authentic Italian, French and Spanish fireplaces, doors, sculptures and other fittings to decorate both house and garden. Back in England, in 1899 he bought Iford Manor with its attractive 18th century Palladian façade, and began to transform the steep hillside in conformity with his ideas. He arranged the grounds – around the grand terrace walk – to echo some of his favourite Mediterranean gardens.

The Garden is open during April & October on Sunday and Easter Monday 2pm – 5pm; from May to September daily 2pm – 5pm except Mondays and Fridays. Homemade teas are available from May to August at weekends and on Bank Holidays. Please note: Saturdays and Sundays are reserved for tranquil visits. Children under 10 years are very welcome during the open week but for health and safety constraints, may not be admitted at weekends. Dogs must be kept on leads.

🏠 historic building   🏛 museum   🏛 historic site   🏞 scenic attraction   🌿 flora and fauna

Malmesbury

🏛 Abbey　🌱 Abbey House Gardens

🏛 Athelstan Museum

The 'Queen of Hilltop Towns' is England's oldest borough and one of its most attractive. The town is dominated by the impressive remains of the **Benedictine Malmesbury Abbey**, founded in the 7th century by St Aldhelm. In the 10th century, King Athelstan, Alfred's grandson and the first Saxon king to unite England, granted 500 acres of land to the townspeople in gratitude for their help in resisting a Norse invasion. Those acres are still known as King's Heath and are owned by 200 residents who are descended from those far-off heroes. Athelstan made Malmesbury his capital and is buried in the abbey, where several centuries later a monument was put up in his honour.

Within the precincts of the abbey are **Abbey House Gardens**, an enchanting place with an abundance of flowers, around 2,000 medicinal herbs, woodland and laburnum walks, fish ponds and a waterfall.

The abbey tower was the scene of an early attempt at human-powered flight when in the early part of the 11th century Brother Elmer strapped a pair of wings to his arms, flew for about 200 yards and crashed to earth, breaking both legs and becoming a cripple for the rest of his long life. The flight of this intrepid cleric, who reputedly forecast the Norman invasion following a sighting of Halley's Comet, is commemorated in a stained glass window. Another window, by Burne-Jones,

Abbey House Gardens

🎭 stories and anecdotes　🐦 famous people　🎨 art and craft　🎭 entertainment and sport　🚶 walks

STANTON MANOR HOTEL

Stanton St Quintin, nr Chippenham,
Wiltshire SN14 6DQ
Tel: 01666 837552
Fax: 01666 837022
e-mail: reception@stantonmanor.co.uk
website: www.stantonmanor.co.uk

Stanton Manor Hotel is a stone-built, country house hotel located in the picturesque Wiltshire village of Stanton Saint Quintin, surrounded by stunning countryside. This beautiful hotel is conveniently situated just a three minute drive from junction 17 of the M4 motorway, at the gateway to the beautiful Cotswold's countryside and a short drive to the nearby town of Chippenham and historical cities of Bath and Bristol in South West England. The house has a rich history and is listed in the Domesday Book. It was once owned by Lord Burghley, chief minister to Queen Elizabeth I, and was rebuilt in 1840. Stanton Manor Hotel has been completely refurbished, and the owners Robert and Linda Davis are on hand to ensure that a friendly and attentive service is extended to guests. Modern facilities and comforts combine easily and unobtrusively with those of the past, which

include magnificent Tudor fireplaces and stone flooring. The hotel's en-suite bedrooms are spacious and individually designed with very comfortable furniture. Four hotel rooms have luxury king-size four-poster beds to complement the stunning New Oriental or Provencal themed rooms. Four of the hotel rooms are suitable for large families.

Head Chef Jean Paul Giraud and his team take pride in creating traditional British cuisine with flair and quality, which is immaculately served in the elegant and light Gallery Restaurant, overlooking the grounds, exhibiting an eclectic collection of art by prominent Oriental artists. All artwork is for sale to customers and guests. Light snacks are available all day in the cozy bar or lounge. The hotel also boasts fully equipped function/conference suites suitable for a range of events, making the Stanton Manor an ideal conference venue. In addition, the hotel is also licensed for civil ceremonies and is planning on launching a new wedding barn by Spring 2007.

---

portrays Faith, Courage and Devotion.

The octagonal Market Cross in the town square is one of many interesting buildings that also include the Old Stone House with its colonnade and gargoyles, and the arched Tolsey Gate, whose two cells once served as the town jail.

In the **Malmesbury Athelstan Museum** in the Town Hall are displays of lace-making, costume, rural life, coins, early bicycles and tricycles, a manually-operated fire pump,

photographs and maps. Here, too, are the ceremonial wheelbarrow and spade used to cut the first sod of the Wiltshire & Gloucestershire Railway in 1865. Among the local notables featured in the Museum are Thomas Hobbes, author of *Leviathan* and tutor to Charles II, and Walter Powell, MP for Malmesbury from 1868 to 1881. In December of 1881 the unfortunate Powell was carried out to sea in a War Office balloon and was never seen again.

🏠 historic building   🏛 museum   🏛 historic site   🌱 scenic attraction   🌿 flora and fauna

Around Malmesbury

museum dealing with the village's history is open on summer Sunday afternoons.

CASTLE COMBE
8 miles SW of Malmesbury on the B4039

The loveliest village in the region, and for some the loveliest in the country, Castle Combe was once a centre of the prosperous wool trade, famed for its red and white cloth. Many of the present-day buildings date from the 15th and 16th centuries, including the Perpendicular Church of St Andrew, the covered market cross and the manor house, which was built with stones from the Norman castle that gave the village its name. One of the Lords of the Manor in the 14th century was Sir John Fastolf, who was reputedly the inspiration for Shakespeare's Falstaff. A small

EASTON GREY
3 miles W of Malmesbury on the B4040

Here the southern branch of the River Avon is spanned by a handsome 16th century bridge with five stone arches. A manor house has overlooked the village since the 13th century; the present house, with a classical facade and an elegant covered portico, dates from the 18th century. It was used as a summer retreat by Herbert Asquith, British Prime Minister from 1908 to 1916, and in 1923 the Prince of Wales was in residence during the Duke of Beaufort's hunting season at Badminton.

THE GALLERY ON THE BRIDGE
The Street, Castle Combe, Wiltshire SN14 7HU
Tel/Fax: 01249 782201

Castle Combe, one of the prettiest villages in the country, is an entirely appropriate setting for **The Gallery on the Bridge**. The premises are as attractive as any in this lovely spot, with small-paned windows, exposed stone walls and old beams and doors – very English and absolutely delightful. Alison Holland has put every inch of space to the best possible use for displaying a truly wonderful collection of fine art, local crafts and interesting handmade collectables.

There are original paintings by artists known locally and nationally, cards and prints of local scenes, a wonderful selection of British potters and ceramicists, some outstanding glass pieces and lots of other beautiful and desirable gift ideas. All the studio glass is produced by individual glass-blowers and each piece is signed by the maker. Castle Combe, which stands on the B4039, 12 miles from Bath and eight miles southwest of Malmesbury, is one of the most visited villages in the region, and no visit is truly complete without taking time to browse in The Gallery on the Bridge.

TOURIST INFORMATION CENTRES

Bedfordshire

BEDFORD
St Pauls Square, Bedford,
Bedfordshire MK40 1SL
Tel: 01234 215226
Fax: 01234 217932
e-mail: TouristInfo@bedford.gov.uk

LUTON
Luton Central Library,
St George's Square, Luton,
Bedfordshire LU1 2NG
Tel: 01582 401579
Fax: 01582 487886
e-mail:
tourist.information@luton.gov.uk

MID BEDFORDSHIRE
5 Shannon Court, High Street, Sandy,
Bedfordshire SG19 1AG
Tel: 01767 682 728
Fax: 01767 681 713
e-mail:
tourist.information@midbeds.gov.uk

Berkshire

BRACKNELL
The Look Out Discovery Centre,
Nine Mile Ride, Bracknell,
Berkshire RG12 7QW
Tel: 01344 354409
Fax: 01344 354422
e-mail:
TheLookOut@bracknell-forest.gov.uk

MAIDENHEAD
Maidenhead Library, St Ives Road.
Maidenhead, Berkshire SL6 1QU
Tel: 01628 796502
Fax: 01628 796971
e-mail: maidenhead.tic@rbwm.gov.uk

NEWBURY
The Wharf, Newbury,
Berkshire RG14 5AS
Tel: 01635 30267
Fax: 01635 30267
e-mail: tourism@westberks.gov.uk

READING
Church House, Chain Street, Reading,
Berkshire RG1 2HX
Tel: 0118 956 6226
Fax: 0118 939 9885
e-mail: touristinfo@reading.gov.uk

WINDSOR
Royal Windsor Information Centre
The Old Booking Hall (Walk-in
visitors only), Central Station, Windsor,
Berkshire SL4 1PJ
Tel: 01753 743900
Fax: 01753 743929
e-mail: windsor.tic@rbwm.gov.uk

Buckinghamshire

AYLESBURY
The Kings Head, Kings Head Passage,
off Market Square, Aylesbury,
Buckinghamshire HP20 2RW
Tel: 01296 330559
Fax: 01296 330559
e-mail: tic@aylesburyvaledc.gov.uk

BUCKINGHAM
The Old Gaol Museum,
Market Hill, Buckingham,
Buckinghamshire MK18 1JX
Tel: 01280 823020
Fax: 01280 823020
e-mail: buckingham.t.i.c@btconnect.com

HIGH WYCOMBE
Paul's Row, High Wycombe,
Buckinghamshire HP11 2HQ
Tel: 01494 421892
Fax: 01494 421893
e-mail:
tourism_enquiries@wycombe.gov.uk

MARLOW
31 High Street, Marlow,
Buckinghamshire SL7 1AU
Tel: 01628 483597
Fax: 01628 471915
e-mail:
tourism_enquiries@wycombe.gov.uk

WENDOVER
The Clock Tower,
High Street, Wendover,
Buckinghamshire HP22 6DU
Tel: 01296 696759
Fax: 0871 2361551
e-mail: tourism@wendover-pc.gov.uk

Gloucestershire

BOURTON-ON-THE-WATER
Victoria Street, Bourton-on-the -Water,
Gloucestershire GL54 2BU
Tel: 01451 820211
Fax: 01451 821103
e-mail: bourtonvic@cotswold.gov.uk

CHELTENHAM
Municipal Offices,
77 Promenade, Cheltenham,
Gloucestershire GL50 1PJ
Tel: 01242 522878
Fax: 01242 255848
e-mail: tic@cheltenham.gov.uk

CIRENCESTER

Corn Hall, Market Place, Cirencester,
Gloucestershire GL7 1EJ
Tel: 01285 654180
Fax: 01285 641182
e-mail: cirencestervic@cotswold.gov.uk

COLEFORD

High Street, Coleford,
Gloucestershire GL16 8HG
Tel: 01594 812388
Fax: 01594 832889
e-mail: tourism@fdean.gov.uk

GLOUCESTER

28 Southgate Street, Gloucester,
Gloucestershire GL1 2DP
Tel: 01452 396572
Fax: 01452 504273
e-mail: tourism@gloucester.gov.uk

NEWENT

7 Church Street, Newent,
Gloucestershire GL18 1PU
Tel: 01531 822468
Fax: 01581 822468
e-mail: newent@fdean.gov.uk

STROUD

Subscription Rooms, George Street,
Stroud, Gloucestershire GL5 1AE
Tel: 01453 760960
Fax: 01453 760955
e-mail: tic@stroud.gov.uk

TETBURY

33 Church Street, Tetbury,
Gloucestershire GL8 8JG
Tel: 01666 503552
Fax: 01666 503552
e-mail: tourism@tetbury.org

TEWKESBURY

64 Barton Street, Tewkesbury,
Gloucestershire GL20 5PX
Tel: 01684 295027
Fax: 01684 292277
e-mail:
tewkesburytic@tewkesburybc.gov.uk

WINCHCOMBE

Town Hall, High Street, Winchcombe,
Gloucestershire GL54 5LJ
Tel: 01242 602925
Fax: 01242 602925
e-mail:
winchcombetic@tewkesbury.gov.uk

Hampshire

ALDERSHOT

39 High Street, Aldershot,
Hampshire GU11 1BH
Tel: 01252 320968
Fax: 01252 311479
e-mail: mail@rushmoorvic.com

ALTON

7 Cross and Pillory Lane, Alton,
Hampshire GU34 1HL
Tel: 01420 88448
Fax: 01420 543916
e-mail: altoninfo@btconnect.com

ANDOVER

Andover Museum, 6 Church Close,
Andover, Hampshire SP10 1DP
Tel: 01264 324320
Fax: 01264 345650
e-mail: andovertic@testvalley.gov.uk

FAREHAM

Westbury Manor, West Street,
Fareham, Hampshire PO16 0JJ
Tel: 01329 221342
Fax: 01329 282959
e-mail: farehamtic@tourismse.com

FORDINGBRIDGE

Kings Yard, Salisbury Street,
Fordingbridge, Hampshire SP6 1AB
Tel: 01425 654560
Fax: 01425 654560
e-mail: fordingbridgetic@tourismse.com

GOSPORT

Gosport TIC, Bus Station Complex,
South Street, Gosport,
Hampshire PO12 1EP
Tel: 023 9252 2944
Fax: 023 9251 1687
e-mail: tourism@gosport.gov.uk

HAYLING ISLAND AND HAVANT BOROUGH

Central Beachlands, Seafront,
Hayling Island,
Hampshire PO11 0AG
Tel: 023 9246 7111
Fax: 023 9246 5626
e-mail: tourism@havant.gov.uk

LYMINGTON

St Barbe Museum & Visitor Centre,
New Street, Lymington,
Hampshire SO41 9BH
Tel: 01590 689000
Fax: 01590 673990
e-mail: information@nfdc.gov.uk

LYNDHURST & NEW FOREST

New Forest Museum & Visitor
Centre, Main Car Park, Lyndhurst,
Hampshire SO43 7NY
Tel: 023 8028 2269
Fax: 023 8028 4404
e-mail: information@nfdc.gov.uk

TOURIST INFORMATION CENTRES

PETERSFIELD
County Library, 27 The Square,
Petersfield, Hampshire GU32 3HH
Tel: 01730 268829
Fax: 01730 266679
e-mail: petersfieldinfo@btconnect.com

PORTSMOUTH
(CLARENCE ESPLANADE)
Clarence Esplanade, Southsea,
Portsmouth, Hampshire PO5 3PB
Tel: 023 9282 6722
Fax: 023 9282 7519
e-mail: vis@portsmouthcc.gov.uk

PORTSMOUTH (THE HARD)
The Hard, Portsmouth,
Hampshire PO1 3QJ
Tel: 023 9282 6722
Fax: 023 9282 2693
e-mail: vis@portsmouthcc.gov.uk

RINGWOOD
The Furlong, Ringwood,
Hampshire BH24 1AT
Tel: 01425 470896
Fax: 01425 461172
e-mail: information@nfdc.gov.uk

ROMSEY
Heritage & Visitor Centre,
13 Church Street, Romsey,
Hampshire SO51 8BT
Tel: 01794 512987
Fax: 01794 512987
e-mail: romseytic@testvalley.gov.uk

SOUTHAMPTON
9 Civic Centre Road, Southampton,
Hampshire SO14 7FJ
Tel: 023 8083 3333
Fax: 023 8083 3381
e-mail:
tourist.information@southampton.gov.uk

WINCHESTER
Guildhall, High Street, Winchester,
Hampshire SO23 9GH
Tel: 01962 840 500
Fax: 01962 850 348
e-mail: tourism@winchester.gov.uk

Hertfordshire

BIRCHANGER GREEN
Welcome Break Service Area,
Junction 8 of M11 Motorway,
Bishop's Stortford,
Hertfordshire CM23 5QZ

BISHOP'S STORTFORD
The Old Monastery, Windhill,
Bishop's Stortford,
Hertfordshire CM23 2ND
Tel: 01279 655831
Fax: 01279 653136
e-mail: tic@bishopsstortford.org

HEMEL HEMPSTEAD
Dacorum Information Centre,
Marlowes, Hemel Hempstead,
Hertfordshire HP1 1DT
Tel: 01442 234222
Fax: 01442 230427
e-mail:
stephanie.canadas@dacorum.gov.uk

HERTFORD
10 Market Place, Hertford,
Hertfordshire SG14 1DF
Tel: 01992 584322
Fax: 01992 534724
e-mail: tic@hertford.gov.uk

LETCHWORTH GARDEN CITY
33-35 Station Road,
Letchworth Garden City,
Hertfordshire SG6 3BB
Tel: 01462 487868
Fax: 01462 485332
e-mail: tic@letchworth.com

ST ALBANS
Town Hall, Market Place, St Albans,
Hertfordshire AL3 5DJ
Tel: 01727 864511
Fax: 01727 863533
e-mail: tic@stalbans.gov.uk

Isle of Wight

COWES
9 The Arcade, Cowes,
Isle of Wight PO31 7AR
Tel: 01983 813818
Fax: 01983 280078
e-mail: info@islandbreaks.co.uk

NEWPORT
The Guildhall, High Street, Newport,
Isle of Wight PO30 1TY
Tel: 01983 813818
Fax: 01983 823811
e-mail: info@islandbreaks.co.uk

RYDE
81-83 Union Street, Ryde,
Isle of Wight PO33 2LW
Tel: 01983 813818
Fax: 01983 567610
e-mail: info@islandbreaks.co.uk

SANDOWN
8 High Street, Sandown,
Isle of Wight PO36 8DG
Tel: 01983 813818
Fax: 01983 406482
e-mail: info@islandbreaks.co.uk

SHANKLIN

67 High Street, Shanklin,
Isle of Wight PO37 6JJ
Tel: 01983 813818
Fax: 01983 863047
e-mail: info@islandbreaks.co.uk

YARMOUTH

The Quay, Yarmouth,
Isle of Wight PO41 4PQ
Tel: 01983 813818
Fax: 01983 761047
e-mail: info@islandbreaks.co.uk

Oxfordshire

BANBURY

Spiceball Park Road, Banbury,
Oxfordshire OX16 2PQ
Tel: 01295 259855
Fax: 01295 269469
e-mail: banbury.tic@cherwell-dc.gov.uk

BICESTER

Bicester Visitor Centre,
Unit 86a, Bicester Village,
Pingle Drive, Bicester,
Oxfordshire OX26 6WD
Tel: 01869 369055
Fax: 01869 369054
e-mail: bicester.vc@cherwell-dc.gov.uk

BURFORD

The Brewery, Sheep Street, Burford,
Oxfordshire OX18 4LP
Tel: 01993 823558
Fax: 01993 823590
e-mail: burford.vic@westoxon.gov.uk

FARINGDON

The Pump House, 5 Market Place,
Faringdon, Oxfordshire SN7 7HL
Tel: 01367 242191
Fax: 01367 242191
e-mail:
tourism@faringdontowncouncil.org.uk

HENLEY-ON-THAMES

King's Arms Barn, Kings Road,
Henley on Thames,
Oxfordshire RG9 2DG
Tel: 01491 578034
Fax: 01491 412703
e-mail: henleyvic@frenchjones.co.uk

OXFORD

Oxford Information Centre,
15/16 Broad Street, Oxford,
Oxfordshire OX1 3AS
Tel: 01865 726871
Fax: 01865 240261
e-mail: tic@oxford.gov.uk

WITNEY

26A Market Square, Witney,
Oxfordshire OX28 6BB
Tel: 01993 775802
Fax: 01993 709261
e-mail: witney.vic@westoxon.gov.uk

WOODSTOCK

Oxfordshire Museum, Park Street,
Woodstock, Oxfordshire OX20 1SN
Tel: 01993 813276
Fax: 01993 813632
e-mail: woodstock.vic@westoxon.gov.uk

Wiltshire

AMESBURY

Amesbury Library, Smithfield Street,
Amesbury, Wiltshire SP4 7AL
Tel: 01980 622833
Fax: 01980 625541
e-mail: amesburytic@salisbury.gov.uk

AVEBURY

Avebury Chapel Centre, Green Street,
Avebury, Wiltshire SN8 1RE
Tel: 01672 539425
Fax: 01672 539296
e-mail: all.atic@kennet.gov.uk

BRADFORD ON AVON

The Greenhouse,
50 St. Margaret's Street,
Bradford on Avon,
Wiltshire BA15 1DE
Tel: 01225 865797
Fax: 01225 868722
e-mail: tic@bradfordonavon.co.uk

CHIPPENHAM

Yelde Hall, Market Place, Chippenham,
Wiltshire SN15 3HL
Tel: 01249 665970
Fax: 01249 460776
e-mail: tourism@chippenham.gov.uk

CORSHAM

Arnold House, 31 High Street,
Corsham, Wiltshire SN13 0EZ
Tel: 01249 714660
Fax: 01249 716164
e-mail:
corshamheritage@northwilts.gov.uk

TOURIST INFORMATION CENTRES

DEVIZES
Cromwell House, Market Place,
Devizes, Wiltshire SN10 1JG
Tel: 01380 729408
Fax: 01380 730319
e-mail: all.dtic@kennet.gov.uk

MALMESBURY
Town Hall, Market Lane, Malmesbury,
Wiltshire SN16 9BZ
Tel: 01666 823748
Fax: 01666 826166
e-mail:
malmesburyip@northwilts.gov.uk

MARLBOROUGH
The Library, High Street, Marlborough,
Wiltshire SN8 1HD
Tel: 01672 513989
Fax: 01672 513989
e-mail: all.tic's@kennet.gov.uk

MELKSHAM
Church Street, Melksham,
Wiltshire SN12 6LS
Tel: 01225 707424
Fax: 01225 707424
e-mail: visitmelksham2@tiscali.co.uk

MERE
The Library, Barton Lane,
(between Castle St. & Church St.),
Mere, Warminster,
Wiltshire BA12 6JA
Tel: 01747 861211
Fax: 01747 861127
e-mail: MereTIC@Salisbury.gov.uk

SALISBURY
Fish Row, Salisbury,
Wiltshire SP1 1EJ
Tel: 01722 334956
Fax: 01722 422059
e-mail: visitorinfo@salisbury.gov.uk

SWINDON
37 Regent Street, Swindon,
Wiltshire SN1 1JL
Tel: 01793 530328
Fax: 01793 434031
e-mail: infocentre@swindon.gov.uk

TROWBRIDGE
St Stephen's Place, Trowbridge,
Wiltshire BA14 8AH
Tel: 01225 710535
Fax: 01225 710530
e-mail: tic@trowbridge.gov.uk

WARMINSTER
Central Car Park, off Station Rd,
Warminster, Wiltshire BA12 9BT
Tel: 01985 218548
Fax: 01985 846154
e-mail: visitwarminster@btconnect.com

INDEX OF ADVERTISERS

INDEX OF ADVERTISERS

INDEX OF ADVERTISERS

INDEX OF ADVERTISERS

Looking for more walks?

The walks in this book have been gleaned from Britain's largest online walking guide, to be found at *www.walkingworld.com*.

The site contains over 2000 walks from all over England, Scotland and Wales so there are plenty more to choose from in this book's region as well as further afield - ideal if you are taking a short break as you can plan your walks in advance. There are walks of every length and type to suit all tastes.

Want more detail for the walks in this book? Next to every walk in this book you will see a Walk ID. You can enter this ID number on Walkingworld's 'Find a Walk' page and you will be taken straight to the details of that walk.

- Over **2000** walks across Britain

- Print routes out as you need them

- No bulky guidebook to carry

Walkingworld routes contain much more detailed instructions and mapping than can be given in a printed book. The walk descriptions have photographs at every major decision point to help you to navigate and each comes with an Ordnance Survey 1:50,000 scale map. Once you have found a walk you like, simply print it out on standard A4 paper and you are ready to go!

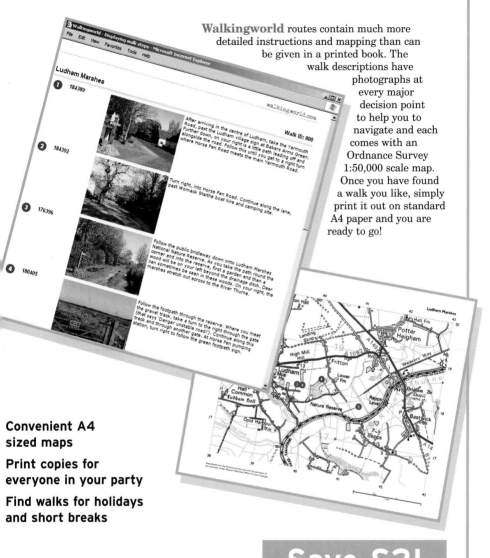

Convenient A4 sized maps

Print copies for everyone in your party

Find walks for holidays and short breaks

A modest annual subscription gives you access to over 2000 walks, all in Walkingworld's easy to follow format. The database of walks is growing all the time and as a subscriber you gain access to new routes as soon as they are published.

Visit the Walkingworld website at *www.walkingworld.com*

ORDER FORM

To order any of our publications just fill in the payment details below and complete the order form. For orders of less than 4 copies please add £1 per book for postage and packing. Orders over 4 copies are P & P free.

Please Complete Either:

I enclose a cheque for £ [ ] made payable to Travel Publishing Ltd

Or:

CARD NO: [ ]   EXPIRY DATE: [ ]

SIGNATURE: [ ]

NAME: [ ]

ADDRESS: [ ]

TEL NO: [ ]

Please either send, telephone, fax or e-mail your order to:

Travel Publishing Ltd, 7a Apollo House, Calleva Park, Aldermaston, Berkshire RG7 8TN
Tel: 0118 981 7777   Fax: 0118 940 8428 e-mail: info@travelpublishing.co.uk

	PRICE	QUANTITY		PRICE	QUANTITY
HIDDEN PLACES REGIONAL TITLES			**COUNTRY PUBS AND INNS TITLES**		
Cornwall	£8.99	....	Cornwall	£5.99	....
Devon	£8.99	....	Devon	£7.99	....
Dorset, Hants & Isle of Wight	£8.99	....	Sussex	£5.99	....
East Anglia	£8.99	....	Wales	£8.99	....
Lake District & Cumbria	£8.99	....	Yorkshire	£7.99	....
Northumberland & Durham	£8.99	....	**COUNTRY LIVING RURAL GUIDES**		
Peak District and Derbyshire	£8.99	....	East Anglia	£10.99	....
Yorkshire	£8.99	....	Heart of England	£10.99	....
HIDDEN PLACES NATIONAL TITLES			Ireland	£11.99	....
England	£11.99	....	North East of England	£10.99	....
Ireland	£11.99	....	North West of England	£10.99	....
Scotland	£11.99	....	Scotland	£11.99	....
Wales	£11.99	....	South of England	£10.99	....
HIDDEN INNS TITLES			South East of England	£10.99	....
East Anglia	£7.99	....	Wales	£11.99	....
Heart of England	£7.99	....	West Country	£10.99	....
South	£7.99	....	**OTHER TITLES**		
South East	£7.99	....	Off The Motorway	£11.99	....
West Country	£7.99	....			

TOTAL QUANTITY [ ]

TOTAL VALUE [ ]

READER REACTION FORM

The **Travel Publishing** *research team would like to receive readers' comments on any visitor attractions or places reviewed in the book and also recommendations for suitable entries to be included in the next edition. This will help ensure that the* **Country Living series of Rural Guides** *continues to provide its readers with useful information on the more interesting, unusual or unique features of each attraction or place ensuring that their visit to the local area is an enjoyable and stimulating experience. To provide your comments or recommendations would you please complete the forms below and overleaf as indicated and send to:*

The Research Department, Travel Publishing Ltd, 7a Apollo House, Calleva Park, Aldermaston, Reading, RG7 8TN

YOUR NAME:

YOUR ADDRESS:

YOUR TEL NO:

Please tick as appropriate: COMMENTS   RECOMMENDATION

ESTABLISHMENT:

ADDRESS:

TEL NO:

CONTACT NAME:

PLEASE COMPLETE FORM OVERLEAF

READER REACTION FORM

COMMENT OR REASON FOR RECOMMENDATION:

....

....

....

....

....

....

....

....

....

....

....

....

TOWNS, VILLAGES AND PLACES OF INTEREST

TOWNS, VILLAGES AND PLACES OF INTEREST

TOWNS, VILLAGES AND PLACES OF INTEREST

TOWNS, VILLAGES AND PLACES OF INTEREST

TOWNS, VILLAGES AND PLACES OF INTEREST

TOWNS, VILLAGES AND PLACES OF INTEREST